RISE AND FULFILMENT OF
BRITISH RULE IN INDIA

RISE AND FULFILMENT

OF

BRITISH RULE IN INDIA

BY

EDWARD THOMPSON

LEVERHULME RESEARCH FELLOW, INDIAN HISTORY

AND

G. T. GARRATT

AMS PRESS

NEW YORK

Reprinted from the edition of 1934, London

First AMS EDITION published 1971

Manufactured in the United States of America

International Standard Book Number: 0-404-06395-0

Library of Congress Catalog Number: 70-137299

AMS PRESS INC.
NEW YORK, N.Y. 10003

'Indian history has never been made interesting to English readers, except by rhetoric.'

The Times, February 25, 1892

'The real truth is that the public mind cannot be brought to attend to an Indian subject.'

THE DUKE OF WELLINGTON, December 21, 1805

PREFACE

A HISTORY of modern India presents in the writing certain technical difficulties, which are mentioned, not to excuse the shortcomings of this work, but to suggest deficiencies which the reader must supply by further study and examination.

1. Without making the book a mere 'charnel-house of facts', it would be impossible to describe the internal history of the many semi-autonomous States, and of the Provinces, which have also developed their own characteristics. Burma, in particular, requires separate treatment. In this history the States and Provinces can only be considered in relation to the Central Government, or to India's life as a whole. Exigencies of space, as well as a desire for unity, have enforced this limitation. Similarly, though we have tried to remind the reader continually that in British India there was an increasingly vigorous intellectual and religious life, influenced profoundly by English administration and literature, yet it was impossible to treat this with adequacy in a book whose range continually tended to make it too bulky for any but a specialist public.

2. The available sources for the period under consideration are predominantly British. Many important official documents and some recent histories were written, consciously or unconsciously, with an eye to certain criticisms which have been made in India and abroad. The growth of Indian nationalism has accentuated a bias which is often unfavourable to Indians, individually and collectively. The point is illustrated in the *Bibliographical Note*. It has been taken by the authors to justify a much greater use of contemporary quotation in the earlier part of this work.

3. The historian's task has been made more difficult by the animosities which have distracted the world during the last twenty years, and by their repercussions, official and unofficial. The mischievous tendency to make historical truth subservient to administrative expediency has been increased by changes in legal practice and procedure, which operate as an effective censorship. An author may be asked to substantiate statements of fact by direct evidence, which would frequently entail collecting Indian witnesses, often illiterate, bringing them to

England, and producing them before a court in which their testimony would be discounted. The freedom with which the Mutiny was discussed during the subsequent two decades would have led, under present conditions, to innumerable *causes célèbres* involving the financial ruin of many concerned. The authors believe that it is as necessary and no more difficult to write objectively about recent events than about those of the last century, and have endeavoured to take this history up to the publication of the White Paper of 1933. But official secretiveness, of which there was little before the Mutiny, combined with this informal censorship, makes it almost impossible to supply the 'penetration, accuracy, and colouring' which Dr. Johnson demanded of the historian.

4. In the spelling of Indian proper names and names of places, and in the anglicizing of Indian words, the system in general use among scholars of all countries has been adopted. We have, however, left certain names and words in the forms familiar to those who have lived in India, and used them constantly. Thus Cawnpore is used instead of Khanpur, ryot instead of raiyat, Punjab instead of Panjab. We have eschewed marks of quantity, as we have written not for Sanscritists and Arabists but for the student of history. An arbitrary line has to be taken between consistency and pedantry. It seems, for example, absurd to use the Hunterian transliteration for the names of those, like the Amir Abdur Rahman or Sir Surendranath Banerjea, who have themselves preferred another form.

By far our hardest task has been to avoid a national or racial bias. We have both had long and close connections with India, and friendships that have given us a feeling of a second nationality; but inevitably our first loyalty is to our own country, one of the last in which free and unregimented thinking is still possible. Yet love of England cannot blind us to the dangers which beset Western civilization, and we are convinced of the immense influence that India, called to a reinvigorated existence, could exert in solving those problems which now oppress the mind of man. We send out this book hoping that it will work for that understanding between the two countries which fate has linked so strongly together.

We should like to thank Mr. J. F. Horrabin for his valuable sketch map illustrating the famines.

CONTENTS

ix

BOOK VIII. 1914-1933

LIST OF MAPS

BOOK I

THE TIME OF TRADING, 1599-1740

'The life of man is so precious, that it ought not lightly to be exposed to dangers. And yet we know, that the whole course of our life is nothing but a passage unto Death; wherein one can neither stay nor slack his pace, but all men run in one manner, and in one celerity. The shorter liver runs his course no faster than the long, both have a like passage of time; howbeit, the first not so far to run as the later.'—

A Discourse of Trade from England unto the East Indies; answering to diverse Objections which are usually made against the same. By 'T. M.'; 1621.

A

CHRONOLOGICAL TABLE

1571. Battle of Lepanto.
1579. Drake's Circumnavigation of the Globe (1577-80). Foundation of the English Turkey Company.
1580. Portugal becomes a Spanish dependency.
1583. Sailing of the *Tyger*.
1588. Defeat of the Armada.
1599. Foundation of the East India Company.
1603. Death of Elizabeth.
1612. Captain Best defeats the Portuguese off Swally, Western India. East India Company's first factory established at Surat.
1615. Sir Thomas Roe sent as ambassador to the Mogul Court.
1620. Defeat of the Portuguese by Persia and the East India Company. Capture of Ormuz.
1623. Massacre of Amboyna.
1627. Shah Jahan becomes Emperor.
1630. Indian Great Famine. Further defeats of Portuguese off Swally.
1633. William Methwold President at Surat.
1635. East India Company and Portuguese establish a truce. Charles I gives charter to Courteen's Company.
1640. Portugal recovers independence of Spain.
1641. Foundation of Fort St. George (Madras).
1642. Permanent peace between East India Company and Portuguese. Civil War breaks out in England.
1649. Execution of Charles I.
1652-54. First Dutch War.
1657. Amalgamation of East India Company and Courteen's Company. A new Charter granted.
1662. Sir George Oxinden President at Surat. Bombay ceded to Charles II.
1665. Bombay handed over to British.
1665-67. Second Dutch War.
1668. Bombay handed over to East India Company. Foundation of French East India Company.
1669. Gerald Aungier President at Surat.
1674. Sivaji the Maratha proclaims himself an independent king.
1680. Death of Sivaji.
1683. Keigwin's rebellion, Bombay.
1686. War between East India Company and Mogul Empire. Temporary ruin of English factories in Bengal.
1687. Madras made a municipality under a mayor. Bombay supersedes Surat as chief Company trading station in Western India.
1690. Foundation of Calcutta. Foundation of Fort St. David (Cuddalore).
1698. Rival Company established in England.
1702. Accommodation come to between two rival Companies.
1707. Death of Aurangzeb. The Calcutta settlement is made independent of Madras.
1714. Surman's embassy to the Mogul Court.
1726. Mayor's courts established in all three Presidencies.
1727. Establishment of Peshwa's power. Rise of Maratha chieftains.
1739. Maratha conquest of Malwa. Nadir Shah of Persia invades India and sacks Delhi.

CHAPTER I

FOUNDATION OF THE EAST INDIA COMPANY

Early trade of East and West: first English attempts to gain share of Eastern trade: Thomas Stevens: sailing of the 'Tyger': Ralph Fitch: foundation of East India Company and Captain Lancaster's first voyage: Edward Monox, William Adams, Richard Cocks: Captain Henry Middleton: Best defeats Portuguese off Swally: pirates: Sir Thomas Roe's embassy: Roe on the Dutch and their policy: Roe's overtures to the Portuguese Viceroy at Goa: Captain Shilling's victories and death: capture of Ormuz: Dutch insolence and hostility: Massacre of Amboyna.

THE commerce of East and West for millenniums moved by the Persian Gulf, across Syria, or up the Red Sea, through Egypt; in the Middle Ages Venice controlled its Western outgoings until the Turks overspread the Levant and taxed and pillaged much of the traffic out of existence. Spain at Lepanto (1571) mastered the Turkish fleet. But as the sixteenth century drew to its close, events continued to push the Eastern trade away from its immemorial routes, and increasingly into one main channel, the perilous but possible sea-way which Vasco da Gama had opened up, rounding the Cape to India (1499). Portugal had succeeded to the primacy of Venice in navigation; and when Spain annexed Portugal (1580), the Dutch, who were in rebellion against Philip II, could no longer buy through Lisbon the spices and the rich stuffs their painters have made so familiar to posterity, and the ancient if loose alliance of England and Portugal finished. Spain considered it her business to be the hammer of all heretics, an ambition which brought her to grief when Holland managed to turn 'her despairing land-revolt into a triumphant oceanic war'.[1]

Between Elizabeth's accession (1558) and Cromwell's death (1658) a fiercely mercantile England hunted for markets, when necessary fighting for them. In 1579, Drake, circumnavigating the globe, reached the veritable Spice Islands, and set up rights of prior discovery which the East India Company, a generation later, were to try vainly to uphold against the monopolising Dutch. He was believed to have entered into treaty engagements with the King of Ternate; and his voyage was the

[1] Sir William Hunter, *A History of British India*, i. 237.

most conspicuous of many exploits that shook his countrymen free of
insularity. When he captured the *San Filippe* (1587), he secured papers
which fired imagination with their witness to the wealth that lay in
commerce with the Indies.

The year of Drake's reaching Ternate was also the year when the
first Englishman set foot in India proper. This was Thomas Stevens,
the Jesuit missionary, whose letters from Goa to his father are supposed
to have done much to arouse English eagerness for the eastward
attempt. Stevens relates the gravity and pomp with which the fleets of
Portugal went out:

' The setting forth from the port, I need not tell how solemn it is, with
trumpets and shooting of ordnance. You may easily imagine it, considering
that they go in the manner of war.'

His own voyage in one of these ships of Lisbon he thought a good one,
since out of a hundred and fifty sick only twenty-seven died.

But the English were to encounter even greater odds, held tres-
passers by Spain and Portugal, who claimed to hold the East in fee from
the Pope, and in the Spice Islands persecuted to death by the Dutch,
their nominal allies. Their ships were of slighter tonnage, in smaller
groups; they were learners and alone, where their predecessors had
stations and helpers along the route and an accumulation of knowledge:

' The English ships, though weatherly and heavily gunned, were small; if
food and water failed, as they often did when they kept the sea for any length
of time, it was chance work replenishing them; every port was armed and
hostile; every ship they met was an enemy and had to be fought or run from
(but the English seldom ran); to reach India was to sail into a nest of wasps;
they sailed as poachers and pirates and so were without the Law, and the
navigation was all sheer guess-work.' [1]

The right of trade with the Levant had been obtained from Sultan
Amurath (Murad) II, in 1579, and a Turkey Company had been formed
in England. In 1583 a ship called the *Tyger* was sent to endeavour to
open up commerce further east still, with India. How keenly men's
eyes were straining abroad we can see from Shakespeare's reference,
twenty years later (one which his audience, aware of that sailing's
significance, took as easily as we should take an allusion to any contemporary long-distance flight or an Everest expedition to-day):

' "Aroint thee, witch!" the rump-faced ronyon cries.
Her husband's to Aleppo gone, master of the *Tyger*.' [2]

[1] J. Courtenay Locke, *The First Englishmen in India*, 5-6.　　[2] *Macbeth*, I. iii. 6-7.

The *Tyger* took her merchants as near Aleppo as the sea permitted. Then five of them—John Eldred, John Newbery, Ralph Fitch, William Leeds and James Story—entered on the overland route to India, which was beset with 'defrauding Turks, blackmailing Arabs or stealthily obstructing Venetians'. Eldred,

' halted between Basra and Baghdad, was to be, as it were, the shaft of the spear, the other four its head thrusting forward into India. Though shaft and head came apart the thrust did in fact go home'.[1]

Portugal had locks at Basra and the Gulf's entry; at Ormuz, Newbery, Fitch, Leeds and Story were arrested, and reached India as prisoners. Here their countryman Stevens befriended them—a generous deed, seeing that he himself, if in England, would have been liable to a traitor's death. Leeds, whose craft of painter made him useful to decorate the numerous churches that Portuguese missionaries were building, became a monk. The other three, with a Dutch merchant's assistance, escaped: the jeweller Story entered Mogul service; Newbery got to Lahore and with 'sheer insolent courage' set off home across Persia, and we do not know what became of him; Fitch wandered over Ceylon and South India and to Burma, 'walking serenely into traps and out again',[2] reappearing in London in 1591. He and Eldred were present when eighty City merchants met in Founders' Hall, September 24, 1599, to establish the East India Company; the Company's Court Minutes contain the note (December 31, 1606):

' Letters to be obtained from King James to the King of Cambaya, governors of Aden, etc. . . . their titles to be enquired of Ralph Fitch.'

In shadow of the imposing fabric of the British *Raj* these foundations appear sordid. We went honourably, thinking it no shame to be merchants. But we are attacked as a folk who came as suppliants seeking leave to trade, and by devious ways of treachery became rulers of a distracted, peace-loving, helpless land. Yet the miracle is not that commerce ultimately expanded into empire, but that for such a vast of time we were traders and nothing else. Of all the European interloping nations we were the last and most reluctant to draw the sword, even in defence. Nor was the name of merchant synonymous, as seems to be suggested, with huckster. Our merchants walked and sailed through deaths Ulysses never knew, and did it with cool good-humour.

The *Tyger* bore Elizabeth's letter 'To the most invincible and most mighty Prince, Lord Zelabdim Echebar, King of Cambaia', stating

[1] Locke, 9.   [2] *Op. cit.* 12, 11.

frankly that trade was the aim. But no Company was formed until in
1599 the Dutch put up the price of pepper from three to six and eight
shillings a pound. Even more than for gold, men were ready to risk their
lives for spices:

‘ The Elizabethans lived on salt meat from autumn to spring; their fresh
meat was of poor quality in general; for the good of the fishermen the Law
compelled them to eat fish more often than they cared about, and with all this
insipid food their craving for pungent flavourings was probably and naturally much stronger than ours. They liked heavily spiced drinks, moreover,
for they had no tea.’ [1]

The East India Company was formed to traffic in the luxuries of the
rich, in spices, silks, gems, bezoar stones, camphor, indigo, sulphur.
Two centuries later, its wealth came through the amenities of the
middle classes; tea had supplanted pepper, cookery books now contained recipes for rice. A resolution was passed ‘not to employ any
gentleman in any place of charge’; and the Company requested to be

‘ allowed to sort their business with men of their own quality, lest the
suspicion of the employment of gentlemen being taken hold upon by the
generality, do drive a great number of the adventurers to withdraw their
contributions’.

There was suspicion of aristocratic disinterestedness and ability alike;
and, although members of the nobility adventured capital in the Company, the influx from what used to be considered the higher classes did
not become considerable until Wellesley’s time.

The first voyages were hardly towards ‘India’ at all (as we understand the term), but further eastward. A commission was granted to
Captain Lancaster, January 24, 1601, to voyage for the Company ‘at
their own adventures Costs and chardges as well as for the honour of this
Our Realme of Englande’. The Realm’s honour was to prove a long-
continuing hindrance. In accordance with the doctrine that to export
specie impoverished a country, Elizabeth gave leave to take only
£30,000, of which £6,000 must carry her arms and effigy,[2] tokens so
valueless that the Company petitioned her successor James for permission to take only £20,000, with no ‘English’ coins at all. Protests to
Elizabeth that her name was unknown in the Orient had been opposed
with the very proper reply that for this very reason these coins must be
used, to the end that her greatness might be blazed abroad.

Captain Lancaster sailed to Achin, in Sumatra, and returned on the

---

[1] *Op. cit.* 4.	[2] Warrant for coinage issued, January 11, 1603.

first Guy Fawkes day (November 5, 1603) with 1,030,000 lbs. of pepper, whose sale was forbidden until King James's own large private stocks [1] were disposed of. Alarmed and exasperated, the Company pointed out that they could not pay their mariners or risk a second voyage; and if they did not send another expedition, their factors [2] left with Eastern princes as hostages might be put to death. With their pepper unsold, they could not even discharge their customs dues to His Majesty. A compromise was arranged, by payment to influential persons. Captain Lancaster was knighted, and a second expedition set out under Henry Middleton, March 3, 1604. Between 1601 and 1618 nine voyages were made, mainly (at first exclusively) to the East Indies, not to India.

The exigencies of a commercial organisation working within a wide range of hazard required frankness of both employer and employed. The Company's correspondence is of unsurpassable interest and individuality. The irascibility of the Directors' sharp comments to their Bantam factors (March 11, 1607)—'at which ignorance of you, to buy such spices, we conceive the Indians do rejoice'—can be matched by the criticism of their agent at Jask (Persian Gulf), in December 1617:

' Touching the pieces and petronels you sent, you were much abused in them, for they were nothing near worth the money you paid for them per invoice. It seems also they took wet in bringing aboard, for many of them were so rusty that we were forced to work off all the damasking to make them clean.' [3]

After Japan was added to the Company's far-flung bazaar (in response to a letter[4] from that remarkable man William Adams, sent October 23, 1611, to 'his unknown friends and countrymen' and to ' the Worshipful Company' in particular), Richard Cocks wrote from that land (1617) that he was amid a people unable to appreciate good things:

' They esteem a painted sheet of paper with a horse, ship or a bird more than they do such a rich picture. Neither will anyone give sixpence for that fair picture of the Conversion of St. Paul.' [5]

The heathen's natural recalcitrance was perhaps heightened by the fact that Japan was passing through a great artistic period.

[1] Probably, as Sir William Foster surmises (*England's Quest of Eastern Trade*, 161), taken out of a Portuguese carrack captured the previous year.

[2] *Factors* is the name of only one rank in the Company's service. But for convenience we propose to use it to signify all their servants in the East.

[3] Sir William Foster, *Letters received by the East India Company*, vi. 279.

[4] *Op. cit.* i. 142 ff.　　　　　　　　　　[5] *Op. cit.* v. 49.

The Company started with separate voyages, changed to a modified joint stock (three voyages being covered by one subscription, in place of new subscriptions for every voyage) in 1614, and a permanent one, 1657. In 1609 their charter was renewed and the monopoly of Eastern trade made theirs in perpetuity. More of the nobility risked capital. Profits, 'though irregular, had been large'.[1] The Company on the whole were 'gentle masters', and their servants in return were zealous and honest in collecting and collating information. Strict cleanliness on shipboard, in which the Dutch were held up as far superior, was enjoined repeatedly, and all were warned to be watchful: 'still expecting and fearing evil, though there be no cause'; 'suspect all, how friendly soever they seem'.

Captain Lancaster had sold iron, tin, lead, and exchanged specie for spices; the woollen goods for which England was so anxious to find a vent, now and later, proved almost unsaleable in a tropical climate, and wasted away in godowns. In 1608 the Company's factors in Bantam and the Moluccas wrote pointing out that the people there were big purchasers of Indian calicoes. To obtain these, to exchange for specie, a trading post in India was essential. Permission was obtained from the Emperor Jahangir, 1608, to settle at Surat, the chief port of Western India; the Portuguese, however, were still too powerful for the leave to become effectual until 1612. Sir Henry Middleton attempted to open up a Red Sea trade; was received with apparent friendliness, but enticed ashore, where his company were taken prisoners (after several had been killed). He himself and a few others presently escaped to their ships, and blockaded Mocha, whose governor received such missives as this (May 18, 1611), in reply to his efforts to placate Middleton and persuade him to sail away without recovering the rest of his men:

'... If you advise the Basha, as you say you will, what is that to me? I am no subject of the Basha's but a servant to the King of England, besides whom I will not be commanded by any king under heaven. And for the referring of matters to the hearing of our betters, as you say, at Constantinople, I know my cause so good that I hope to have remedy against you, but you dare never show your face there. You sent me by the bearer, Nahuda Mahomet, a foolish paper, what it is I know not, nor care not. In God is my trust, and therefore respect not what the devil or you can do with your charms.

At present I cease and rest

As you shall deserve

HENRY MIDDLETON.

' This is all interpreted to the bearer right as it is written.'[2]

---

[1] P. E. Roberts, *History of British India*, 26.   [2] Foster, *Letters*, i. 116.

England does not yet know the quality of the seamen who in the discouraging days of James carried on the Elizabethan tradition. The Company was superbly served. Middleton revenged both his own Arabian imprisonment and the unwillingness of the Surat authorities to allow the factory for which Jahangir had given consent, by holding up traffic between Gujarat and the Red Sea in 1611. Next year Captain Best gave the Portuguese the first of several sound drubbings off Swally, close to Surat. The Mogul Empire, helpless at sea, took note of the new naval power hopefully, willing to think it a match for the Portuguese, against whom it had many grievances. The factory was established that year. In 1614 and 1615, Nicholas Downton [1] won yet greater victories off Swally, announcing his success in a despatch as honourable to its writer as its news:

' The Guzerats ready to embrace a peace upon a parley with the Portugals, doubting of our success; for the force of the Portugals was great, insomuch that it would not have gone well with us if God had favoured their cause. I never see men fight with greater resolution than the Portugals; therefore not to be taxed with cowardice as some have done. . . . If the Portugals had not fallen into an error at the first they might have destroyed the *Hope*, and by likelihood the rest hastening so to her aid. They renew their strength again within ten days; we feared new dangers and prepared accordingly. They set upon us by fireworks. The Portugals with all their power departed from us and went before the bar of Surat. We were afraid they would set up their rest against the town; but they were wiser. Much quicksilver lost for want of good packing. The ships' muskets break like glass; the cocks and hammers of snaphances evilly made. The false making of sold pieces hath disgraced them. The axletrees of your great ordnance made of brittle wood. The tracks must be turned when the timber is seasoned. Match too scanty. Want of iron chains to lay upon our cables to keep them from cutting. Defect in our flesh; our oil most part run out; our meal also spoiled by green casks; so of our pease and oatmeal. No scales nor weights. Much of our beer cast overboard, being put into bad casks.' [2]

The wrath against 'interlopers' [3]—which persisted long after the Company's solely trading days—was justified in the seventeenth century. Efforts in isolation would have been doomed, in seas swarming with enemies. Moreover, the Company were naturally held responsible

[1] He died (1615) 'lamented, admired and unequalled': Orme, *Fragments*, 356.

[2] Foster, *Letters*, 186-7.

[3] English traders who did not belong to the Company's service.

for the acts of all Englishmen,[1] in a period when piracy was the crime commonest in these distant waters. England abounded in skilful seamen, trained in the prolonged wars with Spain and now 'out of a job', thanks to the peace King James was resolute to keep. Sir Thomas Roe, the Company's first ambassador at the Mogul Court, warns his employers (February 14, 1618): [2]

' That these seas begin to be full of rovers, for whose faults we may be engaged. Sir Robert Rich and one Philip Barnardoe set out two ships to take pirates, which is grown a common pretence of being pirates. They missed their entrance into the Red Sea (which was their design) and came for India, gave chase to the Queen Mother's junk, and, but that God sent in our fleet, had taken and rifled her. If they had prospered in their ends, either at Mocha or here, your goods and our persons had answered it. I ordered the seizure of the ships, prizes and goods, and converted them to your use; and must now tell you, if you be not round in some course with these men, you will have the seas full and your trade in India is utterly lost and our lives exposed to pledge in the hands of Moors. I am loath to lie in irons for any man's fault but mine own. I love Sir Robert Rich well, and you may be pleased to do him any courtesy in restitution, because he was abused; but I must say, if you give way, you give encouragement. I had rather make him any present in love than restore anything in right.'

Rich (afterwards Earl of Warwick) was too powerful an offender to be easily penalised. The seizure of his ships led to prolonged dispute; his claim to £20,000 compensation was finally referred to arbitration.

But the Company, though looking austerely on piracy they had not authorised, themselves picked up quick profits by 'rummaging' ships to which their Portuguese rivals had given passes; and we have seen that in their difference with the Governor of Mocha they held up ships from India.

The disadvantages of being represented solely by merchants (a profession which the Mogul Court despised) grew grievous. The Company's first envoys to the Central Government at Agra were unable to stand against the constant objection of the Portuguese that they and their employers were men of lowly rank. The prejudice against gentlemen was reconsidered; in 1615 Sir Thomas Roe, courtier, sent as the Company's and King James's ambassador, entered on four years' magnificent service at the capital of a monarch casual and drunken and on occasion

---

[1] For an account of a piracy (it can be styled nothing else) actually done by an East India Company ship and costing the Company dear in the end, see Thomas Herbert, *Travels in Persia*, 276-7 (edited by Sir William Foster).

[2] Sir William Foster, *The Embassy of Sir Thomas Roe to India*, 451.

indescribably cruel, who had one question only, what presents he brought or could procure in the future. Roe's solemn, stiff demeanour invited impish treatment, such as the Empress's prank when she sent to his bed at midnight a female slave who had offended, 'a grave woeman of 40 years'. Jahangir when liberally inclined would send a male male-factor or a wild boar (tusks to be returned); in June 1616, Roe (whom his employers expected to be liberally rewarded by imperial munificence) noted that his accessions from this source had been 'hoggs flesh, deare, a theefe, and a whore'.[1] But the Court learnt that 'the English were not all obsequious merchants or rough sailors'. He failed to obtain the ex-plicit contracts he worked for, a treaty on Western lines being 'an idea utterly alien to the political system of the Moguls';[2] but his chaplain, Edward Terry, claimed not unfairly, that he was 'a Joseph in the court of Pharaoh, for whose sake all his nation seemed to fare the better', despite the Company's meanness:

' frugality prescribed his allowances, his retinue, and even the present to the Mogul, with little conformity to the sumptuous prejudices of the most magni-ficent court in the universe'.[3]

He was heedless of safety, comfort or esteem, of spirit nobly disdainful as Doughty's when he wandered poor and unfriended among Bedouins.

Roe's *Journal* and correspondence show up not only his integrity but his far-sightedness. The Company were extraordinarily lucky in such a representative. He could write with high controlled indignation to the Emperor himself or his favourite son (afterwards Shah Jahan). His letter of October 19, 1615, to the Governor of Surat, is eloquent of his cruel perplexities and his character and courage:

' The injuries you have offered me, contrary to the faith given by your King, to all civility and law of nations, being a free Ambassador, and con-trary to your own honour and promise, forceth me to send you word I am resolved not to endure it. I come hither not to beg, nor do nor suffer injury. I serve a King that is able to revenge whatsoever is dared to be done against his subjects. . . . I am sorry for nothing but that ever I vouchsafed to send you any remembrance of me, of whom in love you might have received anything, but by this course, of me, nor my nation, I am resolved you shall never get one pice; assuring you I am better resolved to die upon an enemy than to flatter him, and for such I give you notice to take me until your master hath done me justice.'

[1] *Op. cit.* 155.   [2] Foster, *The English Factories in India*, 1618-21, viii.
[3] Orme, *Historical Fragments*, 362.

He saw through the imposing façade of Mogul pomp, saying of Jahangir, in often-quoted words:

' His greatness substantially is not in itself, but in the weakness of his neighbours, whom like an overgrown pike he feeds on as fry. Pride, pleasure, and riches are their best description. Honesty and truth, discipline, civility, they have none, or very little.'

Not least of Roe's perplexities was his knowledge that all his proud carriage was bluff. Behind the English Company was only the cowardly foreign policy of James I.

Every year it became clearer that the Company's destiny was restriction eastward and expansion westward. The trade with Japan amounted to very little; soon that country relapsed into savage xenophobia. The English were to be driven bloodily and ignominiously from the Spice Islands by the Dutch, whose whole Republic

' was virtually an association for the purposes of navigation and trade; the Dutch companies were connected organically with the constitution of the States General. And since in Holland the people at large were merchants and mariners, their commercial policy was stronger, more stiffly resolute, and better supported than that of States ruled by a Court and a landed aristocracy whose aims and interests were diverse and conflicting.' [1]

Roe noted their errors, as viewed from his own employers' rigid standpoint of merchants:

' A war and traffic are incompatible. By my consent, you shall no way engage yourselves but at sea, where you are like to gain as often as to lose. It is the beggaring of the Portugal, notwithstanding his many rich residences and territories, that he keeps soldiers that spends it; yet his garrisons are mean. He never profited by the Indies, since he defended them. Observe this well. It hath been also the error of the Dutch, who seek plantation here by the sword. They turn a wonderful stock, they prowl in all places, they possess some of the best; yet their dead pays consume all the gain. Let this be received as a rule that, if you will profit, seek it at sea, and in quiet trade; for without controversy it is an error to affect garrisons and land wars in India.'

The Dutch were too strong for their nominal allies, whom they pressed steadily and ruthlessly out of Far Eastern seas. The English Company had no choice but to withdraw from a struggle for which they were not yet ready. Meanwhile, it was with the Portuguese, whose

[1] Sir Alfred Lyall, *The Rise and Expansion of the British Dominion in India* (5th ed.), 26.

waning power Roe contemptuously and accurately assessed,[1] that they first came to grips, both off India and in the Persian Gulf.

European nations kept no peace east of Egypt. But (especially when he began to plan a Spanish marriage for his son), King James's policy was peace, and at any price. Roe, under instructions from him, on October 20, 1615, sent the Portuguese Viceroy at Goa a missive which he seems to have considered conciliatory. It reminded the recipient of the repeated thrashings his people had experienced in Elizabeth's time, and warned him that worse would come if they did not eagerly promise to amend their ways now. It was signed 'Your friend or enemy at your own choice, Tho. Roe'; and was unacknowledged and unanswered. The year following this menacing overture, Roe persuaded the Company to open up trade in the Gulf. This involved the extirpation of the Portuguese from these regions, a task begun by Captain Shilling, another of the fine seamen England had available for exploits which the historic muse scarcely noted even in their doing. He won victories off Jask, December 16 and 28, 1620, dying of his wounds, January 6, after lingering 'very godly and patient';

' Here lies buried one Captain Shilling, unfortunately slain by the insulting Portugall: but that his bones want sense and expression, they would tell you the earth is not worthy his receptacle, and that the people are blockish, rude, treacherous and indomitable.' [2]

The Portuguese, seeking to prevent English entry of the Gulf, had begun the actual fighting. Furthermore, the Shah made an alliance with the Company against Portugal a condition of permitting trade, and demanded naval assistance in reducing Ormuz, the island which locks the Gulf. This was provided with deep misgivings. Ralegh's execution was a recent memory to make men wish to proceed cautiously in hostility to Spain, whose Infanta was being wooed by the Prince of Wales. It is amazing that the expedition was ever undertaken; hardly less amazing that it was carried through with impunity. The Indian factors, grumbling and disgruntled men, had some reason for their complaint:

' Indeed (to speak truth) that enterprise was not well entertained on our parts, except upon more certain grounds and better conditions to have enjoyed the command thereof, and not to dispossess Christianity (although our enemies) to place in faithless Moors, which cannot but be much displeasing to Almighty God.'

[1] Roe had been a distinguished seaman and explorer himself, sailing to the West Indies and South America for Henry Prince of Wales and the imprisoned Sir Walter Ralegh. He knew by experience how weak Spain and Portugal were.

[2] Epitaph by the traveller, Thomas Herbert (1606-82).

However, Ormuz was taken, mainly thanks to the Company's naval assistance; in one of the subsidiary actions, the capture of Kishm, the Arctic explorer William Baffin was slain:

'Master Baffin went on shore with his Geometrical Instruments, for the taking the height and distance of the Castle wall, for the better levelling of his Piece to make his shot; but as he was about the same, he received a small shot from the Castle into his belly, wherewith he gave three leaps (by report) and died immediately.' [1]

Persia broke her engagements, the English foolishly handing over the fort; the partial exception in a general dishonouring of engagements was the Shah's promise of half the customs of Gombroon (Bandar Abbas), a concession more evaded than fulfilled, causing constant friction for half a century to come, and dissatisfaction after that. The Dutch, following swiftly into the place of the dispossessed Portuguese, flatly refused to pay duties bringing benefit to their English rivals. The campaign's profits were illusory for the Company, which had acted as the Shah's catspaw; yet Ormuz, still a glittering name when Milton wrote a generation later, had a sheen which cost it dear, for Buckingham, Lord High Admiral, and King James ('Did I deliver you from the complaint of the Spaniard, and do you return me nothing!') each took £10,000 as their tenth of a mythical £100,000 loot. Moreover, this defeat, with the justifiable resentment it engendered, roused the Portuguese as the Swally skirmishes had not done. De Andrade Ruy Freire, their commander taken at Ormuz, escaped in India; he was a seaman of ability, and his exploits, during ten years of peril and not infrequent defeat, were a powerful means of turning the Company's mind towards an enduring peace.

Nevertheless, England's long and honourable record in the Gulf, 'the most unselfish page in history',[2] had begun.

Roe took his duties seriously, as representative of a mercantile company as well as of the King. To avoid draining specie out of England, he urged the capture of the Red Sea traffic ('you must eat the Guzerats out of that trade'); then specie could be obtained from Egyptian merchants in exchange for spices and assorted English and Indian goods. The specie would purchase calicoes in India, which sold readily in the Indies whence spices came, and were already growing popular in England. In fine, he acted much as many think modern consuls should, as trade adviser.

[1] *Purchas His Pilgrimes* (J. MacLehose, 1905), x. 339.
[2] Lord Curzon's speech to trucial chiefs of the Gulf, November 21, 1903.

This led to trouble immediately. By buying up the Gujarat calicoes the Company spoiled Surat's Red Sea traffic; by bringing in Red Sea coral, an importation forbidden to foreigners and kept as a monopoly of Indian traders, they struck it again. This whole Middle Eastern trade was the theme of exceedingly irascible passages between Roe and the Mogul authorities, spreading prejudice in the mind of the Emperor, and still more of his son who was to succeed him as Shah Jahan. It was nevertheless persisted in, being far too valuable to be dropped.

Having demonstrated their naval importance, the Company were able to sell passes, a primitive form of insurance. This system, a source of profit to Portuguese and Dutch also, led to natural irritation when Powers warring among themselves molested shipping which had been granted passes by their rivals.

While India's western approaches were year by year being opened up to their vessels, the Company was losing ground in the Spice Islands, their original market and aim. So long as Spain remained a menace, the Dutch needed British support. But as Spain grew pitifully helpless, the Hollanders, whose mariners were skilled and brave and whose ships were in greater force than the English, chased and sank their allies whenever they could. No doubt the English have earned their reputation for 'imperialism'; but for imperialism at its most ruthless we must go to the Indies and the Dutch record. They beat down native chiefs into granting trade monopolies, and strove to set in force a monopoly whether a grant had been made or not; and

' by fortifying themselves in the place wherever they settle, and then standing upon their guard, put a kind of force upon the natives to sell them their commodities'.[1]

Friction came to war (1618-20) so open and embarrassing that both home governments had at last to take note of it. Roe warned his employers (1618) that the Dutch

' wrong you in all parts and grow to insufferable insolencies. If we fall foul here, the common enemy will laugh and reap the fruit of our contention. There must a course be taken at home, which, by His Majesty's displeasure signified, were not difficult, if he knew how they traduce his name and royal authority, rob in English colours to scandal his subjects, and use us worse than any brave enemy would, or any other but unthankful drunkards that we have relieved from cheese and cabbage, or rather, from a chain with bread and water. You must speedily look to this maggot; else we talk of the Portugal, but these will eat a worm in your sides'.

[1] Edward Terry (Roe's chaplain), *A Voyage to East India* (1777 ed.), 105-6.

The scorn and detestation manifest in these words was no mere jingo-ism, but throughout the seventeenth century was felt fiercely by some of the noblest Englishmen. Holland was the only enemy that stirred the magnanimous spirit of Andrew Marvell to anger.

James Mill strives to set out the imaginable justification of the crowning brutality, when in 1623 ten Englishmen and nine Japanese were arrested, tortured into alleged confession of conspiracy to seize the Dutch fort of Amboyna and assassinate the Governor, and executed with insult and cruelty. The justification amounts to nothing at all; the plot was a figment of savage imbecility and cowardice:

' there were only twenty Englishmen all told on the island, and they unarmed civilians, while of the Dutch there were from four to five hundred, and half of them soldiers in garrison, besides eight large ships in the roadstead'.[1]

No redress could be hoped for under the Stuarts, but wrath smouldered until Cromwell in 1654 obtained under arbitration some belated pecuniary compensation. The outrage, coming as the culmination of years of mounting treachery and enmity, made official war inevitable whenever England found less pusillanimous rulers; as surely as any single deed ever did, it precipitated the clash of nations.

This date, 1623, serves conveniently to indicate the ousting of the English from all but precarious footing in the East Indies, and the sink-ing of the Portuguese star. The Mogul Empire, too, was decaying and had entered on the century and a half of gradual disintegration which was ultimately to bring English, French, and Marathas face to face as contestants for India's sovereignty. The Company, aware of defeat east-ward and with victory of doubtful value won in Persia, held in India six trading stations: Agra, Ahmadabad, Berhampur in Khandesh, Broach, Masulipatam, Surat. Though they clung still to Malaya, with factories at Bantam (Java) and Bencoolen (Sumatra), their face was now turned to India's mainland and away from the islands. They had won a place by the tenacity and valour of their seamen and great ambassador, and had shown the individuality and open fearless dealing which have been the strength of the English in India. Ten years of eclipse were to follow, under nerveless and hesitant men; but the virtue which had gone to their establishment was sufficient to endure until in William Methwold another man arose who could conserve what remained and rebuild the impaired foundations.

[1] *D.N.B.*, article *Gabriel Towerson.*

CHAPTER II

ERA OF PORTUGUESE AND DUTCH RIVALRY

*Company's weakness and difficulties: interference with Indian Red Sea traffic:
famine in India: further victories at Swally: Dutch pressure on Portuguese:
William Methwold: negotiations with Viceroy at Goa: deterioration of internal
polity of Mogul Empire: civil war in England: pirates in Eastern waters:
Methwold's courage: Courteen's Association: 'Golden Farman' from King of
Golconda: changes in character of trade: Malabar pirates: attempts to get footing
in Bengal: coffee and tea: opening up of China trade: internal discipline of Company settlements: Company begins to fortify, at Masulipatam amd Madras:
foundation of Fort St. George: miseries due to English civil war: execution of
Charles I and resulting embarrassments: war with Dutch: quarrels with Mir
Jumla.*

THE factors, who had never relished either Roe's social superiority or
his stiff self-esteem, crabbed his achievement. But his insistence that to
seek territory or fortify was to imitate the uneconomic methods of Portuguese and Dutch was remembered; the Company remained for over a
century essentially a trading concern. Yet the seeds of inconsistency lay
dormant in his other advice, that even merchants could not succeed unless respected because they could enforce respect. 'Assure you', he told
his employers, 'I know these people are best treated with the sword in
one hand and caducean in the other'. Exercised in the naval hand, the
sword entailed the minimum of expense and entanglement. He wrote
(same date: February 14, 1618) to Captain Pring: 'Until we show ourselves a little rough and busy, they will not be sensible'.

It may seem incredible that after Amboyna the English Company
should have continued in 'alliance' with the Dutch, their executioners.
Yet they did. They were so inferior that the alliance was ludicrously unequal. The factors, petty bickering men, merely grumbled; and sought
to hide their loss of prestige in such consolation as the report that the
Tanjore Raja

' having heard the English to be a peaceable nation that seek not to incroach
on other men's territories, was earnest with him'—one Johnson—'to move
into us the favourable opinion he had of our nation and great desire that we
should trade in his dominions. . . . The Dutch have been earnest suitors to the
Naik to fortify in his country, and begun a fort at Tinegapatam; but the Naik
refuseth to have them live in his country, and hath demolished what they had
begun, saying he hath heard how they incroached upon other princes'
dominions and countries, and therefore should not live in his'.

B

So wrote President and Council from Batavia, where they had to abide under the black shadow of Dutch vigour and insolency.

It was true; the Dutch were fortifying—they were exercising all the prerogatives of sovereign power. In their Coromandel station at Masulipatam they even enforced Christian morality, beheading both parties to any irregular union of European and native. The English Company remained sojourners seeking trade alone; they frowned on factors who sought to imitate Dutch pomp and official extravagance; not until 1618 would they extend to even their representative at Surat the Dutch title of 'President'.

The decade following Ormuz and Amboyna was one of poverty and waxing difficulty. Local governors grew more rapacious and faithless, and weaker as protectors. In 1630 came almost unprecedented famine, which did not materially lighten for nearly two years. Both from Indian and European sources comes abundant evidence of its severity:

' an universal dearth over all this continent, of whose like in these parts no former age hath record; the country being wholly dismantled by drought, and to those that were not formerly provided no grain for either man or beast to be purchased for money, though at sevenfold the price of former times accustomed; the poor mechaniques, weavers, washers, dyers, etc., abandoning their habitacions in multitudes, and instead of relief elsewhere have perished in the fields for want of food to sustain them. . . . This direful time of dearth and the King's continued wars with the Deccans disjointed all trade out of frame; the former calamity having filled the ways with desperate multitudes, who, setting their lives at nought, care not what they enterprise so they may but purchase means for feeding, and will not dispense with the nakedest passenger, not so much as our poor pattamars with letters, who, if not murthered on the way, do seldom escape unrifled, and thereby our advices often miscarried on the other side'.[1]

' In these parts there may not be any trade expected this three years. No man can go in the streets but must resolve to give great alms or be in danger of being murdered, for the poor people cry with a loud voice: "Give us sustenance or kill us".' [2]

Dutch and Portuguese were at war; but not English and Portuguese, except in the irregular fashion of the Indies. This fashion, in October 1630, resulted in a completion of the sea-victories by a land triumph

[1] President and Council, Surat, to the Company, December 31, 1630 (Foster, *English Factories*, 1630-1633, 122).

[2] A Dutch factor, Surat, to a member of the Dutch Council, Batavia, December 21, 1631 (*op. cit.* 181).

behind Swally. The English pretended to disperse, 'and marcht about the sandhills'; suddenly uniting, they attacked the Portuguese in imagined safety with their ships close inshore:

' But ours very providently perceiving that but three of their prows could offend them, and these also so ill plied as, for fear of their own, they could not well damnify our people, they fiercely entered amongst them and in the very face of their vessels pursued them into the water chin deep; where with admirable resolution they so prosecuted their fury that even to the frigates' sides they continued the slaughter; and having massacred the greater part, whereof many by small shot and others at handy blows with their swords and musket stocks, returned with a glorious victory and 27 Portingals brought off alive their prisoners.'

English naval prowess was known already; but this was a notable military conquest, achieved with the loss of one very fat man who died of his exertions and of some wounded who recovered—achieved, moreover,

' in the sight of divers Moguls and other these country people, who, in admiration of so strange a manner of fight, have dispersed their letters both to the court and several parts of this kingdom, and were pleased to aver the like battle to have never been seen, heard of, or ever read of in stories'. [1]

These were unhappy times for the Portuguese. The Dutch were ejecting them from the East Indies, Malacca, Ceylon. Shah Jahan, the first Emperor rootedly unfriendly to aliens, succeeded Jahangir.[2] He began hostilities, 1631; and after three months' siege captured their settlement at Hugli, Bengal. More than 4000 prisoners were put to death (refusing the alternative of changing their faith) with Mogul barbarity. Distracted and terrified, Portugal looked about to effect some diminution in the number of her assailants; and remembered her ancient alliance with England, from which she had been warped by annexation to Spain.

In November 1633, after years of fumbling and nerveless administration, the East India Company's affairs again passed under a man of genuine greatness of mind and spirit, William Methwold, the greatest Englishman in India before Clive. He sounded the Jesuits, who had frequent occasion to pass through the English settlement, and they acted as intermediaries. In March, 1634, the Portuguese Viceroy at Goa replied frankly that the recently concluded Treaty of Madrid did not (he thought) apply to the Indies, but suggested an armistice pending word

[1] Letter from Surat to the Company, December 31, 1630.   [2] In 1627.

from Europe; should that prove unfavourable, there might be a longish interval before hostilities were resumed. Methwold then led an embassy, which was received at New Goa with gratifying courtesy, and at Goa by the Viceroy himself. Common dislike and dread of the Netherlanders had wrought to bring the belligerents together.

The truce thus made (1635), after Portugal regained her independance (1640), passed into official peace secured by treaty (1642). The new Viceroy who came in 1635 did not love the English, but explained to his master King Philip that one enemy was preferable to two. Neither truce nor peace was ever really broken; despite rubs and grievances good relations were set up. The English obtained the use of Portuguese roadsteads; the Portuguese could now transport wares not infrequently to Macao and Malacca in English ships, which were normally less liable to stoppage and search by the Dutch.

Though the Portuguese wars were over, other shadows were falling across the Company's course. Shah Jahan, fiercely hostile to the Portuguese, was displeased at this cessation of Anglo-Portuguese bickering; the Shah, too, disapproved. Both these monarchs preferred to wage their quarrels by proxy. The Mogul Empire's internal administration was steadily deteriorating. Company caravans were looted; Company agents were murdered without hope of redress, the reply that the robbers were rebels or Rajputs being deemed adequate defence, whether they were or not. Private trading, always persistent, was now luxuriant. When many employees served for paltry pay or none at all, irregular pickings and the excitement of the possibility of these were the main part of life. Disciplinary action was strongly and openly resented, especially by the seamen.

The Company was doing a considerable carrying trade—doubtfully sanctioned by the Committees, since it enabled Indian merchants to compete, using the Company as wings for transport and protection. When, in June, 1631, a native merchant's goods are found marked with the Company's name, we seem to find ourselves peering into Clive's age. Of course traders wishing to pass their wares under foreign colour would bribe local factors or supervisors to wink at the sleight.

More disturbing yet, Charles and his Parliament were drawing into the long vortex leading to the Niagara of civil war. The King, aware that much of his opponents' strength was in these upstart London merchants, was unfriendly to the Company. Two vessels, the *Roebuck* and the grimly misnamed *Samaritan*, in April, 1635, sailed eastward with his privateering commission. They plundered Surat Indian ships that had

Company passes, and a Portuguese ship similarly insured, torturing the captain and crew of the latter to make them reveal their treasure. The French were making their first appearance (as pirates) in Red Sea and East African waters, so that when this news reached India Methwold hoped that the report of his own countrymen's responsibility would prove false. With characteristic courage he went immediately (April 6, 1636) to the Governor of Surat, whom he found in actual durbar with the chief sufferers: [1]

' I found a sad assembly of dejected merchants, some looking through me with eyes sparkling with indignation, others half dead in the sense of their losses; and so I sat a small time with a general silence, until the Governor brake it by enquiring what ships were lately arrived and from whence, what ships of ours were yet abroad and where, and what was become in our opinion of that one ship which we had so many months since reported to expect out of England.'

Methwold's reply betrayed his ignorance; the Governor

' told me what had happened about Aden, and instantly produced volumes of letters which did all bear witness that an English ship or pinnace had taken the *Tofakee* belonging to this port of Surat and more particularly to Merza Mahmud, a known friend to our nation, as also the *Mahmudee* of Diu. So that now the whole company (which had all this while bit in their anger) mouthed at once a general invective against me and the whole English nation; which continued some time with such a confusion as I knew not to whom to address myself unto to give a reply, until they had run themselves out of breath'.

He and his companion were imprisoned for eight weeks, broken by an interval under surveillance in his own house. The *Roebuck* was caught by a Company's ship at the Comoro Islands, July 1636, but handled delicately because of her King's commission: only part of her booty was recovered.

Charles further gave a charter to a rival group of London merchants, Sir William Courteen's Association, in 1635. They asserted that this involved no interference with the existing Company's trade, and that they would not settle where the latter had factories already, a promise which was very casually observed. The inconvenience and loss of prestige to the Company were immense. ' Squire Courteen's' people, ignorant of the rules of the game, did things that incensed the Portuguese afresh; only Methwold's tact and unfailing courtesy [2] smoothed the

---

[1] Foster, *E. Factories*, 1634-1636, 232 ff.

[2] See F. C. Danvers, *The Portuguese in India*, ii. 243.

trouble over. It was not until 1657 that the mischievous competition was ended by a union.

Bantam in 1630 lost its primacy to Surat, but for some time longer retained control of the struggling and ill-supported stations on the Coromandel coast. These the Company sought to strengthen. In 1634 they obtained from the King of Golconda the famous 'Golden Farman', so named from

' its bearing "the King's great seal, impressed upon a leaf of gold"—possibly also with reference to the valuable nature of its contents' [1]

(though these were summarised by the Bantam President and Council, May 8, 1635, as 'worthless privileges' and their agent censured for his extravagance and pomp, 'two flags and many pikes with pendants, and needless horses, etc.'). The Golconda monarch, 'of his great love to the valiant and honourable Captain Joyce and all the English', freely gave 'that under the shadow of me the King they shall set down at rest and in safety', an assurance repeated in 1639. Unfortunately, this was not easy to accomplish. A good deal was rotten in the state of Golconda; a typical complaint is this:

' The loss we have sustained by these Bramons, by unrecoverable debtors fled to their protection, monies exacted from ourselves and servants, and cloth violently taken from our washers, will amount to little less than four thousand pagodas. And all the remedy our often solicitings at court and elsewhere hath procured is a firman lately come down from His Majesty, wherein the chief kindlers of all these injuries are appointed judges of our cause: the event thereof may easily be conjectured.' [2]

In 1636, Aurangzeb, a boy of eighteen already deeply hostile to all foreigners, and especially Christians, became Viceroy of the Deccan, and the Mogul Empire's steady pressure southward began. His siege of Golconda, 1656, failed, but its extinction was achieved in 1687. *Farmans* from Central Indian kingdoms became worthless.

Bantam was made independent of Surat, 1633, but retained control of the chief Coromandel factory, Masulipatam—where the English, doubly influenced by the Dutch (in its connection with Java, and by the Dutch Company's presence at Masulipatam and Pulicat), were grossly extravagant and imitated the Hollanders' overbearing manners. Fortified by instructions from home, Methwold took Coromandel under his own authority, 1636; the East India Company's affairs in the Malayan Islands become henceforward separate from the purpose of this book.

[1] Foster, *E. Factories*, 1634-1636, xxxiv.   [2] September 26, 1637.

The famine of 1630 caused a dearth of cloth, the weavers having nearly all died. Bengal, which had escaped lightly, beckoned as the only possible source of supply. From 1630 onwards, there were persistent attempts to establish factories in Orissa and Bengal, to gather up silks and cottons from this one comparatively unravaged region, and to benefit by the abnormal prices of rice, ghi, sugar. The famine thus brought the Company into the coastal trade, since communication from Surat had to be by sea, in the disturbed state of the interior. This began a new peril, and many of their ships fell to the Arab and Maratha pirates of the western shores. Both the Company and Courteen's Association suffered losses. Small country-built ships—of which by 1640 the Company had many—were in constant peril. A typical disaster occurred in November, 1638, when the Malabar craft were enabled to draw up by reason of a dead calm,

' insomuch they perceived our ship could not work any way with her sails, they handed their sails and immediately rew all together on board us and lashed fast, notwithstanding we placed ever shot into them and spoiled many of their people. Being lashed on board, they entered their men in abundance, the which we used all means possible to clear; but finding them so resolutely bent, and still encreasing so abundantly, I resolved to blow up our upper deck, and effected it with the loss of not one of our people, yet some hurt, and divers of theirs (namely, the Malabars) slain and maimed. This seemed little or nothing to diminish or quell their courage; but we still continued to defend the opposing enemy by murthering and wounding each other, they being so resolute that they would not step aside from the muzzle of our ordnance when we fired upon them but immediately, being fired, heave in whole buckets of water; insomuch that in the conclusion we were forced to betake ourselves unto the gundeck, upon which we had but two pieces of ordnance. They then cutting with axes the deck over our heads, and hearing the hideous noise and cry of such a multitude, we thought how to contrive a way to send them to their great adorer Beelzebub, which was by firing all our powder at one blast, as many of us as were left alive leaping into the sea, yet intercepted (some) by those divelish hellhounds. We were at that present English 23 (being all wounded, four excepted), blacks 4, and Javaes 4; slain, English 5, Javaes 3, and blacks 13'.[1]

The factories at Hariharpur in Orissa and Balasore in Bengal, established in 1633, struggled on, until a friendly Mogul Governor appointed Gabriel Boughton, a ship's surgeon, his medical attendant in 1645. The tradition that this same Boughton in 1636 healed the Emperor's daughter Jahanara after she had been burned, though mistaken, is old

[1] Foster, E. Factories, 1637-1641, 138 ff.

and respectable, as is the story that he asked no reward except trading rights in Bengal for his people. At any rate, he proved a benefactor to his countrymen, winning prestige which he exercised unselfishly.

Not only was the Company building up local traffic in foodstuffs; in the Gulf and Red Sea it entered the coffee trade, and the factors learnt the excellence of this beverage. In this, as in so many good habits, Oxford led the way; 'a Jew named Jacob opened a coffee-shop in that city in 1649',[1] a Greek following suit in Cornhill three years later. The date of the first notified exportation from India is 1658; in 1659 the Dutch East India Company 'ordered a consignment of coffee for trial, saying that it was beginning to be in demand, especially in England'. The new drink quickly made its way, till the coffee-houses of Dryden's age took the place of the Mermaid and other famous taverns of Ben Jonson's age—

' the Sun,
The Dog, the Triple Tun'.

Another social change began to cast its coming shadow. Pepys, on September 25, 1660, 'did send for a cup of tee (a China drink) of which I never had drank before'.

The factories were destined to become *entrepôts* for Far Eastern commodities as well. Peace with Portugal opened up the attractions of the China trade through Macao; and, since England was usually at least in official amity with Holland, and in any case was far stronger at sea than Portugal, the latter country's nationals found it convenient to send merchandise on East India Company ships. The English could hardly be expected to convey the goods of others past the Dutch prowling and patrolling Malayan seas, without becoming principals in the commerce themselves. Methwold sent an expedition to Macao (April 9, 1635), to bring back gold, pearls, curios, silk, musk, lignum, aloes, camphor, benzoin; and, if there were room, alum, China roots, porcelain, brass, green ginger, sugar and sugar candy. Since the new trade must be carried on in some manner of partnership with the Portuguese, he gave instructions worth quoting as exemplifying the wisdom and tolerance which marked almost all he did. The merchants would get permission to live on shore at Macao, 'to which purpose you shall take a house, and cohabit lovingly together':[2]

' And that no scandal may be given or taken in point of religion (wherein

[1] Foster and Ethel Bruce Sainsbury, *Court Minutes*, 1655-59, xxxiv.
[2] Foster, *E. Factories*, 1634-1636, 105.

that nation is very tender) let your exercises of devotion be constant but private, without singing of psalms, which is nowhere permitted unto our nation in the King of Spain's dominions, except in embassadors' houses.'

A Chinese document exists, which notes that in 1636 'four vessels of barbarians with red hair' arrived from abroad.[1] In this description we may identify our own countrymen, new to Macao.

Almost from the first, the heads of the factories kept much state. Company employees lived and ate together; there were daily prayers; the President was supposed to admonish the younger members. It is often stated that no capital jurisdiction was exercised, either over Englishmen or foreign dependants; and it is true that each successive commission limited the scope of such jurisdiction by keeping it as strictly as possible to cases of murder and piracy. But the steady accrual of authority to Surat (after the disastrous decade following on the capture of Ormuz and the disgrace of Amboyna), and especially to Methwold himself, was shown as early as October 1636, when the master of the *Mary*, rather than take disciplinary action himself, reported an offence alleged against an older seaman with a youth. The President and Council went aboard, a table and bar were set up, a jury empanelled, witnesses examined. The man was convicted, and hanged at the yard-arm.[2]

In 1641 the Dutch and Portuguese example of fortification was at last followed, at Masulipatam, the Company's earliest settlement on the eastern coast of India. Though the expense aroused the anger of the Court of Committees, it had become pikestaff plain that the Company must be able to defend life and goods. In September a settlement was made at Madraspatam, and St. George's Fort begun.

Here for the first time the Company acted as *de jure* as well as *de facto* rulers. Almost on their arrival they discovered that two pariahs had killed 'a common whore for her jewels', throwing the corpse in a river. The deed came to light nearly miraculously, and the local Raja

' gave us an express command to do justice upon the homicides according to the laws of England; but if we would not, then he would according to the custom of Karnatte',[3]

which we may assume was more unpleasant than even that of England.

---

[1] Danvers, *The Portuguese in India*, ii. 261.   [2] Foster, *E. Factories*, 1637-41, 133.
[3] *Op. cit.* 315.

He asked reasonably, who would come and trade here if report made it a resort of thieves and murderers?

' Which being so, and unwilling to give away our power to those who are too ready to take it, we did justice on them, and hanged them on a gibbet',

where they stayed till the Raja's overlord visited Madras, when the bodies were thoughtfully removed lest the sight mar his pleasure. Eight months later a Portuguese swashbuckler who landed drank too much, and slew one of two Company's soldiers sent to rescue a Dane he and companions had wounded in seven places. He was not hanged but shot ('because he pretended to be a gentleman'), despite his people's indignation at such severity to a hidalgo's spirited excesses.

In 1647 the Company had twenty-three Indian stations, with ninety employees whose salaries totalled £4700 annually.

The Company had been eyed askance by the King, brushed aside as irrelevant by Parliament. The Civil War launched them on new miseries; the ship of their fortunes dragged through rocky shallows. Their only comfort was that Squire Courteen's Association had an even grimmer time. War killed the silk demand, and made the home trade precarious in the extreme. The commander of their best ship, the *John*, delivered it to the King's navy, so that Eastern seas saw it no more; it preyed on Commonwealth commerce until wrecked. With the loosening of traditional loyalties in England, Company employees grew untrustworthy everywhere; Bengal, especially, bred roguery, and brought trivial profit and mighty anxiety. Private trade proved inextinguishable. It was found advisable to, sanction it—first, in such small articles as diamonds, and later, by striving to limit it. After all, sailors have always reckoned to make something for themselves 'on the side'. Presently Company's servants were permitted to send home goods, if shipped openly and a percentage paid for carriage and customs and insurance. These privileges proved merely palliatives in the teeming laxity of the times. Repeatedly, when a factor died it was found that he was deep in debt, either to the Company or to country merchants who claimed reimbursement from his employers.

The Company suffered, as we have seen, from the King's dislike of the London mercantile community. Presently it suffered on an opposing count: after the ruin of his cause the Commonwealth's thorough-going sequestrations impoverished its Royalist members. When the 'assault was intended against the City' the Company's guns, meant for its ships, were requisitioned by Parliament for defence.

Both belligerents wanted ready money: and both mulcted the Company. The King, buying up their pepper (practically by compulsion), took over £63,000, not a penny of this price being ever paid. Fifteen years later (1655), a windfall came in £85,000 awarded to them by foreign arbitrators, in settlement of their long-drawn-out account with the Dutch, for Amboyna and other wrongs. They were then pressing Cromwell for a new charter and for restraint of interlopers (who had increased during the civil troubles and were some of them in close friendship with the Lord Protector). When the Company incautiously suggested that the £85,000 should be handed over, they were informed that 'His Highness hath great occasion at present for money'. He borrowed for twelve months £46,000; the twelve months became eternity.

The Company and their more loyal servants could only draw together cautiously, and wait for the long years of national disunion to end. Even this was hard to accomplish; there was growing testiness among the factors, sharp correspondence, demands and assertions of authority by Surat or Batavia, refusals of obedience by inferior agencies. The civil troubles were sedulously made known by the Dutch, who continued to grow to overwhelming superiority and prestige, the English name sinking ever lower. The Company's ship *Endymion* was boarded and robbed of her pepper in 1649; and to remonstrance the Dutch commander

' fell into high terms and swore all Englishmen were rogues and traitors and that he could not esteem them as he had formerly, they having no king; and withal threatened to do the English all the injuries he could, and for the President and Council, he would kick them up and down if they were in his presence'.[1]

Even the Spaniards and Portuguese recovered a disrespectful demeanour, the offending Adam which had been whipped out of them returning. The entire abandonment of the Eastern trade was a contingency which came close to thought and resolution repeatedly.

The Company had foreseen that the King's execution would embarrass them with Oriental monarchs. In especial, they feared the Shah would say that the Gombroon arrangement had lapsed, since made between two kings, of whom one was now dead. There is a story that he heard a traveller relate the event as an eye-witness, whereupon he cried out upon him for a traitor who had watched his lord murdered and clapped him in jail. This may be fable; and it is pleasant to know

[1] Ethel Bruce Sainsbury and William Foster, *Court Minutes of the East India Company*, 1650-1654, 144.

that as late as 1657 some Persians, at any rate, had not heard of the deed (the Dutch must have been culpably slack with their opportunities), for in that year a Persian merchant desiring passage to Surat in an East India Company vessel gave as his reason for preferring this to a Dutch ship, 'that he took the English for a nation of ancient date, which a King governed (as he said); the other a bad caste, and, though powerful, yet not good'.

In 1649 the safe arrival of no less than seven ships seemed an occasion meriting a banquet of congratulation. A rhyming coxcomb, Francis Lenton, the notorious self-styled 'Queen's Poet', gratuitously offered his tribute. He was awarded £3, which we can only call hush-money, for with it went the note that

' the Court did not well relish his conceits, and desired him neither to print them nor proceed any further in making verses upon any occasion which may concern the Company'.[1]

The British connection with India has notoriously been no favourer of literature; but the Company could hardly be expected to welcome bad verses when their world was going wrong.

At last the English in exasperation struck back, in the Navigation Act of 1651, which forbade the bringing of goods into British territory except in English ships manned by a majority of English sailors; an exception was made when goods were of European origin and brought by the ships of the country producing them. This order meant ruin for the Dutch carrying trade.

The Dutch with a persistency that cannot be too admired had pushed unhaltingly forward towards the empire of the whole Asiatic and African seaboard. They had reduced Portugal to the extremity of distress, wresting from her one valuable hold after another, from the Moluccas to Malabar. They spread up the Gulf. Wherever they came they strained all strength to extirpate all trade but their own. Their goods were better than English goods, their home support was firm, their seamanship and shipboard sanitation were excellent, their policy was without hesitations or ruth. That they were universally detested they sensibly ignored as a small matter.

Their news service made them aware (1653) that war had broken out. Keeping this dark, they surprised the Company's vessels, and sailed exultantly into Indian and Persian ports, their prizes in tow. They swiftly swept English commerce off the seas. Cromwell's victories in European waters brought only immaterial compensation to set off

[1] *Op. cit.* 1644-1649, 348.

material loss. Victory in the Channel was a doubtful tale, whereas English shipping captive in the Gulf or in Swally Roads was plain to see.

Meanwhile, the break-up of the Mogul Empire had begun. Bigotry and xenophobia ran through Aurangzeb's administration, and foreign merchants (most of all the English, whose prestige had sunk so low) endured a waxing arbitrariness of oppression and pillage. Bribes became heavier and more constant, in addition to levies and customs duties. The harassed English looked about for some nook of refuge where their persecuted shipping might hide under the guns of fortification, and their personnel fly for safety. A name that crops up in discussions of what was clearly now a necessity is Bombay.

1657 saw the Company's fortunes at perhaps their lowest. All through the Commonwealth years interlopers swarmed; another embarrassment was renewed in the sixties—French pirates whose actions sunk into disrepute the general European name. They were followed in 1668 by a French East India Company trading legitimately.

Interlopers at last saw the folly of ruining the whole commerce. Cromwell granted a fresh charter, and the Company and Courteen's merchants amalgamated and entered on a surly partnership. The new concern bought up the Guinea Company, thereby obtaining gold from Africa and avoiding the drain of specie from England.

The Restoration, 1660, was hailed as setting the Company free from an equivocal position. They needed all the encouragement they could get; they were in controversy with the powerful Mir Jumla, Nawab of Bengal. Madras factors in 1656 had seized a private junk of his, as security for what was apparently a private claim. In the end the Company paid excessively for the alleged loss thus inflicted; and the interim price of his hostility was very heavy. Some madness (worse than ineptitude) was on the Company's servants in these years. Several of them in 1660 provided the Deccan King with mortars against the celebrated Sivaji. The military prowess of English (still more, of Dutch) troops, and of gunners especially, was well recognised; warring potentates had begun the practice of demanding aid of European science and personnel, English gunners had been lent to the Shah and had kept Aurangzeb out of Kandahar. But the Maratha chief was not the man to forget or overlook a wanton addition to his enemies. Raiding Rajapur, he took its factors prisoners; they languished in hill dungeons until ransomed some years later. Since their misfortune was brought on them by their own action, their superiors, both in Surat and London, were extremely annoyed, and unwilling to pay for their release.

Ceylon was the scene of another bag of English captives in 1660. A ship's company were enticed ashore and hospitably treated, and then seized. They too spent years in captivity. These were times when Englishmen were lightly regarded, and treated with contempt and unprovoked cruelty.

CHAPTER III

ERA OF CONSOLIDATION, 1660-1710

Cession of Bombay: Edward Winter: Sir George Oxinden: Sivaji: Second Dutch War: Henry Gary in Bombay: acquisition of Bombay by Company: Gerald Aungier and fortification of Bombay: Restoration in England and effect of Civil War out East: Treaty of Breda: treaty with Sivaji: death of Sivaji: Sir Josiah Child: growth of Bombay: interlopers: rival companies in England: Keigwin's rebellion: Child's war with Mogul Empire: Job Charnock and William Hedges: more interlopers: legends of Charnock: foundation of Calcutta: Hamilton the Indian Herodotus: foundation of Fort St. David: execution of Sambhaji: English and Dutch policies compared: rise of French East India Company: penal practice of English settlements; Elihu Yale: piracy: Thomas Pitt: Sir William Norris: peace between rival Companies: Nawab of Carnatic's interest in Madras: negotiations with Mogul central government: death of Aurangzeb.

IN 1662 Charles II married Catherine of Braganza,

'an event of deep significance to Europeans in the East, for . . . it threw the shield of English protection over the Portuguese, now hard pressed by the Dutch'.[1]

Rumour rioted; its was obvious that if the English were to implement their new engagements, some harbour must be given them. For a time it was believed that all Portuguese India, or Goa at least, was to change rulers. Ultimately only Bombay (and Tangier) came as the Princess's dowry.

The Viceroy of Bombay, passionately supported by his people, flatly refused to hand it over to Sir Abraham Shipman, sent out as King's Governor. Shipman settled uneasily on Anjidiv, an island in the Tapti estuary, where he and most of his men died; it was abandoned in 1665. Charles and his Government at length were stirred to such anger that they threatened to demand the Viceroy's head, as well as an apology.

[1] Sir William Foster, *E. Factories*, 1661-1664, 29.

Peremptory orders came from Lisbon; Bombay became British (1665), the Viceroy giving way with this last protest:

' I confess at the feet of your Majesty that only the obedience I owe your Majesty, as a vassal, could have forced me to this deed, because I foresee the great troubles that from this neighbourhood will result to the Portuguese; and that India will be lost the same day in which the English nation is settled in Bombay.' [1]

Very much less than what was understood by 'Bombay' was handed over, even as it was. The native population seem to have welcomed the departure of the Portuguese, in an address of convincingly sincere irascibility, which singles out their crowning folly of religious persecution:

' None could with liberty exercise their Religion, but the Roman Catholique; which is wonderful confining with rigorous precepts.'

Many considerations move sympathy for the Portuguese, especially in an Englishman's mind. But they deserved their eclipse.

Between 1662 and 1665, Sir Edward Winter was Agent at Fort St. George; an energetic man, as his tomb at Battersea witnesses:

' Thrice twenty mounted Moors he overthrew
Singly on foot; some wounded, some he slew;
Dispersed the rest. What more cou'd Sampson do?'

In that adventure he received a scar that (perhaps intentionally) disfigured his looks and increased his natural extreme tempestuousness.

Like almost everyone else, Winter was more interested in private trade than in the Company's affairs. It is clear that his masters were afraid of him; nevertheless they plucked up courage to send out in 1665 another Agent, George Foxcroft, to succeed him. Winter for a time apparently acquiesced, and then attacked Foxcroft and his Council, killing one of the latter, and arresting the former as guilty of 'high treason'—the grounds of the accusation being remarks (denied by Foxcroft and his associates) which only in the suspicious days of the early Restoration would have been taken seriously. No one except Winter's confederates was on his side; critics pointed out that his own career during Commonwealth times had not been conspicuously Royalist. The nearest factory, Masulipatam, was particularly hostile. Bombay was scornfully against him. Yet this ruthless man held his course until 1668, when, under overwhelming force from England, he allowed Foxcroft to be reinstated. Too powerful not to be forgiven, he retired to

[1] See Shafaat Ahmad Khan, *Anglo-Portuguese Negotiations*; and R. P. Masani, *Evolution of Local Self-Government in Bombay*.

England in 1672. His turbulent arrogance suggests that his mind was unbalanced. He pursued the Company for compensation (apparently for the almost boundless mischief he had done them), and in 1674 Lord Shaftesbury (Dryden's 'Achitophel') as arbitrator awarded him £6000.

We have entered an epoch as slightly known [1] as it was important. In 1662 Sir George Oxinden became President at Surat, a strong man following a weak predecessor who had allowed a quarrel with the Mogul Governor to drag on, to the damage not merely of the Company but of the Indian merchants, who took the coming of a President of sense and character as their chance to offer mediation. With them on his side, Oxinden's firm yet reasonable and conciliatory manner won, and the difference was composed in a pleasing scene:

' So the merchants and we rested on the Marine that night, and the next day went up to Surat in company; were received with acclamations and expressions of joy, the Governor using many expressions of kindness for the future and all the immunities and privileges that former practice could entitle our nation to; excusing himself, protesting what had passed was forced upon him by the rash and inconsiderate actions of a young man whose years were too green for so weighty an employment.' [2]

This happy finish was as well. 'That grand rebel Sevagee' [3] and his scarcely less energetic father Shahji were ravaging India south of the Narmada, 'the whole country being a mere field of blood'.[4] His wars were ostensibly with the Bijapur ruler, but challenged the Muhammadan general empire, which his race were to ruin in little more than a century. The Bombay chaplain, John L'Escaliot, has left a picture of this very remarkable man, omitting neither the valour nor the cruelty:

' His person is described by them who have seen him to be of mean stature (lower somewhat than I am), erect, and of an excellent proportion; active in exercise, and whenever he speaks seems to smile; a quick and piercing eye;

---

[1] Cf. Ray and Oliver Strachey, *Keigwin's Rebellion*: 'The world remains in almost total ignorance of the administrations of Oxinden, Aungier, and Child, administrations that cover a period in which the English Company in India grew from a seed to a sapling, and in which are to be found the origins of our Empire. At the beginning of this period the President of Surat was the local manager of a business concern, and at the end of it he was the head of an executive government with municipalities, law courts, taxation and a standing army'. This admirable summary contains one loose statement; at the end of this period 'the President of Surat' had become 'the President of Bombay'.

[2] Foster, *E. Factories*, 1660-1664, 103.

[3] Practically a 'rubber-stamp' title for Sivaji in Company correspondence of this period.

[4] Surat President's Report, 1662.

and whiter than any of his people. He is distrustful, secret, subtle, cruel, perfidious, insulting over whomsoever he gets into his power, absolute in his
commands, and in his punishments more than severe, death or dismembering
being the punishment of every offence; if necessity require, venturous and
desperate in execution of his resolves.'

In 1664 he sacked Surat, but the stout countenance shown by the
English factors dismayed his followers, after half-hearted efforts to
storm their godowns and residence (threats had been flung contemptuously back). The Company's prestige rose mightily. From now on
the factors refer to Sivaji almost with affection, and certainly with
amusement and admiration. He becomes 'our neighbour Sevagee'; when
he met with a bad setback, in August 1665,

'Our old and dear friend Sevajy hath, we fear, come to some mischance,
having retired his quarters as far as Singapore.'[1]

The Second Dutch War, 1665-1667, proved far less damaging than
the previous war. But it was hard to bear the rejoicing of the Dutch
merchants over de Ruyter's Medway raid and the Great Fire of London.
The Calicut factors were imprisoned by a local Raja for refusing to lend
him money for his own war against the Dutch. Both nations suffered so
heavily (England having somewhat the better of the argument in European waters) that the Treaty of Breda was accepted by all with thank-
fulness. The Dutch began to grow wary of persecuting the English, and
a decline of their overwhelming strength is visible.

In Sivaji, too, a friendlier attitude appeared. He made many overtures, in 1668 going so far as to say he would make good his robberies
from the English. But when he learnt that they expected reparation to
take the form of ready money 'he shook his head and said no more'.
Meanwhile the Company preferred a long spoon in supping with him,
and looked about to find one.

They ultimately found it in Bombay. But so long as this remained
royal property, it was a hindrance rather than a help. The last King's
Governor, Henry Gary, was a strange and troublesome person; his
name is variously spelled, and he was apparently a Portuguese. Also, 'a
Person of a Mercurial Brain, a better merchant than soldier'[2]—'a polite
reference to the lack of personal courage which was one of his prominent
characteristics';[3] 'a sort of recognised institution whose misdoings were
not to be seriously taken', even by 'the stately Court of Committees',[3]

[1] This should be Singhur, a Deccan hill-fort.

[2] John Fryer, *A New Account of East India and Persia* (1698), ii. 30.

[3] Strachey, *Keigwin's Rebellion*, 10.

c

in whose correspondence we find him figuring finally as 'old Gary'. He claimed almost absolute powers of life and death, in exercise of which he hanged one soldier for an affray with another and shot a second for alleged sleeping at his post. According to Alexander Hamilton, he

' condemned a Man to be hanged on a Tuesday, and the Man suffered according to Sentence; but on Friday after, the poor dead Fellow was ordered to be
called before the Court, but he would not comply with the Orders'.[1]

Gary maintained that he alone had the right to give English passes to Indian ships, and his irascibility was a sore trial to the Company in Surat.

However, in 1668, the King, in consideration of a large loan, handed over Bombay to the Company, to be held

' in free and common soccage, as of the Manor of East Greenwich, on payment of the annual rent of £10 in gold, on the 30th September in each year'.

He had always been indifferent to what Pepys calls the 'poor little island', and exasperated by his Governors' demands for money for the garrison and expenses. Another wearying factor was the clerical in-fluence, which was entirely pro-Portuguese and was naturally exercised against the newcomers. The Company accepted Bombay with grum-bling, which may have been part dissembling. They were aware (one supposes) of the qualities and properties which in 1663 had moved Shipman to write:

' The harbour of Bombaim is the noblest that ever I see; the air healthful,
and is exceedingly well seated for trade, and would in two or three years undo
Surat by bringing hither all the trade. For the marchants living at Surat are
under a very great tyranny, their money being liable to be taken away when
the Mogul or his Governor pleaseth, and their persons abused. The customs
in short time would be great.'

Oxinden's successor (1669) as President at Surat, the able Gerald Aungier,[2] advised the Court of Committees that Bombay should be his headquarters as soon as it was adequately fortified.

There were many reasons why fortification was desirable. The Dutch were driving hard for a monopoly of pepper in Malabar (the one impor-tant pepper-producing region in India) to complete a world monopoly.

---

[1] *New View of the Indies*, i. 192.   See also *E. Factories*, 1668-1669, 51.   Apparently both executions were scandalous, one being for a manslaughter whose
alleged victim was very much alive long after, the other for a military offence of
which there was no evidence.

[2] Omitted from the *D.N.B.*

The French were establishing factories on the same coast. Aurang-zeb's reckless and gloomy bigotry was growing, and Hindus were wanting sanctuary. This might have been found in Sivaji's territories if it were not that the 'grand rebel', like Charles and Cromwell, 'had many and great occasions for money'; moreover, his territories were variable, according as his guerilla warfare ebbed or flowed. The President and Council at Surat reported (1668):[1]

' There are many eminent persons that have declared themselves very desirous to live amongst us with their families, might they be secure; saying, except they were assured of that, they did not think it prudent to remove, since it will certainly disoblige that prince whose inhabitants they now are'—

who, like another Prince, might some day be found straddling right across their way and swearing by his infernal den that they should go no further from his City of Destruction, but that here would he spill their soul. The natives of India, it might be thought, were by now inured to living under political systems liable to flux and disastrous reversals; yet these 'eminent persons' pointed out that

' if they should be outed of Bombay ' (i.e. after settling there), 'there would be no place of abode left them'.

Fortification of Bombay would make

' us terrible to our enemies and acceptable to our friends, and keep those few we have more fast and firm to us; which is what you greatly want, for seeing you have hitherto had no place of retirement, or any appearance to counten-ance and own them, hath bin the occasion so many have deserted you and have bin carried away by the Dutch, with great reluctancy, for otherwise they abominate them, well knowing beforehand the slavery they shall be sub-jected to'.

Nor was Mogul persecution the only kind driving men to seek refuge in Bombay. In the very first days of their rule, the Company had de-clined to deliver up to the Catholic clergy alleged apostates. Now, as later, the Holy Inquisition at Goa was a mighty builder-up of the English Empire.

Governor Gary boasted of what he was going to make Bombay, and its rising walls aroused Mogul jealousy and suspicion. The Indian mer-chants of Surat, especially after Bombay was transferred to the Com-pany, were alarmed lest their city should lose its pre-eminence in trade to the upstart. They protested to the local factors against the pro-posed removal of their headquarters to Bombay; the long and profitable connection of Surat and the Company was urged, and the friendship

[1] *E. Factories*, 1668-1669, 82.

between them was invoked. The Company's prowess during Sivaji's irruption induced a dread of helplessness if the foreign merchants departed. Oxinden's funeral, in 1669, was made the occasion for an impressive demonstration of regard, streets and housetops being crowded with respectful spectators.

The Restoration brought relief in the East, as well as in England. But frayed tempers continued, and the quarrels of the Company's servants among themselves were bitter and incessant. The marvel is that any business got done. The grave spirit of Puritan times, which we have seen in a man so tolerant as Methwold, disappeared, and care for outward decorum also. Shem Bridges, chief factor in Bengal, flouted (1669) the instructions for daily prayers:

' that we have divine service once on the Sunday is as much as can be expected in these hot countries; for neither a man's spirits nor voice can hold touch here with long duties'.

He notes that many thought prayers once a week more than they wanted. Why, he asked irascibly, should they be expected to go through a form of prayer on working days, when curious spectators were watching, and all the noise of business, carpenters, cooks, porters, visitors, miscellaneous chafferers, was about them? The Court of Committees tried to exercise a minute and nagging oversight, rendered by distance both exasperating and ineffective. Thus, the St. George establishment are told (October 22, 1686):

' the Tygar you keep at the expence of a Goat a day, besides attendance, we looke upon as a superfluous vain Charge'.[1]

It is strange how rigidly the British administration in India has continued to run in the earliest moulds; a complaint of both British and Indians in its government right up to the present has been that the home authorities have kept, and used far too often, a power of petty interference.

The Treaty of Breda, at the same time as the English were at last obtaining a secure foothold in India, abandoned territorial possession in the East Indies altogether. Even Pulo Run [2] was given up, in part exchange for New Amsterdam (now New York). For forty years it had been acknowledged as belonging to the English Company, although in practice the Dutch—visiting it periodically, cutting down all fruit and pepper trees, and doing a good deal of promiscuous murder—had kept them out of it.

---

[1] The goat would cost perhaps sixpence a day.   [2] In the Moluccas.

'That grand rebel Sevagee', long firmly established, in 1674 enthroned himself as an independent King, the ceremony being witnessed by Mr. Henry Oxinden, a relative of Sir George Oxinden:

' I took notice on each side of the throne there hung (according to the Moors' manner) on heads of gilded lances many emblems of Government and dominion, as on the right hand were two great fishes' heads of gold with very large teeth; on the left hand several horses' tails, a pair of gold scales on a very rich lance poised equally, an emblem of justice; and as we returned at the Palace gate there was standing two small elephants on each side and two fair horses with gold bridles and rich furniture, which made us admire which way they brought them up the hill, the passage being so difficult and hazardous.'

Oxinden returned with a treaty of peace with Sivaji,

' which if punctually observed will be of no small benefit to the Honourable Company's affairs, both on this Island Bombay and their factories which may be settled in Sevagy Rajah's Dominions'.

Sivaji's friendly overtures, intermittently manifest for some time, were partly due to new naval ambitions—he even went on one not very successful sea expedition in person—and his perception that the English were useful as possible allies against the Sidi. The Sidi was the Mogul admiral, in practice a semi-independent personage of piratical habits. His custom was to spend the monsoon period sheltered by Bombay—in the language of the time and country this was called 'going into winter quarters'.[1] These weeks were not, however, given up entirely to idleness; he kept his hand in by looting the Maratha mainland and cutting off its inhabitants' noses. Occasionally his warriors would raise brawls in Bombay itself; a few years later we find them proposing to hold an exhibition of eighty heads recently removed from their owners. This John Child prevented.

Sivaji, who viewed the Sidi's amusements distastefully, spent much time pondering the possibility of seizing Bombay. He and the Sidi did seize two small adjacent islands, Kendry and Hendry. Yet his relations with the English became definitely friendlier. The latter could no longer make any question of the 'grand rebel's' extraordinary qualities—courage, deftness and mobility, to a degree never surpassed in the world's history. The Deputy Governor of Bombay dismisses (February 14, 1678) the Mogul resolution to march to destroy him with the comment: 'But 'tis well knowne that Sevagee is a second Sertorius and comes not short of Haniball for stratagems'.

[1] The Bombay monsoon is, of course, from June to September.

The Company bewail (January 15, 1678) Bombay's poor prospects of trade:

' no considerable augmentation being made therein, nor can be expected can hold so long as the opposite main continues in the possession of so grand a destroyer of commerce as is the Rajah Sevagee; and what we would lament is that we cannot foresee any termination of his government, for he still continues victorious even to a miracle'.

When he died at last (April 3, 1680), and was sent to his reward with accompanying women, male attendants and animals, they stayed doubtful till the end of the year, writing (December 13, 1680):

' Sevagie hath dyed so often that some begine to thincke him immortell. 'Tis certaine little beliefe can be given to any report of his death till experience shews it per the waning of his hitherto prosperous affaires.'

Even this proof did not come immediately. His son Sambhaji began vigorously, waging war on the Portuguese, whom he pushed into extremities of distress, and plotting against Bombay. The Sidi, not backward in the revels, continued his annual sojourn in Bombay harbour; and pirates swarmed up the Malabar coast and congregated in mosquito-clouds round Madagascar.

Sir Josiah Child,

' whose appearance as a city merchant instead of as Emperor of China or the great Mogul seems an error of Providence, ascended his inadequate throne in Leadenhall Street, and reigned despotically over the East India Company for the last twenty years of the seventeenth century'.[1]

Until Sir William Foster proved otherwise, he and Sir John Child in Surat were thought to be brothers; they were linked only in name and knavery. Josiah's irascibility would seem to have been boundless; his letters are tempestuous, and flash into arrogant wrath. The 'supreme gifts' of 'passion and imagination' ' by their magic raise even his knaveries and his follies into the sphere of greatness'.[2] The times, as if conscious of his quality, provided him with a horde of foes. In England, by bribery of superbly insolent openness (he admitted to spending £80,000, buying the Court of Charles II, the King included), he procured official discountenance of interlopers. But he could do

---

[1] Ray and Oliver Strachey, *Keigwin's Rebellion*, i. For a fuller account of this astonishing man, see Shafaat Ahmad Khan, *The East India Trade in the XVII Century*; and P. B. M. Malabari, *Bombay in the Making* (1661-1726).

[2] *Op. cit.* 51.

little against them in India, where so many circumstances, some of the Company's own creation, befriended them. The Company's employees were so badly paid that nothing could prevent private trade beyond what was permitted, especially private trade along the coast. In their fiercely imperious mood the Court of Committees dismissed suddenly and frequently; those dismissed did not always, or even often, return submissively to England. They joined with discarded soldiers—forming a possible reserve of re-employment, a probable source of opposition and rivalry. Henry Gary, for example, when he ceased to be Deputy Governor of Bombay, settled down as a 'planter' (presumably of coco-palms) in the island.

When tenure was so capriciously held, it was not to the advantage of the Company's servants to press hardly on such freelances as Gary or even on arrant interlopers. Bombay was growing fast, its security and tolerance making it an enticing refuge from Inquisition-ridden Goa and from lands ravaged by tramplings of Mogul armies and incursions of the demon Sivaji and his goblin-hosts. From 10,000 when the Company took it over from the Crown, its population grew to 60,000 by 1674. We have noted the pirates of Malabar and Madagascar; we are entering on the golden age of piracy, when freebooters from Europe, sometimes allied with Malabari and Maratha craft, prowled beside India's western shores. The line between interloper and pirate was thin and easily crossed; and between interloper and Company's servant there was neutrality, and sometimes collusion.

In England, too, the interlopers found sympathisers. One of the former, when his ship was seized in the Thames, declared to a committee of the House of Commons (January 8, 1694) that 'he did not think it any sin to trade to the East Indies, and would trade thither till there was an Act of Parliament to the contrary'—an opinion in which Parliament upheld him by a resolution, eight days later, 'that all the subjects of England have equal right to trade to the East Indies, unless prohibited by Act of Parliament'. There was anger among English artisans against import of Indian textiles. Spitalfields silk-weavers demonstrated outside Parliament (1697). The Company was the target of fierce continuous criticism; in Scotland, conscious of poverty and restricted opportunities, there was the resolution—temporarily foiled in the Darien expedition disaster—to muscle in on English monopolies of trade.

Sir Josiah Child, who 'by his great annual presents could command, both at Court and in Westminster Hall, what he pleased', and held that the laws of England are a heap of nonsense, compiled by a few ignorant country gentlemen, who hardly know how to make laws for the good government of their own families, much less for the regulating of companies and foreign commerce',[1]

applied the private arguments which Parliament most readily accepted, and in 1693 procured a new charter. But the Company's foes ferreted out his briberies, and offered the Government a loan of £2,000,000 at eight per cent., from a proposed new Company. The offer was taken. In 1698—the Old Company having still, under their charter, three years' margin of safety before that expired—the New English Company was incorporated.

Long before this disastrous rivalry overtook it, the Company was shaken by the Child policy. Lavish with bribes at home, the Committees—in practice, Sir Josiah—enforced niggling economy abroad. The Surat President was temporarily reduced to an Agent's rank (1680), and salaries were cut. John Child was made Agent over the head of Pettitt, the senior and ablest Member of Council.

He fell heir to a peck of troubles. Aurangzeb had just reimposed the detested poll-tax on all non-Muslims. He anticipated Mr. J. H. Thomas's policy against Mr. de Valera; when the Company protested and refused to pay the tax, their customs dues were raised from 2 per cent. to 3½ per cent. The Hindus were again stirred to exasperated antagonism against Mogul rule; the slumbering war awakened over Western India, most of all under the guns of Bombay itself, where the Sidi hid from the monsoon storms, and diverted himself in forays on the mainland. The Dutch, as Sir John Child observed, were 'huffing and talking bigg'.

In Bombay a strong royalist tradition persisted. Its garrison came reluctantly, and with reservations, under mere mercantile rule, keeping in the mental background possibilities of appeal to the Crown. New retrenchment hit the soldiery hard. Even harder was insistence that the copper coins used in the seven-miles-long territory (known as phedeas, budgerooks, dugonies) must be reckoned against the Portuguese xeraphine—the popular currency—at far more than the exchange actually obtainable. This fiat ran nowhere outside Bombay, while it was outside Bombay that the garrison must purchase provisions and everything else. All logic, as well as quiet sarcastic contempt, was on the side of

---

[1] Hamilton, *A New View of the Indies*, i. 235. For the official evidence of Sir Josiah Child's briberies (apart from statements of his enemies), laid before the Commons' Committee in 1695, see Sir William Hunter, *A History of British India*, ii. 310.

Keigwin, the garrison's commandant, when he urged facts against the Agent's decision. But logic from an inferior carries light guns. Certain allowances were next withdrawn from officers serving in Bombay; protest was answered by cancellation of commissions, only Keigwin (who had not joined in the protest) remaining commissioned, with instructions to work with his sergeants as officers. Patriotism reinforced the arguments of economic stress; meanness was leaving the island defenceless, putting everything in peril. The garrison took Bombay under their own control, and proclaimed it again a fortress owning allegiance directly to the King of England. Their action was to Sir John Child

' a bitter pill that damages all our Joyes, hove us into amazed thoughts, great trouble, and very seveere perplexities'.

In Shakespearian vein he reproved them:

' Oh, Johny Thorburne, thy Ingratitude is of deep dye. . ... Come, one, two or three of you, and looke on your Governour; I am the same that lived amongst you not long agoe,[1] and then had warrs with Sevajee Rajah and great disturbances from the Portuguese, yett protected you all with God's blessing.'

But the rebels proved past the power of elegiac to move them.

We have seen that the population of Bombay had risen sixfold in seven years of Company rule, eloquent testimony to the security which the harassed people of this seaboard, where Mogul and Maratha were in the first stages of their long warfare, discerned within its borders. Keigwin, who in 1679 had defeated a Maratha armada just outside Bombay, tightened up administration and defence. In April, 1684, the Sidi arrived, somewhat earlier than usual, for annual pastime and shelter. To his horror he was ordered to go elsewhere, and had to go: neither was there any hint of reprisal from the Mogul authorities at Surat, an old bogy which had compelled the garrison to acquiesce in his mischievous abuses of the harbour's neutrality:

' from this moment we hear no more of Bombay as the headquarters of the Siddee's winter sports'.[2]

Sambhaji also noted the new spirit and turn of affairs, and wrote off as impracticable his dreams of seizing the fort. Keigwin thus laid two ghosts simultaneously.

[1] He had been Deputy (the Bombay Governor was so styled, as under the Surat President) Governor, 1679; succeeded, when he went to Surat, by his brother-in-law, Ward.

[2] Strachey, 98.

Ultimately he surrendered the island to a fleet sent from home under Sir Thomas Grantham, on terms of a complete indemnification—an even bitterer pill than the first rebellion to Sir John Child, who lamented his escape from a halter. 'Keigwin, that notorious naughty Rascall . . . as Impudent as hell gloring in his Rougery', went off to service in other seas, and died while leading the naval attack on a West Indian isle (Basseterre, St. Christopher's, 1690). His rebellion resulted in the Company's headquarters being moved from Surat to Bombay.

In 1683, with the help of Judge Jeffreys, an appropriate ally, Sir Josiah Child drove into exile on the Continent a rival merchant, Thomas Sandys, who had worked to have the Company's monopoly declared illegal. In 1687 he made his prophetic and often-quoted remark, that the Company should so proceed as to lay

' the foundations of a large well-grounded sure English Dominion in India for all time to come'.

Events were

' forming us into the condition of a sovereign state in India'.[1]

Part of a sovereign state's prerogative is waging war. In 1686, over a quarrel about customs dues in Bengal, war was superbly declared against the whole Mogul Empire, and ten armed vessels and six hundred men were sent to effect the conquest. The first achievement was an indirect one, the temporary ruin of the Company's stations in Bengal.

Bengal, a rich alluvial well-irrigated region, then adequately (and not congestedly) populated, was first exploited by Company settlements at Balasore, Patna, and a few smaller factories. It brought in a far-reaching change in the character of the Company's commerce, gradually and increasingly substituting for luxuries commodities of general use—saltpetre from Patna, and silks, muslins, textiles, from Dacca and the Delta.

In 1682 the Company's Agent was Job Charnock, a name referred to in the correspondence of the Court of Committees as no other is:

' The tone in regard to him is quite unique in the old Court's correspondence.' [2]

He was 'honest Mr. Charnock' ('Among the faithless faithful only he'), 'one of our most ancient and best servants',

' a person that has served us faithfully above twenty years, and hath never, as we understand, been a prowler for himself beyond what was just and modest'.

[1] Despatch to Fort St. George, September 28, 1687.
[2] Sir Henry Yule, *Diary of William Hedges*, ii. xxix.

We shall see that his merits did not always seem so unspotted to those who made his acquaintance in Bengal. Yule, 'from the fragmentary impressions which are alone available', sums up his character cautiously:

' an imperfectly educated, and coarse and wilful, but strong man, who had spent his life in almost isolated positions among natives, and had been deeply tinged with native habits of thought and action, but who maintained a general loyalty to the Company whom he served, though he was by no means so scrupulous as they gave him credit for being'.[1]

Alexander Hamilton, who pounced on any tale with a breath of scandal about it, so retelling it as to pass on his own chuckling pleasure, is the authority for the best-known tradition—how Charnock, taking his file of personal soldiers, went to enjoy a suttee, but found the widow a Brahmin girl of striking beauty whose distress worked on his feelings, so that he rescued her forcibly. They lived together lovingly—Hamilton remarks that she converted him to paganism, and that on the anniversary of her death he used to sacrifice a cock on her tomb. The story has been rejected on two unconvincing grounds—that Charnock would never have dared to rescue a widow dedicated to death, and that an unclean creature like a cock is not a Hindu sacrificial animal. But in Bihar, where Charnock spent many years, low-class Muslims *do* sacrifice cocks to the *manes* of their dead. As for what Charnock would have dared or have not dared, we have the account of a very successful minor battle which he carried through against the police and military forces of Hugli (1686) shortly before Sir Josiah Child's official war broke out. No one who has studied the East India Company records can think that the Mogul local levies—still less any riot the Hindus might raise—had any real terrors for the bolder spirits who served the Company.

The Court of Committees all through this period were in a fever of suspicion and ill temper. In 1681 they sent out William Hedges, one of their own number, as Agent in Bengal (which he reached July, 1682), to exercise a thorough inquisition and set all to rights. His Diary shows him for a busy meddling fool, encouraging Indians to spy on the Company's servants and to tell tales, willing to believe any evil at first hearing. He took a particular dislike to 'honest Mr. Charnock', whose morals he reported as faulty. Charnock had persuaded a Gentoo's woman, whether wife or widow Hedges was not quite clear (possibly the lady saved from burning with her husband's corpse), to run away to him. He kept as personal servant an Englishman of blasphemous and atheistical tenets, also addicted to native women and even less respect-

[1] *Op. cit.* ii. xc.

ably—'a person of a most unquiett turbulent spirritt'. To his complaints Charnock gave, Hedges said, scant attention or reply. But he may have thought a good deal, for Mr. Hedges later asks with surprise 'why Mr. Charnock is so cross to me'.

Hedges's temper was at explosion-point when he arrived; and everything conspired to spoil it further. Interlopers, whom he suspected (with reason) of private relations with the Company's servants, triumphed openly, magnificent in insolence. There was Mr. Pitt (to be grandfather of Lord Chatham), 'no better than a Pyrott', 'a fellow of a haughty, huffying, daring temper'. Pitt and an ally, Captain Dowsell, swung past the Agent in a sloop manned by thirty English seamen and mounting four guns. Another interloper, Captain Alley,

' came up to Hugly in his Barge, rowed with English Mariners in coats with Badges, and four Musicians',

proceeding to the Mogul Chief of Police (*faujdar*)

' in a splendid Equipage, habitted in Scarlet richly laced. Ten Englishmen in Blew Capps and Coats edged with Red, all armed with Blunderbusses, went before his pallankeen, eighty Peons before them, and four Musicians playing on the Weights, with two Flaggs before him, like an Agent. A gawdy shew and great noise adds much to a Public Person's credit in this Country'.

The wise East has never made laws against a man providing his neighbours with as fine and rowdy a spectacle as he can afford.

Since a factor's salary ranged from £20 to £40, and a writer's was £10 only (though allowances made these sums worth much more), the Court of Committees were unreasonable in expecting single-minded service. Hedges, however, in his acrimony went so far as to open letters to the Company in London from their servants in Bengal, high-handedness of a degree that Sir Josiah Child felt should be reserved for him. Though himself a Committee, Hedges was ignominiously dismissed (August, 1684).

The Company having declared war on Aurangzeb, their employees had to flee. Charnock is one of those Englishmen who have cast their shadow on Indian imagination, and attained to an existence above human. A native historian has magnified his passage down the river, ravaging as he went, with boats marching parallel and firing waterside huts and godowns, into a magician's achievement; Job with a burning-glass roasted the whole river-front as far as Chandernagore, and with his sword cut asunder a massive iron chain drawn across to arrest his progress! The final peace is ascribed to him; he appeared majestically before Aurangzeb, who was in straits of famine in his enemies' grip, and offered him food—generosity melting the Mogul's heart, so that he asked how he might requite his saviour, and was told that the English wanted freedom to trade, which he granted.[1]

The Englishmen took refuge first at Chutanuti (part of the modern Calcutta), and then (1687) on Hijli, a malarious and deathly island at the river's mouth, tiger-haunted. Here, out of three hundred two hundred died; nevertheless the tiny garrison repulsed far superior forces.

Captain Heath was sent from England with reinforcements and orders to seize Chittagong, which Sir Josiah thought an important city on the Ganges. Charnock incurred the Committees' displeasure by refusing to bother about Chittagong (yet even their disapproval is expressed apologetically); and watched with disgust while Heath was 'tripping from Port to Port without effecting anything'. The consequence

' of the Company's spirited war policy was the evacuation of Bengal and the loss of the results of half a century's painful toil and effort'.[2]

This is too strongly put. The Company had swept Mogul shipping off the western seas and played havoc with the pilgrim traffic. Aurangzeb consented to peace, February, 1690, on condition that the English engaged 'to behave themselves for the future no more in such a shameful manner', to pay £17,000, and to expel 'Mr. Child who did the disgrace'. The last-named had died a few days earlier,

' having done more for the Company and the honour of his country than ever any Englishman did in India',

an estimate as accurate as most official estimates. A little later in the same year, Charnock returned from refuge in Madras to Calcutta for the third time. This return is taken as the city's foundation (August 24, 1690); we are laconically told 'Rains falling day and night'—the marshes must have presented an unpromising spectacle. Yet the site was well, even if almost accidentally, chosen. William Hedges had noted, seven years previously,

' God Almighty's good providence hath always graciously superintended the affairs of this Company.'

Hamilton tells us that in Calcutta, until his death in 1693,

' Channock reigned more absolutely than a *Rajah*, only he wanted much of their Humanity, for when any poor ignorant Native transgressed his Laws,

---

[1] Sir H. M. Elliot and J. Dowson, *History of India as told by its own Historians*, viii. 378 ff.
[2] P. E. Roberts, *History of British India*, 45.

they were sure to undergo a severe whipping for a Penalty, and the Execution was generally done when he was at Dinner, so near his Dining-room that the Groans and Cries of the poor Delinquents served him for Music'.

The *D.N.B.* pays an enthusiastic tribute to Hamilton as a witness. He is sometimes, however, called the Indian Herodotus:

' Hamilton was a violent partisan and an enthusiastic gossip, and his sympathies, as became his calling, were all against the monopolist company, with the result that his book, *A New Account of the East Indies*, is a perfect storehouse of scandalous libels against John Child in particular and the Company's officers in general.' [1]

He is, nevertheless, far and away our best and fullest source, apart from the Company's own records, for the period 1690-1720; it is surprising how often the student will light on some unexpected outside corroboration of his 'scandalous libels'.[2]

In 1696 the English were given leave by the Nawab of Bengal to fortify themselves against a rebel raja who was advancing south-east from the Burdwan district. The fort which arose, inland from the river's present course, was in 1699 renamed Fort William, in honour of the Dutch King of England. In the same year, three villages, Chutanuti, Govindpur, Calcutta, were rented from the Nawab of Bengal; and the Company became a *Zemindar*, and appointed an Englishman to hold this office and title. Bengal in 1707 was made a Presidency, and independent of Fort St. George (Madras).

Calcutta was the Company's third possession, as distinct from mere trading stations (Madras—Fort St. George—being the first, and Bombay, bought from the British Crown, the second). But Fort St. David (opposite Cuddalore) came almost contemporaneously. The Marathas (who had themselves usurped it) with a gesture of expansive generosity sold the site along with all territory 'within ye randome shott of a piece of ordnance'. Madras sent its longest-ranging gun and instructions that 'it lyes in the gunner's art to load and fire it to the best advantage'. The shots were fired, September 23, 1690, and took in villages known to this day as 'Gundu Gramam' ('Cannonball Villages'). The Company gave their friends the Dutch, who were established well within range on the

---

[1] Strachey, *Keigwin's Rebellion*, vii-viii.

[2] There is evidence, for example—to look back to Hamilton's remarks—that Charnock's 'indianisation' had gone deep enough to impress him with belief in corporal punishment as an inducement to zeal in servants. Cf. his note, June 31, 1686, that certain peons should receive four annas bukshish if they did their work within five days, but a whipping if they were late.

river's southern bank, a cordial invitation to remain and consider themselves esteemed neighbours. The Dutch, however, removed their factory elsewhere.

Sivaji's son Sambhaji had sunk into habits of drunkenness and
brutality. Betrayed (1689) to Aurangzeb, who had against him more
than his political quarrel with Sivaji, Sambhaji was offered life for
apostasy. Maratha courage flared up in the insulting answer that he
would consent if the Emperor gave him his daughter, and in contemptuous reference to Islam. Aurangzeb, long set in morose bigotry,
avenged this by an execution revoltingly cruel even by Mogul standards.
Sambhaji, taken on camel-back to death, vainly besought the Rajput
troopers of the imperial camp to slay him.

Sambhaji had few friends even amongst his own people. But the details of his death roused the Marathas to a flame of detestation. After all,
he was Sivaji's son. Their foe's scorn and hatred had luridly revealed
themselves. There could be only warfare now, till either Mogul or
Maratha was ruined.

Lyall's words begin to be true of the English, as well as of the Dutch,
Company:

' The great Companies of the seventeenth century were the champions and
delegated agents of their respective nations in the competition for commerce
and territory throughout the whole non-Christian world.' [1]

Yet by comparison with their vigorous and hitherto successful rivals
the English Company remained eminently peaceable. On the Malabar
coast they 'were prepared to pay a higher price for pepper, and to buy
it in the open market',[2] while the Dutch policy

' was governed by the single consideration of maximum pepper trade at
minimum expense'.[3]

While the Dutch had long acted on a kind of half-cock offensive,
ready to pass into active belligerence and willing to become embroiled
in local warfare,

' the English Company, in many ways more far-sighted, while keeping itself
strictly outside political entanglements', [4]

did not interfere in any Indian campaign that the Dutch were waging,

[1] *The Rise and Expansion of the British Dominion in India*, 70.
[2] K. M. Panikkar, *Malabar and the Dutch*, 118.
[3] *Op. cit.* 112. To 'pepper trade' we may add 'opium and cinnamon trade'.
[4] *Op. cit.* 120-1.

even when England and Holland were at war, beyond supplying arms and munitions against the Dutch. We may accept Mr. Panikkar's praise as coming from an unquestionable quarter.

Nevertheless, conditions were forcing on the English drastic revision of their policy of unprotected traffic. Their sea-power had ensured them against too high-handed interference and oppression by Mogul governors; and so long as that Empire remained reasonably strong, it gave them fair security inland. But when the Sidi was acting as an almost independent prince, when Malabar and Maratha pirates were attacking any ship weak or isolated enough to offer a chance of prey, when Sivaji and then Sambhaji were pressing the Portuguese hard and ravaging up to the walls of the Company's factories, the Mogul Empire was growing shadowlike and remote, in comparison with these adjutting realities. Without fortification trade was merely an invitation to pillage.

It was in Madras that the Company first developed what its critics would call 'imperialism'—trivially enough at first, and under sufficient compulsion. There were many reasons why from the first Madras was by far the most independent of the settlements, the nearest to exercise of sovereign powers. It was the first to be given by charter from England a mayor's court and be made a municipality (1687). It was in a region hardly even nominally under the Mogul Empire, where petty rajas and a foolish and inadequate Nawab could not afford protection nor effectively resent encroachment. Thirdly, in 1674 François Martin, the real founder of French rule in India, founded Pondicherry, a station obviously destined to provide uncomfortable neighbourhood. Madras became politically alert. It was not possible that such secular foes as France and England should confront each other and not watch for occasions of offence to arise. In 1690 the two fought a drawn naval battle off the Coromandel coast.

The Company's stations in Further India were ceasing to matter; in 1670 the Dutch expelled the English from Macassar, and in 1682 persuaded the King of Bantam to expel them from Java. But after the Revolution had made England and Holland allies against Louis XIV, Dutch animosity began to sink, partly from common interest, partly from Holland's growing weakness against France. This was the period when first disparity of populations resulted in certain countries rising into the category of first-class powers, while others, after long and successful contention, definitely and finally fell back. As the century drew to its close, the Dutch in their relations with Indian administrations resorted (to the waxing inconvenience of the English, who found existence in India very expensive) to bribery more and more, to bullying less and less. They grew aware that such way to greatness as was left to them lay eastward, in the Malayan archipelago where they stood out as unchallenged suzerains and with only paltry chiefs to overawe. The Netherlanders shrink out of Indian affairs.

From 1660 to 1707, as we have seen, 'the Bay' (the Bengal and Coromandel settlements generally) was under Fort St. George. In 1687, Sir John Child, with Bombay as now his headquarters in place of Surat, was 'General' (hence sometimes styled by historians misleadingly 'Governor-General'). Marathas dominated the neighbouring mainland, pirates vexed the seas, the Mogul Empire was at no great distance. In Bengal the English were driven down into deltaic swamps; and afterwards, when peace was restored, were allowed to push up-country slowly and inconspicuously.

In Madras, however, the Company had no more serious threats than those from the Nawab, and from the Portuguese at San Thomé and the French power in its beginnings at Pondicherry. San Thomé was taken by the French in 1672, and lost in 1674 to the Dutch and the Nawab acting together. Meanwhile Madras steadily consolidated its strength; by 1657 it was thoroughly fortified. Its administration acted as sovereign. By the 'eighties we find major native malefactors being hanged, and English ones whipped or burnt in the hand. The last penalty was a favourite one, as it was in Calcutta also, twenty years later. The branding of criminals was not abolished until Dalhousie's time. In the late seventeenth century it was almost invariably inflicted on Englishmen who claimed 'benefit of clergy' after conviction for theft or manslaughter. A century after this it becomes monotonous in the records, especially of Calcutta, where Indians who suffered it were also expelled across the river. But neither Bombay nor Calcutta in the seventeenth century claimed powers of capital punishment, as Madras did. Still less would the English in Calcutta, even a hundred and forty years later, have dared to do what the Governor of Madras did in 1680, when he forbade a suttee which was proposed to grace the obsequies of a rich Hindu merchant.

Elihu Yale,[1] Governor of Fort St. George (1687-92), was the first to see the wide application of the anti-piracy laws which the dread of men's minds, confronted by this menace grown to enormous proportions, made possible. Hamilton's statement that Yale hanged 'for piracy' his

---

[1] Whose name is perpetuated in Yale University.

English groom, a man called Cross, for absenting himself from his duties, 'riding off two or three days to take the air', is usually dismissed as another piece of Hamilton's malicious gossip. We need not hesitate to accept it as fact, if we add that the groom was probably accused by his irate master of meaning to steal the horse. Under Yale's administration courts-martial for 'piracies' sat continually on Indians and Englishmen. In the year of his appointment a Judge-Advocate was sent out from England, and Madras was given a Mayor and Corporation and had a new Supreme Court erected. In government, so far as government consists in machinery for repressing the wicked, Madras was far ahead of any other presidency or agency. We find the records peppered with proof: an Indian is hanged for robbery and his head stuck up in a prominent place; and English sailors who deserted, especially if they used ship's property (a boat or pinance) to make their get-away, plainly were 'pirates', which Yale seems to have interpreted to mean anyone who, while accompanied by a stitch or splinter of property not strictly his, crossed any tract of water. Yale himself generally presided over these Courts, which we need not doubt that his truant groom would find acquiescent in his master's mood. Pirates must have literally abounded in the environs of Fort St. George! That some people were as sceptical of their ubiquity as a few nullifidians in England were of that of witches we may surmise from what happened after a trial in April, 1689, when six pirates were condemned to be branded with a P 'at the Execution Post under the Fort point' and another two to be executed. One of those capitally doomed was reprieved (Yale 'being very buisy' was absent from this particular court-martial); the other was coolly handed over to the *Defence* for Captain Heath to hang at his yard-arm. Heath, who as a naval man might be supposed not to be tender to actual pirates, refused this duty, saying that 'as he had none of the live men, he would have none of the dead'. He was fined 200 pagodas for contempt of court.[1]

After Yale went, this administrative activity slackened, certainly not because piracy slackened. In 1698 the great Captain Kidd himself chased a Company's ship sailing by Madagascar to Madras:

' The Sedgwick, as going, was persued three days and 3 nights by Kidd: being calme weather, and Kidd outrowing her, she narrowly escaped by favour of a Breeze of wind in which she outsailed Kidd. But was taken in her returne near Cape Comorine by Chivers, a Dutchman, in the Algerine Gally of 250 tons, 150 men and 28 Guns and 24 Oars, after 9 houres persuit with

[1] See H. D. Love, *Vestiges of Old Madras*, i. 494.

Sails and Oars. But the Cargo not proving for their turne, and the Captain giving the company a bowl of Punch, they let her go in a good humour, taking only Sailes, Cordage, cable, &c. Stores.' [1]

But Madras ended the century under the government of Thomas Pitt. Himself a notable poacher turned gamekeeper—we have seen him styled by the Company as 'no better than a pyrott'—he held less austere views on the appropriation of other people's property than Elihu Yale had done.

The career of this remarkable man (Pitt) is a startling example of the ease and rapidity with which Company's servant and interloper interchanged places, an ease and rapidity helped by the readiness with which the Court of Committees in this period of bad temper and suspicion dismissed even members of council. In Bengal the Company's officers could do nothing against Pitt; as late as January 15, 1695, only two years before his appearance as a Company's Governor, they wrote that

' Captain Pitt to the last made a great bouncing and have carried himself very haughtily ever since his arrivall in these parts, and has not scrupled to talk very Disrespectfully of your Honours'.

Part of his power came from his purchase of a seat in Parliament, first (1689) as Member for New Sarum, and then (1691) as one of the two Members for Old Sarum, which we may not unfairly call a mythical borough, since almost entirely without inhabitants. Neither his wicked past nor even his disrespectful talk of their Honours prevented the Committees from unanimously electing him Governor of Fort St. George in 1697; and here he remained for twelve years, to the Company's immense advantage. While Governor, he sent home (1702) the Regent diamond,[2] so called because it was sold by him to the Regent of France for £135,000. This handsome little fortune made possible the early success of his grandson, who also was Member for Old Sarum.

It was lucky for the Company that Pitt was in their service and not in that of the rival New Company. The latter made great mistakes, first in loaning practically all their capital to the Crown, secondly in entertaining as their agents in India men dismissed and discredited by the Old Company. Among them was Thomas Pitt's cousin John Pitt, a poor creature beside Thomas. These agents proved incapable as well as dishonest. The New Company determined to copy the precedent set by sending Sir Thomas Roe as ambassador to the Mogul Court, hoping by direct negotiation at the centre to obtain advantages which would

[1] *Op. cit.* i. 589.   [2] He was known as 'Diamond Pitt'.

undermine the Old Company's position. But the man they selected, Sir William Norris, was inexperienced, and had vague notions of even the geography of India; his assistants were men both knaves and fools. After tedious divagations he managed to meet Aurangzeb; but the aged Emperor was hard set in his ways, and in wrath against the English in especial. He demanded a guarantee that the English would patrol the seas so effectively as to kill piracy. This Norris could not give; and he died on the high seas, when returning (1702) broken-hearted at failure.

In 1702 both Companies reached a preliminary armistice, which made provisional union, finally completed six years later. They had familiarised their countrymen with the immense sinews for political corruption furnished by Indian trade; and had been a scandal by their bribery, particularly at election times.

About 1700 the Nawab of the Carnatic, newly appointed by Aurangzeb, suspecting that the Company was very rich, began to take a deep interest in Madras. On his appointment he was presented with blunderbusses, fowling-pieces, looking-glasses, foreign drink, and other commodities, but received the envoy with threats and declarations that the offering was inadequate. He appeared outside Madras (July, 1701) with 10,000 horse and foot, and rejected a second gift. Pitt landed sailors; the Europeans stood to. This sobered the Nawab, who announced that he would accept the present and also dine with Mr. Pitt. A Persian chef was procured, and a snack of some six hundred dishes provided, 'of which the Nabob, Duan, and Buxie, and all that came with him eat very heartily'. They were also 'diverted with the Dancing wenches', and made so very drunk that the Nawab was unable to carry out next morning's programme of inspecting an English ship. When the effects of the previous evening's entertainment had somewhat passed off, he alarmed Pitt by sending word that he intended to march through Madras with elephants and a large body of troops. So the train-bands were beaten up and marines landed once more. Luckily, before he could carry out his intention,

' the Nabob was got into a Portuguez Chappell very Drunk, and fell a Sleep: and so soon as waked (which was about 4 a clock in the afternoon), he Order'd his Camp to March towards the little Mount where he pitch'd his Tents, and sent to the Governour to excuse his not coming to the Garden, and desired him to send him a Dozen bottles of Cordiall waters; which were sent him'.

He reappeared next year, blockading the city, for no special reason except that he wanted loot; and was bought off with Rs. 25,000.

Pitt in 1708 got into communication with the Mogul Central Government, and was granted five villages adjacent to Madras, a gift followed up by the honour of a communication from the Emperor's Vizier couched in very gratifying terms, but drawing his attention to the fact that the Company had not yet sent a present. A list of acceptable gifts was helpfully added. It included:

' Birds of the Sorts of Manila Parrots, Newries, Cocatores, &c., or of any sort that can speak, of a good colour and shape. Birds with Copple crowns, and of other fashions. . . .

' Lacker'd Vessels and Porcelane, Scrutores, Targetts and calamdanes, &c., you may send; also Lackerd Scrutores sett with Mother of Pearle.

' China Ware, what ever is Rare and Fine of any kind or sort, the older the better. The Dishes called Ghoorees, which break when Poyson is put into them, will be very acceptable. You must by all means send some of them.

' Boxes with clock work, China Skreens with clock work, both Painted and with images. Images and Juncks that goe with clock work, &c. Raritys of this kind and fashion will doe.

' Gold and Silver plate, Manilha work (Philigreen); Vessels of Silver, Gold plate enamell'd, Europe work, if to be had, will do.

' Europe fusees; one or two small feild pieces, &c. Gunns will not be amiss. . . .

' A Good Elephant, a Good Horse; Atcheen Horses, the best of the best, and Bengall Horses will also doe.

' Good peices of Ambergrease will do extreamly well, and is the best of all things.

' Clocks and watches that strike or have Chimes you must by all means send.

' Black lead and Red lead pencils of Europe. . . .'

Such marks of favour called for adequate acknowledgment, which was made. The 'Lord High Steward' was informed by Governor Pitt that his letter had been translated, and its contents had given extreme delight. But there were difficulties in the way of answering it adequately.

' Your Excellency writes that there must be presents for all the Princes & some of the Great men. If you mean such as are suitable to their birth and quality, 'tis impossible for us to purchase them with our Company's Estate, who you know are Merchants that run great risques to gett a little, and who often meett with loss instead of gain. So hope, as the presents we intend are Suitable to our circumstances, they will meet with a gracious acceptance from the Great King, and princes, which putts me in mind of what we read in History, That upon many persons making very rich presents to a King there happened a poor man to come with a drop of water, which was as acceptable as any of their presents, being according to his ability. . . .'

A drop of water which included six elephants was therefore collected and sent to Delhi.

In the same month as this letter was written, the Nawab again passed by Madras with an army, drinking 'very hard, and selldome in humour, grumbling very much at the small Amount of our Present'.

' That his final letter to Pitt related to strong waters will occasion no surprise. In a consultation of February, 1709, we find: "Nabob Dowed Cawn having wrott a Letter to the Governour from the Kings Court desireing one thousand Bottles of Liquor; agreed that we now send him 250. And the Governour sends him two large Mastys that he got out of the Europe Ships".' [1]

The last item, of course, was the old stand-by of the English in Oriental argument, from the times of Jahangir:

' A subsequent acknowledgment of "Doggs" by the Nawab shows that mastiffs are meant.'

In 1707 Aurangzeb died. The succession to the Mogul Empire was in the cockpit of civil war for several years, an interregnum of which the Company took advantage to strengthen Fort William.

CHAPTER IV

ANARCHY: DISSOLUTION OF INDIAN
POLITICAL SYSTEMS

Governor Russell's humility: Surman's embassy: piracy: Maratha dissensions: the Angrias: the Ostend Company: rise of Nizam to independent power: the Maratha constitution: rise of Maratha chieftains: Nadir Shah's invasion: Maratha raids over India: the carcase and the eagles.

GOVERNOR PITT's action in corresponding with the Mogul Court direct was followed up from Bengal by the Company's most ambitious enterprise since Roe's ambassadorship. Norris's mission on behalf of the New Company had failed utterly; but the feeling persisted that the Company must get past nawabs and polygars, to the supposed fountain of authority.

In 1711 the President of Fort William addressed the Nawab of Bengal, 'with the humblest submission', laying at his feet 'that life wholly

[1] Love, *Vestiges of Old Madras*, ii. 18.

dedicated to your Service'. Two years later the same suppliant, ingratiatingly describing himself as

' the smallest particle of sand, John Russell, President of the East India Company (with his forehead at command rubbed on the ground)',

approached the Emperor, Farakhsiyar. In 1715 an embassy was sent, under John Surman, which after two years of humble waiting procured at a total cost of over 600,000 rupees a *farman* which confirmed the Company's privilege of free trade in Bengal and their old position at Surat (where they had paid, before Aurangzeb's enhancement, two per cent. customs), on condition of a yearly fee of Rs. 10,000. They might now buy land at Surat instead of renting it; might rent two more villages near Calcutta, and were confirmed in the old grant of 1798, of five villages near Madras (from which the Nawab in 1711 had forcibly ejected them). The *farman* was received with rejoicings in the Presidency centres, broadsides being fired from every available gun. But when this ceremonial was over, the Madras villages had to be re-entered after six hours of bayonet fighting (1717) supported by field-guns. The casualties were slight. As to Bengal, the privileges for a long while were refused implementation.

' Nevertheless, the embassy was a real step in advance. It legalised the whole of the English position in India. In Bengal it placed the local government technically in the wrong so long as the *farman* and orders of the emperor were disregarded, and it consequently furnished the English with a standing quarrel which they might take up at any time. This they at last did after the catastrophy of the Black Hole, and the withholding of the rights won by Surman was the ground put forward by Clive, when he broke with Siraj-ud-daulah and entered upon the conquest of the country. The soldier completed and more than completed what the ambassador began.' [1]

The Mogul, granting other privileges, was firm against that of exercising capital jurisdiction. He refused to permit the Calcutta Government to punish 'Rogues', by which they more specifically meant pirates, who so swarmed in one particular inlet of the Sandarbans that it was styled 'The Rogues' River'. Even Madras in 1718 temporarily hesitated on this head, but only as to the power to inflict death on English male factors. A drunken mate who had murdered a lascar was

' kept in Irons in the Cockhouse upon Rice and water till We can advise Our Honble Masters of the Particulars, and receive their orders how to proceed'.

But Madras did not hesitate as to native offenders; capital powers against

[1] C. R. Wilson, *Early Annals of Bengal*, II. ii., lvii.

them, it was held, arose out of the charter making Madras a municipality (1687), and were steadily exercised.[1] And in February, 1719, a Commission to try pirates came from England; the same year an Englishman was hanged under it.

Piracy had become almost the overmastering fact of these years. As a by-product of the European wars, wherever there was a wild archipelago were swarms of desperadoes sallying out to pillage and hiding from reprisals. We have seen that their favourite rendezvous was Madagascar, 'perhaps the scene of greater continuous misery than any other spot on the surface of the globe'.[2] In the person of Kanhoji Angria peril prowled at Bombay's gates; for half a century he and his successors were largely responsible for depressing the city below its comparatively unharassed compeers, Madras and Calcutta.

After Sambhaji's execution by Aurangzeb, his brother Rajaram led the Marathas, who endured a period of disunion and persecution by the Mogul power. He died in 1700, and his widow, Tara Bai, showing the energy so frequent in the women of her race, became regent. Aurangzeb's successor, Bahadur Shah, released Sambhaji's son Shahu, who had been brought up at the Mogul Court and came profoundly impressed with the greatness of his late hosts and jailors, in a mood not unlike the pro-Norman one of Edward the Confessor, to wage civil war against Tara Bai. It is customary to say the Marathas lost the empire of India by their wars with the British as the century closed; they lost it no less in these internecine conflicts at its beginning.

Sivaji's centralised administration had checked the feudalism which was the Maratha curse. This now revived, leaders espousing one side or the other, fighting for their own hand, jostling for supremacy (under nominal allegiance to whichever representative of Sivaji they acknowledged). Among the chieftains taking Tara Bai's part was the Raja of Kolhapur. Kanhoji Angria regarded himself as a vassal of Tara Bai, and in especial, of the Kolhapur Raja. He therefore ravaged Shahu's territory; and his victim's family in their records concur with the East India Company in calling him 'pirate' *tout court*. This description, which English historians have taken over—'Kanhoji Angria, the famous corsair chief'[3]—is not quite fair or accurate.

Kanhoji's father, Tukoji, served in the Maratha navy originated by Sivaji; the son founded a line of hereditary naval commanders. When

---

[1] See Love, *Vestiges*, ii. 174-5.　　[2] Roberts, *History of British India*, 83.
[3] *Op. cit.* 71.

Shahu, much weakened, came out above his rivals, Kanhoji accepted the situation but gave up nothing, retaining his sea-post and practically independent status. He merely regularised his course, as the Maratha central government at Satara saw it. As Maratha admiral now, he concentrated his hostility against the Sidis, who were soon reduced to being rulers of the petty island of Janjira. He warred intermittently with Portuguese, Dutch and English. The Malabar rocky holds were as thronged with pirates as the Narmada cliffs are with wild bees; these had now found a leader.

Under Sivaji the Maratha armies had been catholic, offering employment to Muhammadans and even untouchables. The navy was even more catholic, being often officered largely by Muhammadans. Kanhoji was no less generously hospitable. In 1713, having captured the Governor of Bombay's armed yacht and another vessel in the previous year, he preferred peace to the English, with restoration of his captures less their guns; for these he suggested that his opponents engage to provide him with powder and shot. He was not alone in regarding warfare in what we should think a queerly professional light. Munitions were marketable commodities; if the English understood their composition better than he did, Kanhoji saw no reason why they should not supply him with them as soon as he and they were no longer technical enemies. But he went further. European gunners were greatly valued by 'the country powers'; deserters were particularly welcome if skilled with artillery. When question arose about restoration of gunners held as captives or as employees, Kanhoji's replies showed that he looked on them as clever artisans entitled to sell their abilities where they wished. On occasion he acted in alliance with—Dr. Sen prefers to say, took into his service—notorious English pirates of Madagascar, Taylor, England and Plantain, with whose help he did not hesitate to 'assail the largest East Indiaman'.[1] But ordinarily he had to act with only his own 'grabs and gallivats', small sailing craft which flocked round a becalmed boat and by sheer pertinacity and numbers strove to overcome it.

The English and Kanhoji made peace, 1713. It might have lasted, if he could have brought himself to restore with the ships whose capture caused the official breach the cargoes as well. He kept these, and both sides accumulated grievances for a new war. Kanhoji, copying precedents, not least set by his European rivals, demanded that merchants who hoped to traverse the seas with impunity must buy his permission. His complaint was that the English not only expected him to let their

[1] *Op. cit.* 71.

own ships go free without passes (to which he had consented), but ships on to which they had laden their goods. They maintained that when the merchandise far outweighed the ships in value, it gave the latter its nationality. He denied this; probably most people to-day would side with him. The final incident was his removal of timber from an indubitably English ship. Like Charles I and Protector Cromwell when they took East India Company money to their own use, he pleaded his needs:

' As I had a great necessity for timber, when the boat came from Surat, I brought her in, in a friendly manner, believing that you observed the friendship without scruples, and what's a little timber? . . . I . . . wrote Your Excellency to let me know the price thereof, and had for answer you wanted timber, which I took well, expecting when mine would come to repay you. In this there is no cause of difference.'

We have it on high ancient authority that friends have all things in common. Bombay, however, had not attained to the lofty highmindedness of Socrates and Kanhoji. It rejected his contention, declared war, and launched hostilities, in an expedition which failed (1718).

The Portuguese suffered most from him; his prisoners from them he usually put to death. He fought a number of naval actions against this enemy, with varying result. But Portuguese powers of recovery had sunk very low, and this protracted warfare must be reckoned one of the main factors making for their rapid continuous decline. They made alliance with the English, who provided a royal squadron of four vessels, under Commodore Thomas Mathews; but the Maratha seafortress of Kolaba beat off the Anglo-Portuguese assault (1720).

In 1729 Kanhoji died, greatly respected and having been long at peace with his suzerain in Satara. He left a brood of sea-faring sons; and in 1737 yet another English attempt on his strongholds was defeated. Next year the Marathas blundered by capturing two Dutch vessels, which resulted in the following year in the arrival of eight Dutch men-of-war accompanied by lighter craft. This armament achieved nothing beyond cowing the Angrias. But the lesson was taken to heart, that the Dutch were too active and irascible to be taken on as foes.

Whatever opinion may be held of Kanhoji's proceedings, those of his successors became practically indistinguishable from piracy. They and he have this importance for us, that they acted as blows which welded the East India Company into a deliberate instrument of war. By 1730 it had become in self-defence against its many foes one of the lesser 'country powers', no longer a mere mercantile enterprise. It had to be watchful to keep, as well as enterprising to gain.

We have seen that there is some colour for difference of judgment as to whether Kanhoji Angria was a simple pirate; and that we may hesitate to accept the Company's opinion, partly because the Company, now at last after years of struggle and exasperation emerging to a place where it felt its grip becoming firm on real power, chose to confound almost any kind of opposition with 'piracy'. It was not interlopers alone who met with high-handed repression.

' The subject that bulks largest in the India Office records during the first thirty years of the eighteenth century is the struggle with the Ostend Company.' [1]

This Company arose out of the desire of the Flemish Netherlands, which had remained under the control of Spain or Austria, to get a share of the Eastern trade which so enriched their independent Dutch neighbours. In this desire, after the Peace of Utrecht (1713), they were supported by the Emperor Charles VI. Single vessels began to make the Indian journey, and a formal charter was obtained in 1722. Dutch and English deserting sea-captains, especially those of the latter who were Jacobites, joined the new Company; and English smugglers worked with them in disposing of their goods.

The Dutch and English companies were so inveterately set in the attitude and habit of monopoly, that this effort of a continental group to share in the Eastern trade was taken as an intolerable outrage. By diplomacy, pamphleteering, through Parliament, with force openly and cynically exerted against all law of nations or of decency, the Ostenders were opposed. The established companies were extolled as almost religious sodalities; if the new-comer succeeded, said a pamphleteer,

' the commerce and riches of one of the bulwarks of the Protestant interest would be thereby transferred to augment the strength of a Roman Catholic State'.

Nothing more plainly shows the enormous strength and importance that by slow accumulation had accrued to the older companies, than the fact that for many years the question seemed certain to bring about European war. The Dutch East India Company captured Ostend ships with as little scruple as they had formerly captured English ones, even when England and Holland were supposed to be allies. In his activities directed towards kidnapping Hume, an Englishman serving the Ostend Company in Bihar, Henry Frankland, Governor of Fort William, by his own admission, in 1727 went

' some lengths that are not so proper to be committed to Black and White'.

[1] Roberts, 62-8—an excellent narrative of the main course of events.

The Ostenders' vessels were shut up in the Ganges, 1730, 'so that they can never come away', one having already been seized; and in 1733 the Fort William authorities suborned a Muhammadan attack on their lonely station at Bankibazar, which had to surrender. This ended the Ostend settlements, except for one which just existed a few years longer.

Mr. P. E. Roberts concludes [1] his admirable summary of what was a wretched and indefensible business, with criticisms that we shall do well to bear in mind in our study of the East India Company throughout the whole of the following century. The crippling of the Ostend Company

'marked the triumph of the narrow policy of restriction and monopoly typical of the century, fortified, in this instance, by national jealousy. Within a few years enlightened statesmen had begun to see that England's action in the matter was not only selfish, but of doubtful expediency. "The abolition of the Ostend Company", said Pitt in 1742, "was a demand we had no right to make, nor was it essentially our interest to insist upon it, because that Company would have been more hostile to the interests both of the French and Dutch East India Companies than to our own".'

The Marathas recovered after Sambhaji's death, helped by the follies of the later Moguls, Aurangzeb among them. Aurangzeb destroyed the Muslim kingdoms of Central India, Bijapur and Golconda, which had acted as buffers between Delhi and Maharashtra; he and his successors by their bigotry and savage cruelty made Sikhs and Rajputs their implacable foes. The Empire became a mere shell empty of puissance. The Nawabs of Bengal and of Oudh were in effect independent rulers. The ablest of all the great Mogul officers of State, Asaf Jah, the Vizier, in 1724 abandoned a hopeless cause and withdrew to his own former province of Haidarabad, nominally as Subadar of the Deccan but actually a sovereign. He and his line will from now on be referred to as Nizams, from his title Nizam-ul-mulk, 'Regulator of the State'. Under him, in a still more attenuated (if that be conceivable) vassalship to Delhi, was the Nawab of the Carnatic, to whom the Company for Fort St. George and Fort St. David owed obeisance, which also, in the political system of India—now one vast fraud and make-believe—was in little more than name.

Asaf Jah died in 1748. He was usually at war with the Marathas, or with some of the Marathas, a preoccupation of immense value to the English, whose South Indian settlements yearly grew more firmly established, havens of trade and quiet in the surrounding cockpit.

[1] 68-9.

The Nizam's dominions to some extent took the place of the barriers which Aurangzeb had destroyed, and kept the Marathas and the central Government at Delhi apart for a few decades longer, though in 1737 the former raided up to the very environs of the imperial city.

Sivaji used a Council, the Astha Pradhan, or Ministry of Eight. Theoretically, their chief was the Pratinidhi, the Peshwa being second. It is not clear when this Cabinet arose. Shahu, Sivaji's grandson, as we have seen, honestly regarded himself as a feudatory of Delhi, a conception which the Maratha chieftains had no difficulty in fitting into the political scheme; two generations later, Mahadaji Sindhia himself procured for his nominal master the Peshwa a *farman* from Delhi, as *Vakil-i-mutluq*. The Astha Pradhan became hereditary officers; and the Peshwa of Shahu, Balaji Visvanath, made his position so outstanding that the Rajas of Satara, Sivaji's descendants, became mere figureheads, treated with immense respect publicly but in fact almost powerless.

' After Shahu the descendants of Sivaji dropped out of sight so completely that all readers of history think of the Maratha government in the eighteenth century as that of the Peshwas.' [1]

With Balaji began the remarkable influence of the Chitpavan Brahmins, a clan that seem to possess innate administrative and political aptitude, certainly not exhausted in our own day, as the examples of Gokhale, Ranade and Tilak show. Shahu died in 1748, the same year as the great Nizam. His importance had largely died earlier; in 1727 he granted his Peshwa, the very able Baji Rao I, son of Balaji, full administrative powers.

The usurpation of power by the Peshwas was not the only factor depressing the Satara family into impotence. In the Maratha wars and far-raiding expeditions, the great Maratha kingdoms surviving into the India of to-day were founded. The Gaekwar's rise dates from about 1724; in 1728 twelve districts north of the Narmada were granted as a fief to Holkar. The Bhonsla family and Sindhia, the latter perhaps the most powerful of all Maratha clans in later years, though preserving an elaborate pretence of humility in their pride as hereditary slipper-bearers to the Raja of Satara, were of the same period. In 1739, after years of raiding and what we may call infiltration, the Marathas completed the conquest of Malwa, or Central India. Baji Rao, the Peshwa, asked the Mogul Emperor to appoint him as Subadar of the vast region wrested from him. The Emperor had no choice but to consent; to make assurance doubly sure, and to grapple what had been illegally gotten as

[1] *Oxford History*, 457.

legally as possible, the Emperor's Subadar of the Deccan (and, incidentally, of Malwa), the Nizam, was asked next year to confirm the appointment. The Nizam pointed out that he himself was Subadar of Malwa,
but graciously made the Peshwa Naib-Subadar, or Deputy Subadar.
Malwa entered upon a process of disruption into feudatory kingdoms;
Holkar, Sindhia, the Puar (a Rajput chief who allied himself with the
Marathas) are still established there, in Indore, Gwalior and Dhar. The
Bhonsla dynasty lost its territory of Nagpur in Dalhousie's annexations. The Gaekwar's territory, Baroda, is outside Malwa.

The wretched Mogul Empire was destined, broken as it was, to endure repeated shocks as the century progressed. Nadir Shah in 1739
invaded it from Persia, and sacked Delhi. 'He revealed to the free-lances
of the north that the power of the Great Moguls had vanished'[1]—a
disservice only slightly offset by his letters to the Peshwa, the Raja of
Satara and other Hindu princes, bidding them 'walk in the path of
submission and obedience to our dear brother' (reinstated after very
thorough pillage), and promising them that if they did not he would
'blot them out of the pages of the book of creation'. The Marathas
whom he thus exhorted, those 'cool and insatiable robbers',

' the only nation of India which seems to make war an occupation by choice,
for the Rajpoots are soldiers by birth',[2]

proceeded to raid India even more widely than before. The Mogul's
immediate territory being temporarily closed to their attentions, in
1740 they occupied the south, ravaging right up to the gates of Pondicherry and Madras. Southern India possessed a permanent witness to
former irruptions, in a Maratha kingdom in Tanjore, established as far
back as the reign of Shahu, Sivaji's father. In 1743 Bengal was invaded,
the Marathas reaching Vishnupur, 120 miles from Calcutta, probably
only with an advance-guard. The Vishnupuris still show where Lal-
madan, a local representation of Krishna, repulsed them with fire-
streams from two long cannon held under his armpits. The English
dug 'the Maratha Ditch' before Calcutta; its manning, however, proved
unnecessary.

The Marathas since Sivaji's days exacted *chauth*, literally a fourth
(of the land revenue), and an extra tenth, called *sardeshmukhi*, from provinces which they overawed without actually occupying. This represented a heavy exaction, and it is not unnatural that the Marathas are

[1] Sir George Forrest, *Life of Lord Clive*, i. 99.
[2] Colonel Mark Wilks, *History of Mysoor*, i. 157.

generally called simple freebooters by English and Muhammadan writers. There is something to be said on the other side, which will be said in its place.

Meanwhile India's internal strength was being ruined by war of one country power against another. Everywhere,

> ' Hercules killed hart-a-grease,
> And hart-a-grease killed Hercules'.

The carcase was in a condition to invite the eagles. As for the administration which cloaked this rapine and pillage and march and counter-march of armies, we have seen that it was a pretence. The Emperor sanctioned the state assumed by his Nizam and his Nawabs of Oudh and Bengal: he sanctioned the conquests of his humble servants the Marathas: the Nizam was the feudal overlord of the Nawab of the Carnatic: the Peshwa was in theory the subordinate of the Raja of Satara: Sindhia, Holkar, the Gaekwar, Bhonsla and Puar were subordinates of both Peshwa and Raja. The time's anarchy is well illustrated by a story first told by Orme. In 1743 the Nizam marched to Arcot, the capital of the Carnatic, where he found that the designation of 'Nawab' had become fashionable and was no longer reserved for the military head of a sub-province, *de facto* ruler under himself (as 'Subadar of the Deccan') and that yet loftier potentate, the Emperor at Delhi. After eighteen 'Nawabs' had been introduced to him in one day, he ordered that the next should be scourged![1]

Before another generation had passed, the English joined the stately pageant, using Nawabs of Bengal and the Carnatic and their titular overlord at Delhi to cover their own exercise of the actual sovereignty. While fate allowed, the French were Nawabs and feudal dependents. As for the wretched ordinary people of India, they

' were becoming a masterless multitude swaying to and fro in the political storm, and clinging to any power, natural or supernatural, that seemed likely to protect them'.[2]

---

[1] Wilks tells the story with a slight difference; it is the *chobdars* (announcers) who are to be beaten on the appearance of the next 'Nawab'.

[2] Sir Alfred Lyall, *Rise and Expansion of the British Empire in India*, 64-5.

BOOK II

FOUNDATION OF THE INDIAN EMPIRE: CLIVE TO WARREN HASTINGS, 1740-1785

' What enterprise that an enlightened community may attempt is more noble and more profitable than the reclamation from barbarism of fertile regions and large populations? . . . What more beautiful ideal or more valuable reward can inspire human effort? The act is virtuous, the exercise invigorating, the result often extremely profitable.'—The Rt. Hon. WINSTON CHURCHILL, M.P., *The River War*, 9-10.

' The Moors, as well as Gentoos, are indolent, luxurious, ignorant and cowardly, beyond all conception; the Country itself is full of great and navigable Rivers, is very woody, enclosed by mountains with narrow passes; in short, everything conspires to render Infantry formidable, and Cavalry (in which the chief strength of Indostan consists) a meer bugbear. The Soldiers, if they deserve that name, have not the least attachment to their Prince, he only can expect Service from them who pays them best, but it is a matter of great indifference to them whom they serve: and I am fully persuaded that after the battle of Placis I could have appropriated the whole Country to the Company and preserved it afterwards with as much ease as Meer Jaffeir the present Subah now does, through the terror of the English Arms and their influence.'
—ROBERT CLIVE, December 30, 1758.

1742. Dupleix Governor of Pondicherry.
1744. War of Austrian Succession.
1746. Naval fighting between French and English off coast of southern Coromandel. French capture Madras.
1748. British repulsed before Pondicherry. Death of Nizam-ul-Mulk and Shahu.
1749. Peace restored by Treaty of Aix-la-Chapelle. Madras restored to British. British interfere in succession to Tanjore State. Death of Nawab of the Carnatic. Dupleix' intrigues and success.
1750. War breaks out in South India, for successions to Nizam and Nawab of the Carnatic. Dupleix (December) becomes titular ruler of the Carnatic.
1751. Clive defends Arcot.
1752. French abandon siege of Trichinopoli. Execution of Chanda Sahib.
1754. Dupleix recalled. Peace between French and English in South India.
1756. Seven Years' War begins. Nawab of Bengal captures Calcutta.
1757. English take Chandernagore. Battle of Plassey. Mir J'afar made Nawab.
1758. Lally in India: he fails to take Madras. Forde overruns the Northern Sarkars.
1759. Forde routs Dutch at Biderra.
1760. Vansittart Governor of Bengal. Final defeat of French in South India, at Wandiwash. Mir Qasim appointed Nawab of Bengal for Mir J'afar.
1761. Defeat of Marathas by Afghans at third battle of Panipat. Fall of Pondicherry. Haidar Ali becomes ruler of Mysore.
1763. Peace of Paris. End of Seven Years' War. Mir Qasim's massacre of Europeans at Patna. Mir J'afar restored as Nawab of Bengal.
1764. Mir Qasim defeated at Buxar.
1765. Death of Mir J'afar. Clive Governor of Bengal.
1767. War with Haidar Ali.
      Departure of Clive. Verelst Governor of Bengal.
1769. Cartier Governor of Bengal. Treaty of Madras ends war with Haidar Ali.
1770. Famine in Bengal.
1772. Warren Hastings Governor of Bengal.
1773. Lord North's Regulating Act.
1774 The Rohilla War.

Governors-General

WARREN HASTINGS. 1774. Establishment of Supreme Court, Calcutta.
                 1775. First Maratha War. Execution of Nandakumar.
                 1778. War with France. French settlements captured.
                 1779. Convention of Wargaon. War with Mysore.
                 1780. Popham captures Gwalior. Haidar Ali ravages the Carnatic. Destruction of Baillie's force.
                 1781. Coote wins battle of Porto Novo. Hastings and Chait Singh, Raja of Benares.
                 1782. Hastings and the Oudh Begums. French naval activity off Madras: de Suffren. Death of Haidar Ali.
                      Failure of French and Spanish siege of Gibraltar: Rodney's victory in West Indies. Resignation of North; the Rockingham Ministry.
                 1783. Treaty of Versailles.
                 1784. Treaty of Mangalore: peace with Tipu. Pitt's India Act.
                 1785. Resignation of Hastings.

CHAPTER I

THE FIRST ANGLO-FRENCH WAR IN THE CARNATIC

Growth of Pondicherry: War of Austrian Succession: de la Bourdonnais: Bourdonnais and Dupleix: fall of Madras: battle of the Adyar: Robert Clive is of a martial disposition: siege of Pondicherry: character of European troops: Dupleix takes up country politics: rival Nawabs of the Carnatic: Clive's swoop at Arcot: battle of Kaveripak: friendship of Clive and Lawrence: cautious warriors: the Trichinopoli fighting: execution of Chanda Sahib.

WITHIN two or three years of the foundation of Calcutta, the French founded Chandernagore (Chandranagar), a few miles farther up the Hugli. At Mahé they obtained a footing on the Malabar coast, 1725; and at Karikal, 1739, a second station on the Coromandel coast, where already they had Pondicherry. Pondicherry, their first, remained their only important settlement. Their East India Company, despite its brief impressive bid for supremacy, was a stiff and hampered effort, strictly subordinated to State policies and home interests—subsidised, regulated, overruled. It never attained to the freedom of a great trading corporation, as its Dutch and English rivals were, with keen pushful shareholders flooding its activities with their energy and expectations. How wealthy the English Company (though inferior to the Dutch) had become we may judge from the fact that by 1750 it had lent or given the British Treasury no less than £4,200,000, whereas the French Company was in constant debt, and liable to pillage and supervision by Court officials.

Pondicherry owed its predominance to three able governors, François Martin, its founder, Dumas, and Dupleix. Up to about 1720 the settlement kept on scrupulously friendly terms with Madras, which extended a tolerant kindness in return. But a change came, a consciousness of growing strength on the one side and distrust of a rival on the other. In 1721 the English authorities at Calcutta, sharing the new feeling of their countrymen in South India, fined a pilot in their service Rs. 500 for taking a French ship up the Hugli, with a promise of a public whipping if he repeated the offence. In 1731 the Company's records contained the first mention of names destined to become menacingly important—de la Bourdonnais and Dupleix. The latter became Governor of Pondicherry and acting Director-General of the French Indies, 1742.

The War of the Austrian Succession, which broke out in 1744, for years had been plainly coming. De la Bourdonnais, Governor of Mauritius, in 1741 urged the French Ministry to equip him to attack English shipping. He was given a squadron; but war was delayed so long that the French East India Company had time to press their objec-

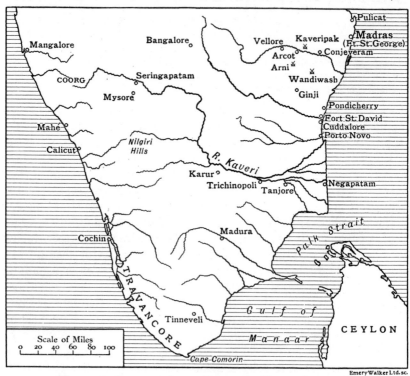

MAP OF THE CARNATIC: ANGLO-FRENCH AND MYSORE CAMPAIGNS.

tions to naval activity near India—objections largely based on their method of trade, whereby each year's enterprise paid for itself. A temporary run of enemy seizures of their ships might ruin a whole group of adventurers.

Both Companies desired neutrality in the East, whatever happened in Europe. But war came (and continued) in such a manner that each belligerent was convinced of the other's bad faith. Dupleix was wroth when an English fleet under Commodore Barnett, a vigorous officer, appeared at the end of 1744 and collected French shipping (and, incidentally, most of the Governor's fortune collected in twenty years of trade and service). Anwar-ud-din, Nawab of the Carnatic, was appealed to, and told the English the French were settled in his country and under his protection. He was brought to understand that Barnett, a King's officer, was not amenable to Company orders. But he stuck to part of his point; Barnett must not attack Pondicherry.

In 1746 Barnett died. Edward Peyton, a poor officer, succeeded him. De la Bourdonnais came from the French islands, a seaman much superior to the English commander:

'His knowledge in mechanics rendered him capable of building a ship from the keel: his skill in navigation, of conducting her to any part of the globe: and his courage, of defending her against any equal force. In the conduct of an expedition, he superintended all the details of the service, without being perplexed either with the variety or number of them. His plans were simple, his orders precise, and both the best adapted to the service in which he was engaged. His application was incessant; and difficulties served only to increase his activity, which always gave the example of zeal to those he commanded.' [1]

But the French suffered heavily in an engagement off Negapatam, 222 casualties to the English 60; fires in ships caused much destruction. Peyton, instead of pressing his advantage, continued his course to Trincomali, in Ceylon, where he repaired damages. De la Bourdonnais was allowed to slip into the shelter of Pondicherry fort. Here, luckily for the English, he conceived himself welcomed disrespectfully, and a quarrel ensued as to precedence of naval officer and Company's servant. Ranga Pillai [2] noted:

'The Governor . . . is aggrieved because M. de la Bourdonnais does not regard himself as his subordinate, maintains a guard of honour of troopers, . . . conducts everything independently, and without consultation with him; whilst M. de la Bourdonnais holds that he is on a par with the Governor, and is consequently entitled to all the honours accorded to that functionary; and that the control of military operations resting wholly with him, he is not bound to consult the Governor in matters connected therewith. . . .'

Again putting out, the French fell in with Peyton in his former haunts off Negapatam. But Peyton sailed for Bengal, refusing action. The English in Madras, thus deserted, in their turn appealed to the Nawab for protection. Both sides (but the French were quicker in

[1] Robert Orme, *Military Transactions*, i. 72.

[2] Dupleix' *dubash*, or confidential native agent. See *The Private Diary of Ananda Ranga Pillai, from 1736 to 1761*, translated and edited by Sir J. F. Price and K. Rangachari.

waking to the facts) still thought the Nawab an effective combatant. He sent orders to the French to leave their enemies alone, but was disobeyed, which the indignant English set down to their own leaders' unwisdom in sending too small a present. Since the word 'present' excited every mind, whatever its nationality, this contemporary belief was probably partly founded.

After a fortnight's siege of sorts, Madras capitulated. The besiegers had not a man killed; and the besieged's losses no authority puts above six, of which four seem to have been Portuguese. Orme comments:

' From this period it is useful to contemplate the progress made by the English in Indostan, both in the science and spirit of war.'

De la Bourdonnais agreed to ransom the town for 1,100,000 pagodas and a private gift of 100,000 (88,000 were paid immediately). Dupleix repudiated the treaty, and prolonged and furious argument followed. He compelled the English to accept articles additional to the capitulation already made; de la Bourdonnais he persuaded to sail to Achin, and then quashed his engagement. 'Dupleix thus justified his patronymic.' [1]

Bent on extirpation, Dupleix embarked on folly so apparent that it is hard to credit that it ever happened. He not only retained Madras, he expelled its English residents and ordered native merchants to remove to Pondicherry. *Delenda est Carthago* now proved a policy more harmful to practisers than victims. As in their controversies with Portuguese and Dutch, the English gained in comparative prestige from their rivals' lack of common sense and ordinary tolerance. The French with 'avaricious exactitude' collected everything they could lay hands on. But merchants obtained leave clandestinely to carry their goods elsewhere than to Pondicherry, for a twenty per cent. commission on their value—which stayed in the hands that received it.

Anwar-ud-din now sent an army to eject the French. Paradis, an engineer officer, routed it in a fight as trivial in casualties as any other in these years of petty fights. Orme's solemn reflection—that it shattered the belief that the country powers were invincibly strong: [2]

' The French at once broke through the charm of this timorous opinion by defeating a whole army with a single battalion'—

has been copied by writers who might be supposed familiar with the early history of the Western nations in India:

' All historians are careful to point out the importance of that fight as

[1] Love, *Vestiges of Old Madras*, ii. 374.   [2] i. 77.

proving the helplessness of an old-fashioned Indian army against an extremely small body of disciplined Europeans.' [1]

What the skirmish really did was to lift Europeans from a temporary (and entirely recent) pusillanimity, and to show the enormous superiority of bayonet and musket over the antiquated pike—still more, over the toy weapons of Orientals.

The Nawab found the event a shock. He had measured

' the military abilities of the Europeans by the great respect and humility with which they had hitherto carried themselves in all their transactions with the Mogul government '.[2]

While he retired to meditate on the light vouchsafed to him, his younger son, Muhammad Ali, went to assist the English, concentrated at Madras, against which the French now marched. Both sides behaved with excessive circumspection. But the English at least put themselves in a posture of defence. The French fell back, and entered on negotiations with the Nawab, who (1747) forgave them, received presents, and was permitted to fly his flag at Pondicherry for one week.

Dupleix' repudiation of the Madras treaty had been reasonably regarded as releasing from parole any who could escape. Robert Clive, a young man of twenty-one, blacked his face and slipped out in Moorish dress. The Company presently record (May 2, 1747):

' Mr. Robert Clive, Writer in the Service, being of a Martial Disposition, and having acted as a Volunteer in Our late Engagement, We have Granted him an Ensign's Commission upon his Application for the same.'

(*January* 27, 1748). 'Be sure to encourage Ensign Clive in his Martial Pursuits. According to His Merit, any Improvement he shall make therein shall be duly regarded by Us.'

Both nations received naval reinforcements, which behaved so warily and inefficiently as to exasperate those they were supposed to be supporting; the French commander, as the weaker in ships, had the more excuse. Receiving a yet further accession under Boscawen, in 1748 the English attacked Pondicherry. There was also a military contingent, under Major Stringer Lawrence, a brave, energetic, experienced King's officer. His arrival (January 1, 1748)

' and the discipline which he at once proceeded to enforce, mark the time from which the Company's troops became an effective military force'.[3]

[1] *Oxford History of India*, 473.

[2] Edward Thornton, *The History of the British Empire in India* (1841), 77, paraphrasing Orme.

[3] H. Dodwell, *Dupleix and Clive*, 23.

His men were from the dregs of England, and his officers he collected largely from Fort St. George, where they were kicking their heels and whiling the days away by incessant gambling. All ranks were mercenary and freelance in spirit; it was Lawrence who first checked their habit of marketing their services where they seemed most profitable. A professional and patriotic soldier, he believed in courts-martial and exercise of what is usually called 'terrible but necessary severity'. Three years later, when Clive stormed a post held by forty deserters to the French, he instructed him to hang their leaders out of hand; and from his first arrival in India he executed spies and informers freely. War became a serious business.

Looking back on these days from the height of his achievement and fame later, Clive told Orme:

' If there be any officers or soldiers in India, remaining of those who were at the siege of Pondichery twelve or thirteen years ago, experience must have convinced them how very ignorant we were of the art of war in those days. Some of the engineers were masters of the theory without the practice, and those seemed wanting in resolution. Others there were who understood neither, and yet were possessed of courage sufficient to have gone on with the undertaking if they had known how to go about it. There was scarce an officer who knew whether the engineers were acting right or wrong, till it was too late in the season and we had lost too many men to begin an approach again.'

English naval and military forces moved on Pondicherry, whose siege they conducted so inefficiently that they lost at the outset Lawrence (as a prisoner, captured 'sooner than follow the Troops in their ignominious flight') and altogether over a thousand men by battle and sickness. The French loss was slight, but included Paradis. A week after the siege had been raised came news of the Treaty of Aix-la-Chapelle, by which Madras was restored.

This failed to bring peace in India, except temporarily. The Nizam-ul-mulk died, 1748, after having rendered to Delhi neither recognition nor tribute for a great while; two of his sons fought to succeed him. Anwar-ud-din was in poor health, and Dupleix was intriguing with Chanda Sahib, a nobleman related to the Nawab. In 1749 the English set the example of overt interference with the politics of India, not very brilliantly, in a dispute for the succession to the principality of Tanjore. Dupleix bettered the instruction almost immediately, sending Chanda Sahib troops with whose aid he routed and killed Anwar-ud-din (1749). It would be tedious to mention all the occasions when large payments were made in the India of this period. This was one; and Dupleix set a precedent which Clive later was to follow on a superb scale (with his *jagir*), obtaining for himself, his wife, and her relations 'a village apiece'.[1] He further obtained from Muzaffar Jang, the Nizam he supported, a grant of the hinterland of Fort St. David. He and his allies proceeded to collect revenue. The Raja of Tanjore was coerced into promising seventy lakhs; most of what he paid had to be given to the French.

At the fall of Madras Dupleix had shown that he aimed at expulsion of the English, a policy which it must be believed he was ready to take up again when opportunity served. He now clearly aimed at their encirclement and isolation. They were to be pinned to their settlements at Forts St. George and St. David, while the French proceeded to suzerainty inland, over the territory where the weavers and merchants who worked for the Company lived. The war that followed was for the English one of self-preservation.

Muhammad Ali, whom we have seen with the English in their retreat at Fort St. David, challenged the nawabship against Chanda Sahib. Muzaffar Jang as subadar of the Deccan ('Nizam') was similarly challenged by Nasir Jang, who appeared (1750) in South India, Lawrence with 300 Europeans joining him. The allies marched against Chanda Sahib, whose French troops decamped in the night, their subaltern officers having collected a month's pay in advance and gone (also in advance), disgruntled at being inadequately rewarded. Both French and English entered on negotiations and intrigues with Nasir Jang, who withdrew to Arcot, the capital of the Carnatic. Thereupon the ablest of the French commanders, the celebrated Bussy, stormed his strongest fortress, Ginji.

None of the four claimants for *subadari* and *nawabi* 'had any relations but that of rebellion' to their alleged overlord at Delhi. Nevertheless,

' two enlightened European nations wasted their ingenuity in volumes of political controversy; rendering homage to virtue and justice, in respectively claiming the reputation of supporting the rightful cause; but adding to the numerous examples of failure in attempting to reconcile the discordant elements of politics and morals; without daring to avow the plain and barbarous truth, that the whole was a trial of strength among bands of foreign usurpers, in which the English and French had as much right to be principals as any one of the pageants whom they supported: but these nations were at peace, and they could only appear in the contest as the mercenary troops of these polished barbarians'[2].

[1] Dodwell, *Dupleix and Clive*, 38.
[2] Wilks, i. 162.

Dupleix intrigued so successfully that in December, 1750, Nasir Jang was murdered. Chanda Sahib, then in Pondicherry, ran through the streets and publicly embraced the Governor. General congratulations followed, which included (as is usual) the Deity; a *Te Deum* was sung in all churches. Muzaffar Jang was invited to Pondicherry, which he entered in the same palanquin with Dupleix. Next day's durbar was a riot of noise and colour, of kettledrums, elephants, flags, jewels, canopies and tapestries. Dupleix was given a robe of honour, titles, a fortress and villages, and a *jagir* (estate) of 100,000 rupees. He was appointed Nawab of the lands between the Kistna and Cape Comorin, with Chanda Sahib under him as Nawab of Arcot. The vast treasure accumulated during Nizam-ul-mulk's long and profitable career was lavishly distributed to the deserving. Dupleix himself was said to have received £200,000 in cash, as well as many valuable jewels.

It was his moment of highest success. But it was a political blunder, similar in kind to that the English Company made when they accepted from Persia a half-share of the Gombroon customs. Just as then the Dutch had declined to accept their rivals as overlords of the Gulf commerce, so now the English could not accept the French Governor as titular head of the province in which they traded. Confronted with threatened extinction, they made their assistance to Muhammad Ali a vigorous reality.

In the ensuing war Bombay took no part, though the strongest of the English settlements. It was contained by the most powerful armies in India, those of the Marathas, who interposed a barrier. Moreover, now as later, Bombay was debarred by provincialism, as well as difficulties, from helping her sister settlements. This quality is the obverse side of an excellence which still sets the city apart—even to-day there is a far friendlier feeling between British and Indians in Bombay than in Calcutta or Delhi:

'Bombay developed a spirit different from the other two Presidencies, a cosmopolitan spirit of co-operation based on mutual respect and necessity instead of a spirit of imperialism founded on military glory and the pride of possession.' [1]

Madras bore the brunt of the first fighting; Bengal became a battle-field later.

The ablest of the French commanders, Bussy, was out of the war that followed. He was sent to Pondicherry in 1751, with 300 Europeans and 4000 sepoys, to support the Nizam (and keep him loyal to the

[1] T. G. Spear, *The Nabobs*, 72.

French). Bussy found Dupleix hard to work with, and did not respect his military policy. Haidarabad State gave him work, and him and his officers exceedingly generous pay and pickings.

A bad President, incapacitated by venereal disease and gambling mania, was succeeded, October, 1750, by a good one, Thomas Saunders,

' a man inferior perhaps to M. Dupleix in splendour of talents, and in all that constitutes the decoration of character, but not yielding to that distinguished statesman in the possession of a sound and vigorous judgment, a clear and quick perception, a constancy of mind not to be disturbed by danger, and a devotion to the cause of his country no less ardent and sincere'.[1]

' Had I anything on earth to expect or anything to fear, he is the man on earth I should dread as an enemy.' [2]

Lawrence was in England. The English fleet had disappeared; the Company looked what Dupleix alleged they were, a handful deserted by fortune and their country, with the victorious French closing round them. They had been plundered so thoroughly that they could not bribe any native supporter. Muhammad Ali, their candidate for the nawabship, was besieged in Trichinopoli.

Clive, now a captain (Company's commission), proposed a reckless diversion—the capture of Chanda Sahib's capital, Arcot, sixty-four miles south-west of Madras. Saunders agreed, and gave him 500 sepoys and 300 Europeans, which left only 100 soldiers in Fort St. David and less than 50 in Madras. Six of Clive's eight officers were new to war; four were from the mercantile service, as he himself was. The tiny force marched to its goal. Presently astonished spies reported that they were moving steadily through a monsoon tempest; the Arcot garrison fled before such obvious demons should arrive. A sergeant with the expedition has left a diary, for soldierly scorn worthy to rank with the narrative of that other sergeant who fought 'against Macbeth's captivity'.[3] He tells us that the force entered Arcot Fort (September 12, 1751)

' without opposition through the town, amidst a million Spectators whose looks betrayed them traytors, notwithstanding their pretended friendship and dirty presents'.[4]

The vanished defenders had left their munitions—quantities of rockets, lead and gunpowder.

Clive won over the populous city to neutrality by forbidding pillage and insolence. Next, for it was always his habit to hunt out his enemy,

[1] Wilks, i. 169-70.
[2] Orme in private letter, March 11, 1758 (Love's *Vestiges*, ii. 489).
[3] See *Macbeth*, I. ii.   [4] Orme MSS., quoted by Forrest, *Life of Lord Clive*, i. 140.

he proceeded to search for the late garrison. The latter had received 5000 reinforcements, hurriedly sent from before Trichinopoli, and were considering the question of storming Arcot Fort. Clive anticipated their decision by sallying out and 'beating up their quarters'. This operation, of which the classic example is the outbreak of Nisus and Euryalus (*Æneid*, ix.), Clive established as a custom. A brilliant band of officers took fire from his example, so that it was soon almost automatic with the English to make a night raid on any enemy whose straggling disorderly camp was within easy march. On this first practice of it, the troops

' about 12 at night marched out with 3 platoons & the Seapoys, observing the most profound silence, well knowing the success of a handfull of men against such numbers entirely depended on not being discovered. The attempt succeeded to wish. ... So great was their confusion that tho' we went through the middle of 'em they fired very few shot amongst us, & those few to no purpose. We made no stay, but returned to Arcot immediately. So privately was this affair conducted that the Inhabitants knowing nothing of our being out upon our return imagined it to be a reinforcement for the garrison. We can no otherwise judge of the enemy's loss than by the terrible shreiks and groans all over the camp. As our people were strictly order'd to keep their ranks less plunder was got than perhaps might have been expected from such an exploit'.

During the siege, which lasted for fifty-three days (September 23-November 14), the besieged sallied out continually, as if overwhelming force were on their side. At last Morari Rao, a Maratha freelance paid to assist Muhammad Ali, moved to admiration after long watching 'on the side-lines', sent word that he was coming to help Clive. This precipitated a general assault, preceded by elephants with pikes on their heads to batter down the gates. These beasts recoiled from the bullets, and dashed their own lines into disorder; the stormers were repulsed at all points. Two days later the siege was raised in confusion. Clive emerged immediately, and at Arni, assisted by the Marathas, won his first battle, the defeated army fleeing wildly: 'except the body of French there were not above 20 or 30 of them in one place'.[1] The Marathas obtained much booty.

The defence of Arcot was a feat of arms immediately famous. Though it would have been impossible except against troops of the most blackguardly character, we must acknowledge the almost superhuman valour of one man. If we follow Clive's adventures, now and

[1] Sergeant's narrative.

afterwards, in Orme's minutely detailed narrative, we shall exclaim that surely no man ever cared so little for his own life. A leader so generous of himself won others to a like vivacity of nobleness. When he marched against Conjeveram, which the French had recovered, the commandant ordered Glass and Revel—who had been wounded and then taken prisoners in a convoy of casualties—to warn their late leader that they would be exposed on the walls if he attacked the pagoda. They did so, 'but added, that they hoped no regard to their safety would induce him to discontinue his operations'. Clive's Indian troops responded to his courage, luck, and considerateness. Their part in the siege was very honourable.

Setting aside writers (still numerous) to whom any criticism of the founders of our Indian Empire is treason, we may note that historians have settled down to idolatrous regard for Warren Hastings but concede flaws in Clive. Luckily there is no need to depress either (though the former's praise is now absurdly promulgated) to extol the other. Prejudice against Clive is hard to maintain while we read of his reckless front towards peril and his constancy in apparent defeat. It is no doubt wrong to admire valour above all things, and we must not do it. But valour such as Clive's, exposed not in proxy but in his person, is a high moral quality.

Clive turned to relieve Trichinopoli, while Dupleix, copying his Arcot example, persuaded his native allies to strike at Madras, a menace which Saunders deflected Clive to meet. Directly Clive drew near, 400 French troops and 4500 Indians entrenched south-west of Madras broke up camp, 'with all the appearance of people greatly alarmed'. Clive following, found them strongly posted in an orchard at Kaveripak. Early in the action he learnt that their rear was unprotected, so, stationing most of his men in a deep watercourse, he led a mixed body far enough to make their task clear: then returned, rallied his troops, who were on the point of abandoning the watercourse, and kept them with difficulty to a holding attack, their contribution to the main assault by the troops he had left. Close on midnight, news came that the enemy's rearguard had been routed and his cannon taken. This action 'changed the balance of French and English influence in India'.[1]

Lawrence returned from England, to find officers with King's commissions and senior to Clive jealous of the young captain who was so popular. He dismissed the allegations of some who 'were pleased to

[1] Orme MSS., Forrest, i. 165.

term fortunate and lucky' Clive's 'uncommon success' at Arcot, holding
that it had come naturally, out of 'an undaunted resolution, a cool temper and a presence of mind which never left him in the greatest danger.'[1]
Between these two there was never anything but mutual trust. When
we contrast their relations with the quarrels of the French leaders, we
see a large part of the reason why the English Company triumphed.
Lawrence later wrote to Clive in England:

' I'm perswaded however distant we are from each other Our Friendship
is unalterable.' (November 30, 1752.)

' For God's sake why do you mention obligations to me, I never thought
you under any and the Proof you have given me that I was not deceived
in my opinion of you from the beginning affords me much satisfaction.'
(February 1753.)

Lawrence brought

' 200 European recruits, just arrived from England, and, as usual, the refuse
of the vilest employments in London, together with 500 Sepoys newly raised,
and as inexperienced as the Europeans. Such a force appeared very unequal
to the enterprise of laying siege to strong forts; and it could hardly be expected that any officer who had acquired reputation would willingly risque
it by taking the command of them; but Captain Clive, whose military life
had been a continued option of difficulties,[2] voluntarily took them on, though
in poor health.' [3]

Clive could already offer the lure which was to draw the mercenary
hordes over ever-increasingly 'to leaders who always paid and usually
won, and whose own countrymen did the hardest fighting.'[4] Yet
those words are anticipating a little. At this date it had been in rapidity
of retreat rather than ferocity of assault that Nordic supremacy
had shown itself. A few months previously, for example, under cover
of night a British force had warily approached the French posted in
Covelong. Next dawn an enemy detachment surprised them with a fire
that killed their officer, whereupon

' his troops fled with a degree of determination which appeared to indicate
that Madras was the point to which they were bent, and that their speed would
not slacken until they arrived there'.[5]

---

[1] Forrest, i. 167.   [2] A sufficient eulogy of any soldier that ever lived!

[3] Orme, i. 261-2. Cf. Sir Charles Petrie, *The Jacobite Movement*, 195: 'The
fighting value of British troops in the middle of the eighteenth century was not
great, and the rank and file, even of the Guards, was recruited from the very dregs
of the population'.

[4] Alfred Lyall, *Rise and Expansion of the British Dominion in India*, 134.

[5] Edward Thornton, *History of the British Empire in India*, i. 150.

While still considerably short of their goal they met Clive, hastening up with reinforcements. With 'great difficulty and some violence' 'this fortunate and popular commander' persuaded them that they had over-assessed the emergency which had so stirred them, and might return with him and their comrades. The siege of Covelong was resumed accordingly. But a shot which struck a rock, so that fourteen men were hit by flying splinters, revived their terrors, and

' it was some time before they could be brought to expose themselves to the danger of similar untoward visitations. The extraordinary regard which these troops manifested for their personal safety was strikingly illustrated in the case of one of the advanced sentries, who, several hours after the alarming incident, was found calmly reposing at the bottom of a dry well. The name of this cautious person is unfortunately not recorded'.

These were 'the debased specimens of manhood' whom Clive and Lawrence had the 'misfortune to command'. The sepoys, for their part,

'might have some advantage over their European coadjutors in point of character, but they had none in respect of experience, being newly raised and unaccustomed to a military life'.[1]

Luckily, the Company's warriors frequently met with adversaries who shared 'a community of feeling' that battlefields were dangerous places which should be evacuated betimes.

Fighting concentrated on Trichinopoli and the Island of Sriringam, famous for its pagodas. Before long,

' the plain of Tritchinopoly having been so long the seat of war, scarce a tree was left standing for several miles round the city; and the English detachments were obliged to march five or six miles to get firewood'.[2]

The detailed story may be read in Orme's brilliantly tedious narrative. By June, 1752, the city was safe, and the French and over 2000 of their native allies were captives. Chanda Sahib surrendered, on promise of his life, to the Raja of Tanjore, and was beheaded. Mill for once speaks fairly when he says:

' Lawrence shows an indifference about his fate which is not very easy to be reconciled with either humanity or wisdom. He well knew that his murder was, in the hands of any of them, the probable, in those of some of them, the certain consequence, of their obtaining the charge of his person. He well knew, that if he demanded him with firmness, they would have all consented to his confinement in an English fort.' [3]

[1] *Op. cit.* i. 159.   [2] Orme, i. 262.

[3] *History of India*, iii. 123-4. Lawrence was present at the council of war which decided who should be Chanda Sahib's jailor.

But life was cheap; and Chanda Sahib an adventurer, though praised by Orme as

' a brave, benevolent, humane and generous man, as princes go in Indostan. His military abilities were much greater than are commonly found in the generals of India, insomuch that if he had had an absolute command over the French troops, it is believed he would not have committed the mistakes which brought on his catastrophe, and the total reduction of his army.'

His conqueror, Muhammad Ali, was contemptible even by contemporary standards. We are destined to grow very weary of him.

CHAPTER II

THE CONQUISTADORES

Clive in England: returns: capture of Gheria: loss of Calcutta: the Black Hole: Clive and Watson sail for Bengal: recapture of Calcutta: Clive and Watson: King's officers and Company's officers: capture of Chandernagore: renewed war with Nawab of Bengal: battle of Plassey: Mir J'afar Nawab: Aminchand, and Clive's forgery: murder of Siraj-ud-Daula: happy days in Calcutta: war in South India: Lally takes Fort St. David: Forde's conquests in the Northern Sarkars: Shahzada invades Bihar: Clive as Kai Lung: rout of Dutch: Lally's defeat at Wandiwash: third battle of Panipat.

EARLY in 1753 Clive sailed for England, where he was lionised. The Directors toasted him as 'General Clive' and presented him with a jewelled sword (which he declined, unless Lawrence also received one). Part of his money he spent restoring his father's fortunes, and squandered the residue on a contested election. Disappointed of getting into Parliament, he returned to India, 1755, commissioned by His Majesty as a lieutenant-colonel, 'in the East Indies only'.

He found the Companies at peace again. Dupleix, who had cost his employers too much, and bemused them with stories of triumphs which unaccountably closed in ruin, had been dismissed, 1754, taking defeat magnanimously, and lamented for his kindness and readiness to scatter, as well as amass, money. His only able officer, Bussy, who had criticised and advised from a distance, continued to reside at the Nizam's Court, routing Marathas for him and doing brilliant service that in the upshot hardly helped France at all. He, as well as Dupleix, showed the

English both what it was wise to do and what it was better to leave undone. He set the precedent which Wellesley followed, long after, of
subsidiary alliances—for this was what the French gave the Nizam, who
handed over (December, 1754), for the expenses of the French corps,
the four Northern Sarkars, a district between the mouth of the Kistna
and Puri, in Orissa.

Clive's first task was to command the land attack on Gheria, the
Angria stronghold, in conjunction with a sea attack under Admiral
Watson. An expedition from Bombay had already (1755)

' destroyed the timorous prejudices which had for twenty years been
entertained of the impracticability of reducing any of Angria's fortified
harbours'; [1]

under Commodore James, Suvarnadroog, 'the Golden Fortress', had
been taken. He secured the Marathas as allies, and the dreaded Gheria
was captured with absurd ease (February, 1756). Clive's men entered
first; and this time the English collected the whole booty. Unedifying
disputes followed between Clive and Watson, as to precedence of one
commission and another, and the share of loot proper to be allotted to a
mere lieutenant-colonel. Watson was not grasping, but he was 'sticky'
on points of the senior service's honour. His integrity is highly praised
by English historians, and shines conspicuously against the time's excessively murky background. It was, however, of a passive rather than an
active kind. Enthusiasm for it seems to us to require a distinct effort of
will.

In Bengal Allahvardi Khan, the Nawab, noted the rising strength of
the English; but rejected proposals to expel them, having the sense to
guess their immense reserves of power. 'It is now difficult to extinguish
the fire on land. Should the sea be in flames, who could put it out?' But
the events in South India so incensed him that

' he threatened the French in Bengal with the seizure of their property.
Incurious and apathetic as Indians may have been, the slaughter of two
Muhammadan princes and the tutelage of a third by the infidel were not
events to be passed over without comment at a Muhammadan court'. [2]

Even Orientals are not blind to the obvious. Captain Rennie, a sea-
captain who wrote before the disaster to Fort William had been completely reversed at Plassey, says

' the principal cause of the war was the knowledge of what had happened on
the coast of Coromandel, for many Moors (and some of distinction among

[1] Orme, i. 406.   [2] Dodwell, *Dupleix and Clive*, 118.

F

them) have come lately from thence and declared that the English and French have divided the country, while their respective Nabobs are not better than shadows of what they should be'.[1]

He testifies also to a growth of casualness and arrogance in the English at Calcutta, who stretched their own trade privileges and rights of asylum:

' The injustice to the Moors consists in that, being by their courtesy permitted to live here as merchants—to protect and judge what natives were our servants, and to trade custom free—we under that pretence protected all the Nabob's servants that claimed our protection, though they were neither our servants nor our merchants, and gave our *dustucks* or passes to numbers of natives to trade custom free, to the great prejudice of the Nabob's revenue; nay, more, we levied large duties upon goods brought into our districts from the very people that permitted us to trade custom free, and by numbers of impositions (framed to raise the Company's revenues, some of which were ruinous to ourselves)—such as taxes on marriages, provisions transferring land property, &c.—caused eternal clamour and complaints against us at Court.'

Allahvardi Khan's adopted son, Siraj-ud-Daula, became Nawab, 1756. He was a mean ruffian, but we need not seek in original sin his reason for attacking the Company. Before his accession they had corresponded with a rival's faction. Then they sheltered a Hindu merchant he desired to plunder, and turned his messenger 'out of the factory and off the shore with derision and insolence'. The merchant repaid their protection by joining another merchant resident in Calcutta, the afterwards notorious Aminchand, in intriguing with the Nawab, especially in the siege which followed. Further, as we have seen, the Bengal governor had witnessed the frightening emergence in South India of alien Powers who possessed footing in his own territories. Both English and French factories in Bengal were being fortified; and while the French to his peremptory command to desist sent a conciliatory reply, the English answered:

' That in the late War between our Nation and the French, they had attacked and taken the Town of Madras Contrary to the neutrality We expected would have been preserved in the Mogull's Dominions; and that there

---

[1] *Reflections on the Loss of Calcutta* (1756). It is important to observe that the goods which (by the concessions Surman's embassy had obtained) went lawfully duty-free along the inland roads and rivers were only those which had been imported by the Company. The President had no right to give his *dustuck*—pass—to goods belonging to individual servants of the Company, still less to natives of Bengal. It was out of the abuse of the *dustuck* system that so much trouble was presently to arise.

being at present great appearance of another War between the Two Crowns,
We were under some apprehensions they would act the same way in Bengal,
to prevent which We were only repairing our Line of Guns to the Waterside.'

The tactlessness of this suggestion that there might be repetition of
the Carnatic business here, and that the Nawab was powerless to protect in his own province, could hardly be improved on. He wrote back
furiously that he was marching on Calcutta immediately, adding in his
own hand:

' I swear by the Great God and the prophets that unless the English consent to fill up their ditch, raze their fortifications, and trade upon the same
terms they did in the time of Nabob Jaffeer Cawn, I will not hear anything on
their behalf, and will expel them totally out of my country.'

MAP OF BENGAL, BIHAR AND OUDH, TIME OF CLIVE AND WARREN HASTINGS.

He seized the Kasimbazar factory (and with it Warren Hastings), and
his host swarmed across the Hugli (June 15). The English fled into Fort
William; the natives fled from its vicinity. Aminchand, detected in
intrigue, was imprisoned by the factors, after a resistance at his house
so desperate that his chief dependent slaughtered his women and fired it
after stabbing himself, though not mortally. Aminchand, 'implacable in
his resentments',[1] had been made an enemy.

In Madras, in October of this year, Orme wrote from the survivors'
stories an account of the siege, from which we can recover its tenseness

[1] Orme.

and terror. An immense curtain of foes moved in on a handful far from assistance and with frightened leaders. The Muslims had European gunners and a French commander. Adopting infiltration methods, they seeped in by houses surrounding the fort. The first night they received a shock, being introduced to South Indian customs by Ensign Piccard, 'who had served on the coast of Coromandel'. Noting silence in their camp, he stole out and beat up their quarters, spiking four cannon without losing a man. The end was sure, however, though delayed by incessant hand-to-hand fighting, which flung back time after time masses of men who came pouring and pouring on, breakers from an inexhaustible sea. Within the gates arose clamour and misery of a horde of Portuguese and half-caste women. It was resolved, at a council of war held late at night, to send all women to the ships; after midnight, a second council saw that retreat on to the water was necessary for everyone. A day of indescribable fright and confusion followed. The boats were overburdened, for

' many of the inhabitants imagined everybody was to shift for himself . . . everyone endeavoured to get on board such vessel as he could, and to be the first to be embarked. . . . Most of those who had crowded into them were drowned, and such as floated with the tide to the shore were either made prisoners or massacred; for the enemy had taken possession of all the houses and inclosures along the bank of the river, from which stations they shot fire-arrows into the ships and vessels, in hope of burning them'.

An act of desertion as impulsive as that of Conrad's 'Lord Jim' followed. A ship's captain set an example of panic, which every 'ship and sloop' accepted; seeing their craft deserting them,

' many of the gentlemen on shore (who perhaps never dreamt of leaving the factory till everybody did) immediately jumped into such boats as were at the factory stairs and rowed to the ships. Among those who left the factory in this unaccountable manner were the Governor Mr. Drake, Mr. Mackett, Captain-Commandant Michen, and Captain Grave'.

Holwell was elected Governor by those who remained, who continued to resist with the desperation that might be expected from foreigners who knew the story of Shah Jahan's extirpation of the Portuguese. Darkness gave a little respite;

' but the night was not less dreadful on that account; the Company's House, Mr. Cruttenden's, Mr. Nixon's, Doctor Knox's, and the marine yards were now in flames, and exhibited a spectacle of unspeakable horror. We were surrounded on all sides by the Nabob's forces, which made a retreat by land impracticable; and we had not even the shadow of a prospect to effect a retreat by water'.

About four o'clock next afternoon (Sunday, June 25, 1756), the enemy sent a flag of truce, under cover of which they presently swarmed in and began a massacre. A few survivors surrendered, and their personal effects were added to the general and indiscriminate plunder in progress.

Everyone knows what followed: how 146 prisoners were thrust into 'the Black Hole', a room which barely contained them standing, and spent a June night raving with heat and thirst. All but some twenty died. Next day Holwell was supported to the Nawab's presence, upbraided for the smallness of the booty found and threatened with blowing from a gun if he did not divulge where a supposed treasure was hidden. He and his companions were then taken to Murshidabad and led through its bazars in triumph. When it was clear that nothing more was to be squeezed out of the English, whose repeated plucking, at Madras and Calcutta, goes some way to explain the extortions of which, when their own day came, they were guilty, the Nawab—who, moreover, seems to have had some confused feelings of pity, which his womenfolk worked upon—released them from actual imprisonment. They carried out of their experience a profound conviction that the real author of their miseries was Aminchand, whom Drake had imprisoned and Holwell forgot to free:

' a circumstance which, in the heat and hurry of action, never once occurred to me, or I had certainly done it, because I thought his imprisonment unjust'.

Five ships of war under Admiral Watson, and six transports under Colonel Clive, sailed from Madras, October 16, 1756. Their journey illustrates the difference since made by man's control of his material and of nature. The north-east monsoon was 'tyrannous and strong', and during twelve days drove the vessels down to Ceylon. Then they beat across the Bay to Tennaserim, and crept up the Burmese coast, straggling into unknown shoal waters at the Hugli's mouth, December 1 and 2, even then having to leave some of their number outside. It was not until December 9 that the spring tides enabled them to go up the river; and not until six days later that they began to reach Fulta (some forty miles down the Hugli from Calcutta), where the refugees and released prisoners were dying of fever, bad water and scarcity of food.

Drake with three colleagues formed a reconstituted Council, to which Clive and Watson were joined. Clive and Watson ignored the civilians and took entire charge, Clive's stiff wrath at his countrymen's treatment and at their leaders' pusillanimity showing from the first. His letters are always most vigorous when the occasion is most menacing. Manikchand, the Nawab's Governor of Calcutta, returned a letter sent to him to forward to his master, rewritten by him into a suitably submissive style. But the days were finished when the English were 'grains of sand' with 'foreheads rubbed on the ground (by command)'. Clive rejected

' your advice in writing to the Nabob a letter couched in such a stile, which, however proper it might have been before the taking of Calcutta, would but ill suit with the present time, when we are come to demand satisfaction for the injuries done us by the Nabob, not to entreat his favour, and with a force which we think sufficient to vindicate our claim'.

However, he consented to write somewhat less belligerently; and Watson suggested to the Nawab an amicable settlement, with 'a reasonable satisfaction for the losses and injuries'. The Nawab preferred war.

The first brush came, December 28. Manikchand attacked the now disembarked troops at Budge-Budge, received a shot through his turban, and lost 150 men. The fort, which was to be stormed at dusk, was prematurely captured by a drunken sailor, who was sent before the admiral:

' The fellow, after having made his bow, scratched his head, and with one hand twirling his hat upon the other, replied, "Why, to be sure, Sir, it was *I* who took the fort, but *I hope there was no harm in it*".....The whole company were exceedingly diverted with his awkward appearance, and his language and manner in recounting the several particulars of his mad exploit. Mr. Watson expatiated largely on the fatal consequences that might have attended his irregular conduct, and then with a severe rebuke dismissed him; but not before he had given the fellow some distant hints, that at a proper opportunity he should certainly be punished for his temerity. Strahan, amazed to find himself blamed, where he expected praise, had no sooner gone from the admiral's cabin, than he muttered these words: "*If I am flogged for this here action, I will never take another fort by myself as long as I live, by God!*" ' [1]

The navy, moving ahead, recaptured Calcutta easily. Clive's commission as a lieutenant-colonel was not taken very seriously, since merely one granted to a successful amateur:

' Thou art outside, and art not of the guild'.

Watson accordingly appointed Captain Eyre Coote, a King's officer, Governor of Fort William. Clive when he arrived was indignant, and threatened Coote with arrest. Thereupon all the King's officers fired up, and Watson sent word he would bombard Clive out of the fort, to which Clive retorted that he would not answer for the consequences, but was staying. Watson offered a compromise, which was accepted. Coming ashore, as indubitably senior to Clive he took over the keys,

---

[1] Edward Ives, *Voyage to India and Historical Narrative* (1773), 101.

thereby washing out 'a Personal Affront, & thro' him to his Ma'ties Authority'. The keys he then handed to Drake and his Council, who officially declared war on the Nawab and put their forces under Colonel Clive. Clive was not too grateful:

' At last the King's troops are put under my command during the Admiral's pleasure (or rather, during mine, if I insist upon my right). It had been better for the service they had never come and I had the like number of Company's in their room.' [1]

He began to recruit from warlike alien Indian races which had come into the province with the Muslim power. This was the beginning of the Bengal Army, which before it perished in the holocaust of the Mutiny was to carry British dominion to the farthest borders of India and beyond.

Drake's 'Select Committee' informed Clive (January 18, 1757) that he was to 'recede from' his independent powers as Commander-in-Chief, and 'strictly comply with and follow whatever plans of military operations the Select Committee of Fort William may point out.' Thinking Drake and his assistants had done enough mischief, he answered in terms that left no room for misunderstanding, that he should do nothing of the sort. In so far as he recognised any superior at all, it was to Pigot, President of Madras, that he reported throughout.

News came that war had broken out in Europe, and the Nawab made the French a highly advantageous offer of alliance, which they refused, dreading to be attacked at Chandernagore. The protracted skirmishing and negotiation drew to a head. The Nawab's intention to storm Calcutta was prevented by a dawn assault on his camp (February 6, 1757), which developed into 'the warmest service I ever yet was engaged in' (Clive) and cost 194 casualties. Thoroughly frightened, next day the Nawab moved out of danger, leaving dead camels, cattle, elephants, and over 500 horses; his human loss was 1300. He offered Clive peace, with jewels, elephant, and robe of honour. Peace was signed, February 9, after peremptory messages from the English leader; and jewels, robes, and elephants were duly sent to Clive, Drake and Watson (and by Watson declined). The Company obtained a promise that Farakhsiyar's *farman* should at last be fully implemented. There was only inadequate material compensation agreed upon, with nothing for private losses.

Clive now pressed the Nawab for permission to attack the French. As their neutrality had been of the greatest value in the recent fighting,

[1] Letter to Mr. Pigot, Governor of Madras, January 25, 1757.

there seems some ground for Mill's opinion that this was shabby. Aminchand, whose property in Calcutta had been temporarily attached (in resentment of his part during the siege), continued busy in intrigue with everyone. He and Nandakumar ('Nuncomar'), *Faujdar* (Military Commandant) of Hugli, were half convinced that Fortune was going to throw her glove to the English, and arranged to persuade the Nawab to stay neutral; Nandakumar was to receive a gift and English interest to keep him in his job. If the English agreed they were to tell the messenger '*Golabke phul*', 'Rose blossom'. 'Rose blossom' was said; and the English moved on Chandernagore. The Nawab, alarmed and troubled, asked Aminchand

' if such an unprecedented act as fighting amongst the Europeans in the river had ever before been known? If any complaints were made to him, would he not have to redress them?'

Aminchand soothed him with fairy tales, drew attention to the menace of Bussy's large disciplined force in the Nizam's country, and stressed English integrity: 'if a lie could be proved in England upon any one, they were spit upon and never trusted'. His information was somewhat out of date, as he was to realise in a notorious incident. However, the Nawab required the English to keep the peace, and the French begged for peace. Clive, who knew pity, reassured both, and promised peace. But Watson, who as a King's naval officer never hesitated to ignore mere civilians, Clive included, was unwilling to leave the French alone; he held that the Chandernagore Council had insufficient authority to guarantee neutrality, and he feared Bussy would come into Bengal. Clive was indignant at being forced into what looked like a breach of faith, as well as renewed war with the Nawab.

Another complication was that Ahmad Shah, an Afghan chief who had sacked Delhi, was rumoured to intend to conquer Bengal. To purchase English help, the Nawab was inclined to throw the French over. He negotiated with Watson, who behaved badly, jealously keeping the matter to himself, apparently as not Clive's business. Presently learning that the Nawab, who not unnaturally was looking everywhere for assistance, had written to Bussy, Watson exploded in the famous menace (which reveals also the stiff self-conceit of his character):

' I will kindle such a flame in your country as all the water in the Ganges shall not be able to extinguish. Farewell: remember that he promises you this, who never yet broke his word with you or with any man whatsoever.'

The terrified Nawab wrote back cringingly, pointing out that the French were 'my tenants, and upon this affair desired my protection'. Reluctantly, seeing no other way, he gave what was construed into leave to attack them:

' You have understanding and generosity: if your enemy with an upright heart claims your protection, you will give him his life, but then you must be well satisfied of his intentions: if not, whatever you think right, that do.'

This settled the matter. The admiral's real zest was in the war against the French, not in these country wrangles. He held that the declaration of war in Europe was a direct command from His Majesty 'to all officers . . . to distress the enemy as far as it is in their power'. After a gallant resistance on land and water for ten days, costing the defenders 200 casualties on the last day alone, Chandernagore surrendered. The conquerors entered a shambles.

Ahmad Shah the Afghan turned his attention from Bengal, and against the Marathas. In Bengal itself a brief halt came in the war. Nandakumar collected bribes impartially from French and English, and preserved a masterly neutrality. Siraj-ud-Daula pestered Clive with letters in varying tenor, and was notified of successes against the French, with the gloss that these were due to the Almighty's blessing and the Nawab's favour. Clive became reckless of what he did; a hard dishonesty enters into his character. There is nothing to choose for humbug between his letters and the Nawab's; to his closest civilian colleague, Watts, the English Agent at Murshidabad, he openly boasts that he is writing 'haughty or submissive Letters as the Occasion required'. To Orme, a few months later, he promises an account of

' Fighting, tricks, chicanery, Intrigues, Politics and the Lord knows what; in short, there will be a fine Field for you to display your Genius in '.

Ethics disappear from his conduct; we see him immersed in a scheme of things which may well strike us, as it evidently struck him, as fantastically unreal, a world of faery whence all moral distinctions had vanished.

The Nawab's temper became hysterical.[1] His ferocity and witlessness kept his Court in terror; and he loathed the English almost to insanity. He struck Jagat Seth, a Hindu millionaire banker, in the face and threatened him with circumcision. Through the indispensable Aminchand, Jagat Seth approached the English, and a plot was formed to make Mir J'afar, a noble, Nawab. When the plot was nearly ripe,

[1] Ghulam Husain Khan, *The Seir Mutaqherin* (Elliot and Dowson), 763.

Aminchand threatened to divulge it unless he were promised 5 per cent. of the Nawab's treasure (estimated at forty million sterling) and 30 lakhs (£300,000). He reduced his demands to £200,000 (substantially what it had been arranged that Clive was to get). Clive drew up double agreements, one on white paper, genuine, one on red paper, fictitious. Both were to be signed by Clive, Watson and the Select Committee; and the sham paper, which embodied his conditions, was shown to Aminchand. Watson's signature to this, however, had been forged by Clive, whose own statement is:

' It was sent to Admiral Watson, who objected to the signing of it; but to the best of his remembrance gave the gentleman who carried it leave to sign his name upon it:—That his Lordship never made any secret of it; he thinks it warrantable in such a case, and would do it again a hundred times: He had no interested motive in doing it, and did it with a design of disappointing the expectations of a rapacious man.'[1]

As to whether Clive was right in supposing (if he did suppose) that he had Watson's sanction to forge his signature, so long as he preserved him from inculpation in the sham treaty by his own hand, the evidence is conflicting. According to a captain who served on the admiral's flagship, Watson learnt only on his deathbed what had been done:

' The Admiral said, that he always thought the transaction dishonourable, and as there was so much iniquity among mankind, he did not wish to stay any longer among them; this was just before his death.'

The same witness deposed that the admiral 'thought it an extraordinary measure to depose a man they had so lately made a solemn treaty with'. However, the plot was pushed forward, Watson concurring.

Clive sent the Nawab a letter summarising the Company's wrongs, and concluding with announcement of the writer's thoughtful intention: ' The Rains being daily encreasing, and it taking a great deal of time to receive your answer, I therefore find it necessary to wait on you immediately'. As he neared Murshidabad, Watts and other captives escaped and joined him. Presently the last decision had to be taken. A council of war voted against action, Clive with the majority. But solitary reflection persuaded him otherwise; he crossed the river Bhagirathi, and halted his force in a large mango-grove at Plassey (*Palasi*, 'the Field of

[1] Evidence of Lord Clive before the Parliamentary Committee.

the Palas-trees' or 'of the Ogre', according as we take the primary or the secondary meaning of the Bengali name). The battle next day (June 23), consisted of two parts: a morning cannonade, followed by a drenching monsoon downpour which damaged the Nawab's ammunition, then an attack precipitated by Major Kilpatrick's keenness, and ending in complete victory at a cost of 65 casualties. Even the defeated lost only about 500 men. As a battle, Plassey was ridiculous. Mir J'afar, who vacillated during the engagement, came timidly round with congratulations and was told he was now Nawab.

At the house of the Seths, the great bankers whose hand was to be in countless intrigues to follow, Clive said to his friend Scrafton, 'It is now time to deceive Omichund'; whereupon

'Scrafton said to him in the Indostan language, "Omichund, the red paper is a trick; you are to have nothing". These words overpowered him like a blast of sulphur; he sunk back, fainting, and would have fallen to the ground, had not one of his attendants caught him in his arms.'

Aminchand was carried home, 'where he remained many hours in stupid melancholy', which passed into permanent imbecility. So Orme, whose heightened narrative obviously has behind it Clive's own excited story of a sleight whose cunning and success greatly pleased him. But Clive's own account before the Parliamentary Committee corrects this: ' the indignation and resentment expressed on that man's countenance bars all description'. And indignation and resentment preserved his intellect; on reflection, he smothered revengeful thoughts and decided to work again with Clive, in a more restricted and less ambitious field of knavery. In his will he left £2000 to the Foundling Hospital in London, which we may interpret as charity or irony, as we will.

The more powerful conspirators did rather better than Aminchand. The Company became *zemindar* of the Twenty-four Parganas, 880 square miles mostly south of Calcutta, with rents estimated at £150,000 (in practice they proved much less). Clive received £234,000. This was the occasion when, in retrospect, he was astonished by his moderation; but Clive was very easily astonished in this regard. His conviction that whatever personal advantage he collected was somehow different from, and altogether holier than, gain seized by smaller men was not quite sane in its cold firmness. Watts received £80,000, Walsh £50,000, Scrafton £20,000. Clive thought that altogether the Company and private persons netted three million sterling. To engineer a revolution had been revealed as the most paying game in the world. A gold-lust unequalled since the hysteria that took hold of the Spaniards of Cortes' and Pizarro's age filled the English mind. Bengal in particular was not to know peace again until it had been bled white.

We may hurry over the crowning scenes. Siraj-ud-Daula was betrayed to Mir J'afar by a man he had once tortured. Mir J'afar gave his English allies the same soothing reassurances that Muhammad Ali had given where Chanda Sahib was concerned; Siraj-ud-Daula, Clive wrote (July 2),

' will be in the City this evening: the Nabob, who is a humane, generous and honest Prince, intends only to confine him and to allow him all the indulgence which a prison can admit of'—

comforting thoughts from which he turns immediately to the more interesting news of the loot. Siraj-ud-Daula, left to his kindly jailor's mercies, was mangled to death with a sabre, flung across an elephant and paraded through Murshidabad streets on the same day as a flotilla bore a load of treasure down to the Ganges for Fort William:

' As soon as they entered the great river, they were joined by the boats of the squadron; and all together formed a fleet of 300 boats, with music playing, drums beating, and colours flying; and exhibited to the French and Dutch, by whose settlements they passed, a scene far different from what they had beheld the year before, when the Nabob's fleet and army passed them, with the captive English, and all the wealth and plunder of Calcutta.' [1]

The loot arrived, July 6, and was received rapturously. 'A world of guns' were fired, the Ladies all got 'footsore with dancing'; and

' a Bumper goes to your health each day in every house from the Admiral's downwards'.[2]

This did not preclude the inevitable quarrels over division, when the soldiers decided that the sailors, who had gone upstream but not far enough to be in the fighting, should not share in the prize-money. This decision Clive quashed, dismissing the council of war.

Eyre Coote, a King's officer, and one who had the misfortune to get across Clive continually, was left up-country to harry the remnants still faithful to the late Nawab and the handful of Frenchmen with them. He failed to catch them, but chased them until his own sepoys would go no further. His officers were severely rebuked by Clive for seeking extra 'batta', despite their allowance being already 'beyond everything heard of in any other Service'. Clive was always very down on anything that savoured of greed.

[1] Luke Scrafton, *Reflections on the Government of Indostan, with a short Sketch of the History of Bengal, etc.* (1770), 93.

[2] Letter (July 5) to Clive from the admiral's aide-de-camp, Captain Latham.

The overwhelming victory of the English disquieted their rivals. France took steps first, sending out land and sea reinforcements, and, to command the army, Comte de Lally, son of an Irish Jacobite. Lally reached Pondicherry, April, 1758, coming to a community fissured with hatreds and fears. His arrogance did not persuade it to support him; French resources had been wasted by Dupleix' schemes, and without money nothing effective was possible in a field so venal and corrupt as Indian politics. Lally was doomed to failure and a felon's death. However, he was lucky in his beginnings. The British admiral, Pocock, though he inflicted losses heavier than his own in several actions, was outmanœuvred by the French, and with naval help Lally took Fort St. David, to Clive's immense indignation. Clive wrote to Pigot: 'I cannot express to you my Resentment and Concern at the Infamous Surrender'.

Clive, one of the most restless, ardent, ambitious men that ever lived, would have drawn Madras under his command if possible. He was already aware that the three Presidencies should be under one, and that this one should be Bengal, 'an inexhaustible fund of Riches'. He sought supreme authority for himself—rightly, since he so obviously towered above his colleagues that to be unaware of his pre-eminence would have been affectation. He saw clearly that nothing but their own restraint need put a limit to the conquests of the English. But he was before his time in his vision and plans; and a piecemeal battle had to continue.

This went well for the English, who were served in South India by a number of brilliant officers, as against Lally and Bussy still apart and destined to co-operate, when circumstances compelled this, only with mutual dislike. They had also brave Indian allies: a famous sepoy leader, Yusuf Khan, and the Raja of Tanjore. The latter, helped by a timely appearance of the English fleet off Karikal, repulsed Lally and did some damage to his troops when they were withdrawing. Lally effected little beyond pillage far and wide, though he came near to success in December, when he captured the native quarters of Madras. But Madras, unlike Fort William in Siraj-ud-Daula's siege, had a gallant and able Governor in Pigot, and an experienced commander in Lawrence. After bitter and protracted fighting, the siege failed (February, 1759) when English ships again drew up; and with its failure sank the last prospects of victory for France.

Clive helped materially in Lally's repulse. But he refused to detach at Pigot's urgency troops he preferred to use in a campaign of diversion in the Northern Sarkars, where a chieftain called Ananda Raz had seized Vizagapatam and raised the English flag. Clive sent him Colonel Forde, as skilful a soldier as any in India. Forde at Condore defeated Bussy's second-in-command, Conflans, who escaped with Lusitanian celerity:

' He is determined not to be taken Prisoner, unless by a Greyhound, for he Supped at Rajamindry the night of the Engagement, which is at least fifty miles from the field of action.' [1]

Forde then stormed Masulipatam, where Conflans was captured. The Northern Sarkars were completely conquered; the Nizam, after his first vexation, decided to cede them to the conquerors and to begin the process of going over to the English side. These operations exercised a profound effect, moral and material, on Lally's campaign farther south.

Meanwhile the Emperor was his Vizier's prisoner, and his son, known as the Shahzada, little better than a condottiere:

' the throne of the Moguls was the sport of servants and strangers, and he who was entitled to occupy it was a wanderer without a home'.[2]

Egged on by the Nawab of Oudh, the Shahzada invaded Bihar, whose Governor, Ramnarayan, at first submitted. But Ramnarayan's eyes were opened when he visited the Shahzada, and found himself absurdly doing the meanest of obeisance to a State obviously in tatters. He invented a pretext for escape back to Patna, where he used evasions till they would serve no longer and then defended the city until Clive could come to his help. Clive while coming up conducted with the Shahzada a correspondence more like the courteous interchanges of Mr. Ernest Bramah's Kai Lung and his brigand captor than anything else outside fiction. First, Clive, 'the Most High and Mighty, Protector of the Great', is advised by the Shahzada gravely to

' make it your business to pay your respects to me like a faithful servant, which will be great and happy for you'.

Clive, while chivying the Shahzada about Bihar's wide confines, expresses deep respect and concern for his welfare, adding a measure of philosophical consolation:

' It is better that one should suffer, however great, than that so many thousands should be rendered unhappy. I have only to recommend Your Highness to the Almighty's protection. I wish to God it were in my power to assist you, but it is not. I am now on my march to the Caramnassa, and earnestly recommend you to withdraw before I arrive there.'

[1] Forde to Clive, January 25, 1759.   [2] Thornton, *History of British India*, i. 410.

The Shahzada accepted his energetic well-wisher's recommendation, and fled expeditiously. The Mogul Vizier, who had the Emperor (the Shahzada's father) in captivity, wrote congratulating Clive:

' The faithful services which you have performed and the pains which you have taken in the late affairs have given me great joy; nor can I sufficiently express your praises for what you have done. Continue to behave with the same fidelity; seize the rebel and send him to court. By the will of God, this service performed, the King will show you the greatest favour, and your honours shall be encreased.'

This letter led to the grant of Clive's notorious *jagir*. The Emperor (under instructions) had already made him a commander of 6000 horse, for his 'services' in making Mir J'afar Nawab of Bengal. The appointment had of course been meant to be purely honorary, but Clive pointed out now that this rank carried a £30,000 salary. He urged the Seths to get something done about it, and they hit on the plan of making over to him the quit-rent of the Twenty-four Parganas. Clive accepted this arrangement, and never saw any hurt in this (or in any other of his acquisitions). He became the Company's landlord, a situation in which the Company acquiesced for a while, partly because they were in fear of this all-powerful servant, partly because they felt that it would be easier to quash a payment to one of their own employees than one to the Nawab. Clive could not stay in India for ever: and he made enemies faster than almost any man that ever lived.

Macaulay thought Clive's acceptance of the *jagir* justified, and many English historians agree with him. We think it necessary to say only that his enormous greed provided an example against which his severity towards others (who took smaller amounts in ways he considered irregular) was entirely ineffective. For the monstrous financial immorality of English conduct in India for many a year after this, Clive was largely responsible. We need not think him hypocritical when later on, in an outburst which has greatly impressed biographers and historians, he besought the House of Commons, while considering his honour, not to forget their own. He honestly thought of himself as a case apart. Horace Walpole (whose own extensive distraints on the public purse, as the son of a distinguished father, were even more adequately sanctioned by political custom than Clive's in Bengal) noted caustically:

' Though Lord Clive was so frank and high-spirited as to confess a whole folio of his Machiavellism, they were so ungenerous as to have a mind to punish him for assassination, forgery, treachery, and plunder, and it makes him very indignant.'

Other questions which Clive overlooked were his right to accept the position of a great noble under the Emperor, and his power to reconcile a double allegiance if policies ever came into conflict.

The Dutch had watched the boats laden with the plunder of Murshidabad filing past their forts with braying of trumpets and 'country musick'—as Scrafton noted, 'a scene far different' from that of the Nawab's return from the rapine of Fort William. Their thoughts had been what we can conjecture—envy, hatred, dread, and contempt. They were no more willing to accept the political predominance of their rivals than the English had been willing to accept French predominance in the Carnatic. Mir J'afar, too, found his dependence irksome. The Nawab and the Dutch at Chinsura intrigued together, and an armament arrived from Batavia, in Clive's words 'crammed with soldiers'. There are times when a public man (he observed later, of this episode) must act with a halter round his neck. War between England and Holland was likely in Europe, and word of it was hourly and eagerly awaited. But this, though a valued formality, was not a necessary antecedent of hostilities: ' the course of events in India, at this period, was not marked by any pedantic adherence to the principles of international law.' [1] The English claimed the right to search all ships coming up the Hugli, lest they should introduce French troops into Bengal, and also as engaged to help the Emperor's Viceroy to keep foreign soldiers out. Clive and the Council answered Dutch protests with assurance ' that we should absolutely and religiously do our duty to the utmost of our strength and power in both capacities.' Two months passed. Then, in November 1759, the Dutch landed troops, and Clive attacked them by land and water. Both assaults were overwhelmingly victorious. Forde, who commanded the land attack, asked to be safeguarded by a definite order. Clive received his note when playing cards, and scribbled the answer:

' Dear Forde, fight them immediately. I will send you the Order of Council to-morrow.'

The battle of Biderra followed, 'short, bloody, and decisive' (Clive). The English lost a dozen men, the Dutch over 400 Europeans and many Malays. Many ghosts, from the days of the Amboyna Massacre, must have felt themselves at last avenged.

The Nawab now decided that Clive's enemies ought to be his also, and moved threateningly against the Dutch. In their helplessness they

[1] Thornton, i. 369.

appealed to Clive; and obtained peace and his protection on acknowledging themselves aggressors, paying damages to get their captured shipping back, and promising the Nawab never to fortify again or to keep more than 125 soldiers.

Lally was finally defeated by Coote at Wandiwash, 1760, when Bussy (who had reluctantly left his semi-princely state and security in the Deccan), was taken prisoner and well entertained by his captors, with whom he was a high favourite. In January, 1761, after a protracted defence, Pondicherry fell, and was treated as the French had treated Fort St. David. Saunders razed the forts and many of the buildings. Peace came in 1763; Lally went home, and after two and a half years' imprisonment was sacrificed to popular wrath over the national humiliation in India, being beheaded. Voltaire, who had enjoyed commenting, on Byng's execution, that the English shot one admiral 'to encourage the others', was enabled to observe that his own people had committed a murder with 'the sword of justice'.

As Clive observed, the English had succeeded in doing to the French everything that the French under Dupleix had set out to do to them.

In 1761, perhaps luckily for the Company, the Marathas met with utter defeat at the third battle of Panipat, against Ahmad Shah, at the fight 'of the black mango-tree'. The Hindu dead were believed to amount to nearly 200,000. The famous report to the Peshwa was:

' Two pearls have been dissolved, twenty-seven gold mohurs have been lost, and of the silver and copper the total cannot be cast up.'

It is matter for amazement that the Marathas should have ever recovered, and have recovered so swiftly. Their nation has shown an almost unequalled resiliency. But they were kept very quiet for some years.

Clive went home, February, 1760. Only thirty-five, he had shown astounding spirit and prowess in both war and peace. Unfortunately, Eyre Coote, with whom he had been so much at odds, had spent a furlough before him; already discontent against the skilful adventurer was spread throughout the Company's directorate and also Parliament. His conduct fostered this discontent. He was perhaps the King's wealthiest subject; and he purchased two hundred £500 shares in the Company, which he distributed to nominees who were to vote as he bade. He entered the House of Commons and engaged in the tremendous corruption of men's consciences that passed for politics in the eighteenth century. He had himself largely to thank that, when the storm

G

broke thirteen years later, even his friend Pitt complained of the floods of easily (and in Clive's case, indelicately, though not quite dishonestly) gathered wealth which had given ostentatiousness and graft an even wider scope than they had already.

CHAPTER III

FIRST SHAKING OF THE PAGODA TREE

Inadequate pay of Company's servants: Holwell and the Nawab: Vansittart: deposition of Mir J'afar: Hastings on Mir Qasim: the inland trading claim: Mir Qasim prepares for war: various atrocities: Mir J'afar restored: mutiny of sepoys: battle of Buxar: Clive's return to India: acquisition of the 'diwani': Clive's grief at scene of moral deterioration: the Society for Trade: Clive persecuted in England: Hastings's return to India: supervisors in Bengal: Muhammad Ali's misrule of the Carnatic: war with Haidar Ali: Clive writes to Hastings: Ramprasad Sen.

As soon as Clive left Bengal,

' there was a general rush of the Company's servants, and of Europeans of all classes, towards the interior trade of the three provinces' [1]

of Bengal, Bihar and Orissa.

It is urged in extenuation that the Company was obstinately unwilling to pay adequate salaries. Even a Member of Council's pay was only 300 rupees a month. When Warren Hastings was Resident at Murshidabad he was paid much less. On the other hand, we must remember that the official salary was 'an insignificant proportion of the total emoluments of a Company's servant'.[2] Even as early as 1750, Dawson, the Fort William President, in addition to Rs. 1600 salary, received Rs. 20,000 under heads of gratuity, *batta,* subsistence allowance, servants' wages. Perquisities, in one form or another, have been a tenacious root of mischief in India. But the Directors would not face decent pay-sheets. They continued to prefer that their servants should recoup themselves by private trade, though they complained that this led to neglect of the Company's interests.

[1] Sir John Malcolm, *Life of Clive,* iii. 88.
[2] E. Monckton Jones, *Hastings in Bengal,* 1772-1774, 35.

Clive's successor, Holwell, never forgot or forgave his Black Hole sufferings. Apart from this, he was untruthful and unscrupulous. He and his colleagues 'treated as a crime'[1] the Nawab's 'poverty, which was extreme':

' their one notion was to grasp all they could; to use Mir Jafar as a golden sack into which they could dip their hands at pleasure'.[2]

When the Seths refused to provide a large 'loan', Holwell wrote to Hastings (who had been sent in 1758, a young man of twenty-five, to the friction-centre at Murshidabad as Resident):

' A time may come when they may stand in need of the Company's protection, in which case they may be assured they shall be left to Satan to be buffeted.'

But it became ever harder for the Nawab and his people to believe that any imaginary Satan could be worse than the Satan already with them. The economics of the time were as crude in theory as they were pitiless in practice. The Directors ceased to send out their 'investment'; their representatives were now supposed to be in the midst of such inexhaustible and presumably natural abundance, flowering out of the soil, that Bengal could pay the expenses of all three Presidencies *and* purchase the commodities sent home for sale! The English on the spot made requisition after requisition on the Nawab's treasury, which was in fact empty—Clive's memory certainly exaggerated when he spoke of passing (after Plassey) through such rows of wealth that the ensuing pillage in retrospect looked to be 'moderation'. The Company's own finances (whatever individuals might possess) were equally exhausted. For the rapine and misery which followed, some of the blame must be borne by the ignorance and unimaginative greed of the people in London.

Holwell was succeeded in July, 1760, by Vansittart, who had come from Madras. Vansittart was a well-meaning man, honest within elastic limits, with a sense of fairness hamstrung by weakness. Mir J'afar, old, tired and lazy, was suddenly discovered to be a bad man, tyrannical, disloyal to the English, incapable. He was all this; but the disloyalty was not only natural, it had been condoned at the time (e.g. his intrigues with the Dutch before Biderra). Holwell, who started the movement for a fresh revolution, found an excuse when a number of ladies of rank, among them the begums of Allahvardi Khan, were drowned in the

---

[1] G. R. Gleig, *Memoirs of the Life of the Right Hon. Warren Hastings*, i. 82.
[2] G. B. Malleson, *The Life of Warren Hastings*, 42.

Ganges: 'these are the acts of the Tyger we are supporting and fighting for'.[1] Hastings replied (June 21, 1760):

' I have hitherto been generally an advocate for the Nabob, whose extortions and oppressions I imputed to the necessity of the times and want of economy in his revenues; but, if this charge against him be true, no argument can excuse or palliate so atrocious and complicated a villainy, nor (forgive me, Sir, if I add) our supporting such a tyrant.'

It is not certain that the Nawab was actually privy to the execution, which was the work of his son Miran. When Vansittart interviewed Mir J'afar, the old man submissively admitted his shortcomings, and was so humble and willing to try to be better that Vansittart was touched and shaken. However, he was compelled to abdicate; and retired to Fort William with as much treasure as he could collect and sixty begums.

His son-in-law, Mir Qasim, who had proposed to Holwell to have his father-in-law cut off, became Nawab. He had offered the gentlemen of the Council a large gift, which Vansittart high-mindedly said was not necessary. He now, however, instructed Hastings to ask for it. The Company received the *zemindari* rights and revenues of Burdwan, Midnapur and Chittagong, as its public reward.

Hastings, who supported the change, wrote of the new Nawab as

' esteemed a man of understanding, of an uncommon talent for business, and great application and perseverance, joined to a thriftiness, which how little soever it might ennoble his own character was a quality most essentially necessary in a man who had to restore an impoverished state, and clear off debts which had been accumulating for three years before. His timidity, the little inclination he had ever shown for war, with which he has been often reproached, would hardly have disqualified him for the Subahship, since it effectually secured us from any designs that he might form against our Government, and disposed him the easier to bear the effects of that superiority which we possessed over him: a consequence which we soon had occasion to experience, since a spirit superior to that of a worm when trodden upon could not have brooked the many daily affronts which he was exposed to from the instant of his advancement to the Subahship.'

Mir Qasim was a genuine patriot and an able ruler, who quickly retrenched expenditure and suppressed disorders. But he was to be driven to the edge of insanity, if not over it.

In 1761 Hastings had become a Member of Council. He and Vansittart maintained (what in his heart no one doubted) that Farakhsiyar's

---

[1] John Zephaniah Holwell, *An Address to the Proprietors of East India Stock,* (1764), 45-6.

farman and subsequent endorsements related only to trade at seaports. As to the Company's earlier practice, when Nawabs still had power, there was no manner of question; Hastings declared:

' Then the trade in such commodities as were bought and sold in the country was entirely confined to the natives; they were either farmed out or circulated through the province by the poorer sort of people, to whom they afforded a subsistence. The privileges therefore claimed by the Company and allowed by the Government, were originally designed by both for goods brought into the country, or purchased in it for exportation; in effect it was ever limited to that; nor can any difference of *power* convey to us a *right* which we confessedly wanted before.'

No Indian ruler would, or could, have granted foreigners leave to wreck his whole system by a monopoly of duty-free trade along every road and river of his kingdom. But Hastings and Vansittart were voted down. Every Company employee continued to assert a right of inland trading free of customs to which the country's natives were liable; and especially in such necessities and common commodities as salt, betel, tobacco. The youngest assistant lived like a king by selling his *dustuck* to Indians. Other Indians, without going to the expense or formality of purchase, merely put the English flag up. The Nawab's revenue disappeared. So did the livelihood of the poorest and meanest classes; the English (who for so many years were to prove themselves the most expensive of all the invaders of India, and in so many ways) could 'undersell the native in his own market'.[1]

An incidental additional disgrace to the English name was the Council's allowing the Nawab to arrest Ramnarayan, Governor of Bihar, who had consistently stood by the Company. The news that he was a prisoner was a deep humiliation to Clive in England. It is fair to add that Hastings thought it wrong to support Ramnarayan,

' the Naib [2] of the Province and an acknowledged servant of the Nabob . . . in an assumed independency in direct violation of the treaty which we had but just ratified with him'.

In 1765 a group of *Zemindars*, greatly daring, sent the Council a complaint that

' the Factories of English Gentlemen are many and their Gomastahs are in all places and in every Village almost throughout the Province of Bengal; That they trade in Linnen, Chunam, Mustardseed, Tobacco, Turmerick, Oil, Rice, Hemp, Gunnies, Wheat, in short in all Kinds of Grain, Linnen and

---

[1] Malcolm, *Life of Clive*, iii. 89.
[2] Deputy (for the Nawab, i.e. of Bengal and Bihar).

whatever other Commodities are produced in the Country; That in order to purchase these Articles, they force their Money on the *ryots*, and having by these oppressive means bought their goods at a low Rate, they oblige the Inhabitants and Shopkeepers to take them at an high price, exceeding what is paid in the Markets; That they do not pay the Customs due to the Sircar, but are guilty of all manner of seditious and injurious acts, for Instance. . . .

' There is now scarce anything of worth left in the country.'

In the same year similar witness was borne by Francis Sykes, who had succeeded Hastings at Murshidabad. His own successor, Mr. Becher, in 1769 summed up the exasperation which the few decent men all felt:

' Since the Hon. Company have been in possession of the Dewannee the Influence that has been used in providing their Investment and under their Name, Goods, on private Account, has proved such a Monopoly, that the Chassars, Manufacturers, etc., have been obliged to sell their Commodities at any price. Those employed to purchase for the English, thought proper to give them. They had no Choice, if any Country Merchant, Armenian or other attempted to purchase; there was an immediate Cry that it interfered with the Company's Investment. . . .

' I well remember this Country when Trade was free, and the flourishing State it was then in; with Concern I now see its present ruinous Condition which I am convinced is greatly owing to the Monopoly that has been made of late years in the Company's Name of almost all the Manufactures in the Country. Let the Trade be made free, and this fine Country will soon recover itself, the Revenues increase, and the Company procure as large an Investment as they can spare Money to purchase. . . .'

Mir Qasim, finding protest and sarcasm alike unavailing, began to retreat up the Ganges. He established his court in a tiger-haunted ruin at Monghyr, and prepared for war, collecting a force 'animated by the strongest feelings of patriotism'.[1] Hastings came to see him, and used his eyes as he went up-country:

' I have been surprised to meet with several English flags flying in places which I have passed; and on the river I do not believe that I passed a boat without one. By whatever title they have been assumed (for I could only trust to the information of my eyes, without stopping to ask questions), I am sure their frequency can bode no good to the Nawab's revenues, to the quiet of the country, or the honour of our nation, but evidently tend to lessen each of them. A party of sipahis, who were on the march before us, afforded us sufficient proof of the rapacious and insolent spirit of these people when they are left to their own discretion. Many complaints were made against them on the road, and most of the petty towns and sarais were deserted on our approach, and the shops shut up from the apprehensions of the same treatment from us.'

[1] Colonel G. B. Malleson, *Life of Warren Hastings*, 67.

Ellis, the Patna Resident, was bullying the Nawab on any excuse that came to hand. Hastings wished to see him, but Ellis found business elsewhere.

The Nawab in desperation declared all trade duty-free to everyone. This ended the English monopoly; and the Council, with the two usual dissentients, told him he had broken the treaty. Hastings protested:

'The Nawab has granted a boon to his subjects, and there are no grounds for demanding that a sovereign prince should withdraw such a boon, or for threatening him with war in the event of refusal.'

In the document which we have already quoted, he declared that 'thus far his conduct will bear the severest examination'. Now, however,

'the hoarded resentment of all the injuries which he had sustained in a continual exertion of patience during three years of his government, now aggravated by his natural timidity, and the prospect of an almost inevitable ruin before him, from this time took entire possession of his mind and drove from thence every principle, till it had satiated itself with the blood of every person within his reach, who had either contributed to his misfortunes or even by real or fancied connection with his enemies became the objects of his revenge'.

He executed the two Seths, and exposed their bodies. Ramnarayan was flung into the Ganges, with a bag of sand tied to his neck. By attacks on the Patna and Kasimbazar factories 200 European prisoners were made, who were butchered (October, 1763) under direction of Walter Reinhard, nicknamed Sumroo (? 'sombre'), the most brutal of the foreign adventurers infesting India. Only Fullarton, a physician who had done many deeds of skilful kindness, was spared.

Mir Qasim was deposed and Mir J'afar brought back (with the usual presents—in which Hastings, true to his earlier habit, declined to participate). A force was despatched into Bihar, under Hector Munro, who had first to quell an attempt of his sepoys to desert. The deserters were surprised asleep, brought back, and then twenty-four were blown from guns. Major Munro's own story has been often quoted:

'Three of the grenadiers entreated to be fastened to the guns on the right, declaring that as they always fought on the right they hoped their last request would be complied with, by being suffered to die in the post of honour. Their petition was granted, and they were the first executed. I am sure there was not a dry eye among the Mariners who witnessed the execution, although they had been accustomed to hard service; and two of them had actually been on the execution party who shot Admiral Byng in the year 1757.'

Mir Qasim, allied with the Nawab of Oudh and the Shahzada (now, by his father's assassination, titular Emperor, Shah Alam), mustered a large army which included 5000 of the Afghans who had recently invaded India under Ahmad Shah Durrani and sacked Delhi. He had guns served by Europeans. The Company with 7000 men, of whom 857 were Europeans, routed him at Buxar in the biggest battle they had yet fought: their loss was no less than 847, but of the enemy 2000 were killed and thousands drowned in flight. A campaign in Oudh followed.

The Company had finally ceased to be a mere trading organisation, and had become in fact (whatever it continued to be in pretence) 'the most formidable commercial republic . . . known in the world since the demolition of Carthage'.[1]

In 1765 Hastings went home. He found himself in bad repute in influential quarters. He had been frank in criticism of people who had powerful and greedy connections, and there was no intention of employing him again.

Appalled by the confusion, dishonesty, and military expenditure which had overtaken their affairs, the Directors felt they had no choice but to send Clive back. They 'began to perceive with dislike' that the huge private exactions from each puppet Nawab

' contributed nothing to the Company's coffers, while they served to drain the country of its resources and form a serious burden on the revenue'. [2]

Clive arrived in Bengal, May, 1765, with 'covenants' which Company servants were to sign, prohibiting them from accepting 'presents' or engaging in the inland trade. Mir J'afar, whose second enthronement cost him promises, supplemented by enforced and one-sided revision, that amounted to £300,000 to the Company, £530,000 to gentlemen of the Council, and £250,000 to the army and navy, in deep distress looked for Clive's coming, but died previously to it.

Clive made peace with the Emperor, who possessed little beyond his title and was glad to grant the Company the *diwani*[3] of Bengal, Bihar and Orissa in exchange for a regular payment of 26 lakhs. The *diwani* was held in abeyance, as Clive had no administration he could trust, and believed it better to lull Dutch and French jealousies to rest by keeping up a pretence that the Nawab was still in power. He had sometimes thought that it would be better for the Crown to take over the Company's conquests, a point much canvassed in England also. But the

[1] Charles Caraccioli, *Life of Clive*, i. 106.

[2] E. M. Jones, *Hastings in Bengal*, 57.   [3] Civil administration.

British Government were unwilling to deepen their own corruption further, by coming into such immense additional patronage. The administration of Bengal was left in the hands of the Nawab's four *naibs* (of whom one was Nandakumar, afterwards hanged during Hastings's governor-generalship, and always hated by Hastings), who were paid salaries of £90,000, £20,000 (two), and £10,000.

Clive's political aims, from which Hastings was to differ strongly, he set out in his final directions to the Calcutta Board (January 16, 1767). This document may be quoted here, as its principles applied from the beginning:

' The first point in Politics which I offer to your Consideration is the Form of Government. We are sensible that since the Acquisition of the Dewanni, the Power formerly belonging to the Soubah of these Provinces is Totally, in Fact, vested in the East India Company. Nothing remains to him but the Name and Shadow of Authority. This Name, however, this Shadow, it is indispensably necessary we should seem to venerate; every Mark of Distinction and Respect must be shown him, and he himself encouraged to shew his Resentment upon the least want of Respect from other Nations. Under the Sanction of a Soubah every encroachment that may be attempted by Foreign Powers can effectually be crushed without any apparent Interposition of our own Authority; and all real Grievances complained of by them, can, through the same channel, be examined into and redressed. Be it therefore always remembered that there is a Soubah, that we have allotted him a Stipend, which must be regularly paid, in support of his Dignity, and that though the Revenues belong to the Company, the territorial Jurisdiction must still rest in the Chiefs of the Country acting under him and this Presidency in Conjunction.'

If the mask were thrown off, he said, ' Foreign nations would immediately take Umbrage and Complaints preferred to the British Court might have very embarrassing consequences'.

This was Clive's famous Dual System. An element of sham runs through all administrations everywhere; but the Indian Government has often almost seemed to have preferred that fiction should occupy the public attention, while fact (a very different fact) got the actual ruling done. Clive made Nawab a boy of eighteen, who was delighted at the prospect of ready money, and said, 'Thank God! I shall now have as many dancing girls as I please!' Clive also rearranged the territory of the Nawab of Oudh. The Emperor, who possessed literally nothing but an empty title (a point which Hastings was to emphasise continually, ringing the changes of scorn, 'a Pageant of our own', 'a mere Idol', and so on), was given the districts of Korah and Allahabad, a disposition of territory which was to prove important in the politics of less than ten years later.

Clive, entering on his second period of power, flew into capitals at the state of Calcutta,

' one of the most wicked Places in the Universe, Corruption, Licentiousness & a want of Principle seem to have possess'd the Minds of all the Civil Servants, by frequent bad Examples they have grown callous, Rapacious & Luxurious beyond Conception, & the Incapacity & Iniquity of some & the Youth of others . . .'

'Rapacity' and 'luxury' are now favourite words of his. He spoke feelingly of 'the unreasonable desire of many to acquire in an Instant, what only a few can, or ought to possess'; and discovered in his colleagues a scene 'shocking to human nature'. All had 'received immense sums' for the latest Nawab's appointment, and were 'so shameless as to own it publicly'. His sensitive nature could hardly bear it:

' Alas, how is the English name sunk! I could not avoid paying the tribute of a few tears to the departed and lost fame of the British nation.'

The Council maintained that to sign the new covenants immediately was unnecessarily precipitate; it could be postponed till the boy Nawab had finished making over his presents. One of them, Mr. Johnstone, was tactless enough to observe, 'With regard to presents in general, we have the approved example of the President, Lord Clive himself', a point he elaborated with considerable skill and felicity of illustration. Clive, who saw himself in a peculiarly noble light, as Galahad (rather than Hercules) come to cleanse the Augean stable, refuted him torrentially.

Clive's attitude and argument were always singularly simple and plain. He thought persons in junior positions ought not to be greedy. But those in senior positions were entitled to collect a great deal:

' My grand object, you know, is that none under the rank of field officers should have money to throw away. When they arrive at that rank, their hands are filled with such large advantages, that they may be certain of acquiring an independency in a few years.' (February 16, 1766.)

He put down presents, so far as they could be put down; and enforced 'cuts', which (as has usually happened in India, when financial stringency has compelled them) were heavy on those who could least support them. Military officers, since the Directors insisted, were deprived of double *batta* (field allowance), which Mir J'afar had given. The result was widespread mutiny, which Clive met as courageously as he met every danger. He broke it, and dismissed some mutineers to England, where they swelled the growing band of his enemies.

The Directors were not yet willing to face proper salaries for their own servants, and Clive disobeyed them by winking at the continuance of inland trading and by establishing for the senior civil and military officers a strict monopoly in salt, calling this 'The Society for Trade'. This the Directors failed to put down until 1768, when Clive was already back in England.

His courage and good intentions deserve the highest praise. Also, he was honest in comparison with nearly everyone else. His 'Society for Trade', whereby senior officers were to gain so generously (a full colonel making an extra £7000 a year, a lieutenant-colonel £3000, a major £2000), was justified in his own mind by the argument that the salt monopoly now belonged to the Company, who, if its profits went to their servants, were merely paying them properly in an indirect fashion. But in the deepest grievances of the people of Bengal, those arising out of the control of their inland trade by foreigners, Clive achieved very little, if anything, as quotations already made have shown.

This is not the place for a full explanation of the way Clive's good and evil deeds working together brought him to ruin in England. To his chagrin, despite a reception full of flattery, he received no honours but an Irish peerage. And in 1772, Sulivan, Deputy Chairman of the Court of Directors, whose supersession had been one of Clive's conditions before consenting to return to Bengal for his last term of service, brought forward a motion in the House of Commons for a Bill[1]

' for the better regulation of the affairs of the East India Company, and of their servants in India, and the due administration of justice in Bengal'.

Clive's actions came in for criticism, and he defended himself in a speech that was an eloquent tribute to himself. He effectively retorted on the Directors, who

' had acquired an empire more extensive than any kingdom in Europe, France and Russia excepted. They had acquired a revenue of four millions sterling, and a trade in proportion',

yet had encouraged the levity and greed of their least reputable servants and let maladministration and corruption proceed apace. The Bill was temporarily shelved, and a Select Parliamentary Committee investigated what had happened in Bengal. Clive was cross-examined, as he complained, like a sheep-stealer, and exclaimed:

' Am I not rather deserving of praise for the moderation which marked my proceedings ? Consider the situation in which the victory at Plassey had

[1] This resulted in 'The Regulating Act', 1773.

placed me! A great prince was dependent on my pleasure; an opulent city lay at my mercy; its richest bankers bid against each other for my smiles; I walked through vaults which were thrown open to me alone, piled on either hand with gold and jewels! Mr. Chairman, at this moment I stand astonished at my own moderation!'

Much of that outburst was rhetorical exaggeration.

The Report, when published, kindled contempt for the Company's mismanagement. But sympathy was growing for Clive. The final scene is well known: certain statements of fact, as to Clive's acquisitions, were carried in the House, but also (without a division) the resolution:

'That Robert Lord Clive did, at the same time, render great and meritorious services to this country.'

With that decision we need not quarrel.

Clive had warned the Directors (August 28, 1767) of what was coming—the jobbery, that besetting curse of Indian administration, which the astonishing evidence of India's inexhaustible riches was to set up: 'the great will interfere in your appointments, and noblemen will perpetually solicit you to provide for the younger branches of their families'. He feared that

'the grasping character of the administration in England would lead to a ruinous interference in the nomination of men to India who had no recommendation but their high birth and great interest'.[1]

It did; and immediately. Directors and Directors' relatives, peers, even the Royal Family, saw no reason why they should not push a young friend or dependent into a service which within an incredibly brief period would bring him back enormously enriched. English politics and morals became corrupted, English ideas of India vulgarised, to an extent and permanency which we do not yet realise. Caraccioli, spokesman of the envious and disappointed military officers whom Clive in his governorship (1765-67) checked from making such wealth as his own, appealed to a vivacious prejudice and jealousy of

'a company of merchants, whose servants have lately exhibited in these realms the magnificence and pageantry of sovereigns to the disparagement of the ancient nobility'.[2]

'The quality' agreed that 'one should have scarcely imagined that such wealth was destined to flow to ravenous upstarts sent at a venture beyond the eastern ocean, by obscure and indigent relations.'[3]

[1] Sir John Malcolm, *Life of Lord Clive*, iii. 85-6.
[2] Charles Caraccioli, *Life of Robert Lord Clive, Baron Plassey*, i. 2.   [3] *Op. cit.* i. 11.

The Proprietors, seeing their employees' gains, demanded higher dividends. The British taxpayer also desired to press up to the pagoda-tree, 'then in full bloom'.[1] In 1767 Parliament held an enquiry into the Company's affairs, and limited the dividend to ten per cent. The Company was ordered to pay £400,000 annually to the Treasury. As it was itself poverty-stricken, however wealthy its servants might be, this benevolence was raised by loans. These in turn deepened its financial distresses; and inevitably it judged, and compelled its representatives to judge, all actions from the point of view of a desperate man being driven towards bankruptcy. The enquiry had a happier result, in Warren Hastings's emergence from obscurity:

'Mr. Hastings being examined at the bar of the House of Commons . . . attracted general notice by his prompt, masterly and intelligent expositions.'[2]

He was sent back to India, 1769, as second at Madras.

In 1769 Mr. Becher, whose frank comments we have already had occasion to quote, left the Calcutta Council without any remaining excuse to pretend to be ignorant that the province's misery was their direct work:

'It must give pain to an Englishman to have Reason to think that since the accession of the Company to the Dewanee the condition of the people of this Country has been worse than it was before; and yet I am afraid the Fact is undoubted.'

He cites humiliating reasons

'why this fine Country, which flourished under the most despotic and arbitrary Government, is verging towards its Ruin while the English have really so great a share in the Administration. . . . When the English received the Grant of the Dewannee their first Consideration seems to have been the raising of as large Sums from the Country as could be collected, to answer the pressing demands from home and to defray the large Expences here'.

His letter, an admirably close and moderate piece of reasoning, led to the appointment of Englishmen as 'supervisors' of the Indian officials and their methods of collecting revenue. The plan proved unsatisfactory, simply because so few Company employees were of any

---

[1] J. C. Marshman, *History of India* (abridged edition), 213. *Pagodas* were coins used in South India, and 'the pagoda-tree' is a term applicable, strictly speaking, only to Madras (where during the last fifty years of the eighteenth century the Company's servants were in every way baser, as well as more venal, than in Bengal).

[2] *Memoirs of Warren Hastings*, by P. C. (*circa* 1820), quoted by Miss Monckton Jones, 102.

experience (Mir Qasim's massacre had been followed by Clive's purges of both army and civilian personnel) or of any character. A supervisorship was seen to be the best scheme devised hitherto for speedy amassing of fortune; no one cared to hold so unremunerative a post as that of Member of Council when graft unlimited might be his as a 'supervisor'. We have Hastings's testimony (January 6, 1773):

' As the collectorships are more lucrative than any posts in the service (the government itself not excepted—whatever it may prove hereafter), we cannot get a man of abilities to conduct the official business of the presidency without violence; for who would rest satisfied with a handsome salary of three or four thousand rupees a year to maintain him in Calcutta, who could get a lac or three lacs, which I believe have been acquired in that space, and live at no expense, in the districts?'

Nevertheless, the scheme, after modification, proved the germ idea out of which later on the Indian Civil Service was to be developed (the 'collector' following the supervisor).[1] The Company, moreover, as the immediate *Zemindar* of the districts of Burdwan, Midnapur, and Chittagong, was coming into intimate touch with the difficulties and complexities of Indian revenue. The three Company districts were happier and better run than the rest of Bengal, because in them Englishmen were not simply invincible demons presenting demand notes, but human beings who saw village life at first hand.

Nature lightened the unhappy *ryot's* problem, in 1770, when such a famine ravaged Bengal that one-third of the natives were believed 'to have perished by sickness and famine'. This was Hastings's own estimate; some English eye-witnesses put the deaths at one-half the population (which was probably about fifteen millions). We may cautiously accept a fifth as the true proportion. The principal Naib, Muhammad Reza Khan, collected the revenue almost fully, adding 10 per cent. (the *najay* cess, a recognised exaction by which the living made good revenue losses which were owing to other taxpayers having been so unpatriotic as to die); and the Company's servants profiteered in necessities.

By the Treaty of Paris (1763), England and France acknowledged Salabat Jang as the *lawful* Subadar of the Deccan, and Muhammad Ali as the *lawful* Nawab of the Carnatic. Wilks, whose italics we have just borrowed, observes: [2]

' Two European nations had thus assumed to themselves the right of conferring the official appointments, and determining the interior arrangements of the Mogul Empire.'

[1] See below, p. 121.   [2] *History of Mysoor*, i. 297.

But a great many things were done in this period whose implications were not noted or understood. Muhammad Ali, however, understood them clearly enough. His position was solely due to English military support, and he decided that this support was capable of aggrandising it immensely further. During a stretch of nearly half a century the administration of the Carnatic was mischievous and corrupt to an even worse degree than that of Bengal in its worst period. He cajoled the Company into an unprovoked attack on Tanjore, that he might make its Raja a dependent; in 1764 he left Muhammad Yusuf Ali, Clive's valiant comrade and the Company's renowned captain of auxiliaries, no choice but to fight in self-defence. It was vain to fight against the Company's protégé, assisted by British forces; and Yusuf Ali, after a gallant and protracted struggle, was executed as a 'rebel': Wherever Muhammad Ali managed to extend his power, his misrule and that of his polygars

' left at an humble distance all the oppression that had ever been practised under the iron government of Hyder',[1]

a contrast which the great missionary Schwartz makes of Tanjore's new condition after conquest. When the century was in its last decade, the Nawab of the Carnatic, a dignified, plausible rascal of engaging manners and venerable appearance, beset with creditors whom he charmingly postponed, was ornamental enough to be forgiven. But in the interim we have it on the statement of a former Keeper of the Madras Government Records,[2] that 'it would be difficult to name a Governor who was neither bribed nor hated by' him. We now see him in his palmier days, when

' the inflated ambition of this political pretender was nourished and incited by the still more absurd and corrupt counsels of his European advisers'.[3]

Muhammad Ali's elder brother, deciding that there were disadvantages attendant on being in too close proximity to the Nawab, renounced the world and set out for Mecca. He took an unusually circuitous route, which brought him to Haidar Ali, the brilliant adventurer now ruling Mysore. After talk with Haidar, to whom he related in detail the mischiefs and territorial extensions which his brother was meditating, the pilgrim found the world still had claims on his services, accepted a *jagir*, and became a confidential adviser. A complex intrigue seethed. The Nizam, an unwilling ally of the English, was guaranteed

[1] *Op. cit.* ii. 103.   [2] Professor Dodwell.
[3] *History of Mysoor*, i. 297.

their support against Haidar Ali and the Marathas, but found it hard to decide which side he preferred to be on; Muhammad Ali thought he would like to supplant both the Nizam and Haidar, who for their part thought his existence unnecessary; the Marathas, now rapidly recovering from the effects of their disaster at Panipat, were inclined to pillage the whole of South India. The whole business was lightened by much conscious humour, which the Marathas, who had so largely brought about the farcical state of Indian politics, seem to have enjoyed most heartily.

The best joke came when Colonel Smith, commanding a force he believed was to support the Nizam, found the Nizam and Haidar in the field against him, with the Marathas benevolently behind the confederates. Smith won a battle at the Pass of Changama (1767), but, having only 7000 men against 70,000, retired. The enemy followed him, to be again defeated, at Trinomali. Haidar then 'rather observed than covered' [1] his own orderly retreat, attended by a troop of French cavalry and his retinue of picked men clad in scarlet and carrying pikes with silver spirals that shone brilliantly. The English victories were of little direct value, since at the very time of their being won Haidar's son Tipu was plundering the Madras Council's country houses. Their indirect value was that the Nizam entered on the course of wavering which was ultimately to make his dynasty the premier one in India, with the title of Faithful Ally of the British Government. When the Bengal Government sent a detachment under a vigorous officer into the Northern Sarkars, his wavering was confirmed into decision. He obtained peace by the Treaty of Masulipatam, 1768; the British unnecessarily agreed to pay him a tribute in exchange for the Sarkars, 'which he neither possessed, nor had the most distant hope of ever possessing',[2] and declared Haidar a rebel and usurper whose territories they meant to conquer and retain, promising the Marathas (who were not even parties to the Treaty) *chauth* on them when this was achieved. The Court of Directors wrote of these extraordinary proceedings:

' You have brought us into such a labyrinth of difficulties, that we do not see how we shall be extricated from them.'

Haidar and Tipu fought on, and fought successfully. They caused Mangalore, after 'a wretched defence',[3] to capitulate; made up for defeat at Mulwagul by a series of victories presented to them by incompetence; ravaged up to the suburbs of Madras, when Haidar coolly nomi-

---

[1] Wilks, i. 320.   [2] *Op. cit.* i. 330.   [3] *Op. cit.* i. 332.

nated an English envoy, and 'practically dictated peace on his own terms'.¹ The Company, whose commitments were now bewildering and contradictory, agreed to support him also against attack. Attack came from the Marathas, two years later (1771), and the Presidency dared not help him. They 'earned at once the bitter animosity of a relentless foe, and incurred the discredit of repudiating their treaty obligations.'

The Directors, who had never ceased to inveigh against 'the general corruption and rapacity of our servants', in 1771 appointed Warren Hastings Governor of Bengal, a post he took up next year. Verelst, who had been in positions of influence all through the worst troubles, and was himself better than most in character, summed up his task thus:

' To reclaim men from dissipation, to revive a general spirit of industry, to lead the minds of all from gaudy dreams of sudden-acquired wealth to a patient expectation of growing fortunes.'

About to enter on this heroic work, Hastings received a long letter from Clive in the rôle of an 'elder statesman', intolerably patronising and self-approving:

' I wish your government to be attended, as mine was, with success to the Company, and with the consciousness of having discharged every duty with firmness and fidelity.'

The man who could seriously believe his government had achieved all *that* was no longer capable of advising the lonely, disdainful spirit he addressed. Hastings's courteous guarded answer indicated that he meant to keep his business to himself. Between him and Clive there was always intense dislike.

We should not forget that the conquered side had a life of their own. There was interaction, and not merely of oppression. It is often cited as a reason for Dupleix' success, that through Madame Dupleix, who had Indian blood in her veins, he had intimate knowledge of the land's people. This advantage, however, the English were not long in sharing with him. Until the austere purging of manners from all intercourse except that of rulers with a subject folk, which followed the Mutiny (and in a less degree had already come with Cornwallis), irregular connections played a part—no doubt in lowering the tone of social life, but also in creating an intimacy of knowledge and sympathy which vanished from better times. And there was English intercourse with bankers like the

¹ P. E. Roberts, *History of British India*, 170.

H

Seths, with mere tools like Nandakumar and the various *naibs*, with brave allies like Yusuf Khan and other sepoy leaders whose names flit into Orme's and Cambridge's generously full stories and into the letters of Clive and Hastings.

There remained the main stream of native life, passive while war and pillage stormed and traversed the land. We have the tale as it looked to contemporary Indian historians, to Ananda Ranga Pillai in the south and the author of *Seir Mutaqherin* in the north, observers puzzled, watchful, seeing the emergence of new modes and different ethics, trying to adjust to known standards the ways of these incalculable strangers whose power seemed so tremendous. We have other records still, of how these years affected those too humble to take the attention of the historic muse. Ramprasad Sen, one of the noblest of lyric poets, was a contemporary of Siraj-ud-Daula and Clive. He was born in 1718, in the district of Nadiya, which is Bengal of the Bengalis, seat of their ancient independent pre-Muhammadan kings. He was a poor man, a poet at the court of the Krishnanagar *Zemindars*. In the time's miseries there was passionate revival of the worship of Kali, the terrible goddess who gives to some strength and abundance and to others a trampled existence. Ramprasad, gazing at the bewildering pageant, exclaims:

' Mother, to some you have given wealth, horses, elephants, charioteers, conquest. And the lot of others is field labour, with rice and vegetables. Some live in palaces, as I myself would like to do. O Mother, are these fortunate folk your grandfathers—and I no relation at all? . . . Some ride in palkis, while I have the privilege of carrying the shoulder-pole'.[1]

On his songs falls the black shadow of ever-constant oppression, and his imagery is drawn from a life pillaged and set to endless toil. 'The Six Passions', 'The Ten Senses', are like *lathials*, club-bearers who strike him down. He dwells in a damaged house, and is terrified of 'those Six Thieves' (the 'Six Passions') who at night come leaping into his court-yard. It is in his poetry that we find the first English word in Bengali— he will take his suit against the neglectful goddess to the courts, where he will win the 'decree'. This brings us just into Warren Hastings's time. His songs, of ineffable pathos and courage, show a true and brave mind kept alive in an oppressed people, waiting for better days.

He died, 1775, drowned while following in trance the clay image of Kali when on the last day of her annual festival it was cast into the

[1] See *Bengali Religious Lyrics* (Edward Thompson and A. M. Spencer; Oxford University Press).

Ganges. What is traditionally his last song addresses the Dark Power he had served:

' Tara, do you remember any more? Mother, as I have lived happy, is there happiness hereafter? . . . Had there been any other refuge, I should not beseech you. But you, Mother, having given me hope, you have now cut my bonds, you have lifted me to the tree's summit.

'Ramprasad says: My mind is firm, and my gift to the priest is made. Mother, my Mother, my all is finished. I have offered my gift.'

CHAPTER IV

WARREN HASTINGS, GOVERNOR OF BENGAL

' Let me have but Existence, and Freedom from Pain, with the full Exercise of my mental Faculties, and I desire no more, till I see the last Sight of Saugur Island.'—WARREN HASTINGS, November 20, 1784.

Hastings's matrimonial embarrassments: prosecution of the naib-dewans: Nandakumar and Hastings: Hastings's early zeal: his difficulties from lack of proper authority: his unique experience fits him for his high post: versatility of his character: Barwell won over: payments to Emperor stopped: ruinous drain on Bengal resources: Nawab of Bengal's civil list curtailed: reforms in penal administration and laws: the Sanyasi rebellion: Rohilla War.

HASTINGS relieved Cartier, April, 1772, 'in the fortieth year of his age and the fullness of his intellectual powers',[1] coming to a province wasted by rapine closing in famine and to officials who saw no reason why they should fear God or regard man. He was burdened by two extra embarrassments, one of his own bringing. On his voyage out to Madras, he had fallen deeply in love with a German lady accompanying her husband, who was a portrait-painter seeking fortune in the land of rajas and nawabs. When Hastings was transferred to Calcutta, the Imhoffs followed him, living together amicably while divorce proceedings were put through in far-off Franconia. Sir James Stephen says [2] that when Hastings was at last able to marry her, in 1777, he bought her from her husband for £10,000; for this figure he gives no evidence, and his (unnamed) authority is not a first-class one. However, it seems likely

[1] *Oxford History of India*, 510.   [2] *Nuncomar and Impey*, i. 24.

that Imhoff's financial position was improved by his cession of his wife. The second Mrs. Hastings [1] was a charming and adroitly attractive woman. Hastings's marriage to her was one of deep, unbroken affection. But it involved him in difficulties which he overcame only gradually, by ignoring their existence. Nothing makes a man more an object of ridicule than an uncompleted sexual intrigue. The new Governor and his friends, notoriously awaiting word of divorce achieved, were for long a byword. Clive, whose dislike of Hastings increased as the latter replied with emptinesses to his gratuitous advice and exhortations, contemptuously said 'that he had never heard of Hastings having any abilities except for seducing his friends' wives'. [2] Mrs. Hastings was a bad influence on her husband's administration. He lay so deeply under her spell that the numerous applicants for jobs knew that her kindness must be sedulously cultivated.

The other embarrassment was forced on him. The Directors instructed him that the Company must 'stand forth as Dewan', and take over the civil administration directly. This was probably meant to be a half-way house towards the Crown's taking over of their conquests, a process which became arrested until the Mutiny precipitated its completion. Hastings was ordered to give proceedings an ethical colour by staging a trial whose ends were really political; he was to prosecute the Naib-Dewans, who could then be deposed for peculation and tyranny. He was further told to use Nandakumar, once a Naib-Dewan himself, but pushed out for Muhammad Reza Khan, as a tool in this monstrous business. So much of shame and mischief sprang from his action, that the despatch merits some quotation:

' We cannot forbear recommending you to avail yourself of the intelligence which Nuncomar may be able to give respecting the Naib's administration; and while the envy which Nuncomar is supposed to bear this minister may prompt him to a ready communication of all proceedings which have come to his knowledge, we are persuaded that no scrutable part of the Naib's conduct can have escaped the watchful eye of his jealous and penetrating rival. Hence we cannot doubt that the abilities and disposition of Nuncomar may be successfully employed in the investigation of Mahomed Rheza Khan's administration, and bring to light any embezzlement, fraud, or malversation which he may have committed in the office of Naib Dewan, or in the station he has held under the several successive Subahs; and while we assure ourselves that you will make the necessary use of Nuncomar's intelligence, we have such confidence in your wisdom and caution, that we have nothing to

[1] Hastings was a widower when he met the Imhoffs.
[2] H. Beveridge, *The Trial of Nanda Kumar*, 106.

fear from any secret motives or designs which may induce him to detect the mal-administration of one whose power has been the object of his envy, and whose office the aim of his ambition; for we have the satisfaction to reflect that you are too well apprised of the subtlety and disposition of Nuncomar to yield him any post of authority which may be turned to his own advantage, or prove detrimental to the Company's interest. Though we have thought it necessary to intimate to you how little we are disposed to delegate any power or influence to Nuncomar, yet, should his information and assistance be serviceable to you in your investigation of the conduct of Mahomed Rheza Khan, you will yield him such encouragement and reward as his trouble and the extent of his services may deserve.'

This letter (and, indeed, the whole affair) might have served as a model to the Ogpu. It disposes of Malleson's statement, often copied: ' That Nandakumar was the evil genius who had suggested to the Court this action is sufficiently proved'.[1]

Nandakumar, since his first appearance in Company affairs, as the Governor of Hugli whom Scrafton in pre-Plassey days bribed into deserting the French at Chandernagore, had continued to be a prime figure in Bengal politics. Clive particularly favoured him, and supported him in one bitter episode when Hastings was compelled to give way to him in an appointment of great financial value. Clive became disillusioned as to his character, which is described as vain, proud, selfish, but faithful to friends and allies; but he regained and kept influence in Verelst's governorship. Hastings always called him 'the basest of mankind'; and, thirteen years after his execution, 'when the hate might be supposed to have been in some measure appeased',[2] wrote:

' I was never the personal enemy of any man but Nuncomar, whom from my soul I detested even when I was compelled to countenance him.'

The reference in those last words is to this episode, when two implacable foes were ordered to work together in what Hastings regarded as iniquitous. He told the Directors (September 1772):

' From the year 1759 to the time when I left Bengal in 1764, I was engaged in a continued opposition to the interests and designs of that man because I judged him to be adverse to the welfare of my employers, and in the course of this contention I received sufficient indications of his ill will to have made me an irreconcilable enemy, if I could suffer my passions to supersede the duty which I owe to the Company.'

There is no parallel in Hastings's recorded writings to his savagery of detestation of Nandakumar, whom he regarded as a scoundrel to the point of being practically vermin. We need not question that a man

[1] *Life of Hastings*, 101. [2] H. Beveridge, *The Trial of Nanda Kumar*, 101.

whose whole life and employment had been spent in such scenes and temptations as Bengal furnished was in many ways as bad as Hastings thought him. On the other hand, at this distance of time we need not count it as part of his criminality that his 'designs' were 'adverse to the welfare of' the foreign adventurers.

The prosecution, distasteful in the extreme to Hastings, ended, as he foresaw, in acquittal. Of the Naib-Dewan of Bihar, Chitab Rai, he wrote, 'Indeed, I scarce know why he was called to account'. His trial ended honourably, with complete exoneration; he was allowed to return to his home, where he died as a result of enforced residence in Calcutta. Muhammad Reza Khan was also acquitted. Hastings wrote the Chairman of the Directors a characteristically thoughtful and fair-minded analysis of the trial. Nandakumar was disappointed of the Naib-Dewanship which he thought would be his by reversion and reward, and left to brood over the contemptuous manner in which he had first been used and then flung aside. It was considered adequate notice that his son was appointed to an influential post in the Nawab's household.

Although Hastings's term of office marks the end of the dual system, he did not return to India with any idea of instituting the direct British-controlled administration which characterised the nineteenth century. The Company held *diwani* and *zemindari* rights—it was supreme ruler and supreme landlord—but the general policy was to farm out these rights under supervision. Hastings had at his disposal the same type of covenanted servant as had served under Clive. Seven years can have made little difference to the personnel, though their discipline was a little better, and their pay and perquisites had been placed on a more regular footing. A letter written by Hastings to the Court of Directors, in 1781, shows his preference for Indian agency in controlling the large area now under the Company's sway.

' The civil offices of this government might be reduced to a very scanty number, were their exigency alone to determine the list of your covenanted servants, which at this time consists of no less a number than two hundred and fifty two, and many of them the sons of the first families in the kingdom of Great Britain, and everyone aspiring to the rapid acquisition of lakhs, and to return to pass the prime of their lives at home.' [1]

If Hastings had wanted to build up a British administration he would have complained of the quality, but not of the number of his subordinates.

[1] Dated May 5, 1781. A *lakh* is 100,000 (rupees).

It is impossible to exaggerate the burdens which lay on one man. He wrote that 'every part' of the Government which had been so long clogged in so many ways was now in full current, yet 'the channels through which the business of it should flow scarcely opened for its conveyance'. He reduced the Nawab's stipend, and appointed native revenue collectors (1774) under a Board of Revenue sitting daily in Calcutta and hearing complaints. English officials, whom at this period he was at pains to pick for ability and character, were sent on tours of supervision. His 'letters to individual Directors glow with indignation'[1] at the scene he surveyed. 'Will you believe', he asks,

' that the boys of the service are the sovereigns of the country under the unmeaning title of supervisors, collectors[2] of the revenue, administrators of justice and rulers, heavy rulers of the people? . . . This is the system which my predecessor, Cartier, was turned out for exposing, and I will be turned out too, rather than suffer it to continue as it is.'

Of the monstrous drain of £400,000 annually to the British Treasury he writes:

' Is it not a contradiction to the common notions of equity and policy that the English gentlemen of Cumberland and Argyleshire should regulate the polity of a nation which they know only by the lakhs which it has sent to Great Britain and by the reduction it has occasioned in their land-tax?'

He found the Mogul land revenue system in the last stage of deterioration. Under Akbar's system the money should have been collected through 'farmers', who remitted the amount—based on a third of the produce—after they had deducted their commission of one-tenth. In Bengal the revenue 'farmers' had become a heterogeneous collection of the descendants of old Hindu chiefs, court favourites, speculators, and former officials and soldiers. These rack-rented their tenants, and were themselves continually pressed by the Nawab, who was virtually an independent ruler. By the middle of the eighteenth century the original basis of land revenue was forgotten. The Mogul revenue staff, the accountants and *qanungos*, had ceased to function, and had gradually disappeared. When the Company's servants began to find their way into the Bengal districts the old village communities had completely decayed. It is doubtful if they had ever functioned to any great extent in Bengal; here, apart from a few large towns, the population was scat-

[1] *Hastings in Bengal*, 181.

[2] He notes in a letter (January 6, 1773) that the supervisors had been 'collectors' for two years, and were now called such.

tered in tiny clusters of huts, wherever a little rising ground lifted them above their water-logged fields. The peasants' salvation lay in their diffusion over this fertile but impassable land, which was almost inaccessible except by the few navigable rivers. These countrymen, and the aboriginal tribes which occupied the less fertile uplands, presented a difficult problem for the rapacious invader, or his more orderly successor the tax-collector. They formed a contrast to the *ryots* in the dry, bare Deccan, which lies open to the invader or the Government's emissaries. The Deccani tends to huddle for safety behind the stone walls of a village. It is comparatively easy to map out his country, assess the value of his land, and collect the revenue village by village. In eighteenth-century Bengal this would have been impossible. It was chiefly practical reasons which led the British to recognise and work through the revenue farmers or *Zemindars* of Bengal, while in Madras and Bombay they attempted a direct assessment of the *ryot*, and to collect the revenue through salaried officials.

The first British administrators naturally regarded the State as the supreme landlord. Though contrary to Hindu theory, this is in accordance with the Muslim idea that the land of the conquered infidel belongs to the conqueror.[1] The status of the revenue farmers raised a more practical difficulty. In Bengal they tended to become independent landlords, a position to which some of the Hindu *Zemindars*, like Vishnupur, could put forward hereditary claims. Hastings strongly objected to the *Zemindar* being accepted as a permanent landlord, and his 'farm' being converted into a fixed rent. During his term of office there was a continual struggle over this question; after his resignation, Lord Cornwallis accepted the Permanent Settlement, a change of policy for which many theoretical arguments were adduced, but which was chiefly due to the failure to operate any alternative system. Hastings had too much to contend against. His Council opposed him on various grounds; the Supreme Court,[2] whose powers had not been properly defined in the Regulating Act of 1773, was continually thwarting him; his European staff were ignorant about land questions, and inclined to be obstructive. Hastings failed, but his policy is important because it marks the first tentative efforts to evolve the district system and the district officer.

[1] The Hindu king claimed a portion, usually a fourth, of the produce, and the disposal of waste lands.

[2] Established 1774.

The 'supervisors', who had been appointed in 1769, had been given a roaming commission to study the revenue system in their districts, a task for which most of them had neither the training nor the inclination. The famine of 1770 finally ruined the old Mogul revenue system, and with it many of the Hindu *Zemindars*. In the general confusion Hastings decided to convert his supervisors into 'collectors', considering that if they received the revenue, district by district, they would exercise more control. In the same year, 1772, the 'farms' were settled for five years. Hastings himself went on tour with a 'committee of circuit', usually assigning the 'farms' to the *Zemindars*, but in some cases putting them up for auction, as at Krishnanagar, 'owing to the subtle and faithless character of the *Zemindar*'.[1] The 'collectors', therefore, had no assessment or 'settlement' work to do, but they were given stringent orders to prevent the *Zemindars* raising rents, and Indian *aumils* were appointed to assist them. The experiment was not a success. If the old Mogul village staff had still been functioning, and the covenanted servants had been of better calibre, these embryonic district officers might have got directly in touch with the tenants, and intervened between them and the oppressive *Zemindars*. Even then the physical difficulties in dealing directly with the villagers would have been great throughout the Deltaic plain. The 'collectors' merely added to the confusion. The famine of 1770, the full extent of which was not appreciated by the Government, led to 'farms' being assessed too high, and some were bought at auction by speculators of poor standing. Defaults were frequent during the next five years, and the Presidency was then put under six Revenue Boards, which superseded the collectors.[2]

The Boards proved no more successful than the collectors, and Hastings, who in 1776 was at last master in his Council, instituted a Metropolitan Revenue Board of senior officials under his own supervision. This body continued to function until Lord Cornwallis took over the administration. Its general policy was to stop the auctioning of 'farms', and work through the *Zemindars*, who were assessed roughly on the fertility of their land. The land of *Zemindars* who defaulted was sold. This was an innovation which, combined with alterations in civil law, made land a commodity to be marketed and mortgaged. Almost unwittingly, Hastings introduced into Bengal that European conception of land which was to have such disastrous consequences throughout

[1] See W. K. Firminger, *Introduction to the Fifth Report*, chapter xi.

[2] The arrears during the five years amounted to 120 lakhs.

India. It would, however, be unfair to blame him for the failure of his revenue policy. He was not responsible for the legal chaos produced by the Act of 1773, and he had a sincere desire to protect the cultivator. But he had to satisfy the rapacity of the Directors in London, who held the usual exaggerated views about the fertility of Bengal, and this forced him to assess land too high. He also lacked any staff, Indian or English, with the knowledge, probity, and will to carry out his schemes.

Much criticism of Hastings is written with a strong bias in favour of the Bengal *Zemindars*. It is absurd to picture them as a group of hereditary landlords, enjoying the confidence of their tenants. A large proportion were adventurers, or the sons of adventurers, who had acquired their position during the anarchy of the early eighteenth century. Many were privy to the gang robberies carried on by dacoits and river pirates. Hastings had strong reasons for objecting to establishing these *Zemindars* as permanent landlords. He failed to produce an effective alternative policy, but it is doubtful whether the descendants of the *Zemindars* have justified the later policy of the Permanent Settlement, either by their services to the countryside or their treatment of the tenantry.

Hastings from the first pressed that all the Company's Presidencies ought to be brought under one head, which obviously must be that of Bengal, the wealthiest of the three and the one to which the other two as a matter of course applied for any subventions which their own deficits required. Moreover, his Council was too large, although it was reduced from fourteen to nine. 'A principle of decision must rest somewhere', he urged. Yet during the two years when he was merely Governor of Bengal, the fact that in theory he was scarcely even *primus inter pares* caused no actual inconvenience, owing to his own complete ascendancy. The immediate administration, especially as regards foreign relations and relations with the Nawab, was in the hands of the Select Committee (which survived throughout the period between Siraj-ud-Daula's capture of Calcutta and the first Governor-Generalship) of himself and two others. But all his councillors were complaisant and trustful, he himself *was* the Government, and it was now that he developed his masterful and solitary habits of mind and action.

Having to resist the pressure of jobbery at home, which had already crowded the services with Directors' and Proprietors' friends and relations, he sought to gather into his own hands as much authority as he could. He himself had to be 'the safeguards'; in all times of transition, a man has to be a cover from the tempest, the shadow of a great rock in a weary land. A Council was too diffuse and garrulous and open to influence and fears:

'A long habit of licentiousness, strong temptations, the cursed encouragements of patronage, and the sturdiness of independence, are too great evils to combat with the weak powers of this Government, which many possess and none can exercise.' [1]

He submitted that the Governor's primacy was precarious in the extreme: 'a moment's contention is sufficient to discover the nakedness of his authority, and to level him with the rest'.[2] He insisted that all Europeans, other than those detailed for actual duty elsewhere, must reside in Calcutta, where the Mayor's Court could enforce decent conduct.

He laboured to bring to the Directors' realisation the fact that 'the Investment' was now unimportant in comparison with the happiness of a people become the Company's subjects. The job was tremendous; the Directors knew little of Indian affairs, and were faintly interested in them, but they did know that public expectation was greedy for dividends. An eye-witness of the debates when Clive's conduct was brought into question in Parliament noted that the whole course of events in India was treated as one undeviating wrong and criminality, but that not one word was ever said about restoring either the lands or the revenues to those who had been dispossessed. Similarly, in every discussion but Hastings's own, it was taken for granted that India's main reason for existence was to provide fortunes—the only point at issue was whether they should be made swiftly or during the passage of some years of service.

This extraordinary man was uniquely fitted for his tremendous task, by experience as well as by his altogether exceptional qualities of intellect, industry, and thoroughness. His had been no sudden rise to power, but a slow apprenticeship which to any less eager and vivid mind would have been insufferably tedious. He had been for long enough overseer of the Company's warehouse and keeper of accounts at Kasimbazar. He knew Bengali and Urdu well, and Persian to an extent which was useful (though not—as biographers and historians all assert, in face of his own modest indication of his actual acquirement—perfectly). He was as insatiably curious as Akbar about everything that could interest a vivid person and brain; his friends knew that no knowledge, whether of

[1] Letter to Sir George Colebrook (October 12, 1773).
[2] Letter to the Directors, November 11, 1773.

the natural kingdom or man's activities, was a matter of indifference
to him. As one noted, whenever he visited Benares, he went 'pundit-
hunting'. In the unexampled burdens of his great service, he kept sane
by taking refuge in his abounding gift of delight. He loved the people
of India, and respected them to a degree no other British ruler has even
equalled. For example, after Siraj-ud-Daula had taken the up-country
factors prisoner in Murshidabad, Hastings's qualities of courtesy and
sympathy procured him freedom within restrictions, and he noted gratefully, long after, that he had learnt in adversity how much kindness and
sympathetic consideration Indians can show. When it was asserted that
his wish to see native officials trusted was unsound, because of Asiatic
incapacity for exercising power decently, he said:

' As I have formerly lived among the country people in a very inferior
station, at a time when we were subject to the most slavish dependence on
the Government, and met with the greatest indulgence and even respect from
the *Zemindars* and officers of the Government, I can with the greatest confidence deny the justice of this opinion.'

His first acts were directed towards establishing general lines of firm
ground in the administrative and political morass. He won over Barwell, the ablest of his councillors, to be a tower of defence in the terrible years that were to follow. Barwell, intolerably loquacious and
addicted to minute examinations, was at first somewhat as Seward was
to Lincoln; like Seward, he learnt how superior were his chief's abilities, and consented gladly to a boundless admiration and service. Re-
tiring from active interference, Barwell devoted his main attention to
his own fortunes, with complete success. Meanwhile, though

' the new government consists of a confused heap of undigested materials
as wild as the Chaos itself: the Collection of the Revenue, the provision of
the Investment, the administration of Justice (if it exists at all), the care of the
Police are all huddled together—we have them all to separate and bring into
order at once. We must work as an arithmetician does, with his Rule of
False, adopt a plan upon conjecture, try, execute, add and deduct from it till
it is brought into a perfect shape'—

the Directors were bent on prosecuting for offences long past, and recovering money long taken to Europe, and were harassing Hastings
with a farrago of queries:

' Are not the tenants more than ever oppressed and wretched? Are our
Investments improved? Has not the raw silk of the cocoons been raised upon
us 50 % in price? . . . as to the expenses of your Presidency, they are at length
swelled to a degree we are no longer able to support.' (April 7, 1773.)

He turned, first, to cut down expenses. The country could not stand the drain of 26 lakhs (unpaid, however, in the famine of 1770) to the Mogul Emperor, with the drain to the puppet Nawab and people in England. Hastings had power to deal with only the two former. The Emperor sent a vakil with a peremptory demand for his money. But he was now in the hands of the Marathas, who had found in Mahadaji Sindhia an able leader. Hastings loathed 'the unprofitable and degrading tendency of political simulation', so esteemed by Clive and his successors in both South and North India, and was determined to clear his path of shams. Necessity was always his master; and now he knew that Bengal was close to starvation. He knew, too, that the Marathas, into whose coffers any payment to the Emperor would go, were the power most to be feared.

'As I see no use in excuses and evasions which all the world can see through, I replied to the peremptory demand of the King for the tribute of Bengal by a peremptory declaration that not a rupee should pass thro' the provinces till they had recovered from the distresses to which lavish payments to him had principally contributed.'

To the Directors he wrote:

'I think I may promise that no more payments will be made while he is in the hands of the Mahrattas nor, if I can prevent it, *ever more*. Strange! that while the revenue of the province is insufficient for its expenses and for the claims of the Company and our Mother Country, the wealth of the province (which is its blood) should be drained to supply the pageantry of a mock King, an idol of our own creation! but how much more astonishing that we should still pay him the same dangerous homage while he is the tool of the only enemies we have in India, and who want but such aids to prosecute their designs even to our ruin.'

The facts and principles which determined his actions were simple. Everyone in India was demanding lakhs from anyone suspected of ability to provide them; the Bengal administration was considered eminent in this class, whereas it hardly possessed a rupee. Having himself to deal with masters who neither understood nor would listen to arguments of poverty, he was inevitably hard in his bargains. He disliked Clive's Treaty of Allahabad, which had given the Emperor the only territory he owned, territory now occupied by the Marathas, whom Hastings always envisaged as the destined enemies of the English. The brigade which Clive had stationed at Allahabad, to be ready for the defence of the Wazir-Nawab of Oudh,

'drew from Fort William in the course of five years not less than two millions sterling. This was a ruinous drain upon the circulating medium of Bengal, to which not a rupee either in bullion or in merchandise returned; and the paltry payment by the Vizier of thirty thousand rupees per month was scarcely felt as a relief, except perhaps by the officers in command of the troops, who reaped no trivial benefit to their private fortunes from the arrangement.' [1]

Hastings accordingly sold Korah and Allahabad to the Nawab of Oudh for fifty lakhs, at the same time as he cancelled the outgoing of twenty-six lakhs tribute for Bengal. He told the Directors:

' I have been happily furnished with an accidental concourse of circumstances to relieve the Company in the distress of their affairs.'

He proceeded to deal with the affairs of another 'idol' of English creation, this time less willingly (under orders from home). The Bengal Nawab's revenues were to be cut down to 16 lakhs; and his expenses were curtailed even further by Hastings in person:

' To bring the whole expenses of the Nizamut within the pale of 16 lacks it was necessary to begin with reforming the useless servants of the court and retrenching the idle parade of elephants, menageries, etc., which loaded the Civil List. This cost little regret in performing, but the President, who took upon him the chief share in this business, acknowledges he suffered considerably in his feelings when he came to touch upon the Pension list. Some hundreds of persons of the ancient nobility of the Country, excluded under our government from almost all employments civil or military, had ever since the revolution depended on the bounty of the Nabob and near 10 lacks were bestowed that way. . . . The President declares that even with some of the highest rank he could not avoid discovering under all the pride of eastern manners, the manifest marks of penury and want. There was however no room left for hesitation.'

He next established civil and criminal courts of appeal in Calcutta, the *Sadr Diwani Adalat* and *Sadr Nizamat Adalat*. Calcutta had its own Mayor's Court, whose powers were uncertain and its jurisdiction supposedly local (though in 1773 the Zemindar of Nadiya, while in Calcutta, was arrested and brought before it, to his great surprise, for a private debt to an English official). This was all that Hastings could achieve for the present, leaving Muslim criminal law in general force. It was in many ways more merciful than English law, which was in the full tide of the century of activity which crowded the penal code with

---

[1] Gleig, *Memoirs of Warren Hastings*, i. 343. The 'Vizier' was the Nawab of Oudh, who was in theory the Emperor's chief minister, a convenient fiction which helped the transfer of the districts.

capital offences. Muhammadan law, however, though in the main easy-going, ran to extremes of ferocity, such as mutilation, 'too common a sentence of the Mohametan Courts', which, 'though it may deter others, yet renders the criminal a burden to the public, and imposes on him the necessity of persevering in the crimes which it was meant to repress'. Since the criminal courts remained in native hands, impalement continued for some years longer; twenty years later, an English officer demands, 'how much longer are we to be outraged by the sight of writhing humanity on stakes?'

For dacoity Hastings had no pity. He knew, of course, how oppression had itself made robbery widespread. But part of his work of bringing tolerable conditions back was to obtain security for honest people. He decreed that dacoits should be hanged in their villages, their families made State slaves, and the villages fined. He was anxious to distinguish between 'the *ryot* who, impelled by strong necessity in a single instance, invades the property of his neighbour' and 'professed and notorious robbers'. The Quran, which was the law-book of the native courts, forbade sentence of death unless there had been murder as well as theft. Hastings was already (and naturally, and in the main rightly) indifferent to strict legality.

' The Mohametan Law is founded on the most lenient principle and an abhorrence of bloodshed. This often obliges the Sovereign to interpose to prevent the guilty from escaping with impunity and to strike at the root of such disorders as the law will not reach.'

For genuine dacoity, then, 'the punishment decreed by this Government' was to 'be superadded by an immediate act of Government'.

The most mysterious episode of this first government of Hastings is the depredations of the Sanyasis, whoever they were. He called them 'the gipsies of Hindostan', one of the few instances of misinformation that he sets down. The extreme reverence of the people for them made their extirpation extremely difficult. They moved, stark naked, in bands: they won successes against isolated bodies of sepoys, and proved hard to hunt down, from the celerity with which they fled into dense jungle. The Sanyasi rebellion is obscure, and a monograph explaining it from the Indian side is needed. It furnished Bankimchandra Chatterji, the celebrated Bengali novelist, with at least part-theme of two of his stories, in which we are shown bandit-heroes who rob from a mixture of patriotic and religious motives. Bengal, especially East Bengal, in Akbar's time, in Hastings's time, in our own time, has always provided this mixture of motives.

Hastings, who neglected no chance of giving the Company's territories better and more defensible borders, expelled the Bhutanese from Kuch-Behar. The same aim of consolidation was one cause of the Rohilla War. Oudh was a buffer State between Bihar and the Marathas; its Nawab 'subsists on our strength entirely'. The province marched with country ruled by Rohillas, Muslims from Afghanistan who had possessed it for about forty years. They and the Nawab and the Marathas entered upon the counterchange of alliance and defiance usual in India, 'all utterly unscrupulous, and each knew that no trust could be placed in either of the others'.[1] To-day, and for long past, Hastings's apologists (as Mr. Roberts observes [2]) hold the field; because Burke's attacks on the Rohilla War were distorted and ignorant, most historians write irritatedly as if all criticism was purely factitious. This is ridiculous, in view of Hastings's own letters and despatches. When critics remark that Nandakumar, for example, could not be expected to be honourable, after having lived through scenes of such hardly paralleled duplicity, they forget that Hastings had lived through them also, with at least this result, that he was not very sensitive to the suffering caused by warfare (as he showed consistently). He accepted it as a necessity; you could not make omelettes without breaking eggs. When the Nawab's projected campaign was postponed for a period, he wrote to Mr. Laurence Sulivan, in words in which we can detect the note so common since, of Indian governmental impatience that anyone should dare to criticise what seemed expedient to 'the man on the spot':

' I was glad to be freed from the Rohilla expedition because I was doubtful of the judgment which would have been passed upon it at home, where I see too much stress laid upon general maxims and too little attention given to the circumstances which require an exception to be made from them. . . .

' On the other hand, the absence of the Mahrattas, and the weak state of the Rohillas, promised an easy conquest of them; and I own that such was my idea of the Company's distress at home, added to my knowledge of their wants abroad, that I should have been glad of any occasion to employ their forces which saves so much of their pay and expenses.' (October 12, 1773).

Much that is sentimental or utterly beside the point has been dragged into this controversy. There has been argument whether the Rohillas were an industrious and artistic peasantry or ruffianly invaders. They were merely alien conquerors, as so many rulers in India were; and were in an unhappy position, between the Nawab of Oudh and the Marathas.

[1] Sir John Strachey, *Hastings and the Rohilla War*, 49.
[2] *History of British India*, 170.

In 1772 they and the Nawab made an agreement, the contracting parties' signatures being witnessed by Sir Robert Barker, commanding on the British frontier, by which the Nawab was to receive 40 lakhs for defending the Rohillas if attacked by the Marathas (who were demanding 50 lakhs from them). The Marathas *did* attack them in 1773, and retreated from a threatening movement of an army which comprised a British section. The Rohillas did not pay the 40 lakhs; as a matter of fact they had not got it, and the chief who held a loose suzerainty among them failed to get any contributions from his fellow-chiefs in response to his whip-round. The Nawab had already sent Hastings an attractive offer:

' Should the Rohilla Sirdars be guilty of a breach of their agreement, and the English gentlemen will thoroughly extirminate [1] them and settle me in their country, I will in that case pay them fifty lakhs of rupees in ready money, and besides exempt them from paying any tribute to the King out of the Bengal revenues.'

Hastings, who was thoroughly entangled in promises to him, lent the Nawab a brigade under Colonel Champion. His correspondence leaves no doubt that his financial straits weighed with him even more than his wish to see Oudh—'my country is in reality the door of Bengal', the Nawab once wrote—a really effective shield between British India and the Marathas. He was so throng with business of many kinds that he often gave imperfect attention to what was proposed, and he was veering and vacillating throughout this expedition,

' to which I had offered my agreement on the consideration of obtaining a saving to the Company of one-third of the expenses of their whole army, and the payment of forty lacs on the conclusion of it'.

The Rohilla leader was defeated and killed, whereupon the allies quarrelled ferociously over the booty. The Nawab with much spirit and wrath insisted that the spoils were his alone, as he was paying a specified sum for the services of the Company's troops. The British field-officers demanded as prize-money twenty lakhs, fifteen lakhs, and the most moderate (their commanding officer reported) ten lakhs, the affair coming as close to actual mutiny as anything short of mutiny could be. Alarmed and incensed, Hastings wrote supporting the Nawab.

[1] 'Extirminate' here did Hastings much harm. It was an over-drastic translation of a word which meant 'extirpate', possibly by mere ejection. The promise to remit the tribute, which Hastings had already stopped, was made by the Nawab as technically Wazir of the Emperor. The spelling 'extirminate' is of course that of the Nawab's translator.

It is customary to assert that the miseries caused by this war were no
unusual matter; that the contrary belief arose out of Colonel Champion's discontent at not being made a brigadier for the campaign, at
being accompanied by a political officer (Middleton), and at the
wrangling outcome of it all. It is also asserted that Hastings is completely exculpated because he wrote, on rumours of excesses, denouncing them and exhorting the Nawab to humanity.[1] He did all this; and
Champion also expressed his revulsion strongly. Nevertheless, that
hardness of heart which even Mr. Roberts admits was in Hastings
appears in his own very able but somewhat cool and unconvincing
defence, containing words often quoted against him:

' I believe it to be a truth that he' [the Nawab] 'began by sending detachments to plunder. This I pronounce to have been both barbarous and impolitic, but too much justified by the practice of war established among all
the nations of the East, and, I am sorry to add, by our own'

(he gives an example of British excesses in 1764). It is undoubtedly
true, as Sir John Strachey says, perhaps not taking very seriously the
sufferings entailed by war (which did not come closer than in their
imaginations, to his generation), that 'there never was an Indian war in
which excesses were not committed'. He goes for a proof of this to the
Mutiny, which (we at once concede) excelled the Rohilla campaign in
both quantity and quality of barbarity and horror. Nevertheless, there
is that indifferent strain in Hastings, which, however excusable in his
difficulties, did exist and functioned repeatedly; also, Hastings knew
uncommonly well what any campaign would inflict, before ever he lent
British services. We may leave this subject with citation of the
appeal of the Rohilla chieftain's widow, which Colonel Champion
forwarded to Hastings:

' To the English gentlemen, renowned throughout Hindostan for justice,
equity, and compassionating the miserable. Hafiz Rahmat Khan for forty
years governed this country, and the very beasts of the forest trembled at his
bravery. The will of God is resistless. He is slain, and to his children not an
atom remains, but they are cast from their habitations, naked, exposed to the
winds, the heats, and the burning sand, and perishing from want of even rice
and water. . . . Yesterday I was mistress of an hundred thousand people. To-
day I am in want even of a cup of water, and where I commanded I am a
prisoner. Fortune is fickle; she raises the humble and lowers the exalted; but
I am innocent, and if any one is guilty it is Hafiz. But why should the children
be punished for the errors of their father? I am taken like a beast, in a snare,
without resting place by night, or shade by day.'

[1] Gleig, *Life of Hastings*, i. 352.

The Rohilla War is one of several affairs in which the pendulum has swung too far in favour of Hastings. The testimony of the British commanding officer, and of other officers with him, cannot be all explained away.

It will be said that we are judging Hastings by expectations unreasonable in the eighteenth century. This to some extent is so. It is an unconscious but impressive tribute to the admiration which he extorts, that his deeds have always been judged by standards which we should never dream of applying to his contemporaries. The Rohillas had done the English no wrong: their right to be where they were was at least as good as the English right to Bengal and Bihar: they resisted bravely, and the British commander (it may be, from ignoble motives and hypercritically) testified to the barbarity of his allies from Oudh and considered the campaign hideously cruel: their chiefs governed well and tolerantly, whereas Oudh from start to finish of its existence as a quasi-independent State was a sink of variegated mismanagement, and Rohilkhand's new administration was iniquitous. Nevertheless, no one would be surprised at finding any other eighteenth-century European statesman sanctioning a war which was to give his country securer frontiers and a lightening of financial embarrassments. This does not alter the fact that to-day the Rohilla War should be beyond defence by any critic with principles.

CHAPTER V

HASTINGS AS GOVERNOR-GENERAL: NANDAKUMAR: MARATHA AND MYSORE WARS

Regulating Act of 1773: Hastings Governor-General: his quarrel with Francis: execution of Nandakumar: Hastings recovers power: Bombay goes to war with Marathas: Convention of Wargaon: Popham takes Gwalior: war with Haidar Ali: his invasion of the Carnatic: Sir Eyre Coote's victories.

THE Company's affairs were so miserable that in 1772, having failed in application to the Bank of England, they asked the British Government for the loan of a million pounds. This caused widespread annoyance and indignation:

' A wealthy nabob, as the retired Indian was in those days called, never returned home without being pointed to as one who fattened on the miseries of his fellow creatures, while it was broadly hinted that the prodigious amount of treasure, which by the Company's misrule went only to enrich individuals, might, and if properly managed would, place the whole people of England in a state of comparative affluence. It is marvellous how attentive mankind are to such as tell them of good things which they ought to possess, yet have not.'

Parliament appointed a Committee of Investigation, which discovered that between 1757 and 1766 its leading servants in Bengal alone had received in presents £2,169,665, in addition to Clive's *jagir*, and that £3,770,833 had been paid in compensation for losses. The result was the Regulating Act, 1773.

Under its provisions Warren Hastings became Governor-General in Bengal, with a Council of four; his only superiority was a casting-vote in case of a tie. The Governor-General in Council had authority to supervise the other two Presidencies; exactly how far this authority extended he was left to find out by experiment. Generous salaries were granted, £25,000 to the Governor-General, £10,000 to each Member of Council. The Company was relieved from its payment of £400,000 annually to the British Treasury.

Hastings's new colleagues were Barwell, already in Calcutta, and General Clavering, Colonel Monson, and Mr. Philip Francis, sent out for the purpose. Francis, who is generally supposed to be 'Junius', was a man 'not destitute of real patriotism and magnanimity',[1] but malignant in his hatreds, preferring to pursue these anonymously. On the long voyage out he obtained control of his two military *confrères*; and six years of incredible vindictiveness, faction, and consistent bad manners followed.

The new Councillors pressed first an item of their charge which related to examination of past demeanours. This action reflected the passionate desire of the Proprietors and Directorate, but to Hastings seemed impertinence. In the notorious strife which ensued, they had a case, though no one is likely ever to take it up with enthusiasm, so completely has his 'sultanlike and splendid character'[2] conquered posterity. It is worth remembering, however, that not these first Councillors only, but all their successors, found him a detested colleague and master. Thornton writes[3] of his 'habitual dissimulation', words which will shock readers to-day, but shocked no one until within the last quarter-

[1] Macaulay.   [2] Heber's phrase.   [3] *History of British India*, ii. 337.

century of ignorant apotheosis. It is justified; Hastings became incapable of giving a straightforward account of any transaction, and he wrapped all he did in maddening secrecy.

However, he was a great man, and his opponents trivial and childish men. They entered on a course of petty oversight and espionage, beginning with the Rohilla War. They had some right when they contended that he had disobeyed orders from home, in waging a campaign beyond his borders and not one of strict defence. He flatly refused to lay open his correspondence with Middleton, his agent in Lucknow, saying that much of it was private. On a rigid interpretation of his rights, he was entitled to take this line, and we can sympathise with his indignation at being treated as on trial for past actions. But 'the majority' [1] felt that their darkest suspicions were confirmed, and that the Governor-General was concealing vast peculations. They recalled Middleton, hoping to get at the facts from his papers. They set themselves to control patronage and to put everywhere supporters of themselves, a course which Hastings was to copy ruthlessly when he regained power.

In January, 1775, the Nawab of Oudh died. 'We three are king', was Francis's own statement; the three now forced the new Nawab to cede the suzerainty of the Benares *zemindari*, and to pay a subsidy of six more lakhs annually, so impoverishing him that he could not pay his troops, and had to suppress a mutiny by a massacre. His predecessor had complained to Hastings of having to deal with Presidents whose reigns were so short, and whose acts were so little binding in their successors' eyes, that the most solemn engagement was liable to be scrapped or drastically revised. Hastings had admitted the force of this protest; he now criticised the rapacity with which men so censorious of him for having waged a war for financial considerations were acting, without even such colourable pretext as he had had. The Directors saw his point, but for the money they needed so badly were willing to wink at anything. Hastings was outvoted on almost every question that arose, and made a ridiculous figure: in Francis's description, 'a timid, desperate, distracted being', 'weary of life'.

All this was changed dramatically, by the most sinister event in British-Indian annals.

The Regulating Act had established a Supreme Court in Calcutta, with a Lord Chief Justice and three puisne judges under him. When this boon was only in prospect, Hastings, dreading the transplantation to

[1] Francis, Clavering and Monson were commonly so called by contemporary Calcutta.

India of 'the complicated system of jurisprudence long the acknowledged and lamented curse of lawyer-ridden England',[1] was not too
pleased. With unwonted fervour of piety he exclaimed:[2] 'If the Lord
Chief Justice and his judges should come amongst us with their insti-
tutes, the Lord have mercy upon us!' They came, however; and in 1774
the inhabitants of Calcutta, and Europeans and their servants throughout Bengal generally, were brought under an enlightened system which
prescribed death for a wide range of turpitude, from murder to stealing
five shillings from the person or 'out of a shop, warehouse, courthouse or
stable'. Hastings held passionately that it was the cruellest injustice to
subject natives of India to laws made for far different social conditions
and enforcing penalties which their own principles considered unreasonable. But in the British mood of determination to right the wrongs
of Bengal, nothing (least of all the opposition of a man so under suspicion as the Governor-General) was allowed to delay the law's
majestic advent. And the Council of Dacca wrote enthusiastically
(1776):[3] 'As British-born subjects we revere and glory in the sublime
system of English penal law'.

The Chief Justice, Sir Elijah Impey, had been a contemporary of
Hastings at Westminster School and, according to Impey's son, his
closest friend. His appointment went far to lessen Hastings's disquiet:
he expressed his delight in cordial terms. Macaulay has stigmatised
Impey as, after Jeffreys, the most infamous name on the roll of British
judges, an opinion not invalidated by the Governor-General's warm
friendship, for Hastings's many qualities did not include austerity in
choice of associates: he accepted many poor and even base ones. In
the arguments of Hastings's worshippers Impey wears a halo of impartiality which would have astonished contemporary Calcutta. By the
testimony of Hickey's *Gazette*, a scurrilous (but evidential) Calcutta
journal, he was regarded as dividing with Mrs. Hastings the disposal of
the Governor-General's patronage:

' A displaced civilian, asking his friend the other day what was the best
means of procuring a lucrative employment, was answered, "Pay your
earnest devoirs to Marian Allypore, or sell yourself, soul and body, to
Poolbundy".'

Pulbundi, 'bridge-builder', was Impey's nickname from a contract for

---

[1] Montgomery Martin, *The Indian Empire*, iii. 323.

[2] Letter to J. Dupré, January 6, 1773.

[3] Sir James FitzJames Stephen, *Nuncomar and Impey*, ii. 21.

roads and bridges which had been given to a near relation whom he had
brought out and given a post in his court. The job had struck even the
venal society of Calcutta as remark-worthy. Macaulay's judgment of
Impey coincides with that of Lord Cornwallis, who wrote to Dundas
(December 28, 1786) after Impey's departure: [1] 'I trust you will not
send out Sir Elijah Impey. All parties and descriptions of men agree
about him'; and again, January 7, 1788, during Hastings's impeachment:[2]

' Without entering into the merits of the case, I am very sorry that things
have gone so much against poor Hastings, for he certainly has many amiable
qualities. If you are in the hanging mood, you may tuck up Sir Elijah Impey,
without giving anybody the smallest concern.'

The two sides of the Nandakumar case have been exhaustively set
out, by Sir James Stephen in an extremely readable book, by Henry
Beveridge in an extremely unreadable and rambling one. Both protagonists succeeded in convicting the other of a good deal of minor
inaccuracy. Beveridge was biased by his conviction that Hastings was
essentially base and persuaded Impey to a judicial murder; Stephen,
though a master of English law, had only a skirting and superficial
knowledge of Indian conditions, and indulges in a good deal of argument which in its context can only raise a smile. His case was strong
where it concerned Hastings's direct instigation, which has not been
proved, and probably never will be proved; it was weak when he went
farther, and tried to show that the whole affair was by no means the
scandalous travesty of decency which the better class of British historians have held.

The main facts, in so far as they emerge at this distance of time and
out of the confusion of controversy, are these. Hastings had many
enemies, and we have seen with what detestation he and Nandakumar
regarded each other. Nandakumar had been further humiliated by the
upshot of the prosecution of Muhammad Reza Khan, in which he was
an unrewarded tool. Now, at a time when the Governor-General's
impotence and persecution by the new Councillors was the one theme
of Calcutta discussion, Hastings forbade Nandakumar his house (which
exercised a hospitality open to all European, and much of Indian,
Calcutta), and showed special favour to one Mohanprasad, Nandakumar's bitter foe. Nandakumar found an ally in Fowke, an Englishman
not in Company employment. Hastings's refusal to produce his corre-

---

[1] *Correspondence of Charles, first Marquis Cornwallis*, i. 249.   [2] *Op. cit.* i. 322.

spondence with Middleton was understood, or misunderstood, to be because that correspondence would show that he had been guilty of accepting bribes in connection with the Rohilla campaign. In his miseries he was regarded as a spent influence, and the Rani of Burdwan began the business of sending the Council accusations of corruption against him. Nandakumar then charged him with taking presents amounting to many lakhs, among them three and a half lakhs from the Mani Begum, whom by a much-criticised action he had placed in control of the Nawab's household. Hastings had to admit that she gave him a lakh and a half when he visited her at Murshidabad, which he (and Sir James Stephen after him) considered 'entertainment money'; it was certainly excessive, considering that Hastings himself had been compelled, under affecting circumstances, to cut down the Nawab's total allowance to sixteen lakhs a year. Whether the other charges were true we shall never know. The new Councillors, crammed with suspicion and dislike, and resenting their inability to see his correspondence, jumped to the conclusion that they were. Hastings left his chair, declaring all meetings without him illegal; he refused to be treated as on trial before his own Council, with as prosecutor 'the basest of mankind', the man whom of all men he most hated. He was perfectly justified in this, but he was unwise not to court enquiry, if he was innocent: he never denied (or never bothered to deny) Nandakumar's charges. We may have some sympathy with Francis when he wrote: 'Nuncomar may have been a most nefarious scoundrel: but, by God! he spoke truth, else why were they in such a hurry to hang him?'

Nandakumar and the triumvirate proceeded to behave with a triumphant cruelty which Hastings scornfully described (March 25, 1775):

' The trumpet has been sounded, and the whole host of informers will soon crowd to Calcutta with their complaints and ready depositions. Nund Comar holds his durbar in complete state, sends for zemindars and their vackeels, coaxing and threatening them for complaints, which no doubt he will get in abundance, besides what he forges himself. The system which they have laid down for conducting their affairs is, as I am told, after this manner. The General rummages the Consultations for disputable matter with the aid of old Fowke. Colonel Monson receives, and I have been assured descends even to solicit, accusations. Francis writes . . . Was it for this that the Legislature of Great Britain formed the new system of Government for Bengal, and armed it with powers extending to every part of the British empire in India?'

Sir James Stephen says justly: 'It is impossible to exaggerate the haste, recklessness and violence of Clavering, Monson, and Francis'. [1]

[1] i. 60.

Hastings and Barwell next prosecuted Nandakumar for conspiracy. Before this had gone far, Mohanprasad charged him with forgery in a will executed five years previously. Nandakumar was tried by twelve British [1] jurymen (after challenging eighteen others), and would almost certainly have been acquitted, the case being hardly even a *prima-facie* one, but for the bad impression made on the judges (who took the unusual course of themselves cross-examining the accused's witnesses, 'and that somewhat severely' [2]) by the excessive zeal of his friends, who provided a mass of perjury. The trial was not so bad as Macaulay states, nor so impartial as Stephen and the *Oxford History* (merely copying Stephen) assert. Nor is Stephen reasonable in dismissing the suggestion that perhaps British jurymen were not the best to consider such a case as this, a perplexing innovation. Hastings does not in any way appear in the records of the trial, and was either a man almost miraculously helped by a *deus ex machina* (in the shape of the Supreme Court) or else so diabolically cunning that Francis spoke without any exaggeration of malice when he called him 'an Asiatic', i.e. a man so steeped in the intrigues of the time that he could hide his hand even when murderously employed. Nandakumar was sentenced to be hanged, a result indecently anticipated by Hastings when it can hardly have seemed distantly possible; 'the old gentleman', he noted (May 18), was 'in jail and in a fair way to be hanged' (the committal had been late at night, May 6).

The *Oxford History of India*,[3] whose disingenuousness in handling this episode cannot be too strongly condemned, says

' it is certain that natives of the country had been sentenced to death for forgery in accordance with the stern law of England long before Nandkumar's case occurred. The dacoits or brigand gangs committed terrible depredations, and when convicted were punished with ruthless severity'.

The dacoits have nothing to do with the argument. Only one case of an Indian being sentenced to death (1765) for forgery, before Nandakumar, is on record; he was not executed, and his condemnation elicited a horrified protest:

' Your petitioners beg leave to set forth the general consternation, astonishment, and even panic with which the natives of all parts, under the domina-

[1] Some of whom may have been Eurasians.

[2] P. E. Roberts, *History of British India*, 188.

[3] 515. Ordinary honesty should have evaded the question-darkening of that phrase 'sentenced to death', leaving the reader to suppose the sentence was carried out.

tion of the English, are seized at the example of Radha Charan Mitra: they find themselves subject to the pains and penalties of laws to which they are utter strangers . . . many things being, it seems, capital by the English laws which are only fineable by the laws of your petitioners' forefathers, to which they have hitherto been bred, lived, and been governed, and that till very lately, under the English flag.'

A case has also been unearthed of an Englishman condemned (1764) for forgery—to a whipping. As to whether the English law could apply to Calcutta, Impey argued that it did, because Calcutta was a place of great commercial activity, and it was to protect business in such places that forgery had been made capital. Yet the severe law did not apply to either Scotland or British North America, neither of them regions sunk in uncommercial barterdom. Moreover, Nandakumar's guilt (if he was guilty) went back to a period four years before the Supreme Court's establishment.

One juryman signed an appeal for mercy, on grounds that everyone to-day would consider overwhelmingly strong, stressing 'the very advanced age of the unfortunate criminal, his former rank and station, both in public and private life'. The Nawab of Bengal, the province's nominal ruler, put in a petition for which Impey snubbed him heavily. It pointed out that 'the custom of this country' did not make forgery capital, 'nor, as I am informed, was life formerly forfeited for it in your own country; this has only been common for a few years past'. It urged Nandakumar's services to the English, particularly when they had needed grain and money for the campaign against Mir Qasim;[1] and begged that his execution might be postponed till the King of England's pleasure might be known. Hanging was certainly a pitiful end for the man who, when the English were suppliants and merchants deserving precious little respect for either character or courage, was a great officer in the land, and who had been in so many prime affairs of State during twenty years.

Clavering, who seems to have been as pure fool as it is possible for anyone to be, having encouraged Nandakumar in the course which concluded in the hangman's noose, simply said he would not look at a petition (presented to him during a garden-party) from a man who had been convicted of such an offence as forgery. Monson and Francis also did nothing, a baseness deeper than that which Hastings showed when

[1] Nandakumar had been a friend and partisan of Mir J'afar, which was one cause of his deep quarrel with Hastings.

his private secretary interfered against a reprieve.[1] Nandakumar was executed, dying with dignity and courage.

According to Macaulay, only idiots and biographers have doubted that Hastings and Impey in collusion got rid of Nandakumar by legal process. This judgment, which has been hooted out of court by writers who have not troubled to study the evidence, is more than the known facts will sustain. But no one can successfully challenge that it was universally assumed that Hastings was the real prosecutor and that Nandakumar was put to death for venturing to attack him. No writer cites any second instance of forgery being punished with death. In Calcutta in 1802, the Chief Justice expressly lamented that the crime was not yet capital.   Meanwhile,

'the offence which had not barred an Englishman's path to a peerage was now to doom a Hindoo to the gallows'.[2]

Nandakumar's fate settled in native minds the question of who was master in Bengal; Hastings had no more trouble from Indian accusation or 'opposition. The triumvirate looked to be baffled men, and beyond doubt *were* cowardly and inconsistent ones, effective only in incitement to faction, shrinking and timorous when incitement had stirred a lion. A further reinforcement of authority came to the Governor-General when Monson died, September 25, 1776. Hastings, a man dry, detached and to himself honest, never pretended regret where he felt none. He wrote immediately to Lord North, noting that this event

'has restored to me the constitutional authority of my station; but without absolute necessity I shall not think it proper to use it with that effect which I should give it were I sure of support from home'.

But the party against him in the Court of Directors, a party steadily increasing with reports from his enemies in India, were given a weapon by his agent in England, Colonel Macleane, whom Hastings had authorised to submit his resignation if events came to extremes. Since Monson's death Hastings was feeling happy and powerful. But Macleane, unaware of this change, produced his authorisation; and despatches reached Calcutta, June, 1777, appointing Clavering in place of Hastings, supposed to have resigned. Clavering tried to take the Governor-General's posi-

---

[1] See Beveridge, 288 ff. The secretary was a young Italian, 'his *protégé*, and he rarely loses sight of him and his interests. "Remember me to my little Belli if he is alive", he writes. "If he is dead, Peace to his little Shade!"' (Sydney C. Grier, *The Letters of Warren Hastings to His Wife*, 119).

[2] Martin, *The Indian Empire*, iii. 334. The reference is to Clive and Aminchand.

tion, and a strife ensued, in which Hastings emerged conqueror by the support of the Supreme Court, which held that he had not resigned. The discomfited Clavering died in August; Hastings remarked with quiet satisfaction:

' The death of Sir John Clavering has produced a state of quiet in our councils which I shall endeavour to preserve during the remainder of the time which may be allotted me. The interests of the Company will benefit by it; that is to say, they will not suffer, as they have done, by the effects of a divided administration. The unsettled state of the government is a great impediment to its operations, and weakens its influence, especially in the management of the revenue.' [1]

When it was known in England that he refused to accept the Directors' supersession of him, there was a great outcry, and George III wrote to North that the dignity of Parliament demanded the recall of Hastings, Barwell, and the Supreme Court judges. But Clavering died; the American War was going badly; the Court of Proprietors, which controlled the Court of Directors, had a pro-Hastings majority, as well as a diffused realisation that in him India, if no other part of the Empire, possessed a man of courage and decision and might as well keep him. So his retention of office was accepted as a fact accomplished. A new Councillor, Wheler, arrived in December, bringing out the prejudice against Hastings which was now so common and joining Francis as an ally. He had, however, less rancour and less vigour than either Monson or Clavering; and in any case, Hastings possessed a majority, with Barwell and his own casting-vote.[2] He had a strong friend even in Caesar's household, in Laurence Sulivan, Chairman of the Court of Directors, with whom he maintained a full and confidential correspondence. Now, though he wrote in moods of despondency that he was 'a pageant':

' I am not Governor. All the means I possess are those of preventing the rule from falling into worse hands than my own, and for these I am an absolute dependant. I came to this government when it subsisted on borrowed resources, and when its powers were unknown beyond the borders of the country, which it held in concealed and unprofitable subjection. I saw it grow into wealth and national consequence, and again sink into a decline that must infallibly end it, if a very speedy remedy be not applied. Its very constitution is made up of discordant parts, and contains the seeds of death in it',

as a matter of fact he acted with a straightforward certainty and effectiveness, which could hardly have been greater if Francis had not continued

[1] Letter to Laurence Sulivan, April 18, 1779. [2] Barwell went home, 1780.

to give a display of impotent opposition. It was well that he did, for the Company's existence in India was to be shaken to its foundations.

Sir John Malcolm observes:

' The history of the Mahrattas, from the time of their great leader Sevajee, to the battle of Paniput, furnished ample ground for the gratification of pride, supposing what occurred to be written in the most plain and unadorned language.'[1]

They began as patriots, making the cause of persecuted Hinduism everywhere in some part their own, 'acting with the concurrence and aid of the Hindu chiefs of the empire, whose just reasons for discontent with the reigning monarch, Aurungzebe, have been noticed'.[2] They exacted *chauth* and *deshmukh*; but did not, 'like more barbarous invaders', ruin prosperity, 'the source from which' revenue 'was drawn, for if they had, it could not have recovered so rapidly, as we find from revenue records that it did'.

' Nor can we deny to the Mahrattas, in the early part of their history, and before their extensive conquests had made their vast and mixed armies cease to be national, the merit of conducting their Cossack inroads into other countries with a consideration to the inhabitants, which had been deemed incompatible with that terrible and destructive species of war.' [3]

By Hastings's time, however, they had become a pest, like every other Power in India. Hastings, the one man who seemed aware of all that was happening and to perceive events yet unborn, with prescience almost superhuman, kept watchful eyes on their progress; and his sanction of the Rohilla War was in part due to his determination to surrender no vantage-ground for the struggle he knew was coming.

The inevitable war came in anything but an inevitable manner. The Bombay Government, isolated and exposed to attack from so many quarters, had long wanted to possess certain neighbouring points, among them the island of Salsette and the port of Bassein. Its chance came, 1775. The Peshwa had been assassinated; his uncle, Raghoba (Raghunath Rao),

' enjoyed the reputation of having contrived his nephew's death; a more indulgent opinion, supported by respectable authority, regards him as intending only to seize the power of his relative, and acquits him of conspiring against his life'. [4]

---

[1] *A Memoir of Central India*, i. 59.   [2] *Op. cit.* i. 61.   [3] *Op. cit.* i. 69-70.
[4] Thornton, *History of British India*, ii. 158.

He became Peshwa for a short time. But a son was posthumously born to the late Peshwa, and when six weeks old was formally invested with the office (1774). Raghoba approached (among other Powers) the Company's Bombay administration for support, and (more fortunate than with his own people) convinced them that he was the rightful Peshwa. He was obstinate at one point of the argument, however; he dared not, and would not, promise them Salsette and Bassein. Bombay got over part of this hitch in the discussion by taking Salsette forcibly, in an unofficial little war. Raghoba, now persuaded, by the Treaty of Surat conveyed to the Company whatever 'right' he may have been considered to possess in the places they coveted.

Unfortunately, his people showed themselves attached to their seaboard. They declined to lose it quietly and without fuss, and Bombay found itself at war with the Maratha confederacy. Their commander, Colonel Keating, won the battle of Aras, which was nearly a defeat. Hastings and his Council then reminded Bombay that Calcutta had come into a vaguely defined suzerainty over the other two Presidencies: they condemned the proceedings as 'impolitic, dangerous, unauthorised, and unjust', adjectives which Hastings elaborated in a long and able minute. One Presidency, he asserted, had involved the whole Company in an unprovoked war against a Power with whom they were even then in friendly negotiation, and on behalf of a man for whom his own people had no use; and they had done this while without even tolerable financial or military resources. His Council went still further. He himself thought that, having begun a war, Bombay must be helped to finish it successfully, but 'the majority' made him conclude peace over Bombay's head, which he did by the Treaty of Purandhar, 1776, Bombay protesting against this assertion of authority by Calcutta.

The Directors with great impudence rejected the treaty. Righteously observing that

' We utterly disapprove and condemn offensive wars, distinguishing however between offensive measures unnecessarily undertaken with a view to pecuniary advantages, and those which the preservation of our honour, or the protection or safety of our possessions, may render absolutely necessary',

they coolly said also (Hastings complained):

' "We approve, under every circumstance, of the keeping of all territories and possessions ceded to the Company by the treaty concluded with Ragobah", and direct us "forthwith to adopt such measures as may be necessary for their preservation and defence". Yet they knew that Salsette, the capital of these territories and possessions, had been taken by force, before any treaty existed that could give them a right to it. . . . And what is the treaty of Surat, with all its antecedent and consequent circumstances, but a series of offensive measures undertaken with a view to pecuniary advantages, and in direct contradiction to their orders?'

Hastings continued that, unless he was 'greatly deceived in my opinion of the temper and dispositions of the gentlemen' of Bombay Presidency, they would break the treaty and renew the war; 'and a wonderful scene of intricacies we shall have opened between us'. They did as he predicted in 1778, and Hastings, with the Directors' full consent,

' renewed the alliance with Raghoba. On this occasion Francis seems decidedly to have been for once on the right, and Hastings and the Court on the wrong, side. The able minutes and protests of the former repay the most careful study'.[1]

Hastings's motives lay in the domain of general politics. He sat loose to principles, as we use the word to-day. His place is not with the proconsuls of our orderly period, but with such men as Akbar; he was himself the government, and like most lonely men who pursue great ends out of sight of their fellows, he grew more and more detached from care for individual welfare, while anxious for the welfare of the whole. He was never much affected by thought of the miseries attendant on a war which, taken by itself, was unjust, if the upshot seemed desirable. Moreover, new complications were entering into his political problems. A French envoy was already at Poona; and news reached him, July 17, 1778, that war had broken out between England and France. The British cause was labouring in low water in America; when they heard of Burgoyne's surrender at Saratoga, Francis (according to Hastings) urged that they should concentrate for the attack he was sure was coming in Bengal. Hastings scouted the possibility of any attack by the French, except by land, and by means of the Marathas, the only Power in concert with whom invasion 'is at present capable of being effected'. He seems to have thought it worth while taking a chance, even one furnished by injustice, of crippling Maratha potentialities for harm to the Company.

His courage and resource were speedily tried. A Bombay army surrendered, and concluded the Convention of Wargaon, January 1779, whose terms—which included a detailed confession of 'war guilt' and prolonged treaty-breaking by the beaten party—'almost made me sink with shame when I read it': 'The wild and precipitate expedition to Poona and the infamous surrender' were 'events lying beyond the reach of human foresight'. Even before he received the text of the

[1] P. E. Roberts, *History of British India*, 192.

treaty, Bombay had the insolence to send him 'a very short letter, which said scarce more than that the army had been defeated and was returned, and that a treaty had been made which they would disavow'. The convention was repudiated.

Meanwhile Hastings decided on his own candidate for the headship [1] of the Maratha confederacy. This was generally conceded to the Raja of Satara, Sivaji's descendant. But the Bhonsla Raja of Nagpur claimed a superior right, and with him Hastings negotiated, while he thrust out into Central India two soldiers of high quality, Goddard and Popham. Goddard was to march right across from Bengal, Hastings knowing well that if the hazardous adventure failed he was ruined. He was able to boast with justifiable pride that it had not failed:

' Its way was long, through regions unknown in England, and untraced in our maps; and I alone knew the grounds on which the facility of its success depended.'

Goddard proved magnificently adequate; he reached Western India, stormed Ahmadabad (February 15, 1780) and overran Gujarat. He established friendly relations with the Gaekwar of Baroda, who was henceforth detached from all the Maratha wars against the Company.

Goddard made a mistake, however, when he tried a dash at Poona. The Maratha Central Government was under the virtual control of Balaji Pandit, the Nana Farnavis (by which name he is better known), the ablest statesman India produced during this century. Aware that the English were in desperate straits in South India, and financially pressed everywhere, so that peace was their necessity, the Nana rejected Goddard's terms, knowing their peremptoriness to be bluff. The Peshwa, a boy of six, he sent to a place of safety, and collected armies which he flung around Goddard, aiming at a second Wargaon. Though Goddard escaped, he lost heavily in men and baggage.

This partial disaster was brilliantly covered by Captain Popham's success, acting in alliance with a small chieftain, the Rana of Gohud, from whose country he drove the Marathas 'with great slaughter, and fairly cleared it'.[2] He stormed Lahar; then by night escalade took Sindhia's famous fortress, Gwalior,[3] 'the key of Indostan', to Hastings's intense delight:

' This is a success which I hope will prove decisive; I look upon it as one of the best concerted and most gallant enterprises that has ever been performed

[1] Titular, that is. The Peshwa, the actual head, was ostensibly only a hereditary chief minister.

[2] Hastings, letter to Sulivan, August 27, 1780.   [3] See map, p. 220.

in India; nearly, if not equal in its advantages to the battle of Plassey. In Europe it cannot miss of its effect. The name of Guallior has been long famous in history. In this country its effect is not to be described. Other congratulations which I have received on the many important successes of our arms were but coldly offered, but scarcely a man mentions this without enthusiasm.'[1]

It will be noted how widely beyond the immediate scope of the Maratha War his mind is straying. He had to think of Europe, where his country was confronted by Spain and France (and presently Holland) in arms together to support a triumphant revolution in the American colonies. And in India he was all but faced by a confederacy whose force must have been overwhelming. We have seen how Bombay treated the Governor-General; the conduct of Madras was yet more discourteous, even more imbecile.

The moral atmosphere of Madras at this time has been stigmatised by Thornton as 'pestilential', an adjective hall-marked by Vincent Smith [2] as felicitously exact. The Governor, Sir Thomas Rumbold, had

MAP OF MARATHA WARS

in time of Warren Hastings, Lord Wellesley and Lord Hastings.

' reached Madras in 1778, and applied himself, with much energy, to the improvement of his private fortune. The Council cheerfully followed so pleasant an example; and unwonted tranquillity prevailed within the presidency, the predominant feature being wilful blindness to the storm gathering without'.[3]

Thus happily united, the Council resolved to stand no nonsense from Calcutta, and sent the Nizam a Resident whom they made to propose

---

[1] Hastings, letter to Sulivan, August 27, 1780.

[2] *Oxford History of India*, 541.   [3] M. Martin, *The Indian Empire*, iii. 348.

arrangements which the Nizam 'declared to be equal to a declaration of war'. As Madras was already involved in a terrible war with Haidar Ali, Hastings, who had ordered the Resident to keep him informed, interfered to prevent this result; thereupon Madras suspended their representative from the service, for 'having betrayed the secrets of his trust to the Governor-General and Council of Bengal'.

Hastings, amazingly keeping his temper, replied by giving him fresh credentials as his own representative. The upshot of this variegated incompetence [1] on an All-India field was a confederacy whereby the two ablest Maratha chieftains, Mahadaji Sindhia and Tukoji Holkar, were to compose their mutual quarrel and to move against Goddard: the Raja of Nagpur was to invade Bengal and Bihar, the Nizam to invade the Sarkars, Haidar the Carnatic. 'I have no doubt', wrote Hastings, that the Nizam was 'the projector of this alliance, and he had sufficient provocation for it'. Nevertheless, he remained passive, partly from inclination to trust the one man in India who obviously had character and the valour to pursue his conclusions to their ends in action. It is hard to resist the conviction, returning upon the mind repeatedly, that no eighteenth-century statesman was greater than Hastings or set amid such a coil and swirl of impossibilities. The threads of a hundred problems, whose hidden beginnings lay out of his control, ran back into his sole hands. The eyes of all India were being increasingly fixed on one man; and that man not only held the Nizam to practical neutrality, he largely disarmed the Bhonsla Raja's hostility also. The war, therefore, though a tempest, was not a cyclone that destroyed.

Popham's seizure of Gwalior had laid open Sindhia's country. Sindhia, however, forced Colonal Camac into a retreat ending in an investment which brought his army close to starvation. In their desperation the British 'beat up' Sindhia's camp, and won an astounding victory. Sindhia, doubly disheartened by losing Gwalior and by this sudden vigour in an enemy whose surrender he was preparing to accept, began negotiations. He did more; he acted as honest broker in a wide plan of pacification, which by the Treaty of Salbai (1781) brought in all the Northern and Central Indian Powers. Raghoba received a pension; the English kept Salsette and Broach but gave up other captures. Nana Farnavis and Sindhia were thoroughly roused to the inevitability of the coming struggle with the Company for the control of India, but had

[1] In which Hastings must be admitted to have shared, by deliberately choosing to allow Bombay's misbehaviour to pass into war with the Marathas.

learnt that they were not as yet equal to it. Also, Sindhia liked and respected the Governor-General. Hastings, with his genuine affection for Indians, untouched with patronage or racial feeling, formed a friendship with the former's vakil,[1] which had incalculably valuable political results. He secured what was to prove a twenty years' invaluable breathing-space; and at the same time procured it that in prestige the British had 'made an advance not to be calculated by words'.[2] Clive was 'the engineer who levelled the ground'; but Hastings first clearly saw how far British sovereignty was to proceed:

'There was no question in his mind as to the power upon which the mantle of Akbar must descend.'

Haidar Ali had sought an understanding with the Company. But their Nawab, whom he knew too well, as did everyone else,

' to believe that any alliance in which he was concerned could possibly be sincere . . . notwithstanding his many perfidies, had possession of the minds of the gentlemen who represented the Company in Madras'.[3]

When war came between England and France, 1778, Haidar was committed at least to benevolent neutrality with the latter, which if opportunity invited would pass into open league. Madras paid no sort of attention to his warning that he meant to protect the French port of Mahé, which was in his territory and necessary to him as his channel of communication with the outside world. Mahé was taken by the English. Then, without troubling him for the formality of permission, the Madras Government marched a force through his country to seize Guntoor (which belonged to the Nizam); at the same time they forcibly stopped a payment pledged to the Nizam, doing all this 'in violation of the treaty of 1768'[4] and kindling to a flame a resentment long smouldering with many grievances. Hastings promised redress, but the offending Government disobeyed him, bringing down on him, 'in terms of great severity and almost of contempt', the Nizam's complaint, so common in these years, of faithlessness and, alternatively, of a good will which was ineffective and worthless. Haidar also sent Sir Thomas Rumbold a scathing characterisation of Muhammad Ali and analysis of the Company's political record since they had first protected him. He concluded: 'I leave you to judge on whose part engagements and promises have been broken'.

---

[1] Lawyer: here envoy. [2] J. B. Malleson, *Life of Warren Hastings*, 309.
[3] *Op. cit.* 312-13. [4] Hastings.

'Incidents' followed rapidly, some grotesque, others painful. In July, 1780, Haidar launched his war, flooding the Carnatic with immense armies which were soon a tide washing the very walls of Madras. In Burke's famous description:

' He drew from every quarter whatsoever a savage ferocity could add to his new rudiments in the art of destruction; and compounding all the materials of fury, havoc, and desolation into one black cloud, he hung for a while on the declivities of the mountains. Whilst the authors of all these evils were idly and stupidly gazing on this menacing meteor, which blackened all their horizon, it suddenly burst, and poured down the whole of its contents upon the plains of the Carnatic. Then ensued a scene of woe, the like of which no eye had seen, no heart conceived, and which no tongue can adequately tell. All the horrors of war before known or heard of were mercy to that new havoc. A storm of universal fire blasted every field, consumed every house, destroyed every temple. The miserable inhabitants fleeing from their flaming villages, in part were slaughtered; others, without regard to sex, to age, to the respect of rank, or sacredness of function—fathers torn from children, husbands from wives—enveloped in a whirlwind of cavalry, and amidst the goading spears of drivers, and the trampling of pursuing horses, were swept into captivity in an unknown and hostile land. Those who were able to escape this tempest, fled to the walled cities; but escaping from fire, sword and exile they fell into the jaws of famine.'

These miseries notwithstanding, the people of the Carnatic, the *Oxford History* admits (and it gives us the measure of the iniquity of the administration of the Madras Government and their Nawab together),

' seem to have preferred Haidar Ali to their own Nawab, and furnished the invader with information which was refused to the British defenders of Muhammad Ali'.

What followed is almost incredible. Sir Hector Munro, victor of Buxar, when within two miles of a force under Colonel Bailie, which he was to relieve, was seized with panic, flung his guns and stores into a tank, and fled to Madras. Bailie was overwhelmed, the few survivors of a grim massacre entering into an imprisonment whose horrors were to become notorious. Sir Eyre Coote, whom Hastings sent hurriedly south with all the soldiers he could spare and fifteen lakhs of treasure, presently reported that Haidar Ali was 'the complete and acknowledged master of the Carnatic, having taken Arcot in October'. With him were 400 Frenchmen under Lally's son; and a French squadron was off the coast. The Madras Government was without revenue, and its sepoys panic-stricken.

Hastings was in such straits that he could not show even elementary regard for political decencies. He asked the Dutch to lend him troops, including a thousand European infantry and two hundred European gunners. He offered them, in addition to expenses, what was not his to give: the province of Tinneveli, in the peninsula's extreme south, exclusive rights in the South Indian pearl fishery, and leave to conquer Cochin. The Dutch and he were both aware that war between their countries was daily expected; but Hastings, who by now had the absolute measure of almost every factor of the Indian situation, was prepared for every risk but those of inaction. If a rupture came,

' so much the better. I am no casuist; but I believe that, in such an event, their soldiers would rather continue to serve us than return to their own colours, and I certainly would not force them to leave us. We, therefore, in that case should have been doubly gainers by what we had, and what our adversaries had thus lost'.

The Dutch, however, hung back, and war between England and Holland closed the negotiations.

The French squadron, despite Haidar's frantic representations that between them they had an unexampled chance to extirpate the Company, withdrew to Mauritius. Coote [1] defeated immense Mysore armies at the battles of Porto Novo, Polilor and Sholinghur, victories partly offset by Tipu destroying a force of 2000, killing 500 and taking the rest prisoners. A vanished age and ended menace seemed to return when Bussy himself landed with 3000 Frenchmen; and a second French navy appeared off the coast, under de Suffren, perhaps the greatest seaman in French annals. But the British survived several indecisive naval fights, and Bussy proved old, ill, and half-hearted. And Hastings not only coaxed the Raja of Nagpur into neutrality, but sent a second force southward to help Coote. Haidar Ali died, 1782 (December); in May, 1784, Tipu and the English made peace on the basis of restoration of captures and prisoners. As Malleson observes, it was obviously a truce, reluctantly accepted by two Powers each unable to destroy the other, but both profoundly convinced that without the destruction of one there was no safety for the other.

[1] A much underrated soldier, largely because Clive's spectacular career so completely outshone his.

CHAPTER VI

INTERNAL POLITICS OF BENGAL DURING HASTINGS'S GOVERNOR-GENERALSHIP

Hastings's pessimism: duel with Francis: Francis's departure: Hastings and the Supreme Court: the Benares incident: the Begums of Oudh: gathering enmity in England: Hastings's impeachment: his services to England and India.

NANDAKUMAR'S death, and still more, the deaths of Monson and Clavering, had flung authority into Hastings's hands, which he used with ruthless ability. 'What I have done', he writes (August, 1780),

' has been by fits and intervals of power, if I may so express it, and from the effects let a judgment be formed of what this state and its resources are capable of producing in hands more able and better supported'.

But this exercise of power was precarious, amid the unremitting threats of the faction in his Council and attacks in England, where Lord North longed to seize the Company's enormous patronage. Through a period of years North was foiled by Hastings's strong party in the Court of Proprietors (who repeatedly passed resolutions forbidding the Court of Directors to pay any attention to parliamentary interference) and by the knowledge that after losing America he had better be cautious about meddling with the one man who looked like saving British interests in India.

Some of the bonds upon Hastings's freedom were to be loosed. Early in 1780 he patched up an agreement with Francis, the most important item of which was thrust in by Hastings's own wisdom and generosity; we need not take Francis's disclaimer as anything more than the pious official clearance at which the Governor-General obviously rated it:

' It was proposed by me as an additional article, for I know by dear experience how much the temper of public business is influenced by the gratification or disappointment of personal attachments on such occasions, that in the distribution of all offices and other emoluments of the service, each party shall be allowed that participation which shall be judged adequate to their respective ranks, and the degrees of weight and responsibility annexed to their respective stations, but Mr. Francis refused to listen to such a condition, lest it should subject him to the imputation of an interested or personal bias in the part which he took in this engagement. . . . I consider it, however, as an engagement on my part, and have declared as much to him.'

This released Barwell, 'who was privy to the treaty in all the stages of it', and he was at liberty to return home,[1]

' with my free consent, and release from any engagement as binding on him from his connexion with me to remain in the service'.

Hastings sanguinely added that Francis's new behaviour was so candid and open that he was sure the old troubles were done with. They were not, however; in July the two fought a duel, in which Hastings, grimly self-controlled, wounded Francis. Hastings's account shows him somewhat ashamed of 'this silly affair', which certainly was an irregular way of conducting affairs of State. Francis recovered, and took his immense accumulation of hatred home, to be busily employed there. The once 'timid, desperate, distracted being' who remained wrote exultantly:

' I have power, and I will employ it, during the interval in which the credit of it shall last, to retrieve past misfortunes, to remove present dangers, and to re-establish the power of the Company, and the safety of its possessions.' [2]

Looking back, four years later (September 13, 1786), in England, he wrote with excusable triumph, in words often quoted:

' When intervals of accidental authority enabled me to act, and I never had more than intervals, I employed them in forming and setting in motion the greatest and most successful measures of my Government. When these were impeded by frequent changes of influence, I still contrived to keep them in existence, and again gave them energy when my power returned. My antagonists sickened, died, and fled. I maintained my ground unchanged, neither the health of my body nor the vigour of my mind for a moment deserted me.'

Unfortunately, his sense of towering abilities exercised in isolation against a world of opposers led him into arrogance and unscrupulousness; and his unparalleled difficulties in waging war on so many fronts and with every source of revenue exhausted fixed him in one aim— remorselessly pursued—as to where and how he could get money. He had to send it to every corner of India—to provide the Madras Government, that sink of iniquity and incompetence, with funds; to finance Bombay; to bribe the Nagpur Raja. Then there were the Court of Directors, whom he savagely but not extravagantly characterised as 'a mine of oppressive rapacity'.

[1] It is natural to think of Barwell as an 'elder statesman'; but, as Busteed points out in his *Echoes of Old Calcutta*, he was only thirty-nine when he took his celebrated fortune home.

[2] Letter to Sulivan, February 21, 1782.

Meanwhile he had won a contest with the Supreme Court. When Hastings observed that he said the seeds of death were in the Bengal Constitution (it is doubtful whether we warp his meaning by using the capital letter), he referred to a state of things which he had foreseen from the beginning, as he foresaw most things. The Company

' as a corporation, and its leading servants in India, both civil and military, were greatly disposed to regard the sovereignty of India as their own private property, and to resent all interference with it by Parliament as a wholly un- warrantable and tyrannical invasion of their rights. They spoke of the sacred rights of the Emperor and the Nabob of Bengal just as the mayors of the palace may have stood up for the rights of the Rois fainéants'.[1]

Hastings by deep-ingrained habit was a whole-hearted Company's man. Parliament in his mind secured an extremely tenuous allegiance, and rightly; and the Supreme Court represented an obvious incursion of the British Government into the Company's domain. Part of the multiple reason put forward by the unfortunate Nandakumar, as to why he should not be hanged under the English (not even British) law against forgery was that he was not a native of Calcutta, or even normally resident there, a plea which would have sufficed him, but for his political offensiveness (as would almost any other part of his demurrer).

The struggle for power between the Council and the Supreme Court, which we must now briefly describe, was of a dramatic nature which has tempted the earlier historians, led by Mill and Macaulay, to ascribe to the chief participants the conventional characters of the theatre. There is no longer any need to search for heroes and villains amongst the nine Englishmen who played the leading parts. Amongst the five members of Council and four judges of the Supreme Court, only two were men of an uncommon type; and in both Hastings and Francis the elements were strangely mixed. The remainder were ordinary men of their race and period, who had been placed in an absurd position by an ill-timed piece of legislation, conceived and drafted in complete ignorance of condi- tions in Bengal. The drafting of the Regulating Act was also bad in itself, containing vague phrases which were bound to cause disputes as

[1] Stephen, *Nuncomar and Impey*, ii. 125. Stephen, though rigidly severe on technical inaccuracies in Beveridge, especially where they turned on legal points, is himself a sufficiently loose writer, and, moreover, was never able to put his mind into the period of which he wrote. When he says 'sovereignty of India', he means 'sovereignty of Bengal'.

to jurisdiction. Seven of the nine Englishmen had only recently come to India, with a distinct bias against the Governor and a strong belief that the whole administration was corrupt. All four judges 'carried with them to India the most inflated ideas of the beauties and benignities of English law'.[1] Possibly the Directors, hoping that the Supreme Court would be a useful instrument for disciplining their servants in Bengal, did not object to the vague drafting of an Act which did not even make it clear whether the 'ordering, management and government of territorial acquisitions and revenues of the kingdom of Bengal, Bihar, and Orissa' came within the jurisdiction of the Court. Two of the judges, Hyde and Lemaistre, began to take cognisance of cases brought against *Zemindars* from all parts of the province. A few educated Indians saw their opportunity and traded upon the judges' ignorance of the country. Macaulay has left a description of the resulting confusion:

' No man knew what was next to be expected from this strange tribunal. It came from beyond the black water. . . . It consisted of judges not one of whom was familiar with the usages of the millions over whom they claimed boundless authority. Its records were kept in unknown characters; its sentences pronounced in unknown sounds. It had already collected round itself an army of the worst part of the native population, informers, and false witnesses, and common barrators, and agents of chicane, and above all, a banditti of bailiffs' followers. . . . Many natives, highly considered among their countrymen, were seized, hurried up to Calcutta, flung into the common gaol, not for any crime imputed, not for any debt that had been proved, but merely as a precaution till their cause should come to trial.' [2]

Hyde and Lemaistre, two of the Supreme Court judges, asserted that the Regulating Act 'had transferred all judicial power from the revenue authorities to the Supreme Court'.[3] The Dewan of the Burdwan *zemindari* put the case for the landlords:

' The inhabitants of the interior country of Bengal are totally unacquainted with the forms and customs of the English law, with the language and phrases of the English lawyers, and with the offices of sheriff and other officers, who are all English. When compulsion is offered to any person in the Mofussil, they threaten with *habeas corpus* and damages, but what an *habeas corpus* is, what are damages, what warrants, what summonses, no one of them can tell. . . . It is a custom in Bengal, whenever the farmers,[4] yet-maundars, and currumcherries have failed in discharging their revenue, to exercise severities upon and enforce payment from them.'

[1] J. W. Kaye, *Administration of the East India Company*, 319.
[2] Essay on Hastings.   [3] *Nuncomar and Impey*, ii. 148.
[4] Farmers of revenue, *publicani*.

Hastings, who himself was 'an Asiatic', in the good as well as harmful sense, a man who profoundly understood the country system and habitually worked by it, agreed with this argument.[1] He stated his opinion that the Regulating Act and Charter gave the Supreme Court no jurisdiction 'over any but British subjects, and natives who are or have been British subjects'; that *Zemindars* were neither British subjects nor the servants of British subjects. He pointed out that the judges themselves had taken this view, that *Zemindars* were not liable to their jurisdiction, and had

' formed an early rule that no summons should issue against any native of the provinces, unless the plaintiff would swear that such native was subject to the jurisdiction of the Court, and add in his affidavit circumstances which rendered him so subject'.

Holding strongly that it was monstrous to subject Indians to alien laws, he himself bailed out the Raja of Vishnupur (whose family was on the borderline between the positions of *Zemindars* and genuine princes), who he found had been 'a prisoner in the common jail' for some months for some default, or alleged default, in revenue payment. His Government were not to

' be parties in dragging the descendants of men who once held the rights of sovereignty in this country, like felons, to Calcutta, on the affidavit of a Calcutta banyan, or the complaint of a court serjeant. . . . I shall pay no regard to rules of construction, or to precedents drawn from the practice in England'.

The inevitable break arose on a point connected with revenue administration. Some thirty Englishmen, out of two or three hundred at most serving the Company in Bengal, acted in vague association under the name of Provincial Courts in the Mofussil. They naturally left the determination of legacies and questions of property to native judges who understood the Hindu and Muhammadan law governing their disposition. Litigation between a rich widow and her nephew in the Patna district was claimed by the Supreme Court as in its jurisdiction, on the grounds that the nephew was a 'farmer' of the revenue, and that disputed points in connection with his revenue-collection ultimately came to it. What this had to do with the nephew in his rôle as a private person seeking to dispossess his aunt of a legacy, only a lawyer perhaps could see. The Court nevertheless took the case up, and

---

[1] The arguments here set together were not made with definite reference to one another, but belong to the same general dispute.

awarded the widow three lakhs damages (which the Company ultimately paid). The chief value of the case was that it showed up the incompetence of the Provincial Courts, and made reform some time or other a certainty. Parliament in 1781 definitely deprived the Supreme Court of any jurisdiction in revenue matters, and legalised the Company's courts.

A second case led to an openly scandalous quarrel. A native of Calcutta, failing to obtain repayment of a loan to the Raja of Cossijura, bethought himself of the Supreme Court. Since the Raja, as a *Zemindar*, was liable to the Court in revenue disputes, it seemed worth while trying to see if the Court would pull him in by this rope into their general jurisdiction. The *Zemindar* hid himself, and the Collector of Midnapur reported that the revenue (which he should have been collecting) was suffering. Hastings and his Council consulted their Advocate-General as to whether the Court was entitled to pursue private debts; the Advocate-General was very doubtful whether 'the few remaining rights of a people to whom we have left but little' should be thus invaded. Hastings therefore instructed the Raja to ignore the Court's process; and when a sheriff's officer and a large body of armed men, among them British sailors, marched and took possession of the Raja's house, he sent sepoys and took the Court's servants prisoners.[1] We may admit that the marching of troops against the officers of the Supreme Court was a disquieting spectacle; and it may be that a lawyer is right in asserting that 'the Council acted haughtily, quite illegally, and most violently, without any adequate reason for their conduct'.[2] But the morality of the proceedings seems to us to lie with Hastings. Sir James Stephen says:[3]

' The explanation of the measures taken by the Council is simple. For a variety of reasons, most of which are quite natural and intelligible, they hated the Supreme Court. It represented an authority which the Company's servants practically repudiated. It represented English law, which they hated both for its defects, which no doubt were then great, and for its merits.'

Their main grievance, he asserts, was

' that the Ijaradars and Zemindars should be interfered with, if, in order to pay their revenue punctually, they squeezed their ryots in a way which English lawyers would describe as oppressive or extortionate'.

That comment does not seem to arise out of the facts. If the *Zemindars* raised revenue oppressively, the fault seems to lie with the Government

---

[1] *Nuncomar and Impey*, ii. 210.   [2] *Op. cit.* ii. 220.

[3] *Op. cit.* ii. 211-12.

which for such a long space of time supported the monstrous and un-natural system of draining 'the surplus revenue'[1] of one country out into another. Hastings was expected to provide money for Madras, Bombay, the China trade, the Company Proprietors, as if he were a wishing-tree that could shower down rupees unendingly. He surely acted reasonably, as well as with characteristic courage, in rescuing his *Zemindars* from the new-fangled Court which understood them as little as they understood it.

Various changes relieved the immediate suffering caused by the introduction of English law and the inauguration of a Supreme Court. The judges slowly learned a little caution, and an Act of 1781,[2] passed after urgent petitions from India, defined and limited the powers of the Court, removing from its jurisdiction all revenue matters when collection was made 'according to the practice of the country or the regulations of the Governor-General in Council'. The appointment of Sir Elijah Impey to preside over the chief Calcutta Court for civil appeals minimised the interference of the Supreme Court with the Indian courts which had been instituted by Hastings. Impey's acceptance of a salaried post under the Company was ill-advised, for he had been sent out to exercise an independent controlling influence, but it was neither unprecedented nor indefensible on the score of good government. Two members of the Council, Clavering and Monson, had accepted the Company's pay as commanders in the army, and one of the judges, Sir Robert Chambers, officiated as a Company's judge at Chinsura. Impey may have felt it his duty to help in reforming the administration of civil justice. In a letter to Mr. Dunning he complains that Mr. Booth, 'who gives law to the whole province of Behar', was a man 'of the meanest natural parts, is totally illiterate in his own and ignorant of any eastern languages, and is one of the lowest, most extra-vagant, dissipated young men in the country. I doubt whether he is of age'.[3] His action, though objectionable on other grounds, was probably beneficial to the working of the civil courts.

Looking back over a century and a half, it is possible to judge the effect of introducing into India our English law, and our legal technicalities, procedure, and traditions. As the Company absorbed province after province, High Courts were established manned by English

---

[1] Hastings's own description of his duty. [2] 21 Geo. III, c. 70.

[3] Mr. Dunning was afterwards Lord Ashburton, and Solicitor-General in 1768. The letter is printed in W. K. Firminger's Introduction to the Fifth Report.

judges, or in later days by Indians steeped in the same tradition. It is an unhappy history, recalling Mephistopheles' description of law as a disease spreading over the land.[1] The disease was to affect Indian life in many ways, but never was the comparison more exact than during those early days in Bengal, when the evils of exotic legislation swept through the land with the virulence of some European malady when introduced into an island of the South Seas. The violence of the first outbreak has been described. The disease then became endemic, and spread through the country, tending always to undermine the independence of the countryman, and to place the uneducated poor at the mercy of the wealthy and literate.

The Mogul courts had not encouraged litigation. Their methods were rough and ready, their officials not over-zealous. Muslim law did not lend itself to much subtlety or chicanery, and Hindus probably avoided the courts when possible. The first activities of the English judges were terrifying and incomprehensible to every Indian, but after a year or two the better educated Hindus saw that there were definite rules guiding the apparently capricious proceedings of the Supreme Court. It was a new ceremonial, meaningless and of almost religious obscurity, but it could be learnt, and the English (whose lack of religion was a by-word) would obey the law scrupulously. A new field was open to the higher caste Hindus, whose subtle minds delighted in the tortuosities of eighteenth-century law. The Brahmin had centuries of experience in dominating his fellows by his knowledge of religious rites and by magnifying their importance. Here was a new form of magic, of immense potency because, if properly invoked, it could control even the Governor-General and that demon force, the English soldiery.[2]

Only the first stages of this development were seen during Hastings's term of office. Bengal was in too much disorder for many of its inhabitants to be affected by any system of civil law. On the criminal side every consideration was overshadowed by the prevalence of dacoities and the close connection between the robbers and the *Zemindars*. This interdependence was abundantly proved in later days, when special departments were created to deal with *thagi*, or gang murders, and dacoities. In Hastings's time it was recognised, and partly accounted for

[1] Es erben sich Gesetz und Rechte
Wie eine ew'ge Krankheit fort,
Sie schleppen von Geschlecht sich zum Geschlechte,
Und rücken sacht von Ort zu Ort.

[2] British soldiers were early promoted to a high rank in Hindu demonology.

the gradual abandonment by him and by his successor of the Indian agencies for police and criminal administration outside Calcutta. Muhammad Reza Khan, who had been Naib Dewan since the time of Clive, and responsible for criminal justice in the province, had been corrupt; but his work was moderately efficient and might have sufficed for the ordinary crimes of an Indian population. Some stronger and more independent agency was needed for offences in which most of the *Zemindars* were involved, and about which it was impossible to collect evidence. Hastings summed up the position in 1774:

> ' I am assured that the Zemindars themselves too frequently afford them protection, and that the ryots, who are the principal sufferers by these ravages, dare not complain, it being an established maxim with the Dakoits to punish with death every information given against them.' [1]

There was no tradition encouraging private individuals to come forward as witnesses, and this evil was to survive throughout the whole period of British administration. Several generations passed before any Government could give adequate protection against the hereditary dacoits, and by that time political terrorism had begun to interfere with the course of criminal justice.

Bengal under the Mogul administration had no police system. The more important *Zemindars* kept a few hired men, 'for the most part adventurers from Upper India, Afghans and Rajputs'.[2] The villagers were accustomed to assign part of the crops to watchmen, who were usually members of some hereditary criminal tribe, a form of insurance well known in the East, or in any country where organised crime is stronger than the forces of order. The larger cities had their organised watchmen, and the courts had their 'runners', but Warren Hastings had no reliable force, apart from the military, with which to stamp out dacoity. His efforts were further hampered by 'the regularity and precision which have been introduced into our courts'. Faced by this widespread conspiracy between landlords and robbers, he abandoned the use of purely Indian agencies for keeping the peace. The Faujdars, who were appointed in 1775 to deal with crime in each district, had proved ineffective. The difficulty was to get cases initiated, and to find Indians in the districts who would investigate robberies and apprehend criminals irrespective of their position. Hastings in 1781 dismissed the Faujdars and appointed covenanted civil servants as magistrates, with

[1] Proceedings of Governor and Council, April 19, 1774. Quoted in Colebrooke's *Digest*.

[2] Sir W. Hunter, *Annals of Rural Bengal*, 324.

power to commit to the nearest Indian criminal court. This was an important change of policy. It paved the way for the extended use of Europeans by Cornwallis, and marked the beginning of criminal administration by district officers.

We must return to our general narrative. Pressed for money, Hastings exercised what in India is an overlord's undoubted right, to claim exceptional assistance from dependents who have, or are suspected of having, money stored up. He was 'well assured', says the *Oxford History*,[1] that the Raja of Benares 'had plenty of both men and money'; he was so assured by his own representatives, whom he had thrust out into every key position, so that the administration was becoming one vast extension of his own masterful will. Their opinions were his own, and their conclusions jumped eagerly with his, even if they sometimes slightly anticipated those which suited his policy. Hastings in 1778 had already, against his own Council, and with great harshness when the Raja asked for a period of delay, exacted an extra five lakhs, which extortion he repeated in 1779, with a half-lakh fine for hesitation. 1780 brought the same demand; the Raja could not suppose other than that his tribute had been arbitrarily and by unilateral action raised by nearly twenty per cent. Faced with the third successive demand, he offered Hastings a private gift of two lakhs. Hastings (who was in such distress for his public needs that he was raising loans, in addition to having stopped the Company's investment for the year) refused this, but then conveyed a hint—which of course was in effect an order— that it should be again offered, when he accepted it. This money he used for the Maratha War, safeguarding himself by revealing the facts to both Sulivan and his own Advocate-General, while at first pretending it was a private contribution of his own. He thoroughly earned (whatever the apologist type of historian may say) the rebuke which the Select Committee of 1783 gave him:

' The complication of cruelty and fraud in the transaction admits of few parallels. Mr. Hastings . . . displays himself as a zealous servant of the Company, bountifully giving from his own fortune . . . from the gift of a man whom he treats with the utmost severity, and whom he accuses in this particular of disaffection to the Company's cause and interests. With £23,000 of the raja's money in his pocket, he persecutes him to his destruction.'

The Raja, who had offered the money on the understanding that he would be freed from the larger requisition, was made to pay every rupee

[1] P. 537.

of the five lakhs, and told to raise a force of cavalry as well. He did not —probably could not—raise all he was commanded, and Hastings, beside himself with rage, swept in person up-country,

' resolved to draw from his guilt the means of relief to the Company's distresses. In a word, I had determined to make him pay largely for his pardon or to exact a severe vengeance for his past delinquency'.

The delinquency rankling in Hastings's mind was the Raja's foolish action at the time when Clavering was seeking to occupy the Governor-General's chair; he had then intrigued with the party he thought were about to become masters. Hastings knew everything and forgave little.

He removed from Benares Fowke, son of Nandakumar's co-accuser of him, whom he had unwillingly left there so long as Francis was in the country, Fowke being of Francis's side; and replaced him by Markham,[1] a boy of twenty-one, ignorant of Persian and everything else that was relevant, but entirely Hastings's creature. The Raja was told to pay a fine of fifty lakhs, concerning which Hastings's biographer coolly remarks, 'a considerable sum, doubtless, but not exceeding one year's rental of Cheyt Sing's zemindarry'.[2] Chait Singh hurried down to Buxar to meet Hastings, who declined to see him except in his own capital, where he meant to humble him before his own people. Arrived at Benares, Hastings still refused to see his suppliant, and wrote an arrogant demand. He

' received a letter from the Raja in self-defence, which an impartial judge can only regard as perfectly respectful, and, considering the way he had been treated, extraordinarily moderate'.[3]

Hastings found it 'not only unsatisfactory in substance but offensive in style', and arrested the Raja. This was too much for the Raja's subjects, who rose and massacred the few sepoys and their officers. Chait Singh fled in terror; Hastings escaped to Chamnagar, where he was besieged half-heartedly, and with a courage wholly admirable and an arrogance and blindness to his own folly and cruelty not admirable, issued his instructions to the nearest British forces. He was relieved, and a campaign followed in which the miserable Raja was defeated and chased into Sindhia's territory. But Hastings obtained no money; even the Raja's treasure, which amounted to only 23 lakhs, or less than half the fine which Hastings had thought to exact, was divided up by the troops who

[1] Son of the Archbishop of York, who 'used intemperate language in defence of Warren Hastings, which was brought under notice of Parliament, 1793' (*D.N.B.*).
[2] Gleig, ii. 404.   [3] Roberts, *History of British India*, 203-4.

captured his fortress of Bijaygarh. Popham excused this action, which annoyed Hastings intensely, by reference to a letter which Hastings explained he had not meant to be taken literally, and by the insistence of his officers. He 'could not withstand the universal clamour and vehemence of his officers for the scramble'. The looters strove to placate the Governor-General by sending

' a very elegant sword as a present to me, and a set of dressing boxes for Mrs. Hastings, all beautifully inlaid with jewels; I returned them all',

taking refuge in dignified sulkiness. But he had written the letter which had served as cover for rapacity.

Hastings was severe on the treaty-breaking which on so many occasions disgraced the English name, once going so far as to say that nothing short of declaring this offence felony would do any good. But the Company had definitely promised the Raja of Benares (July 5, 1775) that so long as he paid his stipulated 22½ lakhs

' no demands shall be made upon him by the Honble. Company, of any kind, or on any pretence whatsoever, nor shall any person be allowed to interfere with his authority, or to disturb the peace of his country'.

A new Raja was now appointed, and his tribute raised to forty lakhs.

Hastings, after all his violence, had been left empty-handed. He was, nevertheless, lifted up with an egoism and complacency worse than those of Clive at his worst. On the suggestion of Sir Elijah Impey, in England, who warned him that there were seditious people who might misunderstand his policy of 'Thorough', as this was reported by the disaffected, Hastings used the Chief Justice to collect numerous testimonials to show how delighted everyone was, including the right-thinking portion of the Benares population. He sent his agent in England a still stronger testimonial to himself, written by himself, which bears on its surface the deep pleasure its writing gave him; and observed (without any reference to anything he himself had ever done) that he feared 'our encroaching spirit, and the insolence with which it has been exerted, have caused our alliance to be as much dreaded by all the powers of Indostan as our arms'. This was a favourite (and just) comment of his; we may quote from another letter:

' Every power in India dreads a connexion with us, which they see attended with such mortifying humiliations to those who have availed themselves of it; and in my heart I always believe, and always did believe, that this was the secret and sole cause of the hesitation of the Government of Berar to accept of our alliance, although I had carefully worded the conditions of it so as to obviate that objection.'

L

Yet he never, now or later, let fall a word of doubt concerning the absolute justice of his proceedings towards the unhappy Raja of Benares: neither did he ever see that his conduct was as foolish as it was insolently tyrannical. He told Laurence Sulivan:

' I feel an uncommon degree of anxiety to receive the sentiments of my friends upon it. I have flattered myself that they will see nothing done which ought not to have been done, nor anything left undone which ought to have been done.'

The man who so acted, and after action so thought and so wrote, was above the reach of human censure as completely as Napoleon or Caesar. He looked about elsewhere for the money which had eluded him at Benares. His glance fell on Oudh, which was in arrears with its tribute. Its Nawab was entirely dependent on the English, and his affairs

' were, as might have been expected, in great confusion. The Nabob, cruelly wronged at the beginning of his reign, . . . sank year by year more deeply into difficulties, from which by any ordinary means escape was now impracticable . . . a more foolish person never occupied a throne: while his private vices are reported to have been as detestable as his weakness was conspicuous throughout. . . . Moreover, his English allies, whether as a government or as individuals, showed him no mercy'.[1]

He was drawn under more stringent terms than even those inflicted on his father; and the Company's servants 'robbed him without scruple, by loans advanced at an exorbitant interest, and pensions and jaghires wrung from him in return'. Here, at least, Hastings stood his friend, and deserves praise. He noted, in that downright fashion of his, that

' every Englishman in Oude was possessed of an independent and sovereign authority. They learned and taught others to claim the revenue of lacs as their right, though they could gamble away more than two lacs (I allude to a known fact) at a sitting'.

He supported the Nawab in trying to abolish this army of thieving foreigners. Then they both thought about the Begums, who had kept the bulk of the last Nawab's treasure, instead of the one-eighth sanctioned by Muhammadan law. They were fortified by a treaty between them and the young Nawab, in 1775, when he had received £560,000 altogether, and with the Company had guaranteed to demand nothing more; but Hastings (who had been outvoted by his Council on this matter) felt no scruples, now that power had come to him, in breaking

[1] Gleig, ii. 405.

the agreement. The Begums were imprisoned, and their eunuchs put in irons and starved, and perhaps whipped. 'By those measures, which any Hindu or Muhammadan government would have regarded as normal',[1] the Begums were made to disgorge a million sterling, and the Company was put in funds by having the Nawab's debts to it paid. Hastings had found, or believed he had found (which in his present infatuation was to him the same as complete proof), that the Begums had assisted the Raja of Benares in his resistance.[2] 'These old women had very nigh effected our destruction'.

Judged by Eastern standards of the time, the episode is not one of the blackest criminality. It is, nevertheless, true that the Nawab would have hung back from such severe measures against respected ladies of his family, and that even Hastings's own British officers did not like the job. The Governor-General, determined to have the money he needed, hounded everyone else on, as strong and as single-minded an autocrat as the world has seen.

Two last comments may finish these discussions. Hastings testified in 1775 that Chait Singh's was 'as rich and well cultivated a territory as any district, perhaps, of the same extent in India'; two years after his expulsion of the Raja, he revisited it, and was 'followed and fatigued by the clamours of the discontented inhabitants', caused (he thought) principally by 'a defective if not a corrupt and oppressive administration'. Secondly, the English key-position in this administration was their Resident; and until Cornwallis effected a drastic change the Benares Residency held an unquestioned pre-eminence for profitable rapacity, being estimated to be worth at least £30,000 a year in bribes. As for Oudh, it is painful for an Englishman to remember its wretched history between this date and the Mutiny, which closed its long sufferings in the wildest agony of all.

During this last period Hastings worked without scruples—a statement easy to prove by the whole tenor of his correspondence, which is excessively bad-tempered. His justification, and it is one so great as to exempt, not his proceedings but his own character from severe condemnation, was his unique perplexities. We must remember all the while what was happening elsewhere. We surely cannot withhold admiration from the man who resolved that in India, at any rate, his country's cause should not fail.

Yet it is strange that writers should express surprise and indignation that disgust, as well as misunderstanding, was accumulating in England

---

[1] *Oxford History of India*, 539.   [2] This is improbable in the extreme.

towards his fall. Hastings had a busy faction, built up by contemporary methods; a friend tells him:

' The Archbishop of York is an active and steady friend, and such as a man should be who is thoroughly grateful for the favour you have shown his son.'[1]

Another champion was Laurence Sulivan, the Chairman of the Court of Directors, to whose son, Stephen, Hastings had granted a four years' contract for the Bengal opium, a privilege which the young man sold for £40,000 to a friend, who then sold it for £60,000. No party were busier in British politics than the Governor-General's; their incessant meddling brought him to his impeachment. It was flattering to be told that the downfall of the short-lived Rockingham Ministry (1782) was ascribed to 'your agents and your power,' and that everyone called the new Government 'Mr. Hastings's Ministry'. But desire to get even with someone who has successfully intrigued against you is a feeling not confined to the East. It is hard to guess from a distance what your enemies are thinking; and Hastings, who was longing for a title and re-wards, noting (with a hit at Clive, whom he despised) that 'my name has received no addition of title, my fortune of jagheers, nor my person any decorations of honours', underrated the detraction set up by the vast army of the disgruntled and the envious, and all whose sons had not been looked after. If his friends were 'sleepless', so were those of Francis. Moreover, his main friend, his agent Major Scott (Waring), was a fool; General Grant wrote to Lord Cornwallis in India (April 6, 1788): 'Scott bullied Burke into the *persecution*', which he did by taunt-ing Burke in the House of Commons, asking when he intended to fulfil certain vague threats he had thrown out, of instituting a searching enquiry into Indian events.

France and England made peace at Versailles, 1783. Fox and Pitt then prepared rival India Bills, both unwelcome to Hastings, whose resignation was practically forced (February, 1785). He went home, where the long-gathering storm, precipitated by himself and his admirers, burst in his impeachment. It began (February 13, 1788) as a colossal show, with royalty and beauty in all their feathers. It soon staled, dragging on until April 23, 1795, when he was acquitted on all charges. Burke and Sheridan undid their cause by savagery and ignor-ance. Hastings steadily built up his own, by the dignity and valour of his bearing; and sympathy grew with growing knowledge of the unique

[1] Gleig, ii. 476. The son was the Markham who, when barely twenty-one, had been given the plum of the service, the notorious Benares Residency.

service he had done his country. Less histrionic than Clive, he defended himself with bare truth when he stated that the administration of Bengal, in all its branches, was his sole creation. 'I gave you all', he said, 'and you have repaid me with impeachment'. In retirement, after the fortunate issue of the trial, he was given a generous pension by the Directors, and lived to old age, happy in intellectual pursuits. In 1813, when he was called up to the House of Lords to give evidence, the assembly, moved by a unanimous impulse of reverence, rose to receive him, a tribute which deeply affected him, as it well might.

There remains the question of his services to India. As the lady who started the 'Dyer Testimonial' in India asked, when Indians unaccountably withheld their subscriptions, 'Have Indians forgotten the days when they were robbed and pillaged by merciless oppressors, before the British bulldog pinned them to the earth?' The lady's use of 'them' was perhaps ambiguous; but her general meaning was clear. No; they have not forgotten. And when they talk about 'the Drain', though they make querulous complaint about sums paid in pensions and interest on money lent for valuable services such as railways and canals, it is likely that at the back of thought is the real rankling in memory of the decades when 'lakhs' were steadily and pitilessly removed from one territory after another. Miss Monckton Jones, in her eloquent appreciation of Hastings, says that

' by unsparing labour, coupled with imaginative insight into native needs, he converted the presence of the English from a bane into a source of healing and strength'.

The labour was certainly unsparing, the insight was imaginative and backed by knowledge fuller and more sympathetic than (one is tempted to say—and surely it is true) that of all other contemporary Englishmen put together. But it was not able to effect what she claimed. Lord Cornwallis found the English still a pest, and Cornwallis's biographer, whose study is as soundly Tory a document as anyone could desire, seems to think this fact too incontestable to need buttressing with quotation.

But we must distinguish between the effect of the English outside Bengal and within Bengal. Bengal was the only region where Warren Hastings's influence was in some degree plenary and omnipresent; he gave this province the unique gift of peace:

' these provinces have continued in an unvaried state of profound peace with armies surrounding them; and the only calamity which at any time threatened their tranquillity was confined to the person of the Governor-General alone, and to the scene in which it originated; and its extreme duration was but thirty-one days'.[1]

How great was this boon, in an India traversed by marauding armies, we can see from Calcutta's rapid and steady growth. Also, despite all the disqualifications imposed by his constant need for money, and by jobbery forced upon him by the necessity to find supporters beside him and to placate people at a distance, Hastings laid the foundations of a better, securer regime than India had known since Akbar. His own oppressions, in certain instances (as we have seen) gross and heavy, were exercised not on the mean and poor but on nobles and quasi-princes. His place is with such great medieval kings as Henry II, who tamed the barons, that the lower orders might begin to have fewer authorities to fear. His rule was popular in Bengal; and he left such an impression as no other Englishman has ever done.

As for his services to England, which naturally pressed upon him as those with first call, and were so accepted by him, these were beyond exaggeration. It is not easy to think of any greater name in the roll of English statesmen, or of any spirit of such exalted courage and self-composure amid every kind of alarm and tumult. It is from Englishmen 'of the left', those most troubled by thought of injustice wrought on weaker peoples in their Empire's mighty course, that he has won the deepest (not the most indiscriminate) admiration. Macaulay, whose essay is not far wrong in the main things, is to-day held up as a defamer; but Macaulay, 'whose own Indian career', as Miss Sydney C. Grier (herself a thick-and-thin extoller, with a deftly drastic way with awkward material) sees, 'had inspired him with a sneaking kindness for Hastings', concludes with moving praise. Mill's tribute is perhaps the most impressive of all, emphasising how circumstantially and fully the events of his life were dragged out to public inspection, and reminding us how very few public men could have survived such a testing as well as he has done. This reflection (which applies also to the actions and motives of those·of us so fortunate as to be private men) must always make us, while unable to evade frank assessment of deeds and their effects, refuse to judge the man austerely and eager to express veneration for the greatness he consistently revealed on the political plane and on occasion showed strikingly in moral ways also.

[1] Hastings, February 20, 1782.

BOOK III

ERA OF SUBORDINATION OF THE COUNTRY POWERS AND CONSOLIDATION OF THE BRITISH POWER

'A tedium inseparable from the professional recollections of retired administrators broods impenetrably above the brightest pages of Anglo-Indian history. Besides, there are so many of them, and almost uniformly bright . . . there is a lack of vicissitudes about them that is almost distressing. That lofty destiny, those prescient forerunners, and the long roll of their inevitable victories sweep past like a political speech to its foregone conclusion. We see the goal; we note the all too steady progress; and our starved dramatic sense cries out for a hitch somewhere.'—PHILIP GUEDALLA, *The Duke*, 69.

CHRONOLOGICAL TABLE

Sir John Macpherson
(acting Governor-
General). 1785.
Lord Cornwallis. 1786.
1787. Reverses of Mahadaji Sindhia and Marathas.
1788. Impeachment of Warren Hastings.
1789. *French Revolution begins.*
1790. Third Mysore War.
1792. Treaty of Seringapatam.
1793. Permanent Settlement, Bengal.
1794. Death of Mahadaji Sindhia.
Sir John Shore. 1795. Acquittal of Hastings. Death of Ahalya Bai. Permanent Settlement, Benares. Defeat of Nizam by Marathas at Kardla.
Lord Mornington. 1798.
1799. Fourth Mysore War. Capture of Seringapatam and death of Tipu. William Carey opens Baptist Mission at Serampur.
1800. Death of Nana Farnavis.
1802. Battle of Poona. Company interferes in Maratha affairs. Treaty of Bassein.
1803. Second Maratha War. Battles of Delhi, Assaye, Laswari, Argaon.
1804. War with Holkar. Defeat of Monson. Capture of Dig.
1805. Siege and storm of Bharatpur fail. Lord Wellesley recalled.
Lord Cornwallis. 1805. (August and September.)
Sir George Barlow 1805. (October.)
(acting).
Lord Minto. 1806. Vellore Mutiny.
1807.
1808. Malcolm sent on mission to Persia, and Elphinstone to Amir of Kabul. Travancore outbreak.
1809. Metcalfe's mission to Ranjit Singh. Treaty of Amritsar with the latter. Mutiny of Madras Company's officers.
1810. Capture of the Moluccas.
1811. Conquest of Java.
Lord Hastings. 1813.
1814-16. War with Nepal.
1817-19. Pindari Campaign and Maratha War.
1817. Battles of Kirki, Sitabaldi, Nagpur, Mahidpur.
1818. Battles of Koregaon and Ashti. First Bengali newspaper.
1819. Pacification of Central India. Foundation of Singapore. Rammohan Roy publishes *The Precepts of Jesus the Guide to Peace and Happiness*. Nawab of Oudh made King of Oudh.
1820. Sir Thomas Munro Governor of Madras.

168

CHAPTER I

LORD CORNWALLIS AND SIR JOHN SHORE

Sir John Macpherson: Dundas: character of Cornwallis: Oudh and the Carnatic: beginnings of Indian Civil Service: reforms in Army: war with Tipu: condition of country powers: Sindhia's foreign troops: Ahalya Bai: Sir John Shore's characteristics: Lord Hobart in Madras: affairs of Oudh.

HASTINGS's departure was followed by twenty months' rule by John Macpherson, senior member of Council, who

' certainly was the most contemptible and the most contemned Governor that ever pretended to govern'.[1]

Reaching India first as a ship's purser, he became involved in the business of native princes, especially Muhammad Ali, 'greatly to his pecuniary advantage';[2] was foisted into Company service; dismissed by the Madras Governor, Lord Pigot; reinstated by the Directors, and sent out to Bengal as Barwell's successor. Provided his own interests flourished, he was indifferent to what was done. Even Hastings, so casual as to the character of those who worked with him, provided they worked submissively, became enlightened:

' a ray of inspiration very early flitted across my imagination more than once, and showed me the naked character of Macpherson'.[3]

Macpherson was known as 'the gentle giant'; 'a very good-humoured fellow',[4] for a while he half-deceived Lord Cornwallis, the next *pukka* Governor-General after Hastings. When Cornwallis was beginning to understand him Macpherson went home, by tortuous devices evading technical resignation. In London he became intimate with the Prince of Wales and collected a party who asserted that he was entitled to have served as Governor-General for the statutory five years, and had therefore large claims on the Company. He was, he hinted, willing to pocket his wrongs, if he might pocket something financially more considerable. During these prolonged intrigues he wrote Cornwallis a letter of masterly disingenuousness and complacency, dwelling with satisfaction

[1] Lord Cornwallis, November 1, 1789. [2] *The Cornwallis Correspondence*, i. 221.
[3] Letter of October 15, 1783. [4] Lord Cornwallis.

169

on the acknowledged truth that he had acted as Governor-General with general and extreme approbation. Cornwallis wrote (November 1, 1788) asking why Mr. Dundas bothered to parley with Macpherson: [1]

' Why does he not tell him, when he talks of grievances and pensions, that he may think himself well off that he is not impeached? . . . that he was guilty of basely degrading the national character, by the quibbles and lies which he made use of . . . that his Government was a system of the dirtiest jobbing . . . that his conduct in Oude was as impeachable, and more disgusting to the Vizier, than Mr. Hastings's?'

To the same correspondent (Dundas), at a later date (August 8, 1789), the Governor-General wrote:

' Macpherson seems to expect that you are to give him a pension, besides all the ill-earned money that he has got under the head of pay and presents. His flimsy cunning and shameless falsehoods seem to have taken in all parties; believe me, that those who trust the most in him will be the most deceived.'

As for Macpherson posing at home as an authority on Indian affairs,

' I do not believe that there is a boy in the service so grossly ignorant in every respect; he does not even know the commonest revenue terms'.

Macpherson was elected to Parliament, but was unseated and fined for bribery, a small setback to so persevering a man. He obtained a baronetcy, a pension, and another seat; and for some years served, in Parliament and elsewhere, the Nawab of the Carnatic and anyone else who would pay him.

The reader cannot remind himself too often that this half-century was the most contemptible and venal in English parliamentary history; and India was now in full enjoyment of all the advantages of close connection with British polity. The last resounding failure of the Jacobite struggles caused the Scots, that sane and realist people, to turn to make the best of their enforced position in that polity, ultimately to the Empire's immense gain. But they brought, along with less restrictedly useful characteristics, the clan spirit of mutual assistance; and they possessed a great captain-general in Henry Dundas, first Viscount Melville, who was Pitt's Indian Manager and for many years President of the Board of Control:

' His Indian and Scottish policies dovetailed very nicely into one another. He managed the Scottish vote at Westminster by the distribution of Government patronage among Scots. As a result, Scotland lost all control of its own

---

[1] The reason, of course, was that Macpherson was a brother Scot.

destinies, but British India enjoyed this priceless boon of government by Scotsmen.'[1]

Certain broad principles were beginning to emerge from the prolonged disorder; even Directors and Proprietors were growing vaguely aware of them. People were seeing that it was idiotic to expect India to be administered either ably or honestly by the scum of Great Britain, or by boys shoved in by influential relatives and then set under someone they despised socially. Pitt's India Act (1784) gave the next Governor-General enlarged powers, which experience had shown he so badly needed, to overrule the inferior Presidencies; and Earl Cornwallis, the first to wield these powers, was England's best at last, after half a century of her worst. He came with such advantages as no predecessor ever had: he was Commander-in-Chief as well as Governor-General, and his rank set him above the necessity of truckling to anybody, however exalted. As Dundas feelingly exclaimed:

' Here there was no broken fortune to be mended! here there was no avarice to be gratified! here there was no beggarly mushroom kindred to be provided for! no crew of hungry followers gaping to be gorged!'

But his chief advantages lay in his own character, in which he was as superior to his age as Hastings had been in ability. His surrender to Washington at Yorktown had not been his fault, and his military experience and talent, while nothing exceptional, were respectable and generally respected. He was indifferent alike to pecuniary gain and adulation, a man of sturdy courage and honesty exceptional in any century, and in his own almost a portent. There is a great deal to be said for government by the right kind of aristocrat.

Macpherson's 'system of mean jobbing and peculation', 'his duplicity and low intrigues', had sunk 'the national character for sincerity and honour'.[2] Cornwallis's main task throughout his term was to reinstate British reputation. He succeeded

' the first honest and incorruptible Governor India ever saw, and after his example, hardly any Governor has dared to contemplate corruption'.[3]

Hastings is widely credited with reforming the administration; as a matter of fact, he achieved practically nothing in this respect, after a first spurt of early promise of some success. Nearly all the esteem now given to him on this head should go to his infinitely less known successor. It is the greatest possible tribute to what Hastings at any rate

[1] D. C. Somervell, *The Observer*, September 10, 1933.
[2] *The Cornwallis Correspondence*, i. 221.   [3] *Op. cit.* ii. 195.

intended, as well as to the cruel reality of his limitations, that Cornwallis, who had such immense trouble undoing his jobs, always spoke tolerantly of him, and with increasing forgiveness.

Macpherson stayed on for a while, and gave the new Governor-General the advantage of his assistance—cautiously and with reservations. Presently the Governor-General decided that nothing Macpherson said was in itself credible. For example, Macpherson affirmed that he knew nothing about an arrangement by which a King's officer (for attractive financial considerations) was lent to the Nizam, a generosity which his enemies, the Marathas, regarded as a breach of the friendliness promised by the English. Cornwallis became satisfied that Macpherson and the late Commander-in-Chief, a gentleman appropriately named Sloper, knew a great deal about the arrangement. Next, the Nawab of Oudh—whose country, as a result of Hastings's energetic intervention in his affairs and his own imbecility, was in the deepest misery—accidentally flung up another item of Macpherson's subterranean knowledge. His tribute of 74 lakhs was in heavy arrears; Cornwallis went to see him, and was shocked by 'the desolated appearance' of his land. The Nawab despairingly said he had no motives for economy while 'uncertain of the extent of our demands upon him'; and that his authority was null, so long as hordes of European adventurers interfered continually. When Cornwallis went into details, and asked why he had not paid for a corps raised for his use, he replied that the corps was mythical. This proved to be so; General Sloper (now in England) and some of his colleagues had thriftily divided its cost. Cornwallis, probably to the Nawab's surprise, accepted this as a valid reason why he should not pay up. More, he reduced Oudh's tribute to fifty lakhs. He ordered that the Company's exemption from duties in Oudh should cease, and also the exemption from duties of the goods of all Europeans residing or trading under the Company's protection. He stopped practices in the camp bazars belonging to Company forces which spoiled the Nawab's revenues. He forbade the Resident or any other servant of the Company to interfere 'in any manner whatever in the internal affairs of your Government'. Even so, the land could not support its disabilities, and the Nawab could not shake off his parasites or his own infirmities of mind and character. Oudh's debt continued to accumulate, and its people remained oppressed. When he had left India, Cornwallis, after referring to

' the ruinous and most inhuman management of the Carnatic and Tanjore country . . . evils which have been long known to me, even to the most minute detail of them',

wrote [1] that 'the Nabob's Government of the Carnatic, with all its vices and horrors, is at least as good as that of the Vizier'.

Nevertheless, this was a new kind of Governor-General, who, instead of pouncing on any pretext to raise his demands, listened courteously to reason, and, for reason shown, at once reduced an intolerable impost. Only a man of lofty social standing, in addition to unique strength of resolution, could have done this elementary justice, against the harpies clamouring for funds and yet more funds:

' To anyone who has read with attention the history of Mr. Hastings's administration, the fact is patent, that the Court of Directors thought only of income, and were not very sedulous in their inquiries as to how it was raised.' [2]

They continually hounded Hastings on into courses which then sometimes, as when he persecuted the Raja of Benares, proved too much for them.

Cornwallis found the Nawab of Bengal 'as poor as a rat'; and he returned the wretched creature's congratulatory gifts for George III on His Majesty's recovery from mental derangement. He returned gifts for himself and everyone else, from whatever quarter they came.

He had much perplexity from two main centres of mischief left by Hastings, 'the Augean stables of Benares and Lucknow'.[3] In 'Benares . . . a scene of the grossest corruption and mismanagement',[4] the Resident, 'although not regularly vested with any power, enjoyed the almost absolute government of the country without control'.[5] His salary was Rs. 1000 a month; he received dishonestly at least four lakhs a year, as well as vast gains from 'the complete monopoly of commerce'. The Raja was 'a fool, his servants rogues, every native of Hindostan (I verily believe) corrupt'.

Cornwallis's first duty was to deal with these scandals. Doing this, he established what has always been recognised as the beginnings of the world-famed Indian Civil Service. The Benares Resident was told he must be content with a salary of Rs. 5000 a month (£7,500 a year as the rupee then stood). The Bengal Civil Service were given enlarged salaries, in addition to a percentage on the revenue, and the principle which has ruled Indian administration to our own day was explicitly

[1] June 26, 1796.
[2] *Cornwallis Correspondence*, ii. 194.
[3] Cornwallis, August 8, 1789.
[4] Cornwallis, November 30, 1786.
[5] Cornwallis, August 14, 1787.

laid down—its members were placed above the excuse for peculation and were expected to abstain rigidly from it. Cornwallis had the satisfaction of writing to the Chairman of the Directors: [1]

'You will see this year what never happened before—that our expenses have fallen short of our estimates . . . the splendid and corrupting objects of Lucknow and Benares are removed; and here I must look back to the conduct of former Directors, who knew that these shocking evils existed, but instead of attempting to suppress them, were quarrelling whether their friends, or those of Mr. Hastings, should enjoy the plunder.'

Unfortunately, he could not touch the internal administration of Madras, which until 1802 continued to be a swamp of misgovernment, greed, incompetence, whose

'whole system is founded on the good old principles of Leadenhall-street economy—small salaries and immense perquisites, and if the Directors alone could be ruined by it, everybody would say they deserved it, but unfortunately it is not the Court of Directors, but the British nation who must be the sufferers'. [2]

Cornwallis was resolute to keep the peace, and told the Nizam and the Marathas that Macpherson had gone beyond his powers in promising to assist them in a war against Tipu Sultan (to whom we had pledged neutrality). This led to some natural vexation, but the sterling truth (honesty is too mean a word) of his character slowly, and then rapidly, won them over to confidence. We have done him wrong in suggesting that he repudiated Macpherson's unjustifiable engagements merely from pacifist policy; he did it mainly because he thought that even Tipu was entitled to 'a square deal'. We are writing of this admirable man with an exhilaration (after the depressing story which has been ours for so long) which we hope is being communicated to the reader.

It was wise, as well as decent, to keep out of what Cornwallis called 'scrapes', for the army was in as unspeakable a condition as the civil personnel. King's officers and the far inferior Company's officers were kept distinct; Cornwallis pressed consistently, but unsuccessfully, for them to be made into one service. The Company's total forces amounted to about 70,000 Europeans and Indians, exclusive of Bombay Presidency's native levies; the whole, it is interesting to note, coming to about half the Indian army of the present day. Europeans were about 11,500 (5500 King's enlisted, 6000 Company's). The latter were of appalling quality: 'the contemptible trash of which the Company's

---

[1] December 16, 1787.   [2] December 31, 1790.

European force is composed, makes me shudder'.[1] H.R.H. the Duke of York gave him such consolation as was possible:

' As for the accounts which You give of the State of the European Troops in the Service of the Company, it grieves me, though it does not in the least astonish me, as It is totally impossible that they be otherwise than the riff-raff of London Streets got together by the Crimps, and the Gleanings of the different Gaols. The Officers are, in general, young men who have ruined themselves and are obliged to fly their Country or very low people who are sent out to make their fortunes, and who will therefore stick at nothing in order to gain money.'

While doing what he could to reform the Europeans, the Governor-General radically overhauled the sepoy establishment also:[2]

' I have abolished their dancing about in various forms to jig-tunes, and have substituted marching to time.'

He acknowledged handsomely, however, that the native army was in far better fettle than the Company's Europeans:[3] 'A brigade of our sepoys would easily make anybody Emperor of Hindostan'.

We have seen with what austerity H.R.H. the Duke of York referred to people whose main eye was towards financial profit. His elder brother, the Prince of Wales, who presently became the First Gentleman of Europe, was less severe. He importuned his friend the Governor-General with monotonous regularity (but increasing diffidence and humility) to look after this or that young gentleman, in no single instance with success. In 1789[4] he pressed what Cornwallis called an 'infamous and unjustifiable job',[5] asking that 'young Treves' should be given the chief criminal judgeship at Benares, 'which is now held by a Black named Alii Cann'. Cornwallis pointed out that Ali Ibrahim Khan, the Black in question, was 'a man of great talent and universally respected', whereas young Treves

' is at the very bottom of the list of the Company's servants (except those of the present year)'.

Bengal was the only Presidency financially sound. It was subsidising Bombay with 40 lakhs annually, a drain possible in times of peace only:

' The income of Bengal exceeds its expenditure by above two millions, and although the other Presidencies are a great drain upon us, yet, on the general state of the finances throughout India, we can, without increasing our debts,

---

[1] August 12, 1787.   [2] July 26, 1788.   [3] December 10, 1787.
[4] May 30.   [5] November 16, 1790.

send home an investment from the different settlements, which costs us £1,300,000, and which will sell in Europe for £2,400,000, which, besides at least a million of profit which the Company receives from the China trade, must I think enable them to pay off at least a million of their debt annually in England.' [1]

But the Governor-General viewed Bombay's whole condition, and indeed existence, with misgiving: [2]

'Of what use is the civil establishment at Bombay? I should conceive that a small factory there, and another at Surat . . . would answer every purpose. Although we have appropriated the whole surplus revenue of Benares and Bahar to the support of Bombay, we are obliged to send many lacs thither from Calcutta.'

As for Madras, under the Hollond brothers, successively governors for brief periods ('in every manner doing infinite mischief both to the interest and reputation of the Company' [3]), it continued to be nothing but a skilled and experienced conspiracy for private aggrandisement.

That Tipu cherished implacable hate was known. Anyone less patient and ready to weigh his own side's shortcomings than Cornwallis was, would have swept down on him long before war actually came. Tipu was a liar so ingrained that he seems never to have risen to perception that a distinction between true and false existed; he could not see that it might sometimes advantage him to keep his word. His letters to commandants besieging forts would instruct them to offer quarter and, when quarter had been accepted, butcher everyone irrespective of age and sex. It was impossible to ascertain what captives he held; and as a preliminary, when war broke out, he would murder any who still survived.

He was keeping British captives now, in defiance of treaty, some having been circumcised into Islam. He had British children trained as janissaries, and others dressed and instructed as Hindu dancing girls. The Nizam, who at this time settled down into his alliance with the Company, and the Marathas, especially Sindhia—who had warmly admired Hastings, and was learning, like the rest of India, to trust the new Governor-General absolutely—were eager for a concerted effort to extirpate a being with no merit but physical courage and variegated intellectual curiosity, and no excuse except that he was probably not sane in his paroxysms.

Tipu was meditating an attack on the Raja of Travancore, an ally

[1] February 23, 1789. [2] November 4, 1788 (letter to Dundas).
[3] August 8, 1789.

of the Company. Told plainly that this would be taken as an act of war, he made it, and made it so badly that he was routed from 'the lines of Travancore', a thirty-mile rampart, December 29, 1789. Cornwallis had contributed to bringing about what he believed was an unavoidable war by stipulating, when he lent the Nizam troops, that they should not be used against the Marathas. Tipu noted the omission of any stipulation regarding himself, and in desperation precipitated the contest he looked on as at hand. 'That mad barbarian Tippoo has forced us into a war with him.'[1]

Madras conducted the war with its usual inefficiency, and a tide of murder and enslavement once more overswept the Carnatic. In December, 1790, Cornwallis himself went to South India and took command. His first care was that the British should be unique among the warring hosts, Mysorean, Maratha, or Nizam's, by being a protection, and not a terror, to the country people. In February, 1791, he hanged nine British soldiers for burning and plundering. As a result, presently, when his guns were roaring before Seringapatam, the enemy's capital, peasants were quietly ploughing within half a mile of them.

He won victories, but the war dragged on, hamstrung by possession of a medieval transport train (and Indian at that). However, in 1792, he routed Tipu almost under his capital's walls. The Treaty of Seringapatam followed, by which Tipu ceded to the allies half his territory, and promised to pay 330 lakhs and to surrender all his prisoners. He had already handed over much of the money and two sons as hostages, when he found that Cornwallis, sometimes a man careless in niceties of phrasing though always sure of his general intention, meant to take Coorg in the territory ceded. Tipu, who planned to make an example of the Coorg Raja and his people—driven by terrible cruelties to the side of the English—was maddened by what he thought a breach of faith. There is no question that Cornwallis would have done grave wrong if he had abandoned Coorg. It is queer that writers who refuse to censure Hastings for rupture of engagements made with cool deliberation, yet speak reprobatingly of Cornwallis's offence, which was at worst a genuine oversight.[2]

The campaign was memorable for the Commander-in-Chief's wide and searching humanity. Tipu's young sons, the hostages, he received with fatherly courtesy and admiration of their gallant bearing. When he found that the iniquitous Madras Government provided no doolies for their native wounded, who were just pitched into blankets, and so

[1] Cornwallis, April 15, 1790.   [2] Cf. *Oxford History of India*, 560.

M

carried away, he blazed out at 'false and cruel economy' and immediately altered the practice. When a court-martial leniently handled a
surgeon who had neglected his wounded and an officer who had beaten
a native creditor, he scarified them with a rigour which reminds us of
Lord Curzon. Nothing more infuriated him than assaults committed
by Europeans on people of the country. And both he and his second-in-
command, General Medows, declined to take their share of the prize-

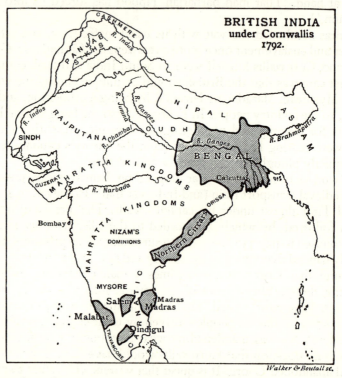

BRITISH INDIA
under Cornwallis
1792.

Walker & Boutall sc.

money when the campaign ended. Medows, whom he justly styled
'generous and noble', was offered the succession to the Governor-
Generalship, but modestly declined it.

The Nawab of Oudh was a puppet, the Nawab of Bengal a mere
poverty-stricken nobleman, their brother of the Carnatic a venerable
rascal whose territory Cornwallis kept urging the Company to annex, if
only for their own sakes, though they cared nothing for the people's
interests: [1]

[1] Cornwallis to Dundas, December 21, 1788.

' the Nabob is anticipating his revenues and ruining his country . . . when his overstrained credit breaks, which I am much afraid will soon be the case, we must expect a very serious defalcation in our Indian resources'.

Tipu, badly hurt, was plotting vengeance, but it was beyond his reach. The Sikhs were not yet neighbours of the English, neither had they yet grown to greatness. The Emperor had been blinded in 1788 by an Afghan, Gulam Kadr, during Mahadaji Sindhia's temporary evacuation of Delhi; Gulam Kadr was captured by Sindhia shortly afterwards, and sent to his victim in a cage and without nose, ears, hands and feet. The Nizam and the Gaekwar were in fact, and usually in form, dependents of the Company.

The Marathas, other than the Gaekwar, were in a position apart. Cornwallis noted [1] their essential weakness, which in the end brought about their ruin:

' The Marathas' power from the feudal constitution of their state can never bear any proportion to their numbers, or the extent of their possessions',

but they 'must always have great weight in the politics of India'. Their history in these last two decades of the eighteenth century is largely that of the rivalry between Mahadaji Sindhia and Nana Farnavis of Poona. The latter aimed at superimposing on the pious fraud whereby the Peshwa (the real head of the confederacy) was nominally merely the Prime Minister of the Raja of Satara, another fraud, whereby his family (nominally servants of the Peshwas) were the real rulers. That the jealousy between him and Sindhia kept short of active civil war we may ascribe to the fact that both men possessed patriotism, great common sense and awareness of realities, both knowing that the English were almost certainly destined to the suzerainty of the peninsula.

As for Sindhia, Grant Duff testifies that, though 'of deep artifice, restless ambition, and of implacable revenge', he was of habits 'simple, his manners kind and frank, but sometimes blustering and coarse'. He was 'of great political sagacity', which perhaps misled him when in 1784, after his unsuccessful war against the Company, he employed a French adventurer, Count de Boigne, to train battalions on the European model for him, and began to encourage Europeans to enter his service (by the end of the century the Gwalior forces had no less than 300 of them in one brigade). The story of these foreign mercenaries is one of the most interesting lesser chapters of Indian history. Brigaded

[1] September 8, 1791.

and trained on Western lines, the Marathas flung away their own natural tactics—they were the most naturally skilled guerillas the world has seen, as Sivaji proved to the Moguls early and Tantia Topi proved to the British later. They came down on to a plane unsuited to them. It is noteworthy that when war broke out afresh against the English, it was not Sindhia's highly trained troops that did most damage, but the still largely 'vernacularised' forces of Holkar, his rival. But for the time being, and in campaigns against Indian opponents, Sindhia gained the advantage; de Boigne defeated for him Muslim and Rajput opponents in 1790 and 1791, and Holkar in 1792. In 1795 Sindhia launched a full Maratha confederation, the last occasion when 'the chiefs of the Mahratta nation assembled under the authority of their Peshwa', against the Nizam, and defeated him at Kardla. This marked the summit of Maratha greatness during an interval when the Company deserted their ally. But the inherent feudalism and separatism of the Marathas scattered them again into sticks easily broken serially.

Between 1765 and 1795 Indore was ruled by the celebrated Ahalya Bai, widow of Malhar Rao Holkar. She was a lady of deep piety, whose munificence benefited distant parts of India; even in Bengal to-day the traveller may journey gratefully for miles along roads shaded by trees that she planted when returning from pilgrimage. Her husband had been killed before she was twenty, and her only son was both wicked and insane. Spared from the funeral pyre by her people (who in this matter exercised a wide though capricious tolerance), she herself sought to banish it, as well as other hateful customs. We have a piteous picture of her anguish when her daughter-in-law insisted on dying the death of a *sati*:

' Ahalya Bai, when she found all dissuasion unavailing, determined to witness the last dreadful scene. She walked in the procession, and stood near the pile, where she was supported by two Brahmins, who held her arms. Although obviously suffering great agony of mind, she remained tolerably firm till the first blaze of the flame made her lose all self-command; and while her shrieks increased the noise made by the exulting shouts of the immense multitude that stood around, she was seen to gnaw those hands she could not liberate from the persons by whom she was held. After some convulsive efforts, she so far recovered as to join in the ceremony of bathing in the Nerbudda, when the bodies were consumed. She then retired to her palace, where for three days, having taken hardly any sustenance, she remained so absorbed in grief that she never uttered a word.' [1]

[1] Sir John Malcolm, *Central India*, i. 190-191.

So great was the veneration felt for her that even Sindhia never thought of attacking her territory; she was semi-deified in her lifetime, and has been exalted to the Hindu Pantheon since. Her dependent nobles, especially Tukoji Holkar, the Commander-in-Chief (who was not related to her), worked loyally as her servants.

Cornwallis held strongly that no man who had been in the ordinary service should be promoted to it. But he was swayed by gratitude to Sir John Shore [1] for his helpfulness; and his praise of him helped to procure his appointment as his successor.

Shore was perhaps the first typical 'bureaucrat'; a thoroughly conventional and, indeed, excessively timid and dependent mind. A friend described him as 'a good well-meaning man, as cold as a dog's nose'. He was a first-rate routine worker, happy at his desk, nervous when necessity drove him into a wider and wilder field. As a young man he had been no worse than others, but for a time no better; and he shared current opinions then, as throughout his life, being indignant at the none too alarming efforts of Clive and Hastings to check dishonesty. He had been at first attached to Francis's party; but Hastings was persuaded to give him promotion, assured him he would prove a friend, and was one. He served Hastings faithfully, and Cornwallis no less faithfully and much more enthusiastically, admiring him intensely, finding in him 'a peace of mind which nothing alarms, being built upon a solid foundation'.[2] His own period of supreme power was an affliction to him, and when it was over he relinquished India as an interest as completely as Doughty in later years relinquished Arabia. Deeply religious, he devoted his retirement to correspondence with such men as Dr. Adam Clarke and to work for the Bible Society, by whom his name is still rightly revered.

As Governor-General, Shore was as scrupulously honest as Cornwallis. But his consciousness of unfitness wrung from him touching admission:

' I sometimes doubt my judgment may not have proved erroneous on the decisions which it has adopted. Often have I wished that Lord Cornwallis were at the head of the Administration here, and that I were his co-adjutor, as formerly: all would then have been easy to him and me. . . . I am not fitted for the scenes which have lately occurred.' [3]

[1] He was made a baronet, 1792, and an Irish peer (Lord Teignmouth), 1798.

[2] February 15, 1789.   [3] March 9, 1796.

Though only a little over forty, he wrote habitually as if he were an old man, and a very exhausted old man. Yet by unswerving rectitude and a deepening conviction of divine assistance—his habit was to withdraw, as Gordon and others who have left a more heroic mark in their countrymen's memory did, to pray alone before any important decision—he won respect and, what was more important, careful service from his subordinates. It should be added that he carried on one of the most admirable features of Hastings's work, in a constant and sympathetic interest in Indian culture. When he entered the service, the Company's officials did not bother to learn anything beyond a smattering of Hindustani; 'broken English being their only medium of communication with their native servants'.[1] But Shore knew Persian; he encouraged Sir William Jones and other excellent Orientalists and succeeded the former as President of the Asiatic Society; he helped Roxburgh the botanist.

Jonathan Duncan, his close friend and, like him, eager for the intellectual advance of the people of India, went to be Governor of Bombay, 1796, to remove 'the accumulated filth of'[2] that 'Augean stable'. 'Augean stable' became a conventional (but far from meaningless) description of practically every place where the Company had held sway. Shore found himself everywhere hampered by former evil deeds whose *karma* was still not worked out to the full. The Company's forces had to fight a battle against the one surviving Rohilla chief. Shore observed to Charles Grant:

' No man can calculate the consequences of a violation of a moral principle; and there is some justness in your suspicion, that the inveteracy of the Rohillas may be traced to the injustice of 1774. Our reputation for justice and good faith stands high in India; and if I were disposed to depart from them, I could form alliances which would shake the Mahratta Empire to its very foundations.' [3]

He was not disposed to depart from justice and good faith; and he was deeply pacific in nature. Some historians, viewing the Marathas as inevitably the enemies of the English, and themselves not too concerned with principles of ordinary straightforwardness, have lamented that he left the Nizam to fight an isolated battle against the Marathas, resulting in his rout at Kardla (1796). But the Marathas had preserved neutrality on many occasions when their hostility would have been hurtful, and had frequently gone beyond neutrality to very valuable friendliness.

[1] *Life of Lord Teignmouth*, by his Son, i. 30.
[2] Sir John Shore, February 13, 1796.   [3] June 22, 1796.

Moreover, Cornwallis's war against Tipu had been costly, and had left that ruler eager for vengeance. Shah Zaman of Kabul had captured Lahore and was threatening Oudh, which was merely a British apanage. The Emperor at Delhi was a blinded, disgraced old man. Shore faced with constant misgiving but complete courage immense clouds that seemed always likely to break in tempest.

His administration can be briefly summarised. He had to meet in late 1795 one of the worst of the periodical mutinous conspiracies of British officers. He temporised and yielded their demands for 'double *batta* or field allowances, promotion by strict seniority, and other personal privileges incompatible with good administration'.[1] The officers had influential friends in England, who worked yet further concessions out of Dundas, President of the Board of Control. Shore's deeply apologetic letters to his old chief in England show how conscious of his weakness he felt, and his failure led to his recall, after wrangling and delay.

He failed also with Lord Hobart, the young and energetic Governor of Madras. Hobart, the eldest son of the Duke of Buckingham, paid little attention to Shore, and gave continual proof of the absurdity of trying to run India by Governor-Generals from the middle classes, while at least one of the Governors was often a man of title and family. When Muhammad Ali died (October, 1795), Shore wanted his revenues to be taken over by the Company, as a first step towards lifting the Carnatic out of its pestilential morass of maladministration. The attempt broke down, because Hobart was precipitate and peremptory, and the new Nawab stood on his dignity. When war began between England and Holland, Hobart sent an expedition which annexed most of the Dutch East Indies (1796). He *dragooned*[2] Tanjore, the unhappy State which was the South Indian equivalent of Oudh, into a treaty foreshadowing its speedy annexation. And when the Governor-General remonstrated feebly, he said openly and often that one of them must go. Shore therefore gave in, soothing himself with the sad observation:[3]

' Lord Hobart seems to me to pursue his objects without any regard to the rectitude of the means or ultimate consequences, to decide with precipitation, and to maintain his decision at all hazards.'

An expedition against Manila, which Hobart wisely stopped at Penang, to meet Tipu's threats—Shore acquiesced in his subordinate's action, and Tipu was overawed by the show of force—introduced to the

---

[1] *Oxford History*, 575.   [2] Shore's own word and italics.   [3] April 26, 1796.

Governor-General's notice the future Duke of Wellington, in a letter from Lord Cornwallis:

DEAR SIR,   'WHITEHALL, June 10, 1796.
          I beg leave to introduce to you Colonel Wesley, who is Lieut.-Colonel of my regiment: he is a sensible man, and a good officer; and will, I have no doubt, conduct himself in a manner to merit your approbation.'

Another event showing the expansion of the Company's affairs was an embassy to Burma.

In February, 1797, the Governor-General made a tour up-country. In Benares he visited the Begum of the late Emperor and her two sons:

' These poor descendants of Imperial dignity maintain the forms of royalty: and we mutually acted parts inconsistent with our real characters; I, the Representative of our Power, professing humility and submission before the dependants on the bounty of the Company; whilst they, who are the objects of charity, and feeling their situation, thought it incumbent on them to use the language of Princes.'

He went on to Oudh, and surprised the Nawab by declining to accept a present of five lakhs of rupees and 8000 gold mohurs. However, relations remained affable:

' The Nabob and myself visit daily, and are in the best humour imaginable with each other. His disposition is naturally good, but irritated by bad advisers, mean associates, and absolute power; which, however, he does not exercise cruelly. He promotes rather than performs bad actions. A few years ago, an Englishman, for his Excellency's amusement, introduced the elegant European diversion of a race in sacks by old women: the Nabob was delighted beyond measure, and declared, that although he had spent a crore of rupees, or a million sterling, in procuring entertainment, he had never found one so pleasing to him. So much for the amusements of Sovereignty! Every evening, almost, he stupefies himself with opium: the effects of which are often felt in the morning, in sickness, vomiting, langour, and dejection of spirits. His confidants are the meanest and lowest people: he dreads the society of men of worth, capable of controlling his conduct.' [1]

Failing in 'the very disagreeable attempt of making an Ethiopian white; and I cannot flatter myself that I have made much impression on his complexion', the Governor-General shrugged his shoulders, and turned his attention away. India was in a deplorable state, but he found refuge in philosophical musings: [2]

' I am now not far from Delhi, once the capital of the largest empire in the

[1] February 19, 1797.   [2] March 25, 1797.

world, Russia perhaps excepted. The present possessor of the throne, the descendant of Tamerlane, lives in darkness, surrounded with empty state and real penury, a pensioner on the niggard bounty of the Mahrattas, from whom he receives less than the Duke of Bedford does from his tenants. He supplicates me on the terms of royalty; and his son is here, a dependant on the benevolence of the Nabob, from whom he receives a comfortable subsistence. Wonderful are the dispensations of Providence, and I feel them in myself!'

Later in the year the Nawab died; Shore had to journey to Oudh again, to see about the succession. Ascertaining that he had (on inadequate information) recognised as Nawab an adopted son whose parentage was unknown and whose character was ruffianly, Shore without the least hesitation deposed him, and with calm courage did it mainly by prestige, allowing himself to dine with and meet alone the man he was ousting. He refused to let the Commander-in-Chief, Sir Alured Clarke,[1] share the risks of assassination. Awed by a coolness so uncanny, the dethroned Nawab did not express his hatred until 1799, when he murdered the Lucknow Resident and some other Englishmen. This peaceful revolution in Oudh was accompanied by the cession to the Company of Allahabad.

Shore, though only forty-six, was

' almost worn out; and shall most gladly resign my station, either to Lord Hobart, or to any other person'.[2]

In March, 1798, he drifted out of the Governor-Generalship as listlessly as he had drifted through it. India was ready for a Wellesley.

CHAPTER II

ADMINISTRATIVE REFORMS

Cornwallis's efforts to reform administration: Nawab of Arcot's debts: Wellesley's College at Fort William: the Permanent Settlement: low moral standards of Company's servants: exclusion of Indians from higher posts; continuance of Muslim penal law: Cornwallis's reform of police system: growth of litigation.

THE forty years which followed the retirement of Warren Hastings were marked by strenuous and moderately successful efforts to reform

---

[1] Who acted after Shore as Governor-General, for a very brief interregnum.

[2] September 13, 1797.

the personnel of the service, and by a tendency to rely more and more upon European civil servants for administration. Macpherson's short but lamentable term of office, followed by Shore's somewhat nerveless one, confirmed the view of the authorities in England that the Governor-General and the Provincial Governors should not be chosen from the Company's servants, and men were brought straight out from England to these posts, a policy which continued after the fear of corruption and insubordination had ceased.[1] Both Clive and Warren Hastings had been hampered by their previous history, and Lord Cornwallis partly owed his authority to the feeling in England that the Governor-General must be one who had 'not graduated in chicanery or grown grey in fraud and corruption'. On his arrival in 1786 he found a new spirit amongst the civil servants in Bengal. His two advisers, John Shore and Barlow, were men of integrity with a real interest in administration. Within two years of taking office Cornwallis was writing to a friend that 'the Company has many valuable servants; the temper of the time is changing'.[2] Probably the chief factor in this change was the prevention of private trading and of private loans to princes, fixed salaries being assigned and the system of commissions abolished. The new salaries were on a very generous scale, though without pensions.[3]

Lord Cornwallis, under Pitt's Act of 1784, exercised far greater powers than Hastings had enjoyed, and was soon able to make his authority felt. He was master in his Council, and had the most drastic powers over the Company's servants, including the right to make each official submit, under oath, an inventory of all his property before leaving India.[4] Cornwallis supplemented this by dismissing and expelling several higher officials, while he was equally strict with the 'inter-

[1] Cornwallis had strong views on this subject, which he expressed in a letter to Dundas, June 18, 1792. 'It is very difficult for a man to divest himself of the prejudices which the habits of twenty years have confirmed, and to govern people who have lived with him so long on a footing of equality. But the Company's servants have still greater obstacles. . . . The wretched policy of the Company . . . has driven all their servants to the alternative of starving or of taking what is not their own and . . . the world will not submit tamely to be reformed by those who have practised it in the smallest degree.'—Ross, *Correspondence of Lord Cornwallis*, ii. 172.

[2] To John Motteau, December 17, 1787.—Ross, *Correspondence*, i. 306.

[3] Limitations imposed by the Act of 1773 suggest the scale of salaries. Six years service was necessary before holding an office of £1500 a year, and twelve before holding one of £4000. The amounts were reduced in 1813, but early salaries were supposed to compensate for loss of trading rights and the tradition of high salaries for senior officials survived when their original purpose was forgotten.

[4] 24 Geo. III, c. 25, cl. 55.

lopers', or private European traders. These, if they wished to live outside Calcutta, had to sign a bond making themselves amenable to the local court of justice. Within a few years the English population of Bengal had been brought under control. The cleansing of the Madras Settlement proved a harder task, and was not accomplished until Lord Wellesley made it his headquarters during the war with Tipu. The administration had been entirely corrupted by the gigantic swindle of the Nawab of Arcot's [1] debts, in which nearly every Englishman of standing was involved. The occasional man who stood out from the ramp paid for it, even when he happened to be a Governor. (Lord Pigot, who opposed it, was arrested by his own subordinates, and died in prison.) This deplorable business must be briefly explained.

Muhammad Ali had early withdrawn from Arcot, and established himself in a superb palace in the outskirts of Madras. Here he lived out his long life, on credit (in the strictly financial sense of the word, and no other) and by roguery; 'nearly every traveller who visited him was favourably impressed'.[2] Even in 1754, he possessed 'a truly majestic countenance tempered with a good deal of pleasantness and good nature'; [3] in 1780, in maturity, he

' looked on a newly arrived European with such a look of majesty blended with sorrow, as one could not behold without compassion and regret'.[4]

He lived lavishly and splendidly, employed Europeans about his person and in the House of Commons, and had a guard commanded by 'a European captain, two lieutenants and six cornets'. 'Asiaticus', who is usually understood to be Warren Hastings's agent, Major Scott (Waring), testifies:

' He keeps a very splendid court, where the English meet with every mark of attention and are often preferred to very lucrative posts about his person.' [5]

A huge mob of creditors and alleged creditors held him in perpetual siege:

' The Nabob receives everybody with politeness, apologizes for his want of punctuality (in paying), which he attributes to the loss of Tanjore, and repeats the hackneyed tale of the cruel treatment which he has received at the hands of Lord Pigot.' [6]

[1] Muhammad Ali was Nawab of the Carnatic, but was usually described as Nawab of Arcot, after the name of his capital. He was thus described by Burke in his famous speech.
[2] T. S. P. Spear, *The Nabobs*, 131.   [3] Surgeon Ives, *A Voyage to India*, 70-1.
[4] Innes Munro, *Narrative of the Military Operations in the Carnatic in* 1780-4, 62.
[5] *Memoirs of Asiaticus*, quoted by Spear, 131.
[6] F. Johnson, *Oriental Voyages*, 74.

Burke styled him 'a shadow, a dream, an incubus of oppression';[1] and a dream he must have seemed, a dignified nightmare, too absurd to be true, too painful not to be true. He and his 'creditors' were 'not adversaries, but collusive parties'; the business was

' under a false colour and false names. The litigation is not, nor ever has been, between their rapacity and his hoarded riches. No; it is between him and them combining and confederating on one side, and the public revenues, and the miserable inhabitants of a ruined country, on the other'.[2]

His 'debts' arose out of a long-continued series of dealings with Company's servants, prominent amongst whom was a certain Paul Benfield, with the Nawab. They 'advanced' sums of money, and received *tuncaws*, assignments of the land revenues of the country over which the Nawab was titular ruler. What actually happened was that the 'creditors' skinned the inhabitants and divided the spoil. The debts, bearing nominal interest at 36 or 48 per cent., became speculative investments, dependent upon whether the Company could be persuaded to recognise their validity and assist in collection. Benfield, for example, while a junior architect in the Company's service, had the effrontery to petition the Madras Council for assistance in recovering the sum of £230,000, which he claimed from the Nawab. From these debts grew up the corrupt 'Indian interest' in English politics, of which Benfield was a prominent organiser. Six Members of Parliament were believed to be in the Nawab's pay, and many prominent politicians invested in the 'debts'. Benfield was twice dismissed, in 1770 and 1778, but on each occasion used his wealth and influence in England to get himself reinstated.

Both Cornwallis and the Directors were anxious to end the scandal of the debts. They knew its effect on the administration, and the ruin which the absentee Nawab was causing in his territories. They were, however, hampered by sinister influences in England, and by lack of support from the two responsible Ministers, Pitt and Dundas. The Act of 1774 provided that the Directors should examine the origin of the debts. These could be divided into three main blocks. Two of these were probably legally valid, but the largest—the so-called Consolidated Loan—would never have stood examination. When the Directors set about this work they were stopped by the Board of Control, which insisted on recognition of the whole debt, and this action was supported by the Ministry. The matter was the subject of a famous speech by

[1] *Works*, Bohn's Standard Library, iii. 179.
[2] *Op. cit.* iii. 193-4.

Edmund Burke in the House of Commons, but the 'Indian interest' had done its work well in that hopelessly venal Parliament. The speech was never answered. The debts, which were discussed with the cynicism of the time, continued, and the Nawab grew more deeply involved each year.

When Cornwallis came to India, he called the debts 'fraudulent and infamous claims', and discouraged their taking over by the Company.[1] He is cited in a despatch of Wellesley's to Muhammad Ali's successor (April 24, 1799):

' These loans have usually been accompanied by assignments of territory to the creditors, whose vexatious management of the revenues assigned has been the continual cause of the most aggravated calamities to the inhabitants of the Carnatic.

' In these transactions the loss has fallen on your Highness, your subjects, and your friends, and the illicit profit has enriched those who (to use the words of your respected father addressed to Lord Cornwallis) "never approach your Durbar for any other purpose than to pursue their habitual views of plunder and rapine." '

Cornwallis could do little except prevent the further spread of this evil amongst the Company's servants. He refused promotion to anyone who was a creditor of the Nawab, and sent Benfield and some others home in 1788. Benfield continued his activities in England, his name appearing or disappearing from the list of the Nawab's creditors as seemed most expedient at the moment.

At last Pitt and Dundas made an arrangement by which, between 1784 and 1804, the debt was paid off by instalments of £480,000 annually. At the end of that period it was discovered that the Nawab and his English friends had quietly accumulated another debt of 30 millions sterling. This a commission of Bengal civilians, who need not be suspected of undue austerity by modern standards, examined between 1805 and 1814, and rejected over 19 millions out of 20 millions. The last of the debt was settled in 1830, with the singular conclusion that less than 3 millions of over 30 millions were found valid. Mr. Roberts remarks that the earlier debt, which had been allowed, was almost certainly no less vulnerable to detailed scrutiny, had that been permitted; and that the finish is the strongest possible

' justification of the censure passed on this vast administrative scandal by

---

[1] Cornwallis wrote to Dundas on November 4, 1788. 'Yet I can have no doubt that we must think alike about them' (the Nawab's creditors) 'and that you only consented that their fraudulent and infamous claims should be put into any course of payment because you could not help it.'—Ross, *Cornwallis Correspondence*, i. 237.

Burke and Cornwallis . . . at a time when all other statesmen conspired to minimize and conceal it'.[1]

The debt which Pitt had paid was a transfer to the Company's 'rebellious servants' of a 'debt contracted in defiance of their clearest and most positive injunctions', a 'most enormous usury', involving in interest alone annual charges of £623,000, 'more than double the whole annual dividend of the East India Company, the nominal masters to the proprietors in these funds'.[2]

The efforts of Cornwallis were chiefly directed towards preventing further corruption and ridding India of the worst offenders. It is regrettable that so much energy, over so many decades, of men so able and noble, had necessarily to be deflected from administration and put into what can only be called sanitary work. The process continued under his successors, and a notable advance was made when Wellesley—who condemned vigorously and constantly the manners and dishonesty of officials still sent out at boyish ages to form their characters in the worst school in the world—founded the Fort William College, in which the young gentlemen were to spend three years in remedying any defects that existed in their education, by studying Indian languages, law and history. Satisfied with having surveyed the absurdities and errors of the existing system in a minute (July 10, 1800), he characteristically neglected to get the Directors' sanction, and just went ahead. The Directors vetoed the scheme, and a long and bitter dispute followed. Wellesley managed to get support from the Board of Control—from Castlereagh in particular—and succeeded in procrastinating suppression for a few years, during which the college played a part with other activities and tendencies of the times, in raising steadily the level of British administration. The Directors, confronted by the Governor-General's contumacy supported by the Board of Control, had the satisfaction of getting in one good shot:

' In our opinion Marquis Wellesley would have best consulted his own dignity, and set an example to the service, at least equal in importance to any lesson it could have derived from the College, by a regular obedience to that authority under which the Law had placed the government of India.'

But such obedience was not in Marquess Wellesley's character. The college survived until 1830; and Haileybury College was founded, 1805, to provide special education for India in England.

---

[1] *India under Wellesley*, 100.   [2] Burke.

A special word must be given to Cornwallis's Permanent Settlement of Bengal, Bihar, and Benares. He put this through with the help of Jonathan Duncan (placed in charge of Benares) and John Shore, especially the latter. In 1790-1 the land revenues of these districts were Rs. 34,53,000 (£420,000) for Benares, and Rs. 2,68,00,000 (£3,400,000) for Bihar and Bengal. Shore, who did most of the hard work of collecting information, wanted to substitute for annual assessments assessments lasting ten years. Cornwallis decided to make an unchangeable settlement and assessment, and to recognise the *Zemindars*, who were hereditary rent-collectors, the Government being the landlord, as the actual owners. This settlement, which to-day hardly anyone will defend, and Indians denounce without measure, up to thirty years ago was believed by most Nationalist writers (for example, Romesh Dutt) to be almost the only good thing the English had done; they were scolded for not having done it everywhere. Its evils were that the *Zemindars* were given a big property not theirs, and relapsed into a selfish, careless class; and the Government obtained a small settled revenue, which should have been an expanding one. Its main justification was that Cornwallis was faced with a country in ruins:

' I may safely assert that one-third of the Company's territory in Hindostan is now a jungle inhabited only by wild beasts.' (Minute, September 18, 1789.)

His arguments were such as we hear to-day, when 'confiscatory' or 'class' taxation is inveighed against. Would a ten-years' lease (he asked the Directors) encourage cultivation, when improvements would result in an enhanced (and uncertain) demand upon those who had made them? He was sure Bengal needed, above everything else, stability and surety; and perhaps he was right.

In this settlement, as in other arrangements which we can now see were mistaken, the English worked on false analogy with their own land. It was easy to see the *Zemindars* as squires.[1] Similarly, Cornwallis enacted that defaulting *Zemindars* could be sold up. This meant that a man's whole family might lose their hereditary position for a temporary difficulty. Great landholders became ruined, including such semi-royal families as Dinajpur, Rajshahi, Nadiya, and Vishnupur, and wrong was inflicted which the people still remember, seeing their impoverished

[1] Lord Cornwallis's Permanent Settlement was 'a measure which was effected to naturalise the landed institutions of England among the natives of Bengal' (Sir Richard Temple, *Men and Events of My Time in India*, 30).

descendants. 'The effect on the peace of the countryside was then disastrous, and probably is still felt.' [1]

A mass of contemporary literature makes it possible to reconstruct the life of Europeans in India during the early days of the nineteenth century. Most of them slipped easily into the lazy, dissipated habits which had already overcome so many northern invaders of the peninsula. The covenanted servants came out as boys of sixteen or seventeen, and until Wellesley's time no arrangements had been made to train them, either at home or in India. It is sometimes contended that they understood the country better than their successors. One source of knowledge they possessed. It was customary to keep Indian mistresses, but it is doubtful whether this brought any great respect for the Indian race, or much interest in its customs. [2] From the time of Sir William Jones, the erudite judge who codified the law for Lord Cornwallis, the Company had at its disposal a succession of keen Orientalists, but they were men who lived apart from the bulk of their fellow-countrymen. The latter did not rapidly alter their habits or their outlook. Many had completely assimilated Hindu ideas of caste, which they combined with a strong objection to the introduction of Christianity into India. The European community bitterly opposed the earlier missionaries, like Carey, partly because they came from the poorer classes, but chiefly because they might have a disturbing effect on Indians. The Vellore Mutiny of 1807 was ascribed to their activities, and the official recognition of Christianity was attacked in language which now seems incredible. [3]

Sir G. O. Trevelyan, writing from India shortly after the Mutiny, has left a description of life in Wellesley's time which can be fully corroborated from contemporary sources, and has an additional vividness because traditions of those times must have still survived. Talking of Mrs. Sherwood's novels, he says:

' Her pictures of a Mofussil station, of a merchant's household in Calcutta,

[1] *Oxford History of India*, 567. Whenever Vincent Smith writes on revenue and administration he is admirable; and his discussion of the Permanent Settlement deserves close study.

[2] Williamson's *The East India Company's Vade Mecum* was a semi-official textbook, published in 1810. It gives details of the cost of such an establishment. The Indian mistress received Rs. 40 a month.

[3] Charles Marsh, a leading Madras barrister, protested solemnly against countenancing 'these low and base-born mechanics . . . crawling from their original destinations, these apostates from the loom and anvil, these renegades from the lowest handicrafts'. It is surprising that he omitted the carpenter's bench.

of an indigo factory among the jungles in the days when Lord Wellesley was Governor-General, are well worthy of careful study. Our knowledge, derived from other sources, fully bears out her vivid descriptions of the splendid sloth and the languid debauchery of European society in those days—English gentlemen, overwhelmed with the consequences of extravagance, hampered by Hindoo women and by crowds of olive-coloured children, without either the will or the power to leave the shores of India. . . . Great men rode about in state coaches, with a dozen servants running before and behind them to bawl out their titles; and little men lounged in palanquins or drove a chariot for which they never intended to pay, drawn by horses which they had bullied or cajoled out of the stables of wealthy Baboos. . . . As a natural result there were at one time near a hundred civilians of more than thirty-five years standing who remained out here in pledge to their creditors, poisoning the principles of the younger men, and blocking out their betters from places of eminence and responsibility.' [1]

Paradoxical as it may seem, this very degeneracy was one of the chief reasons why Lord Cornwallis and his successors tended to keep all the higher offices in the hands of Europeans. The decay of the Mogul Empire was a terrible warning, which was always in the minds of the earlier Indian administrators. Governor-Generals, coming straight from England and shocked by the habits of their countrymen, would naturally think that the only hope of saving the Empire was to bring out trained and uncorrupted men from England. As Cornwallis wrote to the Court of Directors,[2] 'I think it must be universally admitted that without a large and well-regulated body of Europeans, our hold of these valuable dominions must be very insecure'. There is also some force in the argument used by Kaye, that

' it was not so much that Cornwallis and his advisers mistrusted the native, as that they mistrusted the European functionaries. . . . He saw that the native functionary in the hands of his European colleague, or superior, might become a very mischievous tool—a ready-made instrument of extortion—and he determined, therefore, not to mix up the two agencies so perilously together'.[3]

It is unfortunate that the first Indians whom the Company should have taken into its service were drawn from a much-conquered race living in an enervating climate, and lacking the moral fibre which would have enabled them to stand up against individual Europeans or *Zemindars*, even when these should be engaged in illegal transactions. We must date from Cornwallis the definite europeanisation of all the higher

---

[1] *The Competition-Wallah* (1864), 238.
[2] Cornwallis to Court of Directors, August 18, 1787.—Ross, *Correspondence*.
[3] See Kaye's *Administration of the East India Company*, 420.

N

posts in the administration. By the time that the two main arguments in its favour had ceased to have any force the process had gone so far that there were vested interests and much prejudice against its reversal.

In a very short time, the native inhabitants of British India were left without any worthy objects of ambition. Their only chance of rising to anything better than positions of humiliating subordination was service in Indian States, a sphere which rapidly contracted.

This change of policy can be seen clearly in the sphere of justice. Under Warren Hastings and Macpherson the criminal courts, outside Calcutta, were staffed by Muslim officers, administering Muslim law; the official language was Persian, and Oriental punishments, such as mutilation and branding, were habitually inflicted. European Collectors only acted as committing magistrates. Cornwallis, before leaving England, received certain instructions about reforming these courts, but the only alteration in his first Regulations of 1787 was to empower European Collectors to deal with minor offences, and inflict corporal punishment 'not exceeding fifteen rattans, or imprisonment not exceeding fifteen days'. For three years the Governor-General consulted with judges and officials, and on December 3, 1790, he produced the new Regulations, which were to be the basis of criminal administration for the next forty years. The preamble explained the changes as due to 'the numerous robberies, murders, and other enormities which have been daily committed throughout the country'. The old courts were swept away. In their place four Courts of Circuit were set up, each under two judges chosen from the covenanted civil service. By these the Company assumed criminal jurisdiction in Bengal (1790). Cornwallis told the Directors: [1]

' Your possessions in this country cannot be said to be well-governed, nor the lives and property of your subjects to be secure, until the shocking abuses and the wretched administration of justice in the Foujdary department can be corrected.'

Part of this abuse was the principle of Islamic law that no Muslim could be capitally convicted on the evidence of an infidel:

' In order that Hindoos and the classes of people not of the Mahomedan persuasion (who form at least nine-tenths of the inhabitants of your territories) may enjoy equal security of person and property with the Mahomedans, we have thought proper to abolish a distinction, the absurdity of which is too glaring to require a comment.' [2]

[1] November 17, 1790.　　　　[2] August 25, 1792.

In 1793 he established four provincial Courts of Appeal, each under three judges, at Patna, Dacca, Murshidabad, and Calcutta. These judges were also Judges of Circuit; the old Courts of Circuit were done away with. He ordered that there should be two jail-deliveries in every year, and in the cities at shorter intervals still.

Muslim law was still administered, but was modified by the Regulations, in the matter of validity of infidel evidence and in other ways. Restrictions were placed upon the right of the heir of a slain man to pardon the murderer, and imprisonment was substituted for mutilation.[1] There was little interference with Indian customs, even where these clearly offended European susceptibilities, but it is possible to trace the beginning of a revulsion against certain Hindu rites in the evidence given some ten years later, when the working of the criminal and civil courts was reviewed by a commission. The first step in the direction was taken by Lord Wellesley, who made illegal the dedication of children to the sacred water at Saugor Point, and thus established a precedent for the abolition of 'suttee' by Lord William Bentinck.

Apart from minor changes, the general structure of the criminal courts remained unaltered until 1831, when the system was revised by Bentinck. It had degenerated by that time, but in these earlier years it was probably an improvement on the older methods. The Courts of Circuit held their jail-deliveries at regular intervals, and there was not the accumulation of arrears which became such an unhappy feature of the civil courts. The weakness of the criminal administration lay in the detection of crime, and Lord Cornwallis entirely reformed the police system in 1792. Each district was divided into *thanas* under the charge of a *daroga*, and these were under the direct control of the district judge. The *Zemindars* were deprived of all police authority. In 1808 Superintendents of Police were appointed in three districts, and in 1827 this organisation was extended throughout the province. The so-called *thanadari* system has survived till to-day, and is probably the most efficient basis for police work. It has not been successful in Bengal, partly because of physical conditions, partly from the lack of popular support in the eradication of dacoity. This has remained a characteristic of Bengal throughout the British occupation. In 1852 Lord Dalhousie complained that gang-robberies were increasing, and Sir Bhupendranath Basu observed to Mr. Edwin Montagu in 1918 that even in the 'eighties he knew 'very respectable men who went the greater

[1] On the basis of seven years' hard labour instead of the loss of one limb, and fourteen instead of the loss of two.

part of the journey stark naked in order to show the dacoits that they had no money on them'.[1] The prevalence of dacoity was one of the main arguments used in favour of the Partition of Bengal, and the revival of political dacoities during recent years shows how strong is the tradition. Elsewhere the *thanadari* system has been the basis of a cheap and fairly effective police force.

Radical changes were also made in the administration of civil law. The system as left by Warren Hastings had two defects. The Collectors who presided over the district courts were neither skilled in law nor interested in this work, which lay outside and additional to their ordinary routine. Also they might be tempted to misuse their position, either to defend their actions as revenue officials or to further their private interests. Although private trading was forbidden, it had been on too large a scale to cease immediately, and it was known that some Collectors still retained commercial interests through their friends.[2] The only advantage of Hastings's rough and ready system was that it did little to encourage litigation. Cornwallis was actuated by two motives, both unimpeachable in theory. He wished to make civil law cheap and accessible, and have a well-defined law administered by disinterested judges. Accordingly in 1793 he issued a new set of Regulations, re-enacting nearly all his criminal reforms of 1790, but entirely altering the system of civil jurisdiction. He appointed twenty-eight judges in the districts, and further strengthened the four Courts of Circuit, which now became also civil courts of appeal. Below these were a number of Indian *Sadar Amins* and 'Commissioners', the Munsiffs of a later date, and these heard minor civil cases. The judges were European civil servants, entirely divorced from all revenue work, and every effort was made to give them a superior standing to the Collectors. They took over the Collectors' magisterial work, and committed minor cases to the Courts of Circuit. At the same time Cornwallis attempted to codify the existing law and procedure into the form of Regulations, a work in which that remarkable Orientalist, Sir William Jones, was to take a leading part. It was an honest attempt to establish the rule of law by men who had an exaggerated respect for the English legal system and little knowledge of the character of the Indian population.

Lord Cornwallis's reforms did not have the same devastating effect as the Regulating Act of 1773, but they led to a very severe outbreak of

---

[1] *An Indian Diary*, 138.
[2] See H. Beveridge, *A Comprehensive History of India*, ii. 575.

litigation, which was only partially checked by reviving the old system of the deposit-fee, which had been abandoned. By 1802, nine years after the formation of the new courts, the European district judges had heard 8298 cases, but had over 12,000 cases pending, while the Indian Commissioners and 'Registers' had heard 342,184 cases, and had 149,827 cases on their files. It was a period when the law's delays were a proverbial source of misery and oppression in nearly every civilised country, but in Bengal these evils were intensified by the existence of professional informers and witnesses, by the small regard felt for perjury, and by the litigiousness of the *Zemindars*, who found in the law a suitable outlet for their energies. Their combativeness was not absorbed, as in other countries, by the development of their estates or by sport.[1] Reading through a mass of evidence given before various parliamentary committees, one gains the impression that the Cornwallis reforms in civil and criminal law were effective in checking the tyranny of the revenue collectors and preventing violence, but that they encouraged the more subtle oppression of the money-lender and the lawyer; and from their insistence upon formal evidence they increased the difficulty of suppressing organised dacoity.

CHAPTER III

FINAL DEFEAT OF TIPU SULTAN

Lord Wellesley on Sir John Shore: a solitary Governor-General: the subsidiary system: French mercenaries: Tipu's intrigues: the last Mysore War: fall of Seringapatam and death of Tipu: the Nizam's methods of collecting revenue: Wellesley and his honours: campaign against Dhundia Wagh: pacification of Malabar: rivalries of military and civilians: settlement of Mysore.

IN May, 1798, Lord Mornington, whom for convenience, following usual practice, we will speak of by his family name of Wellesley, arrived,

---

[1] Many Indian writers object to the idea that a love of litigation is a national characteristic. A landed aristocracy, unless otherwise occupied, will quarrel amongst themselves, and the above remark applies only to the small proportion of the population who are land-owners. The authors have discussed this question with Indian lawyers, and have no doubt that there is a tendency to regard a law-suit as a kind of tourney, increasing the dignity and standing of the contestants. One might find parallels in Europe, but not to the same extent.

accompanied by his brother Henry as private secretary. He was only thirty-seven years old, and brought to his work a never-surpassed energy; a vigour and centralisation ensued, in which, as in many other features, his rule anticipated Lord Curzon's viceroyalty. His despatches are stiff, verbose, dull, void of sympathy, humour, or imagination. But the mind behind them was merciless in pursuit of a few clear aims.

He found enough to set right, and wrote in a tempest of exasperation of 'the folly of having placed Sir John Shore' (now happily occupied with evangelical affairs in England) 'in the government-general':

' His low birth, vulgar manners, and eastern habits, as well as his education in the Company's service, his natural shyness and awkwardness, added to indolence, timidity, and bad health, contributed to relax every spring of this government from one extremity of the empire to the other; and at the seat of the government established a systematical degradation of the person, dignity and authority of the Governor-General. . . . The effect of this state of things on my conduct has been to compel me to entrench myself within forms and ceremonies, to introduce much state into the whole appearance of my establishments and household, and to expel all approaches to familiarity, and to exercise my authority with a degree of vigour and strictness nearly amounting to severity. At the same time I endeavour as much as is compatible with the duties imposed on me by the remissness of Sir John Shore, to render my table pleasant to those whom I admit to it and to be easy of access to everybody. I am resolved to encounter the task of effecting a thorough reform in private manners here, without which the time is not distant when the Europeans settled in Calcutta will control the government if they do not overturn it. My temper and character are now perfectly understood; and while I remain, no man will venture *hiscere vocem*, who has not made up his mind to grapple instantly with the whole force of government.' [1]

He quickly had every subordinate grovelling. We hear no more of mutinous combinations of officers, such as star the records both before and after him. Lake, his Commander-in-Chief in the Maratha War, is terror-stricken when he has to confess that he has weakly given in to his troops' demand that the treasure taken in Agra be divided as loot. He gibbers his gratitude for a few kind words:

' Your letter of the 30th ult. has quite overpowered me, and left me with a most grateful and feeling heart totally void of utterance. Was I to write till doomsday it would be totally impossible for me to express my sensations upon reading your letter, and can only say in return that my life will be too short to convince you by my attachment to you and yours how sincerely I partake in every circumstance that affords you satisfaction and pleasure, and

[1] Quoted by Roberts, 181, from *Historical MSS. Commission*, MSS. of J. B. Fortescue, Esq., at Dropmore, iv. 383.

if by any exertion of mine in carrying your wishes into effect, it can have in any degree proved to the world the expediency of your measures adopted upon such sound policy and judgment, I shall, to the day of my death, rejoice in the utmost that any act of mine can have added to the lustre of your high and exalted character, both public and private. . . . Your kindness has completely debilitated me, and made me shed so many tears of joy. . . . Pray excuse my saying any more, as my nerves are quite unstrung by your affectionate attention. . . .'

Wellesley himself provides the other half of the picture which such letters from the head of the armed forces suggest:

'In the evening I have no alternative but the society of my subjects or solitude. The former is so vulgar, ignorant, rude, familiar, and stupid, as to be disgusting and intolerable; especially the ladies, not one of whom by the bye is even decently goodlooking.[1]

'It is not possible to give an idea of the pleasure which I receive from your letters in this magnificent solitude, where I stalk about like a Royal Tiger, without even a friendly jackal to soothe the severity of my thoughts.' [2]

Though he pushed his brothers Henry and Arthur with a diligence and rapidity that the Directors (and others) thought resembled jobbery, he discouraged undue familiarity from them. The future Duke of Wellington, in particular, wrote to the Governor-General with a dry reserve contrasting greatly with his frankness to his military friends, such as Close, Malcolm and Munro. He and they grumble among themselves, like the spirits under Prospero.

It is well known that Lord Wellesley established firmly what had existed loosely before, the subsidiary system. In exchange for the protection of a British force, States accepted a Resident and general control over external activities. This force was paid for by cession of territory, which *theoretically* had this value for the State protected, that it became safe from vexatious interference on account of non-payment of tribute. The advantages to the British were set out by Arthur Wellesley as keeping 'the evils of war . . . at a distance from the sources of our wealth and our power'.[3] The system 'enabled the British to throw forward their military, considerably in advance of their political, frontier'.[4]

---

[1] Letter of October 11, 1803 (Montgomery Martin, *The Despatches, Minutes, and Correspondence of the Marquess of Wellesley, K.G.*, iii. 397).

[2] Quoted by Roberts, 180.

[3] Lt.-Col. Gurwood, *The Despatches of Field-Marshal the Duke of Wellington, K.G., during his various Campaigns in India*, ii. 613.

[4] P. E. Roberts, *India under Wellesley*, 36.

That is, the native States became catspaws; the military frontier to an uncomfortable degree they found *was* the political frontier also. The discerning among their statesmen were not unaware of the virtues which the Governor-General found in the system; the Marathas in particular shied off it with a pertinacity which to the Governor-General seemed an exasperating form of bad faith, if not actual treason, a contumacy blocking his benevolent exercise of 'general control over the restless spirit of ambition and violence which is characteristic of every Asiatic Government'.[1]

We have seen that the Nizam, deserted by Sir John Shore, who refused to let him use his subsidiary force against the Marathas, had been defeated by them and their French helpers in 1795. He drew Wellesley's incensed attention by building up his own French force. France and Britain were at war; but it was French revolutionary principles that were dreaded even more than French arms. Sindhia (as we know) had numerous Frenchmen in his employment; but they were comparatively good Frenchmen, royalist and conservatively aristocratic in sympathy, commanded by the Count de Boigne, who had begun in Company service and to the end preserved friendly feelings towards his old masters. The Nizam's Frenchmen were a 'nest of democrats',[2] or Jacobins, as the Governor-General preferred to call them; *Jacobin* then meant what *Bolshevist* means now. Wellesley achieved their disbandment, in October, 1798, by a mixture of boldness and persuasion; and the Nizam, who was beginning to get afraid of his Frenchmen, accepted an increase of his British subsidiary force.

Tipu, shorn of half his dominions, had made 'an honourable and unusually punctual discharge' of his huge indemnity. But he cherished an 'inveteracy '[3] which 'will end only with his life';

' there is sometimes a kind of infatuation about Indian chiefs who have lost a part of their dominions, which tempts them to risk the rest in a contest which they know to be hopeless'.[4]

Mysore had shown itself far the most formidable foe the Company had met; no subsequent wars, not even the Mutiny, were to bring them so close to ruin as Haidar's had done. A quarrel was afoot between two adversaries who regarded each other as vermin fit only for extermination. In 1798 Tipu sent envoys to Mauritius, who solicited French help.

---

[1] Quoted by Lyall, *British Dominion in India*, 244.   [2] Sir John Malcolm.
[3] General Harris, June 23, 1798.
[4] Munro, August 12, 1817.   G. R. Gleig, *Life of Sir Thomas Munro*, 247.

The Governor of Mauritius was foolish enough to issue proclamation of the fact; and 150 French and semi-French rabble went to Mysore as volunteers. Wellesley 'was thus afforded a justification, which he eagerly accepted, for the sternest measures'.[1] For some months correspondence went on, of the most sweepingly dishonest cordiality on both sides. Wellesley was held up from instant war by the lack of equal zeal on the part of his subordinates and the difficulties of the Madras Government, which owed 54 lakhs and 4 lakhs of interest. The latter wrote in terms of perfunctory and conventional loyalty indicating their readiness to co-operate, but made it clear that Bengal as usual must furnish all funds:

' Having made the most urgent and repeated applications to you, upon the state of our finances, it is unnecessary to recapitulate the subject here, but in the discussion of war, a matter of so much moment as money cannot be omitted. It is our duty therefore to apprize you, in the most explicit manner, that we must rely solely and unequivocally, upon your Government, for supplies in specie . . . the scarcity of money here compels us to repeat, in the most unequivocal manner, that our means for equipping, as well as for paying the army, must depend upon the supplies of treasure which your Lordship in council may be able to send from Bengal.

' We shall do ourselves the honour of enclosing, for your information, as soon as it can be prepared, a statement of the monthly expense of our own army in the field, together with a statement of the balance of cash in our treasury.' [2]

This spirit Wellesley crushed, in letters blazing with wrath. Presently his brother Arthur, who had been sent to coach the Madras Governor, Lord Clive,[3] was able to issue a satisfactory report:

' He is a mild moderate man, remarkably reserved, having a bad delivery, and apparently a heavy understanding. He certainly has been unaccustomed to consider questions of the magnitude of that now before him, but I doubt whether he is so dull as he appears, or as people here imagine he is . . . at all events, you may be convinced that he will give you no trouble.'

Arthur Wellesley thought war unadvisable:

' If we are to have a war at all, it must be one of our own creating; a justifiable one, I acknowledge; one which we may think necessary, not on account of any danger which we may immediately apprehend, but one which we

[1] P. E. Roberts, *India under Wellesley*, 44.

[2] Montgomery Martin, *The Despatches, Minutes and Correspondence of the Marquess Wellesley, K.G.*, 215-16.

[3] Son of Robert Clive, Baron Plassey.

suppose may eventually be the consequence of this alliance with the French and in order to punish Tippoo for a breach of faith with us.'[1]

But the Governor-General, in face of so many waverers, stuck to his plans:

' I repeat it, I cannot, consistently with any sentiment of duty, consent to rest the security of the Carnatic, in the present crisis, on any other foundation than a state of active and early preparation for war.'

He used the enforced delay to make the conquest overwhelming:

' Deeply as I lament the obstacles which have prevented us from striking an instantaneous blow against the possessions of Tippoo, I expect to derive considerable advantage from the success of that system of precaution and defence which I have been compelled to substitute in place of an immediate war.'[2]

He ordered the Nizam and Peshwa to get ready to fulfil their engagements of alliance. The former responded, the latter procrastinated. Correspondence continued, flowery in the extreme. Tipu exhorted Wellesley to 'gratify me continually with your messages': Wellesley invited Tipu to share his exultation in the French defeat at Aboukir. At last Wellesley was ready. January 9, 1799, he revealed his full knowledge of the pitifully feeble intrigues of a year previously, and Tipu was warned that ' dangerous consequences result from the delay of arduous affairs'.[3] He was advised, while he still had a chance, to receive Major Doveton, who would explain terms on which a lasting friendship might be established. These terms, though Tipu did not yet know this, included not only final and irrevocable dismissal of all French and the reception of an English Resident, but cession of his Malabar sea-coast and of territory to compensate Nizam and Marathas for the annoyance and expense of preparing for war. Arthur Wellesley objected to these as not merely hard, but unnecessary:

' I think it will be difficult hereafter to prevail upon any French to adventure in this country when it will be known that Tippoo has sent away those whom he took into his service under the terms of the most solemn treaty. In the next place, I don't think that we have any right to expect that he should give up territory without a war, which even the most successful war might not enable us to gain.'[4]

[1] Sidney J. Owen, *A Selection from the Despatches, etc., relating to India of Field-Marshal the Duke of Wellington, K.G.*, 41.

[2] Minute of August 12, 1798 (Martin, 204-6).   [3] Martin, i. 394 ff..

[4] Owen, 52 (January 2, 1799).

Tipu reported that he had 'been made happy by the receipt of your Lordship's two friendly letters'.[1] The news of Aboukir

'have given me more pleasure than can possibly be conveyed by writing. Indeed I possess the firmest hope that the leaders of the English and the Company Bahauder, who ever adhere to the paths of sincerity, friendship, and good faith, and are the well wishers of mankind, will at all times be successful and victorious, and that the French, who are of a crooked disposition, faithless, and the enemies of mankind, may be ever depressed and ruined. . . . Would to God that no impression had been produced on my mind by that dangerous people; but your Lordship's situation enables you to know that they have reached my presence, and have endeavoured to pervert the wisdom of my councils, and to instigate me to war against those who have given me no provocation.'

He goes on to his often-quoted and rather pitiful attempt to wriggle out of what had been discovered:

' In this Sircar (the gift of God) there is a mercantile tribe, who employ themselves in trading by sea and land. Their agents purchased a two-masted vessel, and having loaded her with rice, departed with a view to traffic. It happened that she went to the Mauritius, from whence forty persons, French and of a dark colour, of whom ten or twelve were artificers, and the rest servants, paying the hire of the ship, came here in search of employment. Such as chose to take service were entertained, and the remainder departed beyond the confines of this Sircar (the gift of God); and the French, who are full of vice and deceit, have perhaps taken advantage of the departure of the ship to put about reports with the view to ruffle the minds of both Sircars.'

Colonel Wellesley was shown to have been right in maintaining that Tipu would be only too glad to get out of 'the scrape'.[2] But the Governor-General 'swept away ruthlessly and cavalierly, as disingenuous and insulting, the confused and embarrassed letters written to him by his cowering victim'.[3] The time had struck for swift and strong advance; in England, also, things were going splendidly:

' As to our civil and domestic situation it is equal to the proudest wish of our hearts. . . . No democrat dare show his face—Government popular in every alehouse—Our Commerce and revenue flourishing beyond all former example.' [4]

The waters of Tipu's doom sounded continually nearer. His mind settled

' into a hopeless and fatalistic despair. He could not steel himself to make any

[1] December 25, 1798.   [2] June 28, 1798 (Owen, 42).
[3] Roberts, *India under Wellesley*, 57.
[4] Henry Dundas to Lord Mornington, December 29, 1798 (M. Martin, i. 607).

further sacrifice of his already diminished territories. He resembles a sullen and huddled figure, passively awaiting the *coup de grâce* of a victorious enemy. In the vivid narrative of Wilks the form of Tippu stands out against a sombre and lurid background; the fate-laden atmosphere is almost that of Greek tragedy'.[1]

His adversary, exultant in having at his disposal the 'finest army which ever took the field in India', flung his net. He wrote to Lord Grenville (February, 1799): 'I have had the satisfaction to succeed completely in drawing the Beast of the jungle into the toils'. In the same month two armies invaded Mysore; one under General Stuart, from the Bombay side, routed Tipu at Periapatam, the other—which the Sultan hastily withdrew to encounter—routed him at Malaveli. The latter army pressed on to Seringapatam, an extraordinarily swift movement straight to the heart. The story grows Roman in its deepening and calculated and undeviating ruthlessness; Tipu becomes a Hannibal or Jugurtha at bay. 'The dark obstinacy of the Sultan's mind' grew clouded with omens, a battlefield of conflicting superstitions:

' the moolla and the bramin were equally bribed to interpose their prayers for his deliverance, his own attendance at the mosque was frequent, and his devotions impressive, and he entreated the fervent *amen* of his attendants to his earnest and reiterated prayers; the vain science of every sect was put in requisition, to examine the influence of the planets, and interpret their imaginary decision. To all the period for delusion appeared to have ceased, and all announced extremity of peril.' [2]

Making a last appeal to his implacable hunters, he was told (April 27) that he must surrender all his maritime territories and half his dominions besides, and that half of a ruinous indemnity must be paid with the sending of his ambassadors, who must also be accompanied by four of his sons and four generals as hostages. He responded with 'mixed indications rather of grief than rage, finally subsiding into a silent stupor, from which he seldom seemed to wake'. Wilks's description of his council of war when the certainty of destruction could not by any exercise of imagination be any longer hidden is very moving. Crazed with humiliation, Tipu cried that it was 'better to die like a soldier, than to live a miserable dependent on the infidels, in the list of their pensioned rajas and nabobs'. The 'solemn air and visible distress of their sovereign' [3] wrought on his officers, who called out tumultuously and with tears that they would die with him. On the parapet of the besiegers' trench appeared 'in full view of both armies, a military figure

---

[1] Roberts, 51.   [2] Wilks, ii. 363.   [3] *Op. cit.* ii. 353.

suited to such a scene'. It was Major-General Baird, leader of the stormers, embodiment of vengeful memories and pitiless resolution. The columns swept forward (May 4), and Seringapatam was stormed. Tipu, desperately wounded, was killed by a British soldier anxious to detach the gold buckle of his sword-belt:

' to complete our good fortune his body was found among about 500 others piled one upon the other in a very narrow compass. All his family and treasures fell into our hands that night, excepting Futteh Hyder and Abdul Kaliz. The latter came in and gave himself up the next morning'.[1]

His death glutted the conquerors' passion for vengeance, which had been raised to a fever by news that he had strangled prisoners taken in the present campaign. He was allowed honourable burial, this man who had carried into death such a vivacity of hatred that Arthur Wellesley, standing over him in the flicker of torchlight, could not believe him dead until he had felt his pulse and heart. His sons were treated by the Governor-General with kindness; there was nothing of vengeance or indiscriminate cruelty.

Arthur Wellesley, a young colonel of just thirty, who had not been in the actual fighting, was given the extremely lucrative post of commandant in Seringapatam, a cruel injustice to Baird. 'Before the sweat was dry on my brow, I was superseded by an inferior officer.' Arthur Wellesley described for his brother his taking over. As the fighting had been exceedingly severe, so was the final storming, a setting free of pent-up resentments:

' Nothing therefore can have exceeded what was done on the night of the 4th. Scarcely a house in the town was left unplundered, and I understand that in camp jewels of the greatest value, bars of gold, &c., &c., have been offered for sale in the bazaars of the army by our soldiers, sepoys, and followers. I came in to take the command on the morning of the 5th, and by the greatest exertion, by hanging, flogging, &c., &c., in the course of that day I restored order among the troops, and I hope I have gained the confidence of the people. They are returning to their houses and beginning again to follow their occupations, but the property of every one is gone.'

The Commander-in-Chief (Harris) and six general officers were censured in England for their greedy over-appropriation of prize-money. The Governor-General declined £100,000 offered him, on the ground that it was due to the military; and took only a star and badge of the Order of St. Patrick, made of Tipu's jewels. However, the Directors in 1801 gave him an annuity of £5000.

[1] Colonel Wellesley, May 8, 1799 (Owen, 66).

It was universally acknowledged in India that the storming of Seringapatam was a success equal to Plassey that had established the Company as one of 'the country powers'; this made them in fact the Power paramount. It was admitted that this feat of ruthless planning and rapid execution was the Governor-General's achievement, first of all. From perusal of the contemporary literature we get the impression (which is severely accurate) that 'glory' and 'glorious' were the most esteemed words. European literature of this period differentiated much in the varieties of *homo sapiens*, and 'the man of feeling' was a kind much praised. But the 'feeling' did not move beyond a turgid insincerity of response to natural sights catalogued as 'sublime', or such sentiments as we find in the inventor [1] of Ossian. In all the voluminous matter which the historian of Indian affairs must peruse, only Burke (the much-abused Burke) reveals a genuine remorse for what ordinary people endured.

Tipu's memory has been stereotyped into that of monster pure and simple. But his character was 'perhaps unique in Oriental history'.[2] He had a spirit of innovation and curiosity recalling Akbar's; a new calendar, new scale of weights and measures, new coinage, occupied his energy. But he was a bigot, whereas Akbar and his own father Haidar were examples of extreme tolerance. He was determined to extirpate intoxicants and drugs, even forbidding the growth of henna in gardens. Brave himself, he evoked the extreme of reckless loyal co-operation in others. His industry was as unremitting as that of his great opposer, his anxiety to strengthen his country with Western science and achievement was even free from religious hesitations. He was guilty, repeatedly, and against his British prisoners generally, of abominable cruelty. Yet British officers, grown accustomed to the wretchedness and servility of the peasants in their own province of Madras, were astonished by the flourishing condition of Mysore. It was usual then, as in more recent times, to dismiss poverty as self-induced; the poor are notoriously lazy, shiftless and thriftless. The poor of the East, in particular, are incapable, because of climatic rigours, of real application. Sir Thomas Munro, however, declared of the Madras *ryots* (May 10, 1796): 'They owe their poverty to their government, and neither to their idleness nor the sun'. Sir John Shore testified of Tipu, on the other hand, that 'the peasantry of his dominions are protected, and their labours encouraged and re-

[1] James Macpherson, cousin of Sir John.
[2] Roberts, *India under Wellesley*, 57.

warded'.[1] Mr. P. E. Roberts supports this evidence with other evidence from men 'whose normal sympathies would have been pre-eminently British'.[2] A surprising unanimity on this point exists in his conquerors.[3]

There is equal unanimity about the experiences of the wretched people whom we handed over after each war to our faithful ally the Nizam. John Malcolm has left an eye-witness's (his own) account of that potentate's method of collecting revenue (with British assistance): [4]

' The scene which presented itself to the British officer was beyond all description shocking. The different quotas to be paid by each inhabitant had been fixed; and every species of torture was then being inflicted to enforce it. Men and women, poor and rich, were suffering promiscuously. Some had heavy muskets fastened to their ears; some large stones upon their breasts; whilst others had their fingers pinched with hot pincers. Their cries of agony and declarations of inability to pay appeared only to whet the appetite of their tormentors. Most of those not under their hands seemed in a state of starvation. Indeed, they were so far distracted with hunger, that many of them, without distinction of sect, devoured what was left by the European officer and Sepoys from their dinner.'

This is the forgotten background of that never-pausing transference of lakhs to the use of the rajas' and nabobs' and nizams' masters.

Tipu's hatred of the English made his extermination their necessity, and is usually held to justify the distinction that Haidar Ali had just complaint against the Company (but for whose support of their Nawab there probably would never have been the first two Mysore wars), but that Tipu was the offender in the final quarrel. We do not propose to offer any guidance on this question; the relevant facts have been put before the reader. It is admitted that in every particular except energy and personal valour (in the latter he excelled his father [5]) he was inferior to Haidar Ali. Haidar first discussed a matter, and then decided; Tipu reversed the process. His was a temperament which operated by paroxysm and subsidence.

---

[1] Sir John Malcolm, *History of India*, ii. Appendix II. lx-lxi.

[2] *India under Wellesley*, 59.

[3] Owen sums up, xxvi : 'The flourishing condition of the Sultan's dominions, compared to other native territories, had impressed the English at the time of the conquest'.

[4] Quoted from MS. Memoir by Malcolm (*Life*, i. 17).

[5] Wilks says that, though gallant against Indian foes, Haidar shirked personal encounter with his European ones.

We have seen that Wellesley with a fine disdain abandoned the material spoils to the soldiers. It would have been well if he had let his achievement rest thus. But his haughty and imperious spirit, like Hotspur's, was the most covetous of honour of any alive, and by honour his age understood the outward stars which signified it to the world. He wrote to Lord Grenville:

'You will gain credit by conferring some high and brilliant honour upon me immediately. The garter would be much more acceptable to me than any additional title, nor would any title be an object which should not raise me to the same rank which was given to Lord Cornwallis.' [1]

When all he obtained was an Irish marquisate, he went almost out of his wits:

'I cannot conceal my anguish of mind . . . I will confess openly that as I was confident there had been nothing Irish or pinchbeck in my conduct or in its results, I felt an equal confidence that I should find nothing Irish or pinchbeck in my reward.'

He signed this letter (April, 1800) 'Mornington (not having yet received my double-gilt potato)'. The wounded mind continued, with an iteration dreadful to contemplate, to turn in and upon its own exulceration; he writes (May, 1800) of having 'to remain a country gentleman to the end of my days, talking over Indian politics with Major Massacre and Mrs. Hastings, and the Major Majorum, not forgetting Major Aprorum'. Five months later:

'I attribute all my sufferings to the disgust and indignation with which I received the first intelligence of the King's acceptance of my services, and to the agonizing humiliation with which I have since learnt the effect of my Irish honours in every quarter of India. Never was so lofty a pride so abased; never was reward so effectually perverted to the purposes of degradation and dishonour. . . .' [1]

As this generation knows, the heart-burning which accompanies the distribution of decorations after a campaign is felt most fiercely in the breasts of the highest. Such a mind as this was easy to hurt to the quick.

Tipu's family were removed to Vellore, where they were encouraged to occupy themselves innocuously:

'There ought to be no restriction whatever upon the Princes taking as many women, either as wives or concubines, as they may think proper. They cannot employ their money in a more harmless way; and the consideration of

[1] Quoted by Roberts, from Fortescue MSS. Mr. Roberts's admirable study contains much more evidence of this distress of spirit.

the future expense of the support of a few more women, after their death, is trifling. Let them marry whom they please. Their marriages . . . only create an additional number of dependents and poor connexions, and additional modes of spending their money.' [1]

His Muhammadan chieftains had nearly all fallen in battle, a circumstance greatly easing the pacification.

BRITISH INDIA
under Wellesley
1799.

Walker & Boutall sc.

Two minor campaigns completed the cleaning-up. The first was against a Maratha, Dhundia Wagh, whom Tipu had circumcised and then imprisoned; in the final confusion Dhundia had escaped, and was trying to establish some power of his own. He had the distinction of furnishing Colonel Wellesley with his first independent campaign, one carried through with immense enjoyment and complete success. Dhundia's followers were refused quarter, 'for the purpose of deterring others from similar enormities'; and after he had been slain (September,

[1] Colonel Wellesley, in reply to queries from Captain Marriott, in Mysore (Gurwood, i. 733).

o

1800) his conqueror drew this satisfying conclusion: 'We have now proved (a perfect novelty in India) that we can hunt down the lightest footed and most rapid armies as well as we can destroy heavy troops and storm strong fortifications'.

Malabar was pacified simultaneously. The Nairs—'I am informed, gentlemen, and probably the idlest of that character' [1]—Moplahs, and other turbulent inhabitants of the Wynaad and the Malabar highlands had been for many years in standing revolt against Haidar and Tipu. They now found themselves rebels against the British, and the Iron Duke 'was unsparing in the chastisement of red-handed rebellion': [2]

'It will give you pleasure to hear from Piele of our complete success in the Bullum country. We took the Rajah on the 9th, and hanged him and six others on the 10th....' [3]

Chased into his own homelands, the Raja had been captured starving, when he ventured out in search of food. Three hundred of his headmen were collected for what the editor of the Duke of Wellington's Indian papers has styled 'the edifying spectacle of the public execution of the most guilty', related by Colonel Wellesley 'with grim jocularity': 'They witnessed *the suspension* of the Rajah and their brethren'.[4] Colonel Wellesley, however, stood out against the government of a country permanently by what is called military law:

'I am fully aware that the military gentlemen in Malabar are exceedingly anxious to establish what they call military law. Before I should consent to the subversion of one system of law, and to the establishment of another, I should be glad to know what the new law was to be; and I have never procured from any of those gentlemen yet a definition of their own idea of military law. I understand military law to be the law of the sword, and, in well-regulated and disciplined armies, to be the will of the General.' [5]

In all this he had the assistance of Tipu's Hindu minister Purnaya, who showed great energy in obtaining from the Raja before execution a full inventory of his possessions of all sorts and in keeping his headmen hostages until they had paid up two and a half years' revenue. 'Purneah's abilities have astonished me.' [6]

The Marathas had given no assistance against Tipu, and there is

[1] Arthur Wellesley, September 18, 1800 (Owen, 118).   [2] Owen, xxxv.

[3] *Op. cit.* 141-2, February 13, 1802. See also September 18, 1800 (Owen, 118). The Raja had successfully defied the Mysore sultan for many years.

[4] *Op. cit.* xxxvi., xxxvii. Owen calls the scene 'a sylvan tragedy'.

[5] *Op. cit.* 121.   [6] *Op. cit.* 142.

reason to believe that, if the British success had been less swiftly achieved, the Peshwa would have taken the field beside the Sultan's armies. Wellesley, however, offered the Peshwa a share of the annexed territory, which the Poona Resident was instructed to intimate in the following terms:

' You will proceed to inform him that it is my intention, under certain conditions, to make a considerable cession of territory to him, provided his conduct shall not in the interval have been such as to have rendered all friendly intercourse with him incompatible with the honour of the British Government.'

The conditions amounted to an abrogation of independence. He was to accept absolutely the Company's arbitration of all his disputes, present and future, with the Nizam; to promise the perpetual exclusion of the French, and to make a defensive alliance against any French invasion. A subsidiary force was pressed upon him, but as yet not actually commanded. With this offer Nana Farnavis would have closed, but his master, after 'vexatious and illusory discussion', 'faithless conduct', 'temporizing policy and studied evasion',[1] which pained the Governor-General intensely, refused it. The Nizam took his share of annexed Mysore, but with grumblings stigmatised as manifestations of 'the illiberal, rapacious, and vindictive spirit of which I have perceived so many disgusting symptoms at Hyderabad, even since the fall of Seringapatam'.[2]

Arthur Wellesley advised his brother

' not to put the ·Company upon the Mahratta frontier. It is impossible to expect to alter the nature of the Mahrattas; they will plunder their neighbours, be they ever so powerful. . . . It will be better to put one of the powers in dependence upon the Company on the frontier, who, if plundered, are accustomed to it, know how to bear it and to retaliate, which we do not'.[3]

The Company accordingly took the whole of the Mysore sea-board and big eastern strips. A much shrunken, but still large, Mysore was restored to the Hindu dynasty which Haidar had deposed, and became a vassal State. Purnaya as Dewan governed it vigorously and ably, and strengthened Arthur Wellesley's excellent opinion of him. When the latter left India he sent Purnaya his portrait and an exceedingly cordial letter.

Cornwallis, when he annexed half of Tipu's dominions, was hampered by the almost entire absence of officials conversant with any

[1] Martin, ii. 14 ff. Lord Wellesley's descriptions.
[2] *Op. cit.* ii. 63.   [3] June 23, 1799 (Owen, 72).

Indian language; Madras possessed not a single one. The soldiers were better, in every way; and he had used Read and Munro, two admirable men. Yet when Munro later applied to be made permanent in the work he had begun so ably, Cornwallis at first answered 'that he could not venture to interfere, for it would bring all the civilians on his head'.[1] Wellesley, however, resisted the civilians, fortified by his brother Arthur's objection to 'the Madras sharks':

' I intend to ask to be brought away with the army if any civil servant of the Company is to be here, or any person with civil authority who is not under my orders, for I know that the whole is a system of job and corruption from beginning to end, of which I and my troops would be made the instruments.' [2]

The affairs of Mysore were accordingly settled by a band of Commissioners whose brilliance equalled that of the famous band who settled the Punjab fifty years later. They included Arthur and Henry Wellesley —the Governor-General's persistent pushing of his brothers into one first-rate job after another excited the jealousy of officers less fortunately connected, and was one of the causes which roused in the Directors such disapproval and distrust that they finally recalled him—Colonel Barry Close, whom Arthur Wellesley styled 'the ablest man in the diplomatic line in India',[3] and, as secretaries, Munro and Malcolm. India was at last attracting the services of the best class of British; the growing arrogance of the conquerors, which in the next twenty years was to set such deep estrangement between the races, was for a long while mitigated and its results in certain regions postponed, by the labours of men whom both India and Britain should always remember with gratitude. Such men as Malcolm, Metcalfe, Close, Munro, Elphinstone, Tod were the very crown of all that any country in the whole history of empires can show, and their service was unselfish and filled with respect and understanding of the countries they administered. Several of them began their work in these formative and important years.

[1] Gleig, Life of Munro, 64.

[2] May 8, 1799 (letter to Governor-General). Owen, 69.

[3] Owen, 85.

CHAPTER IV

CAMPAIGNS OF ASSAYE AND LASWARI

Nana Farnavis: Arthur Wellesley on Maratha affairs: Maratha dissensions and wars: the Peshwa re-established by the Company: death of Farnavis: Sindhia and the Bhonsla Raja: Lake's and Arthur Wellesley's campaigns: war with Holkar: Nana Farnavis's widow well deserving of a pension: misfortunes in campaign against Holkar: failure before Bharatpur: the Mogul Emperor and Delhi.

DURING the century's last half-decade most of the great leaders of native India passed away, and relationships changed rapidly. The Nizam, after his humiliation in the brief period of his desertion, emerged as the Company's dependent, by his helplessness promoted to, and held rigorously in, a firm alliance very distasteful to him. Ahalya Bai died 1795; her commander-in-chief, Tukoji Holkar, died 1797. Mahadaji Sindhia, who had formed such a queer friendship (if that be the word) for Warren Hastings, died 1794. The new Sindhia, Daulat Rao, was a lesser man, and the new Holkar, Jeswant Rao, merely a reckless guerilla who boasted that his fortune was on his saddle-bow. A new Peshwa, who was to prove a monster of duplicity and cruelty, Baji Rao II, succeeded in 1796.

The greatest Indian statesman of the eighteenth century, Nana Farnavis, through perilous decades had kept his nation, the Marathas, from falling under the Company's all-conquering sway. Courteously and without giving offence adequate for war, he had put by numerous invitations to walk into the parlour where Nizam, and Nawabs of Oudh, Bengal, the Carnatic, and several smaller rulers, were being entertained. Even when the Nizam excited Wellesley's indignation by flirting with the French, the Governor-General noted approvingly: [1] 'Nana has too much wisdom to involve the Mahratta Empire in such desperate connections'. The Nana, however, was imprisoned by Sindhia, and released only after ten lakhs had been squeezed out of him. He came out broken in spirit and health, to take office under a Peshwa who hated and distrusted him. There was a complete slump in Maratha character at this time, an anarchy and desperate wickedness such as followed Ranjit Singh's death in the Punjab, 1839. As in that instance, it led to the coming of the British.

[1] November 12, 1798.

Wellesley had wished to ensure a moderate, but not excessive, enhancement of the Nizam's and Peshwa's strengths, as a counterpoise to Tipu. We are to-day sensitive about the charge that in India we act on the high Roman maxim, *divide et impera*. In the eighteenth century it was statesmanship's normal aim, and no one saw any hurt in it. Arthur Wellesley notes—and his attitude may be taken as that of everyone else, and the reader saved from wearisome iteration:

' There may be some who imagine that the best thing that could happen to us would be to see the Mahratta government crumble to pieces, and upon its ruins the establishment of a number of petty states. With those who think thus I differ entirely. Not only we should not be able to insure the tranquillity of our own frontiers, and could not expect to keep out our enemy, but we should weaken the only balance remaining against the power of the Nizam. This, it is true, is contemptible at present, but in the hands of able men might be turned to our disadvantage . . . we ought to have such a balance as would always keep the Nizam's state in order. With this view the Mahratta power, as it stood prior to Lord Cornwallis's war, ought to be preserved if possible, and we ought with equal care to avoid its entire destruction and the junction in one body of all the members of the Mahratta empire.' [1]

There are ideas in these words which later fuller knowledge caused the writer to abandon—for example, the belief that 'the Mahratta government' was in any way a unitary State on the lines of such governments as European States. Also, Arthur Wellesley was to come entirely over to his brother's frankly annexationist attitude, and to scoff at the notion that Indian States were independent Powers such as those that spent the eighteenth century rearranging the European chessboard; they both later concurred in an entirely reckless and high-handed disposal of their 'allies' and semi-allies.

Historians darken counsel by angrily stressing the wickedness of the Marathas at this time. There is usually, however, some degree of precedence in scoundrelism; and, as we have seen, the Company possessed a flair for supporting the more villainous of rival claimants. They did so now, in Wellesley's incessant meddling with the Marathas; and did it without the excuse of ignorance. In the despatches and correspondence of everyone, the Governor-General included, 'imbecility' in conduct and 'duplicity' in character are the words automatically ascribed to his Highness the Peshwa. From first to last there is no expression, even of the vaguest, to indicate that anyone was ever so hardy as to hope to find

[1] November 19, 1799 (Owen, 191).

in him a glimmer of ability or elementary decency. Nor was it easy as yet for the people of India to distinguish the Company from the other predatory Powers belabouring them. The Company's administration had known a noble interval under Cornwallis; but so had even Indore, home of the robber Holkar, during the far longer rule of Ahalya Bai. We need not take into account questions of moral turpitude, then, except where they definitely influence the course of events.

The biographer of Elphinstone, who was to be the main instrument of British business with the Marathas during so many years, says of Wellesley's Maratha transactions: 'Our interference in their quarrels must be admitted to have been openly aggressive'.[1]

When Nana Farnavis died (March, 1800), 'with him . . . departed all the wisdom and moderation of the Mahratta government'.[2] He had private virtues equal to his public abilities: 'a man of strict veracity, humane, frugal and charitable'. He died with a mind filled with foreboding for the ruin he saw coming on his people. It came swiftly. By treachery Baji Rao obtained the person of Jeswant Rao Holkar' brother, and amused himself watching him being trampled to death by an elephant. This deed broke up what little chance there might have been of a united Maratha front. Jeswant Rao swept up to Poona (October, 1802), and routed Sindhia and his brother's murderer. The Peshwa fled to Bassein and applied to the British for assistance (December). Colonel Close negotiated the Treaty of Bassein (1803); the Governor-General had found the pretext for interference which he had sought so long and assiduously:

' This crisis of affairs appeared to me to afford the most favourable opportunity for the complete establishment of the interests of the British power in the Mahratta empire, without the hazard of involving us in a contest with any party.' [3]

Wellesley had only one quality of greatness—tremendous driving power and concentration towards an end. He went through his time in India without picking up a single new idea, acting throughout on the analogy of the European governments which he knew before coming out. From first to last remote from the truths of the Indian situation, he judged aloof in doctrinaire fashion, so rigorously repressing any

---

[1] Sir T. E. Colebrooke, *Life of Elphinstone*, 39.

[2] Grant Duff, *History of the Marathas* (Oxford University Press, edited by S. Edwardes), ii. 301. Grant Duff is quoting Colonel Palmer, Resident at Poona.

[3] December 24, 1802 (Martin, iii. 6).

approach other than servile and subordinate, that enlightenment could come to him only within strict limits. Holkar, the most vigorous of all the Maratha chiefs, was of illegitimate birth; therefore Wellesley thought 'Holkar's accidental power' something which could be easily set aside. Holkar was in open revulsion from the Peshwa, Sindhia was mainly exercised far outside his home territories (in a prolonged effort to make himself the actual overlord of the Mogul Empire); both were usually rivals. The Gaekwar had long acquiesced in tepid friendship with the Company; the Bhonsla Raja was wavering between Peshwa and Sindhia, and himself claimed the legal headship of all Marathas; the Peshwa theoretically was merely first minister of the Satara Raja. Yet Wellesley writes of 'the constitution of the Mahratta empire', as if the field of concepts covered by the word 'constitution' were one in familiar Indian use, and as if this loosely feudal congeries were an 'empire'! When war became likely, he stressed the urgency of shattering 'the French state erected by M. Perron on the banks of the Jumna'—as if a gang of mercenaries, cut off by the Revolution from France and without access to the sea, and in any case anxious only to make their plunder safe (which could only be, as they well knew, by the Company's protection), really were part of Napoleon's strength and effort! Everyone but the Governor-General knew the facts, but none dare tell him:

' The more I see of the Mahrattas, the more convinced I am that they never could have any alliance with the French. The French, on their arrival, would want equipments, which would cost money, or money to procure them; and there is not a Mahratta in the whole country, from the Peshwah down to the lowest horseman, who has a shilling, or who would not require assistance from them.' [1]

In point of fact, the Marathas were the least dangerous enemies of the Company in India. Referring to Nizam and Zaman Shah (ruler of Kabul, and now in possession of Lahore, and a great bugbear to the British), Arthur Wellesley wrote: 'I am convinced that, were the Mahrattas to overturn both the Mohamedan powers, we should be more secure than at present'.

All India knew that the Company had not a single willing ally, except the petty Raja of Coorg; that even the Nizam, even when helping to break Tipu, was sullen:

' they all do hate him
As rootedly as I'.

[1] Arthur Wellesley to John Malcolm, June 20, 1803.

Yet the Governor-General, though unable to help seeing, by the Peshwa's 'long and systematic course of deceitful and evasive policy', that his new dependent was irked by the bonds of friendship, nevertheless continued to press the other Marathas, Sindhia most of all, 'to partake the benefits of the defensive alliance', the 'improved system' which by the Treaty of Bassein now included their nominal master. Next, Colonel Wellesley, under no illusions—

' there can be no doubt but that the establishment of our influence at Poonah will be highly disagreeable to the majority of the Mahratta chiefs, and that it will interfere materially with the interests of some and the objects of ambition of all'—

escorted the Peshwa back to Poona, and had opportunity of noting the ravage wrought by Holkar; his description we may accept as holding true of every region occupied by Sindhia, Holkar, or the Peshwa:

' They have not left a stick standing at the distance of 150 miles from Poonah; they have eaten the forage and grain; they have pulled down the houses, and have used the materials as firewood; and the inhabitants are fled with their cattle. Excepting in one village, I have not seen a human creature since I quitted the neighbourhood of Meritch.' [1]

He goes on to say, as he said repeatedly, that sooner or later Holkar was bound to invade the Nizam, if only for subsistence. Indeed, the Maratha War was inevitable, if only because the Company's immense sweep forward had so circumscribed the territory within which that people could levy toll. The Nizam's dominions were their ancient hunting-ground, and now neither furnished *chauth* any longer nor plains for pillage. The robber-State, whose original 'constitution' had been forced on it by necessity and approved by Hindu India suffering under Aurangzeb's bigotry, was in the position of a strong man forced to bay by a far stronger.

Nevertheless, the Governor-General did not wish for a Maratha war. He longed to gain certain advantages, the destruction of 'the French state', the retreat of Sindhia out of Hindustan (which would give the Company a wide connecting band of territory between Bengal and Oudh), a similar retreat of the Bhonsla Raja from Orissa (thereby connecting Bengal and the Sarkars and Carnatic), and the definite recognition of the Company as entitled to settle all disputes between Marathas and Nizam. The queer thing is that he thought he could persuade the Maratha feudal chiefs to enter into these desirable arrangements volun-

[1] To the Governor-General, April 21, 1803 (Owen, 224).

tarily, and that his political thinking was so stereotyped and rigidly bound within European precedents that he believed that a treaty negotiated solely with the detested Peshwa would be meekly accepted by his 'subordinates'. His brother Arthur, writing to his fellow-officers with a freedom that he never ventured upon with 'My dear Mornington' (latterly, far more stiffly, 'Sir' and 'Your Excellency'), very soon had the right sow by the ear:[1]

' The greater experience I gain of Mahratta affairs, the more convinced I am that we have been mistaken entirely regarding the constitution of the Mahratta Empire. In fact, the Peshwa never has had exclusive power in the state: it is true, that all treaties have been negotiated under his authority, and have been concluded in his name; but the chiefs of the Empire have consented to them; and the want of this consent, on the part of any one of them, in this case, or of power in the head of the Empire, independent of these chiefs, is the difficulty of this case at the present moment.'

The Peshwa was 'a cipher, without a particle of power'. General Wellesley had

' long been accustomed to view these different Mahratta governments as powers not guided by any rational system of policy, or any notion of national honour, but solely by their momentary fears or loss or hope of gain.'[2]

There was, however, no question of their universal distrust of the Company, especially since Tipu's fall; and no question of the anger felt by even the smallest jagirdars at the Peshwa's treason in concluding the treaty making him a subsidiary. Resentment of that treaty was the direct cause of war; and it came because Sindhia made the mistake of thinking too much of former successes of the Marathas, in Hastings's time, and under-assessing the Company's enormous advance in strength.

Colonel Collins, a pertinacious but not tactful negotiator, warned Sindhia not to consult with the Bhonsla Raja, who had approached within eighty miles of his camp. Sindhia replied with insulting negligence:[3]

'Dowlut Rao . . . said that he could not at present afford me the satisfaction I demanded without a violation of the faith which he had pledged to the Rajah of Berar. He then observed, that the Bhooslah was distant no more than forty coss[4] from thence, and would probably arrive here in the course of a few days; that, immediately after his interview with the Rajah, I should be in-

[1] To Malcolm, June 20, 1803 (Owen, 243).
[2] To Lieut.-Col. Collins, June 29, 1803 (Owen, 250).
[3] May 29, 1803 (Martin, iii. 163).
[4] A *coss* is two miles (there or thereabouts): the measure varies.

formed whether it would be peace or war. These words he delivered with much seeming composure. I then asked him whether I must consider this declaration as final on his part, which question was answered in the affirmative by the ministers of Dowlut Rao Scindiah. . . . Neither Scindiah, nor his ministers, made any remarks on the treaty of Bassein, nor did they request a copy of it.'

The Governor-General was naturally indignant; but his considerable patience with Sindhia contrasts with his ruthlessness towards Tipu. But there was no trace of the irreconcilable hatred that both parties to the Mysore War had cherished. British and Marathas had on the whole been humane foes, and the Marathas had been sometimes casual yet sufficiently useful allies. War, however, was plainly inevitable, and soon followed, between the Company and Sindhia and the Bhonsla Raja. Holkar held aloof, sulky and conceited; the Gaekwar gave some help to the Company, and the Peshwa, after much procrastination, furnished 3000 men (without any funds to pay them).

The Company sent out four different armies. Those from Bombay and Bengal easily overran Gujarat and Orissa. Lake's army in the north defeated Perron at Aligarh, August 9, and the much-dreaded French officers came tumbling in, as fast as they could escape, and surrendered. Sindhia had to fight on without them, with that army of which Munro said: [1] 'Its discipline, its arms, and uniform clothing, I regard merely as the means of dressing it out for the sacrifice'. The Aligarh 'battle' had been a ridiculous affair, and the operations which ended in Aligarh's capture (September 4) cost altogether only 265 casualties. But the battles of Delhi (September 11) and Laswari (November 1) cost 962 and 824 casualties respectively; of the latter action, Lake wrote: [2]

' These battalions are most uncommonly well appointed, have a most numerous artillery, as well served as they can possibly be, the gunners standing to their guns until killed by the bayonet, all the sepoys of the enemy behaved exceeding well, and if they had been commanded by French officers, the event would have been, I fear, extremely doubtful. I never was in so severe a business in my life or any thing like it, and pray to God I never may be in such a situation again; their army is better appointed than ours, no expense is spared whatever, they have three times the number of men to a gun we have, their bullocks, of which they have many more than we have, are of a very superior sort, all their men's knapsacks and baggage are carried upon camels, by which means they can march double the distance. . . . These fellows fought like devils, or rather heroes.'

[1] But he had the advantage of prophesying after the event (March 6, 1804).
[2] Report to Governor-General (November 2, 1803) (Martin, iii. 445).

After his victory before Delhi, Lake had secured one of the main objectives of the Governor-General, the person of the Emperor, who is regularly listed along with territories, etc., as if he were an inanimate piece of loot. He found him, a poor blind old man, seated under a tattered canopy. This was the 'Shahzada' to whom Clive and Hastings had paid such ostentatious respect.

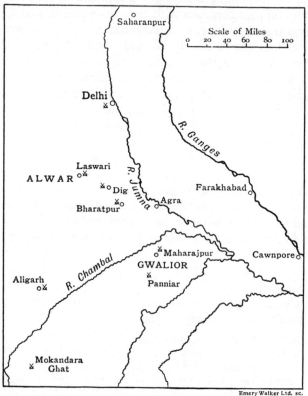

LORD LAKE'S CAMPAIGNS; AND MARATHA WAR OF 1843.

Agra fell without a storm, October 17. Compelled to surrender to his army 24 lakhs taken with its fort, Lake wrote abjectly to the Governor-General: [1]

' The army certainly expected the money, or I would not have given it them, and I think they had deserved it. I hate all money concerns, and sincerely wish I had nothing to do with this; I have ever held money in most sovereign

[1] October 22, 1803 (Martin, iii. 414).

contempt, and shall I am sure do so to the end of my life. I have only to hope I have done nothing which can displease your Lordship, as that would take from me all the satisfaction I have received from our late successes.'

It must be remembered that anything found in a city taken by storm was held to compensate the victors for their perils and exertions; Agra had not been stormed, but these Indian armies were desperate men (the Duke of Wellington has left his opinion on record) and different from the Marathas and other 'free companies' only in discipline of valour. Mutinies were frequent, even among the officers, and provoked quickly, especially by anything that touched what were considered legitimate perquisites.

Meanwhile, the southern army, under Arthur Wellesley, on August 11 stormed Ahmadnagar, and on September 23 won the hardest fight of the combined campaigns, at Assaye, with a loss of 2070 men, the stiffest fight in British-Indian history before the Sikh Wars. There was not much strategy about it:

' Somebody said, "Sir! that is the enemy's line". The General said, "Is it? Ha, damme, so it is!" (you know his manner) and turned. . . . The 74th (I am assured and convinced) was unable to stop the enemy; and I know that the sepoys were huddled in masses, and that attempts which I saw made to form them failed; when "the genius and fortune of the Republic" brought the cavalry on to the right. They charged the enemy, drove them with great slaughter into the Joee Nulla, and so saved the 74th . . . the cavalry, which had then crossed the nulla, charged up its bank, making a dreadful slaughter but affording a most delightful spectacle to us, who were halted on the side nearest the field of battle unable to cross on account of our guns. . . . The General was going to attack a body of the enemy (from their left, I believe), who, when we had passed them, went and spiked our artillery and seized our guns, and recovered some of their own, and turned them all against our rear, which annoyed us a good deal. When the General was returning to the guns there was a heavy fire, and he had his horse killed under him . . . the General passed the night, not in "the pride, pomp and circumstance of glorious war" but on the ground, close to an officer whose leg was shot off, and within five yards of a dead officer. I got some curry and bloody water, which did not show at night, and lay down and slept without catching cold.' [1]

A triumph so overwhelming softened the Governor-General into brotherly cordiality: [2]

' MY DEAR ARTHUR,
        You will conceive the pride and delight with which I received the details of your most splendid victory';

[1] Letter, September 27, 1803; *Life of Mountstuart Elphinstone*, 67 ff.
[2] Letter of October 27 (Owen, 305).

and General Wellesley, having vaguely arranged a suspension of hostilities with Sindhia, proceeded to complete his work by scattering the Bhonsla Raja's forces at Argaon (November 29), where Sindhia's cavalry joined in a half-hearted resistance:

'I had no narrow escapes this time, and I felt quite unconcerned, never winced, nor cared how near the shot came about the worst time; and all the time I was at pains to see how the people looked, and every gentleman seemed at ease as much as if he were riding ahunting.' [1]

War was passing into the knightly amusement which only the Sikh and Gurkha campaigns were to mar with roughness: 'I stopped to load my pistols. I saw nobody afterwards but people on foot, whom I did not think it proper to touch'.[1] Gawilghar was stormed (December 15). The Bhonsla Raja sued for peace, and then Sindhia. The Company gained an immense accession of territorial solidity, the Marathas being driven right off the Orissa coast and the Ganges valley. Both Maratha rulers became subsidiary princes.

Sindhia's overwhelming defeat had been largely due to his wars with Holkar, which had much weakened him; still more, to the Western training he had given his troops, which had resulted in a strengthening of his infantry at the expense of his cavalry. In the wars of this period cavalry were the determining arm. Arthur Wellesley with accustomed accuracy says: [2]

' Scindiah's armies had actually been brought to a very favourable state of discipline, and his power had become formidable by the exertions of the European officers in his service; but I think it is much to be doubted whether his power, or rather that of the Mahratta nation, would not have been more formidable, at least to the British government, if they had never had an European, as an infantry soldier, in their service, and had carried on their operations in the manner of the original Mahrattas, only by means of cavalry.'

He therefore thought (in this, as in an increasing number of questions, differing from the Governor-General) that Sindhia should be allowed to keep European assistance and advice; and 'they should be encouraged to have infantry rather than otherwise'.[2] For the present, the British had routed Sindhia and the Bhonsla, and saved their excellent Peshwa:

' It is proper that the Peshwah should be informed, that, from the highest man in his state, to the lowest, there is not one who will trust him, or will

[1] Elphinstone (*Life*, i. 89).
[2] Letter to Major Shawe, November 18, 1803 (Owen, 356).

have any connexion or communication with him, excepting through the mediation, and under the guarantee, of the British government.' [1]

He 'has no public feeling, and his private disposition is terrible'; was without subjects,[2] except when a British force was actually at his back; and had no desires except money for sensual pleasures, and that what he called 'rebels' should be caught by his protectors and handed over to his vengeance. The Deccan, after ten years of depredation, was in a famine, 'which, in my opinion, will destroy half its inhabitants',[3] for which famine Holkar, 'the most formidable of the three supposed confederates', was mainly responsible.

De minimis non curat lex; and Mars cares as little. Before the campaign against Sindhia, the Governor-General had ordered British subjects in his service to leave him. Some had then served against Sindhia, and the local knowledge and guidance of one in particular had been extolled loudly by both Commander-in-Chief and Governor-General. Holkar forbade his British officers to leave him, and gave them the choice between serving him against their countrymen (which meant military execution if they were captured or he were defeated) and death. They chose death, and were beheaded. Even in watching the fate of kingdoms we may spare a thought to those so pitifully placed, and record the names of men both gallant and unfortunate: Captains Todd, Ryan and Vickars.

This was in December, 1803. Holkar proceeded to drift into a war in which he proved what General Wellesley knew already, that the natural Maratha warfare was far more dangerous than the acquired methods; that acute observer added that Holkar showed further that there was 'no frontier' in India, especially against Marathas. Lake wailed, of the drawn-out hesitations that preceded actual warfare:

' I never was so plagued as I am with this devil; he just, nay hardly, keeps within the letter of the law, by which means our army is remaining in the field at an enormous expense.'

General Wellesley noted the necessity in all Indian wars (and again, particularly against Marathas) of having a part of the people on your side. Lake, too, looked longingly towards their late enemy: 'Sure I am that the only mode of meeting this reptile would be some decisive

[1] Arthur Wellesley, January 24, 1804 (Owen, 365).
[2] Arthur Wellesley, letter to Colonel Close, May 12, 1804 (Owen, 393).
[3] Arthur Wellesley, May 13, 1804.

measure on the part of Scindiah'. Sindhia, however, smarting under recent humiliation and perfectly aware that the effective part of a campaign against Holkar (and the price exacted by that reptile) must fall on him, though he sent a body of horse did not help very cheerfully or earnestly.

'I do not think', General Wellesley wrote to Malcolm (August 24, 1804),[1] 'that the Commander-in-Chief and I have carried on the war so well by our deputies as we did ourselves'. Holkar's war, which ought not to have been 'more than a Polygar war',[2] developed into a series of nasty reverses. Wellesley's deputy and Lake's deputy, Colonels Murray and Monson, were both afraid of Holkar,[1] and both 'fled from him in different directions'. 'Monson advanced without reason, and retreated in the same manner.' He had followed Holkar through the territory of Rajput princes who desired British protection; had stormed a few hill forts, and then, finding himself in the heart of Central India with only two days' provisions, fell back, was pursued, lost his rearguard, held his ground against an attack before Mokandara ghat, moved north again through black cotton country bogged with the heavy rains of July, spiked and abandoned his guns, and concluded a much-harassed retirement by reaching Agra, August 30. General Wellesley's cool analysis of the episode and its 'important military lessons to us all' moved Sir Robert Peel to say that he considered it 'the best military letter he had ever read' and its author 'the most powerful writer in the English language'. He may not have been quite that; but his despatches and letters at this period show that he understood perfectly all that there was to know about Indian warfare. He was much more, but he certainly was what Napoleon called him, a sepoy general—the best sepoy general that ever lived. The inept campaigns of Murray and Monson, in the latter's case the disastrous campaign, went far to undo all that the campaigns of Assaye and Laswari had achieved. The Governor-General showed a noble magnanimity:

'I trust that the greater part of the detachment is arrived at Agra, but I fear my poor friend Monson is gone. Whatever may have been his fate, or whatever the result of his misfortunes to my own fame, I will endeavour to shield his character from obloquy, nor will I attempt the mean purpose of sacrificing his reputation to save mine. His former services and his zeal entitle him to indulgence; and however I may lament or suffer for his errors, I will not reproach his memory if he be lost, or his character, if he survive.'

[1] Owen, 425.

[2] General Wellesley, March 26 (Owen, 420). A polygar was a small South Indian chief, such as the Bullum Raja.

Lake, meanwhile, was almost in despair, following 'this monster' (his usual name for Holkar). Lord Wellesley refused to admit that Holkar had any right to rank as a prince, or anything but a bandit to be hunted down and hanged if caught; and during 1804 there was much talk about supporting 'the just rights' of his legitimate brother, Kasi Rao, who (if we may take Arthur Wellesley's opinion as reasonable) would have made a worthy addition to the Company's protégés:

' He is an infamous blackguard, despised by everybody, full of prejudices, hatred, and revenge, and without one adherent or even a follower. By adopting his cause we shall burthen ourselves with the defence and support of another weak and helpless power, we shall disgust Scindiah's government, and we shall not give satisfaction to the followers and adherents of the Holkar family. The act will be abstractedly generous; but considering that Cashee Rao was concerned in the murder of his brother, it will be to support usurpation founded on murder, and, for the reasons I have above mentioned, highly impolitic.'

General Wellesley found time, amid his greater affairs, to call on Nana Farnavis's widow (according to Lord Valentia, 'really a very pretty girl, fair, round-faced, and apparently seventeen years of age'[1]), in the remote fortress where she had taken refuge; and on his recommendation she was given a pension. 'She is very fair and very handsome, and well deserving to be the object of a treaty.'[2] He offered his escort back to Poona, which was respectfully declined; and wrote her letters which, nearly fifty years later, then a little old woman living in semi-squalor, she brought out proudly, to show to a Governor of Bombay's lady.[3]

The Governor-General had to moderate his private feelings about Holkar. His energy was flagging; he was not 'inveterate' (to use the current term) against Marathas, not even against Holkar; and the Directors were writing letters [4] which, while coldly congratulating him on his successes, made it plain that they understood the Maratha chiefs' want of enthusiasm for the Peshwa. But it is easier to start a war than to end it properly. The unlucky Monson was able presently to send word that he and his immediate superior, General Frazer (who died of wounds received in the action), had managed to bring Holkar to bay under his fortress of Dig (November 13, 1804) and rout him. There was also a cavalry victory at Farakhabad; a glance at the map will give some

[1] *Voyages and Travels to India, Ceylon, the Red Sea, Abyssinia, and Egypt*, 173.
[2] Letter to Colonel Close, May 18, 1804 (Gurwood, ii. 1187).
[3] Lady Falkland. See her book, *Chow-Chow*, edited by H. G. Rawlinson, 135.
[4] See particularly the letter of March 6, 1804 (Martin, iv. 227 ff.).

P

notion of the way that Holkar was ranging over an enormous extent of Northern India, queerly enough with the support of the populations by whose pillage he subsisted. But Monson, having won a great victory, found force of habit too much for him, and fell back 'for supplies':

'He might have spared a battalion or two to have fetched them. . . . It is somewhat extraordinary that a man brave as a lion should have no judgment or reflection. . . . It really grieves me to see a man I esteem, after gaining credit in the extreme, throw it away in such a manner immediately.' [1]

Sindhia, too, was discontented; and he had an accumulating tale of grievances. In February, 1805, he sent the Governor-General a long and unusually frank communication: [2]

'As the war with Holkar, in consequence of the officers of your Excellency's troops thinking too lightly of it, has now run to a great length, and my territory has been exposed to the last degree of devastation, and as . . .'

He and the Bhonsla Raja were thinking that if they had only sunk their differences with Holkar, instead of first being beaten in detail and then serving as catspaws, they might have escaped being thrust into the position of subsidiary rulers. The Raja of Bharatpur had already decided to join the successful freebooter, news which was received with an outburst of rage and contempt. Lake added a 'P.S.' to a letter to General Wellesley: 'The Bhurtpore Rajah has behaved like a villain, and deserves chastisement; a very short time would take his forts'. The Governor-General ordered the annexation of his State. And Monson, though his supersession had been commanded, was allowed to lead assaults on Bharatpur Fort, which after repeated failure cost over 3000 casualties. Bharatpur acquired, and kept for a quarter of a century, a reputation as impregnable.

In April, 1805, Lake made peace with the Bharatpur Raja. But Sindhia grew more and more threatening. His father-in-law, Sarji Rao Ghatkay, 'the worst scoundrel of those evil days',[3] who lived till 1809, when a Maratha chief 'transfixed him with his spear, and thus rid the world of a being, than whom few worse have ever disgraced humanity', obtained a complete ascendancy in his counsels, and in his detestation of the British launched Sindhia on what the Governor-General with reason

[1] Lake to the Governor-General, November 19, 1804 (Martin, iv. 245-6).

[2] October 19, 1804 (Martin, iv. 222).

[3] Oxford History of India, 597.

styled a course of 'menace and defamation'. Sarji Rao was in intimate collusion with Holkar:

' There is no vile act these people are not equal to; that inhuman monster Holkar's chief delight is in butchering all Europeans, and by all accounts Serjie Rao Ghautka's disposition towards us is precisely the same.' [1]

It came close to renewal of war. The Governor-General replied to Sindhia's long letter of complaint with counter-charges, couched in terms of sternest severity, and instructed Lake to prepare for hostilities. Sindhia took fright just in the nick of time; Sarji Rao's influence underwent an eclipse.

An increasing tiredness showed in the Governor-General's writings, and an increasing tolerance and even gentleness in his communications with native princes. His arrangement with the Mogul Emperor was humane and generous, and we may dwell upon it with pleasure. This unfortunate monarch, though indigent and powerless in the extreme, was consistently treated with unique respect. He alone was 'His Majesty', and not merely 'His Highness'; by the eighteenth century, tenaciously holding to the titles of legitimacy and transmitted monarchy, he was scrupulously held to be apart from the temporary tribe of freebooting Marathas and usurping Mysoreans. Wellesley carved out a small kingdom surrounding Delhi for him, and allotted him and his family revenues. The British Commissioner at Delhi was responsible for administration and collections; but both were to be done in His Majesty's name, and Muhammadan courts were to be instituted. It should be noted that events had, as a matter of fact, caused the British to suspect a deeper resentment and enmity in the Mussulman part of India, than in the Hindu. By depressing Mussulman viceroyalties in Bengal and Oudh and the Carnatic, by extirpating Mysore's strong Muslim rulers, they had upset what balance of power existed in India and sunk the Mussulmans towards that decline and dependence which the Mutiny completed, and from which their recovery has been so recent. Wellesley's action in giving the Emperor (who previously possessed nothing) at least revenues and a name of majesty was conciliatory and did something to restore the balance, at least of repute and self-respect. The royalty thus established was deeply cherished by the Muhammadan population. It meant something to be able to see in their midst a court, however idle and merely specious, which recalled their vanished greatness.

[1] Lake to the Governor-General, April 25, 1805 (Martin, iv. 531).

Let us note, too, that in his instructions for the new Mogul State Wellesley inserted this explicit clause, from the law of British India:

' No criminal must in future suffer the punishment of mutilation, under sentences of the courts to be established in the assigned territory. When a prisoner shall be sentenced under the Mahomedan law to lose two limbs, the sentence must be commuted for imprisonment and hard labour for the term of fourteen years; and when the sentence shall adjudge the prisoner to lose one limb, it is to be commuted for imprisonment and hard labour for seven years.'

CHAPTER V

PEACEFUL ANNEXATIONS AND POLITICAL READJUSTMENTS

Tanjore: Surat: Duncan's settlement of Kathiawar: Wellesley and Oudh: annexation of the Carnatic: Wellesley's asperity in despatches to native States: his wisdom in the matter of the Company's trading monopoly: Wellesley recalled.

IT was Wellesley's 'conscientious conviction, that no greater blessing can be conferred on the native inhabitants of India than the extension of the British authority, influence and power'. Dundas, however, wrote (March 21, 1799) of the States which had enjoyed longest the advantages of intimate supervision of their affairs, with a studied moderation which should not deceive us as to the thorough contempt entertained, even in late eighteenth-century England, for the Company's administration and morals:

' The double Government existing in the Carnatic has long been felt as a serious calamity to that country. It enfeebles the natural resources of the country, and, above all, tends to continue that system of intrigue and consequent corruption which has been imputed to the Madras Government so much more than to our other settlements. It is singular to remark, that the country of Oude is the other part of India, where the purity of the Company's servants has been most suspected, and that the same circumstance of a double government has always been assigned as the cause. ... Tanjore ... is exposed in a certain degree, to the same inconveniences which have been injurious to the government of the Carnatic.'

In the case of Tanjore, it would be depressing to recall even a few of the events that justify Mr. Roberts, who never exaggerates, in his conclusion that 'our connection with the country had not, on the face of it, been particularly creditable either to our statesmanship or our good faith'.[1] To take the story up in its closing chapter, in 1786 the Company, acting by the advice of pundits, chose a villainous lunatic as Raja. He was deposed after some years of mischief, and Wellesley inherited a disputed succession:

' After a most tedious enquiry, I brought the several contending parties to a fair discussion (or rather to a bitter contest) in my presence; and after an argument which lasted three or four days, I proceeded to review the whole case. . . . At length the contending parties unanimously concurred in the expediency and justice of the treaty',[2]

which ended Tanjore's existence as even nominally a sovereign State (October 25, 1799) and pensioned the candidate formerly passed over in the madman's favour.

Earlier in the same year the Nawab of Surat died. The Company, by arrangement, since 1759 had defended Surat Fort. So Wellesley annexed the State under a justification anticipating Dalhousie's 'lapse' doctrine; he ruled that, when the Company displaced the Mogul Empire in any district, it acquired the right to settle the fate and successions of principalities formerly under Delhi.

The Governor of Bombay, Jonathan Duncan, carried out the annexation unwillingly. His own practice went to the other extreme; by recognising as 'princes' all *Zemindars*, however petty, who paid tribute to the Mogul, he studded Kathiawar with the multitude of kinglets that are one of the most striking anomalies in the princes' question to-day; His Highness of Bikaner is reported to have stated that one of the Kathiawar 'princes' is sovereign of nothing but a well. Historians condemn Wellesley's action:

' The whole proceeding was characterised by tyranny and injustice';[3] 'the most unceremonious act of dethronement which the English had yet performed as the victim was the weakest and "most obscure" ';[4] 'the procedure was certainly high-handed'.[5]

But it was justified by results, and also by the situation of Indian affairs. When maintenance of a legal right means the community's abiding disadvantage, the paramount Power does well to act illegally.

[1] *India under Wellesley*, 111.
[2] Wellesley to Dundas, March 5, 1800 (M. Martin, ii. 247).
[3] H. Beveridge, *A Comprehensive History of India*, ii. 717.
[4] Mill, *History of British India*, vi. 207.
[5] Roberts, *India under Wellesley*, 114.

Oudh was a more complex problem. Its defence was a Company liability; and in India, as the Duke of Wellington observed, there was no frontier. In Wellesley's early despatches, the threat of Zaman Shah, ruler of Kabul, recurs frequently. He established himself in Lahore, 1796; returned to Afghanistan the next year, but in 1798 reappeared and notified the Nawab of Oudh and the Governor-General that they were to assist him in restoring the Emperor and rescuing him from the Marathas:

' he should consider our not joining his royal standard, and our not assisting him in the restoration of Shah Allum and in the total expulsion of the Mahrattas, in the light of an act of disobedience and enmity'.[1]

Insurrections in his rear caused this hectoring gentleman to retreat again; and in 1800 he was dethroned and blinded by his brother, and became a refugee in British India. Ranjit Singh, later famous as 'the Lion of the Punjab', presently succeeded to more than his power.

Meanwhile Oudh compelled attention from Wellesley. For years it had been drained of 'the maximum tribute which it could afford';[2] it was overrun by rascally Europeans, and 'behind the all too powerful screen of British bayonets' was oppressed and pillaged. The subsidiary system 'meant the sacrifice of independence, of national character, and of whatever renders a people respectable'.[3] But Wellesley's main concern was not for the misery of the people of Oudh; hardly any statesman of the period bothered about the flesh and blood actuality which the abstract maxims of statesmanship concealed. His main concern was the menace from Afghan invasion, to which the rabble which formed the Oudh army was a first line of defence. Therefore, though Oudh was bled white by what it had to pay already—for

' the subsidy demanded from Indian rulers was totally out of proportion to their revenue. In the subsidiary armies the scale of pay was lavish, and the cost of quarters and equipage high' [4]—

he demanded that the Nawab entertain a much larger body of Company's troops, sufficient to be 'at all times adequate to your effectual protection', whose charges could be easily met: 'nothing further is requisite than that you should disband the numerous disorderly battalions at present in your service'.[5]

The cool, breath-taking ignorance behind that advice justifies a

---

[1] Wellesley to Sir J. H. Craig, September 16, 1798 (Martin, i. 262).
[2] Roberts, *India under Wellesley*, 117-18. [3] *Life of Sir Thomas Munro*, 249.
[4] Roberts, 37. [5] November 5, 1799 (Martin, ii. 134).

minute's pause. All the Nawab had to do, to settle all his difficulties finally, was to 'sack' all his own retainers! The Governor-General's brother Arthur, on the other hand, comments continually on what was notorious to every intelligent inhabitant of India, British or Indian— the hardships and harms following from Indian loss of all honourable or lucrative employment:

' Conceive a country, in every village of which there are from twenty to thirty horsemen who have been dismissed from the service of the state, and who have no means of living except by plunder. In this country there is no law, no civil government. . . . This is the outline of the state of the countries of the Peishwa and the Nizam ' (1804).

Even the Governor-General in less lucidly self-complacent moods could see something of the undercurrents of resentment, as when he writes to the Directors (April 22, 1799), on a conspiracy nipped in time at Benares:

' You will observe that the persons concerned in this treason are almost exclusively Mahommedans, and several of them of high rank. It is a radical imperfection in the constitution of our establishments in India, that no system appears to have been adopted with a view either to conciliate the good will or to controul the disaffection of this description of our subjects, whom we found in possession of the Government, and whom we have excluded from all share of emolument, honour, and authority, without providing any ade- quate corrective of those passions incident to the loss of dignity, wealth, and power.'

What 'adequate corrective' *could* be applied, and what thought (if any) lies behind such verbose and confused lucubrations as these (so characteristic of authority when its attention is vaguely drawn to some stirrings of dissatisfaction in the administered sections of mankind), it would be idle to stop to enquire.

By 1799 Wellesley's mind was set on annexing Oudh. Unfortunately, the Nawab somehow or other managed to keep up his huge payments of tribute, and, though endowed with every possible fault from his subjects' side, was embarrassingly loyal. Wellesley therefore merely badgered him to accept 'an improved system' of government; the pro- poser's power and pertinacity made this suggestion an order, though the Nawab knew it meant additional costs for 'protection'. In Novem- ber, 1799, he said he wished to abdicate—he meant, in favour of one of his sons. Wellesley was delighted. His Excellency, he told the Directors,[1]

' appears to have adopted the resolution . . . upon the maturest deliberation.

[1] November 28, 1799 (Martin, ii. 154-6).

Your honourable Committee will observe that his Excellency declares this resolution to have originated in the reciprocal aversion subsisting between himself and his subjects (an aversion, which, on his part, he declares to have grown into absolute disgust), and in his sense of his own incompetency. . . .'

If His Excellency 'should ultimately persevere in this declared intention' —and

' it is my intention to profit by the event to the utmost practicable extent; and I entertain a confident hope of being able to establish, with the consent of the Vizier, the sole and exclusive authority of the Company within the province of Oude and its dependencies, or at least to place our interests in that quarter on an improved and durable foundation'—

then 'it must be deemed entirely and absolutely his own voluntary act'. The Company had long been past-masters of the art of making some vacillating Indian potentate, anxious only to evade decision, sign the order for his own execution. But that Governor after Governor should be capable of such contradictory tangles of argument, and while plainly flaunting his own vivacity of pursuit and inflexibility of will should nevertheless assert that everything was done by the victim's free will, so that his after-wrigglings were arrant treason and 'Oriental' duplicity, helps us to understand why our dealings on the imperial stage have so often been misunderstood by foreigners as hypocritical. What followed was a repetition of earlier pages in Company history. The Nawab was offered a treaty; he pointed out that nothing was said about his successor; he was informed that there would be no successor, whereupon he 'formally withdrew his offer of abdication',[1] and the Governor-General was 'extremely disgusted at' his 'duplicity and insincerity'. The delinquent received a letter remarkable even from the most arrogantly sure of his rightness of all Indian Governor-Generals. Waterloo, no doubt, was won on the Eton milling-grounds; but the Empire's administration was certainly learnt in a less public but even more terrible place. Wellesley, in letter after letter, ruffles like the indignant headmaster about to flog a boy after scathing exposure first of his sinfulness:

' The duty imposed on me by my public station, and the concern which I take in your Excellency's personal honour and welfare, as well as in the prosperity and happiness of the inhabitants of Oude, compel me to communicate to you, in the most unqualified terms, the astonishment, regret, and indignation which your recent conduct has excited in my mind.'

The reader will note that nothing of the time-honoured formula is

_____
[1] Roberts, *India under Wellesley*, 124.

omitted; the castigation is for the castigatee's good, and is obviously going to hurt the castigator worse.

' The conduct of your Excellency . . . is of a nature so unequivocally hostile . . . that your perseverance in so dangerous a course will leave me no other alternative than that of considering all amicable engagements between the Company and your Excellency to be dissolved, and of regulating my subsequent proceedings accordingly. I am, however, always inclined to hope that your Excellency may have been inadvertently betrayed into these imprudent and unjustifiable measures by the insidious suggestions of evil councillors, and being ever averse to construe your Excellency's actions in such a manner as must compel me to regard and to treat you as a Prince no longer connected with the Company by the ties of amity and of a common interest; I trust that my next accounts from Lieutenant-Colonel Scott may enable me to view your Excellency's conduct in a more favourable light, but lest my wishes in this respect should be disappointed, it is my duty to warn your Excellency in the most unreserved terms. . . .'

His Excellency was urged to see to the two really important matters:

' namely, the reform of your military establishment, and the provision of funds for the regular monthly payment of all the Company's troops in Oude.
    ' The least omission or procrastination in either of those important points, must lead to the most serious mischief.'

The troops, at any rate, he was to have, whether he wanted them or not. They were sent, 'and he was simply ordered to find money for paying them'.[1] He was told that he could not alter this decision, though he might

' present reasoned objections, to which he replied, not without dignity:"If the measure was to be carried into execution, whether with or without his approbation, there was no occasion for consulting him".' [1]

This, the reader will see, was impertinence; and he completed the offence by pointing out that the disbandment of his own army threw the soldiers out of employment, and was ill-advised enough to reinforce his argument by appeal to his treaty with Sir John Shore. Wellesley found this behaviour 'highly deficient in the respect due to the first British authority in India'. The culprit was accordingly hauled back to the headmaster's study, and told to be very, very careful. If

' in formally answering his lordship's letter, his Excellency should think proper to impeach the honour and justice of the British Government in similar terms . . . the Governor-General would consider how such unfounded calumnies and gross misrepresentations . . . deserve to be noticed'.

[1] Roberts, 125.

In such documents as these (a good many of them exist) the paramount Power does not condescend to anything so essentially base as argument. The conduct in question is always 'unjustifiable', objections are 'calumnies', and of course 'unfounded'. 'If the party injured', observes Mill,[1]

' submits . . . his consent is alleged. If he complains, he is treated as impeaching the honour and justice of his superior, a crime of so prodigious a magnitude as to set the superior above all obligations to such a worthless connection'.

The upshot of a prolonged and tortuous business, in which the Nawab showed surprising spirit and a hunted animal's sense of territory where he stood some chance of safety, was that in November, 1801, he had to cede the territory that Oudh had obtained by the Rohilla War:

' By a singular reverse of circumstances the Company were able, after having pocketed the price, to seize the territories, and thus obtain possession both of price and subject',[2]

'extremely rich and valuable territory . . . known henceforth as the Ceded Provinces', which Henry Wellesley was sent to govern, an appointment which the Directors considered nepotism, though we can believe that the Governor-General's aim was not merely to give his brother a lucrative post, but to be himself in specially intimate touch with the district. The remainder of Oudh became a State more abjectly vassal than any other in India; but there was this gain, that the subsidy ceased. The Company's gains were immense, in security of financial advantages, in strategy, in quietness.

No serious writer has ever pretended that the episode was from first to last anything but a bullying exercise of overwhelming strength. Wellesley did what little was possible to make things easy for the dispossessed soldiery, and even for the Nawab, to whom he had written so insultingly. But it is hard to follow Mr. Roberts when he says that the Governor-General

' looked through the immaterial barriers of treaties and agreements to the wretched condition of the administration of Oudh, which he so eagerly desired to rectify'.[3]

It is true that he refused to regard Indian States as genuinely independent Powers, and with some reason. But there is no justice in yourself 'looking through the immaterial barriers of treaties and agreements' when you explode with fury at every divagation of others from the rigid

[1] *History of India*, vi. 155.   [2] H. Beveridge, *History of India*, ii. 731.
[3] *India under Wellesley*, 135-6.

letter of any and every promise; and as to the 'eager desire to rectify' the miseries of Oudh—after the richest regions had been carved off and added to Company territory:

' The scandalous and shameless misgovernment of the country continued unabated without the slightest improvement until 1856, when the authorities in England insisted on annexation.' [1]

Wellesley's conduct would have been both more honourable and more profitable to both the Company and the people of India (whose interests still had to wait some time before they were considered by the high contending parties) if he had acted straightforwardly on his convictions and made annexation more sweeping and thorough, instead of trying to persuade himself and others, and to assert—with prohibition of any contradiction by the Nawab—that he was keeping promises and engagements.

On July 25, 1801, the Carnatic at last passed to the Company, one-fifth of the revenues being settled on the Nawab as a pension. The annexation was overdue, and justified by every moral consideration; even Mill thinks that, done frankly, it would have been an excellent action: [2]

' we should have deemed the Company justified, in proportion as the feelings of millions are of more value than the feelings of an individual, in seizing the government of the Carnatic long before; and on the same principle, we should rejoice that every inch of ground within the limits of India were subject to their sway'.

But it was not done frankly or decently. At the taking of Seringapatam Wellesley, to his intense glee, secured documents which he held proved treacherous collusion between the Nawab and Tipu. They proved nothing of the sort, and were merely flowery compliments; and the Nawab was so inconsiderate as to die while his conduct was under discussion. This evasion, however, did not disconcert the Governor-General; his son had

' succeeded to the condition of his father, which condition was that of a public enemy . . . consequently . . . the British Government remained at liberty to exercise its rights, founded on the faithless policy of its ally, in whatever manner might be deemed most conducive to the immediate safety and to the general interests of the Company in the Carnatic'. [3]

Wellesley's despatches form what must be the most question-begging and self-righteous body of literature in existence. 'Rights'

[1] *Oxford History of India*, 591.   [2] *History of British India*, vi. 232.
[3] The words are those of the Governor of Madras, 'by and with the authority of the Governor-General' (Martin, ii. 553 ff.).

'founded on' what? On alleged behaviour strenuously denied by the accused and at this very time under alleged investigation. Clause follows clause, every phrase specious and opposed by pleading protest; the protest is not even noticed, the doubtful statement rises instantaneously into a principle established and beyond query, and deductions or supports to it are thrust forward—in the same infallible and unfaltering fashion!

He put round the Nawab's palace a ring of troops, and on the very day of his death demanded that his successor, a boy under age (who 'had succeeded to the condition of a public enemy'), should abdicate the sovereignty. Himself always loud in denunciation of the impropriety he found in the conduct of Indian princes, he acted consistently as if they were blocks of unfeeling wood, queerly warped into wickedness, but having no other semblance of response or responsibility. It is better to drop a matter so depressing to remember.

There remained the ever-overhanging cloud of the Nawab's 'debts', which we have examined in Book III, Chapter II.[1]

To continue to quote the Governor-General's missives to inferior Powers will only exasperate the reader. It was not easy for the Resident at Haidarabad to carry out his orders (June, 1799) to rebuke 'in the most public and pointed manner' a noble who had spoken disrespectfully of the Company's government. Wellesley thought that the culprit should perhaps be deprived of his pension. The Nizam was commanded to be awakened 'to a just sense of the extensive advantages' his connection with the British had brought him. His enemies had been destroyed at little expense to him, and 'from a weak, decaying, and despised state, he has recovered substantial strength . . . and resumed a respectable posture among the princes of India'. His dominions, 'formerly the most vulnerable', were now secure. All true; but hardly tactful. Fortunately, the Residents at the two courts most subject to the Governor-General's asperity were men whose revulsion from the duties so overbearingly inculcated upon them would induce them to soften his speech in deliverance. Major Kirkpatrick at Haidarabad lived and acted as an Indian; Colonel Palmer at Poona constantly condemned the scorn of Indians, which was now the rule. They were treated, he said (1802), 'with a mortifying *hauteur* and reserve'; 'in fact, they have scarcely any social intercourse with us'.

When he moved out of the domain of the Company's relations with Indian States, Wellesley could show a detached wisdom in advance of

[1] See pp. 187 ff.

his time. He tried, without success, to persuade the trading concern who employed him, to abandon a spirit of narrow monopoly that was extremely harmful to British interests. A very small proportion of India's trade with the West was by means of Company vessels; foreign countries, and America in especial, were thrusting into it. English traders, forbidden to do what traders of any nation but their own could do, worked through this foreign shipping. So did Company employees, secretly. Wellesley and Dundas urged that the Company should set aside some vessels for the use of non-Company British trading, to keep immense sums now being lost to aliens. Thus might 'that pre-eminence of wealth and power' (in India) 'which has proved so important to the general interests of the British Empire' be preserved and increased. But selfish views prevailed, especially those of the shipping interest, 'under a most false and erroneous idea that it is prejudicial to their interests'. His far-sighted policy offended the Directors almost more than the expense of his wars did.

Warren Hastings, watching with mixed feelings while Wellesley did all that he had desired to do but for which he had lacked the means and personal position, noted the unwisdom of the latter's habitual scorn of the Company Directors: 'If I was in his confidence I would tell him that civility costs little'. England has never been able to regard India as a matter which came close to her own necessities, except in 1857; and the British Government, occupied with the Continental struggle, could not bring itself to believe that large armies and glorious wars were necessary in India. Assaye faded before the sun of Austerlitz: even Tipu was not the Corsican: the defeat of French men-of-war off Malacca by merchantmen that they intended to plunder, though gratifying to national pride, was not Trafalgar. These Indian wars were costly. These princes that we engaged to support seemed more deserving of being left to such fate as the devious twist of events might bring them. Wellesley was recalled (1805) under a cloud, even amid mutterings of impeachment. But no one wanted to renew the idle show which the persecution of Hastings had provided. The Directors concurred in his observation that 'the disturbances occasioned by Jeswunt Rao Holkar and his adherents have proved a vexatious and painful interruption of tranquillity';[1] saw through his half-hearted assurances that that matter was now practically settled; and were weary of the whole business. Lord Cornwallis was sent back, though in age and failing strength, King Log in place of King Stork.

[1] Letter, March, 1805.

CHAPTER VI

LORD MINTO'S ADMINISTRATION

Death of Lord Cornwallis: Sir George Barlow's administration: abandonment of Rajput chiefs to Marathas: death of Krishna Kumari: character of a 'bureaucracy': Vellore Mutiny: Lord Minto's arrival and character: some 'little wars': Metcalfe's embassy to Ranjit Singh: conquest of Java: a missionary controversy: ecclesiastics and dacoits: the Governor-General's establishment: Sir Charles Metcalfe: the 'white mutiny'.

LORD CORNWALLIS, whose return had been fitfully imminent ever since he left, and whom Pitt 'regarded as an infallible cure for all ills',[1] governed for two months, dying October 5, 1805, at Ghazipur, where he was buried in accordance with his injunction, 'Where the tree falls let it lie'. An excessively sick man, he sought only peace, for which it is the custom to censure him. But the man who has himself seen the squalor and ugliness of war, how wretched in defeat, how melancholy in triumph, is less enthusiastic about it than the man who knows it merely as a sequence of exciting rumours and happy intrigues. The old warrior was so weary of pomp and the trappings of regality, that he rejected the titles of 'Excellency' and 'Most Noble', and all the grandeur of Wellesley's time.

The charge of pusillanimity is brought against him and his immediate successor, Sir George Barlow (who had been senior member of his Council), for abandoning the Rajputs to the Marathas (as Cornwallis and Sir John Shore had formerly abandoned the Nizam, and for the same reasons). It is a shameful enough story; yet these inevitable recoils follow on policies of aggression and vigour beyond a Government's power to sustain. In essentials it does not differ from such later abandonments as those of Assyrians or Druses, after they had been encouraged to show friendliness to British effort in the World War. Wellesley had sown native India with distrust, and piled up indebtedness. It is generally overlooked that it was actually in his time that the process of withdrawal began, in those last days when there was a distinct flagging of energy and outward thrust. When the Maharaja of Jodhpur did not choose to accept the Governor-General's conditions of protec-

[1] *Oxford History of India*, 604. The same comment is made by Marshman (*History of India*, 279): 'Lord Cornwallis was Mr. Pitt's invariable refuge in every Indian difficulty'.

tion, Sindhia had received what looked uncommonly like a direct invitation to handle him in his own way—the Raja being delivered over to Satan, that he might be taught not to blaspheme:

'The British Government has no intention to interfere in any manner between your Highness and the Rajah of Jodepore. . . . Your Highness will act according to your pleasure towards that Raja.' [1]

His Highness did.

Even more did Holkar and his Pathan ally, Amir Khan, act according to their pleasure towards the Rajput chiefs. Holkar, after being harried into the Punjab—the Sikhs neither helped his pursuers nor molested him, but watched the double incursion, and drew conclusions which kept peace between Ranjit Singh and the Company until his death (1839)—was given generous terms by Barlow. His persecutors withdrew to their own territory, leaving the Marathas, hemmed in between Sikhs and Company, to pour out their profligacy of pillage on the confined Rajput area. The oppressed openly put up the plea that the Company had in fact succeeded to the paramountcy of the Moguls, and were under obligation to succour the weak. But the plea went unheeded. Inward decay worked with outward pressure, as commonly in such circumstances. The Rajput rulers were degenerates, and all the barbaric cruelty miscalled Rajput chivalry—such as widow-burning, often on a terrific scale (the saner and humaner Marathas disdained while not actually prohibiting the rite)—was allowed to keep this attractive race on a childishly savage level.

There is generally some one incident, when the affairs of any nation have sunk into squalor, which to men's imaginations seems to fling a torch up against the truth. It came now, in the death of Krishna Kumari, the lovely Udaipur princess, in 1810. When internecine war, fomented by Sindhia and Amir Khan, broke out about the hand of the girl-princess, her father accepted the suggestion that she should drink poison and in that fashion bring his people peace. Her patience and valour and the pity of her passing—though to us this will seem a merciful anticipation of death on some warrior's funeral pyre—have never ceased to stir Indian memory.

Sir George Barlow, after some vacillation, was not permanently appointed. He is usually considered (and was considered at the time) to prove once more the utter unfitness of any Company man to take up the supreme authority. A Governor-General of these antecedents was

[1] April, 1805.

apt to be ill served, from the jealousy of his late equals above whom his new authority had raised him. Also, the Company's administration was already shedding—except in 'frontier' regions, such as the annexed parts of Mysore and Malabar (as, later, in the Punjab of the Lawrences) —its earlier improvised and vigorous character, and was accumulating all the merits and shortcomings ascribed to 'bureaucracy'. The Company man now, said Thomas Munro,

' learns forms before he learns things. He becomes full of the respect due to the court, but knows nothing of the people. He is placed too high above them to have any general intercourse with them. He has little opportunity of seeing them except in court. He sees only the worst part of them, and under the worst shapes; he sees them as plaintiff and defendant, exasperated against each other, or as criminals; and the unfavourable opinion with which he too often, at first, enters among them . . . is every day strengthened and increased. He acquires, it is true, habits of cautious examination, and of precision and regularity; but they are limited to a particular object, and are frequently attended with dilatoriness, too little regard for the value of time, and an inaptitude for general affairs, which require a man to pass readily from one subject to another'.[1]

Barlow had willingly seconded Wellesley's imperial schemes; he was equally ready to support the Directors' new opposite policy of re-trenchment and retreat.

The main event of his brief administration was the Vellore Mutiny. The Madras Commander-in-Chief ordered the sepoys to wear a special and obnoxious turban, trim their beards as directed, and give up caste marks. These 'ill-judged regulations'[2] were considered important enough to risk empire for; Munro told the Governor, Lord William Bentinck:[3]

' However strange it may appear to Europeans, I know that the general opinion of the most intelligent natives in this part of the country is, that it was intended to make the sepoys Christians.'

To us, conscious of our absolute impartiality in religious matters, this general opinion seems silly in the extreme. But in a country which remembered Tipu Sultan's measures to make Hindus Mussulmans it spread easily. A regiment declined to obey the new orders; and when two ringleaders were awarded 900 lashes apiece, the sepoys rose and massacred two European companies. Gillespie raced in with his galloper guns, stormed Vellore, and rescued the besieged survivors.

[1] Gleig, *Life of Sir Thomas Munro*, 279-80.
[2] Munro.   [3] August 11 and September 4, 1806.

The inevitable crop of executions followed. In every detail the episode is a little rehearsal of the Mutiny of 1857, and it thrilled British India with a horror unparalleled until that later event swept it into oblivion. Since Tipu's family and the concomitant swarm of hangers-on of Indian royalty and semi-royalty resided at Vellore, their complicity was suspected, and they were certainly an aggravating factor in what was mainly a Hindu revolt.

Lord Minto, the new Governor-General, passed through Madras when the business was finishing. Like most men who have ever come to India fresh from the outside world, he was surprised by the atmosphere which he found:

' The mutual ignorance of each other's motives, intentions, and actions, in which Europeans and natives seemed content to live, had forcibly struck Lord Minto during his short residence in Madras in 1807. "I do not believe that either Lord William or Sir John Cradock had the slightest idea of the aversion their measures would excite. I fully believe that their intentions were totally misapprehended by the natives." ' [1]

He considered that the Directors made a mistake in recalling the Governor and his Commander-in-Chief; since the chiefs of army and administration were dismissed, the sepoys executed under their orders would be regarded as justified, and be made into martyrs. Here, again, we hear a familiar argument; and are reminded that in almost every period of British-Indian history all strata of opinion have been simultaneously present, the 'diehard' and the 'bolshy', the modern and the medieval.

A devoted friend of Burke, Minto had been one of the managers of Warren Hastings's impeachment. He was a quiet, humane, experienced man: 'of as courtly manners as Lord Wellesley; but though he is less lively, he is far more finished and elegant'.[2] His term was one of steady progress. He modified the policy of non-intervention carried to extremes, but never resumed Wellesley's high-handedness. When Amir Khan, in 1809, invaded Berar, he observed, with that dryness and cool lack of emotion which make his despatches such a welcome change from Wellesley's:

' It has not perhaps been sufficiently considered that every native State in India is a military despotism; that war and conquest are avowed as the first and legitimate pursuit of every sovereign or chief, and the sole source of glory and renown; it is not therefore a mere conjecture deduced from the natural bias of the human mind, and the test of general experience, but a cer-

---

[1] *Lord Minto in India*, i. 369.   [2] Elphinstone, August, 1807.

tain conviction founded on avowed principles of action and systematic views, that among the military states and chiefs of India the pursuits of ambition can alone be bounded by the inability to prosecute them.'

After what may be felt to be this 'glimpse into the obvious' he goes on to note that British interests should be the factor deciding

' whether it was expedient to observe a strict neutrality amidst these scenes of disorder and outrage which were passing under our eyes in the north of Hindostan, or whether we should listen to the calls of suffering humanity';

and referred to the Directors, who replied that they thought non-interference could be carried a great deal too far, a change from their feeling of only a year or two back. Minto had meanwhile chased Amir Khan out of Berar, and occupied his homelands and capital. The Company then relaxed its grasp, and the freebooter was left at liberty to harry people not actually its allies.

Minto's rule was marked by a number of 'little wars', reducing turbulent chiefs in Bandalkhand, and punishing a Travancore outbreak (due to offended religious susceptibilities) in which thirty European soldiers were murdered. He had next to give some attention to Ranjit Singh, who had established a Sikh State in the Punjab and, after conquering the smaller Sikh chiefs north of the Satlej, was threatening those on its southern bank. Charles Metcalfe was sent to him to negotiate an understanding. Metcalfe, in the last Maratha War, when only nineteen, had been General Lake's political officer. Now, at twenty-four,[1] he had won golden opinions, including Lord Minto's: 'he really is the ugliest and most agreeable clever person—except Lady Glenbervie—in Europe or Asia'.

The Sikh Power was regarded as an extension into India of the block of great Central Asian States, vaguely known and distrusted, Afghanistan, Persia, the Turkestan khanates. Russia was beginning to emerge as the main foreign bugbear, but had not yet ousted France from this position, despite Napoleon's naval disasters. The Company kept nervously looking towards Persia and the frontier lands. Malcolm was twice sent to Persia, the first time making a good impression, the second time erring by arrogant demands that the envoys of France and Russia (the latter obviously in a far better position to damage Persia than the far-off Indian Government) be dismissed. It is only fair to remember that in his second visit he was hampered by the presence of a rival embassy, sent direct from England; the Shah not unreasonably kept asking which

[1] Ranjit Singh was three years older.

embassy he was to attend to. Elphinstone (who was one of the great four who are England's glory in the next twenty years—Malcolm, Metcalfe, and Munro (who belonged to an earlier generation) are the other three) was sent to Kabul, 1808, but merely reached Peshawar, where he set up with Shah Suja, the Afghan Amir, who was dethroned shortly afterwards, cloudy but friendly relations which had a deplorable sequel in Lord Auckland's time.

Metcalfe's embassy proved the most difficult and most successful of all. Ranjit Singh was jealous and suspicious; it was true that his aggrandisement had been swift and great, but it was nothing to the progress he had seen made by the Company. Though the young envoy impressed him, he plainly hinted that he did not want him. Metcalfe followed the Sikh ruler about; and his patience and firmness, seconded by Minto's firmness, won, after immense delay. In December, 1808, when Ranjit Singh was sunk in a prolonged debauch, he sent him a severely worded warning that the British Government insisted on taking under their protection the Cis-Satlej Sikh States—Nabha, Sirhind, Faridkote, Patiala. Reading it, the Raja staggered as from 'sudden shock'; the dreaded foreigners were henceforward camped on his doorstep. He spoke humbly to the bearer, Metcalfe's confidential *munshi*; but immediately fled from politics to a Mussulman dancing-girl, conduct which so pained the priests of the Golden Temple at Amritsar that they laid the shopkeepers under an interdict (*hartal*): 'There was a great strife between the Temporal and the Spiritual power; and the former was worsted in the encounter'.[1] Ranjit fled to Lahore, followed by the pertinacious young envoy. Ranjit grew 'careworn and thoughtful'; Hindus were sitting *dharna*[2] at his gates, his people were beseeching a peaceful settlement. His ministers

' tried to reconcile Metcalfe to the eccentricities of their chief; but the English gentleman had answered with becoming firmness that, although the eccentricities were sufficiently apparent, he could not admit that they furnished any justification for his conduct'.[3]

Brought to bay, Ranjit demanded *why* he should have to give up places he had already captured. Metcalfe told him, because the British Government intended to protect them. After a final interview, Metcalfe to his

[1] John William Kaye, *Life of Lord Metcalfe*, i. 289.

[2] Mr. Gandhi's method of putting pressure on those who differ from him, by fasting until they see their error.

[3] *Life of Metcalfe*, 290.

astonishment saw the Raja, with 'surprising levity', a phrase which indicates the psychological dullness which went with such high qualities in so many Company's men, riding his favourite horse, round and round his courtyard. The *Times*, in December, 1839, gave this incident the proper journalistic picturesqueness by making him gallop madly over the confined space; Metcalfe said 'prancing'. Ranjit Singh by his body was trying to expel the demons of anger and perplexity. More interviews followed. Then Metcalfe lost temper and prepared to leave. General Ochterlony appeared on the Satlej; other troops were moving up in support of his contingent. Again Ranjit Singh turned to his courtesans, from which 'pleasant forgetfulness Metcalfe roused him by a missive, which flashed the sunlight into his sleeping face': [1]

' The Maharajah is revelling in delight in the Shalimar gardens, unmindful of the duties of Friendship. What Friendship requires is not done, nor is it doing.'

He demanded his dismissal. Ranjit replied humbly 'that the delights of the garden of Friendship far exceeded the delights of a garden of roses', and Metcalfe got his treaty, a treaty of immense value, since it kept the peace over so many years between the two greatest armies in India.

In 1765 Clive had put down a mutiny of the officers of the Bengal army; since then 'scarce a decade had passed without an open struggle between the military and the civil power'.[2] Mutinies were periodic, and the mutineers usually won, which 'justified the belief that representations made by numbers and supported by clamour would not fail'.[3] In 1808 the Bombay officers almost mutinied because it was found that a cavalry regiment might be more conveniently raised at Madras. In Madras next year the Government, driven by the Directors, who 'threatened to take the pruning knife into their own hands',[4] asked their Quartermaster-General to draw up a report on a system which gave the commanding officers of regiments tent allowances for their men, whether they were in the field or in cantonments. He found the system was regularly abused, whereupon the officers called on the Commander-in-Chief to bring him 'to a court-martial for aspersions on their character as officers and gentlemen'.[5] The Commander-in-Chief complied; but Barlow, who had gone to Madras as Governor, countermanded his action. Then the former, whose soreness at his exclusion from a place

---

[1] *Op. cit.* 306.　　[2] *Lord Minto in India*, 197.　　[3] *Op. cit.* 202.
[4] Marshman, *History of India*, ii. 240.　　[5] *Lord Minto in India*, 207.

on the Council made him unwearied in forming a party for himself, confronted Barlow with a mutiny. The officers in many large stations

' talked of fighting against a tyrannical Government in defence of their rights to the last drop of their blood. Seditious toasts were given at the mess tables, and drunk with uproarious applause. From day to day tidings went forth from one excited station to another—tidings of progressive insubordination which fortified with assurances of sympathy and support the insane resolves of the scattered mutineers. . . . The moral intoxication pervaded all ranks from the colonel to the ensign'.[1]

At Masulipatam the officers put their commanding officer under arrest and seized the fort; Seringapatam followed suit. Malcolm, sent to Masulipatam, wrote back

' that there was not a Company's corps from Cape Comorin to Ganjam that was not implicated in the general guilt—that is not pledged to rise against Government unless what they call their grievances are redressed'.

Haidarabad next rose. 'All concealment was thrown off', and 30,000 men, it was threatened, would march on Madras. Public funds were seized, correspondence interrupted—'in a word, civil war had commenced'. Then Barlow for once acted with some approach to vigour. He demanded from all officers a signed pledge of obedience, on pain of being sent inland if they refused. When not one-tenth consented to sign, he appealed to the sepoys to stand firm to their allegiance; they did so, and though Sir James Mackintosh wrote to John Malcolm that [2] 'were he asked whether the deposition of a Governor by military force or an appeal to private soldiers against their officers be the greater evil, I am compelled to own that I must hesitate', the sepoys' loyalty left the mutineers stranded. They had never allowed themselves to doubt that they would have their regiments with them. Lord Minto on going to Madras received 'a penitential letter'. As every decade proved, there was a wide difference in the punishment meted out to mutineers, according to whether they were sepoys or British officers; only a handful of ringleaders were now court-martialled, having first been offered their choice of trial or dismissal. The courts-martial resulted in several being cashiered. Much bitterness remained, and the Company officers sent to Coventry the King's officers, who held them 'mighty cheap'.[3] Barlow's handling of the episode was considered un-

[1] *Op. cit.* 197.
[2] J. Kaye, *Correspondence of Sir John Malcolm,* quoted in *Lord Minto in India,* 216.
[3] Lord Minto.

satisfactory. It finished whatever chance he had had of being appointed Governor-General, and he went home in 1812.

Inside India, Minto's regime was one of quiet consolidation, with vigorous action against turbulent chieftains. The ablest of these, Jeswant Rao Holkar, went mad in 1808, and for three years was kept bound with ropes and fed with milk, dying October, 1811. Outside India, Lord Minto's government was one of brilliant conquest. As part of the war with Napoleon, he captured the islands of Bourbon and France (Mauritius). Whenever Napoleon compelled a European State into his system, England 'took charge' of that State's foreign possessions. Thus she possessed for a few years the Moluccas and Java, the Governor-General himself accompanying the latter expedition and being present at the Dutch rout at Fort Cornelis, near Batavia. Gillespie of Vellore led the storm, which Minto describes (August 28, 1811): [1]

> 'It really seems miraculous that mortal men could live in such a fire of round, grape, shells, and musketry long enough to pass deep trenches defended by pointed palisades inclining from the inner edge of the ditch outwards, force their way into redoubt after redoubt, till they were in possession of all the numerous works, which extend at least a mile. . . . The slaughter was dreadful, both during the attack and in the pursuit. . . . We have upwards of 5000 prisoners, including all the Europeans left alive. . . . There never was such a rout.'

Java passed into British keeping, and the great Stamford Raffles was appointed lieutenant-governor. These dark slavery-ridden East Indian regions certainly needed cleaning up. Minto abolished execution by torture, and the brutal custom of compelling the families of the condemned to witness the malefactor's death, and afterwards selling them into bondage. Java entered on a period of prosperity and humane administration. It was returned to the Dutch when general peace was made, at the end of the Napoleonic wars.

Lord Minto's most criticised action was that which he took against missionaries. The Company's territory being closed to them, they were established in the Danish settlement at Serampur, whence they issued pamphlets which were distributed in British India. Minto forbade propagandist preaching in Calcutta, and William Carey, the great Baptist leader, agreed to a censorship of their publications. In the latter demand

---

[1] *Lord Minto in India* (*Life and Letters . . . from* 1807 *to* 1814), edited by his great-niece the Countess of Minto, 291.

Minto was not as unreasonable as clamour in London represented. To the Chairman of the Directors he wrote:

' Pray read especially the miserable stuff addressed to the Gentooes, in which, without one word to convince or to satisfy the mind of the heathen reader, without proof or argument of any kind, the pages are filled with hell fire, and hell fire, and still hotter fire, denounced against a whole race of men for believing in the religion which they were taught by their fathers and mothers, and the truth of which it is simply impossible it should ever have entered into their minds to doubt. Is this the doctrine of our faith? ... If there are two opinions among Christians on this point, I can only say that I am of the sect which believes that a just God will condemn no being without individual guilt. ... The remainder of this tract seems to aim principally at a general massacre of the Brahmins of this country. A total abolition of caste is openly preached. A proposal to efface a mark of caste from the foreheads of soldiers on parade has had its share in a massacre of Christians. ...'

As that last sentence reminds us, Vellore had gone deep and into bitter remembrance.

In 1808, when England and Denmark were at war, Serampur was occupied by the Company. The Serampur missionaries were Baptists, and the Governor-General found them easier to persuade to be reasonable than he found the Rev. Claudius Buchanan, one of his own Presidency chaplains. Buchanan printed a memoir urging:

' An archbishop is wanted for India—a sacred and exalted character, surrounded by his bishops, of ample revenue and extensive sway. ... We want something royal in a spiritual and temporal sense for the abject subjects of this great Eastern empire to look up to. ... When once our national Church shall have been confirmed in India, the members of that Church will be the best qualified to advise the State as to the means by which from time to time the civilisation of the natives is to be effected.'

So firmly did Mr. Buchanan believe in the efficacy of the mere sight of his sacred and exalted characters, that he was said to have exclaimed, 'Place the mitre on any head. Never fear, it will do good among the Hindoos!' Clearly, long before Keble's sermon on 'National Apostasy' gave a date for the start of the Oxford Movement, there was a widespread *preparatio evangeli*.

Minto dealt also with characters whom no one has called sacred or exalted. In Mogul times, in Warren Hastings's time, in Lord Curzon's time, in our own time, dacoity—robbery with violence—had been rife in Bengal, especially in East Bengal, where natural conditions make it almost ineradicable. Dacoits are people who need not excite our pity:

' It is impossible to imagine, without seeing it, the horrid ascendancy they

had obtained over the inhabitants. . . . They had established a terrorism as
perfect as that which was the foundation of the French republican power, and
in truth the *sirdars*, or captains of the band, were esteemed and even called
the *hakim* or ruling power, while the real Government did not possess either
authority or influence enough to obtain from the people the smallest aid
towards their own protection. . . . Men have been found with their limbs and
half the flesh of their bodies consumed by slow fire, who persisted in saying
that they had fallen into their own fire, or otherwise denying all knowledge
of the event that could tend to the conviction or detection of the offenders.
They knew, if they spoke, they would either themselves or the remaining
members of their families be despatched the same evening. By these measures
such a vigorous efficient government was erected by the banditti in these
districts, that they could send a single messenger through the villages with
regular lists of requisitions from the different houses and families—some to
furnish grain, some forage, some horses, some two sons to join the gangs,
some labourers to carry the plunder, or to bear torches, or to act as scouts;
some were to send a wife or daughter to attend the gangs.' [1]

Governor-Generals occupied with disposal of patronage or with vast
imperial designs had been too busy to be vext. But Minto

' was not a little shocked, and could not help feeling some shame, when I
became fully apprised of the dreadful disorders which afflicted countries under
the very eye of Government; and for many months past it has been one of
the principal objects to put this monstrous evil down. . . . I am happy to say
that hitherto the success has even exceeded my expectations. In Nuddeah,
which was the principal seat of this evil, there has not been a single dacoity
during the last months; and it is in that one district that the computed average
of persons put to death in torture was seventy a month. Nine sirdars have been
executed at one spot, and the impression of that example was remarkable.
The people had come to think it impossible that the leader of an established
gang should be punished, or at least capitally punished, and they looked on
with fully as much awe as satisfaction on this proof of the supreme power of
Government'.

The 'gangster' operates very similarly in East and West, and requires
the same conditions for success and impunity.

This quiet, unassuming man has had much less than his due of praise.
He was firm when firmness was wanted: he tightened up Government
when it had been rendered intolerably lax, and yet there was no return
to the bullying arrogance of Lord Wellesley. He was amused by the
pettifogging pompousness which he found enwrapping his position,
and 'in the log kept for the benefit of the family circle at home' (who,
we may hope, were worthy of it) he ridicules it with the mild ribaldry it
merits:

[1] Letter to Lady Minto, 1809.

' The first night I went to bed at Calcutta I was followed by fourteen persons in white muslin gowns into the dressing-room. One might have hoped that some of these were ladies; but on finding that there were as many turbans and black beards as gowns, I was very desirous that these bearded handmaids should leave me . . . which with some trouble and perseverance I accomplished, and in that one room I enjoy a degree of privacy, but far from perfect. The doors are open, the partitions are open or transparent also, and it is the business of a certain number to keep an eye upon me, and see if I want the particular service which each is allowed by his caste to render me. It is the same in bed; a set of these black men sleep and watch all night on the floor of the passage, and an orderly man of the body-guard mounts guard at the door with Sepoys in almost all the rooms, and at all the staircases. These give you a regular military salute every time you stir out of your room or go up or down stairs, besides four or five with maces running before you. I have gradually got rid of this troublesome nonsense, but enough remains and must remain to tease me and turn comfort out of doors. . . .'

An ease and informality of intercourse came into Government correspondence, between the Governor-General and his higher officers. Government House became a habitable region: 'no other circle in Calcutta contained prettier women or abler men'.[1]

Young Charles Metcalfe, in April, 1811, entered on his great work as Resident at Delhi, where he found the Mogul's family a heavy trial. As with Tipu's family at Vellore, there were rumours that the young bloods committed murder and robbery; they were reported to have killed an old woman behind the walls of what Kaye calls 'that great sty of pollution',[2] and we are given this glimpse of what must be called their amusements: [3] 'oiling their naked persons, then rushing with drawn swords among the startled inmates of the Zenana, and forcibly carrying off their property'.

Ought the palace to be allowed to continue the slave-trade, which Metcalfe had prohibited in Delhi (where also he prohibited suttee)? 'The truth struggled out but dimly from the murky recesses' of the labyrinth of buildings where a swarm of several generations of the royal family co-existed, plotting and fighting among themselves. Blind old Shah Alam was dead, and his successor complained that 'the tribute' paid him by the Company was insufficient. The young Englishman who had to reconcile his responsibility for a great city with his anxiety to respect fallen majesty found support in an administration so cordial and so full of common sense and sense of the absurdity of the whole

---

[1] *Lord Minto in India*, 349.   [2] *Life of Lord Metcalfe*, i. 351.   [3] *Op. cit.* i. 344.

Indian scene (that comforting reflection which has kept the wiser Indians and wiser British alike sane). When Metcalfe lost two valued assistants, promoted elsewhere, Minto answered his protests by a 'ragging' which showed how complete was the confidence in the Resident who was left to carry on with new and raw help:

'You will perceive that I entertained none other' [intention] 'than that of promoting the views in the service of two young gentlemen, whom, without knowing either personally, I esteemed and admired extremely. . . . With regard to the *Resident at Delhi*, I may as well confess that, having always had a very mean opinion of his abilities, and thinking him a very unamiable character and dull companion, I did entertain a secret wish to bring him into disrepute, by depriving him of his most able and experienced coadjutors. . . .

'As the whole ship's company of the *Hussar* are your slaves, I may venture, without consulting them, to send you everything that is kind from the whole, of all ages, and both genders.

'Believe me ever, my dear Metcalfe,
(being entitled to this familiarity by the *contract*),
Faithfully and affectionately yours.'

It is less than a decade since Lord Wellesley's rule finished, yet we seem to have moved forward a whole century! Minto's achievement was that he came to a government militarised and still medieval, and gave it the amenities of a civilised administration.

CHAPTER VII

THE NEPAL WAR

Racial relations: treatment of Eurasians: condition of native India: the Nepal War.

THE Earl of Moira, whom, anticipating a little, we will call by his better-known name, Marquess of Hastings, was nearly fifty-nine when he became Governor-General. Hitherto distinguished chiefly for being 'on terms of the closest and most expensive intimacy with the Prince Regent',[1] he departed from all the probabilities by rendering over nine years' service of a quality which has been underrated. He was shrewd,

[1] *Oxford History of India*, 620.

patient, independent, holding his opinions modestly and under continual revision; from his diary, as from his actions, emerges the image of a man experienced and humane. He proved once more that an astringent despair, if accompanied by rigid views of duty, can achieve almost as much as hope itself:

' I feel a bond that will never allow me to relax in effort as long as my health will suffice. I at times endeavour to arouse myself with the hope that I may succeed in establishing such institutions, and still more such dispositions, as will promote the happiness of the vast population of this country; but when the thought has glowed for a moment it is dissipated by the austere verdict of reason against the efficacy of exertion from an atom like me. The Almighty wills it; it is done without the mediation of an instrument. The notion of being useful is only one of those self-delusions with which one works oneself through the essentially inept vision of life'.[1]

He attacked his own ignorance by at once undertaking an extensive tour up-country, during which he comments repeatedly, in the strongest, most contemptuous terms, on the racial estrangement which was to run its deepening course until the tardy improvement in our own post-War world. But he was unable to do more than by example confirm in courtesy those who had no temptation to fail in it, thereby staving off the worst insolence on one side and the worst humiliation on the other, for a few years longer. He could not re-establish friendly intercourse. He and his wife, Lady Loudoun, managed to do a little for the self-respect of Eurasians. Learning that the ablest freelance in India, the celebrated Captain Skinner—who, after quitting Sindhia's service in 1803, had served the Company, and 'much distinguished himself by his enterprise, his intrepidity, and his judgment',[2] qualities much to seek in the conduct of military affairs at this time—was again in the market for any native State, disgruntled at being liable to 'find himself under the orders of possibly a very inexperienced youth', Hastings 'requested' him to 'assume the honorary title of Lieutenant-Colonel', and

' apprized him of my intention to propose to Government that such a rank in the Irregulars should entitle the officer holding it to rank as youngest field-officer of the line, and to command accordingly all captains and subalterns'.[3]

The veteran was extraordinarily moved by this act of consideration.

' To understand this warmth of feeling, one ought to know the excessive depression in which the half-castes are held by the Company's servants. Till Lady Loudoun gave a private hint that colour never would be noticed, half-

---

[1] *The Private Journal of the Marquess of Hastings*, January 1, 1816.
[2] *Op. cit.* i. 293.　　　　　　　　[3] *Op. cit.* i. 294-5.

caste ladies, though of the best education and conduct, and married to men in prominent stations, were not admitted to the Government House.'

Yet (whatever might be done for a Skinner) the lot of Eurasians, who did the immense mass of the actually indispensable work of administration in the uncovenanted services, remained what it has been to our own day—the most inexcusable stain in even the records of Anglo-Indian snobbery. A Governor-General's sister exclaims, twenty years later: [1]

'The "uncovenanted service" is just one of our choicest Indianisms, accompanied with our very worst Indian feelings. We say the words just as you talk of the "poor chimney-sweepers", or "those wretched scavengers"— the uncovenanted being, in fact, clerks in the public offices. Very well-educated, quiet men, and many of them very highly paid; but as many of them are half-castes, we, with our pure Norman or Saxon blood, cannot really think contemptuously enough of them.'

During his tour Lord Hastings was shocked by repeatedly discovering men rotting in jail for ancient offences which seemed to him long over-expiated. This resulted in an important reform in procedure. Believing that the Company's personnel could now be trusted to wield magisterial as well as administrative functions, he joined the offices of magistrate and collector. Thus British India for minor offences was given something of the 'non-regulation' methods which obtained in such regions as Delhi, the most effective in newly annexed districts, the most popular with those who administered and in the main liked by those who were administered unto—swift and summary, and dispensing with much formality and highly paid roguery.

Had it been possible, he would have done away with the whole legal hocus-pocus. He wrote (November, 1817):

' Nothing can more strongly mark the prematurity of our attempt to force upon the Indian population our judicial system than the abhorrence which every man of family among the natives entertains against being summoned, even as a witness, into one of our courts. On this account, it is almost impossible to obtain the testimony of any of them in criminal cases, where they have been present at the perpetration of the act. They will, in the preliminary examination, admit their having been present, but will stoutly swear that they did not happen to notice what was going forward, and can say nothing on the subject. With the lower classes the system is equally unpopular. The security which they enjoy in person and property is duly estimated by them; but that they refer entirely to the principle of Government. The inconvenience, the

[1] The Hon. Emily Eden, *Up the Country*, 140 (June 9, 1838).

expense, and the delay which they experience in our civil proceedings, make them unreservedly lament that they are not subjected to military decisions.' [1]

But the contrast between the abundance of wisdom wrested from experience and the slight prevalence of that wisdom in human affairs, despite the many enlightened men in influential places, is one of the most powerful reasons for pessimism. It remains mildly mysterious how the legal system, so condemned by the wisest and noblest of the conquerors, became securely fastened down on India. To-day, when the unemployed Indian lawyer is so abused that the uninstructed reader might judge—*does* judge, in fact—that he wilfully ate of poisonous fruit and is suffering in his person the proper penalty of foolishness, it is worth remembering how reluctantly India accepted Western justice. We are told that during Lake's Laswari campaign, whole populations fled in terror, not from 'the brutal and licentious soldiery', but from the 'High Court' which was believed to be accompanying them!

In language strangely prophetic,[2] Lord Hastings, who saw 'around me the elements of a war more general than any which we have hitherto encountered in India', immediately diagnosed the almost universal hatred of the Company. It was useless to pretend that native States were sovereign Powers so long as the British kept in them subsidiary forces. These subsidiary forces made tyranny safe, and constantly had to put through dirty jobs for contemptible rulers; those rulers hated their overlord, and oppressed their subjects. With every year Hastings's certainty

[1] *Private Journal*, ii. 229.

[2] ' In our treaties with them we recognise them as independent sovereigns. Then we send a Resident to their courts. Instead of acting in the character of ambassador, he assumes the functions of a dictator; interferes in all their private concerns; countenances refractory subjects against them; and makes the most ostentatious exhibition of this exercise of authority. To secure to himself the support of our Government, he urges some interest which, under the colour thrown upon it by him, is strenuously taken up by our Council; and the Government identifies itself with the Resident not only on the single point, but on the whole tenor of his conduct. In nothing do we violate the feelings of the native princes so much as in the decisions which we claim the privilege of pronouncing with regard to the succession to the musnud. We constantly oppose our construction of Mahomedan law to the right which the Moslem princes claim from usage to choose among their sons the individual to be declared the heir-apparent. It is supposed that by upholding the right of primogeniture we establish an interest with the eldest son which will be beneficial to us when he comes to the throne. I believe nothing can be more delusive. He will profess infinite gratitude as long as our support is useful to him; but, once seated, his subsequent attachment will always be regulated by the convenience of the day. He, too, will in his turn have to feel our interference in the succession as well as in minor instances.' (*Private Journal*, i. 47 ff.)

of the 'disgust and estrangement' set up by these relations deepened. Whatever the princes had been when Wellesley began his vigorous dealings with them, they were now—except Ranjit Singh and the Gurkha Maharaja, who were both outside the Company's sphere—vassals in fact, and vassals in a condition of smouldering disaffection. Most of Lord Hastings's time was occupied with the wars he foresaw, and with efforts to set on to some plane of logic and honesty the Company's relations with such States as survived. He sought opportunity to bring them all where they would accept control of their armies, and submit their mutual quarrels to British arbitration. Before he succeeded, there was to be desperate kicking against the pricks.

Looking over India, he surveyed a dreary scene; and in his despondent conclusions the best British opinion concurred. Sir John Malcolm found in Haidarabad [1] (1817)

' a broken and oppressed race. I am, indeed, disposed to believe that no country was ever more miserably governed. What, indeed, can be expected when the prince is a melancholy madman, and the minister a low Hindoo, who owes his power to the support of our Government, and pays the price of subservience to our Resident for continuance in office? Where power is without pride there can be no motive for good government. I am told it is impossible to maintain our connexion on a better footing. I can only reply, it is impossible there can be a worse. . . .'

Metcalfe was urging the Governor-General to abolish the mischievous fiction of 'the King' in Delhi; the Mogul establishment, whose pomp was as inflated as their importance was small, were abominable neighbours to his authority. Lord Hastings acknowledged that

' nothing has kept up the floating notion of a duty owed to the imperial family, but our gratuitous and persevering exhibition of their pretensions—an exhibition attended with much servile obeisance in the etiquettes imposed upon us by the ceremonial of the court'.[2]

But he had his hands too full to handle a problem so intricately bound up with questions of legal and historical right. Never can Governor-General have felt more distracted, as he listened to the representations of his ablest servants, each convinced that his particular trouble was

---

[1] An incident in the summer of 1814 had shown how completely Haidarabad, as well as Oudh, had become dependent. The Nizam's two youngest sons were in the habit of ranging the capital with a gangster band. The Resident tried to round them up; they barricaded themselves in a palace; he blew its gates open 'with some six-pounders he had with him' (Prinsep, i. 264). Then the princes were banished, and some of their boon companions executed.

[2] *Private Journal*, i. 320 (January, 1815).

the one most desperately needing settlement. Munro was pleading for drastic reorganisation of India's internal polity, and in a long letter [1] lamented the subsidiary system's

' inevitable tendency to bring every Native state into which it is introduced, sooner or later, under the exclusive dominion of the British Government. . . . Even if the prince himself were disposed to adhere rigidly to the alliance, there will always be some amongst his principal officers who will urge him to break it. As long as there remains in the country any high-minded independence, which seeks to throw off the control of strangers, such counsellors will be found. I have a better opinion of the natives of India than to think that this spirit will ever be completely extinguished; and I can therefore have no doubt that the subsidiary system must everywhere run its full course, and destroy every government which it undertakes to protect'.

' This very Peishwah will probably again commit a breach of the alliance. The Nizam will do the same; and the same consequence, a farther reduction of their power for our own safety, must again follow.'

' The usual remedy of a bad government in India is a quiet revolution in the palace, or a violent one by rebellion, or foreign conquests. But the presence of a British force cuts off every chance of remedy, by supporting the prince on the throne against every foreign and domestic enemy. It renders him indolent, by teaching him to trust to strangers for his security; and cruel and avaricious, by showing him that he has nothing to fear from the hatred of his subjects. Wherever the subsidiary system is introduced, unless the reigning prince be a man of great abilities, the country will soon bear the marks of it in decaying villages and decreasing population.'

Readjustment of relations had to be postponed, however, for in 1814 border raids and boundary disputes passed into a war with Nepal. This for a time was 'regarded as a mere affair with a troublesome Raja of the frontier'.[2] When its magnitude emerged, the Governor-General himself organised four distinct attacks 'on a frontier of about six hundred miles. . . . But, unfortunately, four out of five generals employed displayed extraordinary incompetence in different fashions'.[3] The first to so distinguish himself was General Gillespie, of Vellore and Java fame, who on October 30 was killed trying to storm the Kalunga stockades. At a second attack on them (November 27), the troops hung back and sacrificed their leaders. The two attempts cost 740 casualties, 'considerably more than the entire number' of the defenders of 'this petty fortress'.[4]

---

[1] *Life of Sir Thomas Munro*, 247 (August 12, 1817).

[2] Henry T. Prinsep, *History of the Political and Military Transactions in India during the Administration of the Marquess of Hastings*, 1813-23, i. 133.

[3] *Oxford History of India*, 621-2.   [4] Prinsep, i. 92.

It was invested and cut off from water, and its confined space subjected to intensive bombardment, measures resulting in its evacuation three days after the repulse of November 27. The Gurkha commander and the seventy unwounded men of his 'defiant garrison' [1] slipped unnoticed through the besieging lines, leaving Kalunga 'in a shocking state, full of the mangled remains of men and women killed by . . . our batteries'.[2]

It is pleasant to remember that this terrible campaign was marked not only by great suffering but by mutual kindness. The Gurkhas were such an enemy as the Company had never encountered:

' None ever displayed so much bravery in action or so much system, skill, and conduct, so much prudent caution, and so much well-timed confidence. None other ever possessed a country so easily defended, and so difficult to the invader.' [3]

They gave, as well as extorted, respect. Burial of the dead was 'a courtesy they never refused . . . and not the only one we experienced at their hands'.[4]

The invaders fought blind, while all the eyes were with their foes, who moved easily round them in the dense forests and towering hills. Gillespie's rout was followed by others. On December 25 a European storming party was chased from Jaituk, and the sepoys following them even outstripped them, fleeing so expeditiously that they were back in their camp, the whole force having lost 500 men, by ten o'clock in the morning.[5] General Wood was defeated at Jitgarh. Yet another army lost two detachments amounting to over a thousand men, the Gurkhas rushing their camp and burning the tents, and pursuing the fugitives in every direction. The loss of officers was unprecedented; they were so often left unsupported. Only the fourth army, General Ochterlony's, by sheer caution, building roads and bringing up heavy guns, had escaped serious humiliation, and its leader

' was steadily pursuing his plan by slow and secure manœuvres, but had yet gained no brilliant advantage over his equally cautious antagonist'.[6]

The impression made in India was deep and wide. Metcalfe, than whom no one was now more influential with the Governor-General, wailed (January 15, 1815):

' We have met with an enemy who shows decidedly greater bravery and greater steadiness than our troops possess; and it is impossible to say what

---

[1] *Life of Lord Metcalfe*, i. 393.　　[2] Prinsep, i. 94.　　[3] Metcalfe, January 15, 1815.
[4] Prinsep, i. 107.　　　　　　　　[5] *Op. cit.* i. 99.　　[6] *Op. cit.* i. 130.

may be the end of such a reverse of the order of things. In some instances our troops, European and Native, have been repulsed by inferior numbers with sticks and stones. In others our troops have been charged by the enemy sword in hand, and driven for miles like a flock of sheep. In a late instance of complete rout, we lost more muskets by a great number than there were killed, wounded and missing. In short, I, who have always thought our power in India precarious, cannot help thinking that our downfall has already commenced. Our power rested solely on our military superiority. With respect to one enemy, that is gone. In this war, dreadful to say, we have had numbers on our side, and skill and bravery on the side of our enemy. We have had the inhabitants of the country disposed to favor us, and yet overawed, notwithstanding our presence and partial success, by the character of our enemy.'

One division (Gillespie's, and then Martindell's) had lost a third of the numbers with which it had set out from Meerut. The failures were instantaneously reflected in the attitude of the Maratha chiefs and Ranjit Singh's armed watchfulness at Lahore. It was now that the seeds of the next Maratha War were sown.

The British, for whom 'an uninterrupted course of easy victory' had bred 'precipitancy and want of caution',[1] set themselves to learn from their brilliant teachers. The Gurkhas, on their part, erred by being satisfied with a successful defensive war. Pushing home no advantages, they 'were abundantly satisfied with repulsing an attack or cutting off an outpost'. When the British themselves erected stockades, the war became one of 'continuance, that is . . . length of the purse', and of strong points.

Ochterlony, who changed all this, received no help from his brother commanders. Gillespie's successor, in particular, had managed to infect his whole army with his own imbecility, thereby reinforcing the enemy's decisive individual superiority. A distressing incident took place at Chamalgarh, where two hundred Gurkhas, being surrounded by two thousand irregulars, resolved to die fighting. This heroic expedient proved unnecessary: the mere sight of the stout countenance which they showed caused their besiegers to flee precipitately, 'this unlooked-for result of their intrepidity' giving the victors

' so much confidence, that they never afterwards failed to attack a post of irregulars, whenever placed within their reach: and even when stockaded, they generally succeeded'.[2]

But Ochterlony plodded on, despite minor defeats, and did well enough to overrun Kumaon; and in May, 1815, the Gurkhas made overtures

---

[1] *Op. cit.* i. 135.   [2] *Op. cit.* i. 160.

R

for peace. Negotiations failed on the Company's demand to have a Resident at Khatmandu; and an intercepted letter from the Gurkha leader to his prince showed why he was willing to risk everything rather than this. He insisted—and this attitude is one of the reasons why the independence of Nepal survived, when that of other kingdoms, also formidable in battle, went down—that if a treaty were made, it must be honourably kept. 'Lands transferred under a written agreement cannot again be resumed', though 'if they have been taken by force, force may be employed to recover them'. It was better to make no peace, he argued, but to let the war sleep for two years, while the British, in temporary possession of the malarious Terai, were steadily weakened by climatic ravages. The prayers of Brahmins, if these were bought by promises of *jagirs* in the event of victory, would be weakening them still further. Then the war could be strongly reawakened.

The writer of this letter was thinking along lines now common to all native India:

'After the immense preparations of the enemy, he will not be satisfied with all these concessions, or if he should accept of our terms, he would serve us as he did Tipu, from whom he first accepted an indemnity of six crores of rupees in money and territory, and afterwards wrested his whole country. If we were to cede to him so much country, he would seek some fresh occasion of quarrel, and at a future opportunity would wrest from us other provinces. . . . When our power is once reduced, we shall have another mission, under pretence of concluding a treaty of alliance and friendship, and founding commercial establishments. If we decline receiving their mission, they will insist; and if we are unable to oppose force, and desire them to come unaccompanied with troops, they will not comply. They will begin by introducing a company; a battalion will soon after follow, and at length an army will be assembled for the subjection of Nipal. You think that if for the present the lowlands, the Doon, and the country of the Satlej were ceded to them, they would cease to entertain designs on the other provinces of Nipal. Do not trust them! . . . if you had in the first instance decided upon a pacific line of conduct . . . the present contest might have been avoided. But you could not suppress your desire to retain these places' (Butwal and Sheoraj), 'and by murdering their revenue officer excited their indignation, and kindled a war for trifles. . . . In this place I am surrounded, and daily fighting with the enemy. . . . I must gain two or three victories before I can accomplish my object of attaching Ranjit Singh to our cause. On his accession . . . the chiefs of the Deccan may be expected to join the coalition, as also the Nawab of Lucknow. . . . If we are victorious, we can easily adjust our differences; and if we are defeated, death is preferable to peace on humiliating terms. . . .'

Fighting was resumed early in 1816, and Ochterlony won important victories. The Gurkhas hurriedly made peace, at the price of loss of territory and acceptance of a Resident. A more valuable result yet was the lasting character of the agreement. The contending parties had learnt mutual respect, and understood the limits to which each could be pushed with safety. Even during the last stages of the actual fighting Gurkhas began to enter the British army. Now their Government allowed such recruiting; and 'Johnny Gurk' began the career which was to bring him fame in such distant lands.

CHAPTER VIII

FINANCIAL PROBLEMS

Financial difficulties: demands on the Bengal revenues: land problems: salt and opium: public works and education: Metcalfe as Machiavelli: the Company has recourse to an old and tried friend: His Majesty of Oudh.

LORD HASTINGS on arrival had found the Bengal Government in one of its periodic states

' of great pecuniary embarrassment. The Directors were so urgent with me to send home treasure that I overcame the reluctance of my colleagues, and we remitted gold pagodas to the amount estimated by ordinary exchange of £300,000. Should the price of gold in England be still what it was when I left Europe, this bullion will be sold by the Directors for not less than £450,000. We have, however, in consequence been on the brink of great distress.

' The Embassy in Persia, though wholly appointed by the Crown, is entirely supported by the Government of Bengal; such being the arrangement made by ministers with the Directors, or rather imposed on the latter. Without any means of curbing the prodigality of the ambassador, or of determining the propriety of expenditures quite unconnected with the interests of India, we are bound to answer the bills drawn upon us by Sir Gore Ouseley. Of course they come both heavily and unexpectedly. The Governor of the Isle of France and the Governor of Ceylon have both had the privilege granted to them of drawing upon us, furnishing us in return with bills on the English Treasury, which we often cannot negotiate. Java is a still worse drain than the others. Instead of the surplus revenue which, for the purpose of giving importance to the conquest, was asserted to be forthcoming from that possession, it could not be maintained without the treasury as well as the troops of Bengal. Just now, in the height of our exigencies, we receive an intimation from the Lieut.-Governor that he cannot pay his provincial corps unless we allow him 50,000 Spanish dollars monthly in addition to the prodigious sums which we already contribute to his establishment'.[1]

The China tea investment also had to be financed from Bengal.

This crisis makes a convenient pause, to consider the principles of East India Company finance, a subject so intricate that only a cursory survey can be attempted. Until the Charter Act of 1813 no attempt was made to separate political and commercial accounts, and further complications arose from repeated additions of new territory, from military operations which were partly debited to the British Exchequer, from continual changes in the method of keeping accounts for the three Presidencies, and from the lack of a uniform currency.[2] This last problem was a continual embarrassment to the earliest settlers, for in Mogul times each prince had his own coinage, and none of these circulated throughout the peninsula. There were three mints in Bengal in 1765. These the Company abolished, and began issuing rupees from a mint in Calcutta, and after 1773 produced a 'sicca' rupee of standard weight but bearing the name of the Mogul Emperor, Shah Alam, and the date 1779.[3] Their rupees gradually ousted other rupees from Bengal, and replaced the copper coinage which was current outside Calcutta. In other parts of India the position was equally complicated, and was further confused by the recognition of such gold coins as the Madras *pagoda* and the Bombay *mohur*. It was not until 1835 that a uniform silver currency was established throughout India.

Until 1833 the Governor-General had to serve, financially, two masters. He was responsible to the Directors of a large trading company carrying on business under difficult circumstances. He was also a colonial administrator in charge of mixed forces, the King's and the Company's, always liable to be involved in wars with neighbouring princes, or with representatives of some European Power. The latter character predominated from the time of Cornwallis. Each successive Governor-General had financial disputes with the Directors, and in 1805 these were so acute that, apart from questions of general policy, they must have led to Wellesley's resignation. The Company's insistence that part of the revenue should be expended on goods for export

---

[1] *The Private Journal of the Marquess of Hastings* (February 1, 1814), i. 40-41.

[2] For further information see P. Banerjea's *Indian Finance in the Days of the Company*.

[3] Del Mar, *History of Money in Ancient Countries*, 111. It is difficult to understand why this date was chosen, and retained over a long period.

is an example of this conflict of interests. The matter has also some theoretic importance because it raises the question of 'tribute' and the 'financial drain', which were the subject of later controversies.

On taking over the *zemindari* rights of Bengal the Company had incurred certain financial responsibilities to the British Exchequer. Parliament insisted that territorial acquisitions belonged to the Crown, and the yearly payment of £400,000 demanded from the Company represented a form of rent. At that time the acquisition of land was considered a certain source of revenue, an idea which has led to confusion of thought even up till to-day. A government is not a landlord, and in extending its territory it increases the cost of its administration and its liability to be drawn into a war. These items may easily convert an apparently prosperous area into a 'deficit province'. The eighteenth-century English had not learnt that lesson. When taking over the reputedly fertile area of Bengal it was felt that the revenues should supply a surplus which could be remitted home. The Company arranged that this should take the form of goods to be sold in order to meet interest charges on home debts and the Exchequer demands. Each Governor-General was expected to devote a portion of his revenue to the purchase of commodities, which would be sent to England as part of the 'Investment', the early name for the cargoes which were exported to be sold for the benefit of the Company. About twelve million pounds were expended in this way between 1766 and 1780, and as part of the money realised by the sale of these commodities was paid to the British Exchequer it formed a kind of 'tribute', though only indirect. The demands of the Exchequer ceased in 1773, but the system of investing part of the surplus revenue in commodities for export was revived, after the lapse of some years, as a purely commercial transaction. Between 1793 and 1813 some twenty-five million pounds worth of goods were sent to England in this way, and the money was used to meet the interest on the growing 'home debts' of the Company.[1] Wellesley and his successors protested against the system, and it was finally abandoned in 1813.

This is the only time when anything which could be correctly described as 'tribute' was taken from India by the British Treasury, and it is important to differentiate two periods. Until 1780 the need for surplus cargoes was partly due to the demands of the Exchequer, but during the second period, from the 'nineties onwards, the extra com-

---

[1] By 1786 the Company had a nominal capital of £3,200,000 and debts in Europe of £11,800,000, besides an Indian debt of over eight millions.

modities went to defray the interest on debts incurred during the French war. The Directors were not yet reconciled to the modern idea of raising loans to meet war-time expenditure, and the complicated system described above was really due to this hesitation. Almost exactly the same result would have been obtained if the home debt had been reckoned as an Indian debt, bearing interest at about eight per cent. The surplus cargoes would have represented interest charges. Force of circumstances brought about this change, against the wishes of the Directors. The period from 1793 to 1813 covered the Mysore and Maratha wars of Cornwallis and Wellesley, and deficits piled up until the Government debts in India had risen to over thirty millions in 1814, an increase roughly equivalent to the Indian revenue spent on buying extra goods for export. From 1813 onwards trade relations between British India and England began to assume a more modern form. The balance of trade was no longer strongly in India's favour, and this checked the steady flow of bullion from Europe eastwards which had characterised the sixteenth, seventeenth, and eighteenth centuries. An important factor in this change was the raising of Indian loans for war expenses and then for productive purposes, such as railways and canals. At first these were taken up almost entirely in England, though by the time of the Mutiny Indian investors had begun to purchase them. Other home charges steadily increased during the first half of the nineteenth century, as the British administration spread over the whole peninsula, and became more complicated and expensive. In the time of Cornwallis this process was only just beginning, and it will be convenient to study the financial system while there was still only the bare framework of an administration, and before the series of internal wars which we connect with the names of Wellesley and Lord Hastings.

A rough budget worked out for British India in, say, 1790 will make it easier to appreciate the interaction of financial policy and administration.[1] Cornwallis had had four busy years, but the war with Tipu was still to come. The revenue was made up of four main items. The land revenue was by far the most important, bringing in some four million pounds, of which over three-quarters came from Bengal. The salt monopoly produced about half a million, the opium trade £80,000, and customs perhaps half that amount. A police tax was collected and employed locally, and the beginnings of the Excise department appear in the *abkari* regulations laid down by Cornwallis for taxing the sale of

---

[1] No such budget was, of course, prepared. The three provinces kept separate accounts, and their form was not that of a modern budget.

liquors. The complete dependence of the Government upon the land revenue remained a feature of British India for many years. It was recognised as an evil, but it is difficult to see what alternative was possible, and it is worthy of note that the two other practical sources of income—salt and opium—have been the subject of bitter attack up to the present day. Apart from customs, the chief resources of a modern government are income tax and death duties, both of which present special difficulties in India because of the Hindu joint family system. In the eighteenth century there was little ascertainable income apart from land, and another fifty years were to pass before Peel, in 1842, tentatively and experimentally introduced an income tax into England. The first Indian income tax was to follow still later, in 1860, but even under far more settled conditions it has been found very difficult to bring the money-lender and trader within its meshes. Death duties have never been imposed.[1] In 1857, the last year of the Company's rule, land revenue made up half of the Government's receipts, and salt, opium, and customs brought in more than two-thirds of the remainder.[2]

The incidence and collection of land revenue are bound up with peasant life, and import duties with the prosperity of the craftsmen. They will be discussed in a later chapter. The salt and opium monopolies have had long and controversial histories, with certain points of resemblance. Both commodities had been taxed under Muslim rule, and these taxes were retained by the British when other inland duties were abolished. The method of direct collection proving unsatisfactory, Warren Hastings in each case assumed the monopoly, and farmed out the right of manufacture. This led to the abuses usually connected with the farming system. Large profits were made by speculators, the actual salt-makers and poppy cultivators were oppressed. In 1780 Hastings instituted a salt office, with agents who arranged for the manufacture of salt, and sold it to wholesale dealers at prices fixed from year to year. In 1799 Wellesley abandoned the contract system for opium, and substituted a single agency under a covenanted civil servant. Both monopolies became part of the permanent revenue system.

[1] Probate duties are now charged, but these are not estate duties. They are really a court fee, and only applicable when there is a will, which is exceptional amongst Hindus. Muslims are not liable. The charge is about 3 per cent.

[2] Land revenue, £15,317,337; customs, £2,148,834; salt, £2,131,346 (against charges of £605,880); opium, £6,864,209 (against charges of £629,480). Total receipts, £31,706,776.

Much nineteenth-century criticism of the salt and opium policies was based on the idea that any State enterprise which makes a profit is tyrannous, and was especially objectionable in the case of a 'foreign' government. There is to-day less belief in the virtue of free competition, especially in the production of articles in which purity is of great importance. The real charge against the Government's salt policy was that too much profit was taken on supplying an essential to life, and against the opium policy that the Government was engaging in an immoral business. At the end of the eighteenth century neither criticism had very much force. The salt monopoly ensured a plentiful supply of good quality, and the profit up to 1788 was under Rs. 1 as. 8 for 80 lb.[1] As the average yearly consumption per head was under 12 lb., the charge was not a very heavy burden, and there is no reason to believe that salt would have been retailed cheaper under a system of open competition. Subsequently the salt trade became more complicated. From 1817 there was a small import from England, the salt being loaded as ballast, and private manufacture was allowed under licence. Later governments were tempted by the elasticity of this source of revenue to raise their charges to meet unexpected calls, and the duty was as high as three rupees per 80 lb. during the first Afghan War. After the Mutiny the salt duties were open to far greater objection. The imposition of income tax in 1860 had shown the possibility of differentiating taxation so as to fall chiefly on the rich, and thus provided a strong argument against continuing a tax on an essential food. Opium was on a different footing. It was at best a luxury, and was intended chiefly for export to China. The Government made very large profits on the trade, but the high price was mostly paid by Chinese, and was virtually a luxury tax upon them. The moral aspect was hardly considered. It was not an age much given to interfering with other people's domestic habits, and opium-eating—as contrasted with the exotic indulgence in opium-smoking—has never been considered in India as a dangerous vice. Both Indians and English would probably hold it less baneful than alcoholism.

The expenditure side of the 1790 budget would have been under two main heads, military and civil. Attempts were made to keep the expenses of the army, then about 70,000 strong, to a million and a half pounds, but the struggle with Tipu Sultan upset these plans, and by 1793 the army had risen to nearly ninety thousand men, and the cost to three million. During Wellesley's time expenses rose immediately,

[1] Pramathanath Banerjea, *History of Indian Taxation*, 253.

and by 1813 the army had a strength of about two hundred thousand.[1] A considerable part of these military expenses were not paid out of revenue, but in peace or war the army must have absorbed about two-thirds of the total receipts. Civil expenditure came under very few heads, for it was only about the middle of the nineteenth century that governments, even in Europe, began to develop the 'social services'. The main item was salaries for officials, but the expenses of revenue collection were usually deducted before remittance, and it is almost impossible to estimate the amount of this charge. It is certain that the immediate effect of Lord Cornwallis's judicial and other reforms was a heavy increase in these expenses. The old system, whereby the Company had paid its servants small salaries, but had connived at irregularities, had at least been cheap. With a very inelastic revenue each successive Governor-General was continually hampered by financial difficulties, even before the Mysore War, and the police system was rendered ineffective by the very small amounts available for salaries.

The other branches of Government activities were still in an embryonic state at the end of the eighteenth century. The first public works were military, but Lord Cornwallis was interested in the repair of the many minor irrigation works of Bengal, most of which had been allowed to degenerate during the anarchy of the past century. Local committees were appointed, and pressure put upon *Zemindars* to undertake this work. The Marquess of Hastings was one of the first statesmen to emphasise the importance of better communications, and from about 1820 there was considerable activity in the *maramat* department, while the trunk roads were put in hand after the Charter Act of 1833. There was at that time little knowledge of hydraulic engineering, and the effort made under Lord Amherst to revive the old Mogul Jumna canal only proved that the original alignment had been wrong.

Mass education was at that time not considered the duty of a government. In England it was entirely in the hands of the Churches, and it was not until 1833 that the first Government grant of £20,000 was given to the two leading societies engaged in this work. 'Free and compulsory' education did not, of course, follow till after 1870. A few European countries were earlier in recognising governmental responsibility, but most were later. It is an anachronism to imagine that in 1790 any Indian or Englishman would have thought it to be the Govern-

[1] Martin, ii. 101 ff., letter of the Right Hon. Henry Dundas to the Earl of Mornington, March 18, 1799. The whole letter deserves careful study and fuller quotation than we can find space for.

ment's duty to undertake or even assist the work of the little temple and mosque schools which existed in many of the villages. Higher education was considered in a different light. Government interference was justified by the need of men trained for Government service. The Calcutta Madrasa was founded in 1781, and a Sanskrit College was founded in Benares in 1792, but little more was done until after 1813. Under the Charter Act of this year the sum of £10,000 was appropriated yearly for the 'revival and improvement of literature and the improvement of the sciences', the wording of which shows clearly that it was intended to assist in higher education. The amount remained unappropriated for some years, though in 1816 the Hindu College was founded in Calcutta, chiefly through the energies of David Hare and the Chief Justice, Sir Hyde East. The grant was, however, the basis of the struggle which took place under Bentinck between the 'Orientalists' and the English school, and which finally settled the future of higher education in British India.

The Nepal campaign heavily deepened the Government's financial distress, to which we return. The Directors noted (October, 1815)

' with extreme concern that the effects of the Nepaulese war are so strongly felt in your financial department as to induce the apprehension that the advances to be issued to our European investment will be reduced to a very small sum indeed. . . . If the advances for the investment are to be withheld, the sales at this House for India goods will soon be brought to a stand'.

The Company's administration therefore had recourse to the Nawab of Oudh, their old and (in every sense of the phrase) much-tried ally. His government 'since the forced cessions of 1801, had been conducted systematically on a principle of selfish avarice, which aimed to draw as much as possible from the country, at the smallest possible charge'.[1] It is perhaps not easy to explain how his aim differed from the Company's; but Anglo-Indian writers are so sure that there *was* an immense difference, that we may take it that there must have been, and that the passage of time has blurred our chances of perception of it. Possibly part of the difference lay in his wasteful expenditure of what he wrested from his people, whereas the Company built up an admirable military machine; Metcalfe, whose mind was as clear as the Governor-General's own, and whose advice was very congenial to Hastings, wrote that they ought:

' 1st. To make it the main object of all the acts of our Government to have

[1] Prinsep, i. 217.

the most efficient army that we can possibly maintain, not merely for internal control or the defence of our frontier, but also for those services in the field which our army is perpetually called on to perform on emergencies when we have not time to increase it to sufficient strength.

' 2nd. If our resources should, at any time, be unequal to the maintenance of an ample force, not to cripple our strength by attempts to reduce our force within the limits of fixed resources at the imminent peril of our dominion; but to endeavour to raise our resources to meet the demands on us for force.'

If the revenues of British India proved inadequate,

' we ought to draw forth new resources; and if these be impracticable within our own dominions, we must look to increase of territory by conquest over our enemies in the interior of India. There is no doubt that opportunities will arise for effecting such conquests, for with the utmost moderation and justice upon our part, misunderstandings and wars in the course of time will be occasionally unavoidable'.

As the further aims of British policy, Metcalfe listed:

' To enlarge our territories in the interior of India on every occasion of war as much as possible consistently with justice and policy, moderation to our enemies, and due attention to our allies.

' 4th. To apply the net revenues of conquered countries to the maintenance of additional force, and the acquisition of additional force to the achievement of new conquests, on just occasions—thus growing in size and increasing in strength as we proceed, until we can with safety determine to confine ourselves within fixed limits, and abjure all further conquests. . . .'

No one in any country at this date considered that the revenues of conquered countries belonged to those who paid them.[1] They were at the conqueror's free disposal, to spend—as Metcalfe urged—on bigger and better armies, which were to conquer bigger and better lands, which in turn were to pay for bigger and better armies again—or else to put into the annual investments (as the Directors urged), and send home thus as a disguised tribute. And the Nawab himself, whatever we may think about his subjects' case, was undoubtedly deeply beholden to the Company, as without outside support Oudh could never have gone on and on being scandalously misgoverned for decade after decade, and by Nawab after Nawab. He had won additional security by removal of the menace of the Gurkhas at his doors, and it was not unjust (as justice went in the India of those days) that he should pay towards that war.

His administration, moreover, needed improvement, even as seen

[1] See Appendix A.

from the distance of Calcutta. As far back as 1810, he had been urged to

'assimilate the administration of Oudh to that of the British provinces ... dividing the territory into districts, with revenue and judicial officers, acting under separate controlling authorities at the capital'.[1]

He betrayed as his chief characteristics 'extreme folly and timidity', which were heightened by his Resident, Major Baillie, who interfered high-handedly and continually. In 1814, while Lord Hastings was on his way to a personal meeting, the Nawab died; when the Governor-General reached Lucknow, he found that Baillie had zealously forced on the new Nawab the reforms desired, and that 'all the most lucrative appointments ... were filled by the Resident's own moonshees and dependents'.[2] Full conviction of what had been happening did not come to Hastings till a year later, when he immediately removed Baillie. Meanwhile, in October, 1814, His Excellency of Oudh was privileged to contribute a large loan to equip the Company's armies against Nepal. In the Governor-General's absence from Calcutta, his Council used part of this in an unauthorised fashion, which led to a second application to the Nawab, 'the financial officers being unable to devise any other remedy'.[3] His Excellency was slack in response, offering only fifty lakhs, which was refused, his offer being 'assumed to be made from an imperfect acquaintance with the extent of the embarrassment for which we sought relief'. The gaps in his knowledge were repaired, and an additional crore collected from him. In recognition of his helpfulness the Nawab was allowed to take the title of King, thereby outraging Muslim loyalty to the Mogul dynasty:

' "His Majesty" of Oude makes me sick. If the King of Delhi was in fact an absurdity or a mockery (I do not admit it was either), it had its root in a wise conformance to usage, in a generous consideration of the feelings of fallen greatness. It was the veneration of a great power that had passed away; and the superstition that continued to give homage to the shrine which we had addressed to propitiate our rise, was sanctioned by the example of the wisest among nations. There was little except goodness in it. The expenditure was duly repaid in the return of impression. . . .'[4]

[1] Prinsep, i. 218.   [2] *Op. cit.* i. 222.   [3] *Op. cit.* i. 227.
[4] John Malcolm to Gerald Wellesley (Kaye, *Life of Malcolm*, ii. 378).

CHAPTER IX

THE PINDARI AND MARATHA WARS

The Governor-General's dealings with the Maratha States: influence of Metcalfe: three types of native State: destruction of the Pindaris: murder of Gangadhar Sastri and imprisonment and escape of Trimbakji: the Peshwa's attack: battles of Kirki, Yeraoda, Koregaon, Sitabaldi: war with Holkar: battles of Mahidpur and Ashti: settlement of Central India: changing racial relations: administrative changes: the Palmer scandal: suttee.

THE Maratha States deserved the eclipse about to overtake them. Their original revolt against Mogul tyranny and bigotry was so successful that even to-day its victories are written on the map, in great Maratha principalities far outside the Deccan, which is ethnically Maratha territory. But these principalities, so valued an element in modern India, could not be established as we know them, except on the ruins of the system which preceded them and was their beginning. That system in 1817 was solely rapacious, except for the Gaekwar's dominions (which had settled into an administration more or less of the kind we know now as an Indian State). Holkar's and Sindhia's 'States' were merely the range within which they normally pillaged; their boundaries were liable to sudden extension or retraction, according as the pillagers' armed power waxed or waned.

For exemption from their attentions, these chieftains claimed tribute from many princes who had moved into the British sphere. Sindhia had claims on Bhopal, whose Nawab had assisted Goddard's march in Warren Hastings's time and thereby set up connections with the Company. By Maratha political notions, the claims were good ones; Sindhia 'having been in the habit of . . . levying contributions on this territory as his peculiar and exclusive prey, he conceived no one else had any right to interpose. This is the meaning he attached to the word dependency'.[1]

The Nepal War and the Burmese threat seemed to provide a good occasion for reasserting rights of pillage. But, warned by Lord Hastings, he withdrew (December, 1814); and the Nawab, whose conduct had been marked by double-dealing, was effectively protected.

It became increasingly clear that a new Maratha war was pending. Relations became strained in 1815, when, following on its interference

[1] Prinsep, i. 243.

for Bhopal, the paramount Power took charge of differences between the Nizam and Peshwa, the latter having claimed *chauth* as due under an agreement concluded after the Nizam's defeat at Kardla. Two sets of circumstances brought about the final break. The first was the continual application of the miserable Rajput kingdoms to be taken under Company protection. The granting of this request was precluded by the unnecessary treaty of 1805, whereby Sir George Barlow had pledged the British not to come between Sindhia and his prey in this quarter. The second precipitating factor was the inroads of the Pindaris, a name loosely applied to those banditti-cavalry which reinforced all Indian armies. Hordes of these swarmed in Central India, and their numbers had been augmented by the successive annexations of the Company, driving into the continually contracting region of native India those who had found employment as soldiers of Tipu or the Nizam. The Pindaris, Malcolm noted, were now 'what the Mahratta power was in the decline of the Mogul Empire of India. Let us take warning, and save the British Empire from the downfall which its predecessor sustained, chiefly from the hands of the predecessors of the Pindarrees'. As those words show, the political possibilities were remarkably well understood. Such Pindari leaders as Amir Khan were themselves almost established as independent princes inside the territory of Holkar or Sindhia, and seemed at the start of a career very like that of these chieftains themselves, not so long ago. There was, however, much obscurity as to their relationship with the leading Maratha States. They certainly appeared in the field with Sindhia and Holkar, and in varying degrees obtained protection from them; yet Sindhia and Holkar exercised little, if any, authority over them.

From contemporary documents, and the tradition preserved by men who, like Kaye, had talked with officers who passed through this last great Maratha war, we can recover the intense excitement with which the British anticipated the hoped-for conflict. But the immediate move was against the Pindaris only, whose depredations into Bengal, and still more, into the Northern Sarkars, were increasing, and were accompanied with terrible cruelty. They forced bags of hot ashes over the faces of those they suspected of concealing riches, and carried off young girls, tied on horseback 'like calves',[1] three or four together. Whole villages committed suicide to escape them. At last Hastings, in defiance of the Directors' veto (while urging them to remove it, which, in consideration of his horrible evidence, they did), prepared his wide net to

[1] Hastings, *Private Journal*, April 15, 1816.

sweep this curse out of being. He gathered two armies amounting to 120,000 men, the northern under himself, the southern under Sir Thomas Hislop, with Malcolm as the latter's principal political officer. The Gwalior Resident was told to make Sindhia 'sensible to the benefits' he would 'derive from frank co-operation', and the Maratha chiefs were ordered to allow free movement through their territories and to assist in every way this drive against general nuisances. Sindhia's Minister 'shrugged up his shoulders and said, "The weakest must obey the stronger"', which the Governor-General thought 'a curious avowal of incapacity for effectual resistance'.[1] Hastings with justice (he was not a man to cherish illusions) noted that the Maratha leaders were in correspondence together, and 'We must not look to the security of honourable pledges from them, but be satisfied with carrying point by point through gentle intimidation'.[2] Sindhia was made to yield up for temporary occupation two forts. Hastings was not a Wellesley, and he felt compunctions over the humiliation he felt bound to impose:[3]

' He subscribes to all the conditions which I dictated, and has swallowed a bitter drench in so doing. I should have thought myself oppressive had he not been so thoroughly false a fellow. The engaging to co-operate in the extirpation of the Pindarries, whom he has fostered—to whom he has plighted protection, and who really have hitherto constituted a material part of his strength, must be deeply mortifying'.

But he hardened his heart, determined to 'rivet such shackles upon Scindiah and Holkar as that all the treachery they are at this moment meditating will be impotent. In fact, the downfall of the Mahrattas is achieved'. A fact so patent as that last was not lost on the Marathas themselves. Nor on anyone else.

' Let the reader place before him any map of India, and contemplate the expanse of country lying between the Kistnah and the Ganges rivers. Let him glance from Poonah in the south-west to Cawnpore in the north-east; mark the positions of the principal Native Courts, and think of the magnificent armies—the very flower of the three Presidencies—which were spreading themselves over that spacious territory, closing in upon Hindostan and the Deccan, and compassing alike the Pindaree hordes and the substantive States in their toils. The sportsmen of the day, indeed, regarded it as a grand *battue* of the princes and chiefs of India; and we cannot be surprised if those princes and chiefs looked upon the matter in the same light, and thought that the Feringhees, after a long season of rest, were now again bracing themselves up for vigorous action, and were putting forth all their immense military

[1] *Private Journal*, October 11, 1817.   [2] *Op. cit.* September 30, 1817.
[3] *Op. cit.* November 7, 1817.

resources in one comprehensive effort to sweep the native principalities from the face of the earth.

'The Mahratta was roused. He had been uneasy. He was now alarmed. The whole history of our connexion with India shows that for a native prince to apprehend danger is to precipitate it by his own conduct. He is more often ruined by his fears than by anything else. . . . He commits himself to hostility before he is aware of it; and when all is over—when, prostrate and helpless at the feet of his conqueror, he declares that he had no intention to provoke the war which has destroyed him, there is often more truth in the words than we are wont to admit. It is said, in such cases, that our diplomatists are duped and over-reached, because they have not perceived hostile designs before they were formed, and known more about the future movements of our enemies than was known, at the time, to themselves. It is not a want of good faith, so much as a want of consistent counsel and steadfast action, that has brought so many of the princes of India to the dust.

'So it was, it appears to me, with the Peishwa and the Rajah of Berar. They were alarmed by the gathering and the advance of our armies. They did not believe that these immense military preparations had been made simply for the suppression of the Pindarees. They thought that whatever the primary and ostensible object of the campaign might be—a campaign conducted by the Governor-General himself in person, at the head of the Grand Army—it would eventually be directed against the substantive Mahratta states. And this was no baseless suspicion. The probability of another Mahratta war, as the sequel of the Pindaree campaign, was the subject of elaborate State papers and the small gossip of our camps. Statesmen solemnly discussed it at the council-board, and soldiers joyously predicted it at the mess-table. Had the whole scope of our policy been fully understood at the Mahratta Courts . . . they would not have suffered their fears to hurry them into aggression. But they only knew that we were putting our armies in motion from all points, and that in every cantonment of India the talk was about the probability of another war with the Mahrattas. . . .' [1]

When Mr. P. E. Roberts remarks [2] of Lord Hastings's dealings with native Powers, 'Full justice has not perhaps always been done to the moderation of British policy throughout this epoch. Seldom have forbearance and firmness been more happily combined. Those bad rulers, the Peshwa and Apa Sahib, were again and again given chances to reform', we must wonder that so judicious a historian should write with what appears unconscious irony. The Peshwa, it may be said in passing, was where he was at all only because we had seen to it that he was there, whether his own people wanted him or not. Lord Hastings's treatment of native princes looks moderate and courteous, because we remember

---

[1] J. W. Kaye, *Life of Sir John Malcolm*, ii. 187-9.
[2] *History of British India*, 288.

Wellesley's extreme of high-handed contemptuousness. For what he did, there was justification in the facts of the Indian situation—which were that all Central India was in anarchy, and the rulers with whom he dealt so rigorously were silly or wicked (the Peshwa was both). But this does not alter the fact that the princes near enough to feel the weight of British might were rounded up like wild beasts—that rebellion (if it was rebellion) was made humanly certain, and then punished. Malcolm thought the Maratha chiefs

' had at least as good a right to prepare for contingencies as we had. If, when the British Government first took up arms, and calculated the scale on which it would be expedient to conduct its military operations, the contingency of a Mahratta war was duly provided for, and that provision is to be considered demonstrative only of wisdom and forethought, we must surely be blinded by our national self-love, if we would denounce as treachery, or as folly, a like provision on the part of the Mahrattas, who were in much greater danger than ourselves. We surely cannot expect all the world to dismount their guns whilst our own are loaded and primed, and the portfire is burning in our hands'.[1]

It is often said that Britain acquired her Indian Empire in a fit of absent-mindedness; the epigram has served to support our useful reputation with foreigners for stupid stolidity, but has been overworked. From Clive's time onwards, British India never lacked minds seeing and planning far ahead. There was no trace, even momentary, of absent-mindedness in such rulers as Warren Hastings, Wellesley, Lord Hastings, or Dalhousie.

Metcalfe had the Governor-General's ear to an exceptional degree; and his influence, so inadequately noted by historians, outweighed the representations of men who desired to see the native States given more, not less, independence. As Resident in Delhi, he saw only the abundant seamy side [2] of these country regalities, beginning with the dilapidated Mogul 'Empire' at his door; his increasing scorn of them worked with Hastings's own desire to sweep away the whole system of outdated pretence. They had discussed Central India together during the Governor-General's original tour up-country; and in a memorandum Metcalfe divided existing States into three classes:

' Substantive states, ardently desiring our overthrow, and ambitious to aggrandise themselves. . . .
' military powers not substantive states . . . living by plunder and devasta-

---

[1] *Life of Sir John Malcolm*, ii. 189-190.

[2] He was much pestered by this or that prince begging to be allowed to make war on some neighbour.

s

tion—the enemies of all regular governments, more especially hostile in spirit to us. . . .

' petty states . . . subject to the continual plunder and oppression of the two former classes, who in consequence look up to us for protection, and are, therefore, well-disposed towards us.'

The division, though admirable, presented difficulties. Holkar and the Nagpur *raj*, both ranking with Sindhia as 'substantive states', were so reduced that they were in danger of splitting into predatory fragments; Amir Khan and others were partly of the freebooting class, partly dependents of Sindhia, partly on the point of themselves emerging as 'substantive states'.

The preliminaries of the Pindari campaign were pushed forward. The petty States, mostly Rajput, whose protection was desirable both for their own sake and for the revenues they would afford to prosecute the war which was bound to come against the Marathas, were taken into the British system, Hastings announcing to Sindhia and Holkar that the treaty of 1805 was abrogated. The Maratha Powers were told again that no neutrality in the drive would be permitted. If they hung back to the extent of themselves becoming enemies, so much the better:

' The war in this case would require greater exertions, but would also be attended with better prospects of solid advantage. The territories of Scindiah, Holkar, or the Rajah of Berar, would afford a recompense for the expenses of the war, and an increase of resources for the payment of additional force.'

So Metcalfe to the Governor-General; and Metcalfe's biographer surmises that 'perhaps the expectation entertained that some previous reluctance or some subsequent infidelity would embroil us with the substantive states in such a manner as to enable us to make certain new distributions of their territory was not, in some quarters, much unlike a hope'.[1]

---

[1] *Life of Metcalfe*, i. 456-7. That this surmise was soundly based, no one at the time would have bothered to deny. When Sindhia accepted the terms dictated to him, the Governor-General thought it necessary to apologise to the army for their disappointment: 'His Highness engages to afford every facilitation to the British troops in their pursuit of the Pindarees through his dominions, and to co-operate actively towards the extermination of those brutal freebooters. In consequence, the troops and country of his Highness are to be regarded as those of an ally. The generous confidence and animated zeal of the army may experience a shade of disappointment in the diminished prospect of serious exertion; but the Governor-General is convinced that the reflection of every officer and soldier in the army will satisfy him that the carrying every point by equity and moderation is the proudest triumph for the British character'.

Cf. Kaye: 'These threatening appearances at the Native Courts were regarded fearlessly by all—hopefully by many' (*Life of Malcolm*, ii. 187).

The Pindaris most vigorous leader, Chitu, routed by a surprise attack, was chased into jungle where he was, appropriately enough, eaten by a tiger. Other leaders surrendered. The worst, Amir Khan, who had been a fiend for twenty years, made his peace before operations commenced, and became an orthodox chieftain. An admitted sirdar of Holkar, he was given a principality sliced out of his feudal superior's domains, and recognised as Nawab of Tonk.

The longed-for Maratha War followed, but was partial, not general, Sindhia being immobilised by the effective severity of the Governor-General's arrangements and Holkar—who had the best *casus belli* of any, in the cool generosity to Amir Khan at his expense—entering it with characteristic belatedness. It came first with the Peshwa, and out of a long-standing trouble. The Gaekwar had sent to Poona as ambassador Gangadhar Sastri, a europeanised and tactless Brahmin: 'though a very learned Shastree, he affects to be quite an Englishman, walks fast, talks fast, interrupts and contradicts, and calls the Peshwa and his ministers "old fools" and "damned rascals", or rather "dam rascal" '.[1] The Peshwa, who alternated his time between debauchery of the obscenest description and steady pursuit of political aims, had fallen completely under the influence of Trimbakji, a base creature. By Trimbakji's instructions, with the Peshwa's connivance, Gangadhar Sastri was murdered in open street (July 14, 1815), at Pandarpur, most sacred of Maratha places of pilgrimage. Indian opinion was outraged by a Brahmin's slaughter, especially there; the British Government was indignant that an envoy, and, moreover, an envoy representing one of its extremely few really faithful dependents, had been murdered. Elphinstone, Resident at Poona, was told to demand Trimbakji's surrender. After long evasion, this was obtained. But Trimbakji, ill-guarded, escaped by a mixture of daring and cunning which delighted his own people and went far towards removing the odium which had attached to his criminal actions:

' The principal agent of communication was a Mahratta horse-keeper, in the service of one of the officers of the garrison, who passing and repassing the window of Trimbukjee's place of confinement, when in the act of airing his master's horse, sang the information he wished to convey, in an apparently careless manner, which the Europeans, for want of sufficient knowledge of the language, could not detect. The difficulties of this escape were exaggerated into an exploit worthy of Sivajee.' [2]

[1] Elphinstone (*Life of Elphinstone*, i. 275).
[2] James Cuninghame Grant Duff, *A History of the Mahrattas*, edited by S. M. Edwardes, ii. 442.

His late jailors, who did not share the popular enthusiasm, forced on the sullen Peshwa a new Treaty of Poona (May, 1817). This was a hard one, as even the following statement (which might serve as a model of how many question-begging assertions could be crammed into little space) half admits: 'The rights of war are proverbially severe. The Peshwa's conduct gave us unquestionable right to exact penalties for acts of scarcely disguised hostility, as well as to demand security for the future'.[1] It had not yet come to war; nevertheless, the Peshwa was treated as a beaten foe, commanded to close down abruptly all correspondence with other States, release all dependent rajas from submission, acknowledge complete subservience to the Company, abandon his claim to titular headship of the Marathas, acknowledge in set terms his belief in Trimbakji's guilt, and cede territory to support the subsidiary force. His resentment smouldered, five months later, into an attack which excites indignation and surprise in orthodox historians. We may admit that he was 'a perjured, vicious coward', whose 'usual game' was 'perfidious intrigue'.[2] But even a Washington or John Nicholson, supposing such characters capable of emergence in Oriental races, might have been restive under such terms as had been 'riveted' on him in face of watching India. The truth is, we see in Anglo-Maratha relations the jarring of opposite codes of ethics and conduct. One side is swift in severity of judgment and punishment of vacillation and duplicity, even if it were duplicity arising out of humiliation and conscious helplessness—the other is still on a childish level of caprice and casualness, and a sub-childish level of silliness and cruelty. To the Marathas the British seemed ruthless, to the British the Marathas seemed contemptible. We may pity those who, like Gokla, the Peshwa's general, had to throw away their lives out of loyalty to a master whose follies they saw yet could not prevent, while they thought his independence worth even the supreme sacrifice, now that all India was rapidly sinking into servitude.

Elphinstone remained serene in the heart of the gathering storm; playing cards with lady friends, reading and confiding to his diary his 'reactions' to Sophocles and Thucydides and Walter Scott, rising at four and, after two hours Greek, riding out to the Briton's pastime of slaying; inflexibly just as he saw justice; aware of peril but above it; watchfully equable, though the clouds that gathered concealed lightning that might strike with death. Grant Duff, his only companion through

---

[1] *Life of Elphinstone*, i. 305-6.   [2] *Oxford History of India*, 631, 688.

it, has left an unforgettable picture [1] of the last night of watchfulness (October 28, 1817):

'The British cantonment and the Residency were perfectly still, and the inhabitants slept in the complete repose inspired by confidence in that profound peace to which they had been long accustomed; but in the Peishwa's camp, south of the town, all was noise and uproar. Mr. Elphinstone had as yet betrayed no suspicion of the Peishwa's treachery, and, as he now stood listening on the terrace, he probably thought that, in thus exposing the troops to be cut off without even the satisfaction of dying with their arms in their hands, he had followed the system of confidence, so strongly recommended, to a culpable extremity: but other motives influenced his conduct at this important moment. . . . Apprised of the Governor-General's secret plans and his intended movements on Gwalior, which many circumstances might have concurred to postpone, Mr. Elphinstone had studiously avoided every appearance which might affect the negotiations in Hindoostan, or by any preparation and apparent alarm on his part, give Sindia's secret emissaries at Poona reason to believe that war was inevitable. To have sent to the cantonments at that hour would have occasioned considerable stir; and in the meantime, by the reports of the spies, the Peishwa was evidently deliberating; the din in the city was dying away; the night was passing; and the motives which had hitherto prevented preparation determined Mr. Elphinstone to defer it some hours longer. Major J. A. Wilson, the officer in command of the European regiment on its march from Bombay, had already been made acquainted with the critical state of affairs, and was hastening forward.'

If anyone wonders why the British passed to the supreme control of India, this scene, happily preserved by the vivid memory of one of its two participants, should remove his difficulty—Elphinstone listening from his veranda to the mad tumult of the city close to which his handful of troops slept unwarned, risking their lives and his deliberately on the chances of peace and lest he should mar the train of action which his Governor-General was laying elsewhere.

Next day, after ascertaining that attack was a matter of hours, Elphinstone stationed 250 men at the Residency, and moved out the rest of his tiny army to Kirki, four miles away. His sepoys stood fast against seduction and threats; and after further fruitless negotiations, on November 5 the Company's troops were invested. Again the scene is preserved by an eye-witness: [2]

'Those only who have witnessed the Bore in the Gulf of Cambay, and have seen in perfection the approach of that roaring tide, can form the exact idea presented to the author at sight of the Peishwa's army. It was towards the afternoon of a very sultry day; there was a dead calm, and no sound was

[1] Grant Duff, ii. 472-3.   [2] *Op. cit.* ii. 477.

heard, except the rushing, the trampling and neighing of the horses, and the rumbling of the gun wheels. The effect was heightened, by seeing the peaceful peasantry flying from their work in the fields, the bullocks breaking from their yokes, the wild antelopes startled from sleep, bounding off, and then turning for a moment to gaze on this tremendous inundation, which swept all before it, levelled the hedges and standing corn, and completely overwhelmed every ordinary barrier as it moved.'

The Peshwa's heart failed him, seeing the enemy standing firm in the floods that swept around them. The attack, launched by his gallant general Gokla, failed miserably; 2800 men, of whom 800 were Europeans, with a loss of 86 killed and wounded, repulsed 18,000 horse and 8000 foot, with a loss of 500. The Peshwa vented his rage and disappointment on the Residency, which was gutted, not one stone being left upon another. He had shot his bolt; after Kirki he 'never rose above the character of a heartless and desperate fugitive'.[1]

A relief force advanced swiftly on Poona, and routed the Peshwa on the 16th at Yeraoda, since famous as the site of Mahatma Gandhi's periodic 'retreats' in jail. Poona fell, and the chase of the Peshwa began. He caught Captain Staunton's 800 at Koregaon, 'the Indian Thermopylae',[2] where for eight hours, frantic with thirst, they held out against attack after attack by thirty times their number. 'Their situation towards evening was very hopeless.'[3] But the Peshwa withdrew, and in the darkness Staunton evacuated the shattered mud hovels, carrying off as many of his wounded as he could. The Marathas, a magnanimous people, lost heavily, but 'have the generosity, on all occasions, to do justice to the heroic defenders of Korygaum'.

Meanwhile, the Peshwa's secret ally, the Raja of Nagpur, had attacked his own Resident, Jenkins, in the first of a series of events that were almost exact repetition of those at Poona. In fighting which began on the evening of November 26, 1817, and lasted for eighteen hours, the Marathas were repulsed from Sitabaldi, two hills near Nagpur, with a ridge yoking them. The victory cost the defenders 333 killed and wounded, more than a quarter of their number. On December 19 the Raja was again routed in front of his capital, which presently surrendered.

Holkar's durbar had continued in 'everlasting turmoil', the normal condition of that turbulent court. Its real ruler was Tulsi Bai, who had been a concubine of Jeswant Rao Holkar—a woman profligate but intelligent and educated, of exceptional beauty and endowed with the

[1] Prinsep, ii. 82. [2] Colonel Tod's phrase.
[3] Grant Duff, ii. 486.

vigorous qualities that have so often showed in the women of her blood. She offered secretly to place herself and the young Holkar, a minor, under British protection. Her own people, discovering this, put her to death; and presently Indore, in the indeterminate casual manner of most of its wars, found itself in hostilities with the British southern army. On December 20 Sir Thomas Hislop forded the Sipra, and defeated the Marathas at Mahidpur. Again, Holkar's troops showed themselves the most dangerous of all Maratha adversaries. The victory cost 778 men, including 38 British officers; and though Holkar lost 3000 men, mainly in the pursuit, many of his infantry managed to retreat in good order, despite the enemy's cavalry strength. Mahidpur

' is the only action in the third Maratha war in which there was any considerable European element in the British forces engaged. Other battles, such as Kirkee, Sitabaldi, and Koregaon, were won almost entirely by native troops under the command of trusted British officers'.[1]

The war was now nearly over. Gokla, aware that all was lost, died fighting in the last battle, the cavalry skirmish of Ashti (February 20, 1818). A number of fortresses remained to be captured, the last, Asirgarh, surrendering in April, 1819.

The Governor-General's comprehensive settlement left Holkar and Sindhia with approximately the territories they have to-day, but now definitely and finally part of the British system, with powers and limits plainly indicated. The Bhonsla Raja was deposed, and lost his lands north of the Narmada; he fled to the Sikhs, and a minor took his place, with the British in real control. The Peshwaship was abolished; Baji Rao, by Malcolm's precipitate generosity, was given a large pension, the refusal to continue which was the action which gave mortal offence to his son, 'the Nana Sahib'. At Ashti, the Raja of Satara was among the captives; rescued from the Peshwa's control, he was re-established in his kingdom, with additional sanction from the all-powerful Kompani Bahadur. Elphinstone, as Commissioner, seated him on his throne 'with great pomp' (April, 1818); and the Raja 'published two proclamations, the one announcing his connexion with the British Government, the other making over entire powers for the arrangement and government of his country' to Captain Grant (Grant Duff), the future historian of his people. In 1817 the Rajput States, in quick succession, were formally made protectorates. In 1819 the Rao of Kachchh (Cutch), who had also

[1] *Op. cit.* ii. 503 (editor's comment, in Oxford University Press reissue).

'been caught in the wide sweep of the net of treaties',[1] kicked against the meshes, and after a brief war was deposed for an infant. The Company thus reached the Indus mouth, and only the Punjab remained independent.

Hastings encouraged Stamford Raffles in founding Singapore, 1819. The Dutch were exceedingly vexed, but were placated, a few years later, when the Company exchanged its Sumatran settlements for the Dutch possessions still left in India.

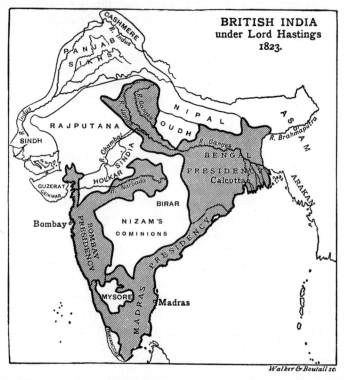

BRITISH INDIA
under Lord Hastings
1823.

Walker & Boutall sc.

Probably peace has never descended anywhere more gratefully than on the wasted regions of Central India. Sir John Malcolm, who played so prominent a part in the ending of tumults, wrote shortly afterwards:[2]

'With the means we had at our command, the work of force was comparatively easy; the liberality of our Government gave grace to conquest, and men were for the moment satisfied to be at the feet of generous and humane conquerors. Wearied with a state of continued warfare and anarchy, the loss

[1] *Oxford History of India*, 639.   [2] *A Memoir of Central India*, ii. 264-8.

even of power was hardly regretted: halcyon days were anticipated, and men prostrated themselves in hopes of elevation. All these impressions, made by the combined effects of power, humanity, and fortune, were improved to the utmost by the character of our first measures. The agents of Government were generally individuals who had acquired a name in the scene where they were employed: they were unfettered by rules and their acts were adapted to soothe the passions, and accord with the habits and prejudices of those whom they had to conciliate or to reduce to obedience. But there are many causes which operate to make a period like this, one of short duration; and the change to a colder system of policy, and the introduction of our laws and regulations into countries immediately dependent upon us, naturally excite agitation and alarm. It is the hour in which men awake from a dream. Disgust and discontent succeed to terror and admiration; and the princes, the chiefs, and all who had enjoyed rank or influence, see nothing but a system dooming them to immediate decline and ultimate annihilation. . . .

' The same classes of men do not fill the same places in society, under our government, as they did under a Native prince; nor are men actuated by similar motives. Our administration, though just, is cold and rigid. If it creates no alarm, it inspires little, if any emulation. The people are protected, but not animated or attached. It is rare that any native of India living under it can suffer injury or wrong; but still more rare that he can be encouraged or elevated by favour or distinction. Our rules and regulations constitute a despotic power, which is alike imperative upon the governors and the governed. Its character impels it to generalize, and its forms, as well as principles, are unyielding.'

The Governor-General's own observations in Bengal and his enlightening tour through the up-country corroborated Malcolm's testimony from Central India. 'Our people', he wrote, 'are too dry with the natives, who give us high credit for justice, but I fear they regard us in general as very repulsive'.[1] When Munro from Madras pleaded passionately [2] with him against the now settled policy of granting no employment but the most mechanical and trivial to even the ablest Indians, we seem to be listening down a prolonged lapse of time, to Henry Lawrence's criticism, on the eve of the Mutiny, of the absurdity of expecting men endowed with feelings and ambitions to rest content with a clerkship in administration or a corporal's authority in the field; or to the complaint of Rabindranath Tagore [3] in our own day, that his country's Government had become like patent foods, something 'untouched by hand'. But the generation whose memory went back to an

[1] *Private Journal*, i. 338.
[2] See Appendix B, 'Opinions of Sir Thomas Munro and Bishop Heber'.
[3] In his *Nationalism*.

era when British and Indians met on terms of equality and often of friendship was passing fast. Munro's course was nearly run; he and others like him were growing into survivals, venerated as having been fine men in their prime but recognised as now not quite up-to-date.

We come to the one really perplexing and distressing part of Lord Hastings's career. We have seen how heartily historians reprobate the misgovernment of 'those bad rulers, the Peshwa and Apa Sahib'.•Unfortunately, the countries of princes meritorious enough to retain the paramount Power's support were no happier than theirs. Haidarabad was

' a great congeries of diseases. Nothing seemed to flourish there except corruption . . . the wretched people were dragooned into submission, and the required payments extorted from them at the bayonet's point or the sabre's edge'.[1]

Monotonous iniquity, unchecked, unmitigated, reigned. Outside the swing of the sword was mere banditry. The 'State' was as little of an ordered system as any Maratha one, the only difference being that it was more steadily and pitilessly pillaged, and for the benefit of aliens. The Nizam's contingent were so highly paid that employment in his service, civil or military, was eagerly sought 'by the officers both of the King's and the Company's army. The Resident was importuned with applications for these comfortable staff appointments, and large sums passed annually into the pockets of our own people'.[1] The joyous catchword was, 'Nizzy pays for all'. At last a firm of money-lenders, William Palmer & Co., came to the distracted ruler's help. They lent him, mainly to pay his costly troops, £20,000 a month, in return for assignments of £300,000 a year on his revenues, that is, at 25 per cent. interest. The system was that used with the Nawab of the Carnatic; and the Nizam dealt with rascals even more impudent.

Throughout these transactions the Governor-General showed 'strong domestic attachment and excessive vanity'.[2] 'Influenced by the fact that one of the partners was married to a ward of his, a young lady whom he regarded as his daughter',[3] he sanctioned without enquiry all that the Palmer combination (a firm 'without office or establishment' [2]) did, and displayed a ferocity and tenacity of rage at opposition, which are explicable only on the supposition that India and age had worn

[1] *Life of Metcalfe*, ii. 10 ff.   [2] M. Martin, *The Indian Empire*, iii. 421.
[3] *Oxford History of India*, 639.

down his principles and mental soundness. In saying this, we give due weight to the possibility that he may at first have thought the arrangement justified as making the contingent's pay secure; no administration was ever so incubus-ridden as the Company's, with black financial care seated behind the horseman, while on every wind that blew from England the clamorous voices of Directors and shareholders cried out for dividends.

Sir William Rumbold, husband of the Governor-General's ward, was adventurer pure and simple, and 'had accompanied his Lordship to India with the not very rare or unintelligible design of making as much money as he could'.[1] Too old to make it by soldiering or in administrative service, he had toured native India in quest of a centre for operations; had looked longingly at Oudh, but it was oversupplied already with people like himself—at Delhi, but with Metcalfe there he decided it was no good—at Mysore, but it was too close to the recently purged Carnatic. Haidarabad therefore secured the advantages of his presence. His firm soon had a stranglehold on the State, when a piece of cruel ill-luck befell it, in Metcalfe's arrival as Resident (1820).

Metcalfe came at a time when all of even his valour and honesty were to be hardly strained. Lord Hastings, entirely cynical where Nizzy's plucking was in proposal, forced the Resident to insert in a revised treaty imposed on the Nizam the following article, which he brought in the Governor-General's own handwriting:

' His Highness the Nizam, contemplating the great benefits which he has reaped from the late military operations, in the security of his dominions, and in the advantages accruing to his revenue, is anxious to manifest his sense of such a boon by a gratuitous contribution. In this view his Highness desires that he may be allowed to furnish sixteen lakhs of rupees (payable at the rate of four lakhs yearly till the amount be completed) for public purposes connected with the city of Calcutta or its vicinity . . . the sum shall be applied in such portions and for such objects as the Governor-General in Council may direct.'

The European quarters of the British capital were to obtain from the gratitude of the Company's one Faithful Ally lights, water and roads. A graceful gesture, but the Directors disallowed it—Lord Hastings thought, because they paid undue attention to what seemed to them 'the inconsistency of exacting from the resources of the State such a sum when we represent its finances to be embarrassed in such a degree as to require the aid of a British house of agency'. It may have been so.

[1] Kaye, *Life of Metcalfe*, ii. 45.

Metcalfe succinctly summarised Sir William Rumbold's ambition as 'to make a large and rapid fortune in the style of the old time, by other means than his own personal labour'. It is an ambition which society everywhere considers entirely respectable, if achieved along accepted lines and within the law. The Palmers only misjudgment was in underestimating Metcalfe's courage. He was appalled to discover everywhere 'decay and depopulation', and to find foreign financiers exercising control superior not only to the Nizam's, but to the paramount Power's. He quickly came to suspect that he was understood to be bribed into complicity; 'fruits, dinners, &c., &c.', were sent to the Residency, he reported, 'in such quantities as to give them the appearance of regular supplies, instead of being merely complimentary'. His predecessor's entire household had been in collusion with the Palmers and the Nizam's officers, and his own servants, of whatever race, expected Metcalfe to continue the arrangement. Recusancy was assumed to be unthinkable, with the Governor-General's son-in-law by adoption at the head of the enterprise; and Metcalfe's duty was excessively hard, to one who had been in such intimate friendship with Lord Hastings. Moreover, he had had close relations with the Palmers themselves. William Palmer was brother of one of his dearest friends, and son of General Palmer; Sir William Rumbold had been his guest in Delhi, and nursed by him through serious illness. Nevertheless, when in 1820 the firm proposed to the Nizam a sixty lakhs loan, he pointed out that the loan would be 'a mere fiction', made up by a transference of the existing debt, with eight lakhs commission to the lenders for their kindness added to it. It was true that interest on this swollen sum was being reduced to 18 per cent. But as to further accommodation, the Palmers 'went on with confidence lending afresh at their usual rate of interest, above 25 per cent'.[1] Sir William instructed him to keep quiet, and to use his influence to keep the Governor-General's Council quiet. As he very reasonably asked,

' What can the Government care whether the arrangement be more or less beneficial to us, provided it bestows upon the Nizam's Government the great advantages that have been held out?'

The firm represented that the Resident was backing the proposal, and Lord Hastings was fooled (it must be admitted, fooled very easily) into what looked like Government guaranteeing. 'The accumulation of wealth' in the firm's books, 'from the immense interest which they

[1] *Op. cit.* ii. 44.

charged, seemed to be boundless'. European officers eagerly put their money into so splendid a ramp, and these resources, combined with the Nizam's payments for his mainly mythical loan, 'was such as to supply the most wasteful expenditure on the part of the members of the firm, and was nevertheless overflowing'. Happy days had come again in Haidarabad.

But Metcalfe was miserable and indignant. In 1821 he proposed to open in Calcutta a loan at 6 per cent., to liberate the Nizam, though at enormous cost, from meshes that meant ruin. He was deeply concerned also for what always was close to his heart, the credit and dignity of his own people and Government. The Palmers replied with effrontery on a scale that moves into the region of musical comedy. They pretended to acquiesce, but claimed 6 lakhs 'compensation' for being paid: 'the sudden liquidation of the loan to the Nizam would inflict a very serious injury on the firm'.[1] Racked with unhappiness—he repeatedly said that if he had suspected what was happening, nothing would have induced him to come to Haidarabad—and anxious to close a business so humiliating, Metcalfe agreed to this. Rumbold nevertheless wrote the Governor-General an urgent private representation (or rather, misrepresentation) of the Resident's hostility. The Governor-General's wrath was hot and implacable. But Metcalfe stuck to his guns. Few letters so stiff and unyielding, while perfectly respectful, have ever been written to a Governor-General; and the writer's integrity throughout this intensely painful episode cost him Lord Hastings's friendship, and furnished him with a host of unscrupulous foes at home as well as in India. It probably kept him out of the Governor-Generalship later on. We may excerpt a few of his 'laments'. As to the Palmers, he says,

' I lament their connexion with some of the most profligate and rapacious of the governors of districts, through whom their character, and what is of more consequence, the British name, become involved in detestable acts of oppression, extortion and atrocity. I lament the power which they exercise in the country, . . . enforcing payment of debts, due to them either originally or by transfer, in an authoritative manner not becoming their mercantile character; acting with the double force of the Nizam's Government and the British name. . . . I lament the monopoly established in their favour by the sanction and virtual guarantee of the British Government, because it deprives the Nizam's Government of the power of going into the European money-market, where, with the same sanction, it might borrow money at less

[1] *Op. cit.* ii. 51.

than half the rate of interest which it pays to Messrs. Palmer and Co. I lament the political influence acquired by the House through the supposed countenance of your Lordship to Sir Wm. Rumbold, because it tends to the perversion of political influence for the purposes of private gain.'

He scouted the accusation that his opposition was due to personal spite. But Lord Hastings, whose administration in his last years went all to pieces, took the side of the Palmers.

Metcalfe became an object of ridicule in Haidarabad. But he was not the man to accept such a position. The Resident, he meant to be recognised as such; and to protect the people and British reputation. He found a cautious but convinced sympathiser in John Adam, the senior member of the Governor-General's Council; Adam was particularly shocked by Metcalfe's proof that the officers of the Residency, in his predecessor's time, had been in the gang, even if the Resident was not (and he probably was). Hastings himself, having incurred the Directors' censure for the affair, resigned, 1821, lingering listlessly in India until the end of 1822. Though a reconciliation was patched up between him and his brilliant and too fearless servant, after his return to England he kindled enmity against Metcalfe.

The Palmer controversy rose to heights of scurrilous partisanship unequalled since the time of Warren Hastings's trial; 'Sir William Rumbold's levies'[1] beating up all the prejudice they could. John Adam, who acted as Governor-General for seven months, until Lord Amherst arrived in August, 1823, disallowed the more flagrantly dishonest items of the Palmer claims. The firm were paid to the extent of eighty lakhs, a sufficient tax on Indian resources; and withdrew, a year later, by the simple process of going bankrupt,

' not from any run . . . but merely from want of funds to meet ordinary demands' (Minute in Council, C. T. Metcalfe, December 11, 1828).

But their affairs haunted India for long enough, and Sir William Rumbold remained active and dissatisfied.

The episode lowered Metcalfe's opinion of human nature, as he sorrowfully recorded, but gave him that contemptuous assessment of the worth of popularity (of which no man won more, and by entirely worthy means) which accompanied his courage to the end. The uncomplaining gallantry with which he supported through years the cancer which killed him is a story too deep for tears; but his stand against his own countrymen, and his friend the Governor-General in particular,

[1] *Op. cit.* ii. 90.

called for no less of character, and should be gratefully remembered by all who love the memory of brave men.

Lord Hastings's attitude is almost inexplicable, unless we take into account the influence exercised by a woman loved as a daughter and roused to hard anger and greed. Even so, it remains difficult to understand, for he himself was incorruptible to almost a prudish degree. Indeed, if anyone doubts that there was justice as well as urbanity in Lord Minto's partial recantation of his earlier severity of judgment:

' The loose principles which formerly prevailed amongst the Company's servants . . . deserved . . . a little more indulgence perhaps than, as one of its sworn enemies and persecutors, I was disposed to show it. Peculation and abuse were not merely tolerated; they were in a manner established and authorised by the parsimony of the Company in the regular remuneration of its servants'—

and, we may add, established and made almost inevitable by the pestilential sycophancy of the country—let him read Lord Hastings's *Private Journal*, with its reiterated narration of the way enormously valuable gifts were pressed upon him, despite his firm, courteous, and continued refusal. He and Lady Loudoun never took a thing; and it was almost superhuman to stand out when the donors were so unwearyingly silly in their determination to put the all-powerful British in their debt.

Lord Hastings refused to abolish suttee, and made the mistake, in 1813, of ordering that a police officer must be present at a widow-burning. This regulation was interpreted as giving official sanction to the cowardly and detestable rite; and Hastings himself finally admitted that it had increased 'these sacrifices'. As against 378 suttees officially reported in Bengal in 1815, 839 were reported in 1818. It was about this time that British notice was widely and often drawn to the seamy side of Hinduism, which in practice had become a thoroughly loathsome thing. The contempt engendered became an increasingly powerful factor making for ruthlessness in the attitude of the stronger towards the weaker people. The impartial historian, whatever his race, must admit that much of the scorn entertained for the practices and thought of the people of India at this time was deserved. The Governor-General brought out with him the European mind, jaded from experience of world-shaking revolutions followed by the dragging Napoleonic wars and from the Prince Regent's disillusioning friendship. He was perhaps unfortunate in having his closest contact with Bengal, whose inhabitants, sunk in centuries of oppression, had not yet begun their striking mental recovery. He regarded them with pity, but also with contempt; and there are periods in the history of every nation when both are merited:

' Every day more and more satisfies me that I formed a just estimate of those who inhabit Bengal at least. They are infantine in everything. Neat and dexterous in making any toy or ornament for which they have a pattern, they do not show a particle of invention; and their work, unless they follow some European model, is flimsy and inadequate. Their religious processions constantly remind me of the imitation of some public ceremony which English children would make. One sees seven or eight persons gravely following a fellow who is tapping on a kind of drum that sounds like a cracked tin kettle, and though nobody looks at them they have the air of being persuaded that they are doing something wonderfully interesting. The temples they build are just such as would be constructed by schoolboys in Europe, had they the habit of dealing in brick and mortar. The edifices are rarely above four feet high, exclusive of two or three steps on which they are raised, and contain some rude and shabby carving or delineation of their gods. If this be the rate of the men, one may easily conceive what that of the women must be. Never enjoying even female society, their lives are passed in the extreme of listlessness. It is this which produces so many instances of women burning themselves.' [1]

As for suttee, though the Government of Bengal dared not suppress it, Metcalfe in Delhi, following the discountenancing of it by its Muslim rulers, prohibited the rite. The Marathas also, who exercised—this is one of the paradoxes attaching to these freebooters—a genuine if capricious humanity, were in advance of the British administration:

' The Mahomedan rulers endeavoured, as much as they could without offending their Hindu subjects, to prevent it; and the Mahrattas, since they acquired paramount power in this country, have by a wise neglect and indifference, which neither encouraged by approval, nor provoked by prohibition, rendered this practice very rare. In the whole of Central India there have not been, as far as can be learnt, above 3 or 4 Sutties annually for the last 20 years.' [2]

Only in Rajasthan and Bengal did this cruelty persist on a large scale within the British sphere of influence; and in both countries the men had lost their natural heritage of independence, and were at the mercy of oppressors.

[1] *Private Journal*, June 23, 1814.
[2] Malcolm, *Central India*, ii. 207.

BOOK IV

PRE-MUTINY PARAMOUNTCY: ERA OF REFORMS AND SUPPRESSION OF INHUMANITIES

'If I do well I shall be blessed, whether any bless me or not.'—JOHN SELDEN.

CHRONOLOGICAL TABLE

Governor-General.

JOHN ADAM (acting).	1823. (January-July.)
LORD AMHERST.	1823. (August.)
	1824. War with Burma. Barrackpur mutiny.
	1826. Sack of Bharatpur. Treaty of Yandabo ends Burmese War.
	1827. Death of Sir Thomas Munro.
LORD WILLIAM CAVENDISH-	1828.
BENTINCK.	1829. (December.) Abolition of suttee in Bengal. Beginning of suppression of *thagi*.
	1830. Abolition of suttee in Madras and Bombay.
	1831. Raja of Mysore deposed, and State taken over in trust. Burnes's journey up Indus. Meeting at Rupar of Governor-General and Ranjit Singh.
	1833. Renewal of Company's charter.
	1835. Macaulay's minute on education.
SIR CHARLES METCALFE (acting).	1835. Dost Muhammad Amir of Kabul.
LORD AUCKLAND.	1836.
	1837. *Accession of Queen Victoria.* Colonel Low prevents revolution in Oudh. Famine in Hindustan.
	1838. Tripartite treaty between Shah Suja, the Afghan pretender, Ranjit Singh, and the Company.
	1839. New treaty forced on Sind Amirs. Death of Ranjit Singh. Invasion of Afghanistan and capture of Ghazni (July) and Kabul (August). Raja of Satara deposed.
	1840. Surrender of Dost Muhammad.
	1841. Murder of Burnes and Macnaghten.
LORD ELLENBOROUGH.	1842. Retreat from Kabul. Sale's defence of Jalalabad. Pollock's advance; reoccupation of Kabul. Restoration of Dost Muhammad.
	1843. Conquest of Sind. Defeat of Gwalior troops at Maharajpur and Panniar. Suppression of slavery.

CHAPTER I

LORD AMHERST AND LORD WILLIAM BENTINCK: THE OPENING UP OF THE NORTH-WEST

John Adam and the Press: Lord Amherst Governor-General: first Burmese War: the Barrackpur mutiny: sack of Bharatpur: Oudh: the Noozeed case: Lord William Bentinck Governor-General: Bird's Land Settlement of the North-West Provinces: charter renewal, 1833: Bentinck and native States: British travellers in Central Asia: Avitabile: Alexander Burnes.

JOHN ADAM's brief sway was remarkable only for his action against the Press. There had been Calcutta English journals since 1780. In Warren Hastings's time they were scurrilously personal, revelling in the wide range of material afforded by a settlement as non-moral as any cinema-crazed community of to-day. Checks were supplied by duels, assaults on editors, or vigorous executive action whenever Mrs. Hastings or her friends got too annoyed. In Cornwallis's time the Press was fairly well behaved; no one wanted to libel a Governor-General so respected and so respect-worthy. Wellesley and Minto maintained a thorough over-sight; and under them

' this dread of the free diffusion of knowledge became a chronic disease, . . . continually afflicting the members of Government with all sorts of hypo-chondriacal day-fears and night-mares, in which visions of the Printing Press and the Bible were ever making their flesh to creep, and their hair to stand erect with horror. It was our policy in those days to keep the natives of India in the profoundest possible state of barbarism and darkness, and every attempt to diffuse the light of knowledge among the people, either of our own or the independent states, was vehemently opposed and resented'.[1]

Lord Hastings followed, holding opinions liberal in the extreme and completely contemptuous of misrepresentation; he thought that India should be educated, and the Press left free to say what it liked. Munro for once was on the illiberal side, considering a free Press incompatible with despotic government.

It must be remembered that the British community in India was below the level of responsibility of even the eighteenth-century public

---

[1] Kaye, *Life of Metcalfe*, ii. 247-8.

in England. It was not a question of whether seditious lawyers and 'babus' should be allowed to write at large, but of whether every attempt of Government to cut down perquisites or economise on administration—and every personal grievance against executive action or merely against some individual—should be open to the imaginative letters of disgruntled anonymity. ' "Brutus" was, not improbably, a rising member of the Civil Service' [1]—some junior civilian who found the pagoda-tree a little higher than his friends had led him to suspect; 'and "Cleophas" a liberal-minded major on the general staff', who remembered better times before these jacobins came to ruin everything. These gentlemen, in Mr. Winston Churchill's admirable phrase, 'stood no nonsense from facts', and lived in a society which saw no reason why anyone should stand any nonsense from them.

Adam's action, however, was stupidly taken, on narrowly bureaucratic grounds. The editor of the *Calcutta Journal*, James Silk Buckingham, had brought out with him a sense of absurdity; and India had increased his natural light-heartedness. Madras had been unfortunate in its Governors, with the fine exception of Munro; a gentleman who occupied this position, 'to the regret of the public',[2] was given an extension of his term. Buckingham announced the news inside a black border, to Adam's exceeding wrath. Government had a fervent partisan, one Bryce, a Church of Scotland minister; Bryce started a rival journal, trouncing Buckingham in a manner which the Supreme Court, appealed to by the trouncee, decided was libellous. When Bryce was consoled with the lucrative post of Clerk to the Stationery Department, Buckingham was amused, and said so; he pictured the reverend gentleman entangled in tape and envelopes when he should be pondering sermons. Thereupon Adam, 'one of the old oligarchy of Calcutta—an honest, uncorrupted, good-hearted and very able man, with a mind warped by the chronic condition of bureaucracy, to which he had been so many years condemned',[3] rose from his desk, and 'smote heavily', in regulations 'which took all the pith and manhood out of the journals of the day'. Buckingham's licence to reside in India was cancelled; he was 'deported, ruined, and became for years a continual running sore in the flesh of the East India Company and the British Parliament'. He got into the House of Commons, 1832, and the Company found it wise to allow him a pension of £200 a year.

[1] *Life of Metcalfe*, ii. 249-50.
[2] Higginbotham, *Men Whom India Has Known*, 42.
[3] *Life of Metcalfe*, ii. 249-50.

Metcalfe disapproved of Adam's action. But this was the one period when Metcalfe did not matter.

Between the Company and Burma unsatisfactory relations had persisted for over thirty years. When Burma conquered Arakan, 1784, there was an influx of refugees into the Bengal delta, which already swarmed with pirates, mostly Portuguese and Mugs (mixed Bengalis and Arakanese). Burmese troops made no scruples about following them up, and Sir John Shore for the sake of peace surrendered their prey on condition that they retired with it. In Wellesley's time there were armed clashes, but he was too occupied with bigger wars to attend to the business. Fugitives continued to pour in, begging piteously not to be sent back; the Burmese continued to chase them in British territory. The Court of Ava informed the Company, in 1817, that if they did not return to their doom 'the vagabond Mugs . . . the Lord of the Seas and Earth would be obliged to reassert his authority over such places as Dacca and Murshidabad—undoubted apanages of the crown of Arakan'.[1] Lord Hastings was the wrong person to address such a menace to. However, war did not come until Lord Amherst's time.[2] It broke out in 1824.

To-day it seems strange to read, in the *Life of Henry Lawrence*,[3] that there was 'a panic that the Burmas had taken Chittagong, and were pushing up to Calcutta in their war boats'. But after years of overrunning their neighbours the Burmese were filled with conceit, and had conveyed their good opinion of themselves to others. The encounters between them and the Company's troops, though trivial, had been numerous, and the latter had generally got the worst of them. The Company began now with defeat, in Kachar (February, 1824). Then Maha Bandula, the most famous Burmese general, 'mopped up' a detachment at Ramu in May. The eastern frontier seemed threatened, and Bandula carried a set of golden fetters for the Governor-General.[4] But the British struck from the sea, occupied Rangoon (May, 1825), and proceeded to win victories. It was an absurd war, against an enemy who did much tom-toming, and tattooed his body with ferocious beasts to make himself invulnerable, but also dealt skilfully in underground pits behind stockades. It was a cruel war also. The Burmese refused to

---

[1] Anne Thackeray Ritchie and Richardson Evans, *Lord Amherst* ('Rulers of India'), 73.

[2] 1823-28.   [3] Edwardes and Merivale, 35.

[4] Major Snodgrass, *Narrative of the Burmese War*, 277.

grant or accept quarter. When they took prisoners—and there were some British reverses, whose repercussions in India were important—they executed them, the British frequently coming upon the sight of the hung-up bodies. Maha Bandula, hastily recalled from the Bengal frontier to meet the invaders, awoke to the fact that pitilessness was a game which might have two players; the campaign became tolerable in consequence. Sickness wrought great mortality, so that both sides were glad when peace was made (Treaty of Yandabo, February, 1826); the British were then getting uncomfortably near the Burmese capital. Maha Bandula, a genuinely remarkable man, though with barbarous methods of instilling courage into his men, had been killed by a rocket a year previously. No one will grudge the Burmese Court its official version of events: [1]

' White strangers of the west fastened a quarrel upon the Lord of the Golden Palace. They landed at Rangoon, took that place and Prome, and were permitted to advance as far as Yandaboo; for the King, from motives of piety and regard to life, made no preparation whatever to oppose them. The strangers had spent vast sums of money in their enterprise, so that by the time they reached Yandaboo their resources were exhausted, and they were in great distress. They then petitioned the King, who in his clemency and generosity sent them large sums of money to pay their expenses back, and ordered them out of the country'.

The large sums of money were an indemnity of one million sterling. Assam, Arakan, and the Tenasserim coast were annexed.

'Exaggerated reports of the strength and ferocity of the Burmese troops' [2] had swept through India:

' The peasants on the frontier fled in dismay from their villages; and every idle rumour was magnified so industriously by timid or designing people, that the native merchants of Calcutta were with difficulty persuaded to refrain from removing their families and property from under the very guns of Fort William'.

It was just such a disquiet as some of us remember on a smaller scale, when the *Emden* was working havoc among Indian shipping and shelling Madras. It brought about at Barrackpur, the Governor-General's place of residence near Calcutta, another rehearsal of the Great Mutiny. We are told that the sepoys had got above themselves, by reason of 'their pride in the successes that had been achieved in the campaigns

[1] W. E. B. Laurie, *Our Burmese Wars*, i. 60.
[2] Snodgrass, *Narrative of the Burmese War*, 74.

against Pindaris and Marathas',[1] which 'bred a spirit of insubordination', such as perhaps their more observant members noticed from time to time in their European comrades, particularly the officers. Moreover, an attempted invasion of Burma through Arakan was accompanied with pestilence and appalling mortality. The sepoys, high caste men, were furnished with precisely the same grievance that had repeatedly been held to justify mutinous behaviour of Company's officers, a heavy financial loss. Coolies, carriers, drivers, were offered higher pay than the infantry, to induce them to enlist for service which was dreaded; sepoys were told they must continue on the lower rates for which they had contracted. They 'also had a real material grievance owing to the impossibility of obtaining land transport, which had to be provided by the men themselves under the rules then in force', while the requirements of Government had gathered up most of the available beasts.

Vincent Smith remarks: 'As usual, the genuine grievance was made the occasion for raising the cry of religion in danger'.[2] The grievance, at any rate, was seen and admitted by many regimental officers, who tried to help the men from their own pockets. But 'strait-laced officialdom at headquarters was inflexible. . . . The men were under engagement to provide their own carriage, and government declined to relieve them of the responsibility'.[3] The 47th Native Infantry refused to move or to ground arms, and remained on the Barrackpur parade-ground,

' as described by some who witnessed the scene . . . dazed by excitement . . . men not so much bent on mischief as possessed by some fatal infatuation . . . "with ordered arms in a state of stupid desperation, resolved not to yield, but making no preparation to resist" '.[4]

After warning, guns were opened on them, making the parade-ground a shambles. The survivors

' fled in all directions, and were instantaneously dispersed. Above 800 muskets and uniforms were found in the adjacent fields and roads. The Court-martial sat immediately. The ringleaders (six) were hanged the next morning. Many

---

[1] *Lord Amherst*, 149.

[2] *Oxford History of India*, 649. But religion (as Hindus understand religion) *was* in danger; 'the usage of caste compelled each man to take his own set' (*Lord Amherst*, 148) of cooking utensils, for which no transport could be obtained. As for Vincent Smith's 'as usual', the extreme rarity with which disaffected elements raised the cry of 'religion in danger'—the most effective cry possible, for which plausible excuse always existed—is admiringly commented on by distinguished soldiers all through the troubled times which continued with scant intermission ever since Lord Wellesley's governor-generalship.

[3] *Lord Amherst*, 150.   [4] *Op. cit.* 153.

hundreds since have been found guilty and sentenced to death, but this was commuted to hard labour for fourteen years on the public roads. Five other ringleaders were executed afterwards, and one man whom the mutineers regarded as their Commander-in-Chief was hung in chains in front of the lines. . . . All the officers (native) were dismissed the service and their guilt proclaimed at the head of every regiment in their native language. . . .

'. . . our situation was awfully alarming. Lord Amherst resolved not to leave the house, and I determined not to quit him. Sarah behaved heroically, and, though ill, declared she would remain, and kept up her spirits, as we all did as well as we could.'[1]

It is generally considered that the episode should be judged retrospectively, through the lens of what happened thirty years later:

'It did not appear that the Sepoys had contemplated active resistance, for though in possession of ball-cartridge, hardly any had loaded their muskets. Sir E. Paget was much blamed for resorting at once to the extremest measure; but the events of 1857, which began at the same station of Barrackpore, throw a truer light on the gravity of the crime of military mutiny.[2]

'The punishment was just, but the fate of the regiment was unspeakably pathetic . . . the name of the regiment was effaced from the list of the army. . . . Those who blame the rigour shown in 1824 may, perhaps, ask themselves whether lenity might not have been misconstrued. No one felt more keenly than the Governor-General the pain of the spectacle',[3]

though he did not obtrude himself too closely upon it. However, 'nothing cheered and pleased him more than the proof he was hereafter to receive of the return of a better feeling among the soldiers . . . the 39th Native Infantry and the 60th Native Infantry volunteered services to go anywhere that Government ordered them'.

In 1826 took place the one considerable military action of Lord Amherst's administration inside India. The Bharatpur Raja died, 1825, perhaps without assistance; his nephew murdered the regent and took prisoner the new prince, who was six years old and, but for the swift interposition of Sir David Ochterlony, Commissioner at Delhi, would probably have joined 'the long list of Indian princes born too near a throne to escape death by a poisoned opiate, or the dextrous hand of an athlete'.[4] He was not delivered up when Ochterlony demanded; the long-desired *casus belli*, aggravated by much vaunting defiance, was

---

[1] Lady Amherst's *Journal*.

[2] Sir Herbert Edwardes and Herman Merivale, *Life of Sir Henry Lawrence*, i. 59.

[3] *Lord Amherst*, 153-4.   [4] M. Martin, *The Indian Empire*, iii. 426.

furnished against the grim fortress which India believed impregnable. This time the British commander, Lord Combermere, before storming blasted a tremendous breach: his men rushed in through the smoke and terror. The enemy suffered a loss of 8000, cut off by the cavalry almost to a man; the British casualties were 600. Lord Combermere's enthusiasm for financial gain attracted some comment; Metcalfe observed that, while he was ostensibly acting as the young Raja's protector, that child was plundered of even his brass pots. The General awarded himself 6 of the 48 lakhs of treasure found, which has been censured by even recent historians as overstepping proper bounds.[1] But to a Government generally moving from one triumphant campaign to another, the army had long been all-powerful; experience had proved repeatedly the danger of coming between it and its captures. And we who live on the wrong side of the World War can surely be happy in the spectacle of bygone jollity, of men happy and victorious, women gay and unbothered:

' It may cheer the present generation to hear of past illuminations and rejoicings which are almost like those in a fairy tale, in which everyone is victorious and comes home unharmed. On the king's birthday, April 24, there is a grand entertainment at Government House; Combermere and Bhartpur in lamps on the right, Campbell and Ava in coloured lamps on the left, wreaths round the pillars, George IV in the centre also in lamps, with the appropriate accompaniments of star and crown. In the great ballroom were transparencies representing Lord Combermere leading the young Raja into Bhartpur, followed by his staff, while a figure of Victory waved a laurel wreath. Also Sir Archibald Campbell on horseback with his steamer in the background, the Dagon Pagoda, and a nymph-like figure scattering olive branches,—India, Peace, Victory and other appropriate inscriptions were liberally scattered about, and the company danced till 3 o'clock morning.
' Rejoicings, alas, do not last for ever . . .' [2]

We must turn to finance. ' "Adapt your revenue to your ruling requirements" was the contention of Sir Charles Metcalfe. "Adapt your military requirements to the exigencies of economical finance" was the unceasing burden' [3] of those mean-spirited men, the Directors. 'And in a sense the Directors were right. The disaffection created by

---

[1] 'The glory of the achievement was dimmed by the excessive rapacity for prize-money displayed by Lord Combermere' (*Oxford History of India*, 653). Cf. Marshman (*History of India*, 356): 'The laurels of Bhurtpore were tarnished by the rapacity of the military authorities'; he considers 'rapacity' open to criticism before it becomes 'excessive'.

[2] *Lord Amherst*, 158.   [3] *Op. cit.* 33.

excessive or inappropriate imposts is no whit less dangerous than weak battalions, and the problem of finance pressed very heavily on the minds of those responsible.' Luckily the King of Oudh again proved a very present help, in 1825 and 1826 providing a million and a half sterling, thereby 'soothing the anxieties of the conscientious but impecunious John Company'.[1] Another helper was the Maharaja of Gwalior. Daulat Rao Sindhia died, 1827; and his wishes as regards an adopted child and his favourite wife's regency were respected, in consideration of a loan of eighty lakhs, whose interest was to be spent on a British subsidiary force.

His Majesty of Oudh had monetary anxieties of his own, Oudh having continued for forty years the prey of European harpies. As far back as 1798 Sir John Shore had refused to include in a treaty a clause making the Company the guarantor of alleged loans, which in the usual manner—dishonesty and 36 per cent. usury—had 'swelled to an amount calculated to excite a feeling of astonishment at the vast amount of rank vegetation springing from so inconsiderable a seed'[2] as the alleged original assistance. Successive Nawabs, harassed by pimps, pandars, dancing girls, and 'conscientious but impecunious John Company' ever busy with new wars, had accepted the aid of generous-minded Europeans; and in return had dispensed bonds 'with truly oriental magnificence. Had these securities been satisfied in due course, the Vizier would have set an example altogether new in India'. But, as Thornton observes, finding a theme adequate to his vivacity of ironical meiosis, the Wazir 'did not thus violate the principles upon which Eastern rulers ordinarily administer their pecuniary affairs'. Each Wazir (later, King) knew that he was dealing with venomous crooks, and he himself was usually a crook in his own fashion. Oudh for close on a century resembles a still living carcase on which thousands of bloated insects were battening.

The 'creditors', decade after decade, pressed for settlement of their steadily mounting claims, which no amount of such piecemeal composition as was progressively obtained could wipe out. The nature of these claims was by now pretty generally understood, and a Committee of the East India Company recorded (May 31, 1822) that 'loans at such an exorbitant rate of interest cannot justly be considered in any other light than as gambling transactions'. But better times were coming for the

[1] Op. cit. 182.
[2] Thornton, History of the British Empire in India, vi. 2-3.

creditors. As one by one the men who remembered when there were still native States not without qualities that called out respect—when a Gurkha war was a frightening campaign, and Bharatpur a still unconquered fastness, when Englishmen and Indians met as foes but as foes who still had hours of friendly equality—as Munro, Scotland's noblest gift to India, died, as an Elphinstone and then a Malcolm went, as Webbe and Graeme Mercer died, and Metcalfe was withdrawn into the Calcutta Secretariat, already a man touched with mortal disease and lingering on only until his place could be filled, a certainty of immeasurable superiority settled on British minds. It was felt that Indians had no particular rights beyond that of accepting the government provided for them, without demurs as to cost or kind. That this cost was immensely swollen by the voracity of unofficial Europeans troubled the best officials, and made them (Metcalfe was here an exception, for entirely liberal reasons) steadfast against lifting the licence on non-Company personnel or allowing 'colonisation' on any scale. But most took it in the light-hearted spirit of the old saying, that 'Nizzy pays for all': 'this was a period when the good fortune of those who were desirous of preying upon the people of India was in the ascendant'.[1] Nevertheless, the Oudh creditors received a series of checks in 1834, when Lord Ellenborough, supported by the Duke of Wellington (who was exceedingly well informed as to what lengths adventurers habitually went to, and held strong views about what he called 'these gentry'), asked a number of questions which were resented but not satisfactorily answered. Ultimately, 'after much tedious argument', during twenty years—and with this we may dismiss an unsavoury topic—'political influence procured a decision more favourable to the claims of the European money-lenders, against various native debtors in Oude, than was consistent with the honour of the British government'.[2]

The partial check which rapacity experienced in 1834 was due to some extent to its victory in 1832, a triumph so astounding that it set men thinking. During the worst times of the Madras corruption, various officials trumped up claims against the *Zemindar* of Noozeed, some based on bonds given by him, when in prison, to his jailor, Mr. James Hodges. The claims were so obviously worthless, even in those days, that they were left alone, after the *ʒemindari's* affairs had been finally settled in 1803, for thirty years. Nevertheless, the House of Lords in 1832 accepted them, though opposed at every stage by the whole power of the East India Company. The connoisseur of malversation should look into

[1] *Op. cit.* vi. 9.   [2] Montgomery Martin, iii. 422.

this once-notorious case; it would teach him something of the possibilities of really skilful dishonesty.

Opposition to acceptance of the whole claim (a million and a half sterling) against Oudh was due also to slowly growing perception of the value of Oudh as an unofficial treasury whenever the Company needed special subventions. Its annexation was always an event hovering more or less close to materialisation; and, referring to this possibility, Sir Robert Peel in 1834

' solemnly deprecated . . . the commencement of the exercise of sovereignty, by appropriating eleven hundred thousand pounds sterling of the property of the territory to the liquidation of a claim, for which it did not appear that the British State had ever made itself in the slightest degree responsible'.[1]

The Nepal War had acquainted British officers with the pleasure and health of Himalayan sojourning. Lord Amherst in 1827 started the custom of summering at Simla, which perhaps is his strongest title to remembrance. The three Governors-General who followed Lord Hastings were less powerful than the brood of vigorous soldiers with 'the knack of executive success', whose valour and spirit of conquest were within a quarter of a century to make the Company's dominion into an empire as superb as any the world has seen. There might be discontent beneath the surface, but it was discontent absurdly helpless. Courage, enterprise, physical and moral strength, were all on the rulers' side.

Lord William Cavendish-Bentinck arrived, July 4, 1828, and began with unpopularity, having to enforce stringent economies. These were of course accompanied with threats of mutiny by the military personnel, but had far-reaching administrative results, and after a considerable interval were saving half a million sterling in civil affairs and (rather more quickly) a million in the army. He abolished the Provincial Court of Appeal and Circuit, 'which had become proverbial for their dilatoriness and uncertainty of decision',[2] a gain financially and judicially. He licensed the direct passage of opium from Central India (where then, as now, certain States grew it largely) to Bombay, diverting it from Karachi; the British Government secured the profits which the Amirs of Sind lost. This action 'practically ensured a valuable contribution, paid for by the Chinese drug-taker, to take the place of the

[1] Thornton, vi. 20.

[2] Demetrius C. Boulger, *Lord William Bentinck*, 61.

alleged payment to the Company by the English tea-drinker'.[1] R. M.
Bird put through the Land Revenue settlement of the North-West (the
modern United) Provinces, Allahabad being given a separate Board of
Revenue. Most important of all, the urgency of economy led to the
extension of 'the uncovenanted services', already begun by Lord Amherst, a wide devolution of important administrative and judicial duties
to an Indian personnel, as far less costly than a solely European one.

The Company had lost its monopoly of the Indian trade in 1813.
Another twenty-year period closed in 1833, and opinion in England was
setting steadily and increasingly against renewing the charter. Probably the charter would have gone, if it had not been that by 1833
Lord William Bentinck's immense reforms in moral and social practices
had made a very different and far better impression abroad than the
surfeit of victories which in the dawning of modern thought and
modern ethics were wearying and even disgusting people. The Company's activities put up 'a better show', and what would probably have
been denied to a Wellesley or Hastings was granted to Bentinck. The
China trade monopoly, however, went the way of the old Indian one.
It had been grudgingly continued, and as the Burmese operations
opened up the Far Eastern trade increasingly, and its profits were seen
to be 'far in excess of its dimensions',[2] the demand that it be thrown open
proved too strong to be resisted. China has disappointed the West in
recent years, but in 1830 its people were satisfactory beyond their
neighbours; 'the capacity of the Chinese for consuming opium and
paying silver then seemed to be unlimited'. Moreover, the East India
Company was accused of profiteering in tea, a commodity which bulked
largely in their annual profit of over a million sterling from the Chinese
trade.

It is interesting to note that practically all the items which make up
the present-day controversy (or, rather, the controversy of a yesterday
that is only just finished) were established by 1830. The home remit-
tances amounted to three millions sterling, which the Company
covered by the profits of Chinese and Indian goods sold in London.
Five years of Lord Amherst's administration had seen average annual
deficits in the Indian revenues of close on the same sum; and the rule of
Lords Hastings and Amherst together had resulted in a total deficit of
nearly nineteen and a half millions. Bentinck turned the deficits into
what was a two millions surplus when he left, showing what was

---

[1] *Op. cit.* 121.   [2] *Op. cit.* 10.

possible if wars were avoided and revenues used for the ordinary administrative routine.

The Company had done England service, immensely augmenting commerce, adding to national pride, weakening and humiliating France and Holland. It drew dividends from its possession of India, and would have to be bought out if deprived of India. The Act of 1833, passed after discussion before 'empty benches and an uninterested audience' of the House of Commons and a less languid treatment by the House of Lords, reprieved the Company for twenty more years. The Proprietors' dividends became definitely chargeable on Indian territorial revenues, but were backed by collateral British Government stock.

The *Calcutta Gazette* (October, 1833) hailed the charter's renewal by calling for 'a general illumination and a display of fireworks', which were granted, and brought much satisfaction to a populace always agreeably avid for *tamashas*. The new regime came into force in the spring of 1834.

Bentinck's orders, arising naturally out of the need and demand for economy, were to leave native States alone. This he could not altogether do. In suppressing *thagi* he obtained the help of Oudh, Haidarabad, and Gwalior, the Maratha durbars behaving much more amicably than during Lord Hastings's drive against the Pindaris. He failed in his attempts to apply pressure on the Central States over the opium trade, however, and had to fall back on the arrangement whereby the Malwa opium was sent through British Indian ports. Mysore since Purnaya's retirement in 1811 had been robbed and terrorised till a peasants' revolt came in 1831; the Company suppressed this, and took the country over in trust,[1] almost certainly the only possible course. An Oudh minister who tried to reform administration was unsupported by the Power whose citizens were largely responsible for that kingdom's drawn-out wretchedness, and he was driven out. The Raja of Coorg, a murderous ruffian who refused to hold any relations with the British, was deposed after considerable fighting, in which the Governor-General acted as Commander-in-Chief, and Coorg was annexed. The Political Commissioner in Delhi was murdered, and the culprit, a chieftain, hanged, to the menace of a rising. Jaipur, after disturbances amounting to civil war, the murder of a British officer and the wounding of the Resident, and the child-raja's death, possibly by poison, was given a

---

[1] It was restored in 1868.

Council of Regency for a new child-king. Gwalior broke into internecine quarrels, Indore sank into disorder, Baroda became truculent and hostile, Udaipur drifted towards the condition which was presently to stir Henry Lawrence's contempt and his scepticism of Tod's rose-coloured pictures of the Rajputs.

All this completed the working out of the modern relationship of princes and paramount Power in its main technique, except for Haidarabad, which (as befitted its long and practically unbroken alliance) was treated as a case apart. Haidarabad sank now into chaos of the worst kind, left to its ruler's devices, which tended only towards show and luxury.

The peninsula and all Hindustan conquered, the Company looked earnestly to their western borders. Ranjit Singh, 'the Lion of the Punjab', was sinking fast to decrepitude. In October, 1831, Bentinck drew him into a camp of several days' duration, at Rupar, on his marches; 'those sons of glory, those two lights of men', displayed themselves on an Oriental counterpart of 'the Field of the Cloth of Gold',[1] and concluded a treaty of perpetual amity, which, as a matter of fact, was to last for another seventeen years—a long period for such treaties.

It was in Bentinck's time that the major bugbear of the century entered Indian politics. Russia, steadily encroaching on Persia and Turkestan, made the Indian Government cast roving eyes abroad, seeking fresh alliances with buffer States, pondering annexations which would provide a better frontier. Cutch was theirs already; and in 1825 Sind had been awed by the presence of 'a hostile demonstration'[2] on its frontiers. In journeys, sometimes open, sometimes in disguise, the Company were assiduously collecting geographical and military information concerning their neighbours. There had been Elphinstone's mission to Kabul, Malcolm's two missions to Persia. Central Asia was not as bigotedly closed to British infiltration as it afterwards became (thanks, mainly, to the two Afghan Wars). From 1819 to 1825, Moorcroft and Trebeck, two men not in any covenanted service, but spurred by adventurous courage and curiosity, explored (as horse-dealers and merchants, predecessors of Kipling's Afghan in *Kim*) Ladakh, Kashmir, Afghanistan, Balkh, Bokhara. Moorcroft died in the vast snowy loneliness behind the Hindu-Kush, disappointed that he had not stirred the Indian Government to overcome their apathy and fear of annoying the

---

[1] See Emily Eden, *Up the Country* (Oxford University Press, 1930), 186.

[2] Kaye, *History of the War in Afghanistan*, 175.

Sikh Power. He wrote to Metcalfe, who as Resident in Delhi had helped him and sympathised:

'It is somewhat humiliating that we should know so little of countries which touch upon our frontier; and this in a great measure out of respect for a nation that is as despicable as insolent, whose origin was founded upon rapine, and which exists by acquiring conquests it only retains by depopulating the territory.'

His view of the Sikhs was largely coloured by the prejudice he found in Afghanistan. Ranjit Singh, after rising to supreme power among his people, had steadily pushed back the border tribes and their suzerain in Kabul, in 1834 wresting from them Peshawar. He was aided by soldiers broken in the downfall of Napoleon, most prominent being Avitabile, 'the ferocious Neapolitan', whose methods revolted Henry Lawrence, his guest during some of the Afghan War:

'All that can be said in his favour is, that he has savages to deal with— but why should he deal with them as a savage? He might be as energetic and as summary as he pleased, and no one would object to his dealing with a lawless people in such manner as would restrain them in their practices; but he might spare us the scenes that so frequently occur in the streets of Peshawur, equally revolting to humanity and decency.' [1]

Avitabile blew from guns, impaled, flayed alive, left men naked and honey-smeared in the sun to die. Yet Lawrence thought him, though 'just the picture of one of Rubens' Satyrs, one of the world's master-minds'; and to his wife he added, 'Remember . . . that I have eaten of his salt, and that he has been civil to me. We must therefore, in telling the truth, do so in mercy'. But the Sikhs added, to cruelty ruthless as their foes', fighting qualities which make Moorcroft's adjective 'despicable' ring queerly in our modern knowledge of them.

Moorcroft was before his time, but only a few years before it. The time came suddenly, bringing with it the man. Alexander Burnes at the age of sixteen arrived in Bombay, 1821; and 'at a period of his career when the majority of young men are mastering the details of company-drill, and wasting their time in the strenuous idleness of cantonment life',[2] was a noted linguist, and while yet in his teens the official Persian translator to the Sudder Court. In 1831 he was sent up the Indus, from the 'enlightened desire' of Lord Ellenborough, President of the Board of Control, 'to ascertain' that river's 'commercial possibilities'. The

[1] Henry Lawrence, An Adventurer in the Punjaub, chapter ii.   [2] Kaye, i. 175.

Sind Amirs were told that they were to throw open their river. Burnes's ostensible mission was to take a present of fine English horses to Ranjit Singh.

Metcalfe, in a Minute of Council (October, 1830), contemptuously called the camouflaged expedition 'a trick unworthy of our government, which cannot fail when detected, as most probably it will be, to excite the jealousy and indignation of the powers on whom we play it'. The Amirs watched with dismay; one spectator at the riverside lifting his hands and crying 'Sind is gone, since the English have seen the river, which is the road to its conquest'. But Burnes went on, and was received honourably by Ranjit Singh, who was delighted with the horses. Returning, at Ludhiana he met a former Amir of Afghanistan, Shah Suja, whom his own people had driven out in 1809 and repulsed twice in attempts since; Shah Suja spoke warmly and longingly of the joy it would be to him to be back in Kabul, with an English Resident and the English using his country as a high-road between Europe and India. Full of enthusiasm, Burnes obtained passports from the Indian Government for an overland journey 'to England', a journey which took him over Afghanistan, the Central Asian khanates, Persia, and by sea back to Bombay. In justice to the man who was destined to play so prominent a part in the silliest and most unjust war ever waged by the Indian Government, it is fair to say that he stated emphatically that Shah Suja lacked both energy to recover his throne and tact to keep it, while he found the ruling Kabul chief, Dost Muhammad, a far superior man, and his people 'simple-minded, sober', 'of frank, open manners, impulsive and variable almost to childishness'.

Burnes's travels made a tremendous impression. In India, and then in London, he was lionised excessively; fashionable ladies besought him to honour their gatherings, statesmen and scholars listened eagerly to him. Special missions to Sind (1835) and Kabul (1837) followed. All this he enjoyed immensely. The rest of his career will emerge in the course of narrative. Kaye observes pityingly:

' It was the hard fate of Alexander Burnes to be over-rated at the outset and under-rated at the close of his career.'

CHAPTER II

RACIAL ESTRANGEMENT AND CHANGING OF HINDU THOUGHT AND AMBITIONS

The widening gap: fears of old-time officials: Metcalfe and intelligent and influential native gentlemen of Calcutta: William Carey: Rammohan Roy: Henry Vivian Derozio: Dr. Richardson: the Brahmo Samaj: the Bengal Renaissance: Michael Dutt: the education controversy: introduction of travel by steam: Malcolm and the Bombay Supreme Court: Metcalfe as acting Governor-General.

BENTINCK's entertainments were magnificent; and 'he achieved fame by permitting Indians to drive to the Governor-General's house in carriages',[1] at a time when superiority on one side, and timidity on the other, had grown to such lengths that

' on going to a station no Englishman thought of calling on the notables of the district, as was once done as a matter of course; instead, certificates of respectability were required of the notables before they could be guaranteed a chair when they visited the officer. . . . In Calcutta many writers expected every Indian to salute them.'

Lord William did something, by precept and example, to mend matters. But it was a passing improvement only; and racial relations in Bengal continued what they are still—the amazement of the society of India's saner regions. Elphinstone was scornfully aristocratic even among his own people. But he knew well that India had its own aristocracy, whose friendship was worth regarding. He told Malcolm (May 24, 1819):

' The picture you draw of the state of India, as it is likely to be for the next four or five years, makes me regret that you are likely so soon to leave it. It has sometimes struck me that the fault of our younger politicians—who have never seen the Indian states in the days of their power—is a contempt for the natives, and an inclination to carry everything with a high hand.'

Towards the end of Lord Hastings's time, he wrote what many felt about conditions in Bengal:

' Sir Henry Strachey, in his report laid before Parliament, attributes many of the defects in our administration in Bengal to the immeasurable distance between us and the natives, and afterwards adds that there is scarcely a native in his district who would think of sitting down in the presence of an English

---

[1] T. G. P. Spear, *The Nabobs*, 140. See the whole chapter, 'Racial Relations'.

gentleman. Here every man above the rank of a hircarra sits down before us, and did before the Peshwa; even a common ryot, if he had to stay any time, would sit down on the ground. This contributes, as far as the mechanical parts of the society can, to keep up the intercourse that ought to subsist between the governors and the governed: there is, however, a great chance that it will be allowed to die away. The great means of keeping it up is for gentlemen to receive the natives often, when not on business.' [1]

Admitting the degradation, and in many things depravity, which had overtaken the native populations, there was, nevertheless, in Bengal a stratum of Indian life where liberal sentiments were cultivated, and modern enlightenment was beginning to marry with ancient culture and courtesy. There is pathos in the Address given to Metcalfe in 1835, when he was preparing to close his superbly beneficent career, 'signed by more than five hundred of the most intelligent and influential native gentlemen resident at the capital'; and in the understanding and sympathy of his reply:

' Our opportunities of estimating the private qualities that have earned you the love of your countrymen have necessarily been few. But it would be a reproach to our hearts and understandings, if we did not come forward to proclaim our sense of the inflexible regard for equal justice, and utter contempt for abuse, corruption, and chicanery, which have uniformly marked your official career.

' I greatly lament that a difference in religion and customs should operate, as it does, in a great degree, to prevent the benefits of social intercourse between the native and European communities in India; and consequently to preclude that personal intimacy, and that knowledge of private character, which are the chief cements of mutual attachment. You can neither share in our convivial enjoyments nor take an interest in our amusements; and it is much to be regretted that nothing has yet been devised, which, being suited to the habits and tastes of both parties, might lead naturally to that frequency of intercourse, which is so much to be desired, as tending to unite all in the bonds of affection. I trust that time will effect this desirable result, and remove the obstacles which retard it.'

The process Metcalfe prayed for had already achieved notable (though by Government unsuspected) progress. William Carey, ex-cobbler and Baptist missionary, settled at Serampur in 1799, finding in Danish territory the toleration refused in lands under Company control. For over forty years he laboured with a practical wisdom and a catholic enthusiasm for every kind of enlightenment, which both recall John Wesley. He and his colleagues introduced printing; and Bengali prose

[1] *Life*, ii. 82-3.

saw its birth in the translations and treatises of pandits working under
their direction. Bengal itself also produced a great man. Rammohan
Roy (1774-1833), while yet a boy, saw the unwilling death of his
brother's widow on her husband's pyre; emotional and intellectual
revolt stirred together, and he found himself driven out on a path as
lonely as any ever trodden by a valiant spirit. To his knowledge of
Sanskrit, Persian, Arabic, he added English, Greek, Hebrew, that he
might read the Bible; and he sought out such European acquaintance as
was possible to a native of Bengal. In 1820, he published *The Precepts
of Jesus the Guide to Peace and Happiness*, and was soon involved in a
controversy with the Serampur missionary Dr. Marshman, to whom
his rejection of Christ's deity was a heresy outweighing his close
approach to Christianity in other matters. But he found allies in the
Unitarians of England, and gathered a band of Bengalis theistically
minded like himself, who formed the nucleus of the Brahmo Samaj; he
ravaged orthodox Hinduism with his attacks on suttee, idolatry, and the
manifold mischiefs and errors of contemporary religion. There are noble
strains in Hindu thought, and India has never lacked saints and mystics;
but Hinduism at this time was an insanely wicked system, enjoining
a multitude of revolting practices. Rammohan Roy's courage by 1820,
or even earlier, 'raised such a feeling against me that I was at last
deserted by every person except two or three Scotch friends, to whom
and to the nation to which they belong I will always feel grateful'. He
thought Bentinck's prohibition of suttee premature and inexpedient.
But his support of the action in England (which he visited in 1830, and
where he died, 1833), in private and before the Select Committee of the
House of Commons examining Indian affairs, was invaluable in procuring the rejection of the appeal of over five hundred leading Bengalis
to the Privy Council, against the prohibition.

Elphinstone in 1822 noted

' the wonderful improvement of the natives that begins to be discernible, in
Bengal especially. There is a Bengalee newspaper, which discusses all subjects, and is interesting even to English readers, though of course often
puerile and often mistaken.

' Ram Mohun Roy, wisely retaining the name and observances of a Hindoo,
is writing books in favour of Deism, and many natives begin to discover
curiosity and interest about the form of their government as well as its proceedings, together with a strong spirit of reform as applied to the science,
religion, and morals of their nation. Amidst all this there is a great deal of
cant, affectation, and imposture, Bengalees talking about liberty and phil-
anthropy, and declaiming against the efforts of the Tories to crush the infant

liberty of the press . . . but even to use this sort of language without understanding it is a wonderful advance, and from admiring the sound, people
must come to relish the sense.'

The dog was beginning to walk on his hind legs like a man—remotely;
he did not do it well, but he was beginning to do it.

Bengal had other spirits swift and brave, and filled with intellectual
fire. A half-caste Portuguese, Henry Louis Vivian Derozio, in 1826, at
the age of seventeen, joined the staff of the Hindu College,[1] Calcutta
(now the Presidency College). Derozio's life flamed out quickly.
To him truth and beauty were a passion, and their attainment worth
infinitely more than the keeping of life. His own verse, a flood
romantic, flushed, luxuriant, was valueless; but his enthusiasm and
selflessness swayed his students wildly. Such an emancipation seemed
to be coming to intellectual Young Bengal that the orthodox compelled
his dismissal. His defence, though unavailing, was noble:

' Entrusted as I was for some time with the education of youths peculiarly
circumstanced, was it for me to have made them pert and ignorant dogmatists
by permitting them to know what could be said upon only one side of grave
questions? . . . I never teach such absurdity.'

He started a daily paper, *The East Indian*, but before he could make a
new career, cholera killed him, December 23, 1831.

The Hindu College had found another remarkable teacher, Dr.
Richardson. Thanks to such men as these, Bengal not only gained the
intellectual primacy of India, but possessed it so firmly established that
even to-day the largest half of current literature in such a language as
Gujarati is translations from Bengali; there is no Indian vernacular
which does not still exist in a state of considerable dependence
on this the most vigorous of them all. The Derozio school cared
nothing for nationalism, despising everything Indian, awake to one
fact only, that at last intellectual freedom had come, and that nothing
else mattered. Movements long spent in Europe found renewal here:
the French Revolution and its ideas, the late eighteenth-century
philosophers, such poets as Shelley and Byron. More than vigorous, they were often reckless, against superstition; students would
fling beef-bones into the houses of the orthodox, would go round
shouting, 'We have eaten Mussulman bread', would stage ceremonies of
mock-conversion to Islam. They showed great earnestness for social
reform; and when Dr. Alexander Duff founded in 1845 what is now the

[1] See p. 266.

Scottish Churches College, he won swiftly from the highest Hindu families a group of converts whose after-career proved them of outstanding
ability and character. Among them were Lalbihari De, whose *Folk Tales
of Bengal* and *Bengal Peasant Life* enjoyed a long spell of use in schools;
and Kalicharan Banerji, Registrar of Calcutta University, one of the
founders of the National Congress (*circa* 1885), a man influential in
Bengali literature. Krishnamohan Banerji, another man destined to
matter greatly in his country's life, in 1833 left the Derozio group,
with their scorn for all religion as superstition, and was baptised. For a
while it looked as if Bengal, led by its young intelligentsia, was at the
start of a mass movement into Christianity recalling the early centuries
of Christian missions in Europe. Macaulay's belief that enlightenment
would kill Hinduism and bring in Christianity, so derided now, in its
context was a reasonable guess. But as with the Oxford Movement,
that contemporary drift of Anglicanism towards Rome—one stirring
similar hope, alarm, and rage—a Dr. Pusey was found in Hinduism,
in Debendranath Tagore, father of the poet, and the consolidator,
practically the real founder, of the Brahmo Samaj. 'Wait a bit! I will
stop all this', he said, when he heard of Duff's success. In his *Autobiography* he tells us how he went from house to house cementing opposition. The Brahmo Samaj did what orthodox Hinduism was powerless
to do; providing a half-way house where men could worship without
idolatry and the cruelties which passed for religion, it stayed the exodus.
The Brahmo Samaj to-day is a dying institution. But for seventy years
its influence was all-pervading in every higher walk of Bengali life, and
it produced a succession of men for whom the only adequate adjective is
'noble'. Without them, Bengali intellectual and spiritual life would have
been almost negligible, whereas with them it was a beacon to the rest of
India, which Bengal saved by her example, as she was saving herself by
her exertions. The great house of the Tagores, in their more influential
members, were Brahmos, a galaxy of genius and accomplished talent;
they were supported by a society intensely individual, highly and
variously cultured, energetic in effort, upright in conduct. Christian
missions continued to win an occasional convert who mattered, notably
Madhusudhan Datta, better known by his baptismal name of Michael—
the greatest poet of nineteenth-century Bengal, author of the epic, *The
Death of Meghnad*, introducer of blank verse and the sonnet. But the
Brahmo Samaj provided what awakened consciences asked, without
compelling an absolute break with Hindu society.

With these spiritual movements secular reforms were also working. The early 'thirties, the period of the working of renewed revolutionary activity in Europe and of the beginning of electoral democracy in England, saw the passing from the Indian scene of the great figures, alternately soldiers and statesmen, moving at ease amid the frightened (yet with them trustful) princes of the land, self-confident, happy, athletic, preferring the saddle to the Councillor's seat, when on campaign hunting in the intervals between battles. A very different man was about to appear. The 1833 Act provided for an additional member of the Governor-General's Council, to codify the laws. As this, Mr. Thomas Babington Macaulay came, in 1834. He had thoughts on other than legal matters, and is perhaps best remembered in connection with India by his famous Minute on Education.

We must retrace our steps a little. The idea of State-controlled, State-organised machinery for universal education was as foreign to the English civil servants of his day as it would have been to the group of Indians like Rammohan Roy, Dwarkanath Tagore, and others who led the reformist movement. It is true that a system of that kind had been instituted in Prussia after 1806, but in almost every other country the primary responsibility for bringing up a child lay with the parent and the Churches. Government participation in England was confined to grants-in-aid, and these, which were on a small scale, did not involve any State control until 1856, when the Vice-President of the Council of Education was made responsible to Parliament. Forster's Education Act was to follow fourteen years later, but this did not destroy the dual system. A considerable part of English elementary education is still in Church schools. State interference is small both in the Public Schools and Universities. The English certainly did not bring to India any predilection for a unified secular educational system, yet this was what was actually developed during the twenty years preceding the Mutiny and was defined in the Directors' despatch of 1854, which determined the organisation of education throughout British India. Looking back over nearly a century of educational effort, the evils of a State system are sufficiently obvious, the failure of a secular Westernised education is writ large over India, but it is difficult to see what alternative lay before Bentinck and those who worked with him and after him. The Government entered unwillingly into the field of elementary education because the existing facilities were inadequate and there was no other body with the necessary driving force to undertake this work. It decided to support a modern Western type of higher education, but only after a long controversy, in which many English opposed and many Indians supported the view which Bentinck finally adopted. Both decisions followed inevitably from the decay of Hinduism and the disordered state of the country.

The state of education in India before the British occupation is, unfortunately, a favourite subject for political dissertations. This has led to a certain confusion of thought about the various types of indigenous teaching, of which three were of importance in the eighteenth century. The ideal training for the Brahmin youth is of great antiquity, and represents an extremely high standard of education. After assuming the sacred thread at the age of eight, the boy would spend fourteen years away from his home under the personal supervision of his *guru*, or in the forest *asram*. Such an upbringing was always confined to a very small and highly privileged class, and was probably only common in the hey-day of Brahminism, before the spread of Muhammadanism. This was not a type of education in which the Government could take part, though the traditional relation between *guru* and *chela* might be an inspiration to University teachers, as it has been to Rabindranath Tagore in his *asram* at Santiniketan. Two other institutions catered for a wider but still limited range of boys. These were the Muslim and Hindu schools which were common in the towns and larger villages. Both suffered during the eighteenth century from the continual disorders which disturbed most parts of the peninsula, but they were found in many districts when they came under British rule, and their work and scope are described in early reports. Most of them were of a very primitive nature, being usually attached to a temple or mosque. This meant the exclusion of the lower castes and the primitive tribes, and it is typical of the early attitude of the Government towards elementary education that almost the first elementary State schools were for the children of Bhils, Khonds, and of criminals whose parents could not send them to religious schools. The Muslim schools taught the Quran and some Persian to a few elder boys, but there is little evidence about the standard of teaching. In the Punjab, which was annexed later, indigenous education was surveyed with a more modern eye.

' The Hindu schools were rare, being either colleges in which Brahmin boys learnt Sanskrit and received a half-religious, half-professional training, or elementary schools where sons of Hindu shop-keepers were taught to keep accounts and read and write the traders' scripts. The few Gurmukhi schools that existed were of a purely religious character. The best feature of the indigenous schools was that they were not confined to the religious and mercantile classes, but were open to the few agriculturists who cared to attend them.'[1]

These schools continued to function, and some of them have survived till to-day. They had the usual weaknesses of isolated religious schools, and they only reached a very small proportion of the population. In 1835 Bentinck instituted an enquiry into the state of indigenous education in Bengal and Bihar, and found that under five per cent. of the male population attended these schools, but that 'certain classes of the native population, hitherto excluded by usage from vernacular instruction, have begun to aspire to its advantages.'[2] The more accurate survey of the North-West Provinces some ten years later showed that 'of a population which numbered in 1843 23,200,000 souls, and in which were consequently included more than 1,900,000 males of a school-going age, we can trace but 68,200 as in the receipt of any education whatever'. In all the recently acquired territory adult literacy was proportionately far lower than amongst the young.

The evidence does not suggest any widespread system of what would now be called popular education, but a fair amount of local effort by Hindu pandit or Muslim maulvi, and this would be supported, here and there, by grants from local princes. The training of elder Hindu boys, confined to a small section of the population, was obscurantist and ineffective.

' The ancient scriptures of the country, the famous records of numerous Hindu sects, had long since been discredited. The Vedas and Upanishads were sealed books. All that we knew of the immortal Mahabharata, Ramayana, or the Bhagavad Gita, was from the execrable translations into popular Bengali, which no respectable young man was supposed to read.'[3]

Persian, Sanskrit, and Arabic were taught, all of which were, from the Indian standpoint, 'dead' languages, though Persian remained the language of the courts until the time of Lord William Bentinck. Vernacular learning and vernacular literature were at a very low ebb, and were not considered a suitable medium for instruction.

' Though the past had produced very much that was noble and popular in vernacular literature, such as the Hindi work of Tulsidas or the Marathi of

[1] See Trevaskis, *The Land of the Five Rivers*, 179. The quotation is from a Punjab Administration Report.

[2] *Third Report on the State of Education in Bengal.*

[3] For an account of the decay of Hindu learning prior to the revival which took place after the Mutiny, see P. C. Mazumdar's *Life and Teachings of Keshab Chandra Sen*, from which this quotation is taken.

Tukaram, the existence of which the opponents of vernacular ignored, it was certainly true, as they urged, that very little was being produced at the time.' [1]

Such, roughly, was the position which confronted the Committee of Public Instruction which had been set up in 1823, and to which Bentinck looked for advice on education, and it was in this body that the struggle took place between the 'Orientalists' and the 'Anglicists' which culminated in Macaulay's famous minute, and the initiation of a policy which was to have such a profound effect on the future of India. Two points were in dispute—the type of education to be given in such colleges as received public assistance, and the best method for encouraging popular elementary education. The dispute which took place over the first question has rather obscured the importance of the policy adopted for the second.

The battle between 'Anglicists' and 'Orientalists' was fought out over the allocation of the Government grant to a few colleges in Bengal. Some of these had been founded under European initiative—such as the Muslim Madrasa at Calcutta, which was founded by Warren Hastings, and the Sanskrit College at Benares, which owed much to Jonathan Duncan. All of them, however, except the *Vidyalaya*, the Hindu College, were definitely Oriental in character. The *Vidyalaya*, which finally became the Presidency College, was founded in 1817 by a group of reformist Hindus, led by the English secularist watchmaker, David Hare. These Hindus, of whom Rammohan Roy was the most prominent, were anxious for a new type of education. They believed that the teaching of science would help to abolish certain social evils in the Hindu system, that it would make it easier for Indians to take their part in Government service, and that practical and engineering training would help to make their country prosperous. The Committee of Public Instruction was divided, but not along racial lines. Several Europeans were keen Orientalists, including Wilson, the principal of the Hindu College; others took the line, which was ultimately adopted by Bentinck, that if the Government contributed money it should be invested in some form of 'useful' training. The discussion was closely connected with the 'suttee' controversy, and the Orientalists suffered a severe blow because Wilson had doubted the wisdom and practicability of abolishing the practice. Bentinck finally gave his decision that the 'object of the British Government should be the promotion of English

[1] Arthur Mayhew, *The Education of India*, 84.

literature and science'.[1] The 'Anglicists' had won the day. As a foretaste of the expected revolution in Hindu mentality, the Medical College was opened to Indian students in 1837, and the orthodox Hindus heard to their dismay of Brahmins dissecting human bodies 'with even more than the indifference of European professional men'.[2]

Once it had been decided to encourage a modern type of education in the colleges, the use of English as a medium of instruction followed inevitably. The choice lay between English and either Sanskrit or Arabic. There was at the time a strong prejudice amongst educated Hindus against the use of the vernaculars for higher education, an attitude which had an exact parallel in medieval Europe. William Arnold, writing in 1840, notes the Punjabi scholar's strong objection to the use of Urdu.[3] Bentinck was guided solely by practical considerations. He believed that science would be the subject most taught, and, as between English and a 'dead' language, he preferred the former. He certainly had no feeling against the vernacular languages, and he gave a great impetus to their study when he abolished Persian in the law courts and substituted the vernacular as the official language in all except the highest courts. He was, however, anxious to foster the growth of a small educated class, who would know English and through that knowledge bring Western ideas to India. There was much talk at that time of what has been called the 'filtration' theory. Macaulay emphasises this idea in his minute of February, 1835. 'It is impossible for us, with our limited means, to attempt to educate the body of the people. We must do our best to form a class who may be interpreters between us and the millions whom we govern; a class of persons, Indian in blood and colour, but English in taste, in opinions, in morals, and in intellect. To that class we may leave it to refine the vernacular dialects of the country, to enrich those dialects with terms of science borrowed from the Western nomenclature, and to render them by degrees fit vehicles for conveying knowledge to the great mass of the population.' These ideas held the field for some twenty years, and led, especially in Bengal, to an excessive concentration on a modernised higher education. Looking back after a century of it, it is easy to see why Bentinck and his officials were too optimistic. The Hindu system divides the population into water-tight compartments, most unsuitable for filtration. The educated *Zemindar*

[1] The decision was given in a resolution dated March 7, 1835. Macaulay's well-known minute recommending this course was dated February 2 of that year.

[2] C. E. Trevelyan, *On the Education of the People of India*, 1838, p. 33.

[3] Director of Education in the Punjab. See p. 318.

did not return to his village and educate his tenants, or even undertake scientific farming. Science has not taken the place in education which was expected in 1830, and the higher castes have shown an overwhelming preference for literary and legal studies, which they are not likely to impart to others. The reformist movement amongst the educated classes was based on the Brahmo Samaj, and almost disappeared in the revival of Hindu orthodoxy, of nationalist sentiment, which followed the Mutiny. Yet Macaulay's forecast [1] has come partly true. We have formed a definite English-speaking 'class of persons', though they have no desire to act as interpreters for the Government. The vernaculars have become of greater relative importance, but it is the vernacular Press rather than the text-book which has penetrated into the villages. The dialects may not have been 'refined', but they have certainly been 'enriched' by the assimilation of foreign words and foreign idiom.

Steam was an event almost more revolutionising than education itself. In August, 1830, Bentinck decided in favour of the Red Sea route over the slow Cape one, for letters and tidings. After his governor-generalship, giving evidence in 1837 before a Select Committee of the House of Commons, he brought forward an argument for steam communication by the shortest route, which reads now like a prophecy which has been ironically fulfilled:

' It is through the means of a quite safe and frequent communication between all India and England that the natives of India in person will be enabled to bring their complaints and grievances before the authorities and the country; that large numbers of disinterested travellers will have it in their power to report to their country at home the nature and circumstances of this distant portion of the Empire. This result I hope will be to rouse the shameful apathy and indifference of Great Britain to the concerns of India; and by thus bringing the eye of the British public to bear upon India it may be hoped that the desired amelioration may be accomplished.'

In every way the West made it clear that it had come to remain. From 1830 onwards the Government possessed a summer capital in Simla, which had been in part annexed after the Gurkha War and in part purchased from the Maharaja of Patiala. Darjeeling was bought from the Raja of Sikkim in 1835. Bentinck also established the hill station of Ootacamund, in the Nilgiris of South India.

The mood and methods of the old brigandage were changing into those of modern industrialism and capitalism. The process of readjust-

---

[1] See Appendix C for Macaulay's Minute.

ment proved painful, as every such process must in intensely conservative circles. When in 1835 the five chief mercantile firms of Calcutta failed, the financial dislocation, following on the Palmers' failure in Lord Amherst's time, hit the Company's servants specially hard. It was difficult to know how money could be safely kept, in a country where commercial morality had been so low during so many decades.

CHAPTER III

ADMINISTRATION UNDER LORD WILLIAM BENTINCK

Bentinck and the new spirit in England: reaction against Hinduism: Bentinck's reforms: judicial changes: police: suppression of thagi and suttee: effect of these campaigns on administration: Sir Charles Metcalfe.

THE arrival of Lord William Bentinck marked the beginning of a new era in numerous ways. His seven years' rule proved a peaceful interlude between two periods of severe and costly campaigning, and thus made it possible to achieve reforms which were long overdue. Helped by his previous experience in Madras and a more efficient staff of officials, he consolidated and reorganised the administration which since the time of Cornwallis had been hastily adapted to the newly conquered countries. His own instincts were those of a Liberal reformer. He believed in peace, retrenchment, and reform, in free competition, free trade, and a strictly limited sphere of State action. In Sir Charles Metcalfe he had an admirable chief of staff who supplied the local knowledge and some of the driving force behind the reforms. These touched nearly every side of Indian life and formed the basis of the paternal government of the Victorian era. Bentinck initiated new policies in the spheres of finance, justice, and education. Freedom from war gave him a larger European staff and greater confidence in taking unpopular measures. He was able to turn his attention to the civilisation of savage tribes and the abolition of certain religious and social customs, such as suttee, the *meriah* sacrifices, and female infanticide.

This epoch is important from another point of view. Bentinck and the younger officials who came out in the 'twenties brought with them some of the new spirit which was causing a religious and social revival in England. For some years Wilberforce and Fowell Buxton had been exposing the horrors of slavery, and Sir James Mackintosh had been inveighing against the barbarities of the criminal code. They were beginning to have their effect. By 1830 over a hundred felonies had been removed from the category of capital offences, and English law became little more bloodthirsty than Muslim. In 1833 slavery was abolished throughout the British colonies. The Poor Law of 1834 helped to restore the working man's self-respect. In 1833 also, Keble preached his sermon on National Apostasy, and Newman published the first of the *Tracts for the Times*. They started a movement which was to have considerable influence upon many of the pre-Mutiny officials. A new leaven was working within the small English community in India, a new school of officials and officers began to make its influence felt. It was to show itself in a revolt against the lax morality common amongst Europeans in the East, against the patronage of idolatry by the Government, and against certain Hindu customs.[1] The English began to believe that they had a moral mission in India, that they represented a higher civilisation, a better religion. The younger men came out to India and received an impression of a country where crime flourished, and the mass of the people were steeped in a form of savagery which they connected with the Hindu religion.

Trevelyan, writing in the middle 'thirties on Indian education, talks of 'suttee, Thuggee, human sacrifices, Ghaut murders, and other excrescences of Hinduism and expressly enjoined by it'.[2] This was the view of many contemporaries, and the moral was only emphasised by the horrid example of the older generation of Englishmen, with 'their black wives running about picking up a little rice, while their husbands please them by worshipping the favourite idol'.[3] Evangelical activities in England were beginning to have their repercussions in India. Phrases like 'churchwarden to Juggernaut' and 'wet-nurse to Vishnu' embarrassed a Government which held that the policy of complete impartiality required the attendance of the Company's officers at

[1] The reactions of a younger civil servant to his older fellow-countrymen are shown in that curious novel *Oakfield*, written by Matthew Arnold's brother, W. D. Arnold, who died (1859) after a few years in India. See Matthew Arnold's commemorative poem, *A Southern Night*.

[2] C. E. Trevelyan, *The Education of the People of India*, 1838, p. 83. Trevelyan, later Sir Charles Trevelyan, was a prominent official of the Mutiny period. He was a brother-in-law of Macaulay.

[3] A. Mayhew, *Christianity and the Government of India*, 48.

Hindu and Muslim religious festivals. Government offices were still closed on such days, but open on Sunday, and a cocoanut was officially broken at the beginning of the monsoon. The question was to become still more acute under Lord Auckland, when Sir Peregrine Maitland, the Commander-in-Chief at Madras, resigned his post rather than punish a British soldier who refused to take part in a ceremonial parade in salutation of a Hindu deity. These ideas were beginning to affect the expatriated Englishman when Bentinck came to India. They had their counterpart in that reformist movement amongst certain sections of educated Hindus of which Rammohan Roy was the leader. Hinduism at that moment was at a low ebb, and the more enlightened Indians turned Westward for inspiration. Many Englishmen of that period would have subscribed to Macaulay's view, written in 1836, that 'if our plans of education are followed up, there will not be a single idolater among the respectable classes in Bengal thirty years hence'. The revival of orthodox Hinduism did not become vigorous or wide-spread[1] till after the Mutiny. When Bentinck arrived, nearly thirty years were still to pass before that catastrophe. His reforms started an era of great administrative activity, somewhat marred by the secularist complacency of the early Liberalism.

One of Bentinck's first tasks was both dangerous and unpopular. Since the Charter Act of 1813, which separated the Company's political and trading activities, there had been a rapid increase in the expenditure under the former head. By 1827 this had risen from about sixteen million yearly to over twenty-five million, and the difference was only partially covered by receipts from the newly added territories. There was a deficit of a million in the last year of Lord Amherst's term of office, and Bentinck sailed for India with definite instructions to cut down civil and military salaries and allowances, and reduce expenditure generally. The army was mulcted of half its *batta*, the extra allowance which the officers had come to regard as a permanent addition to their pay. Special committees examined and reduced the expenditure of each Presidency, cutting down the irregular military forces and part of the civil establishments. The work required great tact and firmness. These Bentinck possessed, but he never recovered from the odium engendered by those early years and to most Englishmen he remained 'the clipping Dutchman' until he retired.

---

[1] The 'counter-reformation', led by Debendranath Tagore (the poet's father) against Dr. Duff's success in Christian propaganda in the 'forties, was local.

The judicial system had been little altered since the time of Corn-wallis, and the Provincial Courts of Appeal were showing signs of deterioration. The administrative side of the civil service has usually attracted the ablest men, and this tendency was especially marked when new areas were being brought under control. The Courts had become, in Lord William Bentinck's words, 'resting-places for those members of the service who were deemed unfit for higher responsibilities'. The general standards of administration had improved, but the Courts re-mained hopelessly in arrears, both with the civil appeals and also their gaol-deliveries. The Courts were now abolished, and their criminal jurisdiction transferred to the Commissioners of Revenue. This experi-ment was a failure, and the Sessions duties were then allotted to the civil judges, who were instructed to hold a monthly gaol-delivery, and thus became the forerunners of the present District Judges. Their magisterial powers had, of course, to be transferred, and were given to the District Collectors, a 'blending of Somerset House and the Old Bailey' which survives in spite of obvious theoretical objections. The main features of district administration—the District Magistrate, who is also collector of revenue and head of the police, the Sessions Judge with criminal and civil jurisdiction—were thus established. The concentra-tion of power in the hands of the European District Magistrate was originally justified by the difficulty of initiating cases against gang-robbers, many of whom were protected by *Zemindars*, and by the need of a single authority in times of disorder. The system received a new lease of life in the Mutiny, and has continued since, though the revenue work is more stereotyped, and the District Magistrate has become more like a French *Préfet*, co-ordinating in each locality the many activities of a modern government.

Bombay, after Elphinstone's departure, saw a temporary revival of that struggle between a High Court, created in 1823, and the Executive, which had so disturbed Bengal forty years earlier. The Court claimed jurisdiction over every person in Bombay territory, then extended far beyond the port and adjacent islands. On October 6, 1828, the Pre-siding Judge told the world where, in his opinion, the Governor stood:

' Within these walls we own no equal, and no superior but God and the King. The East India Company, therefore, all those who govern their pos-sessions, however absolute over those whom they consider their subjects, must be told, as they have been told ten thousand times before, that in this court they are entitled to no more precedency and favour than the lowest suitor in it.'

Malcolm, the Governor, was properly determined not to be beaten down, 'not by honest fellows with glittering sabres, but quibbling, quill-driving lawyers', and won support from the Governor-General and Lord Ellenborough, President of the Board of Control. The latter wrote from London, in February 1829, that 'their law is considered bad law; but then their errors in matters of law are nothing in comparison with those they have committed in the tenor of their speeches from the bench'. The dispute was temporarily settled by the appointment of Malcolm's own Advocate-General as Chief Justice, a timely reminder that patronage still went to those who supported the Company, and the Privy Council rejected the claims of the Supreme Court. The controversy aroused much talk, because Malcolm's indiscretion allowed a private letter of the Board of Control's President to get into the Press, with the result that 'Lord Ellenborough, of whom little before had been known in India, suddenly became famous'.[1] But the Privy Council's action settled the trouble for the time being; and Malcolm, whose qualities were better fitted for a solely Oriental stage than for one systematised and in process of modernisation, was able to leave the cares of his governorship, and pass to activities in which he was perfectly at home, riding through Kathiawar to Cutch, where he harangued Rajput chiefs and dewans on the horrid custom of infanticide. He was respectfully listened to; and returned, hunting and slaying by the way,[2] in the manner of the old joyous times when even a campaign had been for its leaders more than half play, with battle and the chase alternating and easily passing into one another. Meanwhile, the establishment of the 'rule of law' had suffered a temporary setback, from which there was a quick recovery. Malcolm was typical of a vanishing age, and even he knew that his beliefs and principles were doomed to defeat:

' I have tried to deal some heavy blows at these costly and dangerous fabrics yclept Supreme Courts; but they are too essential for the objects of power and patronage, and to feed the rising spirit of the age, for me or any man to prevail against them.' (October 19, 1828.)

[1] Kaye, *Life of Malcolm*, ii. 532.

[2] 'Thirty-one hogs slain in the last two days by the spears of our party; and I have had an opportunity of showing the boys that his honor's dart is as sure and as deadly as the best of them.' (March 7, 1830.)

' I am just returned from Cutch in high health, having, besides the inspection of our western frontier and the revision of establishments, had glorious hunting and shooting—wild hogs, elks, deer, foxes, hares, black partridges, and quails, almost to a surfeit. It has been a great treat.'

x

A weakness of the Cornwallis Regulations had been the very cautious and limited use of Indian judges for civil cases. From time to time their jurisdiction had been slightly increased, but the first real extension was made in 1827, when more subordinate judges were appointed and *Sadar Amins* were empowered to try suits involving double the former amount. In 1831 Lord William Bentinck established a superior type of Indian civil judge authorised to try cases involving property to any amount, and with salaries rising to £720 a year. The principle of appointing more Indians to positions of importance was discussed before the Parliamentary Committee of 1832-3, many witnesses arguing that this was the only method of keeping down arrears of work, and avoiding a more expensive administration. The next ten years saw the appointment of Indian deputy-collectors in 1837, and deputy-magistrates in 1843. In the latter capacity they were able to pass sentences of imprisonment up to three years. In this way some real recognition was made of the principle contained in the famous 87th clause of the new Charter Act of 1833. 'Be it enacted that no native of the said territories . . . shall by reason only of his religion, place of birth, descent, color, or any of them, be disabled from holding any place, office, or employment in the said Company.' Up to the time of the Mutiny the employment of Indians was being extended at a moderate rate. In 1857 there were some 256 Indian officials drawing over £360 a year, and 2590 held various appointments of a lower grade. Nearly every civil case was by this time being tried originally before an Indian judge.

The tracking and apprehension of criminals has always proved a more difficult task than the organisation of criminal justice. Cornwallis had taken the management of the 'police' into Government's hands, and introduced the *thanadari* system, with Indian *darogas* in charge of each police district, but the rank and file of the police force were the village watchmen, 'an enormous ragged army who eat up the industry of this province'.[1] The idea of an organised disciplined body of men had hardly been conceived in any part of the world. It was considered a great innovation when Sir Robert Peel reorganised the London Metropolitan Police in 1829, the year after Lord William Bentinck had become Governor-General, and England had her first 'Peelers'. In 1830 few governments thought it their duty to provide a 'patrolling' police force

[1] Hunter, *The Annals of Rural Bengal*, 335. He was writing in 1860, before the new force was organised.

with recognised stations, any more than they would have thought it incumbent upon them to provide universal juvenile education. Regular policemen were first found necessary in the large cities, but in other countries, as in India, the expenses were entirely defrayed by the residents. The extension of this system into country districts, and the co-ordination of the various forces, has proved a very slow process which is far from complete even in countries like the United States, where a sheriff may still have to summon a posse of fellow-citizens to pursue a criminal. Bentinck did not alter the *thanadari* system, but he organised what might be described as a 'flying squad' to deal with the specific crimes of *thagi* and dacoity. His successor, Lord Auckland, improved the pay and standing of the *darogas*, but the village watchmen remained dependent upon the other villagers for their support, and shortly before the Mutiny it was recognised that, while the special department was doing excellent work, the *thanadari* system was functioning very badly. The matter was under discussion in 1856, when a minute by the Governor of Bengal sketched out a policy which would have turned the watchmen into regular Government servants.

The suppression of *thagi* was a notable achievement of the pre-Mutiny era. The *Thag*, or more accurately *phansidar*, was a member of one of those hereditary criminal castes which have always been a feature of Indian life. Some of these, like the *Chapperbunds*, and the *haran shikaris*, still survive to worry the police officer by their cunning thefts. The *phansidar*, or 'noose-holder', was unusual because his invariable method of procedure was to murder before robbing. Working in gangs, which were bound together by strict religious vows to the goddess Kali, the *phansidars* would ingratiate themselves with travellers, and then strangle them and bury them. They formed a powerful confederacy operating over the whole of the north of India, and supported by many landowners, through whom they disposed of their booty. For some years after the British occupation their activities were screened by the Maratha and Pindari Wars, but the existence of the professed *Thag* had been established by Lord Hastings's administration, and in 1829 a special department under Colonel Sleeman was appointed to deal with them. The methods by which these gangs were finally dispersed, and a description of their habits and curious mentality, have been recounted in two classic works.[1] Some idea of their depredations can be gathered from Sleeman's report of 1840, when the number of

---

[1] *Confessions of a Thug*, by Colonel Meadows Taylor (first published, 1839); *Rambles and Recollections*, by W. H. Sleeman.

'ascertained well known and bloody Bhils' in Oudh alone was given as 274, and of the twenty approvers one confessed to 931 murders in 40 years, and another to 508 in 20 years. Over 1500 *Thags* were apprehended in the first six years.

In 1837 Colonel Sleeman was also entrusted with the suppression of dacoity, but here the task was much more difficult. Many Indians of all classes must have known about the operations of the *Thags*, and in some cases assisted them and profited by them, but a far larger and more influential section of the population were accessary to the dacoities. There were parts of India where dacoity was as much a national pastime as bull-fighting in Spain. It was considered by its participants as an honourable profession.

' Whilst talking over their excursions . . . their eyes gleamed with pleasure, and beating their hands on their foreheads and breasts, and muttering some ejaculations, they bewailed the hardness of their lot, which now ensured their never being able again to participate in such a joyous occupation.' [1]

They could not be hunted down with the ruthlessness employed against the *Thags*, and for some years they were protected by the insistence of the law courts upon proof of specific offences, when all that could normally be proved was that a prisoner belonged to a gang of dacoits. This was partially corrected by an Act of 1843, but the difficulty of obtaining evidence still proved a great hindrance, and the professional dacoits learnt to operate near the borders of Indian States, where their pursuit was made harder by questions of jurisdiction. In Western India the most persistent robbers were the Bhils, whose settlement and reclamation by Outram was a wholly admirable work.

The Government's duty was clear in the case of *thagi*, and also of dacoity. It was impossible to justify murder for the sake of robbery, even though the perpetrators might claim to be religious devotees. Other savage customs presented greater difficulties. The religious element was stronger, the element of gain was less. As our officials spread over the country, they were brought into touch with new sides of Indian life, about which their predecessors had been ignorant or indifferent. Some of these offended strongly against all European ideas of civilisation. The three most important, not only in themselves but in the way they affected the Englishman's idea of India, were the *meriah* human sacrifices in Orissa, the prevalence of female infanticide, and the

---

[1] Colonel Sleeman's Bhudduck Report, 1849, quoted by Kaye, *Administration of the East India Company*.

custom of 'suttee' or widow-burning, which was common throughout
Bengal and Northern India. The first was confined to certain backward
sects, but the other two were practised by the highest castes, and the
last was enthusiastically approved by all classes.

The *meriah* sacrifices of Orissa were first noticed·in the report of an
official (Russell), May 11, 1837. Their suppression was a slow business,
not completed until the end of Lord Dalhousie's time, if then. The main
work was done by General Campbell. The sacrifices were to the spirit
of natural fertility, a sanguinary form of the *Iti* or *Itu* worship still
existing in rural North India. At Chinna Kimedy she took the form of
an elephant, at Gumsur and Boad of a bird. The Khonds who practised
the rite sometimes allowed *meriah* girls to live until they had had
children by Khond fathers. These children were reared for sacrifice, and
were well treated. Before being put to death they were exchanged for
similar children in another village, apparently because their own village
had ties of affection with them. The sacrifices were always in public.
They took varying forms, all inexpressibly cruel, consisting of the
cutting of the flesh off the living victim.

Campbell was away on the Chinese War, 1842-7, and had to take up
the work of suppression afterwards with renewed vigour. His task was
pursued with immense patience and kindness. In Chinna Kimedy the
people were suspicious, since it was rumoured that he himself was collecting *meriahs* to sacrifice to the water-spirit, because a tank he had
made had dried up; also, that his elephants needed periodical meals of
human beings. He began by giving cotton cloth and strings of bright
beads to those who had female children (he was simultaneously trying
to extirpate infanticide), and threw open his tent to full examination.
('It is the house of a god!' his astonished visitors exclaimed.) He tried
also, with scant success, to introduce vaccination. In 1853, towards the
end of his long campaign, he discovered that this formula was being
used in the now *meriah*-less worship:

' Do not be wrathful with us, O Goddess, for giving you blood of beasts
instead of human blood! Vent your anger on this gentleman, who is well able
to bear it. We are guiltless.' [1]

Between 1837 and 1854, 1506 meriahs were rescued.

The killing of girl babies was commonest amongst the warlike castes
in Central and Western India, and is a natural development of a primitive

[1] *Narrative by Major-General John Campbell, C.B., of his Operations in the Hill
Tracts of Orissa for the Suppression of Human Sacrifice and Female Infanticide.*
Printed for Private Circulation, 1861.

civilisation in which an unmarried woman is considered as unchaste, and a fair proportion of the men are killed in war. Some castes carried the habit to extreme lengths. The Rajkumars kept very few of their female children, and the custom was prevalent throughout Rajputana. It was extremely difficult for the early administrators to deal with this problem. The systematic murder of children was an affair of the zenana. The mother was usually the executioner. She either did not feed the child, or 'rubbed a little opium on the nipples of her breasts'. Considering the extreme privacy of the zenana, it was impossible to deal with specific cases, and the only practical method was to bring Government pressure to bear upon the leaders in areas where the very small proportion of female babies showed that the custom was in force. One economic reason for female infanticide was the high dowries demanded amongst certain castes, such as the Mairs. In Kathiawar the Political Agent, Willoughby, instituted an 'infanticide fund' from which presents were made to members of the Jharijah tribe who preserved their daughters, while maximum sums were fixed for dowries. As the country became more settled it was possible to keep better registers of births, and infanticide became more and more localised, and even before the Mutiny had tended to disappear amongst all except a few castes.

'Suttee' presented a more difficult problem, and the subject has had far more publicity outside India. *Sahamarana*, the 'dying in company with' one's husband, is a very ancient Indian rite. The Anglo-Indian word 'suttee' is from *sati*, the woman who performs the rite, usually by immolating herself on the funeral pyre. It seems to have been confined to the higher castes of the Hindus, though the weavers of Tippera practised a still more objectionable variant in burying their widows alive. The Moguls attempted to discourage the custom whenever it came under their notice. Tavernier says that 'the Governors, who are Mussalmans, hold this dreadful custom of self-destruction in horror, and do not readily give permission'.[1] Manucci describes a case at Agra, in which the woman was rescued, and the Brahmins complained, whereupon Aurangzeb 'issued an order that in all lands under Mogul control, never again should the officials allow a woman to be burnt'.[2] It was discouraged in the neighbourhood of Delhi, where Metcalfe when Resident was able to prohibit it, but was common amongst the Brahmins of Bengal and throughout the Hindu States. When a prince died

[1] *Travels in India* (Oxford University Press), ii. 162 *et seq.*

[2] Manucci, *A Pepys of Mogul India* (Murray), 124.

there was something approaching a holocaust. In 1780 sixty-four women burned at the death of Raja Ajit Singh of Marwar. As late as the middle of the nineteenth century, during the anarchy of the last days of Sikh rule in the Punjab, such wholesale 'suttees' were frequent. Wives and concubines were burnt in numbers after the deaths of Kishari Singh and Basanta Singh. Suchet Singh's death was reputed to have been followed by the burning of ten wives and three hundred concubines. For some years the various Europeans who came to India noticed and disapproved of the practice, but could not prevent it except in small compact areas. The French prohibited it at Chandernagore, the Danes at Serampur, the Portuguese at Goa.

From the Hindu point of view *sahamarana* was an extremely popular semi-religious spectacle. It was attended by large crowds, and re-dounded to the credit of the deceased husband and his family. There was no opposition to the practice from Indians until about 1820, when a few educated and Westernised Hindus, led by Rammohan Roy, started a reformist movement. The higher Muslim officials disapproved of 'suttee', but, like the earlier British servants of the Company, they had no police force at their disposal and no means of preventing such occurrences. Occasionally English officials would interfere when a case came to their notice. Mr. Brooks, Collector of Shahabad, forcibly prevented a suttee in 1789. The Collector of Gaya, in 1805, stopped the burning of a girl of twelve. It was only when the administra-tion became better organised, and more Englishmen began to move about the country, that the extent of these and other practices was fully understood. William Carey, the missionary, brought the subject of widow-burning before the Bengal Government by carrying out an unofficial census of 'suttees' occurring within thirty miles of Calcutta. He placed the figures—there were 438 in 1803—before Lord Wellesley, who had already forbidden one religious practice, that of exposing children at Saugor Point, and was disposed to take the same action about widow-burning. Unfortunately he referred the matter to the Supreme Court.

The Supreme Court displayed its accustomed pedantry, and advised the Government to be guided by 'the religious opinions and prejudices of the natives', and for the next twenty-five years a vacillating policy was followed. The Government took the advice of leading Hindu pandits, who replied that the practice was 'recognised and encouraged by the doctrines of the Hindoo religion', and for some years attempts were made to regulate the 'suttees', and 'to allow the practice in those cases in which it is countenanced by their religion, and to prevent it in others in which it is, by the same authority, prohibited'.[1] The effect of this action was to legalise the purely voluntary immolation of a widow who was over sixteen and not pregnant, and in pursuance of this policy the police were ordered to get early information of an intended 'suttee', and to see that the widow was neither drugged nor forcibly burned. It was a lamentable procedure, for the police officer would almost invariably be a Hindu or a Muslim of the poorer classes, and in either case would not be too critical, while his presence would give an impression that the Government's approval had been obtained. This official sanction had one good effect. As more European officers came out to undertake magisterial and police work in the districts, they began to investigate these cases, and to discover the sordid economic reasons as well as the sheer love of cruelty which formed the background to so many cases of *sahamarana*.

By the 'twenties there was a strong move for prohibition amongst the officials in the more settled areas. The evidence of Mr. Ewer, the Superintendent of Police in Lower Bengal, had great weight. It may be quoted at length as a fair description of most 'suttees.'

' There are many reasons for thinking that such an event as a voluntary Suttee very rarely occurs; few widows would think of sacrificing themselves unless overpowered by force or persuasion, very little of either being sufficient to overcome the physical or mental powers of the majority of Hindoo females. A widow, who would turn with natural instinctive horror from the first hint of sharing her husband's pile, will be at length gradually brought to pronounce a reluctant consent because, distracted with grief at the event, without one friend to advise or protect her, she is little prepared to oppose the surrounding crowd of hungry Brahmins and interested relations. . . . In this state of confusion a few hours quickly pass, and the widow is burnt before she has had time to think of the subject. Should utter indifference for her husband, and superior sense, enable her to preserve her judgment, and to resist the arguments of those about her, it will avail her little—the people will not be disappointed of their show; and the entire population of a village will turn out to assist in dragging her to the bank of the river, and in keeping her on the pile.' [2]

Bentinck's Regulation prohibiting widow-burning was not issued until 1829. Both Lord Hastings and Lord Amherst had considered this

[1] Government resolution of December 5, 1812. Reply to an enquiry from an official in Bandalkhand.

[2] Ewer's evidence is given in Peggs' *India's Cries to British Humanity* (Second Edition, 1830), 14. See also Edward Thompson, *Suttee*, passim.

step, but had deferred action, partly from fear that such an order could not be made operative, but chiefly because they thought it might lead to disaffection in the sepoy army, then on active service, and to disturbances in the recently ceded districts. Nothing of the kind actually occurred, but men like Sir Charles Metcalfe, while concurring in the prohibition, believed that it might 'produce a religious excitement, the consequences of which, if once set in action, cannot be foreseen'.[1] Rammohan Roy himself considered that the order was premature.[2]

In Bengal and Bihar there was opposition to the Regulation, but it took only a legal form. An appeal was made to the Privy Council, and after many delays heard and dismissed. The enforcement of the Regulation was made effective throughout the provinces within a year or two. It took another generation before the practice was abolished in all the Indian States. In Southern India *sahamarana* would seem to have been dying out before the Regulation was made, but over Bengal, Bihar, and parts of what are now the United Provinces the prohibition was directly contrary to public sentiment, and the tradition in favour of the rite has survived even until modern times. The not infrequent cases when widows commit suicide in their own homes are commented upon with approbation in the Indian Press, and the occasional cases of widow-burning which have occurred in the last thirty years have always aroused great popular enthusiasm. In the last recorded case, in August, 1932, events seem to have followed very much the course described by Mr. Ewer, over a century before.[3]

This long campaign to suppress certain types of indigenous crime had a notable effect on British administration. The English officials of the early Victorian period were convinced that they had to deal with a degenerate race, and this impression was only intensified when, passing beyond the old Mogul Empire, they came into contact with the savage hill chieftains of the Himalayan foothills. There is no more need to pass final judgments on early Hindu morality than upon, say, the mercantilist theory. Able apologists have from time to time defended the

[1] *Life of Lord Metcalfe*, J. W. Kaye, 1858, ii. 78.

[2] Miss Collet, *Life and Letters of Raja Rammohan Roy*, 146.

[3] See *The Times*, September 2, 1932. 'A brahmin of Fatehpur Sikri died on Monday. His widow was determined to commit suttee, but was dissuaded. A mob collected at her house and demanded that she should burn herself. The police locked the woman in the house, but the mob broke in and dragged the woman to the burning ghat. The mob was erecting a pyre when the police fired, killing three persons and wounding five, and rescued the woman.'

sahamarana rite,[1] and future generations may hold that female in-fanticide is a lesser evil than the unchecked growth of population which has characterised these later years. The point which must be emphasised is that from about 1830 onwards English officials were imbued with the idea that they were, in Macaulay's phrase, undertaking the 'stupen-dous process' of reconstructing 'a decomposed society'. They ex-pressed their contempt for the older type of Company's servant by saying they were 'Hinduised', and this attitude developed into a kind of racial aloofness which became more marked as English women began to settle in India with their husbands. There is a definite change of outlook between the earlier administrators, like Munro, Elphinstone, and Malcolm, and their successors who in 1849 set to work in the newly annexed Punjab. The latter were more ruthless, more spiritually arrogant, and less disposed to delegate any real responsibility to Indians. The tendency to isolate themselves from the Indians was to become still more marked after the Mutiny. This new attitude was visible in every department of our administration. The annexationist policy of Lord Dalhousie was largely inspired by the difficulties which he encountered when urging the abolition of 'suttee' and female in-fanticide in the Indian States. Part of the opposition to using Indians in an executive capacity was due to a fear of weakening the administration in its struggle against such barbarities. Men like Elphinstone and Munro had envisaged an India in which the British did little more than keep the peace. Leaving the administration in Indian hands, they would have trusted to education to cure such evils as they believed to exist. The next generation of officials was conscious of the clash between two civilisations, one of which they believed to be improving, and the other to be in the last stages of degeneration.

On Lord William Bentinck's going, in March, 1835, Sir Charles Metcalfe acted as Governor-General for a year. He abolished the Inland Transit Duties, a great assistance to commerce, and removed the restrictions on the Press. The latter action aroused the Directors to boundless indignation, and settled all question of his confirmation as Governor-General, which had long been canvassed with much vacilla-tion. He stuck to his opinions with characteristic courage; and though the objection to officials being appointed to the supreme place was

[1] See, for example, Ananda Coomaraswamy, *The Dance of Siva*. Modern writers, however, adopt a very different line of argument from that of the orthodox Hindus who opposed Bentinck in such papers as the *Chandrika*.

upheld (when for once it might wisely have been waived), he was considered good enough for two colonial governorships, of Jamaica and Canada.

CHAPTER IV

FIRST AFGHAN WAR

Miss Emily Eden: a popular potentate: and an attentive creature, his Majesty of Oudh: Low suppresses a revolution: Shah Suja: Eldred Pottinger and Herat: the Tripartite Treaty: the Sind Amirs: the Khan of Khelat: occupation of Kandahar: death of Mehrab Khan: growing perplexities: surrender of Dost Muhammad: murder of Burnes and Macnaghten: retreat from Kabul: our Sikh allies: Sale and Pollock: Lord Ellenborough Governor-General: Roman proclamations.

GEORGE, Lord Auckland, the new Viceroy, a bachelor, was accompanied by his sisters Fanny and Emily. The latter was to write a commentary, witty, vivacious, skilled in perception of all that lay on the surface, the best book ever written by any foreigner merely visiting India, perhaps the best journal of any kind in our language. It shows us a great Whig noble—a languid, gracious, punning gentleman—completely unaware of anything that passed beneath the ludicrous aspect of absurd rajas, queer peoples outlandishly dressed and quaintly mannered, little pushing officials and their scheming flirting womenfolk. He and his sister are revealed in their intimacy of amusement at the bourgeoisie and bureaucracy surrounding them. Miss Eden's political views are all 'snap judgments', based on what those nearest to the Governor-General (and, necessarily, often farthest from the scene involved) told him. When in the second phase of the Afghan War disasters come thick and fast, ignorant jauntiness gives way to reckless fierceness eager for vengeance.

Auckland, however, began well enough, with the usual long leisured tour up-country. He was away from Calcutta from October, 1837, to March, 1840, a stretch of time which brings home the slowness and difficulty of travel even after steam had come in, and the reality (and on occasion, the value) of 'the time-lag' which has so completely disappeared from modern politics. He was enabled to mix freely with

English society and selected natives; his sister reports that he came away 'in a great state of popularity in the Upper Provinces; all these people talked of him with such regard and admiration.'[1]

Less satisfying was the fact that the huge entourage passed through ghastly famine. Auckland gave freely from his private purse, and instituted an enquiry into preventive measures; the Indian Government's beginnings of famine policy, which were to grow slowly into effectiveness, date from this time. It is significant of the way Governor-General and sister moved throughout in a rose-hued mist, that Miss Eden tells us they rejected experienced officials' advice to stop the tour, lest their horde of followers deepen the land's distress. Her characteristically Whig reply was that these followers were a blessing, since good for trade! Neither of them ever came to suspect the extent to which those curses of India, officialdom's dependents, pillage countries through which their masters pass.

The Governor-General was much beset by the King of Oudh, an 'attentive creature',[2] as he had reason to be. Three months before the tour began, close on midnight of July 7, 1837, the Lucknow Resident, Colonel Low, was waked and told that the King was dying. He wrote to the Brigadier commanding the Oudh subsidiary force, to hold a thousand men in readiness to march at a moment's notice; and went to the palace. He found the King's body still warm, blood flowing freely when the Residency surgeon opened a vein; but there was no other sign of life. Part of Low's force was already present, and he placed seals on the treasures, and guards everywhere. The night, a very dark one, was studded with torch-bearers. For the new King, an uncle of the just-deceased monarch, a statement was drawn up, 'that he was prepared to sign any new treaty for the better government of the country that the British Government might think proper to propose'.[3]

The late King had assured Bentinck that his putative son was not his. 'The Padshah Begum', mother of this putative son, now installed him, and made a furious assault on the palace. Low, an intrepid man, demanded to see her, and pushed through a dense crowd witnessing the installation of 'the pretender'. Dancing-girls were swaying and chanting; swords, spears, matchlocks, muskets were being flourished in a forest of torches. The excited mob, 'more like demons than human

---

[1] Emily Eden, *Up the Country*, 391.　　　　　　[2] *Op. cit.* 51.

[3] Major-General Sir W. H. Sleeman, K.C.B., *A Journey through the Kingdom of Oude in 1849-50*, ii. 154.

beings',[1] a menacing 'dance of the imps', closed round Low and two companions, shouting angry and obscene abuse, threatening them with swords and guns thrust in their faces, firing muskets. The Begum haughtily refused to withdraw her candidate. Low was seized by the neckcloth, dragged forward, and commanded to congratulate the new King on pain of instant death. He remained steadfast through insult and imminence of murder; and the Begum's vakil, who had the sense to look ahead to what would follow if the Resident were killed, shouted loudly that the Begum's order was that Colonel Low should be allowed to withdraw; and himself led him out. Low, going out, was passed by Colonel Roberts, a brigadier in the Oudh service, who presented his offering to the boy and 'then went off and hid himself, to wait the result of the contest'. For contest there clearly must be; and there was as much reason for pusillanimity as there ever is, seeing that Oudh furnished so large a proportion of the Company's sepoys.

The subsidiary force arrived, and Low told its commander the work was 'now in his hands'. The palace gates were blown in, and sepoys stormed the halls. The late King's favourite wife, 'a modest, beautiful, and amiable young woman, who had been forced to join the Begum, in order to give some countenance to the daring enterprise', was let down from a height of twenty-four feet, on a rope of clothes made by a female attendant whose arm was shattered by grapeshot as she followed. By nine o'clock the palace was cleared of insurgents, the King officially sanctioned brought out of hiding, 'and the Resident exerted himself to soothe and prepare him for the long and tedious ceremonies of the coronation, while the killed and wounded', in all over a hundred, were removed, and the palace cleaned for the ceremonial.

After forcing Oudh to accept a new and harder treaty, Lord Auckland betrayed his gravest fault. He was incompetent and casual, and his administration has been more generally condemned than that of any other Governor-General. But all this is trivial beside his habit of suppressing and garbling documents. The treaty was rejected by the Directors, but Auckland told the King merely that *one* clause, that saddling Oudh with 16 lakhs for an additional subsidiary force, had been disallowed. By what Mr. Roberts generously calls 'an inexcusable piece of carelessness',

' the treaty was actually included in a subsequent government publication and was referred to as still in force by succeeding Governor-Generals. Upon Lord

[1] *Op. cit.* ii. 161.

Dalhousie was thrust the invidious task of explaining to the King that the treaty, which he and former Governor-Generals had believed to be in force since 1837, had really been abrogated two years after that date, and of expressing a tardy regret that the communication of this fact had been inadvertently neglected. Such miserable and unpardonable mismanagement obviously gave too much ground to those who held that the annexation of Oudh was "a gross breach of national faith".[1]

'Neither Lord Hardinge in 1847 nor Colonel Sleeman in 1854 knew that the whole treaty had been annulled. It was left for Lord Dalhousie to discover the truth, as confirmed by Low himself, then a member of his Council, and to acquaint the India House with the extent to which Lord Auckland had evaded their commands.' [2]

When Auckland visited Oudh, the King, a rheumaticky, almost bed-ridden creature, hovered round him, seeking release from the more onerous clauses of the treaty. The Governor-General regarded his attendance as a boring jest, and played with him languidly. There was, for example, a magnificent breakfast at Lucknow, on Christmas Day, 1837, when 'G.' (George Eden, Baron Auckland)

'sugared and creamed the Nawab's tea, and the Nawab gave him some pilau. Then he put a slice of buttered toast (rather cold and greasy) on one plate for me, and another for F., and B. said in an imposing tone, "His Royal Highness sends the Burra lady this, and the Choota lady that", and we looked immeasurable gratitude. At the end of breakfast, two hookahs were brought in, that the chiefs might smoke together, and a third for Colonel L., the British resident, that his consequence might be kept up in the eyes of the Lucknowites, by showing that he is allowed to smoke at the Governor-General's table. The old khansamah wisely took care to put no tobacco in G.'s hookah, though it looked very grand and imposing with its snake and rose-water. G. says he was quite distressed; he could not persuade it to make the right kind of bubbling noise.' [3]

Superb presents (which by law now went into the Company's resources, when they could not be declined) and the usual round of fights between elephants, rhinoceroses, tigers, followed.

Kaye puts it down to Simla, 'where our Governors-General, surrounded by irresponsible advisers, settle the destinies of empire without the aid of their legitimate fellow-counsellors, and which has been the cradle of more political insanity than any place within the limits of

[1] *History of British India*, 355-6.
[2] L. J. Trotter, *Lord Auckland* ('Rulers of India'), 29.
[3] *Up the Country*, 55.

Hindostan',[1] that Auckland, who is credited with being a pacific man, ever launched the first Afghan War.

The Durani Amir of Kabul, Shah Suja, lost his throne, 1809, and after many adventures, which included two attempts to reconquer it, had settled down as a Company's pensioner at Ludhiana. Lord William Bentinck would have been glad enough to see him re-established, but explained that it was not the British habit to interfere in other States' affairs. His supplanter, Dost Muhammad, when Lord Auckland reached India, sent his congratulations:

'The field of my hopes, which had before been chilled by the cold blast of wintry times, has by the happy tidings of your Lordship's arrival become the envy of the garden of paradise. . . . I hope that your Lordship will consider me and my country as your own.'

On this Kaye allows himself the comment: 'He little thought how in effect this Oriental compliment would be accepted as a solemn invitation, and the hope be literally fulfilled. Three years afterwards Lord Auckland, considering Dost Mahomed's country his own, had given it away to Shah Soojah.'[2]

We have seen that a sprinkling of officers brilliant and daring, with a disinterested love of enterprise that of itself would have sent them forward, were moving, sometimes openly, more often disguised as Muslim devotees, horse-copers, and the like, beyond the Punjab. One of the most gallant, Lieutenant Eldred Pottinger, in 1838 encouraged the Afghans of Herat, when in despair of holding out against a Persian army, and saved the city. British prestige stood high in Afghan regions. Dost Muhammad himself was eager for a British alliance, and for a great while refused to make terms with Russian envoys. But Burnes, who was sent to Kabul, could effect nothing because his hands were empty, both literally and metaphorically. His presents were of slight value. Nor could he offer anything of political worth. Dost Muhammad was sore over Ranjit Singh's capture of Peshawar (1833), and wished the British to press for its return. This Auckland rightly refused to do. But there was nothing else that the Company would or could offer, beyond the distinction of fighting their battles against the Russian Empire as well as his own. Inevitably, after long reluctance, Dost Muhammad had to begin to compose his differences with Russia and Persia, now acting together on his borders.

[1] *History of the War in Afghanistan*, i. 312.
[2] *Op. cit.* i. 170.

This natural course of self-preservation served as sufficient excuse for hostility. Macnaghten, secretary to the Indian Government, was sent to Lahore, and on June 26, 1838, the Tripartite Treaty between the Sikhs, Shah Suja, and the Company was signed. The British intention was that they should hover as a vast menace, at Shikarpur on the Indus, while Shah Suja, supported by the Sikhs, entered Afghanistan amid the welcome of a delighted nation. Ranjit Singh, further sunk in physical than in mental decrepitude, in the end managed to reverse the method entirely; it was the Sikhs who contemptuously held the passes for a remnant of the shattered British forces to straggle back. For the present he visualised (without enthusiasm) the only kind of attack on the Khyber he thought possible—a thrusting forward of Sikhs, and yet more Sikhs, over the bodies of those first slain, until sheer weight of casualties and numbers bought the passage.

Miss Eden's exultant pages tell how in the autumn 'G.' himself, with a huge attendance, came to Ferozpur, close to the Sikh borders, where tremendous junketings took place. Amid a wild tumult of clanging weapons under the fiercer crash of massed artillery and the skirl and blare of military music, the elephants of Maharaja and Governor-General were brought alongside;

'and Lord Auckland, in his uniform of diplomatic blue, was seen to take a bundle of crimson cloth out of the Sikh howdah, and it was known that the lion of the Punjab was then seated on the elephant of the English ruler. In a minute the little, tottering, one-eyed man, who had founded a vast empire on the banks of the fabulous rivers of the Macedonian conquests, was leaning over the side of the howdah, shaking hands with the principal officers of the British camp, as their elephants were wheeled up beside him. Then the huge phalanx of elephants was set in motion again' [1]

towards the Durbar tent, where presently 'the imbecile little old man' (imbecile only in the physical sense) was tottering between the support of the Governor-General and the Commander-in-Chief, Sir Henry Fane, a superb giant of a man, an undesignedly cruel contrast.

As yet the British had no intention of fighting themselves. 'England was to remain in the background jingling the money-bag.' But the money-bag had to be filled first with something to jingle; and it was not reasonable to expect England to find this metal. The Sind Amirs were cast for the part of providers, Oudh being penniless and Bengal fully occupied with financial performances. Their country had once been in

[1] *Op. cit.* i. 389 ff.

(exceedingly loose) dependence on Afghanistan. It was decided that they should pay Shah Suja twenty lakhs, which he was to divide with Ranjit Singh. When Ranjit Singh demanded more than ten lakhs, this was arranged by the easy expedient of raising the Amirs' contribution to twenty-five lakhs, of which he was to have fifteen.

The Amirs at this juncture did what in some phases of British rule might have been awkward. They objected to the revival of financial claims by a man exiled from his throne thirty years previously, and produced his formal renouncement of these claims. Colonel Henry Pottinger, the Company's political agent in Sind, submitted that the 'question' of the Amirs being fleeced for the Afghan pretender's benefit was

' rendered very puzzling by two releases written in Korans, and sealed and signed by his Majesty, which they have produced. Their argument now is, that they are sure the Governor-General does not intend to make them pay again for what they have already bought and obtained, in the most binding way, a receipt in full.'

The Governor-General and his advisers, however, had got beyond such pedantry. Pottinger was told to warn the Amirs that

' the interests at stake are too great to admit of hesitation in our proceedings; and not only they who have shown a disposition to favour our adversaries, but they who display an unwillingness to aid us in the just and necessary undertaking in which we are engaged, must be displaced, and give way to others on whose friendship and co-operation we may be able implicitly to rely'.

The treaty by which they had been cajoled into opening the Indus to navigation, in consideration of the Company's solemn promise to convey no military stores along it, was to be set aside 'while the present exigency lasts'. As the Amirs began to betray a sullen reluctance, Pottinger was ordered to assure them that 'neither the ready power to crush and annihilate them, nor the will to call it into action, were wanting, if it appeared requisite, however remotely, for the safety of the Anglo-Indian Empire or frontier'.

Macnaghten afterwards complained

' that no civilised beings had ever been treated so badly as were the British by the Princes of Sindh. If it were so, it was only because no civilised beings had ever before committed themselves to acts of such gross provocation. . . . The Ameers . . . viewed all our proceedings . . . with mingled terror and indignation. Our conduct was calculated to alarm and incense them to the extremest point of fear and irritation; and yet we talked of their childish distrust and their unprovoked hostility'.[1]

[1] *Op. cit.* i. 403.

Y

As the huge British armies moved through Sind, devastating and eating up, the wealthiest group of the Amirs, in particular those of Haidarabad, became openly disgruntled, almost hostile. Their recalcitrance was eagerly seized upon, and part of the army was detached to bring them to a better sense of their privileges and duties:

' Down the left bank of the Indus went Cotton with his troops, glorying in the prospect before them. The treasures of Hyderabad seemed to lie at their feet. Never was there a more popular movement. The troops pushed on in the highest spirits, eager for the affray—confident of success. An unanticipated harvest of honour—an unexpected promise of abundant prize-money —was within their reach.' [1]

But Macnaghten, appalled to see a tremendous military invasion about to degenerate into a freebooting expedition against puny folk, wrote frantic letters to Burnes, to Colvin, to Sir Willoughby Cotton, to Auckland himself. Just in time the Haidarabad Amirs, terrified at the majestic vengeance marching their way, accepted a fresh treaty, by which they were to pay annually three lakhs for the subsidiary force which it was at last to be their privilege, as it had long been that of other Indian States, to support. Cotton, 'to the extreme disappointment of his troops',[2] abandoned 'a pretty piece of practice for the army' and returned to the main business.

The Amirs, to whom it was pointed out that 'friendship, alliance, and unity of interest' with the Company were far better than the independence to which they were so foolishly attached, and that their mulcting, though grievous, was trivial when it was considered what 'vast advantages' they would obtain (arrival of trade and traders, employment for thousands of their meaner subjects, increased demand for grain, etc.), were told further 'that henceforth they must consider Scinde to be, as it was in reality, a portion of Hindostan, in which the British were paramount and entitled to act as they considered best and fittest for the general good of the whole Empire'.[3]

These arguments, coming from a Power which was daily giving proof (as it pointed out) of 'moderation and disinterestedness', carried conviction; the Amirs answered that

' their eyes were opened. They had found it difficult to overcome the prejudice and apprehension of their tribes, who had always been led to think the only object of the British was to extend their dominion. Now they had been taught by experience English strength and good faith.'

[1] *Op. cit.* i. 412.　　　　　　　[2] *Op. cit.* i. 417.
[3] See Major-General Sir F. J. Goldsmid, *James Outram*, 170 ff.

It is not to be supposed that there had been no misgivings, no protests. On the contrary, every reputable authority outside India was
aghast at what was afoot. Wellesley and his brother, the Duke of Wellington, Elphinstone, Bentinck, all condemned it. Alexander Burnes,
whose life was to go in the enterprise, and whose share in the business
has been considerably misjudged, had urged that

'it remains to be considered why we cannot act with Dost Mahomed. He
is a man of undoubted ability, and has at heart a high opinion of the British
nation; and if half you must do for others were done for him ... he would
abandon Russia and Persia to-morrow. . . . I think there is much to be said
for him. Government have admitted that he had at best a choice of difficulties; and it should not be forgotten that we promised nothing, and
Persia and Russia held out a great deal.'

Moreover, London had persuaded the Russian Government to withdraw their envoy, who returned to St. Petersburg and blew his brains
out; and Persia raised the siege of Herat (September 9, 1838). There remained, therefore, no shadow of an excuse, ethical or political, for per-
sisting in the enterprise. But Lord Auckland in October issued a minute,
in which 'the views and conduct of Dost Muhammad Khan were mis-
represented with a hardihood which a Russian statesman might have
envied'.[1] Burnes was told that his job was merely to go ahead through
the Amirs' country, making requisitions for the army that was following and aweing the people by threats of their destruction if they were
backward in assistance.[2]

Diverted from passage through the Punjab, by Ranjit Singh's objections, the British moved through Sind and entered Baluchistan by the
Bolan Pass, March, 1839. The Khan of Khelat, who had formerly been
generous fool enough to protect Shah Suja, was made another unwilling accomplice. 'An able and sagacious man',[3] Mehrab Khan talked
reasonably to Burnes (who was now merely a subordinate tool), and
told him what others kept on telling the invaders, that Shah Suja was
detested and despised and that, though Dost Muhammad could no
doubt be conquered, 'we could never win over the Afghan nation by it'.[4]
Burnes told Macnaghten that the Khan's country had been swept, as by
a razor, clean of grain and greenstuff, some of its inhabitants being reduced to 'feeding on herbs and grasses gathered in the jungle . . . the
small quantities we have procured have been got by stealth'.[5]

[1] Sir Herbert Edwardes.   [2] For maps see below, Book VI.
[3] Kaye, i. 424.   [4] Burnes to Macnaghten: Khelat, March 30, 1839. MS. Records.
[5] Burnes to Macnaghten, April 2, 1839.

Kandahar was occupied in April, the Afghans with deepening resentment watching this restoration of their oft-rejected monarch by a host of *Kafirs*. A clash came at Ghazni, which was stormed in July. Dost Muhammad fled from Kabul, which was occupied in August. The Ghazni carnage was dreadful; and Shah Suja butchered fifty *Ghazi* prisoners. From this incident dates the abhorrence of him which soon became intense, and was understood, if not shared, by many of his British supporters. 'The day of reckoning came at last; and when our unholy policy sunk unburied in blood and ashes, the shrill cry of the *Ghazee* sounded as its funeral wail.' [1]

When Shah Suja entered Kabul, 'it was more like a funeral procession than the entry of a King into the capital of his restored dominions'.[2] His public acknowledgment in Kandahar had been a similar failure. Macnaghten had set apart a large space 'for "the populace restrained by the Shah's troops". But the space remained almost empty, and 'no Afghan of repute came forward to pay his reverence to the popular idol of Macnaghten's fancy'.[3]

In Simla, however, things were seen in a far more satisfactory light. In May 'G. got the official accounts of the taking of Candahar, or rather how Candahar took Shah Soojah, and *would have* him for its King. There never was anything so satisfactory'.[4] Presently 'G.' became an earl, Sir John Keane, the Commander-in-Chief of the Indus army, a baron, Macnaghten a baronet, and 'a shower of honours fell upon the civil and military services'.

Meanwhile the punishment of the wicked had continued steadily. Raging because the march of such a host had not been a picnic, and unable to see 'that the army of the Indus was at least as much the cause, as it was the victim, of the scarcity in Beloochistan',[5] British Indian opinion had fallen into 'the fashion' of attributing 'to the wickedness of Mehrab Khan all the sufferings' which accompanied the campaign. His friendly offices had made possible the passage of the Bolan Pass; and, while he pointed out that no one wished the return of Shah Suja, nevertheless he himself had sheltered the latter, five years previously, when he fled from his rout at the battle of Kandahar. On the morning of November 13, a British-Indian force appeared before Khelat, and stormed it—news which was received with delight. Macnaghten heard it when dining with General Avitabile, Commandant of Peshawar.

---

[1] Kaye, i. 462. [2] *Op. cit.* i. 479.
[3] L. J. Trotter, *Lord Auckland*, 86. [4] Emily Eden, *Up the Country*, 290.
[5] Kaye, ii. 29.

All rose and gave 'the "three times three" of a good English cheer'.[1] On December 3 Miss Eden saw an aide-de-camp 'fidgetting about behind G.'s chair with a note in his hand':

' it turned out to be an express with another little battle, and a most successful one. The Khan of Khelat was by way of being our ally and assistant, and professing friendship: did himself the pleasure of cutting off the supplies of the army when it was on its way to Cabul; set his followers on to rob the camp; corresponded with Dost Mahomed, &c.

' There was no time to fight with him then, and I suppose he was beginning to think himself secure; but G. directed the Bombay army, on its way home, to settle this little Khelat trouble. . . . It was all done in the Ghuznee manner— the gates blown in and the fort stormed—but the fighting was very severe. The Khan and his principal chiefs died sword in hand, which was rather too fine a death for such a double traitor; and one in six of our troops were either killed or wounded, which is an unusual proportion. . . . Also there will be a great deal of prize money.'[2]

A better authority than Miss Eden sums up the humiliating story:

' For former hospitality, and for protection from sanguinary pursuers, the gratitude of Shah Shooja, under British influence, awarded to Mehrab Khan the loss of his poor capital and a soldier's death. After his honourable fall documents were found which proved the manner in which the Khan had been betrayed and his endeavours to negotiate frustrated; nevertheless it was thought advisable to consummate the threat formerly made, and to place Shah Nawaz Khan, to the exclusion of the son of the fallen chief, upon the masnad of Khelat.'[3]

The day after the battle a British officer (Lieutenant Loveday) looked on pityingly as

'a few of Mehrab Khan's servants brought the body of their master for burial—a fine-looking man. There was one little hole in his breast, which told of a musket-ball having passed through. He had no clothes on, except his silk *pyjammahs*. One of his slaves whispered me for a shawl. Alas! I had nothing of the kind, but luckily remembered a brocade bed-cover, which I had bought in my days of folly and extravagance at Delhi. I called for it immediately, and gave it to the Khan's servants, who were delighted with this last mark of respect, and wrapping up the body in it, placed their deceased master on a *charpoy*, and carried him to the grave.'

The army had reached Kabul, only because Macnaghten lavishly corrupted those Afghans he could reach. The campaign ravaged Indian finances. Withdrawal, however, was impossible; for repression,

---

[1] *Op. cit.*, ii. 25.   [2] *Up the Country*, 348-9.
[3] Sir Henry M. Durand, *The First Afghan War and its Causes*, 227-8.

for punitive measures, for all the abundant dirty work, British officers were indispensable. So the troops were brought in to the capital, and cantoned for winter on an open plain. Meanwhile, Burnes wrote: 'Bad ministers are in every government solid grounds for unpopularity; and I doubt if ever a King had a worse set than Shah Soojah'. At their head was the Wazir, a man 'old and enfeebled by age. His memory was gone; so were his ears. For some offence against his Majesty in former days, he had forfeited those useful appendances.'[1] Such vigour as remained to him was concentrated into two channels, oppression of the people and loathing of the British. With this valuable assistant the latter had wrought what was almost a miracle, an immense revolution in Afghan feeling, hitherto divided but now become one flaming patriotism. British officers sent for their wives from India.

The Tripartite Alliance was about to lose all but nominal adherence of its Sikh component. Ranjit Singh's body, which had been so long rotting for death, ceased to breathe, June 27, 1839; and a handful of enthralled Europeans watched his barbaric obsequies. Miss Eden, appalled, exclaims:[2]

' Those poor dear ranees, whom we visited and thought so beautiful and so merry, have actually burnt themselves ... they were such gay young creatures, and they died with the most obstinate courage.'

Her brother instructed his representative at Lahore to express horror. Horror could be notified only 'unofficially', and was rebutted with polite hint that it was an impertinence.

We descend fast into the shadows of the most sombre and terrible years India has ever known; the terrors of the Afghan slaughters and the Sikh anarchy begin the tale which the violation of Sind, the clash of British-Sikh arms, and the Mutiny are to continue and conclude. Miss Eden's delightful vivacious commentary is soon to be as irrelevant as the piping of linnets in a bombardment. If, contemplating the straightforward wickedness of Lord Auckland's Afghan policy and its dreadful close, we marvel that so inept and recklessly unscrupulous a Power should yet have survived, we may keep faith in an ethical governance of the world (should we desire to keep such faith), by turning our eyes upon the cruelty and cowardice of native India.

But our immediate interest is that Ranjit Singh 'was the only man in the Sikh empire who was true at heart to his allies, and all genuine co-

---

[1] Kaye, ii. 18.   [2] *Up the Country*, 310.

operation died out with the fires of his funeral pile'. From now on, the British were in the position of a man who has a wolf by the ears and dare not relax hold. What troops could be withdrawn were withdrawn; it became increasingly plain that no others could be withdrawn. Afghanistan was in for a military occupation whose finish no one could see. British money-bags were emptying; the Commander-in-Chief, Sir Jasper Nicolls, experienced old soldier of another unsuccessful war, that against the Gurkhas, at the Governor-General's board kept on stressing the impossibility of endlessly spending at the rate of a million and a quarter sterling a year, on such an enterprise and such a ruler. The rest of the Council seconded him. Lord Auckland, gentle but disinclined for descent into serious controversy with common mortals, shirked and evaded the issue. Sir Alexander Burnes, growing daily wise with a mournful knowledge, a male Cassandra, and like Cassandra doomed to share the ruin he foresaw, remained in Kabul, as he complained 'in the most nondescript of situations': [1]

' It appears to have been his mission in Afghanistan to draw a large salary every month, and to give advice that was never taken. This might have satisfied many men. It did not satisfy Burnes. He said that he wanted responsibility; and under Macnaghten he had none. . . . He probed, deeply and searchingly, the great wound of national discontent—a mighty sore that was ever running—and he felt in his inmost soul that the death-throes of such a system could not be very remote.' [2]

Macnaghten, meanwhile, was becoming lost to all ethical considerations, and moral blindness was bringing its inevitable companion, intellectual obsession. Exasperated because he saw questioning in the faces of all but himself, as the hazards and follies of the excursion grew appallingly apparent, he blamed Government's attention to reports of people afflicted with 'the imposthume of too much leisure', who cursed the enterprise, as keeping them away from delectable India, 'in a land not overflowing with beer and cheroots'. He plotted wilder adventures yet, and urged that 'we have a beautiful game on our hands if we have the means and inclination to play it properly'. That game was to attack Herat and bring it under Shah Suja's immediate sway; and to annex the Punjab, an action of whose necessity and righteousness men were freely talking, for the Punjab was the only considerable source of revenue still outside British control. Lord Auckland was to 'insist'

' upon the concession of our rights from the ruler of the Punjab. . . .In addition to the demands already made upon the Sikhs, they should be required, I

[1] Kaye, ii. 137.   [2] Op. cit. ii. 64 ff.

think, to admit unequivocally our right of way across the Punjab, and in the event of their denying this right, they should be convinced that we can take it.'

Dost Muhammad remained at large, a figure intangible and almost immaterial, flitting through the wild scattered borders of his land. His supporters ('rebels' Macnaghten called them) inflicted petty galling defeats on the invaders; the invaders sometimes routed some trivial detachment of his troops. But while the defeats of the British grew ever more menacing, and each time their prestige shrank visibly, their enemy's defeats were unimportant. 'I am like a wooden spoon', he said; 'you may throw me hither and thither, but I shall not be hurt'. On September 18, 1840, Macnaghten despondently wrote: 'At no period of my life do I remember having been so much harassed in body and mind as during the past month. . . . The Afghans are gunpowder, and the Dost is a lighted match. Of his whereabouts we are wonderfully ignorant.' He talked of hanging Dost Muhammad 'as high as Haman', of 'showing no mercy to the man who was the author of all the evil now distracting the country'. Shah Suja, long checked from aweing his subjects in complete Afghan fashion, was delighted, yet surmised, 'I suppose you would, even now, if I were to catch the dog, prevent me from hanging him'.

The dog, however, was not yet caught, and his teeth were presently fastened in his pursuers' flesh. On November 2, on a clear crisp morning of autumn, Dost Muhammad turned at bay. He and his men were poorly mounted, but they were desperate. From his blue standard the native levies fled; and the Afghans charged home on the British cavalry. It was a precursor, in pitiful and useless gallantry, of the Khyber and Maiwand. But the ex-Amir, left victor on the battlefield, knew himself no match for these powerful interlopers. Victories such as this could only stir the Feringhis to such an effort as would crush him and his people beyond rising again. He rode through night and the following day, twenty-four hours in the saddle; and, the day after the battle of Parwandara, Macnaghten on his evening ride outside Kabul was hailed by a horseman, who told him Dost Muhammad was behind, to surrender. Dost Muhammad himself then rode up; dismounted, cool and debonair as if from his bed; saluted the British envoy and gave him his sword. Macnaghten, who had desired to hang him, was moved and deeply respectful. He returned the sword, and they rode side by side, the ex-Amir asking eagerly about his family. He remained about ten days in Kabul, conversing freely with Macnaghten, who was stirred to chivalrous esteem and admiration by the Afghan's story of his life as a fugitive and his undaunted bearing. His own people, who had remained aloof from His Majesty Shah Suja, crowded to the prisoner's tent burning to show their affection and respect. Shah Suja refused to see him, since he was not allowed to hang him; he 'would not be able to bring himself to show common civility to such a villain'. But Macnaghten delighted to honour 'the dog'; and when the Dost was sent to India, wrote, in almost the only words of candour that emerge from the self-deception with which he had enmeshed his mind:

' I trust that the Dost will be treated with liberality. His case has been compared to that of Shah Soojah; and I have seen it argued that he should not be treated more handsomely than his Majesty was; but surely the cases are not parallel. The Shah had no claim upon us. We had no hand in depriving him of his kingdom, whereas we ejected the Dost, who never offended us, in support of our policy, of which he was the victim.' [1]

Lord Auckland received the captive generously and respectfully, 'and burdened the revenues of India with a pension in his favour of two lakhs of rupees'.[2]

The British increasingly established themselves. Bungalows were built, gardens were laid out. The Afghan climate suited Feringhi energy. There were race-meetings, jackal and fox hunting, shooting parties, fishing, amateur theatricals. We are told of the 'infinite astonishment' of the people when they saw British officers skating on their lakes. With resentment they noted all the signs of a permanent occupation. This energy was wonderful, and boded no good, conjoined with such ambition; 'the manliness of the Feringhee strangers quite put them to shame'. It put them to shame also in perilous fashion, shame which 'for two long years' burned 'itself into the hearts of the Caubulees'.[3] Afghans of highest family had their harems raided and their women dishonoured.

Then the country cause was given a martyr. Akram Khan, a chieftain who refused to come in, was betrayed for a price, and by Macnaghten's instructions, exercised through nominal Afghan authority, blown from a gun as a rebel.

All through 1841 the storm gathered. Khelat had been recovered from the puppet khan; Duranis, Ghilzyes, and other formidable tribes

---

[1] The reference is to Shah Suja's sojourn as a pensioner in British India, before his restoration.

[2] Kaye, ii. 98.   [3] *Op. cit.* ii. 143 ff.

were rising in revolt. Macnaghten for his services and success was appointed Governor of Bombay, and prepared to leave, rejoicing that everything was 'quiet'. The British, who had occupied a line on the Bala Hissar, the famous fortress overlooking Kabul, gave up their barracks to the aged King's harem and established themselves in an indefensible 'sheep-pen' on flat plain, by a refinement of stupidity putting their arsenal elsewhere. Lord Auckland, having in General Nott an adequate soldier to his hand, preferred to make commander-in-chief in Afghanistan, on Sir Willoughby Cotton's retirement, General Elphinstone, of whom Miss Eden reports (February 6, 1840): ' He is in a shocking state of gout, poor man ! one arm in a sling and very lame, but otherwise is a young-looking general for India'.[1]

Macnaghten, happy in promotion and preparing to go, made light of the warnings from every outpost. At the very time when a formidable conspiracy was meeting constantly in Kabul, he wrote (of a grim little fight which came close to disaster) that he 'hoped the business . . . was the expiring effort of the rebels', and accepted Burnes's congratulations on 'my approaching departure at a season of such profound tranquillity'. The congratulations must have been ironic; to a native agent's disclosures of peril about to break, Burnes 'stood up from his chair, sighed, and said he knows nothing but the time has arrived that we should leave the country'. That very evening (November 1, 1841), at the house of a chief whom Burnes had called a dog and threatened with the loss of his ears, the conspirators made their plans. Next day Kabul was in commotion, and among the first whom the mob murdered was Burnes.

A massacre followed, of British officers and their families, caught in their pleasant homes. The insurgents were in terror that retribution would come at any moment, and slew and plundered with their eyes watchful for a way of escape. But a British-Indian army remained unmoving, half an hour's march away. Towards evening General Elphinstone wrote to Macnaghten: 'We must see what the morning brings, and then think what can be done'.

Hereafter hardly one act of the British fell below an almost incredible level of imbecility. No disgrace, no humiliation, was wanting. Elphinstone and his troops looked on while the Afghans stormed the fort where the commissariat was stored. The rank and file and junior

[1] *Up the Country*, 389.

officers—who hitherto had kept their morale—when they saw their supplies being looted by enemies not four hundred yards away, carrying off their prize 'as busily as a swarm of ants', begged to be allowed to prevent their own starvation. General Elphinstone considered the effort too dangerous, and to Macnaghten (who at least pressed for energetic action) pointed out that his men 'have been all night in the works, are tired, and ill-fed'. On November 13 came a solitary gleam, when Macnaghten took the responsibility on himself and overcame the General's reluctance so far that a detachment attacked a force which was cannonading their cantonment, and rendering it almost untenable. A desperate fight came close to overwhelming disaster; for the first time the British soldiery showed that panic terror which was to make this campaign unique in our annals. Called on to advance, as one of their own officers witnesses,[1] 'with a few gallant exceptions, they remained immovable, nor could the Sepoys be induced to lead the way where their European brethren so obstinately hung back'. At the action's outset, their bayonets had been charged down by the impetuous Afghan cavalry, and ruin had shaken them by the throat. Lady Sale, watching, felt 'her very heart' 'as if it leapt to my teeth when I saw the Afghans ride clean through them. The onset was fearful. They looked like a great cluster of bees, but we beat them and drove them up again.'[2] One enemy gun was spiked and another smaller one brought back; and the day closed with the keening of Afghan women, and the hillsides dotted with the flitting torches of the burial-parties. This 'was the last success, even of a doubtful and equivocal character, which the unhappy force was destined to achieve'.[3]

On December 11 Macnaghten concluded a treaty, whose preamble with humiliating blandness observes:

' Whereas it has become apparent from recent events that the continuance of the British army in Afghanistan for the support of Shah Soojah-ool-Moolkh is displeasing to the great majority of the Afghan nation; and whereas the British Government had no other object in sending troops to this country than the integrity, happiness, and welfare of the Afghans, and, therefore, it can have no wish to remain when that object is defeated by its presence ...'

Shah Suja was to be given his choice of accompanying the British or remaining on a pension; Dost Muhammad was to be released; the Army of Occupation was to become immediately an Army of Evacuation.

[1] Vincent Eyre. See his *Journal, passim.*
[2] *A Journal of the Disasters in Afghanistan,* 1841-2, p. 98.　　[3] Kaye, ii. 223.

Macnaghten began trying to set one group of chieftains against another, using the weapon of corruption which had formerly served so well. Akbar Khan, Dost Muhammad's son, enticed him to a conference, and shot him with a pistol given by Macnaghten the previous day and accepted with profuse gratitude: 'the Envoy has deeply paid for his attempt to outdiplomatize the Affghans'.[1] As the price of safe-conduct to Peshawar, the British were compelled to accept a new and even worse treaty: surrendered hostages: paid individual chiefs large sums: and promised to order the evacuation of Jalalabad and all forts held inside the Afghan border.

The Afghans, however, kept no treaty. Demand upon demand was added, as each was yielded. In the end, all coin in the treasury, all surplus muskets, all the guns except six, ammunition, waggons, stores, all were given up. Afghan insolence rose, British depression deepened. Pottinger, who had succeeded Macnaghten as 'Political', was overruled in Council when he 'would have snapped asunder the treaty before the faces of the chiefs, and appealed to the God of Battles'.[2] A rejoicing and fiendish rabble pillaged and insulted and haunted 'a herd of broken-spirited slaves', who on January 6, 1842, set out through the snow.

Sale, who at Gandamak controlled the eastern passes, under Elphinstone's peremptory instructions withdrew to Jalalabad, where presently he was conducting a second 'Defence of Arcot'. Sale, in his own words later, having to choose 'between the alternatives of being bound or not by the convention, which was forced from our Envoy and military commander with the knives at their throats', chose rightly. He and his force had been no party to the compact, and they saw no signs of the Afghans keeping any scrap of the faith they pledged. For the sake of his wretched brethren in Kabul, he deemed it his duty to stay at this advanced post, to succour them as early as possible.

Meanwhile 4000 fighting men and 12,000 camp-followers were enduring the miseries of frost-bite, starvation, and constant attack. The retreat was a mere movement of deer into whose midst wolves kept rushing, picking off a weakling here, striking down another there. Akbar Khan from time to time appeared on the flanks, and demanded (and obtained) more hostages for Sale's evacuation of Jalalabad. The entry of the Kabul Pass was marked by a massacre. Here Elphinstone

[1] Lady Sale, *A Journal*, etc., 3.　　　　[2] Kaye, ii. 326.

ordered a halt, and would not stir from his decision. Eldred Pottinger, a prisoner spending the night under a roof, thought of the wretches camped without cover, fire, or food, and persuaded Akbar Khan to promise to take over the British women and children who still survived, and convoy them safe to Peshawar. Akbar Khan, whose own family were in British India, agreed, for he wanted the ladies as hostages. Accordingly, eleven women passed into his keeping, their husbands and children accompanying them. The retreat continued (January 10); at the close of that day, one prolonged butchery, only 450 Europeans remained alive. All baggage was lost, every sepoy was dead, of the 12,000 camp-followers a raving, clogging mass of over 3000 lived.

From these, under cover of night, the fighting men plotted to escape. But the wretches heard them move on, and 'in the wildness of their fear' surged after them, drawing a massed Afghan fire. Next day the remnant almost reached the Pass of Jagdalak, where they cowered behind ruined walls. The last three bullocks were taken from the camp-followers and killed, the European soldiers devouring the flesh raw, slaking it down with handfuls of snow. Two days of desperate fighting, with intervals of negotiation, followed. Generals Elphinstone and Shelton, with a third officer acting as interpreter, were received by Akbar Khan round a blazing fire, and given hot tea, being afterwards kept as hostages.

Akbar Khan probably wished to save the few survivors. But the hillmen, beasts of prey then as now, were determined none should escape. The retreat continued into the Jagdalak Pass, where nearly all of the 150 fighting men who lived were killed. Next day, 25 officers and 45 men reached Gandamak, and were all but about twenty massacred while entering upon invited negotiations. Sixteen miles from Jalalabad, six, all officers, were alive. On January 13 the Jalalabad garrison, straining their eyes from the ramparts, saw one reeling pony in the distance, stumbling forward, with a rider bowed on its neck. It was Dr. Brydon. So closed in 'awful completeness', 'sublime unity', the most terrible disaster that ever overtook a British force.

When the truth, after preliminary rumour, came home in all its certainty, Auckland knew one spasm of courage, in his Proclamation of January 31, 1842:

'. . . A faithless enemy, stained by the foul crime of assassination, has, through a failure of supplies, followed by consummate treachery, been able to overcome a body of British troops, in a country removed, by distance and difficulties of season, from the possibility of succour. But the Governor-General in Council, while he most deeply laments the loss of the brave officers and men, regards this partial reverse only as a new occasion for displaying the stability and vigour of the British power, and the admirable spirit and valour of the British-Indian army.'

The flash went out, and he sank into such despondency that many who received his letters at this period out of pity destroyed such a revelation of a spirit crushed and despairing. One good thing, at any rate, was done. The crisis called for the best soldier, not the most senior; and General Pollock, though a Company's officer, was preferred to the King's officers, and placed in command of the troops at Peshawar. In their distress the British called on the Sikhs to implement their part in the Tripartite Treaty, by which their allies were entitled to call on them for help in case of need. They hung back. And on January 10 a sepoy battalion mutinied, demanding increased allowances and coats and gloves before advancing through the cold to Kabul. The other troops fell in, and everything was set for another Barrackpur massacre. Fortunately there was in Peshawar a man as humane as he was intelligent:

'It was so dark we could hardly distinguish one another. There was a general hum and whisper. We stood there in a great suspense. An order came for the portfires to be lighted. We could just see Lawrence on horseback, dark and prominent against the sky, vehemently urging, and riding here and there. At length we were ordered back. Lawrence had shown the madness of firing on the regiment at such an hour, when we could not discern the different corps, and of exposing to the Sikh army our internal discords. . . .

'The following day the matter was arranged under Lawrence's counsel, and the Sepoys accepted their pay. I have heard Sir Henry dwell on the dangers of that night, and the difficulty he had to prevent Wild from the suicidal measure of ordering the other Sepoy regiments to compel the 64th. There may have been a deeper danger than we knew; for there is little doubt that all the Sepoys were equally averse to the advance.' [1]

Pollock arrived in Peshawar, February 5; and quietly settled down for two months, while he infused his own confidence and serenity into men who had been handled with imbecility for so long. On April 5 and 6 he forced the Khyber by flanking methods, seizing commanding points instead of merely thrusting through its terrible jaws. On the 16th he relieved Jalalabad. On the 20th he moved forward again, and on September 8 he crowned lesser victories by a resounding

[1] Colonel J. R. Becher, quoted in *Life of Henry Lawrence*, i. 300.

one in the Jagdalak Pass; five days later, at Tezin, sepoy and Briton, at last reknit into terrible comradeship, so defeated Akbar Khan that he knew his cause was doomed. Meanwhile, Nott also was fighting his way towards Kabul. Ghazni was recaptured, September 6. Pollock reoccupied Kabul, September 16, Nott joining him next day. On October 9 and 10 the great bazaar was destroyed, 'an inexcusable act of vandalism';[1] perhaps it was, but the consideration which decided its blowing up was the fact that Macnaghten's mutilated body had been exultingly exposed there. Far worse was the deliberate sacking of Kabul, not in the heat of entry, but as a last-minute policy:

' Guilty and innocent alike fell under the heavy hand of the lawless retribution. . . . Many unoffending Hindoos, who, lulled into a sense of delusive security by the outward re-establishment of a government, had returned to the city and reopened their shops, were now disastrously ruined. In the mad excitement of the hour, friend and foe were stricken down by the same unsparing hand.'[2]

Having covered their name with detestation everywhere, on October 12 the British evacuated the shattered capital. Lord Ellenborough, an exuberant orator and a writer of the high Roman kind, who had succeeded Lord Auckland, February 28, 1842, on October 1 issued his pæan:

' . . . Disasters unparalleled in their extent, unless by the errors in which they originated, and by the treachery by which they were completed, have, in one short campaign, been avenged upon every scene of past misfortune; and repeated victories in the field, and the capture of the cities and citadels of Ghuznee and Caubul, have again attached the opinion of invincibility to the British arms.

' The British arms in possession of Afghanistan will now be withdrawn to the Sutlej.

' The Governor-General will leave it to the Afghans themselves to create a government amidst the anarchy which is the consequence of their crimes.'

Here the reader will probably find himself compelled to pause, at contemplation of the impudence and mixed reasoning of this puerile outburst. Both qualities persist to the end:

' To force a sovereign upon a reluctant people would be as inconsistent with the policy as it is with the principles of the British Government, tending to place the arms and resources of that people at the disposal of the first invader, and to impose the burden of supporting a sovereign, without the prospect of benefit from his alliance'—

truths as self-evident as those with which the American Declaration of

---

[1] P. E. Roberts, *History of British India*, 324.   [2] Kaye, ii. 369.

Independence opens. Now that they are recognised, late though it be and after unexampled punishment for blindness:

' Content with the limits nature appears to have assigned to its empire, the Government of India will devote all its efforts to the establishment and main-tenance of general peace, to the protection of the sovereigns and chiefs its allies, and to the prosperity and happiness of its own faithful subjects.

' The rivers of the Punjab and Indus, and the mountainous passes and the barbarous tribes of Afghanistan, will be placed between the British army and an enemy approaching from the West, if indeed such an enemy there can be, and no longer between the army and its supplies.

' The enormous expenditure required for the support of a large force, in a false military position, at a distance from its own frontier and its resources, will no longer arrest every measure for the improvement of the country and of the people.'

In those last words the brazen countenance at last shows some signs of almost shame. The long-delayed internal improvement of much-pillaged India was postponed further by this iniquitous campaign. Hardly anything, and certainly nothing adequate, could be done until after the Mutiny; and then that outbreak crippled Indian finances for many a year longer:

' It is upon record, that this calamitous war cost the natives of India, whose stewards we are, some fifteen millions of money. All this enormous burden fell upon the revenues of India, and the country for long years afterwards groaned under the weight. The bitter injustice of this need hardly be insisted upon.' [1]

The war, moreover, had been waged for solely British purposes, a wild parrying of an imagined stroke by Russia, that dread of statesmen in London and Calcutta.

This was all silly and humiliating enough. But on November 16 the Governor-General issued what the Duke of Wellington styled a 'Song of Triumph', his notorious Address to 'All the Princes and Chiefs', 'My Brothers and My Friends', congratulating them because General Nott had torn away from the tomb of 'Sultan Mahmud, that victorious Lord',[2] the gates which in his lifetime (it was alleged) the victorious Lord had brought from Somnath, in Gujarat. The tomb's guardians wept and protested; but no one else was destined to care:

' Our victorious army bears the gates of the temple of Somnauth in triumph from Afghanistan, and the despoiled tomb of Sultan Mahomed looks upon the ruins of Ghuznee.

[1] *Op. cit.* iii. 398.   [2] FitzGerald's *Rubáiyát of Omar Khayyám.*

' The insult of eight hundred years is at last avenged. The gates of the temple of Somnauth, so long the memorial of your humiliation, are become the proudest record of your national glory, the proof of your superiority in arms over the nations beyond the Indus.

' To you, Princes and Chiefs of Sirhind, of Rajwarra, of Malwa, and of Guzerat, I shall commit this glorious trophy of successful war.

' You will yourselves, with all honour, transmit the gates of sandal-wood through your respective territories to the restored temple of Somnauth.

' The chiefs of Sirhind shall be informed at what time our victorious army will first deliver the gates of the temple into their guardianship, at the foot of the bridge of the Sutlej.'

The 'People of India', also 'My Brothers and Friends', received their own separate Address.

These Proclamations at first were thought to be a hoax, but were discovered to be genuine. As for the 'gates', they were found to be modern, and not those of Somnath at all; and were finally left to repose in the armoury at Agra.

Lord Ellenborough in December staged a colossal military show at Ferozpur. This was meant partly as a warning to the Sikhs, whose help was 'crabbed' and whose reluctancies were angrily discussed, that their turn would come next if they were not careful. All was noise, excitement, flutter—fine dresses, fine warriors, fine horses—elephants decorated, caparisoned and painted—triumphal arches, gigantic marquees, tinsel, bright-hued cloths, festoons and awnings, 'polyglot emblazonments' of the victorious army's battles, field-days, banquets, speeches and applause. Forty thousand troops and a hundred guns were manoeuvred under the eyes of the Governor-General, the Commander-in-Chief, Sir Jasper Nicolls, Pertab Singh the Sikh heir-apparent, Dhyan Singh the Sikh Prime Minister, and a host of happy ladies. The year which began in disaster 'opportunely closed in gaiety and glitter—in prosperity and parade'.[1]

The Governor-General had intended to compel Dost Muhammad to salaam at his durbar; but this Roman insolence and cruelty was too much for some who had stood enough of what Kaye calls his 'Napoleonic' histrionics. Dost Muhammad was allowed to pass quietly out of India, and reached Lahore, January 20, 1843, where the Sikh durbar received him with genuine honour. He rejoined a people in whom he found 'scarcely a family . . . which had not the blood of kindred to revenge upon the accursed Feringhees. The door of reconciliation

1 Kaye, iii. 396.

z

seemed to be closed against us; and if the hostility of the Afghans be an element of weakness, it seemed certain that we must have contrived to secure it'.[1] He was enthusiastically welcomed back, and proceeded to give his country again a government wise by contemporary standards, and less ruthless by far than that of its neighbours of the Punjab and the Central Asian khanates.

So ended an episode whose

' one consolation—if indeed it can now be called a consolation—was that we had learned a lesson which we could never need to be taught again'.[2]

Unfortunately for the prophet, history, which as a matter of fact rarely 'repeats itself', did so with tragic closeness in the second Afghan War of 1878-80.

CHAPTER V

THE CONQUEST AND PACIFICATION OF SIND: SUPPRESSION OF GWALIOR ARMY

The Amirs' candle burns at both ends: Napier and Outram: battles of Miani and Daba: various comments on the war: Napier settles the new province: the last Maratha War: battles of Maharajpur and Panniar: dismissal of Lord Ellenborough: Lord Ellenborough on future relations with native States.

' THE conquest of Sind followed in the wake of the Afghan War and was morally and politically its sequel ' [3]—in Sir Charles Napier's expression, ' the tail of the Affghan storm'. Part of the story has already come in the narrative of that campaign. The rest can fitly come mainly in the conqueror's own words.

Lord Ellenborough had reprobated in advance the mischievous activities of anyone who should rob India of peace, and warned such that the full majesty of British strength would move against them. In 1841 the Company, having 'acquired by degrees that secondary moral force which belongs to utility irrespective of abstract justice',[4] by

---

[1] *Op. cit.* iii. 399.   [2] R. Bosworth Smith, *Life of Lord Lawrence*, 156.

[3] P. E. Roberts, *History of British India*, 325.

[4] Sir Charles Napier (Sir William Napier, *The Conquest of Scinde*, i. 92).

virtue of that secondary moral force decided that it should annex Shikarpur, on Sind's northern border and its largest city. The Amirs reluctantly assented. As the British had already seized and kept Karachi, Sind's only port, in the extreme south, 'the Ameers' candle was burning at both ends'. The Amirs were suspected of still harbouring ungrateful feelings, so Sir Charles Napier, recalled from Europe, 'a small dark-visaged old man . . . with a falcon's glance',[1] 'always more under the influence of excitement than of reason',[2] in September, 1842, was sent to Sind, with the widest possible powers of war and peace. He was a veteran trained under the Duke of Wellington, and imbued with all the master's love of discipline and promptitude; and Lord Ellenborough, when sending him, warned the Amirs, in these 'explicit and honourable' terms, 'stimulated by the lofty ambition of saving India from ruin':[3]

' On the day on which you shall be faithless to the British Government sovereignty will have passed from you; your dominions will be given to others, and in your destitution all India will see that the British Government will not pardon an injury received from one it believed to be its friend.'

The dark-visaged old man with a falcon's glance carried these instructions:

' If the Ameers, or any one of them, should act hostilely, or evince hostile designs against the British forces, it was the Governor-General's fixed resolution never to forgive the breach of faith, and to exact a penalty which should be a warning to every chief in India.'

Major Outram, 'the Bayard of India', who acted as his 'Political', after cherishing natural enough resentment and suspicion from his memories of a certain lack of enthusiasm in the Amirs' co-operation during the Afghan War had come to feel that their offences were trivial in face of their provocation and the wolf's obvious intention first to charge them with muddying his springs and then to devour them. In February, 1843, he wrote to Napier that he was

' unable entirely to coincide in your views, either as respects the policy or justice of, at least so suddenly, overturning the patriarchal government to which alone Sind has been accustomed . . . I say *patriarchal*, for, however we may despise the Amirs as inferior to ourselves, either in morality or expansion of intellect, each chief certainly lives *with*, and *for*, his portion of the people;

[1] Description by his brother, Sir William Napier, *op. cit.* i. 22.

[2] J. C. Marshman, *History of India* (abridged edition), 435.

[3] *Conquest of Scinde*, i. 97, 98.

and I question whether any class of the people of Sind, except the Hindoo traders . . . would prefer a change to the best government we could give them. . . .

' It grieves me to say that my heart, and the judgment God has given me, unite in condemning the measures we are carrying out for his Lordship as most tyrannical—positive robbery. I consider, therefore, that every life which may hereafter be lost in consequence will be a murder. . . .' [1]

However, Outram was instructed to force on the Amirs a new treaty. They argued that, 'having never broken the old agreements into which they had entered with the British Government, there was no necessity to impose upon them new and objectionable terms as punishment for an offence they had not committed'. Napier held otherwise, and so did Ellenborough. 'Certain vague charges of disaffection . . . based on evidence now generally recognized to have been unsatisfactory',[2] had been brought against them, the only serious item being a letter which the best scholars in India said was probably a forgery but which Napier, who had the advantage of total ignorance of any Indian language, decided was genuine.[3] The main proof, of course, was in the Governor-General's declared conviction that the Amirs could not possibly be genuinely devoted to the Company—a conviction which must be admitted as based on sound reasoning. Napier's own standpoint was disarmingly honest. He wrote in his Diary: 'We have no right to seize Sind, yet we shall do so, and a very advantageous, useful, humane piece of rascality it will be'.[4] Outram's testimony, to which he stood throughout, despite his first prejudice which made him willing to support considerable tightening of the treaty so long as the Amirs were left sovereigns, was: [5]

' The information I obtained during my voyage up the Indus, and my previous knowledge of the chiefs of Sind, satisfied me that the reports of their warlike preparations were unfounded, probably promulgated by themselves, in the hope that our demands would be less stringent, if we supposed them in any way prepared for resistance. . . . I well knew that they themselves were quite conscious of their inability to oppose our power; that they had no serious intention of the sort; and that nothing but the most extreme proceedings and forcing them to desperation would drive them to it.'

Napier destroyed the Amirs' magazines and grain stores, and their

[1] *James Outram*, 316.   [2] P. E. Roberts, *History of British India*, 327.

[3] Marshman, *History of India*, 432.

[4] Sir W. Napier, *The Life and Opinions of General Sir Charles Napier*, ii. 218.

[5] *James Outram*, i. 298-9.

fortress of Imamghar. All these actions he considered peaceful arguments. The Amirs, terrified, gave way to Outram's persuasions, and
signed a treaty promising to abandon the right of coining money
(which was to be issued by the Company henceforth and to bear
on one side the effigy of the British sovereign), and to fuel Company
steamers on the Indus. But they implored him to leave Haidarabad,
before their people got out of hand. The outbreak came, three days
later (February 15, 1843), when Outram escaped to a steamer. On
February 17, at Miani, Napier routed a horde of Baluchis:

' Thick as standing corn, and gorgeous as a field of flowers . . . they filled
the broad deep bed of the Fillaillee, they clustered on both banks, and
covered the plain beyond. Guarding their heads with their large dark shields,
they shook their sharp swords, beaming in the sun, their shouts rolled like a
peal of thunder, as with frantic gestures they rushed forwards . . . with
demoniac strength and ferocity. But with shouts as loud, and shrieks as wild
and fierce as theirs, and hearts as big and arms as strong, the Irish soldiers
met them with that queen of weapons the musket and sent their foremost
masses rolling back in blood',[1]

while the guns swept the river-course diagonally, tearing the dense
crowd with an appalling carnage. Napier's courage and generalship
were both admirable. A desperate fight ended in complete victory, at
the cost of 275 casualties; the enemy lost 6000.

' The ferocity on both sides was unbounded, the carnage horrible.
The General, seeing a 22nd soldier going to kill an exhausted Belooch chief,
called to him to spare: the man drove his bayonet deep, and then turning,
justified the act with a homely expression, terrible in its truthfulness accompanying such a deed: "This day, General, the shambles have it all to themselves".'

Napier next summoned Haidarabad to surrender. Vakils sent to ask
his terms were told: 'Life, and nothing more. And I want your decision
before twelve o'clock, as I shall by that time have buried my dead, and
given my soldiers their breakfasts'.[2] Haidarabad was yielded in haste;
its booty, a star drawing envy ever since Alexander Burnes brought
British India the report that the Amirs had twenty millions sterling
hoarded, proved disappointing. The Khairpur Amir was routed at
Daba (March 24), a repetition of the previous battle, the losses of both
sides almost exactly as before. The nullas and hamlets were crammed
with dead and dying: 'All the fallen Beloochs were of mature age, grim-

[1] *The Conquest of Scinde*, ii. 311-12.
[2] *Op. cit.* ii. 320-1.

visaged men, athletic forms: the carcass of a youth was not to be found'.[1] But, 'contrary to all expectation', thirteen unwounded prisoners were taken, as against three at Miani; 'and this slight approach to mildness gave the General infinite satisfaction, for the ferocity on both sides had pained him deeply'.[2]

Napier continued to roar up and down. His voice became a bellow:

' If you come in and make your salaam, and promise fidelity to the British Government, I will restore to you your lands and former privileges, and the superintendance (*sic*) of the dawks. If you refuse, I will wait till the hot weather is gone past, and then I will carry fire and sword into your territories, and drive you and all belonging to you into the mountains; and if I catch you I will hang you as a rebel. You have now your choice. Choose!'

The chief so exhorted chose to make his salaam. But 'his barbarian pride would not bend'. He came with six attendants, and his demeanour was reported by the colonel who received him as haughty. He was accordingly told to come in again, with proper humility: 'Come here instantly. Come alone and make your submission, or I will in a week tear you from the midst of your tribe and hang you'. 'Had he hesitated, the General would have been upon him within the time specified.'

Sind was annexed, the Amirs exiled; Napier received £70,000 prize-money, and the Governor-General strained even his throat of eloquence in crowing over what had been achieved:

' The army of Scinde has twice beaten the bravest enemy in Asia, under circumstances which would equally have obtained for it the victory over the best troops in Europe. . . .

' To have punished the treachery of protected Princes; to have liberated a nation from its oppressors; to have added a province, fertile as Egypt, to the British empire; and to have effected these great objects by actions in war unsurpassed in brilliancy, whereof a grateful army assigns the success to the ability and valour of its general; these are not ordinary achievements, nor can the ordinary language of praise convey their reward.'

Outram refused his £3000 prize-money; told Napier, for whom he cherished warm affection (which was returned): 'I am sick of *policy*; I will not say yours is the *best*, but it is undoubtedly the shortest —that *of the sword*. Oh, how I wish you had drawn it in a better cause!'; and went home to plead for the Amirs. Mr. Gladstone afterwards revealed [3] that Sir Robert Peel's Cabinet, of which he and the

---

[1] *Op. cit.* 390.   [2] *Op. cit.* ii. 407.
[3] *Contemporary Review*, November, 1876.

Duke of Wellington were both members, disapproved, he believed unanimously, of the conquest. 'But the ministry were powerless, inasmuch as the mischief of retaining was less than the mischief of abandoning it, and it remains an accomplished fact.' Even Napier once wrote in his Diary: 'My present position is not, however, to my liking: we had no right to come here, and are tarred with the Afghan brush'. In England, Elphinstone's contemptuous comment was:[1] 'Coming after Afghanistan, it put one in mind of a bully who has been kicked in the streets, and went home to beat his wife in revenge'. The conqueror's 'sardonic pun',[2] 'Peccavi' ('I have Sind'), is one of the few things in connection with British-Indian history that have lodged in the common mind.

Having conquered Sind, Napier entered on its pacification. Like many great soldiers, he regarded 'the frocks' with scorn. 'Having fixed notions of government' (as of most matters) he rejected the civilian element and its opinions, observing that

' the mercantile spirit weakens if it does not altogether exclude noble sentiments. . . . The bravery and devotion of the troops . . . have expanded the original small settlement on the Hooghly to a mighty empire; and yet on every accession of territory the soldier has been treated as unfit to govern what his sword had won; on each new acquisition a civil establishment has been fastened, incongruent with the military barbarism of the people to be governed but fulfilling the conditions of patronage and profit. . . . For those civil servants have much higher salaries and allowances than the military servants have. . . .

' In this manner a vicious circle of policy is completed, and a solution furnished of that seeming paradox, that while the instructions issued by the directors for the government of the East have always been moderate and opposed to aggrandizement by war, their empire has been continually augmented by arms and little or nothing has been affected for the welfare of the people.'

The civil servants he styled 'ignorant of great principles, devoid of business habits', wasteful and greedy for jobs and ease, run by nepotism, grossly overpaid and demanding swollen costly establishments. They

' have worn out originally vigorous appetites and feeble minds while enjoying large salaries and the adulation of black clerks. . . . Despising and avoid-

[1] Letter to Metcalfe: *Life of Elphinstone*, ii. 374.
[2] Roberts, *History of British India*, 330.

ing the society of the natives, they yet pretend to know the characters of those natives, and call themselves the Statesmen of India!'

He set up a cheaper administration than the bureaucracy considered proper. The Court of Directors he dismissed as 'but cunning fools, and I am a man whose daily occupation is to deal with the lives of my fellow-men'. To the administration of India generally he called 'Hands off Sind!'; and he set the model which the world-famed Punjab Tradition was to copy and amplify a few years later. To the chiefs and nobles he restored their swords, 'with this stern though flattering admonition': [1]

' Take back your sword. You have used it with honour against me, and I esteem a brave enemy. But if forgetful of this voluntary submission you draw it again in opposition to my government, I will tear it from you and kill you as a dog.'

He had absolute powers of life and death without trial, and did a deal of hanging, justified by the region's profligacy of murder. Felons were suspended bearing labels in three languages (as in an ancient example) explaining the reason for their doom. Lord William Bentinck had abolished flogging in the native army; Napier ignored this change, flogging freely, as a sane alternative to shooting or dismissal, the penalties lavishly meted out in those hard times. He held that 'the human mind is never better disposed to gratitude and attachment than when softened by fear'; and he used to observe: 'It will not do to let their barbaric vanity gradually wipe away the fear cast on them by the two battles'. The properly behaved were sometimes allowed to salaam to Queen Victoria's picture, which was kept 'covered with a curtain from the gaze of private men and retainers'.[2] It is no marvel that the Conqueror of Sind has been so long the hero of boys' stories, and his simple philosophy that of all those who 'know how to deal with Orientals'. His nickname with the tribes was 'Shaitan-Ke-bhai', 'Satan's brother'.

The civil service were chagrined, not unnaturally. Nevertheless,

' if we would speak true,
Much to the man is due'.

By his single fiat he abolished slavery. The occasional suttees of Sind (mainly a Muslim region) were peremptorily stopped. When the Brahmins protested that the burning of widows was a religious custom,

[1] Sir William Napier, *History of General Sir Charles Napier's Administration of Scinde*, 14.

[2] *Op. cit.* 17.

he replied cheerfully that in that case they must prepare the pyre, of course. But

' my nation has also a custom. When men burn women alive we hang them, and confiscate all their property. My carpenters shall therefore erect gibbets on which to hang all concerned when the widow is consumed. Let us all act according to national customs'.

No more widows were burnt. When a chief interceded for a man who had merely killed his wife, a trivial fault, Napier replied that she had done her husband no wrong. 'No! but he was angry! why should he not kill her?' 'Well, I am angry', said Napier. 'Why should I not kill him?' —and did kill him. There is something to be said for a despot whose hand is heavy on cowardly savagery. He did a magnificent work; and Providence, as the Sindis were quick to note, approved him, by sending abundant showers at the very beginning of his rule.

Moreover, the moralities are mixed. Utterly indefensible as the conquest of Sind was, when the argument got away from legality and international ethics a deeper defence revealed itself (as Napier felt, and sometimes expressed in his rough, roaring fashion). The Amirs' rule was hard on minorities not of their faith; and it was as barbarous as any other of these childish Eastern administrations. Napier found one wretch a prisoner in a cage, where he had been so long that he could not live in any other way. It is interesting to remember that within the last half-dozen years a similar case was discovered in Sind, the victim of an ecclesiastical sentence, whose promulgators were defended by a much-admired Muslim nationalist lawyer. Outram, like Henry Lawrence, was apt to see one side only, that of native potentates who liked and trusted him and impressed him with their charm; a side of their activities, one deeply diabolical, lay necessarily out of the sight of the courteous, fair-minded English gentleman to whom his own country's reputation for good faith was a passion. Napier also saw one side only, being impatient of princely rights. A time will come when the historian of British India will be able to take both sides into account.

Sind's revenues proved insufficient; but that was because a large army was kept in the province, ready for the expected Sikh War. Watching at the Punjab marches, and convinced that a Punjab War must come, Napier compared himself to Cato with his 'Delenda est Carthago'.

Towards the close of 1843 Lord Ellenborough achieved another war, the last Maratha one. This arose out of the political situation, which drove all independent and martial spirits into what was the only State, outside Nepal and the Punjab, with any genuine autonomy left. Gwalior, a scene of confusion, had an army of 40,000 men and a strong artillery force. The Governor-General's interference was justified by expediency only, and was precipitated by his anticipation of war with the Sikhs, whose friendly Maharaja, Sher Singh, was assassinated, September, 1843. Fearing a possible junction of Sikh and Maratha troops, in a minute (November 1) he took occasion to proclaim that the British Government could not tolerate 'the existence within the territories of Sindhia of an unfriendly government nor that those territories should be without a government willing and able to maintain order'.[1] He suddenly remembered that Wellesley's treaty with Sindhia in 1804 provided for a subsidiary force in Gwalior. The provision had been allowed to lapse; but the British Government was about to surprise native India by discovering a tender regard for treaties. Two British armies marched on Gwalior, the Governor-General accompanying the larger one under General Sir Hugh Gough, the Commander-in-Chief. This on December 23 crossed the Chambal, and thereby invaded Gwalior. Queerly enough, it was taken for granted that the matters at issue would be settled peacefully, the mere presence of British arms disposing the Marathas to kindly thoughts. The Gwalior army was not taken seriously. Lord Ellenborough, relating the event in a letter to the Duke of Wellington (January 21, 1844), begins: 'I little expected ever to have to write to you about a battle in which I had myself been present—however, so it is'.

The Marathas under cover of night moved from the place where they were known to be, and entrenched at Maharajpur,[3] with their batteries before them. The Commander-in-Chief regarded them as a rabble, and his Adjutant-General observed that all he needed was a horse-whip. Ladies accompanied the 'promenade', on horseback and on elephants. The gay party was about to breakfast, when masked batteries opened on them; later, from the long millet and sugar-cane, 'literally, batteries were put up like covies of partridges'. A hugger-mugger haphazard battle followed, of 12,000 Company's men against slightly more Marathas. The British had left their heavy guns behind, and their field pieces were soon silenced; so 'the troops were, according to the usual tactics of Sir Hugh, launched on the batteries, which were served with desperation as long as a gunner was left'.[2] The Company lost 800 killed and wounded, and the enemy

[1] *The Indian Administration of Lord Ellenborough*, edited by Lord Colchester, 412.
[2] Marshman, *History of India*, 440.   [3] See map, p. 220.

about 3000. On the same day (December 29, 1843) General Grey won a battle of a less arduous kind, at Panniar.

Gwalior was not annexed, but passed under British rule for the next ten years, the prince being a minor. Gwalior Fort was put in control of a Company contingent, which in the Mutiny cast off their officers and joined the rebellion. The State army was reduced to 3000 infantry, 6000 cavalry, and thirty-two guns.

Lord Ellenborough returned, rejoicing, and reached Calcutta in March. On the 15th of June, 1844, to his astonishment, he heard that the Court of Directors had revoked his appointment, and dismissed him. This was their retort to his consistent contempt for them: to the absence of respect in his communications: to his gasconades and histrionics: to his scorn of the civil service and exclusive affection for the army (he often mourned that he was not a soldier): and to his military obsession generally. 'His administration presented only a succession of battles.'[1] His exuberance and verbal intoxication had undone him; the man of the Gates of Somnath Proclamation, and many others only less ridiculous because less prominent, was regarded as a dangerous mountebank. The army was intensely annoyed, and emitted a number of speeches and addresses which from Indians would have been held wickedly seditious. The Fort William officers gave him a feast, which the Duke of Wellington refused to censure:

' I who am thus called upon to notice this affair as a serious offence against discipline and a breach of military orders, have served the public now for nearly half a century, and I believe I may safely say that neither in these times nor in any other did there ever exist an officer half so feasted and "festivated", or who received half the number of testimonials from those under his command that I have.'

Lord Ellenborough had excellent qualities, a freedom from nepotism unusual in office-holders of any age and particularly of that, 'patriotic distribution of his patronage', immense energy. But excitability had its usual effect, of disguising genuine powers of mind. These on occasion could find conspicuously wise and independent utterance, as in his letter to Queen Victoria (January 18, 1843):

' The anomalous and unintelligible position of the local government of India excites great practical difficulties in our relations with native chiefs who in an empire like ours have no natural place, and must be continually in apprehension of our design to invade their rights and to appropriate their territories. All these difficulties would be removed were your Majesty to be-

---

[1] *Op. cit.* 441.

come the nominal head of the empire. The princes and chiefs of India would be proud of their position as the feudatories of an empress; and some judicious measures calculated to gratify the feelings of a sensitive race, as well as to inspire just confidence in the intentions of their sovereign, would make the hereditary leaders of this great people cordially co-operate with the British Government in measures for the improvement of their subjects and of their dominions.

' Lord Ellenborough can see no limit to the future prosperity of India if it be governed with due respect for the feelings and even the prejudices, and with a careful regard for the interests, of the people, with the resolution to make *their* well-being the chief object of the Government, and not the pecuniary advantages of the nation of strangers to which Providence has committed the rule of this distant empire.' [1]

The measured criticism underneath those closing words should be noted; like many who came to India from outside—and this detachment is the clinching argument for having a Viceroy from England, instead of a 'man on the spot', for the best man on the spot cannot escape that strangling loop of prejudices and stock opinions which besets Anglo-India—Lord Ellenborough was disquieted by tendencies which seemed to him unethical in their brutally direct selfishness.

However, the British civilian community viewed his supersession 'as an act of unquestionable wisdom',[2] while recognising that he had merits.

[1] *The Indian Administration of Lord Ellenborough*, edited by Lord Colchester, 64-5.

[2] Marshman, 441.

BOOK V

FROM THE SIKH WARS TO THE END OF THE MUTINY

'Though Justice against Fate complain,
And plead the ancient rights in vain—
    (But these do hold or break,
    As men are strong or weak).'

ANDREW MARVELL, *An Horatian Ode upon Cromwell's
Return from Ireland.*

CHRONOLOGICAL TABLE

SIR HENRY
HARDINGE. 1844.

1845. Sikh army crosses Satlej. First Sikh War. Battles of Mudki, Ferozshah, Aliwal, Sobraon.

LORD DALHOUSIE. 1848. Second Sikh War. Battles of Chilianwala and Gujarat.

1849. Punjab annexed.
Moplah rising.
Annexation of Satara.

1852. Second Burmese War.

1853. Sir John Lawrence Chief Commissioner of the Punjab.
Bombay-Thana railway opened.
Annexation of Nagpur.
Renewal of Company's charter.

1855. Sonthal rising.

1856. Annexation of Oudh.

LORD CANNING. 1856. War with Persia.

1857. Treaty with Amir of Afghanistan.
Outbreak of Mutiny at Meerut (May).
Delhi recaptured (September).
Havelock reaches Lucknow (September).
Sir C. Campbell finally relieves Lucknow (November).

1858. Storming of Jhansi (March).
Proclamation on Oudh (March).
Reduction of Oudh.
Proclamation of peace (July).
Government of India transferred to Crown.

CHAPTER I

FIRST SIKH WAR

Annexationist trend of thought: the Punjab during the Afghan War; anarchy after Ranjit Singh's death: the Sikhs cross the Satlej: battles of Mudki, Ferozshah, Aliwal, and Sobraon: a noble 'sati': Gulab Singh: beginning of 'the Punjab Tradition': John Lawrence's methods and views: Henry Lawrence on native States under British tutelage.

THE new Governor-General, Sir Henry Hardinge, came when men were much exercised over what seemed the inevitable unification of India. The best, as well as the crudest, minds played with annexationist dreams. Henry Lawrence, Resident in Nepal, wrote[1] in 1845 that 30,000 men could take that 'magnificent country' in two months, without chance of failure:

'We should then have a splendid frontier in the snowy mountains, and a line of sanataria from Darjeeling to Almora.

'I see the advantage to *us* of taking the country whenever the Goorkhas oblige us to do so; but I have no wish to hasten the measure, for it is only justice to them to say that, bad as is their foreign and Durbar policy, they are the best masters I have seen in India.'

The contradiction in Lawrence's conclusion, one implicit in Indian affairs, was to impress him increasingly, until he became the despairing but resolute foe of the time's popular policy.

The Sikhs had watched the Company over a long period steadily, and often rapidly, advancing. In the Afghan campaign British troops surged across the Punjab, and used it as lines of communication. It could hardly be unknown that British high officers had freely advocated annexation or partition of the Punjab, on grounds of military convenience—which, if the Kabul occupation had proved permanent, would have become necessity.

Ranjit Singh and his successors had been repeatedly warned off countries whose integrity and independence the Company alleged it important to preserve, only to see these annexed afterwards. It was Russia's provocation to Japan when she kept her out of Port Arthur, to

[1] *Life*, i. 482.

367

take it herself. Ferozpur, once regarded as definitely in their sphere, was now an extensive cantonment, where British manœuvres had twice taken place on an elaborately and menacingly magnificent scale. Shikarpur, which Ranjit Singh had vainly tried to obtain as reward for help in the Afghan War, was British, as was the whole lower Indus, to which this important mart formed a gate.

It was the Afghan War—from which so many vivid contemporary pictures have come down, of the Sikhs contemptuously and half-heartedly protecting the retreat of an army convicted of inefficiency unexampled in British annals, while continuing to use the Punjab high-handedly for its purposes—which made war a certainty sooner or later. According to Colonel Steinbach,[1] after the Kabul disaster the Sikh sirdars were all for attacking the British, but were restrained by Maharaja Sher Singh. Every British statesman and soldier was watching for this eventuality; Sir Charles Napier, whose iron blows at Miani and Daba were deeply remembered, was massing on Sikh marches, making no secret of his expectation of war. When the disorder of the Punjab increased, the British strengthened frontier posts and prepared for emergencies—measures explicable but misinterpreted as preludes to invasion. Last of all, Major Broadfoot, who had been prominent in the Afghan War and in 1841, obsessed by conviction that he was moving through a populace intent on destruction of him and his troops, all but precipitated war [2] in the Punjab, was sent to Lahore as British Agent, November, 1844, to the people he had irritated and alarmed. 'The Sikh authorities did not derive any assurance of an increasing desire for peace, from the nomination of an officer who, thirty months before, had made so stormy a passage through their country.'[3]

Broadfoot began by taking under Company protection the remaining Cis-Satlej possessions of the Sikhs, as liable to formal incorporation when the present Maharaja died or was deposed. Without the preliminary of announcing what he had done, he proceeded to act as if the districts were British territory. Finally, when a small body of Sikh horse crossed the Satlej without his,permission, on their way to a town belonging to their Government, he ordered them to recross:

' and as he considered them dilatory in their obedience, he followed them with his escort, and overtook them as they were about to ford the river. A shot was

---

[1] The adventurer who wrote *The Punjaub*.

[2] See J. D. Cunningham, *A History of the Sikhs* (edited by H. L. O. Garrett), 238 ff., for Broadfoot's surprising conduct and Avitabile's dismay.

[3] *Op. cit.* 278-9.

fired by the English party, and the extreme desire of the Sikh commandant to avoid doing anything which might be held to compromise his government, alone prevented a collision.'[1]

His actions, and similar activities on the Sind-Punjab frontier by Sir Charles Napier, were held by the Sikhs to amount to war.

Since Ranjit Singh's death the Punjab's condition had beggared description. A succession of Maharajas and pretenders died suddenly and violently. The Rajas of Jammu (southern Kashmir), a Rajput family who had risen from being ordinary foot-soldiers to be Ranjit Singh's most influential officers, by assassination or battle lost Dhyan Singh, his son Hira Singh, and his brother Suchet Singh. Gulab Singh, who survived, was intent on establishing the virtual independence his clan had founded in the north, and carefully kept out of the war with the British.

The Sikh army frankly usurped the State. They had their committees, much like Cromwell's army, and were pretorian in behaviour, making and unmaking Maharajas. Many of their leaders, now and during the war, were in traitorous correspondence with the British. Among these was the Wazir, Jawahar Singh. The army *panchayats* sentenced him to death, summoning him to appear before them (September 21, 1845). When he came, he was told to stand aside from the boy Maharaja, and a file of soldiers shot him. The act 'partook of the solemnity and moderation of a judicial process, ordained and witnessed by a whole people'.

Rani Jindan, his sister, who was Regent, in a passion of grief and indignation drove his wretched women, two wives and three slave-girls, on to his pyre. The army forced them to march in procession between its ranks, snatching from their trays of distribution the jewels and gifts which are held sacred from a *sati*, even ripping out their ear-rings, answering their entreaties with jest and ribaldry. After the pyre was burning, soldiers tried to rescue the gold fringing of the victims' trousers. In her agony one of the *satis* rose amid the flames and predicted that within a year the Khalsa would 'be overthrown, and the wives of the men of the army would be widows'.[2] A *sati*'s last words are prophetic, and these were terribly fulfilled: 'For a crime so terrible and open, the slaughter of the Khalsa a few months later seemed a just retribution'.[3] The sympathy which otherwise we might give to the Sikhs for their patient endurance of forty years' pressure and the valour

[1] *Op. cit.* 281. [2] Sir Lepel Griffin, *Ranjit Singh*, 65 ff.

[3] Edward Thompson, *Suttee*, 98.

2 A

of their last tremendous stand, dies when we contemplate such savagery. Their religious brotherhood had become admirable only in war; and its destruction was a feat morally desirable.

Rani Jindan and other Sikh leaders became terrified of the army which arrogated powers of summary execution of its nominal chiefs. Foreign war is a well-known expedient of desperate Governments. If the army of the Khalsa crossed the Satlej, like Crœsus it would 'destroy a great kingdom', whether its own or another Fate's

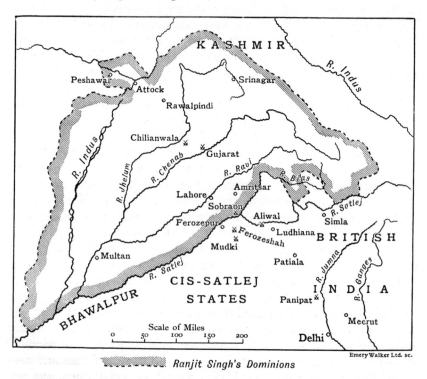

Emery Walker Ltd. sc.

▨▨▨▨ *Ranjit Singh's Dominions*

enigmatic lips declined to say. A very little persuasion would precipitate this consummation, in either possible form welcome; especially since the Sikhs were convinced that war, undeclared but in being, already hovered on their frontiers. The soldiery assembled round Ranjit Singh's funerary memorial, and vowed fidelity in the battle they were about to wage. Then, half in tumult and half in awe, they surged forward: and on December 11, 1845, commenced to cross the Satlej, taking by surprise the British, who had never visualised a beginning so overt, but rather a dragging civil war upon which the Company would at last interfere, in magisterial manner imposing order. The Sikhs were absurdly underrated, 'called a "rabble" in sober official despatches'.[1] Nothing worse than a steady counter-thrust, pausing for a few unstrenuous battles, was anticipated.

The Sikhs, for their part, having taken up a position close to Ferozpur, halted, in solemn dread at their own daring. They had immense advantages, of enthusiasm which made every Sikh consider 'the cause as his own, and he would work as a labourer as well as carry a musket; he would drag guns, drive bullocks, lead camels, and load and unload boats with a cheerful alacrity, which contrasted strongly with the inapt and sluggish obedience of mere mercenaries, drilled, indeed, and fed with skill and care, but unwarmed by one generous feeling for their country or their foreign employers'.[2] But they were now face to face with the Power that had struck down mighty empires, their coevals when it reached this land. They waited, therefore, an army listening in silence to the beating of its own heart.

All India paused from every other occupation to watch the clash between the aliens and the last surviving kingdom (except Nepal). In Nepal, Henry Lawrence's Diary notes (October 2), when war was regarded as a certainty, awaiting only the formalities of declaration, that the Maharaja 'has ordered all the Pundits to examine their books, and inform him whether the British will be victorious'. 'Much anxiety', he reports, eighteen days later, 'is expressed as to the expected fall of Lahore, when Nepaul will be the last free State in India'.[3]

At Mudki, twenty miles from Ferozpur, a Sikh detachment of probably 2000 foot and perhaps 10,000 cavalry, supported by 22 guns, assailed two British divisions (December 18). They were repulsed, but less decisively than Indian armies usually were. The Sikhs were practically deserted by their commanders, Lal Singh and Tej Singh, who were both in correspondence [4] with the enemy. John Lawrence's biographer makes the observation [5] which in this war was to become a commonplace, that if the issue had depended on the sepoys, who ate the Company's salt, and fought for no other reason, Mudki would

---

[1] Cunningham, 288.   [2] *Op. cit.* 292.   [3] *Life of Henry Lawrence*, i. 481.

[4] They 'assured the local British authorities of their secret and efficient goodwill' (Cunningham, 291).

[5] R. Bosworth Smith, *Life of Lord Lawrence*, i. 185.

have been a defeat. The British lost 872 men, among the killed being Sir Robert Sale of Jalalabad:

'The last two hours of battle were a series of dogged stands and skirmishing retreats on the part of the Sikh troops, of sharp struggles, gun captures, and pursuits by the British, over five miles of the worst ground that ever two armies fought for. Night closed the contest, or rather the pursuit, and the British army was left in possession of the field and nineteen of the enemy's guns.'[1]

The British troops effected a junction with Sir John Littler's Ferozpur division, and attacked the Sikhs at Ferozshah, just before sunset, December 21. The most terrible battle of British-Indian history ensued. 'The resistance was wholly unexpected, and all started with astonishment. Guns were dismounted, and their ammunition was blown into the air; squadrons were checked in mid-career; battalion after battalion was hurled back with shattered ranks.'[2] Sir Hugh Gough, the British commander, had chosen the year's shortest day and its last hour of daylight, for his favourite (and only) plan of attack, the frontal assault. 'Cold steel' was his prescription for every emergency, and he sent the troops to the muzzles of the Sikh guns. A very little of the enemy line had been captured, when darkness closed on what was named 'this night of terrors'. The British were

' half outside and half within the enemy's position, unable either to advance or retreat. Regiments were mixed up with regiments, and officers with men, in the wildest confusion':[3]
' generals were doubtful of the fact or of the extent of their own success, and colonels knew not what had become of the regiments they commanded, or of the army of which they formed a part'.[4]

Sir Henry Hardinge (who had commanded at Albuera) testified that he had 'never known a night so extraordinary as this'. He spent it, like another Henry, moving through his disheartened troops, scattering

'A little touch of Harry in the night';

and when day dawned on the full extent of ruin, he exclaimed, 'Another such victory, and we are undone!' He and Gough collected a broken division, and attacked the Sikh batteries in reverse, capturing them. The enemy were withdrawing, when a second Sikh force appeared, under Tej Singh, from whose front Sir John Littler's force had slipped away. This opened a cannonade, 'which at once dismounted our feeble

[1] Herbert Edwardes (*Memorials*, i. 37).   [2] Cunningham, 295.
[3] *Life of Lord Lawrence*, i. 186.   [4] Cunningham, 295.

artillery', and then mysteriously withdrew from before men 'drooping from hunger, not having tasted food for thirty-six hours' and having 'fired away almost their last round of ammunition'. The Sikh cause was doomed, having traitors in command.

The British loss was 2415, among the slain being Major Broadfoot. Heavy material damage had been sustained also, and Hardinge sent John Lawrence, Collector at Delhi, an urgent note in his own handwriting, to send up all the transport he could. The British were short of ammunition, heavy guns, food; and dared not fall back. Exaggerated fears were felt for Delhi's safety, which Cunningham compares to 'the nervous dread of Augustus when he heard of the defeat of Varus and the destruction of his legions'. The extent of the shock may be gauged by the Governor-General's issuing a Proclamation inviting Sikhs to desert, promising rewards and pensions, and 'the immediate decision of any lawsuits in which the deserters might be engaged in the British provinces'.

Sir Harry Smith at Aliwal (December 28) drove a Sikh force back across the Satlej, with the loss of 67 cannon and many drowned as well as slain, the British losing only 589. Then the end came, February 10, 1846. The British stormed strong entrenchments resting on the Satlej, at Sobraon. The treacherous Sikh commander, Tej Singh, fled early, and managed to break the bridge of boats, 'accidentally or by design'. His troops were thereby hampered in following him. But for a long while few sought to follow him. They 'everywhere showed a front to the victors, and stalked slowly and sullenly away',[1] like Socrates after Delium; or, emulating the white-haired Sham Singh, rushed on death. He, the noblest of the sirdars, had hated the dreary course of wickedness which led his nation to disaster, and like Falkland before Newbury, was resolute to be out of it by nightfall. He had sworn on the *Granth* not to leave the field alive. Dressed in white, and on his white mare, he rode everywhere, encouraging the waverers. When all was lost he led some fifty of his men against the 50th Regiment, and was killed.

Fighting every inch of ground, the Sikhs were forced back upon their bridge, which gave way; and the river, which was in flood, was filled with a struggling mass. The British artillery crashed down on the swollen waters; and as the triumph 'became full and manifest', the victors,

' defiled with dust and smoke and carnage, stood mute indeed for a moment,

[1] *Op. cit.* 315.

until the glory of their success rushing upon their minds, they gave expression to their feelings, and hailed their victorious commanders with reiterated shouts of triumph and congratulation'.[1]

The British loss was heavy, over 2400; that of the Sikhs was immense, at the lowest computation 5000, and usually estimated at several thousands more.

After the battle, Sham Singh's servants obtained permission to search for their master's body, and found him 'conspicuous by his white dress and long white beard ... where the dead lay thickest'.[2] They placed it on a raft, and swam with it across the river, reaching his home on the third day. His widow, as soon as she heard that a battle had been fought, had already burnt herself. This high-hearted act of valour out of an antique and barbaric world, the rite at its noblest, fitly concluded the story of martyred wives in the Punjab. Debarred from her lord's body, still on its journey, the heroic woman, a bride for ever, had died clasping the clothes he had worn at their wedding. This, says Griffin,[3] followed by the *Oxford History of India*, 'was the last *sati* in the Punjab,[4] and the pillar which marks the spot where it took place is still standing outside the walls of Attari'.

By the treaty of peace the Sikhs lost all their cis-Satlej lands, as well as the Jullundur Doab. Their army was reduced to 20,000 infantry, 12,000 cavalry. Since their treasury was empty, half the million and a half indemnity imposed was secured by annexing Kashmir and selling it to Gulab Singh, who had remained neutral to see which way victory would go. Suggestions were made of colonising Kashmir, the only part of India climatically fitted for European residence. But this would have been impossible unless the Punjab also were permanently occupied.

Of Gulab Singh John Lawrence wrote: 'Well known as he is, both in Jullundur and Lahore, nobody has ever yet been heard to say a word in his favour'. Henry, holding 'an embarrassingly low opinion'[5] of this man whom he had to support, mourned over his duty of ordering the Sikh durbar 'to make over, in the most marked and humiliating manner, the richest province in the Punjaub to the one man most detested by the Khalsa'. Herbert Edwardes, 'who was closeted with him daily', looking back later, testified that he was 'the worst native I have ever come in contact with, a bad king, a miser, and a liar'. All that can

---

[1] *Op. cit.* 315-16.   [2] Griffin, *Ranjit Singh*, 67.   [3] *Op. cit.* 65.

[4] This is erroneous. See *Life of Henry Lawrence*, ii. 80.

[5] *Life of Henry Lawrence*, ii. 73.

be said in justification of the transaction is that Gulab Singh was already in effective occupation of the Jammu part of the dominions now cynically sold to him, and that the Indian Government needed money, and at no time has been squeamish about how it obtained it.

The doctrine that human beings have rights, even the right of choosing their rulers, was still in the region of mischievous radicalism; and the historian cannot afford to be too critical of transactions dictated by

' Necessity, the tyrant's plea'.

Yet this selling of a Muslim people to a family extravagantly Hindu has resulted in rebellion even in our post-War world, which British power had to suppress; and the scandal of the Kashmir transfer was felt even at the time, in an uneasy subconscious fashion.

Its first-fruits also were rebellion. The writing of Indian history is overrun with cant. The Kashmir Muslims, 'who looked forward with horror to the rule of Golab Sing, declared like one man in favour of' [1] revolt; and the *Oxford History* expresses astonishment that the British force which put revolt down 'was actually supported by a contingent of 17,000 Sikhs who had been fighting in the campaign just concluded'.[2] The facts can be gathered from the men who did the job. Henry Lawrence, who 'trusted to carrying the thing through by expedition, and by the conviction that the British army was in our rear to support and avenge us',[3] never forgot

' that ticklish occasion when I took the Sikh army to Cashmere, and when I was obliged to tell Lal Sing's vakeel that if anything happened to me, John Lawrence was told to put Lal Sing in confinement'.[4]

This is, the Resident took forward a deeply reluctant force, while his brother stood by with a pistol pointed at the chief minister's head, comforting his conscience with reflection that the Muslim Governor of Kashmir, who was leading the rebellion, was little better than the new Maharaja: 'If Golab Sing flayed a chief alive, Imamuddin boiled a Pundit to death; they are certainly a pair of amiables'. Henry Lawrence and Herbert Edwardes put the affair through.

The campaign over, a regency was established in Lahore, under Henry Lawrence, 'in peaceful possession of viceregal authority over the

[1] John Lawrence.   [2] 696.   [3] *Life of Lord Lawrence*, i. 225.
[4] Quoted by Kaye, *Lives of Indian Officers*, ii. 298.

province'.[1] For assistants he had the most celebrated company of British officials and soldiers that the Empire has ever produced. The 'Punjab Tradition' began.

' What days those were! How Henry Lawrence would send us off to great distances; Edwardes to Bunnoo, Nicholson to Peshawur, Abbott to Hazara, Lumsden somewhere else, etc., giving us a tract of country as big as half of England, and giving us no more helpful directions than these, "Settle the country; make the people happy; and take care there are no rows!" ' [2]

The men who with powers of life and death quieted a kingdom long given over to turbulence, suppressed suttee, strove against infanticide, hunted down the robber and murderer, exulted now and always, and naturally enough, in their strength and freedom, and despised the men of tamer India, who had to abide by 'the Regulations'. Their work was superb; and in the days of the Mutiny, enforced by a terrific rigour, it stood. They were, almost without exception, profoundly religious, in a manner compounded of Cromwell, the Thirty-Nine Articles and the public schools of England. It has been remarked that it was almost an accident whether Dr. Arnold's pupils entered the Church or the Army. The muscular Christian whom Kingsley and others were holding up to admiration was to be increasingly triumphant in this new vigorous India; men like Edwardes, Montgomery, John Lawrence, did whatever they did to the glory of God. Nevertheless, there remained still a few who clung to old ethics. The Mutiny had not yet touched righteousness with exalted hysteria, and, so long as Henry Lawrence remained in the Punjab, the native nobles received consideration.

Yet how great the work was! And it was such as only men imbued with deep evangelical religion, convinced that they were there to fill their hasting day from dawn to sunset with service to an ever-watching King, could have carried through with such unflagging passion. No wonder that they were impatient of trammels on their activity—that they brushed aside as irrelevant the surmise that even fallen chiefs had feelings! Inevitably, when States or dynasties tumble, those who stand highest in them must share their fortunes. You cannot impose a fresh administration, and continue nobles and military leaders in positions that conciliate their self-respect. Henry's business kept him much outside Lahore, and John was largely the actual ruler. He used to tell sirdars and holy men whom he found in fiefs granted on conditions of

[1] Edwardes and Merivale, *Life of Henry Lawrence*, i. 411.
[2] *Memorials of Edwardes*, i. 58.

feudal service: 'We want neither your prayers nor your soldiers, and we cannot afford to pay for either'. He was a far abler man than Henry, and his ambition was to build up a prosperous revenue-paying peasantry; he did not share in Henry's feelings of pity for leaders brought low by the event of battles that had shaken India. He

' was brusque of speech. . . . He used, with a merry twinkle of his eye, to say very sharp things to the Punjab chiefs, under which they winced, although he was half in fun. . . . In his endeavours to reduce expenditure he insisted on all orders for disbursing money being brought to him for his counter-signature, a proceeding to which the Durbar greatly objected, and, perhaps, not without some reason, as it was virtually the assumption of the highest power in the State'.[1]

He would ask the Durbar Vakeel, when papers were brought for signature, 'What new roguery is there to-day?' It is hard for the great to realise that their dependents may not be their equals in sense of humour. John used

' to *tutoyer* the chiefs. . . . The Durbar, though they had a great respect for his force of character, did not regard him with as much affection as they did his brother. He was unpretentious in his habits, and used to sit in his room with his shirt-sleeves turned up over his arms and a cigar in his mouth, dictating orders'—

an easygoing efficiency in which there was no great harm, doubtless, and in which he was not much different even from Henry, for none of these men had either time or inclination for 'frills'. Henry, however, always had time for courtesy and gentleness; whereas John, like such famous juniors as 'Nikal Seyn', practised a method much like Bunyan's Moses: 'It was but a word, and a blow, and he knocked you down'. In later days, when time had mellowed his methods, and he was Lieutenant-Governor of the Punjab, a Sunday pastime of Europeans in Lahore was to hang about outside the church to watch their ruler, before driving home, hammer his coachman.[2] He left a tradition of equal zest in secular matters. Robert Cust tells of his first memory of him, 'his coat off, his sleeves turned up above his elbows', handing out land-agreements and insisting that each one of these great children before going should repeat aloud 'the new trilogue of the English Government':

' Thou shalt not burn thy widows; thou shalt not kill thy daughters; thou shalt not bury alive thy lepers.'

[1] *Life of Lord Lawrence*, i. 242 (Lewis Bowring's reminiscences).
[2] See Sir Henry Cotton, *Indian and Home Memories*, 65.

They marvelled at this strange new dispensation with its incomprehensible inhibitions. One chieftain, who, 'you will scarcely believe it . . . publicly petitioned me for permission to destroy all their female children, which it seems they have hitherto done', offered to practise continence, never again entering his harem—but lost his lands rather than obey.

John's protection of lepers arose out of an appeal which in his early days, in the Gurgaon district, had profoundly stirred him:

' Hail, cherisher of the afflicted!

' Be it known to your enlightened mind that your devoted servant has been a leper for many years. My limbs have fallen off piece by piece; my whole body has become a mass of corruption. I am weary of life; I wish to die. My life is a plague and disgust to the whole village, and my death is earnestly longed for. It is well known to all that for a leper to consent to die, to permit himself to be buried alive, is approved by the gods, who will never afflict another individual of his village with a similar malady. I therefore solicit your permission to be buried alive. The whole village wishes it, and I am happy and content to die. You are the ruler of the land, and without your leave it would be criminal. Hoping that I may obtain my prayer, I pray that the sun of prosperity may ever shine on you.   ' RAM BUKSH, Leper.'

He had rushed from his office to where the petitioner was lying under a tree, one corrupted mass, armless, legless. The request was of course refused, to the distress of the sufferer and his friends. John's mind kept on the incident for days; he said at last, to 'an intelligent native who had . . . witnessed the scene' and been perplexed by the Presence's rejection of the petition, 'I have no power to grant the permission, even were I willing'. 'You will find that the village will bury him alive without leave.' And so it happened, the whole village attending a deed done in all solemnity. John punished the community's leaders, but leniently.

From such experiences John Lawrence learnt, as many another of his race did, to feel a deep pity for a people so tormented, so wayward and strange, yet in many ways so noble. We are told—and indeed it was notorious—that he 'never weighed his words too carefully. If he thought a man a knave or a fool, he generally called him so to his face. If he had to strike at all, he struck a knock-down blow.'[1] But the best of this generation immediately preceding the Mutiny never sank for one moment to the brutal vulgarity of that minority which, then as now, have sullied the splendid fame of our race. His biographer witnesses that in thousands of his letters, all hastily written, there is no single

---

[1] *Life of Lord Lawrence*, i. 176.

instance of an expression which could wound the most sensitive Indian, least of all of 'the opprobrious term which is the very first to come to the mouth of too many young officers, or casual visitors in India'.

Unfortunately the seeds of lifelong estrangement were sown between the two great brothers. Feudal obligations, which had sat lightly and brought public estimation, were commuted for money obligations; nobles were told that they must pay cash, instead of keeping retainers for times of crisis. *Jagirs* were cut down, and in many cases regranted only during the lifetime of their present holders. All this was inevitable. The Khalsa had been beaten in war, and its pride must shrink. This process troubled John comparatively little; but experience was already slowly changing Henry Lawrence till he passed out of sympathy with his bright vigorous companions, though not out of their admiration. It was a puzzle to Robert Montgomery to recall in after years his old friend and master's conviction—and he served in Nepal, Punjab, Rajputana, and just-annexed Oudh—that the people were happier under their own rulers than under the Company. It was manifestly absurd and impossible; yet Henry, with opportunities greater than any other man's for knowing, believed it. He wrote in 1846:

' If ever there was a device for ensuring mal-government, it is that of a Native ruler and minister both relying on foreign bayonets, and directed by a British Resident; even if all three were able, virtuous, and considerate, still the wheels of government could hardly move smoothly. If it be difficult to select one man, European or Native, with all the requisites for a just administrator, where are three who can and will work together to be found? Each of the three may work incalculable mischief, but no one of them *can* do good if thwarted by the other. It is almost impossible for the minister to be faithful and submissive to the British Government; and how rarely is the European officer to be found, who, with ability to guide a Native state, has the discretion and good feeling to keep himself in the background. . . .'

He is moving into the loneliness that encompassed his spirit long before he died; and to the humility, so hard to parallel in his generation, which his gravestone has made familiar to the world:

' Here lies Henry Lawrence, who tried to do his duty '.

The men of this time were deeply impressed by the kindness of the Company's treatment of the Sikhs. Edwardes, that infallible Greatest Common Intellectual Measure, exclaimed: 'I know not in all history a parallel to the generosity displayed by the British Government'. Of the first Sikh War, Mr. P. E. Roberts

remarks: [1] 'The Sikhs by their absolutely unprovoked violation
of British territory could have looked for little else than the complete loss of their independence'. The *Oxford History*, it is needless
to say, is equally severe [2] on the war which 'the arrogance of the army
of the Khalsa' forced on the peace-loving aliens. Yet the people guilty
of such atrocity were left 'independence': that is, a British officer
over a Council of eight Sikh 'yes-men'; British garrisons (costing the
Punjab 22 lakhs a year) in their forts; an infiltration of the most
masterful men that even our imperious race has ever produced. This
arrangement was to last eight years, a long time for a people proud and
restive under control, a time in which new vested interests and accomplished facts would grow up into sturdy plants.

Lord Hardinge's departing action was to cut down the Indian army:
'I never could understand why he was in such a damned hurry', the
Duke of Wellington said afterwards. The reason of course was
financial; generation after generation of paying for conquests and up-
keep of armies had bled the country white. The nationalist's complaint
about the cost of 'Defence', like many of his charges, is based not on
present-day facts so much as on memory of an injustice rankling
through two centuries. The curtailed forces were massed between
Meerut and the Satlej, in readiness for the expected second Sikh War.
It broke out in 1848, when Henry was in England and John was serving
under a temporary Chief Commissioner.

CHAPTER II

THE SECOND SIKH WAR: DALHOUSIE AND THE PUNJAB

Discontent of Sikh aristocracy: Lieutenant Edwardes wins fame: irritation in
India at war's renewal: war 'with a vengeance': Sleeman's views on causes of
renewed war: unsatisfactory victories: annexation of the Punjab: Dalhousie and
the Lawrences: Henry Lawrence's dismissal: Nikal Seyn and the beginnings of
a legend.

WAR arose out of the Sikh aristocracy's discontent at the fine mesh of
British administration which had overspread their land, and the

[1] 338.   [2] 690.

tightening up which the need for more money necessitated. Mulraj, the semi-independent Governor of Multan, got into trouble over revenue payments, and his accounts were demanded. After procrastination, he offered to resign, an offer at once accepted. Two young English officers sent to take over were murdered in a sudden outbreak. Mulraj fled dismayed, but recovered himself and went into open revolt.

It was now that Lieutenant Edwardes, busy in revenue settlement of the trans-Indus district of Bunnoo, won fame. He dropped his work to raise a band of what he styled 'bold villains ready to risk their own throats and cut those of anyone else'; and,

' availing himself of the hostility which he knew to exist between the different races in the Punjab, enrolled 3000 Pathans; thus following the reverse of the process which afterwards stood us in such good stead during the Mutiny. He armed the Mussulmans of the frontier against the Sikhs and Mussulmans of Mooltan, as we afterwards armed the Sikhs against the Mussulmans and Hindus of Delhi.' [1]

With these and a Muslim battalion under General Van Cortlandt, an experienced soldier of fortune in Sikh employ, he flew at Mulraj, defeated him at Kineri (June 18) and Sudosain (July 3), and began a temerarious siege of Multan, feeling 'like a terrier barking at a tiger'. A Sikh force sent by the Resident deserted to the enemy, and Edwardes had to raise the siege.

Dalhousie, who in January had succeeded Hardinge as Governor-General, was hesitating [2] for perhaps the only time in his career; Henry Lawrence in England exclaimed that he and Lord Gough had decided 'to have a grand *shikar* in the cold season!' Insurrection spread, and the old soldiers of the Khalsa flung down their tools and brought out their weapons. Dost Muhammad, brooding over ancient wrongs, joined them, on condition of receiving back Peshawar; this was the only occasion in history when Sikh and Afghan were allies. At last Dalhousie acted, leaving Calcutta in October, 1848, after the promise: 'Unwarned by precedent, uninfluenced by example, the Sikh nation have called for war, and on my word, sirs, they shall have it with a vengeance'.

The war's renewal caused intense irritation, which deepened into the

[1] *Life of Lord Lawrence*, i. 253-4.

[2] Edwardes wrote to Lord Hardinge (November 14, 1848) in criticism of the delay, 'insurrections cannot be postponed, like tea-parties, with a note, nor enemies be bound over to keep the peace until it is quite convenient to you to fight'.

resolution to have done with serious challenge once for all, that the job of government and civilising might be got on with, and this endless diversion of internal campaigning finish. It must be owned that Sleeman, who a few years later was to admit mournfully:

> 'Few old officers of experience, with my feelings and opinions on this subject, now remain in India; and the influence of . . . a school . . . characterised by impatience at the existence of any native State, and its strong and often insane advocacy of their absorption—by honest means, if possible—but still, their absorption . . . is too great over the rising generation, whose hopes and aspirations they tend so much to encourage',[1]

who complained, moreover, that 'There is no pretext, however weak, that is not sufficient, in their estimation, for the purpose [of annexation]; and no war, however cruel, that is not justifiable, if it has only this object in view',[1] chose a bad time (September, 1848) to approach Lord Dalhousie with a long remonstrance.

> 'The native aristocracy of the country seem to have satisfied themselves that our object has been to retain the country, and that this could be prevented only by timely resistance. The sending European officers to relieve the chief of Mooltan, and to take possession of the country and fort, seems to have removed the last lingering doubt upon the point; and Molraj seems to have been satisfied that in destroying them he should be acting according to the wishes of all his class, and all that portion of the population who might aspire to employment under a native rule. This was precisely the impression created by precisely the same means in Afghanistan; and I believe that the notion now generally prevalent is, that our professed intentions of delivering over the country to its native ruler were not honest, and that we should have appropriated the country to ourselves could we have done so. . . .
> 'Satisfied that this was our error in Afghanistan, in carrying out the views of Lord Ellenborough in the Gwalior State I did everything in my power to avoid it, and have entirely succeeded, I believe; but it has not been done without great difficulty. . . . I had another reason for believing that Lord Hardinge's measures were wise and prudent. While we have a large portion of the country under native rulers, their administration will contrast with ours greatly to our advantage in the estimation of the people; and we may be sure that, though some may be against us, many will be for us. If we succeed in sweeping them all away, or absorbing them, we shall be at the mercy of our native army, and they will see it; and accidents may possibly occur to unite them, or a great portion of them, in some desperate act . . . the best provision against it seems to me to be the maintenance of native rulers, whose confidence and affection can be engaged, and administrations improved under judicious management.

[1] Letter to Sir James Hogg, January 12, 1853; and letter to same, January 2, quoted together.

' The industrial classes in the Punjaub would, no doubt, prefer our rule to that of the Seiks; but that portion who depend upon public employment under Government for their subsistence is large in the Punjaub, and they would nearly all prefer a native rule. They have evidently persuaded themselves that our intention is to substitute our own rule; and it is now, I fear, too late to remove the impression. If your Lordship is driven to annexation, you must be in great force; and a disposition must be shown on the part of the local authorities to give the educated aristocracy of the country a liberal share in the administration.

' One of the greatest dangers to be apprehended in India is, I believe, the disposition on the part of the dominant class to appoint to all offices members of their own class, to the exclusion of the educated natives. . . .'

The native aristocracy, 'who know that they are not fitted for either civil or military office under our system, and must be reduced to beggary or insignificance' under it, had 'given up all hope of ever having any share in the administration . . . when they saw all offices of trust by degrees being filled by Captain This and Mr. That'.

Lord Gough was defeated at Ramnagar, November 22, launching a cavalry charge across a sandy river-bed two miles wide and under heavy gunfire. He fought a second minor action, December 3, at Sadulapur, from which the Sikhs retired in unbroken order. Enjoined by the exasperated Governor-General to caution, he remained for six weeks inactive. Then, on January 13, he fought the drawn battle of Chilianwala. His 'spirit of defiance and antagonism'[1] being roused by a few dropping shots from Sikh field-guns—'Indeed, I had not intended to attack to-day, but the impudent rascals fired on me. They put my Irish blood up, and I attacked them'[2]—after a little over an hour's shelling, the effective half of which was the enemy's, at three in the afternoon he flung two infantry brigades blindly at dense jungle. The Sikh commander had thoughts of retreating, when he saw the British, in his own words, panting like dogs in chase. He turned a shower of grape on them, beginning a discomfiture which masked musketry fire completed: the 24th Foot lost 482 men and their colours, a remnant being saved by General Colin Campbell. Mimosa scrub splintered into fragments the cavalry, who were additionally handicapped by being commanded 'by a superannuated general, who could not mount his horse without assistance, and who was irascible and wedded to ancient notions of cavalry manœuvres'.[1] In this happy condition, they were routed by

[1] Marshman, *History of India*, 464.
[2] His remark to a brigadier, according to Lord Dalhousie.

Sikh cavalry, and made their celebrated backward charge over their own infantry and through their own artillery and wagon lines. The Sikhs accompanied them, and took four guns. When night fell the British had lost 2446 men and the colours of three regiments. Sikh soldiers traversed the tangled battlefield, butchering the wounded.

Only the Commander-in-Chief was delighted with his feat. He was astounded when George Lawrence seemed dissatisfied:

'What? not a victory! do you not consider it a victory to drive back the enemy, to spike 30 or 40 of his guns, and occupy the ground you had gained?' 'Yes, but they say you did *not* occupy the ground you had gained, and that the guns you had taken and spiked were retaken in consequence; and that they took up a position stronger than before.'

The Governor-General sent the Duke of Wellington an account written with all the expansiveness of extreme vexation. The Duke's criticism was directed at what was widely felt to be Lord Gough's worst disability as a general, his inability to realise that artillery were anything more than fireworks, adding majesty to a battlefield but not seriously interfering with the business of the infantry of either side. After explaining what *he* would have done with his guns, harking back now to Sobraon, the Duke exclaimed: 'The fire of that battery would have gone right in among them, so that, by Heavens, I would not have left a cat there with room to stand. . . . Ah, the truth is, they are not masters of their game.'

After fighting Chilianwala, Lord Gough proposed a six miles retirement, to get better fodder. Henry Lawrence, newly returned from England, dissuaded him from a course that would be interpreted as admission of defeat. To Lawrence, Dalhousie wrote despairingly:

'Everything . . . as far as the Commander-in-Chief is concerned, grows worse and worse . . . the best news which I now hope for is, that his Excellency has not had his "blood put up", but has waited the few days which will give him reinforcements, that will enable him to make sure work of the next action. I have written to him to-day on his future proceedings in terms which I am aware will be very distasteful to him, but which it is both necessary that I should employ as a caution to him, and prudent that I should address to him in relief of my own responsibility.'

Next day, in the same strain of exasperation, he tells the same correspondent:

'It is already too notorious that neither you nor anybody else can exercise any wholesome influence on the mind of the Commander-in-Chief; if you could have done so the action of Chillianwallah would never have been fought as it was fought. . . . All that we can do will hardly restore the prestige of our power in India, and of our military superiority, partly from the evidence of facts and partly from the unwise and unpatriotic and contemptible croaking in public of the European community itself all over India, high and low.'

Sir John Hobhouse, President of the Board of Control, reported that 'the impression made upon the public mind' by the news of Chilianwala was 'stronger than that caused by the Kabul massacre. The result has been that, in eight-and-forty hours after the arrival of the mail, it was determined to send Sir Charles Napier to command the Indian army.' To Napier the still more aged Duke of Wellington had said, 'If you do not go, then I must'. But before Napier arrived, Gough, overruled to give his matchless artillery full play at last, at Gujarat (February 21) won overwhelming victory. He gave his troops a full day for battle, instead of an hour or two before darkness; not a musket fired until a terrific storm raging through two and a half hours had beaten down the brave Sikh gunners. The battle, which cost the victors only 776 casualties, ended in a pursuit by the cavalry for fifteen miles. The Sikhs lost everything.

' They are dropping their guns and tumbrils along the road, getting rid of every encumbrance to hasten their flight. They were, as an army, one vast mass of fugitives, all crowded together in one heap. . . . The loss of their entire camp; every tent taken, of chief and soldier; all their ammunition, which is now being blown up in every direction. . . . The army is in high spirits. It was like a beautiful field-day, the whole day's work.' [1]

The chase allowed no chance of rallying. On March 12 there was a general surrender of Sikhs. Thirty-five sirdars laid their swords at Sir Walter Gilbert's feet; and the army of the Khalsa, man after man, flung tulwar, shield, matchlock on the cairn of weapons, salaamed to his lost glory in that glittering pile, and passed through the British lines, no longer a soldier but a conquered peasant. *Aj Ranjit Singh mar gya*.[2] Hardest of all was the giving up of their horses by the cavalry.

A series of forgotten episodes were the defences made by Lawrence's isolated assistants. George Lawrence was again made a prisoner by Afghans. But with the Afghans were Sikhs, a race 'to whom treachery and ingratitude are not naturally congenial'; [3] they thanked him for the kindness they had received from his family, apologised for putting

---

[1] Letter of Sir Colin Campbell to Henry Lawrence (quoted from *Life of Henry Lawrence*, ii. 121-2).

[2] 'To-day Ranjit Singh is dead!'—the exclamation of one old warrior, as he put his palms together in one last salutation to the piled arms.

[3] *Life of Lord Lawrence*, i. 258 ff.

2 B

upon him even the restraint of 'an honoured guest'; and presently sent him on parole, as their ambassador to British headquarters. Another of this heroic Punjab band, Lieutenant Herbert, held a dilapidated post with a handful of Pathans who refused to leave him until Dost Muhammad himself appeared; and when the Dost came, and they learnt that he held their wives and children, then, unwillingly going, 'they expressed their sorrow that they could do no more'. Yet others, Reynell Taylor, James Abbott, held out by the aid of men who ought, strictly speaking, to be now their enemies. These, surely, are episodes honourable to both races, part of the long chain of kindness between Briton and Indian, which has made even the political quarrel by now partake of the nature of a family affair!

Dalhousie, aged thirty-five, was the youngest of the Governors-General. Gough's strategy and its results had quickly shaken him into his true character, that of the most masterful ruler between Wellesley and Curzon, resembling both in the ready acerbity with which he 'ticked off' inferiors; like others who have been in a position to enjoy the exhilarating exercise of frankness without having to suffer frankness in return, he 'was apt to pique himself on his own resolution in performing that painful function of official duty—the correction and reprimand even of distinguished officers, when necessary'.[1] He brought from England a prejudice against Henry Lawrence: and the latter, when he wrote from Lahore, expressing certain misgivings, received an ominous reply. 'You say you are grieved at all you saw and heard at Lahore; so am I—so I have long been; but I don't know whether our griefs are on the same tack.' Sharper raps were to follow.

To John Lawrence, Dalhousie took immediately, finding in him a decision untroubled by any nonsense of seeing both sides of a question. Henry presently made the mistake of 'funking' a meeting with the Governor-General, sending John in his stead. John and Dalhousie formed a friendship which grew ever closer, and melted the stern young autocrat even to playfulness, as in such letters as this (1856):

' MY DEAR OLD BOY,
'I have just received your letter, and as I shall be in Calcutta to-morrow evening for good, I will not give you the trouble of coming out here, but will see you, and with *sincere pleasure*, on Tuesday forenoon. As for my health, Jan La'rin,[2] I am a cripple in every sense.'

[1] *Life of Sir Henry Lawrence*, ii. 125.
[2] A shot at the Indian pronunciation of John Lawrence.

Henry's treatment was very different. Between Chilianwala and Gujarat he had been instructed to draft an invitation to the Sikhs to lay down their arms. He drafted it too gently, and was snubbed with ferocious severity. We must quote; the pedagogue with cane in hand has his own peculiar intonation, which no lesser breed can hope to convey:

' In my conversation with you a few days ago I took occasion to say to you that my mode of conducting public business, in the administration with which I am entrusted, and especially with the confidential servants of the Government, are, to speak with perfect openness, without any reserve, and plainly to tell my mind without disguise or mincing of words. In pursuance of that system, I now remark on the proclamation you have proposed. It is objectionable in matter, because, from the terms in which it is worded, it is calculated to convey to those who are engaged in this shameful war an expectation of much more favourable terms, much more extended immunity from punishment, than I consider myself justified in granting them. It is objectionable in manner: because (unintentionally, no doubt) its whole tone substitutes you personally as the Resident at Lahore, for the Government which you represent. . . . This cannot be. . . .' [1]

It is no wonder that timidity (for no man likes to put his head where there is a probability of its being smacked) entered into Henry's approaches to this haughty master. It was little mitigated even by the gracious intimation, a fortnight or so later [2] than the smart correction which we have cited: 'Be assured, if ever I lose confidence in your services, than which nothing is farther from my contemplation, I will acquaint you of the fact promptly enough', an assurance which doubtless brought some comfort, though it can hardly have been needed. Henry was pleading against annexation and confiscation of lands, to which Dalhousie thundered back, that nothing but lives and subsistence were to be promised. Lawrence urged the Sikhs' chivalrous treatment of their prisoners, and of the ladies in particular. But by making these captive at all, the enemy had

' shown themselves unmitigated ruffians . . . that they have not ill-treated them into the bargain, rescues them from irrecoverable infamy and nothing more. . . . Nothing is granted to them but maintenance. The amount of that is

[1] February 1, 1849. Cf. *Private Letters of the Marquess Dalhousie* (J. G. A. Baird), 52. February 5, 1849: 'I have . . . shaken him for it. . . . Lawrence has been greatly praised and rewarded and petted, and no doubt naturally supposes himself a King of the Punjab; but as I don't take the Brentford dynasty as a pattern, I object to sharing the chairs, and think it best to come to an understanding as to relative positions at once. It will soon be settled'.

[2] February 18, 1849.

open to discussion, but their property of every kind will be confiscated to the State. . . . In the interim, let them be placed somewhere under surveillance; but attach their property till their destination is decided. If they run away our contract is void. If they are caught I will imprison them. And if they raise tumult again, I will hang them, as sure as they now live, and I live then.'

This was while the bear had not yet been quite captured. After Gujarat, the Punjab was annexed (March 29, 1849).

The province passed under the most unselfishly rigorous rulers it had ever known. How simple and unpretentious its new masters were was ludicrously revealed by the incident of the celebrated Koh-i-nor diamond. This Ranjit Singh had persuaded Shah Suja (when his guest) to hand over, and it came to the Company, among the Sikh crown jewels, as spoils of victory. It was entrusted to John Lawrence, who put it in a waistcoat pocket and forgot all about it. When Dalhousie presently wrote that Queen Victoria had ordered it to be sent to England immediately, John said, 'Send for it at once'. 'But *you* have it.' John used to say that this was the worst scrape he was ever in. He concealed his horror till business was finished, and then sent for his bearer. Luckily, this individual, though 'it was nothing, sahib, but a bit of glass', had preserved the box when he went through his master's pockets. John lost no further time in despatching it to become part of the British crown.

The Punjab was governed by a Board of Three, Henry being chief. Gang robbery had to be put down; and, to their amazement, the new Governors found thuggee, extirpated in British India, surviving. Suttee had to be suppressed: a people to be disarmed: fallen chiefs treated with a compromise between the opposing views of the Lawrence brothers: cantonments selected for British troops: the Sikh army disbanded, and some re-enlisted as Company soldiers: Mulraj tried: roads built. There were the beginnings of that warfare against the tribes on the frontier, which has since been so heavy a trouble.

In all the main work of revenue settlement, John proved the abler. His knowledge of revenue matters was immense; his energy insatiable. But the two together did work greater than either could have done alone. It was done, however, with growing friction.

Henry, who had to bear the brunt of Dalhousie's meddling, found it increasingly hard to endure. In 1851 (June 13) he burst out in a letter to John:

'I am at a loss to understand the Governor-General. . . . Bad enough to snub us when we were wrong, intending to do right; but to be insulted by assumptions and tittle-tattle is too bad. The remarks, too, on the last batch of Jaghires, on which we all agreed, are not pleasant. I am heartily sick of this kind of letters. One works oneself to death, and does everything publicly and privately to aid the views of a man who vents his impertinences on us, in a way which would be unbecoming if we were his servants.'

But there was worse trouble inside the Board. In May, 1852, its third member, Robert Montgomery, 'half-jestingly' said he was 'regular buffer between two high pressure engines'. The two brothers took to writing to Montgomery, instead of direct to each other. Henry was bitter because every attempt he made to conciliate the old jagirdars and ruling class was opposed; he was 'sorely' and 'daily' vexed by John's conduct:

'Independent of feelings of humanity, I look on the manner in which these people are treated as most impolitic. The country is not yet settled; troubles may arise at any hour, almost, in any direction, when the good will of such men . . . would be of consequence.

'And the annoyance was that these were *not* great questions of policy rarely occurring, and for which there might be one struggle, but they were, daily, small questions each immaterial in itself, but the whole amounting to a great grievance. For instance, we were well agreed as to the proper mode of defending the frontier, and of keeping the peace generally; we were in unison as to light assessments, simple laws, and general non-interference in village concerns and prompt energetic measures in putting down the first germ of disturbance. But we differed much as to the treatment of the old Durbar officials, military and civil, and especially as to rewards to those who had served us well during the war. We also differed *in practice*, though not much in theory, as to the employment of the people of the country, and indeed as to nominations of officials generally. I wished to employ Punjaubees wherever they were at all fit. I also wished to help sons of old officers. My brother, on the other hand, stood out for giving all the uncovenanted berths to natives employed in the settlement, which was tantamount to excluding Punjaubees and young gentlemen altogether. The opposition I met on all such questions, and as to the treatment of Jagheerdars, was a daily vexation. The chiefs and people of the Punjab had been accustomed to come to me for relief, aid, and advice. Now I could literally never say or do anything without almost a certainty of my order or wish being upset or counteracted by my colleagues.'[1]

Dalhousie had long ago made up his mind which brother to keep. As far back as December 22, 1849, announcing Henry's return, he had written:

'I shall not be sorry when he goes; because, although he has many fine qualities, I think his brother John, take him all in all, is a better man, fitted in

---

[1] Henry Lawrence, March 6, 1853, to Sir James Hogg, one of the East India Company Directors.

every way for that place; while Sir Henry's opinions are so strong, and differ so widely from mine and the opinion of most other people, that unless they were overborne or much modified by his colleagues, we should come to a deadlock in a month. This antagonism of opinion has, as I suspected, brought the brothers into violent collision very often during the present season in the discussions of the Board; and John Lawrence is a good deal distressed by it, and would not unwillingly get away.'

As those last words show, an understanding existed between Lord Dalhousie and John, which it is not pleasant to remember; it was widely resented when Henry's dismissal came. In December, 1852, both brothers offered their resignations, and asked for the Haidarabad Residency. Henry's was accepted, in a letter insultingly disingenuous. The Governor-General explained that his supersession was because he had been originally an artilleryman:

' Although the Regulations do not prevail in the Punjaub, and although the system of civil government has wisely and successfully been made more simple in its forms, still we are of opinion that the superintendence of so large a system, everywhere founded on the Regulations and pervaded by their spirit, can be thoroughly controlled and moulded, as changes from time to time may become necessary, only by a civilian fully versed in the system of the elder provinces and experienced in its operation. All the world unites in acknowledging the talents and merits of Sir Thomas Munro. I cannot, there-fore, illustrate better the strength of my own convictions on this head than by saying that if Sir Thomas Munro were now President of your Board, I should still hold the opinion I have expressed above regarding the office of Chief Commissioner.'

Henry's exposure of this sophistry is clear and convincing: [1]

' With all deference to the Governor-General, I think he has gone twenty years too fast, and that already we have too many trained civilians and too much of the Regulations in the Punjaub; that what is then wanted is the very simplest form of law, or rather of equity, and that the proper men to carry it out are such as Edwardes, Nicholson, Taylor, Lake, Becher, and civilians of the same stamp—men who will not spare themselves, who will mix freely with the people, and will do prompt justice, in their shirt sleeves, rather than propound laws, to the discontent of all honest men, as is done in Bengal, and even in the pattern Government of Agra. The expression a trained civilian puzzles me; the fact being that I have done as much civil work as my brother and twice as much as many civilians who are considered trained men. I, too, have held every sort of civil post during the last twenty-one years, and *have trained myself* by hard work and by putting my own shoulder to the wheel. . .'

Nevertheless, he was removed—not to Haidarabad, but to Rajputana, a

[1] Letter to Sir James Hogg, March 6, 1853.

far inferior post, though his pay was kept at its Punjab level, as a special consideration. This was a snub he never forgot to his dying day. John became sole head of the Punjab, with the title of Chief Commissioner.

How deep the estrangement went we can read in Henry's farewell letter to his brother: [1]

' As this is my last day at Lahore, I venture to offer you a few words of advice, which I hope you will take in the spirit it is given in, and that you will believe that, if you preserve the peace of the country, and make the people high and low happy, I shall have no regrets that I vacated the field for you. It seems to me that you look on almost all questions affecting Jagheerdars and Mafeerdars in a perfectly different light from all others; in fact, that you consider them as nuisances and as enemies. If anything like this be your feelings, how can you expect to do them justice, as between man and man? . . . I think we are doubly bound to treat them kindly, *because they are down*, and because they and their hangers-on have still some influence as affecting the public peace and contentment. I would simply do to them as I would be done by.'

The efficiency with which John wrought, now and in the storm of 1857, is part of the legend of our race. But the people of the Punjab mourned, and Henry's going 'was a long, living funeral procession from Lahore nearly to Umritsur'. They knew that the other would bestow material benefits, but that this man was one of the lessening band who remembered that they had once held their heads high as an independent people. John's famous challenge, 'Will you be governed by the pen or by the sword? Choose!' was in its times and context intelligible. But only an insensitive arrogance could have selected it to perpetuate on his statue in a great city (Lahore).[2]

John's difficulties were increased, too, by the passionate personal love Henry roused in the unlikeliest quarters, and the feeling that he had not been quite loyal as a brother. John Nicholson, in particular, a man whose ways made him as much an embarrassment as a strength, resented the change. While Henry, in whose 'hands he was himself like a little child',[3] was in the province, he was useful. But to John, with whom he exchanged strong dislike, he refused to be amenable:

' he could brook no official control. Obstinate, haughty, and imperious, no regulations could bind him; they were made only to be broken. "The autocrat of all the Russias", he was called not inaptly by his brother officers; and the natives, not less naturally . . . were disposed to worship him as a god. . . .

[1] January 20, 1853.
[2] This inscription has at last gone (1927), after repeated mutilations of the statue.
[3] *Life of Lord Lawrence*, i. 508-9.

Many of his deeds, had they been done in other parts of India, would have caused a general rising, or his dismissal from the service—not without reason. He was one day, as I have been told by Colonel Urmston, who was then Assistant Commissioner at Peshawur, riding through a village, attended by a single orderly, and he observed in passing a mosque that the Moulla, instead of salaaming to him, looked at him with a gesture of contempt or hatred. When he got home he sent his orderly to fetch the Moulla, and then and there shaved off his beard!' [1]

The much-admired laconism of this note (to John Lawrence) is the egoism of the man aware that he is 'a regular card' and proud of it:

' SIR,—I have the honour to inform you that I have just shot a man dead who came to kill me. Your obedient servant, JOHN NICHOLSON.'

In 1855 Neville Chamberlain asked him for information, and received a tempest of refusal. John wrote:

' I have got an official letter from Chamberlain, putting twenty queries on each of the four raids to Nicholson! Now, if anything will bring "Nick" to his senses, it will be these queries. He will polish off a tribe in the most difficult fortress, or ride the border like "belted Will" of former days; but one query in writing is often a stumper for a month or two. The "pen-and-ink work," as he calls it, "does not suit him".'

This was in July. In December Chamberlain wrote: 'He has only to come within reach for me to extend both hands towards him, and, in doing so, I shall be doubly glad, for I shall know that the Government, of which we are the common servants, will be the gainer'. But 'Nick' was obdurate. Pressed by John Lawrence to co-operate with Chamberlain in a necessary border expedition, he stormed that he would leave the Punjab. John had decided that he should, when the Mutiny interposing gave all three their lasting fame, and left the legend of their close friendship to crown that other legend of 'Nikal Seyn'.

Nicholson's temperament was one of those operating through their passions and not their reason. It was John's mood (his methodical ways apart) that jumped with his, and not Henry's. But it was Henry whom he loved and worshipped, as a being almost more than mortal. And it was Henry who, men felt, had been jockeyed out of the position his by long right; he was now eating his heart out in one inferior job after another, first in Rajputana, and then, just before the Mutiny broke, in the immense and depressing disorders of Oudh, away from his gallant people of the great garrison province.

[1] *Life of Lord Lawrence*, i. 508-9.

CHAPTER III

DALHOUSIE'S ADMINISTRATION AND ANNEXATIONS

An outworn system: Dalhousie and Napier: premonitions of the Mutiny: Dalhousie's doctrine of lapse: Satara: Sambalpur: Karauli: Jhansi and Nagpur: the Nizam: Bhawalpur: Oudh: the palace at Delhi: the Peshwaship: the second Burmese War: understanding with Afghanistan: the Santal rebellion: irritation spreading through both British and native India: war with Persia: summary of Dalhousie's administrative achievements.

DALHOUSIE entered on an outmoded system, which in fact broke down under his vigorous administration. The East India Company Proprietors entitled to vote numbered now 1800, each possessed of at least £1000 stock. Lord Derby summed up their duties and privileges thus: 'They receive the dividends upon their stock, and elect the members of the Court of Directors'. They also attended ceremonial dinners.

The Directors theoretically still possessed unlimited power, except that the Board of Control might overrule them. This exception, so important, was reinforced by the Board of Control's power of 'secret' communications with the Indian Government. The President of the Board was in the Cabinet, a precursor of the Secretary of State of post-Mutiny times. 'Thus the Court of Directors was tied hand and foot by the Board, which signified the President, while he in turn signified the Government or Crown.'[1] The system lasted a few years longer (till alarm and indignation over the Mutiny made the Company's end inevitable), only because Dalhousie, unlike Wellesley, always treated his nominal chiefs with courtesy. Even when matters were strained, he kept his dignity.[2]

He had first to become master in his own household. History does *not* repeat itself; yet British-Indian history seems to possess a static quality. We see, with deep variations yet with striking repetition of mood and action, resemblances in Wellesley, Dalhousie, Curzon;

---

[1] Sir William Lee-Warner, *Life of Lord Dalhousie*, i. 104 ff.

[2] Cf. his letter to the President of the Board of Control, June 29, 1854: 'My experience has taught me that men who correspond over a space of 10,000 miles should watch their pens; for ink comes to burn like caustic when it crosses the sea. I therefore repress the inclination to say what I feel, and will merely reply that I am open to no blame; and will prove it.'

similarly we see crises and oppositions recur. The quarrel of Dalhousie and Napier appears a parallel to that of Curzon and Kitchener. If Wellesley also did not quarrel with his own military power, that was because it was largely represented by his brother.

Dalhousie's Commander-in-Chief, Sir Charles Napier, from old scars that had changed his physiognomy or warped his physical efficiency, had gone far towards realising Tod's famous description of the Mewar chief who was 'a fragment of a warrior'. But his energy, fire, and egoism flared as destructively and grandly as ever:

' He is wonderfully well preserved for a man of sixty-seven, still more so when it is recollected what a life of hardships he has led, what climates he has braved, how riddled and chopped to pieces with balls and bayonets and sabre wounds he is. His hair is now quite gray; and allowing it to grow as it will, he combs it back straight off his forehead to the back of his head. Under bushy eyebrows gleam a pair of piercing and brilliant eyes. . . . His nose, highly aquiline by nature, was made still more so by a bullet at Busaco, which went in at his right cheek, through his nose, shattering it as it passed. . . . Sir Charles's manner is peculiarly young and gay. He is full of anecdote, such as his varied life was likely to supply; full of fun and full of cleverness. I never had a more agreeable inmate in my house' (Lord Dalhousie).

Since Cornwallis's time we have heard the constant grumbling of civilian and military that one service got all the jobs and honours. This ever-present squabble was renewed with particular fierceness, John Lawrence and his friends 'grousing' that only 'a red coat' was considered, Napier furious at the all-encroaching civilians. He said he would rather by far have been Governor of the Punjab, the province whose frontier fortresses peered towards those Central Asian plains where England and India (it was held) must grapple one day in the world's mightiest struggle, the rehearsal of Ragnarok and Armageddon. The dominant school of thought was divided as to whether it were better to await Russia behind strong natural walls, already British, or to annex Afghanistan, press boldly on, and bring the Muscovite to bay in his own deserts. Napier preferred the latter course; there were no limits to the regions into which he would march devastatingly. He found the new Governor-General utterly unawake to his chances and duties:

' I like this young man, for he is seemingly a good fellow, but he has no head for governing this empire and drawing forth all its wondrous resources! What the Koh-i-noor is among diamonds, India is among nations. Were I emperor of India for twelve years, she should be traversed by railroads and have her rivers bridged; her seat of government at Delhi, or Meerut, or Simla, or Allahabad. No Indian prince should exist. The Nizam should be no more heard of, Nepaul would be ours, and an ague fit should become the courtly imperial sickness at Constantinople, while the Emperor of Russia and he of China should never get their pulses below 100!

'Would that I were king of India! I would make Muscowa and Pekin shake. . . . The five rivers and the Punjab, the Indus and Scinde, the Red Sea and Malta! what a chain of lands and waters to attach England to India! Were I king of England I would, from the palace of Delhi, thrust forth a clenched fist in the teeth of Russia and France. England's fleet should be all in all in the West, and the Indian army all in all in the East. India should not belong another day to the "ignominious tyrants", nor should it depend upon opium sales, but on an immense population well employed in peaceful pursuits. She should suck English manufactures up her great rivers, and pour down those rivers her own varied products.'

He raved at the civilian government of the Punjab, and those incompetent Lawrences. He found Dalhousie 'as weak as water and as vain as a pretty woman or an ugly man'.

Napier inhabited a cinema world of his own creation. Everywhere, he roared, revolt and war were preparing. Gulab Singh was gathering for an invasion of British India, the Sikhs were casting cannon daily in the jungles and hiding them in holes. Mutiny, mutiny—it was being concerted on all sides, and anyone but these fools who were ruining India could have heard its mutterings. As for his own strategy, it was superbly simple. He thought in fifties, apparently; he would, if given his way, have placed 50,000 men on the Narmada, 50,000 on the Brahmaputra, 50,000 beyond the Satlej. Then, when ready, he would overrun Afghanistan and Southern China, and parcel them out among his legions. A war of acrimonious papers was waged between him and the Governor-General, with the Lawrences writing to the latter, sometimes with contempt, sometimes in wrath. John wrote sceptically of the wonderful Sind methods which were always being flung at his head:

' What a system for such a man as Sir Charles to advocate! Judicial—you flogged and fined up to 500 rupees without record or power of appeal. I fear some of your men must have done much harm. There was a Mr. —— under me in the Jullandur who had been in Scinde, and I saw some terrible cases of oppression by him in this way, to which I speedily put a stop. . . . '

' To suppose that a man ignorant of the manners, customs, habits, and language of a people, with untrained men under him, could really have governed a country as he thinks he did Scinde, seems to me an impossibility. He has always had one great advantage, namely, that he tells his own story. A man may make a good many mistakes, and still be a better ruler than an Ameer of Scinde.'

The last sentence hits the nail squarely. Napier's despotism had been experienced by a people used to caprice and certain of one thing only, that man was born to oppression as the sparks fly upward.

As for Napier's suspicion of mutiny all around, in 1850 alarm was caused by rumour that a Sikh regiment had refused *batta* for its share in putting down a trivial rebellion. The Governor-General enquired, and learnt that what happened was that they had refused to take 'blood-money' for fighting against their own countrymen. 'They said they had done their duty and were content with that they had received.'[1] Marvelling, he dismissed the incident as 'highly creditable'. The final storm came over this *batta* business, which from first to last has raised so many tumults in India. Early in 1850 Napier, with the excuse that Dalhousie was then at sea, on his own authority cancelled a regulation disallowing certain special grants for dearness of provisions. When corrected he stuck to his guns, asserted a right to have so acted and his intention to repeat the action if he saw necessity. The Governor-General wrote to Sir John Hobhouse, President of the Board of Control: 'I have been exceedingly vexed, and with reason'. The war continued. Napier put in memorandums, one of which his opponent characterised privately as 'the most discreditable paper that ever was traced by the pen of a public man'. Napier proceeded to accuse the Governor-General of 'most extraordinary and most disingenuous' reasoning. He resigned, and left his command in December, 1850, going home to die, but to achieve in posthumous publications an explosion hardly less than those which had accompanied him through life. Especially was it believed that he had foreseen the Mutiny; and his countrymen, who naturally admired the old hero, set him on the same plane of exalted esteem as Nelson, Wellington, and Lord Roberts.

Napier asserted that all princes regarded us with 'venomous hatred'; and in this, as in his assertions of mutiny everywhere, there was enough of truth. There were disquieting incidents in a number of native regiments. But it is certain that his random and abounding accusations of disaffection everywhere and in everyone had behind them no genuine prescience. He threw such a cloud of missiles that some hit some mark. A far more striking example of prophecy was Henry Lawrence's playful forecast[2] written in 1842, which even to details, as in its prediction of events at Delhi and at 'Meerut itself, at all times unquiet', reads like a forgery composed after 1857. John, also, in his parting shot[3] at his adversary, showed that the gift of prophecy was in the family:

[1]*Life of Dalhousie*, i. 353.   [2] *Life*, i. 445 ff.   [3] October 29, 1853.

' I think poor Charlie Napier will probably make an ass of himself in his posthumous work. Like Falstaff's sack, which bore so large a proportion in his daily expenditure compared with bread, there will be in Napier's work very much about himself, and little about India. He was so eaten up with passion and prejudice that his really good qualities had not fair play.'

In 1842, when the title of Nawab of Surat was abolished, Lord Auckland declared his intention

' to persevere in the one clear and direct course of abandoning no just and honourable accession of territory or revenue, while all existing claims of right are at the same time scrupulously maintained',

words which Lord Dalhousie echoed early:

' I take this opportunity of recording my strong and deliberate opinion, that in the exercise of a wise and sound policy the British Government is bound not to put aside or neglect such rightful opportunities of acquiring territory or revenue as may from time to time present themselves.'

He changed the map with a speed and thoroughness no campaign had equalled.

He was, however, not quite the sweeping annexationist he is usually made out. He made attempts to distinguish between States possessed of independent or quasi-independent power before the Company's rise to paramountcy, and those which were its creation. The right of adoption was disallowed to the latter class; [1] if their rulers died without male heirs of the body, they were held to have 'lapsed' to the Company. Under this ruling, a number of important States were gathered in, one after another, till Indian opinion thought the foreigner looked on sovereignty as a tree whose fruits must all ultimately fall to his basket.

---

[1] Sir John Malcolm, who understood 'adoption' and the Indian attitude towards it better than anyone else, twenty years before Dalhousie's time (November 14, 1829) expressed this opinion: 'Adoptions, which are universally recognised as legal among Hindoos, are not a strict right (any more than direct heirs) where grants of land are for service. . . . But while a few have been permitted to adopt, others are denied the privilege; and while we declare their direct heirs are entitled to succeed, we lie in wait (I can call it nothing else) to seize their fine estates on failure of heirs, throwing them and their adherents and the country into a state of doubt and distraction. . . . The Bengal Government, influenced by, if not composed of, men bred in Calcutta, take a mere fiscal view of the subject, and believe, I imagine, our chiefs and Jagheerdars to be like the Baboos and Bengal Zemindars. . . .' As this passage suggests, British-Indian history would have taken a very different, and probably far happier, course if Calcutta had not been the capital.

The story of Satara's annexation has been told too fully for effectiveness in a wordy, cantankerous book,[1] hard to read. Major Basu's version is, however, amply in accord with contemporary British testimony, and, despite his silly trick of digging at the word 'Christian' on every page, almost in every paragraph, is adequate polemic and a case hard to dispose of.

Elphinstone and others had used the Satara Raja, at the time of the last war with the Peshwas, as a means to localise and lessen the campaign and our enemies. There had been previous communication between the Raja and the British; and there is some reason to believe that the Raja understood that he had been promised complete restoration to the power once his ancestor Sivaji's. On the other hand, the British regarded him as a helpless tool, almost a prisoner, of the Peshwa. But they found him a valuable tool, and consciousness of this fact rankled afterwards. The course pursued may be indicated by a quotation from Thomas Munro's letter to Elphinstone, March 29, 1818:[2] 'The limits of his principality may be left undefined for the present. He should be required to summon Bajee Rao and his principal chiefs to his presence, and in case of their not obeying, to proclaim Bajee Rao and all who adhered to him rebels'. This the Raja, whose person was wrested from the Peshwa at the battle of Ashti, did, and it helped to huddle the war to a finish.

He was disappointed in the extent of the principality awarded him, though the British—who soon forgot his very real service in denouncing the Peshwa as an unfaithful servant who had forfeited all right to obedience himself, and underrated his assistance as much as he overrated it—considered their action generous, the giving of something to one whose own power to obtain it was nil. He was left also with a genuine grievance in the matter of certain *jagirs* where he was promised feudal suzerainty, a promise which lapsed by some of the accidents due to changing personnel and policies in an administration that was manned from far overseas. Over his disappointment, and especially this definite loss, he brooded.

Pratap Singh was a ruler of exceptional ability and probity. The main complaint his English overlords had against him was one inherent in geographical conditions, and one which in times less unscrupulously realist and imperialist would have been ignored. It was exposed in a

[1] *Story of Satara* (*The Modern Review* Office, Calcutta, 1922).
[2] Gleig, *Life of Sir Thomas Munro*, iii. 237.

minute (January 30, 1837) by Sir Robert Grant,[1] Governor of Bombay, after the trouble had started:

' An opinion is now very commonly entertained that the erection of Sattara into a separate principality was a mistaken proceeding. It is at least clear that this principality includes the finest part of the Deccan, and by its position most awkwardly breaks the continuity of the British territory. There are those, therefore, who will hail the present crisis as affording an excellent opportunity of repairing the error alluded to, by pulling down the inconvenient pageant we have erected.'

Of particular annoyance to the British authorities was the habit of Hindus who had widows they wished to burn, of taking them into Satara territory, where the anti-suttee regulation did not hold, much as an interrupted prize-fight in old times would move across a county boundary.

Grant's minute contained another passage which deeply interested the surviving princes when Parliament incautiously ordered the Satara papers to be published:

' I am aware that it is the probable course, or, if I may so speak, the natural history of such an Empire as ours in India, that it gradually absorbs all the petty and dependent states attached to it, nor is there any reason to suppose that Satara will not at length share the common fate.'

He noted at the same time that the Portuguese possessions were

' absolutely valueless, except as the shattered and fading memorials of past glory; to us they are most inconvenient neighbours, by breaking the continuity of our dominions, and by furnishing in very supposable cases rallying points for the discontent and disaffection of our own subjects . . . certainly it is our obvious policy to seize the earliest opportunity of barring up this most inconvenient and possibly mischievous inlet'.

In December, 1835, the East India Company took the exceptional step of sending Pratap Singh a jewelled sword worth £3000 for his 'exemplary fulfilment of the duties' of 'his elevated situation', which had filled their minds with 'feelings of unqualified satisfaction and pleasure'. He did not receive the sword, however, for early in 1836 his Resident reported that he believed the Raja was trying to seduce British sepoys stationed in Satara from their allegiance. The Bombay authorities prosecuted the enquiry 'with an eagerness that embarrassed the Government both at Calcutta and at home'.[2] After close examination of the evidence, Lord Auckland's Government decided (1837) that

---

[1] Author of 'O worship the King all-glorious above' and other well-known hymns.

[2] Colebrooke, *Life of Elphinstone*, ii. 387. Elphinstone, in retirement, took a deep interest in the affair, having been so largely concerned in the re-establishment of Satara.

there was 'little or nothing in the evidence recorded . . . to inculpate the Raja'. He should, however, be warned that suspicions had arisen, and advised to conduct himself warily to prevent such episodes, painful for both sides. Then the business might be dropped. Grant was not willing to drop it, and did not drop it. But he died, 1838, and others had to continue his researches. Further accusations of anti-Company intrigue with neighbouring Rajas, notably of Jodhpur, and with the Portuguese, were brought against the Satara ruler. The evidence did not seem considerable to many contemporary British officers who deserve respect. The Raja used titles which indicated that he considered himself the head of the Maratha people, and in general rather more important than the paramount Power considered him. But in India (where titles had always been cheap, and the Company had never scrupled to go on giving them to Nawabs and Rajas who had been stripped of every shred of power and territory) this one proven offence (if offence it was) did not justify annexation. In 1839 the Bombay Government

' took the singularly infelicitous step of inviting the accused prince to acknowledge the truth of the accusation, and renew in more stringent terms the treaty alleged to be broken. Intimation was given that, on his failing to criminate himself, he would be dethroned. The terms were indignantly rejected, and the dethroned prince went into exile.' [1]

That is, he preferred to be dismissed, rather than accept pardon for actions that had not been proved or even examined in fair court. He resided at Benares, until his death in 1847, conducting a campaign of protest both in India and England, with many British sympathisers, both soldier and civilian, and regarded as a martyr by Indian opinion. He quite possibly was guilty—he and the Portuguese may even have come to know Sir Robert Grant's statesmanlike plans for them, and have taken counsel together, as threatened men sometimes do; and it is very probable that he was not an enthusiastic subject of the Company, or sure of his own future under their expansive mood. But there is no justification for the way our historians assume a doubtful case as proved, as when the *Oxford History of India* compresses his story into

' the Raja of Satara . . . engaged in a long-continued series of foolish treasonable intrigues with the Portuguese and other people. The Bombay government made every effort to convince the Raja of his folly, and gave him opportunities for repentance; but he refused to listen, and was necessarily deposed, his brother taking his place.' [2]

[1] *Op. cit.* ii. 387.

[2] 674. It is worth noting that Kaye (*History of the Sepoy War*, i. 72) thinks his deposition justified.

That brother, Apa Sahib, a worthless debauchee, had been adequately described by Grant Duff in 1819: 'an obstinate, ill-disposed lad, with very low vicious habits, which all the admonition of the Raja cannot get the better of'. He was, however, amenable, and he introduced some needed measures, such as the abolition of suttee. He died in 1848, on his death-bed adopting a son and successor. The Company were now in the full tide of their annexation-on-any-pretext fever, and Sir John Hobhouse, President of the Board of Control, had already sent Dalhousie, newly arrived and with his mind still fluid on the Satara business, 'this obvious incitement to annexation': [1]

'. . . The death of the ex-Raja of Satara certainly comes at a very opportune moment. The reigning Raja is, I hear, in very bad health, and it is not at all impossible we may soon have to decide upon the fate of his territory. I have a very strong opinion that on the death of the present prince without a son, no adoption should be permitted, and this petty principality should be merged in the British Empire.'

Satara was annexed, and the adoption swept aside, a blow to such reputation for straightforwardness as the Company still possessed: [2]

' I do not remember ever to have seen Mr. Elphinstone so shocked as he was at this proceeding. The treatment of the Sattara sovereignty as a jageer, over which we had claims of feudal superiority, he regarded as a monstrous one; but any opinion of the injustice done to this family was subordinate to the alarm which he felt at the dangerous principles which were advanced, affecting every sovereign state in India.'

The Satara family was the family of Sivaji, with peculiar claims to Maratha and Hindu reverence. The testimony of Sir John Low, a member of Dalhousie's Council, may serve to show how deeply such Indian opinion as existed was wounded:

' The confidence of our Native Allies was a good deal shaken by the annexation of Satara. . . . When I went to Malwa, in 1850, where I met many old acquaintances, whom I had known when a very young man and over whom I held no authority, I found these old acquaintances speak out much more distinctly as to their opinion of the Satara case; so much so, that I was, on several occasions, obliged to check them. It is remarkable that every native who ever spoke to me respecting the annexation of Satara, asked precisely the same question: "What crime did the late Rajah commit that his country should be seized by the Company?" ' [3]

---

[1] Sir William Lee-Warner, *Life of Lord Dalhousie*, ii. 158.

[2] *Life of Elphinstone*, ii. 388.   [3] Minute of Colonel Low, February 10, 1854.

2 C

It was held, soundly enough, that the merits or demerits of Apa Sahib or the boy he adopted were not relevant. The only question was, Had he been the Company's faithful vassal? He notoriously had —he lacked his predecessor's self-respect as conspicuously as he lacked his other qualities. The matter continued to exacerbate both British and Indian minds, and must be considered one of many incidents that forced on the Mutiny. When that event came, this affair had been ceaselessly agitated for twenty years, with much ensuing resentment. Native India thought the annexation high-handed in the extreme, and despaired of seeing *any* ancient rights or engagements respected.

The last chapter was written in the Mutiny. The agent who had spent fourteen years of exile in London trying to get justice for the family, fled from Satara with a price on his head. There was disaffection and a tiny rising, which cost the lives of four native policemen. Then a group of over twenty—which included a son and another relative of the lawyer who had caused so much trouble, both through the House of Commons and in India—were blown from guns.

Sambalpur, a gain of only 4693 square miles and a £7000 revenue, lapsed in 1849. Since 'a pestilential climate, with no roads or comforts', it was left to Indian subordinates, who raised extra money by a 25 per cent. increase of the land tax, an increase doubled in 1854. Complaints went unheeded. In 1857, mutineers wrested from a British prison the nearest heir to the lapsed sovereignty, who had been serving a life sentence since 1840. His people welcomed him back, but he led a desperate hunted life, with one interval of renewed imprisonment, until caught finally in 1864.

Karauli, a Rajput State, escaped annexation (1852), largely because Henry Lawrence, then Agent for Rajputana, pleaded on its behalf; partly, too, in deference to Indian reverence for the Rajput clan and name. Dalhousie wrote:[1]

'It is not worth creating any alarm about; and perhaps after all it may be politic to let alone these Rajput states, even though we have strict right on our side. . . .

'. . . I have received a letter from Colonel Low, in which he urges the *policy* of recognising the adoption with reference to Rajputs' feelings, so earnestly that I think it right to send you an extract from his letter. He is a temperate and safe man, and his views will probably incline you still more to the liberal view which I have anticipated that the Court would take. On the

[1] *Life of Dalhousie*, ii. 168.

question of *right*, I would not have deferred to him; on the question of *policy* as regards Rajputana I do not wish to insist upon my opinion against his.'

The Court of Directors demurred, but in the end Karauli was spared. It remained steadfastly loyal in the storm, so helpful that its Chief's salute was raised to 17 guns, and his State's debt of £11,000 remitted. Rajput States stood fast in the Mutiny. The Rajputs had come under British

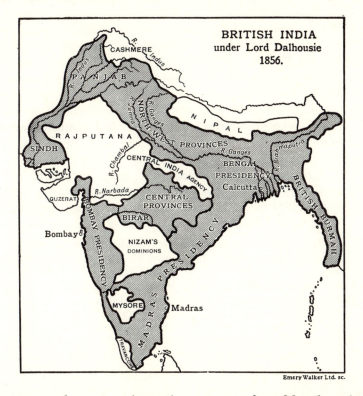

BRITISH INDIA
under Lord Dalhousie
1856.

Emery Walker Ltd. sc.

protection in the main voluntarily, to escape from Maratha subjugation; to this day a steady regard has persisted towards them from us, in which Tod's enthusiastic book has helped. The Marathas, those stiff opponents, have been less fortunate, and it is only now that esteem is belatedly growing up.

Two Maratha States, Jhansi and Nagpur, lapsed in 1854. The sequel of Jhansi's annexation, its beautiful young Rani's 'inveteracy' during the Mutiny, is known to everyone. Against the annexation of Nagpur, historically one of the leading four Maratha States, Low wrote two desperately earnest minutes of protest. But Dalhousie 'had no difficulty' (with the Directors and himself) 'in proving' that Nagpur was a dependent State created after its ruler's share in the last Maratha War. Facts, too, were against Nagpur; it consisted of no less than 80,000 square miles, whose annexation

' would not only give the Company a revenue of forty lakhs of rupees, but it would consolidate their scattered dominions, and enclose Hyderabad in a ring fence. The road between Calcutta and Bombay would lie almost entirely in British territory, and, in short, "the possession of Nagpur would combine our military strength, would enlarge our commercial resources, and would materially tend to consolidate our power".' [1]

The settlement, as commonly happened, was marred by unfortunate incidents.[2]

The Nizam, who passed into 'a ring fence', had a somewhat narrow escape from elimination. His dominions had never been much more happily governed than Oudh. But there was nothing between him and the paramount Power except money differences and debts, and the Governor-General was a man just and scrupulous, far inferior to Wellesley in ability to work himself up into passionate acceptance of his own case; he could see other points of view:

' The monthly subsidy for which the Resident maintains a perpetual wrestle with the Diwan, and which transforms the representative of the British Government, by turns, into an importunate creditor, and a bailiff in execution, is the pay of the contingent. Were that source of demand and dispute once adjusted, there is no Native State in India whose relations with the British Government would, as far as we know, be more friendly and unruffled. The Nizam has been our ally for much more than half a century. This Government disclaims not only the intention but the wish of doing any act by which the independence of the Nizam can be in any way impaired.' [3]

The districts known as the Berars were put under British control, their revenues to be taken in settlement of claims and for payment of the subsidiary force, all surplus to be paid to the Nizam's treasury.[4] The Nizam remained nominally their sovereign. In this manner, Dalhousie saved the Company's ancient ally, and re-established him as what he is to-day, the only genuinely independent prince in India.

[1] *Op. cit.* ii. 178 ff.

[2] See Kaye, *History of the Sepoy War*, Book I, chapter 2; and for a partial defence, Lee-Warner, *Life of Lord Dalhousie*, ii. 181.

[3] Minute of March 30, 1853.   [4] Treaty of May 21, 1853.

Dalhousie's reign was a crowded season of removing anomalies and of unifying and consolidating India. Nationalist opinion to-day is not sore about his actions, for the princes seem a survival adverse to the modernist dreams of a United Independent India. It would rejoice, had he gone further, and absorbed every State. But we are concerned only with the effect in that vanished semi-feudal age, an age of European princedoms such as we have forgotten entirely, and of public opinion everywhere which thought the people largely negligible, and only aristocratic 'rights' important. Some outbreak was certain, unless all Indians were willing to be relegated to inferiority for ever.

Yet with a State that was not Maratha and had unquestioned title-deeds of internal independence, Dalhousie could be forbearing, as we have seen. In 1852 a Muslim State, Bhawalpur, was allowed to have a disputed succession, which next year passed into civil war, resulting in the rebel's victory and enthronement. The Governor-General rejected John Lawrence's strong plea for interference, and was a wise Gallio; the troubles did not concern British India, unless fighting slopped over the border: This incident [1] shows how much rope was left native States within their limits; it is only by degrees that their rulers, long afterwards, have been told that they must not torture to death, or even inflict capital punishment too readily and capriciously. For example, the next Nawab of Bhawalpur, after Dalhousie's time, was allowed to execute three uncles, who might have cherished kingly ambitions.

Dalhousie's quick humanity made him protest beyond strict political rights, against suttee, which persisted on a shocking scale in some of the Rajput States. But the most ancient and inveterately traditional of them all, Udaipur, persisted in these sacrifices at its rulers' funerals (in 1861 the last *legal* widow-burning in India outside Nepal disgraced it).[2] Though the Governor-General could not coerce Udaipur, when suttee occurred in Dungapur, a Rajput State temporarily under British regency, he treated it as a crime, and punished it far more heavily than it is punished to-day.

We come to the last chapter but one of Oudh's misrule and misery. We have seen its Nawabs taken from nominal dependence on the Mogul to dependence on the Company: tossed a province and new subjects by Hastings, in the subjugation of the Rohillas: robbed by authority and without authority: made 'kings' by Lord Hastings: forced by Auckland to accept a treaty whose annulment was concealed from them: sub-

---

[1] *Life of Dalhousie*, ii. 117 ff.   [2] See Thompson, *Suttee*, 108 ff.

jected by successive rulers to that iniquity which revolts us to-day, 'unilateral' denunciation distortion and revision of solemn treaties:

' Most assuredly Warren Hastings, Lord Teignmouth, Lord Wellesley, Lord Hastings. and Lord Auckland, would never have acted in private life as they did in the capacity of governor-general towards prostrate Oude.' [1]

Under the aegis of British protection, Lucknow was infested for close on a century with pimps and panders, musicians, robbers and Europeans. Contemporary accounts show a populace armed and swaggering, and crowded streets where 'elephants and camels are the common labourers',[2] blocking traffic. The buffalo-hide shield, studded with brass knobs, is flung up on the left shoulder: fiercely-moustached Rajputs and Pathans, black-bearded Mussulmans, 'self-sufficient citizens', flaunt matchlock and tulwar. Midway ran the silvery streak of the river, between sprawling glittering palaces and those parks which still make Lucknow uniquely beautiful.

' Elephants in scores, tigers, rhinoceroses, antelopes, cheetahs or hunting-leopards, lynxes, Persian cats, Chinese dogs, might all be seen sunning themselves in this park, either in their cages, or stretched listlessly on the grass, as commonly as sheep and cows in an English meadow.' [2]

The visitor was 'transported suddenly into some of the scenes . . . read in childish history and novels'. Such lunacy, even in the East, would have been swept away by revolution long before, but for the terrible puissance outside Oudh's borders, protecting its rulers.

Oudh, nevertheless, remained important. It had been loyal, slavishly so, to its engagements, and the paramount Power had no legal excuse for annexation. It remained, a vast and awkward gap in the Company's dominions. Larger than Switzerland, Saxony and Wurtemberg together, 'stripped as it has been of its rupees and its most valuable provinces by successive governors-general, Oude is still more populous than any of the German states . . . except Prussia and Austria'.[3] But at last something had to be done, within or without the cover of treaty rights. In 1847 Lord Hardinge warned the King that he must mend his atrocious government, or the British Government would take steps to see it mended. In 1848 Sleeman was sent to Lucknow by Dalhousie as Resident, to undertake 'the reconstruction of a great, rich, and oppressed country . . . a noble as well as an arduous task . . .'; [4] in 1849

---

[1] *Calcutta Review*, iii. 376.
[2] W. Knighton, *The Private Life of an Eastern King*, 6, 5, 3, 5.   [3] *Op. cit.* 9.
[4] Sleeman, *A Journey through the Kingdom of Oude*, 1849-50 (1858 ed.), xviii.

he was instructed to make a tour and report on conditions. He found them fantastic in iniquity. His least trouble was with infanticide, the common practice of the Rajputs in the kingdom, practised with the indecency that so easily goes with ruthlessness. Yes, his colloquists told him, of course they killed their female children; they buried them alive, or after smothering them with the first fæces passed from the bowels, and on the thirteenth or fourteenth day afterwards the priest came and ate a meal in the room which had been both birthplace and tomb, thereby becoming a 'sin-eater'.[1] Lucknow, that 'overgrown city', was 'a perpetual turmoil of processions, illuminations, and festivities'.[2] The King had settled down to a continuous Eisteddfod, his sole companions fiddlers and buffoons, his ambition 'limited to the reputation of being the best drum-beater, dancer, and poet of the day',[3] aspirations admirable in a private individual but out of place in a ruler, and in any case not likely to appeal to an Indian official. Most of his fellow-artistes were Doms, outcastes of the most scavenging and despised kind. Sleeman's sombre narrative is lit up with humorous interludes, all verging on grimness. There were, for example, the activities of 'the King of the Fairies' (*djinns*), an enterprising Muslim who precipitated by means of a false ceiling messages from elfland, enjoining gifts to that region through himself, its representative.

The King's pastimes needed money, to procure which royal forces scoured the land. The peasantry grew swift-footed and long-sighted. They sometimes hit back, Oudh being full of sepoys, 'the great nursery of soldiers for the Company's army. The forces of the Bengal presidency come almost exclusively from Oudh.' But these armed groups were an added element to the universal lawlessness. Sleeman was often assured that annexation would be welcomed, if there were any way of evading our dreaded courts. In this desire he sympathised deeply, but, like others, unavailingly; when Oudh was ultimately annexed, little notice was paid to his witness that our legal methods wrought more harm than all other evil agencies together.[4]

' The quality of testimony, no doubt, like that of every other commodity, deteriorates under a system, which renders the good of no more value *in exchanges* than the bad. The formality of our Courts here, as everywhere else, tends to impair, more or less, the quality of what they receive. The simplicity of Courts, composed of little village communities and elders, tends, on the contrary, to improve the quality of the testimony they get; and in India, it is

---

[1] Cf. Mary Webb's *Precious Bane.*   [2] Sleeman, i. 275.
[3] Sleeman in 1852.   [4] *Journey through Oude,* ii. 68-9.

found to be best in the isolated hamlets of hills and forests, where men may be made to do almost anything rather than *tell a lie*. A Marhatta pandit, in the valley of the Nerbudda, once told me, that it was almost impossible to teach a wild Gond of the hills and jungles the *occasional* value of a lie! It is the same with the Tharoos and Booksas, who are, almost exclusively, the cultivators of the Oude Tarae forest, and with the peasantry of the Himmalaya chain of mountains, before they have come much in contact with people of the plains, and become subject to the jurisdiction of our Courts. These Courts are, everywhere, our *weak point* in the estimation of our subjects; and they should be, everywhere, simplified, to meet the wants and wishes of so simple a people.'

To sum up:

' A want of sympathy or fellow-feeling between the governing and governed is common in all parts of India, but in no part that I have seen is it so marked as in Oude. The officers of the Government delight in plundering the peasantry, and upon every local Governor who kills a landholder of any mark, rewards and honours are instantly bestowed, without the slightest inquiry as to the cause or mode. They know that no inquiry will be made, and therefore kill when they can; no matter how, or for what cause.' [1]

Yet the region tormented with this madness was nobly endowed:

' I have seen no soil finer; the whole plain of which it is composed is capable of tillage; it is everywhere intersected by rivers, flowing from the snowy chain of the Himmalaya, which keep the moisture near the surface at all times, without cutting up any of the land on their borders into deep ravines; it is studded with the finest groves and single trees, as much as the lover of the picturesque could wish; it has the boldest and most industrious peasantry in India, and a landed aristocracy too strong for the weak and wretched Government; it is, for the most part, well cultivated; yet with all this, one feels, in travelling over it, as if he was moving among a people suffering under incurable physical diseases, from the atrocious crimes every day perpetrated with impunity, and the numbers of suffering and innocent people who approach him in the hope of redress, and are sent away with despair.' [2]

Sleeman was strongly against annexation, and warned Lord Dalhousie in writing 'that the annexation of Oude would cost the British power more than the value of ten such kingdoms, and would inevitably lead to a mutiny of the Sepoys', a prediction he died just too soon to see fulfilled. He held, as others of his way of thinking did, that the native States were 'breakwaters, and when they are all swept away, we shall be left to the mercy of our native army, which may not always be

[1] *Op. cit.* i. 334-5.   [2] Sleeman, letter to Sir Erskine Perry, February 2, 1850.

sufficiently under our control'. Also, that they had an educational value; Indians, looking first on the quiet and security pervading the Company's dominions and then on the lunatic caprice and misery of such States as Oudh, would feel how lucky those in the former were. He knew, too, how valuable as a safety-valve native India was; the ambitious and energetic, who could serve only as subordinates on a pittance and without self-respect in British India, here could rise to places of responsibility or, at any rate, power and esteem. Those 'whose habits unfitted them' to occupy niches of humility and lowly service could here swagger with tulwar and matchlock.

But his report was too convincing, and was borne out by the Governor-General's own experience. In December, 1851, Dalhousie journeyed on Oudh's borders, in the North-West Provinces, then under Thomason's beneficent rule, and noted:

' The district profits considerably by its proximity to Oudh, since the disturbances in that unfortunate land very frequently produce an emigration of good cultivators from some village that can stand squeezing no more. The other day the whole of the cultivators of one village, two hundred in number, fled into the Shahjehanpur district, and were all eagerly hired by the zamindars at once.[1]

' All day I heard a heavy cannonading going on, and marvelled to think that we should be able to hear the artillery practice all the way from Cawnpore. Before the evening I discovered it was our neighbours in Oudh collecting their revenue! Nothing more common, the people say, all along this border.' [2]

Yet with amazing patience Dalhousie procrastinated. It is an example of the queer illogicality with which British-Indian history is written, that the annexation of Oudh has been so often reprobated, when actions flatly unethical are glossed over. This is because the Mutiny followed. There is not much open to criticism in the Oudh annexation, details apart; and as to details, 'it is impossible but that offences should come', and it is the historian's business not to stress the unavoidable that is also trivial.

In 1854 Outram was sent to Lucknow as Resident. He reported that there had been no improvement. His account, 'excellent, clear, concise, temperate in its tone, and decisive in its conclusion', reached Dalhousie at Coonoor in the Nilgiris, March 15, 1855; Oudh's administration was an orgy of massacre and corruption set to music.

[1] Sir William Lee-Warner, *Life of Lord Dalhousie*, ii. 317.

[2] *Op. cit.* ii. 319 (Diary entry, December 30, 1851).

Even yet Dalhousie pondered and hesitated. Wellesley's treaty of 1801, a gross injustice at the time and in its attendant bullying, now stood the erring kingdom in good stead; it enjoined that reforms must be carried out by the Nawab's own officers, and Dalhousie believed in promises being kept. On January 2, 1856, a Court of Directors' decision reached him; he was to offer the King a kind of 'Vatican' sovereignty, the title of King, adequate funds, and full jurisdiction short of death over the Lucknow palace, parks (and menageries). Outram, who had been recalled to Calcutta for conference, was sent back to Lucknow, reaching it January 30, with a British brigade close behind. He went to the palace, to find its guns dismounted in mourning, and a disarmed guard of honour saluting with empty hands signifying helplessness. The King placed his turban between his hands, and broke down when reading the treaty he was to sign. Given a few days' grace, he refused to accept the new position (February 7), was deposed, and went to Calcutta, where he resided, agitating and protesting, one more centre of pity and resentment.

Dalhousie's pledge of generous grants to those brought low was ignored, and in Canning's brief pre-Mutiny rule they were 'reduced to great pecuniary straits, with all the humiliations attendant upon such a state'.[1] Those who had sung and revelled starved; and with them starved royalty and nobility. An unsympathetic Chief Commissioner succeeded Outram the Resident, and chose to occupy a palace 'expressly set aside for the King's family'. Oudh was flooded with disbanded troops, under a new regime in which robbery was liable to heavy penalties. Not less than 40,000 Company's sepoys had their homes in the province, and they and their families, a large fraction of the total population, were troubled in their minds.

Dalhousie's words in his Diary [2] are movingly sincere:

' I believe the work to be just, practicable, and right. With that feeling on my mind, and in humble reliance on the blessing of the Almighty, I approach the execution of the duty gravely; and not without solicitude, but calmly and altogether without doubt.'

It seems hard, after careful weighing of three-quarters of a century of criticism that has followed the event, to see how he could have acted other than he did. But the mischief arose from the fact that now Indians, except within a restricted and threatened area, were debarred from hope of any post, civil or military, of any importance.. Tolerant of

[1] Lord Stanley, October 13, 1858.   [2] January 9, 1856.

much misrule and misery (explained by religious philosophy, as these were), the people of India until recently never attached as much weight to actual material improvement as we have imagined. They could see only that a very rich province, long pillaged and longer coveted, had been swallowed up, and an ancient family exiled, 'who, whatever may have been their offences towards their own subjects, have not been unfaithful to the British Government'.[1] This claim, which to the Directors appeared a mainly formal one, to them was essential: if the British both annexed when there had been the test of strength in war, as with the Punjab, and when there had been nothing but decades of slavish submission, where did anyone stand? As for the sufferings under native rule, there were two sides to this question: [2]

' General Lowe, whom I have always known as a most indulgent judge of native governments and an enemy to annexation . . . used, in the particular case of Oude, to maintain that the people preferred their present misrule to our strict and meddling system, and the insolence and extortion of chuprassies and other petty officials; yet, after having been ten years and more Resident at Lucknow, he is now one of the most decided as to the impossibility of maintaining the present Government. Sleeman (the most vehement advocate of annexation) [3] is said to be in general a still greater friend to native governments.'

However, Oudh was annexed, and its teeming disorders dispersed rather than grappled with. As for the few surviving States, they drew into themselves, watchful, frightened, thinking such thoughts as even Englishmen have occasionally known:

' Another year! another deadly blow!
Another mighty empire overthrown!
And We are left, or shall be left, alone.'

Dalhousie ended other long-standing anomalies, as well as petty kingdoms that had outlived their real independence. In 1852 he secured the Delhi heir-apparent's promise to leave his palace (which was wanted for British military uses) when he succeeded his father; and 'regretted that the silly sentimentality of the Court [4] interposed any impediment to taking the crown as well as the palace'. We may doubt the wisdom of this yet further attenuation of a faded majesty venerated

---

[1] Court of Directors, November 21, 1855.

[2] Mountstuart Elphinstone, May 4, 1856 (*Life*, ii. 395).

[3] This, as we have seen, is mistaken. But it was the common belief.

[4] The Court of Directors.

even in its relics; and again, may ponder, with the coming shadow of 1857 falling on our narrative. The same shadow falls with another name, the Peshwa's. He died, 1851, and the pension granted him by Malcolm was not renewed to his adopted son, the notorious Nana Sahib. Dalhousie argued:

'In thirty-three years the Peshwa received the enormous sum of more than two and a half million sterling. He had no charges to maintain, no sons of his own, and has bequeathed twenty-eight lacs to his family. Those who remain have no claim whatever on the consideration of the British Government. They have no claim on its charity, because the income left to them is amply sufficient for them.'

We may envy the people of India, and wish that the same reasoning might be used of British pensions granted for events in the far past and continued age after age. There seems no cause to cavil at it. In 1855, the Nawab of the Carnatic died, and the title was discontinued, his uncle, who succeeded, being now styled merely Prince of Arcot and becoming a nobleman. The same year, the 'rajas' of Tanjore died out, as their power had died long ago. In this, as in the Nawab's case, Dalhousie intended a generous financial settlement. It was not his fault that the usual thing happened to the Ranis' personal property. One by one, princedoms whose ghosts had long haunted the Indian scene were exorcised and vanished.

A major campaign outside India was the second Burmese War, 1852. Frontier incidents had been accumulating since the first war; and in November, 1851, the foreign merchants of Rangoon made a detailed complaint of grievances. Dalhousie sent Commodore Lambert to express his 'confidence' that the Court of Ava would right these, and would disclaim breaches of treaty. A party of naval officers (January 6) went to the Rangoon Governor's house; told to wait outside, they pressed on to the foot of the steps, where they were informed that His Excellency was sleeping and could not be disturbed. A long stand in hot sun tried their tempers, as did the discovery that His Excellency was amusedly watching through a lattice. Lambert in reprisal seized a vessel belonging to the Burmese King, and blockaded the rivers. Dalhousie remained patient, and sent a second letter. The Commodore's ship, bearing it, was fired on, but easily silenced its assailants. John Lawrence meanwhile had asked, 'Why did you send a Commodore to Burma if you wanted peace?'; and Dalhousie himself remorsefully admitted (January 23, 1852) that 'these Commodores are too combustible for negotiations'.

At length a thrasonical answer arrived from the Rangoon Governor,

' commanding the forces, and appointed to go and rule a large territory and brave army, after due prostration at the royal feet, and after taking counsel with Meng Tarahgyee Phooyah, who is all-powerful Lord of the Universe, Master of the Tshat-tang elephant, and all White Elephants, and Lord of Life, he who is like unto the Lotus-flower'.

The British officers were reproved for having invaded his privacy while he was sleeping, and for having been drunk when they did it.

Dalhousie's next communication went to the point. By April 1,

' if, untaught by former experience, forgetful of the irresistible power of the British arms ... the King of Ava shall unwisely refuse the just and lenient conditions which are now set before him, the British Government will have no alternative but immediate war'.

War followed; it had minor setbacks, but no repetition of the mistakes of the former war. At first the British suffered more from pine-apples, which were one hundred for a shilling, than from Burmese missiles. The Shwe-Dagon pagoda, in Rangoon, was stormed, April 14, 1852; other pagodas and strong points were stormed, till in October the Burmese generalissimo, son of the Bandula who had fought so well in the first war, was ordered to appear before the Golden Foot in woman's dress,[1] for having been defeated. He preferred surrender to the British.

The war ended without treaty, the British annexing Pegu and the Burmese King, who explained that he was not at liberty to sign away territory, formally notifying the invaders (June, 1853) that he would allow them to remain in his country, and forbid his generals to molest them. His people, cut off from the sea, were almost starving; he asked that the Irawadi blockade might be lifted, and free trade established between his nation and the British.

The war had been marred by one sinister incident. The 38th Native Infantry, afraid of losing caste, had 'respectfully but firmly' refused to go to Burma by sea, though willing to march anywhere by land. It was technically within its rights, and the Governor-General acted with characteristic humanity:

' I could not fail to remember the melancholy incident in the same station of Barrackpore on the same occasion of the march of troops for a Burmese war, when from some misunderstanding and want of judicious and temperate

---

[1] William F. B. Laurie, *Narrative of Events during the second Burmese War, from August, 1852 ...* , 89.

handling, the Native troops were at length massacred as mutineers. Bearing that sad scene in mind, I felt that while I should never advise the Government to permit open disobedience of its orders, to truckle to its Sepoys, or in any the slightest degree to compromise its own authority; yet if it were practicable to modify existing orders, so as to avert an occasion which stupidity or error might make use of for a manifestation of discontent, or even of open mutiny, it would be a wise act for the Government to avoid such occasion for misapprehension, and so to preserve the men from the certain consequences of their own folly.'

The battalion had declared its willingness to march; and 'we thought it right that they should march'. They marched, therefore, though the hot weather had come, to Dacca, and relieved a less scrupulous unit there, which sailed for Burma.

Ever since the close of the second Sikh War, in which Dost Muhammad had attempted to wreak belated vengeance for his former sufferings at our hands, the question of an understanding with Afghanistan had been pondered. John Lawrence, who wrote, 'The best attitude, perhaps the only safe one, with Orientals, is that of complete superiority', and

' I look upon a Sikh chief as in every respect a more honourable and trust-worthy man than an Afghan. Falsehood and villainy are the natural char-acteristics of an Afghan, and their rulers are probably much worse than the majority of their people';
' All thinking men would say that it must, indeed, be a terrible crisis—Russia must be a frightful foe—when the lords of the East—the English—backed by France and Turkey, hold out in this fashion the right hand of fellowship to Kabul!' [1]

represented one attitude, that of standing on dignity for the Dost's impertinence in interfering in the Sikh campaign. The Dost answered this by suspicion; 'I know that the English will never forgive me'.

Herbert Edwardes, the chief warden of the marches,[2] was the first who made negotiation possible. Of a frank and adventurous nature, he was ready to see unofficial emissaries. When a treaty was finally made, March, 1855, though Dalhousie preferred that John Lawrence should actually carry it through and sign it, the main credit was Edwardes's. It was perhaps fortunate that negotiations were not hustled through, but protracted until almost the eve of the Mutiny. Dost Muhammad in that immense upheaval kept to his side of the fence.

Next year (May 14, 1854) the Khan of Khelat was brought within

[1] March 24, 1854. The Crimean War broke out, 1854.
[2] He became Commissioner of Peshawar, October, 1853.

the Indian system, and became a subsidised prince. The western frontier was now closed, except for the border tribes who kept it in a condition of constant petty warfare.

Inside India the Santal rebellion, 1855, at the time was taken as a portent, and aroused much of the alarm and savagery of repression which were to blaze out less than two years later. This was partly because it came so close to the capital. The Santals (Sonthals), aborigines who in a state of nature live by the chase, a people of extreme simplicity and lovableness, were suffering (as they continue to suffer) from Hindu infiltration. This meant change of habits and a whole train of perplexities. Their lands became alienated, they were entangled in debts to people far cleverer than themselves. They were under foolish local officials, who would not help them: 'The facile reply that the Santals should appeal to the civil courts, or prove their charges of oppression before the criminal courts, was the answer of the father who should offer his son a stone when he asked for bread'.[1] No one dreamed of insurrection by 'a race so gentle and harmless, with courts of justice ever open to them'; moreover, courts of British justice—which 'are open to everyone (like the Savoy Hotel)'. Planters, who were having trouble with the Bengali peasant, praised these 'laborious and patient' people; railway contractors delighted in them. Then, without warning, a Santal inundation swept over the outlying regions of Bengal, reaching to within a hundred miles of Calcutta, cleaving open skulls of European and Indian alike, pouring out poisoned arrows, burning huts and bungalows. All ended, however, as it was bound to end, in massacre and executions. The blood of the martyrs—if we may for a minute forget their wrong-doing and remember only that except by such an outbreak no redress could ever have come to them, for mere grumbling and representation has never brought humanity anything—proved the seed of better conditions. Their land was made into a 'non-regulation' district, and they shared with the Punjab the privilege of exemption from the blessings of justice as dispensed in the law-courts, experiencing in their stead straightforward protection.

Dalhousie, like the rest of Calcutta, was deeply impressed by this sudden fire out of the heart of aboriginal darkness:

'This Santal outbreak has taught us a new and cogent lesson; and I trust very much that Her Majesty's ministers and those who talk of drawing troops from India so glibly and confidently . . . will lay that lesson to heart.'

[1] *Life of Dalhousie*, ii. 62 ff.

As these words show, a vague uneasiness was troubling men's minds; there was growing through many years an underground irritation of the sort that so often contributes to exceeding passion of anger, when at last its dimly suspected justifications seem to leap up in open menace. The irritation was felt by both sides. Its centres were in Oudh, swarming with pillaged landowners and unemployed soldiery; in the Marathas, who felt that Sivaji's family had been wronged, and their rightful Peshwa (by adoption of his predecessor) deprived of the pension which kept a memory of ancient grandeur alive; in Delhi, where an ancient family knew that their tenure of the palace which was itself a city, within whose walls they could fool themselves that they were still regalities, was running out, and that a foreign soldiery would take their place there; and wherever (which was everywhere in North India—it is easy to see why South India was untouched by the Mutiny, which was as much outside its interests and passions as an outbreak in Poland or China, almost) European society had been exacerbated by the intense angers of the civilian-military quarrel which Napier had brought to a head.

In January, 1856, Lord Dalhousie went; but his going was followed by three events 'in rapid succession',[1] all part of the swiftly rising rapids that were sweeping tranquil India to the catastrophe. An order was issued, July 25, 1856, which made all units liable for general service, beyond the seas as in India; henceforward, refusal for caste prejudices was mutiny pure and simple. War was declared against Persia, November 1, 1856; India was deprived of a large part of its shrunken forces, not long after public opinion had been disquieted by the Crimean War, in which the clash which Government had anticipated for decades, with increasing apprehension and gravity, had come at last, and (rumour said) with not any great success to England. The Persian expedition, which was commanded by Outram and Havelock, won battles easily enough. But men remembered another war, that with Afghanistan, which arose from the same obsessing dread of Russia; that one also had begun with victories, over which a pack of fuss was made at the time, but had passed into overwhelming disaster. Many agreed with John Lawrence when he scoffed (January 30, 1857) at this eternal Russian bugbear: 'I believe there is no man now alive who will ever see a Russian army in India, and no Asiatic army could stand for a day before our troops in the open field'. Again Indian troops were being

[1] *Op. cit.* ii. 360.

sent far beyond their borders, to similar destruction! Moreover, India was left very low in British troops.

Lastly, on January 23, 1857, General Hearsey [1] (surely the most suggestive name that even a novelist could invent!) reported that there was 'an unpleasant feeling' about cartridges which the men believed were smeared with cow and pig lard. What followed is known to the world.

It is natural that we should look back on Dalhousie's reign as a time of territorial expansion. But it was also one of intense and beneficent activity. Sir James Thomason, perhaps the greatest of Indian provincial governors after Munro, ruled the North-West Provinces, 1843-53. Wise, patient, pacific, he gathered no laurels of war; but he won a personal regard from wilder spirits such as only Henry Lawrence won. His administration was looked on as a mine whence the Punjab could 'dig' first-rate men for its own more exciting service. Even to that promotion they went, however eagerly, yet with sorrow at parting from such a master; Thomason's farewell letter to Sir Richard Temple on going to the Lawrences, Temple wrote in his retirement, ' still shines like the evening star in my recollection'.[2]

Thomason moved continually about his province, always with a mind at leisure to listen and be interested,

' till at length there was hardly a place or a road in an area of 70,000 square miles, scarcely a clan or tribe in a population of 30 millions, with which he was not acquainted'.[3]

He was the bureaucrat at his best and noblest; a machine of ungrudging effort. He would

' set himself laboriously to learn how each kind of complex business should be performed from beginning to end, from the lowest to the highest step; having done that, he would reduce all his knowledge to lucid statement, so that what had perhaps been hard to him might be made easy to others. When he had thus instructed his officers of all degrees, he was extraordinarily patient and watchful in seeing that they acted up to his instructions.' [3]

In such a subordinate Dalhousie found a man who even foreran him in enthusiasm for the people's advancement. So much was done, in the

---

[1] Sometimes spelled 'Hearsay'. The Hearseys were a very famous Anglo-Indian family.

[2] Sir Richard Temple, *Men and Events of My Time in India*, 45.

[3] *Life of Dalhousie*, ii. 360.

North-West Provinces, in the Punjab, throughout India generally, that we can understand the vexation which accompanied deeper feelings when the Mutiny came. The mere record of the Lawrences' achievement in one year, which was called out from John by Napier's criticisms, is staggering. Theirs was a system which did not admit of leave. The need was too enormous, the work too exciting; men must persist until they broke down. When Dalhousie had mentioned that his near relation, Lord William Hay, wanted leave, John had answered:

' If Lord W. Hay is left to our mercies, we must, in duty bound, refuse him leave. We have agreed not to recommend any leave unless when men are sick. There is still much to do, and will be so for the next two years. Every day is of value, and the best officer cannot work too hard or too long for the public interest.'

A tyranny of duty drove on the best men, as fiercely as any taskmaster's whip. After thirty years in which men's lives had gone in such work as extirpating thuggee and suttee, infanticide and slavery, we need not wonder that respect for Indian civilisation was low. The slavish superstition which made men refuse to cross the sea, lest defilement came, pressed on Dalhousie

' the necessity for commencing the movement intended to uproot the absurd and unmeaning system, under which the whole Bengal army is practically no better than a collection of local corps, and to substitute for it a system of enlistment for general service of every man who may hereafter be recruited for any arm within its ranks'. (August 2, 1854.)

Dalhousie sanctioned Thomason's plans for an engineering college at Rurki and kept up at his own cost the girls' college founded in Calcutta by J. E. Drinkwater Bethune, a member of his Council, who died 1851. He pressed on the Directors educational expenditure. He established for Bengal, hitherto a charge of the Governor-General, and too apt to be neglected for general responsibilities, a separate lieutenant-governorship. He established a Central Legislative Council. He even dreamed of a time when Indians might rise to authority themselves. He laid practically all the foundations of modern India; and it is only when we look at the promise of this period and remember the prolonged setback which followed the Mutiny—an experience like the American 'Reconstruction' era after the Civil War—that we realise the tragedy of that episode, which substituted harsh judgment and bitterness for understanding and eagerness. He greatly increased the expenditure on public works, so much so that we may look on the gain of four and a half millions sterling to the revenue from his annexations as one for the good of India as a whole. The Grand Trunk Road was begun; canals were vastly extended, and the mighty Ganges Canal was finished in 1854, after eight years of work and the spending of £1,400,000, of which sum all but £170,000 was provided during his period of office. Its 525 miles (at this date) exceeded 'all the irrigation lines of Lombardy and Egypt together'; and Thomason, not a man to boast, claimed that it was 'unequalled among the efforts of civilised nations'. Dalhousie insisted, against strong opposition, that such benefactors as outstanding public engineers, though neither in red coats nor among the 'heaven-born' civilians, should be knighted. Prisoners were put under inspectors, first by Thomason in his territory, then by degrees in every other province; even criminals were acknowledged to have rights of protection. The final extirpation of the *Meriah* abominations was in Dalhousie's time. He introduced railways, the first line being opened in 1853, and a more important one, between Calcutta and the Raniganj coal-area, in 1854. India saw (1853)

' the splendid sight of fifty Parsee ladies riding in a special train upon the rail from Bombay to Tanah'.[1]

He introduced the electric telegraph, and supported the man responsible, against every sort of official nonsense and red tape, having him directly under himself, and not under the Military Board. The Punjab was given a network of military roads, immensely valuable to its people. The inefficient postal arrangements were abolished, and the cheap half-anna rate of pre-War days established. The forests were conserved and tea-planting encouraged.

Macaulay's 'filtration theory' in education had worn very thin before the Mutiny, and a new policy was laid down in the Directors' despatch of 1854, which is usually ascribed to Sir Charles Wood, the President of the Board of Control. The Bombay Government had already acknowledged the relative importance of elementary education, and by 1852 had 233 vernacular schools with over 11,000 pupils, as against 14 Government colleges and English schools with 2000 scholars. The Bengal Government, following the older theory, had 30 colleges with 5000 pupils, but only 33 elementary schools. The despatch of 1854 was a justification of the Bombay policy. This difference of outlook was typical of a change which was taking place throughout the administration. As province after province came under British rule the new Governments took more direct responsibilities. The *ryotwari*

---

[1] William F. B. Laurie, *The Second Burmese War, Pegu*, 280.

system of direct assessment succeeded the *zemindari* method of farming out the land revenue. When the Government began to embark upon large development schemes, roads, irrigation canals, and buildings, these were constructed as far as possible by public departments. The whole of British India was divided up into districts, and subdivided into areas under Indian officials, *Tehsildars*, *Mamlatdars*, etc. The district officer had an ever-increasing number of duties thrust upon him, especially in those early days in the Punjab, where sixty picked men, of whom Nicholson is the most famous, brought immense energy to their work. 'The sound of his horse's hoofs was heard from Attock to the Khaibar', as a frontier tribesman said of Nicholson. The Englishman is at his best in dealing with a primitive people, and this ruthless progress and efficiency, imposed directly from above, was typical of Dalhousie's administration.

He came to an official world sunk in routine. The Commander-in-Chief spent the whole year in the hills, involving the State in heavy expense by his residence there and by 'the enormous quantity of transport which he required when he moved about';[1] the reader with Indian experience can fill in details. By personal example Dalhousie reformed those who could be reformed,[2] and encouraged those who, in the Punjab and elsewhere, were moved by a zeal like his own. Though haughty and imperious, he was no stickler for state; a note to his private secretary, at midnight of March 29, 1849, says:

'If you are up and have your breeches on come here. If not, without them.'

He worked unpausingly through the sorrow of his wife's death and his own deepening pain. An affection diagnosed as gout settled into malignant disease of the shin-bone, afterwards extended to his throat. He had to be much at sea or in the hills, and when he left India dragged himself on board with crutches. He had then long outlived any desire but for retirement, and praise and rewards were vanity to his spirit, which continued unflagging in unselfishness, in care for his friends, in uprightness and courage and witty vivacity. India has been the scene of abundant valour, but of none more moving than this man's. All things weighed, he was the greatest of the Governors-General after Warren

[1] *Life of Dalhousie*, i. 113.

[2] This did not include the military administration, whose head continued to live on the heights.

Hastings; and as a man he has a place all to himself, his pluck and intellect making of steadfast conscientiousness a thing of exceeding loveliness,

> ' Not harsh and crabbèd, as dull fools suppose,
> But musical as is Apollo's lute'.

CHAPTER IV

PEASANTS AND CRAFTSMEN UNDER THE COMPANY

Importance of peasantry: pressure on soil: comparative fertility: eighteenth-century conditions: landlords and tenants: land revenue policy: rule of law in the villages: landless workers: craftsmen and the British connection: luxury trades and export market: policy of the Company: effect of British occupation.

With Lord Dalhousie's departure the Company's rule virtually ended. He had done much to transform its character, and his successor, Lord Canning, was soon embroiled in the Mutiny. Before describing that disastrous prelude to the formal introduction of Crown Government, it will be convenient to consider the influence of the British connection upon the manual workers. Unfortunately it was not until recently that any scientific enquiries were made into Indian economic and social conditions, and these have been limited in scope, referring to parts of the peninsula only. The historian searching for evidence of change, of improvement or deterioration over long periods, is driven to statistics of doubtful validity, to official reports which are seldom written from the required standpoint, and to chance observations of travellers and contemporary writers whose mental background and standards of comparison are difficult to estimate. There has been much tendentious writing about the condition of Indian villagers during the eighteenth and nineteenth centuries by authors who, consciously or unconsciously, have wished to suggest either that a golden age of peace and prosperity existed before the British came, or that the whole of India was plunged into anarchy and misery from which it was saved by the British connection. The honest historian must confess that, while it is easy to produce evidence to support either proposition, there is extremely little upon which to form a fresh and unbiassed opinion. A few preliminary generalizations may be permitted.

Throughout the period under consideration the measure of Indian prosperity was the condition of her peasantry. Not only did they form nearly three-fifths of the population, but the great majority of the rest worked for these directly, as farm labourers, or indirectly, as village servants, and as carpenters, smiths, etc. The rulers and the religious lived ultimately off the peasant's surplus produce. The *ryot's* first need is several acres of tillable land, containing sufficient phosphates, nitrates and potash. Probably fifteen acres of dry land, or five acres of irrigated, form a sound 'economic' family holding. The *ryot* also wants some draught cattle to help him cultivate. He is not much interested in other stock, partly because India is not a natural dairy country, but chiefly because the population is largely vegetarian, and the pig, an easy animal for the peasant to keep, is forbidden to Hindu and Muslim. Like most countrymen, he has no love for intensive farming, and slightly despises the *mali* or market gardener, who grows vegetables near a town. His object is to grow enough food for his family, food which will keep for a year; and also something which he can exchange, or sell for cash, either grain, fibre, dye, or drug. His first two considerations are his acreage and the fertility of the soil. There is some evidence to show that the *ryot* was better off in both these respects a century and a half ago, though the deterioration, which had already begun by the Mutiny, had only an indirect connection with the British occupation.

The first census was not taken till 1872, and the results, which surprised everyone, discount the value of rough estimates of population which were made previously.[1] It is, however, safe to assume a considerable increase in population between 1750 and 1850, especially in Southern India. During the latter part of the century it was the subject of frequent comment in official records. The spread of population was not relieved by any large-scale irrigation works until Dalhousie's last years. It was due to the establishment of peaceful conditions amongst a people used to war, and possessing high natural fertility. The efforts to reduce female infanticide must also have had some influence. It is certain that the cultivators were becoming a larger proportion of the population. In the eighteenth century there were more aboriginal and out-caste tribes not settled on the land. Village servants and craftsmen were comparatively more numerous, and far more men were in military ser-

[1] The figure of 206,162,360 was much higher than was expected. See App. D.

vice of some kind or another.[1] The cultivator was also less tied to the soil. In Bengal many *ryots* preferred to take their land on the seasonal or *paikasht* tenure, rather than on the permanent or *khudkasht*. With no great pressure on the land, occupancy rights had little value, and the *ryot* was freer to bargain with the *Zemindar*. He was also less exposed to the wiles of the money-lender, for he could only borrow money on his personal security, and in those lawless times the money-lenders plied a dangerous and uncertain trade. In the Deccan the drainage of men for military service was perhaps greater than in Bengal. The researches of Dr. Mann suggest that the average size of holdings was reduced to less than half during the seventy years preceding the Mutiny.[2] With a larger proportion of sons staying at home the evil of 'fragmentation' or 'morcellement' became more noticeable, each separate plot being divided up amongst the heirs of a dead man, until the village land was broken up into tiny irregular plots. Hindu and Muslim laws of inheritance both encourage this tendency. Efforts are now being made to counteract excessive subdivision, undoubtedly an important factor in lowering the standard of living.

The question of soil deterioration has been the subject of controversy. The official view is that 'most of the area under cultivation in India has been under cultivation for hundreds of years, and had reached its maximum stage of impoverishment many years ago'.[3] Undoubtedly India is a very old arable country; the new areas brought under canal irrigation or reclaimed during the last century are a small fraction of the land normally cultivated. Wastage of natural fertility has probably gone on for centuries, for religious prohibitions prevent the use of certain excrements, and make it difficult to manage stock so as to produce farmyard manure.[4] It is, however, probable that the natural yields per acre were higher when the holdings were larger. Cropping would be

[1] In political criticism of military expenditure it is often forgotten that even before the Mutiny the regular Indian army gave employment to a very small part of the population. The present proportion of about one in 2000 is far less than in most parts of Europe. The extension of the Indian Empire led to the disbandment of large bodies of irregular soldiery.

[2] H. H. Mann, *Land and Labour in a Deccan Village*, 45.

[3] Evidence of Agricultural Adviser to Government of India, *Report of Royal Commission on Agriculture in India*, 76.

[4] The use of cow-dung for fuel is common throughout India. It is often claimed that this unfortunate habit has arisen from the difficulty of obtaining firewood owing to forest restrictions. This may be partly true, but the custom seems to date from long before the Forest Acts, and is prevalent where firewood is plentiful.

less continuous, there would be more fallowing, and possibly more
'green manuring'. This would be enough to account for the tradition of
greater fertility. There would have been rather higher returns per acre,
with considerably fewer mouths to feed.

This is confirmed by some incidental references in early writers. Thus
Tavernier, describing his journeys in seventeenth-century India, remarks that 'even in the smallest villages, rice, flour, butter, milk, beans,
and other vegetables, sugar and other sweetmeats, dry and liquid, can
be procured in abundance'.[1] The general impression gained from such
sources is of a village life in which the cultivators and craftsmen stood
out more definitely than at present from a mass of unsettled and out-
caste humanity. There was a larger 'kulak' element, to use a word
familiarized since the Russian revolution. Female infanticide and frequent wars, raids, and disturbances helped to prevent any rapid increase
in the population. It was a more dangerous, but probably a more interesting life. The *ryot*, with his larger holding, would not be so likely to
suffer from that curse of modern village life, under-employment. His
son, in those unruly times, might rise to almost any position if he left
his village to join the army of some aggressive princelet. A shepherd's
son might become a Holkar. A trooper, even in the nineteenth century,
could rise to be ruler of Kashmir. The one chance in a million may not
interest the economist, but it would form the subject for endless talk,
night after night, under the village pipal tree.

It was not a peaceful or well-ordered rural India through which the
English spread from Calcutta, Madras, and Bombay. There were patches
of moderately good government, but always under some ruthless and
efficient prince, like Ranjit Singh in the Punjab, or Haidar Ali in Mysore. The whole area was covered by a network of semi-feudal estates,
but the feudal system was in the last stages of decay. The Mogul
Emperors had used these territorial magnates, half landlords and half
officials, as the easiest channels through which to collect revenue and
armies, and had added largely to their numbers. As their rule relaxed,
these *Zemindars*, *Talukdars*, *Jagirdars* and their like struggled to
establish themselves as hereditary rulers, or at least as hereditary landlords. They seem to have been as incapable of organised action as the
Polish nobility in the sixteenth century. The most they could inspire
was a feeling of personal loyalty amongst their tenants, or, in the case
of the important princes, amongst their feudatories. Nothing but a
state of anarchy could explain the ease with which the English overran

---

[1] *Travels in India* (Oxford University Press), 1925, i. 238.

the country with ludicrously small armies. Only occasionally (as in Rohilkhand, or later, in the Punjab) did the English meet with men imbued with a feeling of local patriotism, and fighting for a country rather than an individual. Many villages, especially in the Deccan, had an ancient system of self-government by *panchayats*, or 'councils of elders'. These enforced caste rules, maintained village wells and 'tanks', and exercised some control over minor offences. Their authority, based solely on religion and tradition, seems to have weakened rather than strengthened the countryman's powers of resistance.

Princes and *Zemindars* proved themselves, as a whole, ineffective as leaders, but rapacious as collectors of revenue, providing nothing for the rent they received. As province after province came under British rule, the first problem was how to deal with all those superior holders whom we may loosely call *Zemindars*, claiming rights over the land apart from the cultivators themselves. Mention has already been made of this difficulty in Bengal. It arose in Madras, the Deccan, and the North-West Province, as these were absorbed by Lord Wellesley and Lord Hastings. The two main questions were whether their vague territorial rights were to be acknowledged as equivalent to those of a landlord, and what financial arrangements were to be made with the *Zemindar* about land revenue, or with the *ryot* if the *Zemindar* was not recognized. Both were the subject of prolonged controversy in England as well as in India, and official practice has varied from one decade to another. In Bengal, the north of Madras, and later in Oudh and part of the North-West Province, the rights of superior holders were admitted, and the revenue was collected from them. This is the true *zemindari* system and is so styled. Over most of Madras and the west of India very few superior holders were recognized, and assessments were made directly upon the cultivator. This is the *ryotwari* system.[1] In the *zemindari* areas many revenue farmers of no long standing were elevated into landlords. In the *ryotwari* districts of Madras the Polygars, revenue officials 'whose actual condition had become changed to that of military rulers during the revolutions of power in the Deccan', were disregarded by Lord Wellesley.[2]

A change in the official outlook took place about the end of the eighteenth century. Sir John Shore and Thomas Law, the Collector of

---

[1] The correct spelling is *raiyatwari*, but the words *ryot* and *ryotwari* have become familiar.

[2] Fifth Report, 1812, p. 143.

Bihar, were in favour of encouraging 'a class of native gentlemen proprietors, who will gradually establish themselves in good houses, with
the various comforts of life'.[1] Cornwallis shared their view that agriculture needed landlords. To the Whig of that period it seemed right
that land should be rack-rented, and that a landed aristocracy should be
the leaders of the country. The keener officials of a later date, like Sir
Thomas Munro, could see little use in a parasitic land-owning class, and
since his time the tendency of the Civil Service has usually been towards
a direct assessment on the cultivator or upon the village community.
The *ryotwari* system entails harder work on officials, and requires a more
intimate knowledge of the country. It fitted in better with the euro-
peanized and more efficient type of administration which was built up
during the nineteenth century.

Other factors turned the balance against the *zemindari* system, except
in those areas, like Bengal, where by reason of physical conditions direct
assessment was very difficult. Each year of ordered government proved
more clearly the complicity of the *Zemindars* with the various robber
and murder gangs which infested the country, and experience showed
that it was almost impossible to give effective legal protection against
a rapacious landlord. The joint family system also does not help the
development of a landed aristocracy taking a direct personal interest
in their estates.

Controversy about the *zemindari* and *ryotwari* systems has often been
confused by the dispute over permanent and variable assessments.
There is no connection, for *zemindari* or *ryotwari* assessments can either
be made in perpetuity, or revised after a period of years. But it so happened that the one great permanent settlement was made by Lord Cornwallis in Bengal, the typically *zemindari* area. It was also extended to
a small part of Madras, but in the other provinces, as they came under
British rule, the land revenue was left as a revisable charge, and has remained so until to-day.[2] In most *ryotwari* areas each district is examined
every twenty or thirty years, and the land revenue is re-assessed by a
'settlement officer'. The arguments for and against a permanent settlement have filled volumes of official and unofficial literature. The subject
touches Indian administration at many points—the need for a more

[1] Mr. Law to the President and Members of the Revenue Board, October 4, 1778.
Quoted by Kaye, *op. cit.* 178.

[2] In 1927-8, 52 per cent. of the assessed area was held by *ryotwari* proprietors, and
18 per cent. by permanently, 30 per cent. by temporarily settled *Zemindars*. *India*,
1929-31, 128.

elastic revenue, the financial relations between the provinces and the central Government, the connection between land revenue and the incidence of famine, the respective rights over land of the State, the landlords, and the *ryots*. The controversy broke out afresh after the Mutiny, and during Curzon's term of office. It is likely to be a political issue under the new constitution; but during the period now under consideration the permanence of the assessment, though of interest to the *Zemindars*, was less important than the amount demanded.

The origin of land revenue can be traced to the share of one-sixth of the produce taken by Hindu kings. In practice this was usually raised to a fourth. The Muslims claimed the conqueror's right to take the infidel's land, and though this was remitted on payment of a land tax the idea of the State's rights being limited to a fixed proportion of the produce had virtually disappeared before British administration began. The Moguls had farmed out the revenue, exercising little control over the relations between the revenue farmers and the cultivators. The English when they came to Bengal saw little difference, as we have noticed, between this and their own landlord system. They assumed that the State was supreme landlord, and that for every parcel of ground there must be someone vested with a proprietary interest in the land with whom the Government could settle. Land revenue was considered as a rent rather than a tax, and the eighteenth-century Englishman was obsessed with the idea that no harm could follow from taking the highest rent obtainable. The crude economic theories of the time justified the belief that the money raised in this way represented the difference between the best land and the worst.

The history of the pre-Mutiny assessments is a series of unsuccessful efforts to extract an 'economic rent', which was frequently identified with the 'net produce'. The original auctioning of the Bengal revenue farms was an attempt to get as large a share as possible of the 'net produce'. The failure of this system led to the Permanent Settlement. In Madras and Bombay the original assessments were usually based on four-fifths of the estimated 'net produce'. This proved far too high. The first attempt to assess the North-West Provinces failed in the same way, and was abandoned in 1832. A new system had to be introduced whereby 'fair' rents were ascertained by empirical methods. The modern settlement officer has to examine the previous history of the area, the type of soil, the rainfall, communications, and markets. The 'net produce' principle was never applied to the Punjab, or Oudh, which came later under British rule. There is no doubt that much suffering was caused, both in Madras and Bombay, by the heavy assessments imposed during the first quarter of the nineteenth century, when the Government were striving to meet war expenses from revenue, and their staff was untrained, and sometimes (as at Coimbatore) was also corrupt. Even in the Punjab, where the British assessments reduced the former Sikh demands, 'it would seem that cash payments and rigidity of collection largely set off the advantage to the cultivator'.[1]

English theories about land, and the orderly collection of revenue in cash and on exact dates, were injurious to the *ryot* in several ways. The Whig idea that the payer of Government dues must have a proprietary interest in the land presented the *ryot* with a very embarrassing gift. Before the establishment of British rule he had no occupancy right, certainly none of which he could dispose. Under the new system, 'when a *ryot* has occupied and paid rent for land for two years, he is considered as its proprietor, and is, in fact, saddled with the rent of it as long as he can pay'.[2] When there was plenty of waste land, this right was chiefly a liability, and the peasant in the *ryotwari* areas often had to pay for land he was not cultivating.[3] Later, as population increased, occupancy right grew more valuable, and became the basis of the money-lender's influence, and of the immense agricultural debt of modern India. The peasant gained a proprietary right which he could sell or mortgage for cash, at a time when the village was being placed on a monetary basis. The British system hastened what was probably an inevitable change, but it meant the ascendancy of the village shop-keeper, who developed into a grain dealer and usurer. The *ryot* found himself in the position of the small peasant in nearly every part of the world. He was forced to dispose of part of his produce to meet a cash demand, and had only one channel through which to sell. He had to think of wealth in terms of money instead of as cattle or grain; money was a medium of which he knew little, which exposed him to the wiles of the shopkeeper and silversmith, the demands of the priest, and the depredations of the robber.

A subtle change in village life followed the introduction of British law. The Cornwallis Regulations were extended from Bengal to Madras

[1] H. Calvert, *Wealth and Welfare of the Punjab*, 122.

[2] Revenue letter from Court of Directors to the Government of Madras, January 22, 1822.

[3] Buchanan, *Journey from Madras* (London, 1807), ii. 309. Dr. Buchanan was deputed by Wellesley to tour South India in 1800. He is very critical about the stringency of the early assessments.

in 1802, and the British criminal and civil code followed gradually behind their armies. Much of the physical brutality of the old regime was
eliminated.

'The Tehsildar was stripped of his *ketticole* or hand torture, the stone
placed on the head in a burning sun, the stocks, and other of the former
insignia of office, by the display and occasional use of which he had been
enabled to saddle the ryots with the rents of such land as he deemed proper.' [1]

In theory the poorest Indian could seek redress in the courts. In practice
it was some decades before this had much effect. Criminal law has little
meaning unless enforced by an effective police force, or by organised
public opinion. India had neither. Until 1820 British energies and most
of the available personnel were absorbed in the Pindari and Maratha
wars. It was only from about 1830 that organised efforts were made to
deal with the robber and murder gangs, the dacoits and *thags*.

The evil traditions of eighteenth-century disorder were to last for
many years in the tyranny of the petty official, the criminal associations
of many *Zemindars* and independent princes, and in the rough lawlessness of most employers and landlords, whether Indian or English. The
possibilities of the new civil law only percolated slowly down to the
villages, and then would mean little except to the money-lending shopkeepers and the *Zemindars*. The right of distraint on a debtor by order
of court, the transferability of land, these were new ideas, and for many
years they merely served as a cumbrous and expensive substitute for
the '*ketticole*' and the stocks. The Whig philosophy, which believed
that ultimately no harm would arise from demanding a 'natural' rent,
could foresee no hardship in applying the idea of free trade in land and
commodities to India. It was some years, after the passing of the new
Regulations, before the Government prevented a *Zemindar* in Bengal
from distraining on the cooking pots and plough of a defaulting tenant.
Complete free trade in land was to last for much longer, justified
by the comfortable theory 'that the replacement of an owner who has
shown himself to be thriftless and incompetent by one with superior
intelligence and greater command of capital cannot be otherwise than
beneficial', a theory which dominated English policy throughout the
nineteenth century. From time to time it was modified by legislation
intended to prevent the exploitation of the *ryot* by the money-lender,
the inevitable result of the free disposal of land in a primitive agricul-

---

[1] *Report of Madras Board of Revenue*, quoted by Kaye, *Administration of East
India Company*, 225.

tural community; but this quotation, taken from an official memorandum published in 1895, illustrates the persistence of a theory which made the rule of law a very doubtful blessing to the cultivator.

The landless countrymen — shopkeepers, craftsmen, labourers, village servants, and outcastes—still number about two-fifths of the rural population. In earlier days the proportion was higher. The British occupation affected them in different ways. The shopkeepers gained most from the introduction of the cash nexus and the rule of law. They reaped the reward of literacy and a sedentary life. Village servants and labourers, restricted by caste conventions which tie them to certain occupations, have never been much more than village slaves. The British Government has seldom interfered with the caste system, but a rule of law before which men are theoretically equal has done something to improve the status of the lower castes, though they are still forbidden the use of village wells and temples. After 1840 the construction of canals, railways and roads absorbed many landless workers, who received cash wages comparing favourably with the returns from a peasant's holdings, but the growing pressure on the land blocked the easiest means of escape for menial castes. They had normally to follow their hereditary calling though their numbers might far exceed the demand for their services. The congestion which can occur in a prolific sub-caste may be brought home to the European reader by considering what would have happened if the smiths had been confined to their hereditary profession. The landless poor may have gained a little self-respect, but not much material advantage from British rule.

Craftsmen may be divided into two groups; those making the simple commodities needed in the villages, and the far smaller section who produce luxury articles for the wealthy or for export. Weavers are still a feature of Indian village life, numbering over three millions, and making a full quarter of the cotton goods consumed. For the century before the Mutiny they had almost a monopoly of the local market. Indian steam mills were just beginning to compete, and imports from abroad were unimportant. Cotton goods of this rough class were exported by the East India Company, though in small quantities. From 1820 the current of trade was reversed. Piece goods from the longer-stapled American cotton were sent from England, but again the total amount was insignificant, and reached only a small part of the peninsula. After 1860 the position changed rapidly. By that time twelve mills had opened in Bombay; while foreign trade and overland communications were developing rapidly. The hand-loom weaver found himself competing with the foreign and indigenous machine-made article at the moment when the American Civil War temporarily quadrupled the price of raw cotton. The decay of village weaving began under Crown Government.

The craftsmen engaged in making 'luxury' goods were affected in a different manner. They were concentrated in the larger towns, working in guilds, and each trade bore a close resemblance to the medieval 'mystery', in the manner of its regulation and insistence upon certain standards. Their customers were chiefly the princes and landed aristocracy, but there had been a certain export trade from the very earliest days of European civilisation. The delicate muslins from Dacca, silk *bandanas* from Murshidabad, brocades from Ahmadabad, shawls from Kashmir, brass ornaments from Tanjore, enamelling, damascening, and *bidri* work from the Punjab were all intended primarily for a leisured aristocratic class in India, and being exported to Europe helped to build up the unhappy European tradition of the 'gorgeous East'.[1] The anarchy of the eighteenth century, the partial monopolisation of foreign trade by the East India Company, the social changes in India due to British rule, were bound to influence these crafts, but it would seem that most of them were decaying even before the battle of Plassey.

The export trade suffered first. Information about the extent and character of the old caravan trade through Aleppo is not very reliable, but when the western European countries captured the Eastern trade in the seventeenth century the business consisted in the exchange of bullion, metals, and woollen goods, for spices, cotton and silk goods, indigo, and other tropical products. Bullion formed two-thirds of the exports from Europe, and manufactured articles about a third of the returning imports. The total trade was much affected by frequent wars in Europe, but towards the latter end of the seventeenth century English imports from the East averaged about half a million pounds, and England had become the *entrepôt* for much of the European trade. About half the imports and nearly all of the manufactured goods were re-exported.

By 1700 the total imports from India to England amounted to £787,731, and the Dutch imports were rather over £100,000. The end of the seventeenth century marks the highest point in the export of silk and cotton goods. It was an extremely profitable business for the Company, and in 1672

'several artificers such as throwsters, weavers, and dyers were sent over by the Company with great quantities of English patterns, to teach Indian

[1] Indian muslins found their way to ancient Greece, under the name of *gangetika*.

weavers new methods of manufacturing goods suitable to English and European markets'.[1]

The export of manufactured goods began to decline during the first half of the eighteenth century. The fifty years which preceded Plassey were marked by a growing movement in all European countries against Indian imports. The most powerful argument, especially applicable in war-time, was the 'mercantilist' objection to exporting bullion, but there was also a strong feeling, much exploited by the enemies of the Company in England, that good money was being sent out of the country in exchange for mere luxuries.[2] There were other factors, of which the most important was the growth of silk and cotton manufactures in Europe, but opposition to Eastern imports was based on the need for sumptuary laws as much as on the idea of 'protection'. From the beginning of the seventeenth century there was a struggle between the Company and the Government, which culminated in the total prohibition of Indian silks and painted calicoes in 1720. After about 1710 the greater part of the Company's Eastern manufactured goods was intended for re-export to Europe, a trade which continued for many years after the English had become territorial rulers, but steadily declined as other countries developed their own manufactures.

The ruin of this *entrepôt* trade occurred rapidly towards the end of the eighteenth century, and during the early nineteenth century. Certain historians have given the impression that after the occupation of Bengal the export of manufactured goods from India was deliberately discouraged. This idea seems to be due to mistaken chronology. The British Government continued, but did not intensify, its old policy of protection and prohibition. The English consumption of cotton goods had never been an important factor. The cold climate and small population of eighteenth-century England prevented it being a good market. The Company did its best to encourage the lucrative re-export trade.

---

[1] Bal Krishna, *Commercial Relations between India and England*, 1601-1757, p. 140. The reader is referred to this valuable monograph for further information.

[2] This was a very old complaint against Eastern trade. Gibbon, writing of the later Roman Empire, says, 'The objects of oriental traffic were splendid and trifling. . . . As the natives of Arabia and India were contented with the productions and manufactures of their own country, silver, on the side of the Romans, was the principal, if not the only instrument of commerce. It was a complaint worthy of the gravity of the Senate, that in the purchase of female ornaments, the wealth of the state was irrecoverably given away to foreign and hostile nations.'—*The Decline and Fall of the Roman Empire*, chap. ii. He refers to a speech by Tiberius given in Tacitus, *Annals*.

There are even signs that it wished to hamper the English production of cotton goods, which had begun to compete in the foreign market. In 1786 orders were given that 'for prudential reasons . . . no more cotton yarn was to be sent from India to England either as part of the Investment or in private trade'.[1] These efforts had little effect. The French revolutionary wars, which completely dislocated the European markets, were followed by a period of economic nationalism, of high tariffs and low purchasing power. The Company strove to combat these tendencies in England, but was powerless abroad. Markets were lost in the New as well as the Old World, and the opening of the Eastern trade to private merchants in 1815 made no difference. Exports to America fell from 13,633 bales in 1801 to 258 in 1829, those to Denmark from 1457 to 150 in the same period. Indian exports to England were gradually reduced to certain tropical products, to spices, drugs, dyes, and fibres, the most important being tea and coffee, indigo and lac, cotton and silk. A similar tendency is to be found in the trade of the Danish Company throughout the period.

The movement of bullion eastwards decreased rapidly for a quarter of a century after Plassey, though it began again towards the end of the century;[2] but it is difficult to estimate the effect upon the craftsmen. We have no real knowledge about the distribution of the bullion which came to India in the early eighteenth century, and very little about the condition of the weavers who worked for the export trade at that time. The Company in its earlier days merely bought through the usual agents, and when they substituted their own *gomastas* it would seem that this was more to get the type of article required than to drive a still harder bargain with the weaver. The Company's servants were not good masters, but they only followed the existing custom when they got the weavers into their debt by means of advances, and then kept them working. They followed what had become the practice in India during

---

[1] Bengal public letter from Court of Directors, April 12, 1786. Further quotations from this important letter are given in Aspinall, *Cornwallis in Bengal*, 181.

[2] Between 1758 and 1783 bullion from England amounted to just under £400,000, but from 1784 to 1807 over £8,000,000 was exported in bullion. India, of course, did not 'begin to pay for imports in food grains', as stated by R. C. Dutt in his *Economic History of British India*, 296. Except for small quantities of rice and sugar, no food was exported from India to Europe until the opening of the Suez Canal. This, combined with the extension of irrigation in the Punjab, led to the development of the wheat trade from 1870 onwards. Previous exports of wheat had been less than 800 tons yearly. The journey round the Cape made it impracticable to send bulky and perishable articles.

2 E

its disorders, and were probably neither better nor worse than other Indian employers, though there was certainly some desertion of weavers from their factories. Verelst, in 1767, talks of weavers 'deserting their profession to seek for subsistence from a less precarious calling', but this was mentioned as a result of the decreasing demand for export which had already begun to operate.[1] There is no satisfactory evidence as to whether the English either lowered or raised the standard of treatment of the weavers by those who employed them or bought from them. It was not a subject which much interested their contemporaries. The Company did its utmost to keep alive a decaying industry, but it probably paid as little as it could for its commodities, and the type of covenanted servant in the eighteenth century was not likely to enquire too closely into the actions of his agents.[2]

Exports never absorbed more than a small fraction of the luxury trades. Changes in fashion and the anarchy of eighteenth-century India were far more potent factors in the decay of craftsmanship than the loss of the European and American markets. Industries which cater for the wealthy and for the courtier must be the first to suffer during such troubled times as followed the accession of Aurangzeb, and continued until the establishment of British rule. The specialised craftsmen of those times were dependent on a very limited market, usually the patronage of a court, or the pilgrim traffic. The lack of roads and bridges, the prevalence of dacoity, and the multitude of internal customs discouraged the movement of goods, most of which were hardly known outside a small area. During the eighteenth century, when one State after another suffered a temporary eclipse or fell into the hands of some adventurer, the withdrawal of all patronage would damage many crafts irretrievably; and the process continued when courts such as that of the Nawabs of Oudh at Lucknow finally disappeared. Apart from these violent dislocations of industry, there was a steady decrease in the demand for this very elaborate Oriental work, much of which was only suitable for a feudal method of living. The new types of wealthy Indian, the business

[1] Letter to Directors, March 17, 1767.

[2] It is unfortunate that a story about the cutting off of weavers' thumbs has been used to typify the Company's treatment of those engaged in the silk trade. The matter is discussed in a recent work, *Economic Annals of Bengal*, by J. C. Sinha, where it is shown that the story takes two forms, neither of which can be justified by any evidence. The idea was probably originally based on a quotation from a contemporary book, *Considerations on Indian Affairs*, by W. Bolts, who was dismissed from the Company's service and returned to England to carry on a campaign against its monopoly.

men, the europeanised officials, the successful money-lenders, were not good patrons, and even in those Indian States which have been least touched by European influence the ancient crafts have long been in a moribund condition. The British occupation hastened, but not very markedly, a process which had already taken place in Europe.

CHAPTER V

NATURE AND ORIGIN OF THE MUTINY

Importance of Mutiny in Indian history: previous disaffection in army: relation of Mutiny to other wars: origin of revolt: the dispossessed: Hindu grievances: Muslim discontent: state of Bengal army: immediate reasons for outbreak: greased cartridges: Barrackpur mutiny.

AN extensive literature has grown up round the Mutiny. Every incident has been described at length, the most minute engagements and the conduct of comparatively obscure individuals have been the subject of long controversies. The fierce light thrown upon each detail has put the whole struggle out of focus. Further distortion followed because most accounts have been written from the English standpoint after racial antagonisms had been aroused by accusations of atrocities and of treachery. The conventional view of the Mutiny was developed during an era when European ascendency and the superiority of Western civilisation were not seriously challenged, when many features of the Company's rule had been forgotten, and when few Englishmen had any experience of war. The present generation should be able to see the events of 1857 and 1858 in better perspective.

They were more important in their indirect results than in themselves. There was much hard fighting, including many exciting and some appalling incidents, but all on a very small scale. It was a domestic affair. No seaport was seriously threatened, and no foreign Power intervened.[1] Afghanistan, under Dost Muhammad, was strictly neutral. Nepal allowed her Gurkhas to be freely recruited, and a Nepalese force, under

---

[1] A possible exception was Persia, with which the Government had been at war until May 1856. Persian envoys, probably unofficial, visited Bahadur Shah at Delhi.

the Minister Jang Bahadur, joined Sir Colin Campbell before Lucknow. The frontier tribesmen remained comparatively quiet, watching the outcome of the struggle. Less than a third of the peninsula was seriously disturbed, though there was general excitement, due partly to the widespread belief that 1857—the centenary of Plassey—would mark a change in Indian history.

The Mutiny may be considered either as a military revolt, or as a bid for recovery of their property and privileges by dispossessed princes and landlords, or as an attempt to restore the Mogul Empire, or as a peasants' war. From every aspect it was localised, restricted, and unorganised. Only one of the three provincial armies rebelled, and it is doubtful if a quarter of the sepoys were ever in arms against the Government. Estimates of rebel forces at Delhi and elsewhere suggest that, as each regiment mutinied, many sepoys drifted back to their villages. No important prince threw in his lot with the rebels, and many, like Patiala, actively helped the Government. Of the thousands of landlords who had lost their property through the Inam Commission, or through changes in Oudh and the North-West Provinces, only the *Talukdars* of Oudh made any concerted attempt to help the mutineers, and they did not decide for some months. Of the fifty million Muslims in India scarcely three out of every ten thousand can have rallied to their restored Emperor. In a few areas, which had suffered from very high assessments, the villagers helped the mutineers, but nowhere was there anything approaching a *jacquerie*. The ordinary administration continued to function everywhere south of the Narmada, and in most of Bengal and the Punjab. Troops, Indian as well as British, were sent from Madras and Bombay to join in the work of repression. In the recently annexed Punjab the Bengal army regiments mutinied or were disarmed, and the Cis-Satlej districts were affected; but a mobile column under Nicholson was spared to help in the siege of Delhi, and many Sikhs and Muslims were enlisted. Even in the North-West Provinces, where the severest fighting took place, only an insignificant section of the population took any active part.[1]

The Mutiny resembled some medieval civil war, or the early campaigns in Bengal. Minute armies operated amongst a population which was probably sympathetic with one side, but was disarmed and chiefly anxious to be left in peace. When the Meerut garrison mutinied and marched to Delhi there were scarcely 40,000 effective British troops in

[1] The North-West Provinces, part of the modern United Provinces, must not be confused with the present North-West Frontier Province.

India.[1] When Havelock marched to the relief of Lucknow, through a country treated as hostile, he had under two thousand men, an army smaller than Clive had taken to Plassey.[2] Within four months a portion of the 40,000 British troops, with the help of some Madras regiments, a small force of Gurkhas, and the hastily raised Sikh and Muslim levies, had broken the back of the rebellion. Delhi was recaptured, Lucknow relieved, and all serious hopes of a successful revolution had been abandoned. Reinforcements from Europe arrived, and joined in hunting down those in arms against the Government, but they were not sufficient to alter the scale of the fighting.

It is not immediately obvious why the Mutiny should have had such a powerful influence upon later generations of Indians and English. Both races had seen fierce and even desperate fighting during the preceding half-century. Sixteen years earlier the Indian army had suffered an overwhelming disaster in Afghanistan. Subsequently the Government had been engaged upon the conquest of Sind, the two Sikh wars, and the second Burmese war. Nor were mutinies unknown in the Company's army. As early as 1766 a regiment of the newly raised Bengal army rebelled, and twenty-four ringleaders were blown from guns. The outbreak at Vellore, in 1806, was more serious, and had certain analogies with 1857. There were the same rumours of India being forcibly converted to Christianity. Leather cockades[3] took the place of greased cartridges, and the intrigues of Tipu's children formed a parallel to those of the Nana Sahib and the King of Oudh. Three years later came the famous White Mutiny, one of numerous occasions when the Company's European troops set an example of organised insubordination. During the next fifty years there was periodic disaffection in the Indian army, chiefly due to disputes about pay and prospects, and about liability to serve either abroad or in those outlying parts of the country which were then being brought under the Company's rule. The first Burmese war led to the mutiny amongst high-caste sepoys at Barrackpur, who feared they would be sent overseas. After massacre by gunfire, the regiment was disbanded.

[1] Immediately before the Mutiny the British troops, including invalids and some non-combatant services, numbered 45,522. Indian troops amounted to 232,224. The total population of India was probably about two hundred million.

[2] Havelock's 'field state' before his first engagement was 1404 Europeans, 561 Indians.

[3] The cockade of cow or pig skin might endanger the caste of a Hindu or affront the religion of a Muslim.

This severity discouraged such manifestations for some years, but the Afghan war was followed by a marked deterioration in discipline. Four Bengal regiments refused to march to Sind, and in 1844 two regiments mutinied on the Sikh frontier. Similar trouble, mostly about *batta* or allowances, occurred in the Madras army. After the second Sikh war Napier believed that twenty-four regiments were on the point of rising. In 1849 four regiments refused to draw their pay, and one regiment was sent to Multan in a state bordering on mutiny. In 1850 the 66th Infantry rebelled, but were crushed by some Indian cavalry, and the regiment was disbanded. The general feeling of insecurity was not lessened by the open dispute between the Commander-in-Chief and Lord Dalhousie, which ended in Napier's resignation and his alarmist statements about the condition of the army. Subsequently, in 1852, the 38th Regiment refused to march when ordered to Burma. These facts were possibly ignored in England. It was a point of honour amongst British officers of the sepoy regiments to resent vehemently any aspersions on the discipline of their troops, but the deep impression made by the Mutiny can hardly be ascribed to the unprecedented disloyalty of the native army.[1]

Two factors differentiated the Mutiny from the host of 'little wars' which the English fought in Asia and Africa during the nineteenth century. In most of these the final issue was never seriously in doubt, but for four months during the summer of 1857 it seemed that the Mutiny might develop into a real war of independence, which would make reconquest impossible.[2] By September it was clear that the Indians who

---

[1] The absence of serious disaffection in the Indian army after its reorganisation has obscured the extreme dissatisfaction with which most officers, especially of the British army, viewed the state of the Company's forces. This could not be expressed openly. 'An officer would be persecuted, hunted down, ruined, who dared to tell the truth': Russell, *My Diary in India*, i. 267. Lord Dalhousie had no illusions on this subject. 'The discipline of the army, from top to bottom, officers and men alike, is scandalous', he wrote in a letter to the President of the Board of Control, and he repeatedly urged the need for more European troops. See Lee-Warner, *Life of the Marquess of Dalhousie*, ii. chap. viii.

[2] Paradoxically it is an article of faith amongst Indian nationalists to describe the Mutiny as a war of independence. This may be due to the proscription of Savarkar's *War of Indian Independence of 1857*, a book which states the Indian case with force, but with little critical acumen. It is a poor compliment to Indian courage and ability to treat this revolt as an organised national movement. It was repressed by a minute force. Its leaders, when in a position to prove their competence as rulers, were a failure. Historical accuracy, as well as respect for Indian ability, makes it requisite to stress the small part taken in the revolt by the better elements in the country.

were in revolt were incapable of working to any settled plan, or of subordinating themselves to a national leader. Their prestige was waning, and their commanders had proved themselves incompetent except in guerilla warfare. The course of the revolt had, however, shown the weakness of the English hold on India. This aspect of the Mutiny was never forgotten, and its memory was to influence every branch of the administration. Even more important was the nature of the fighting. Colonial wars against disorganised levies and uncivilised governments are invariably conducted with considerable savagery and degenerate into something like the suppression of a servile revolt. Non-combatants, including women and children, are ill-treated and occasionally murdered, their houses and villages are burnt. Prisoners are executed, and sometimes mutilated; or are tortured either by prolonging the agony of their death or by some act the religious significance of which might endanger their future immortality.[1]

Such disregard of the elementary rules of civilised warfare characterised nearly every campaign fought by European Powers outside Europe. The English public knew little about these happenings. They had forgotten that wars, unless fought by highly disciplined troops obeying strict conventions, involve looting and house burning, much indiscriminate slaughtering, sieges which cause intense suffering to women and children, occasional rape and other bestialities. Information could only come from officers who might feel sufficiently strongly to risk their professional career, or from the few newspaper correspondents who might be present and were prepared to take the unpopular line of criticising their countrymen's conduct of a war.[2] The Indian revolt occurred in a settled country; English as well as Indian women and children were implicated; and the course of the Mutiny was closely followed by millions of educated Indians. From the first it was fought with peculiar savagery. The rebellious sepoys knew they would get no quarter if captured. Those in arms against the Government soon learnt that it was not only death they had to fear. The British troops were 'sewing Mohammadans in pig-skins, smearing them with pork-fat before execution, and burning their bodies, and forcing Hindus to defile themselves'.[3] The mutineers rapidly lost their military discipline, and

---

[1] The Hindu is specially susceptible to this kind of suggestion, as he believes that dismemberment or ceremonial defilement ruin his prospects after death.

[2] The second Afghan war illustrates these points.

[3] Russell, *My Diary in India*, ii. 43. The author was correspondent for the *Times*.

collected round them a rabble of Pathans, as well as the worst elements from the slums of Delhi, Cawnpore, and Lucknow, and from the criminal tribes. On the British side the Company's own British troops included some of the toughest and most hard-bitten soldiers in the world.[1] The suggestion has been made in recent histories that the conduct of the fighting underwent a complete change after the massacre of Cawnpore. This event caused a great stir in England, and added to the ferocity with which the revolt was suppressed; but the lines along which mutineers and unfriendly non-combatants were to be treated had been decided within three weeks after the outbreak, and the war was from the first fought without any regard for the ordinary rules of civilised warfare. It will be necessary to revert to this subject in the next chapter.

Apart from the feelings aroused by the nature of the fighting, the year 1857 is rightly considered as a turning-point in Indian history. By revealing the instability of the Company's rule, the Mutiny completely altered the system of government and the outlook of the administration. It is important therefore to consider not only the conditions which now appear to have engendered the revolt, but also the contemporary views of its origin. The end of Lord Dalhousie's administration had been marked by a vague but general feeling of unrest. Nearly every class had been affected by recent innovations, by social and administrative changes, by the expensive thoroughness of the Government, and by the impact of Western ideas. The princes and the landed classes had the strongest reasons for fearing this reformist spirit. The Englishman in India is often impelled by his conscience as a good administrator to advocate measures which would seem extremely socialistic to his compatriots in England. Few members of the Civil Service viewed with equanimity the congeries of feudal States which had been allowed to survive under inefficient and sometimes degenerate chiefs. Equally obnoxious to the revenue officers were the landed estates within British territory, held on uncertain tenure by descendants of the Mogul revenue collectors. These men, though virtually landlords, had little of the public spirit which might justify their kind in Europe. On such points Lord Dalhousie, the Liberal, was at one with John Lawrence. They had no wish to extend the frontiers of India, but they wanted within the

---

[1] They must not be confused with the regular 'Queen's regiments' which were in India or were sent as reinforcements. The Company's European troops were specially recruited, no questions being asked so long as the men were physically fit. They had much in common with the French Foreign Legion.

peninsula a free peasantry, directly under a unitary government, standardized and homogeneous except for a few large States, which would remain nominally independent, but under some kind of tutelage.

With this ideal in view Dalhousie took every opportunity of mediatizing the smaller subordinate States and expropriating landlords with doubtful titles. For the first he used his legal prerogative of not recognising the right of adoption, and annexed Satara, Jhansi, Nagpur and other minor States, as already described. His second object he achieved by appointing the Inam Commission, which had the unpopular duty of investigating titles of landowners and confiscated some twenty thousand estates in the Deccan. Theoretically the general policy was justifiable. Small States are an anachronism. India has suffered (and may suffer more) from the reversal of policy after the Mutiny which has perpetuated hundreds of tiny principalities. Indian agriculture cannot really support the parasitic millions, landlords and princelets, who have survived under post-Mutiny conditions. Dalhousie's action was, however, too drastic. The Government had certain disabilities for carrying out such reforms. It was foreign and expensive, and had been at no pains to enlist public support. Few Indians would feel that a measure of confiscation, though it brought revenue to the State, was necessarily a contribution to the common weal. The tradition of the 'tribute' was to survive for many more decades. Innate conservatism and ancient loyalties, which delay agrarian reforms in Europe, were reinforced in India by racial feelings. The vast scale of these operations, the linguistic and legal complications, and the general illiteracy, led inevitably to individual cases of gross injustice which the Government did little to rectify. No attempt was made to mollify the feelings aroused. Much of the bitterness caused by the final and greatest annexation, that of Oudh, could have been avoided by adopting the advice of Sleeman and Henry Lawrence, who proposed that the land revenue should be devoted to local administration, and the balance given to support the royal family.

The effect of these dynastic and territorial expropriations was to leave, scattered over the country, a large number of princes and landowners who felt themselves deeply aggrieved, and whose followers and retainers saw themselves threatened by ruin. Some of the dispossessed were conspiring against the Government before the Mutiny, and supplied the only effective leadership after its outbreak. Chief amongst them were the ex-King of Oudh's very capable adviser, Ahmad Ullah, the 'Moulvi of Faizabad'; Dandu Pant, adopted son of the former

Peshwa, who claimed unsuccessfully to be allowed his father's pension, and became notorious as the Nana Sahib; Nana Sahib's nephew, Rao Sahib, and his retainers, Tantia Topi and Azimulla Khan; the Rani of Jhansi; the octogenarian Rajput, Kunwar Singh, whose estates had been lost owing to the unjustified severity of the Board of Revenue; Firoz Shah, a kinsman and dependent of the Mogul 'Emperor' Bahadur Shah. This list of the dispossessed and their followers contains the name of nearly every capable rebel leader, except Khan Bahadur Khan, who was a pensioner.

A larger section of the population had less specific grievances against the British. The higher castes saw a new civilization being introduced which lowered their standing and threatened their sodality. The Government was universally suspected of wishing to convert India to Christianity, the first step being the destruction of caste and of the traditional Hindu family life. Amongst the sedentary classes secular education, extended by then to both sexes, was undermining the influence of the family priest. Inventions, such as the railway and the telegraph, suggested to the lower castes that the foreigners possessed occult knowledge hidden from the Brahmin. Their old and holy land was being disturbed, and even the sacred Ganges was tapped for irrigation purposes. In the new factories and in railway carriages the castes were working and sitting cheek by jowl. The introduction of an efficient but common messing system into the gaols was considered another attack on caste. The unwarranted optimism of certain missionaries lent some colour to this belief, which was sedulously fostered by active opponents of the Government. The abolition of suttee, though it had been in force for over twenty years, had never been accepted by the orthodox, and further legislation aroused their indignation. The Religious Disabilities Act of 1850 protected the civil rights of converts from Hinduism. The Hindu Widows' Remarriage Act of 1856 removed legal obstacles to these unhallowed unions. These Acts caused the greater anger and alarm because they entrenched upon the customary Hindu law of inheritance, suggesting that the Government was prepared to destroy the civil law of the Hindus as it had previously disregarded their conceptions of criminal justice.[1]

Most contemporary histories, letters, and diaries dilate upon the

[1] As, for example, in refusing to allow a money payment in murder cases, or to recognise caste distinctions in punishing offences. Few Hindus accepted the view, so contrary to the laws of Manu, that the murder of a Sudra by a Brahmin was an offence comparable with the murder of a Brahmin by a Sudra.

racial bitterness displayed by the Muslims, who were usually assumed to be the real instigators of the Mutiny. It is difficult to explain the view, held almost universally amongst the British, that the 'mild Hindu' was suffering from some temporary aberration, but that the Muslim was our implacable foe. Undoubtedly the upper class Muhammadans had their grievances against a Government which had superseded the Mogul Empire, and then introduced educational standards favourable to the Hindu. Muslim domination in previous centuries had been based on a small number of Central Asian immigrants, backed by many million converts, drawn from the lower castes. Neither section found life too easy under the new regime. The Muslim *ryots* were the chief sufferers from the supremacy which English law gave to the Hindu moneylender. The disabilities of educated Muslims were enhanced by the religious ordinance which made their children spend some years in learning the Koran. It does not, however, seem that Muslims took a leading part in the Mutiny.

Possibly too much importance was attached to the machinations of the Wahabi sect, whose wandering Moulvis were active before as well as after the Mutiny. There is no evidence to suggest that the restoration of Bahadur Shah was part of an organised Muslim plot. Sepoys, Hindu as well as Muslim, seem to have regarded him as the rightful Emperor, though it is doubtful whether many seriously believed that the Company's 'treason' justified rebellion, though this was afterwards asserted.[1] From the first the mutineers treated Bahadur Shah with contempt. Firoz Shah, the most enterprising member of his household, was in Persia when the Mutiny began, and returned to lead only some of the revolted soldiery from Indore and Gwalior. Khan Bahadur Khan, a Government pensioner, set himself up as Viceroy at Bareilly, and established Muhammadan rule in Rohilkhand. Apart from these two, few Muhammadans of any standing were openly against the Government. Haidarabad, the leading Muslim State, was the scene of much intrigue, but under the guidance of the Nizam's Minister, Salar Jang, neither its inhabitants nor its troops took any part in the Mutiny. The bulk of the mutineers were Hindu.

India has always contained important groups with grievances against the Government, and too much weight can be attached to these vague causes for discontent, many of which could be paralleled at any period of the British occupation. Without a lead from the soldiers it is unlikely

---

[1] See F. W. Buckland's *The Political Theory of the Indian Mutiny*, and subsequent controversy in the *Transactions of the Royal Historical Society*, vii.

that any dissident group would have organised an armed revolt, though probably the grievances of the *Talukdars* and of the disbanded State soldiers in Oudh were sufficiently acute to have led to a local and easily suppressed rising.[1] Even when the mutineers won their first successes, and there were hardly any British troops between Calcutta and Delhi, the *Talukdars* held their hand for some months. On the other hand, discipline was deteriorating so rapidly in the Bengal army that, apart from the greased cartridges, almost any incident might have caused an outbreak.

The Bengal army was not recruited in Bengal, but in the North-West Provinces, and in certain States. Oudh alone contributed 40,000 men. Many of the sepoys belonged to 'twice-born' castes, and were allowed a deference neither conducive to discipline nor compatible with military efficiency. In this, and also in retaining the rule of promotion by seniority, Bengal was more conservative than Bombay or Madras. The army was a survival of the sepoy force raised experimentally to over-awe the Company's first neighbours, and its organization had never been brought up to date. It was totally unsuited for defending the new and turbulent North-West Frontier, for garrisoning distant and in-salubrious parts of India like Sind, or for service in Burma and over-seas. These limitations were recognised by the Government, but instead of reforming the old army they relied upon building up a new army drawn from Sikhs, Punjabi Muslims, Gurkhas, and races not formerly available. The one departure from this policy was in 1856, when Lord Canning, finding it almost impossible to get regiments to serve in Burma, made a fundamental change. He insisted upon a General Service Enlistment Act, under which all future recruits had to undertake to march wherever ordered. The Bengal sepoys saw their privileged position being undermined, and they had other grievances arising out of the Government's new economy and efficiency. Invalid pensions were no longer paid to those unfit for foreign service, and postal privileges were curtailed. The annexation of Oudh was doubly unpopular. Many sym-pathised with the ruling house, and sepoys from an Indian State had certain privileges not enjoyed by those from British India.[2] Those who came from the North-West Provinces were affected by the recent agrarian disputes, and by Thomason's heavy land assessments.

[1] The disbanded State army numbered about 80,000 men. They had already rioted in parts of Oudh before the mutiny at Meerut.

[2] For these advantages see Kaye and Malleson, *History of the Indian Mutiny*, i. 254.

As members of 'twice-born' castes the sepoys fully shared the general suspicion of European innovations and of the supposed Christianizing enthusiasm of the Government. As professional soldiers they could not but be alarmed by certain developments in the Punjab and elsewhere. Formed at a time when the Company was only one of many 'war lords', the Bengal army had become a kind of military sub-caste, with exaggerated ideas of their own importance and of British dependence upon their aid. They strongly objected to being merely part of an imperial army, drawn from all the races of the peninsula, with no potential enemies except beyond the frontier. The temptation to mutiny before this new army came into being was intensified by the small number of British troops in Eastern India, and by ludicrously distorted ideas about the strength of England.[1] Throughout the vast area normally garrisoned by the Bengal army there was hardly one British soldier to twenty-five sepoys. The remainder had been withdrawn for the Crimean war, or for service in the Punjab. No British regiment was stationed in Oudh, in spite of its disturbed condition, nor at Delhi, though the old Emperor still personified the Mogul tradition and his palace, with its 5000 retainers, overlooked the magazine. This great ammunition 'dump' of Northern India was in the charge of two officers and six British sergeants. Between Calcutta and Allahabad the only British regiment was at Dinapur. The dissidents could point to this weakness, and play upon the sepoy's ignorance by suggesting that England could not spare any troops for reinforcements but was dependent upon the new Indian army, to which many of their keenest officers had been drafted.

At the end of 1856 the Bengal army was sullen, insubordinate, and on the verge of rebellion. 'A consciousness of power', wrote the Commissioner of Meerut, 'had grown up in the army which could only be exorcised by mutiny, and the cry of the cartridge brought the latent spirit of revolt into action'.[2] When the Government introduced the new Enfield rifle, its use, which entailed biting a greased cartridge, provided exactly the type of grievance best calculated to bring discontent to a head. The sepoys believed with some justification that the grease was made from cow or pig fat, and without any justification that this was a deliberate attempt to break the caste of the Hindus and affront

---

[1] It was widely believed that most Englishmen had already migrated to India.

[2] Letter to Colvin, dated September 24, 1857. *Enclosures to Secret Letters from India*, 455-6.

the religion of the Muslims.[1] In spite of this incitement and the shadowy activities of emissaries of the King of Oudh and the Nana Sahib, the army only drifted slowly from insubordination to armed rebellion. The cartridges had been issued to several regiments before their use led to disturbances and incendiarism at Barrackpur. The agents of the King of Oudh, then living at Calcutta, probably helped to foment this trouble in the 34th Infantry, but the first refusal to obey orders occurred in the 19th Infantry at Berhampur on February 26, 1857. There were no British troops there, but the regiment marched quietly down to Barrackpur and was disbanded under the eyes of a British regiment, hastily brought from Rangoon. The 34th was also disbanded, but not till May 6, though their offences had been far more serious. Lord Canning, misled by the pathetic confidence which the British officers placed in their sepoys, treated this double outbreak as an isolated case, and allowed five weeks to pass before enforcing the order upon a regiment which had then got completely out of hand, the guard even refusing to help when their adjutant was shot and other officers were threatened by a sepoy—the Mangal Pandi, whose exploit gave the mutineers the nickname of 'pandies'. The delay and mildness of the punishment may have encouraged the growing insubordination amongst the sepoys; but the first act, which converted spasmodic mutiny into armed rebellion, occurred at Meerut after a refusal to use the cartridges had been followed by a court-martial, and by the severe sentences of ten years' imprisonment upon eighty-five troopers of the 3rd Cavalry.

[1] The first cartridges sent out for instructional purposes were covered with lard. The mistake was recognised and mutton fat substituted, but explanations were complicated and delayed. Anson, the Commander-in-Chief, wrote to Canning, 'I am not surprised at their objections to the cartridges, having seen them. I had no idea they contained, or rather are smeared with, such a quantity of grease, which looks exactly like fat.' Lord Roberts himself refers to 'the incredible disregard of the soldiers' religious prejudices'.—*Forty-one Years in India*, i. 94.

CHAPTER VI

THE MUTINY

Meerut mutiny: Delhi: weakness of rebel organisation: the Punjab: support from the south: nature of fighting: Cawnpore: fall of Delhi and relief of Lucknow: punitive campaigns of Colin Campbell and Rose: guerilla warfare.

ON Sunday evening, May 10, the day following the degradation and imprisonment of the Meerut troopers, the three Indian regiments at that station shot their officers, broke open the gaol, and after releasing their companions set out with their arms along the road to Delhi, some thirty miles away. The moment was propitious, and no serious attempt was made by the British troops to cut off their retreat.[1] The general confusion was increased by a crowd from the Meerut bazaar, which came, plundering and burning, into the cantonment. The next morning the first mutineers had reached Delhi. Some went to the palace and proclaimed Bahadur Shah Emperor. Others approached the three Indian regiments, which mutinied, murdered their officers, and joined in killing any Europeans they could find. An attack was made on the magazine, but the Englishmen in charge, finding themselves overwhelmed, blew up what they could. It was a courageous deed, which incidentally caused heavy loss to their enemy; but a considerable amount of ammunition remained undestroyed. Within twenty-four hours of the outbreak, Delhi was held by over five thousand armed soldiers. They had as their nominal leader the aged Bahadur Shah, whose name still conjured up to millions the past glories of the Mogul Empire.

The opening of the rebellion was remarkably successful, but it was soon apparent that no one opposed to the Government was capable of pressing home the advantage, though the British position in Northern India was sufficiently precarious. The hot weather had set in. Anson, the Commander-in-Chief, and his staff were at Simla. The available British troops were insignificant in number, and not mobilised. Neither transport nor supplies were ready. British forces in 1857 were little more mobile than a hundred years before. Communications were still rudimentary. Roads were few and bad, and not more than two or

[1] There were two British regiments, one infantry and one cavalry, at Meerut, and some British artillery. General Hewett, who was in command, has been much blamed for not despatching troops to Delhi before the mutineers had consolidated their position.

three hundred miles of railway had been laid. The Calcutta line ran 120 miles to Raniganj, the Bombay line only as far as Thana. The one recent improvement had been the linking up of the chief cities and garrison towns by telegraph lines. For some reason these wires—which sepoys afterwards allowed were 'the strings that hanged us'—were never systematically cut. If any able and energetic Indian had enjoyed the confidence of the sepoys he could have established a rebel government over most of British India between the Narmada and the Satlej, and destroyed or masked the few British troops in that area. This would have emboldened and attracted the dissident and wavering elements amongst the States and the neighbouring provinces. Three weeks elapsed, and then came a fresh crop of military revolts and civil disorder in nearly every garrison town throughout the North-West Provinces, Oudh, and Central India. But there were still no signs of leadership or of well-ordered plans. Over a large area the machinery of government was destroyed, but nothing set up in its place. The first instinct of the sepoys was to take the road to Delhi. Usually, but not always, they killed their own British officers, but they did not attack British regiments. In three or four cases a leader had sufficient force of character to win over the mutineers, and use them locally. The Nana Sahib called back the Cawnpore mutineers to surround Wheeler's little force of four hundred Englishmen, and at Lucknow the rebellious troops remained to fight and finally blockade Sir Henry Lawrence with a thousand British soldiers and seven hundred 'loyal' sepoys. The Rani of Jhansi, widow of the Raja whose State had been annexed, persuaded the mutinied garrison to accept her as leader and defend her capital. Khan Bahadur Khan at Bareilly set himself up as Viceroy. At a later date Kunwar Singh collected the Dinapur mutineers to carry on a guerilla warfare in Bihar. Over the rest of the area in revolt the sepoys either drifted towards Delhi or formed themselves into marauding bands.

The first weeks gave evidence of fatal weaknesses amongst those in arms against the Government. Regional and religious disunity showed itself in the absence of any co-ordination amongst the leaders. Even at Delhi, neither of the rival commanders, Mirza Mughal and Bakht Khan, were able to control the troops, which by the middle of June numbered some thirty thousand.[1] Even where a local leader asserted himself, religious differences caused trouble. Khan Bahadur Khan was soon

[1] A council of twelve, the 'Bara Topi', became the nominal rulers. In view of the controversy mentioned on page 443, it may be noted that Bahadur Shah was not directly or indirectly represented.

involved in disputes with the Hindu landowners of Rohilkhand. The sepoys, freed from discipline, were joined by Gujars and other criminal elements. The general disorder did the rebel cause great harm by frightening the princes and the propertied classes. Another factor was the consciousness of inferiority which affected sepoys when opposing European troops. It did not prevent them fighting bravely, but showed itself in a lack of enterprise in attack. The advantage gained by the capture of Delhi was rendered nugatory by the delay which allowed two small British forces to combine and occupy the Ridge, overlooking the city. Anson had died on May 27; but his successor, Sir Henry Barnard, marched down from Karnal and was joined by Archdale Wilson from Meerut. The combined forces amounted to less than five thousand, but after a successful action at Badli Serai on June 8 they were able to establish themselves within gunshot of Delhi. The moral effect was incalculable. The rebel capital was nominally under siege, though there must have been more than six times as many men under arms in the city than on the Ridge. The presence of this small British force prevented any serious attempt to establish a rebel government, and it was soon apparent that the revolt, even if successful, would only lead to anarchy and the rule of 'war lords' of the type familiar in eighteenth-century India or modern China. The withdrawal of British authority from any area, such as the Doab, was followed immediately by the revival of old feuds, by outbursts of religious fanaticism, and by the unrestrained activities of the criminal tribes.

The failure to establish a reputable authority on the rebel side was one powerful factor which prevented the spread of the rebellion. Another was the personal character of the Bengal sepoys. Their arrogance had made them cordially disliked in every part of India to which they had been sent. Troops which mutinied in the Punjab, or even in Southern Bengal, were attacked by the surrounding villagers. The peasant rising was confined to those parts from which the Bengal army was recruited, and there was no difficulty in enlisting men to fight against the mutineers from the areas in which they had been stationed. The most important as well as the most striking instance was the attitude adopted by the Sikh community. It was only eight years since the defeat of the *Khalsa* army and the annexation of the Punjab. Everything depended on this new province. The Viceroy could do little from Calcutta, except arrange for reinforcements from England, and indicate, not very effectually, the lines on which the campaign was to be fought and the general policy to be adopted south of the Narmada. If British

2 F

rule in the Punjab had collapsed, as it had done in the North-West Provinces, nothing could have prevented the troops on the Ridge from being isolated, and probably the whole of Northern India would have been submerged. The prospects of the Punjab going against the British seemed considerable. The new administration had been vigorous and efficient, but hardly popular. The attitude of the frontier tribes was uncertain. The garrison contained only ten thousand European troops (most of whom were in the Peshawar valley), about thirteen thousand Punjab Irregulars, and thirty-six thousand sepoys of the Bengal army. The Sikhs might well have seen in the rebellion an opportunity of regaining their hegemony, or might, like the Pathans, have waited for the outcome of the struggle. So uncertain was the position that John Lawrence, the Chief Commissioner, was prepared to withdraw his troops from the Peshawar valley, and cede that area to the Amir, but the proposal was vetoed by Lord Canning. The fact that the initiative in the rebellion came from the Bengal army seems to have been decisive. Sikhs and Punjab Muslims joined the Government's hastily formed levies. The population generally supported the authorities in disarming and guarding the Bengal troops at Lahore, Peshawar, and Multan, and in pursuing those regiments, at Mardan, Jallandhar, and elsewhere, which succeeded in mutinying and absconding. The state of the province soon made it possible to send reinforcements to Delhi. Nicholson, in charge of a movable column, completed the disarming of Bengal troops at Jhelum and marched to the Ridge at the end of July.

The Government at Calcutta had the double task of keeping open the road to the north, and of relieving Cawnpore and Lucknow. The efforts which it made were on so small a scale as to be almost absurd, but however much it may be blamed for the peace-time distribution of forces, there is hardly sufficient evidence to criticise its later policy. The affair was without precedent, and information, especially about the army, came through unreliable channels. Lord Canning's advisers succumbed at first to the official's temptation to minimize unpleasant facts. The Viceroy was over-optimistic in refusing offers of volunteers from Calcutta, which might have enabled him to release a British regiment, but he was deceived by the three weeks' lull which followed the Meerut outbreak and was naturally loath to assume that sepoys at Benares, Dinapur, and Allahabad would follow suit.[1] The second wave that

---

[1] In replying to the first offer Lord Canning referred to 'the passing and groundless panic'. The news from Meerut *did* cause panics amongst Europeans at both Simla and Calcutta, two curious incidents which gave rise to later controversy.

swept through the Bengal army made him unwilling to move the few troops at his disposal without some definite objective, before he knew at what points the rebels were concentrating, and how far the rebellion might spread.

The position in June was very obscure. Several princes, like Holkar in Indore, wavered when the troops garrisoning their States mutinied. Muslim fanatics were concentrating in Haidarabad, and it needed all the courage and astuteness of Sir Salar Jang to prevent an outbreak. One regiment mutinied as far south as Kolhapur, and disturbances occurred in Bombay and in the southern Maratha country. The valley of the Ganges was threatened at several points. Lack of decision prevented the disarming of sepoys at Dinapur, and three regiments escaped with their rifles to form the nucleus of Kunwar Singh's guerilla force. At Benares an attempt to disarm the Bengal regiment led to a confused struggle, but some Madras troops, which had marched from Calcutta under Colonel Neill, restored order locally. Neill then pushed on to Allahabad, where the Indian garrison had rebelled but the fort was still held by Captain Brasyer and a detachment of Sikhs. This became the advance base for operations from the south, and here Neill was joined, on June 30, by Havelock, with orders to relieve Cawnpore and Lucknow. Major Renaud was sent forward on the same day with four hundred British and four hundred Indian troops, Havelock and Neill following about a week later with 1000 British soldiers, 130 Sikhs, and twenty volunteers. In the interval news had come that Wheeler had surrendered at Cawnpore, and that his garrison had then been treacherously destroyed.

By the end of June the rebellion had spread over a large area, but the rebels had done little to consolidate their position. Large armed forces were collected at Delhi and Lucknow, but no attempt had been made to organise the civilian population, or to place the rebellious area in a state of defence. The British had now begun to take the aggressive, with Nicholson and Chamberlain in the north, Havelock and Neill in the south; but the smallness of their forces shows how very narrow was the margin which enabled them to attack rather than defend. The comparative inertness of the rebel leaders is the more surprising because from the first the fighting was of a peculiarly brutal character, no quarter being given on either side. The post-war generation is wisely suspicious of 'atrocities', and it is necessary to discount much conscious and unconscious working up of a war atmosphere. The mutinous conduct of regiments prior to May 10 had been punished according to the normal peace-time procedure. The outbreak of armed rebellion coincided with the first murder of European civilians, men and women, at Meerut and Delhi. The British immediately replied by adopting similar standards, which were applied not only to the Bengal army, but to any Indians known or suspected to be unfriendly. Mutineers if captured were executed, and also subjected to what the *Times* correspondent described as 'spiritual and mental tortures to which we have no right to resort, and which we dare not perpetrate in the face of Europe'.[1] After the abortive rising at Peshawar on June 10, forty prisoners were taken out and publicly blown from guns, and this became the regular punishment for suspected mutiny.[2] Within a fortnight of the Meerut outbreak, and before the second group of mutinies, Nicholson in the Punjab was writing to Colonel Edwardes—'Let us propose a Bill for the flaying alive, impalement, or burning of the murderers of the women and children at Delhi. The idea of simply hanging the perpetrators of such atrocities is maddening.'[3] Lynching mentality, as seen to-day in the Southern States of America, soon degenerates into a kind of racial mania. Every Indian who was not actively fighting for the British became a 'murderer of women and children'. Even the servants with the British troops at Delhi were treated 'with outrageous harshness. . . . A general massacre of the inhabitants of Delhi, a large number of whom were known to wish us success, was openly proclaimed. Blood-thirsty boys might be heard recommending that all the native orderlies, irregulars, and other "poorbeahs" in our camp should be shot.'[4]

Townsmen and villagers near the centres of rebellion were victims of this lust for blood. Colonel Neill, after suppressing the mutiny at Benares on June 4, extended martial law into the surrounding district.

' Volunteer hanging parties went into the districts, and amateur executioners were not wanting to the occasion. One gentleman boasted of the numbers he had finished off quite "in an artistic manner", with mango trees for gibbets and elephants for drops, the victims of this wild justice being strung up, as though for pastime, in the form of figures of eight.'[5]

[1] Russell, *My Diary in India*, ii. 43.

[2] Cf. a letter written by Lieutenant (afterwards Lord) Roberts to his mother, June 11, 1857: 'We have come along this far, doing a little business on the road, such as disarming regiments and executing mutineers. The death that seems to have most effect is being blown from a gun.'—*Letters written during the Indian Mutiny*.

[3] Kaye and Malleson, *History of the Indian Mutiny*, ii. 301.

[4] See *The Chaplain's Narrative of the Siege of Delhi*.

[5] The two quotations are from Kaye and Malleson, *History of the Indian Mutiny*, ii. 177 and 203. The reference in the second extract is to papers presented to Parliament, February 4, 1858.

Similar events followed the capture of Allahabad a week later. Martial law was strengthened by the Act of June 8, which enabled the Executive Government to proclaim any area to be in a state of rebellion, and to give capital powers to a Commission. By June 20, at Allahabad ' soldiers and civilians alike were holding Bloody Assize, or slaying natives without any assize at all, regardless of sex or age. It is on the records of our British Parliament, in papers sent home by the Governor-General of India in Council, that "the aged, women, and children are sacrificed as well as those guilty of rebellion!" They were not deliberately hanged, but burnt to death in villages—perhaps now and then accidentally shot.' [1]

Neill himself was not responsible, either at Benares or Allahabad, for the way in which his successors administered martial law, and only partially for the drastic manner in which Renaud, with the advance force, interpreted his instructions to 'attack and destroy all places *en route* close to the road occupied by the enemy, but touch no others'. Havelock's main force followed along a stretch of dreary waste, in which every village had been burnt, and from which every inhabitant had disappeared except those who had been caught and hanged by the roadside.[2]

It has been necessary to describe the nature of the fighting during the six weeks following the Meerut outbreak in order to place in proper setting the terrible events at Cawnpore. These occurred later, about the end of June. General Wheeler had not expected that the mutinous sepoys would return to besiege the few European troops which he had, and he had collected the European and Eurasian population in an entrenchment poorly suited to withstand a siege. The epic story of the three weeks' defence, from June 6 to the 27th, has often been told. It ended by General Wheeler's surrender on an ambiguously worded safe-conduct to Allahabad by river. The troops were attacked when embarking, and nearly all of them killed. The women and children were taken to the Nana Sahib's palace. About a fortnight later the Nana Sahib, who had had himself declared Peshwa, learnt that Havelock was rapidly approaching Cawnpore, and had defeated his troops at Fatehpur and in two other engagements. The two hundred and eleven women and children were then brutally murdered by some palace servants.

The two massacres must be considered separately in view of the importance which they acquired. The first was the work of mutineers,

[1] See note 5 on previous page.

[2] There can be no doubt about the recklessness of these executions. *Parliamentary Papers*, xliv. pt. i. 23. Also see Russell, *My Diary in India*, ii. 402.

and, however reprehensible on general grounds, it was in keeping with a struggle in which no quarter was expected, and any trick seemed justifiable. It may be compared with the means by which Cooper, a Punjab civilian, captured and slaughtered some hundreds of unarmed sepoys belonging to a regiment which had been disarmed at Lahore. After escaping during a dust storm, these men were attacked by villagers, and took refuge on an island in the Ravi. About three hundred surrendered to Cooper and a few policemen, thinking they would be tried, but after being secured in a bastion they were taken out next morning and shot. Forty-five were already dead of suffocation.[1]

The massacre of the women and children at Cawnpore was a diabolical act, but it was not the work of the rebel troops, who refused to have anything to do with it. Nor is there the slightest evidence for the stories of rape and mutilation which were circulated at the time.[2] The slaughter seems to have been due to a panic, or possibly to a desire on the part of the Nana Sahib's retinue to compromise their half-hearted leader. It followed and was probably inspired by the savage punishments inflicted at Benares and Allahabad, and by Renaud's advance guard. Its results were altogether lamentable. In India and in England the news gave a welcome and almost religious sanction to any act of savagery which the Government troops might perpetrate. Townsmen were slaughtered wholesale at Cawnpore and later at Lucknow and Delhi.

' At the time of the capture of Lucknow—a season of indiscriminate massacre—such distinction was not made, and the unfortunate who fell into the hands of our troops was made short work of—sepoy or Oude villager, it mattered not—no questions were asked; his skin was black, and did not that suffice? A piece of rope, and the branch of a tree, or a rifle bullet through his brain, soon terminated the poor devil's existence.' [3]

In England, to quote a contemporary writer, 'everyone chuckled to hear how General Neill had forced high Brahmins to sweep up

---

[1] See Cooper's own account in his book *The Crisis in the Punjab*, 152 *et seq*: 'They were possessed of a sudden and insane idea that they were going to be tried by courtmartial after some luxurious refreshment.' 'The doors were opened and behold. Unconsciously the tragedy of Holwell's Black Hole had been re-enacted. . . . Fortyfive bodies dead from fright, exhaustion, fatigue, heat, and partial suffocation, were dragged into light.'

[2] See Colonel Williams' valuable synopsis of evidence taken at Cawnpore. Printed in *Annals of the Indian Rebellion*.

[3] Lieutenant V. D. Majendie's *Up among the Pandies*, 195. This ingenuous account of the Mutiny operations by a subaltern is of considerable importance in this connection.

the blood of Europeans murdered at Cawnpore, and then strung them in a row without giving them the time requisite for purification'.[1] From Cawnpore can be traced the widespread belief that one European life, especially that of a woman or child, is worth the lives of innumerable Indians. Educated Englishmen came to India with ideas drawn from the Press of that period, invariably depicting the Indian as a cowardly slayer of women. How this was likely to appeal to the rank and file is illustrated by Trevelyan's story of an unfortunate incident amongst the drivers attached to a newly landed regiment. 'I seed two Moors talking in a cart. Presently I heard one of 'em say "Cawnpore". I knowed what that meant; so I fetched Tom Walker, and he heard 'em say "Cawnpore," and he knowed what that meant. So we polished 'em both off.'

Another two months saw the end of the aggressive rebellion and the beginning of the punitive campaigns. Delhi fell after a series of operations carried through with marvellous courage. The siege train arrived on September 6; a week later the Kashmir gate was blown in. The city and fort were then captured after six days' fighting. Nicholson, the moving spirit in a very hazardous enterprise, was mortally wounded.[2] The rebels retreated, leaving behind Bahadur Shah. The ex-Emperor was arrested by Hodson, who also shot three of his sons. The city was sacked as ruthlessly as had been Cawnpore in July. Most of the male population, which had not already fled, were slaughtered, though many were known to have been friendly to the British cause, and few can have actively helped the rebel force. 'All the city people found within the walls when our troops entered were bayoneted on the spot; and the number was considerable, as you may suppose when I tell you that in some houses forty or fifty persons were hiding.'[3] The rebel soldiers had purposely left behind large quantities of liquor, easily accessible to the incoming troops; and this ruse, while it facilitated their retreat, led to appalling excesses against their compatriots during the final stages of the capture of the city and fort.

[1] G. O. Trevelyan, The Competition Wallah, 284.

[2] The scale of the fighting round Delhi may be judged by the casualties. The siege cost 992 killed and 2795 wounded. This was more than the total casualties suffered during Havelock and Outram's campaigns, Sir Colin Campbell's relief of Lucknow, his subsequent action at Cawnpore, Sir H. Rose's campaign in Central India, and Whitlock's campaign in Bundelkhand.

[3] Letter in the Bombay Telegraph. Quoted by Montgomery Martin, The Indian Empire, viii. 449. In view of these events the blame attached to Hodson for pistolling the princes seems hypocritical. They had been active members of the rebel army, and had surrendered without safe conduct.

Meanwhile Havelock, with his minute force, continued to win victories. After being joined by Outram he fought his way into Lucknow on September 25. These two events, the fall of Delhi and the relief of Lucknow, finally established the superiority of the Government's troops, even when at a great numerical disadvantage. The rebels never again showed the same vigour. Their nominal leader, Bahadur Shah, was captured, they had no headquarters, and their last hope of ultimate victory disappeared as they found reinforcements were steadily arriving from England. After September the British campaign became more orderly, while the rebels were divided into groups under such leaders as the Rao Sahib, Tantia Topi, Khan Bahadur Khan, Firoz Shah, Kunwar Singh, and the Rani of Jhansi. For another nine months these were systematically hunted down. Sir Colin Campbell operated in the North-West Provinces and Oudh, Sir Hugh Rose worked from Bombay through Central India. They were helped by columns under Colonel Greathed from Delhi and General Whitlock from Mhow. At first the hardest fighting fell to the share of Sir Colin Campbell. Lucknow had to be relieved for the second time in November, and he had only just succeeded in clearing the city and evacuating the non-combatants, when he had to hurry back to Cawnpore, where General Windham was hard pressed by some 20,000 men under Rao Sahib and Tantia Topi. Outram with 4000 men was left at Lucknow, where he successfully held the Alambagh against forces estimated at over a hundred thousand. Lucknow had therefore to be relieved for a third time, in March, 1858.

Tantia Topi's force was drawn from the Gwalior garrison. Sindhia's own State troops had remained loyal to their master, and still defended the treasury and arsenal, but the Government troops mutinied in June. This powerful army might have played a decisive part against the weakened British forces, but it did little for five months. It was now faced by Campbell's better equipped army and was defeated on December 6. Joined by a force of Gurkhas under Jang Bahadur, Campbell then returned to Lucknow, relieved Outram, and began campaigning in Oudh and Rohilkhand, driving Khan Bahadur Khan and his Ghazi followers out of Bareilly in May. These operations in Oudh continued until the end of the year. Ahmad Ullah and the Begum of Oudh fought with great determination round Shahjanpur, until the former was treacherously murdered by a brother of the Raja of Powain, from whom he was seeking help. The Begum ultimately fled to Nepal. This resistance in Oudh developed into a war of local independence. The *Talukdars*, who had previously adopted an attitude of benevolent neutrality towards the mutineers, were driven into active rebellion by a singularly injudicious Proclamation issued by Canning at the end of March, which declared that, except in a few specified cases, the *Talukdars'* lands would be liable to forfeiture.[1] This Proclamation was so opposed to the usually conciliatory attitude of the Governor-General that it is probable that he did not fully appreciate its significance, and merely wished to give the administration a free hand in the future settlement of Oudh. Ahmad Ullah was able to arouse the territorial patriotism which was so markedly lacking over most of India during the eighteenth and early nineteenth centuries; but his army had not the training of the sepoys who followed Tantia Topi and the Rao Sahib. The Moulvi fought with great courage, and fully deserved this tribute from a contemporary historian: 'He had not stained his sword with assassination, he had connived at no murders; and he fought manfully, honestly, stubbornly in the field against the strangers who had seized his country'.[2]

Interest in the Central Indian campaign turned on the siege of Jhansi and the combined activities of the Rani and Tantia Topi. Sir Hugh Rose, after capturing Ratgarh and relieving Saugor, reached Jhansi on March 21. He had not completed the investment before he was called upon to meet a determined effort to relieve the city. Tantia Topi, after his defeat three months previously, had collected his forces at Kalpi and now marched on Jhansi. He was again defeated on the Betwa river, and Rose then stormed Jhansi, though the Rani managed to escape and joined Tantia Topi. Their forces were once more defeated at Kunch, but the indomitable Rani tried a final gamble, and marched with Tantia Topi into Gwalior, hoping that the State troops would at last join them. Sindhia went out to oppose them, but his army would not fight, and the rebels seized the town and fort. Rose saw the danger of a Maratha rising and, making a last effort, defeated Tantia Topi at Morar and Kotah, after which the Rani was killed when riding, dressed as a sowar, with her cavalry. Gwalior was retaken on June 20, and on July 8 Canning proclaimed peace, though nearly all the leaders were still at large. The Nana Sahib, the Begum of Oudh, and Firoz Shah escaped from India during the autumn of 1858. Tantia Topi was given up by Man Singh, a rebellious princelet who hoped to recover his fief by this betrayal. He was

---

[1] This Proclamation brought a strongly censorious letter from Lord Ellenborough, then Secretary of State for India. He sent this without Cabinet authorisation, and resigned.

[2] Kaye and Malleson, *History of the Indian Mutiny*, iv. 381.

tried and hanged for waging war against the king.[1] The Rao Sahib was arrested and hanged three years later.

Thus ended an episode, lamentable in its origin, distinguished by great courage but by few other virtues during its course, and ending in a manner which left the seeds of much future trouble. On the British side the valour and endurance of soldiers and civilians were marred by crude racial passions, and by gross ingratitude to many Indians who assisted them. Indians must also recognise certain failings in the conduct of those who took arms against the Government; the indecision which kept large numbers inactive when they might have been most effective, the selfishness and lack of national pride which prevented their leaders working together or sacrificing their own personal ambitions.

[1] Not, as frequently stated, for complicity in the Cawnpore murders. The justice of the sentence was severely criticised. See Kaye and Malleson, v. 265. This, like the criticism of Hodson, seems based on a form of snobbishness. Actually, if not theoretically, everyone who joined the mutineers was treated as deserving capital punishment. Hodson laid himself open to other charges affecting his personal integrity, and if he had survived might have been tried for giving guarantees 'in a very unaccountable manner'. These are fully discussed in Kaye and Malleson. See also G. Campbell, *Memoirs of my Indian Career*, i. 247.

BOOK VI

POST-MUTINY INDIA IN THE ERA OF PATERNALISM

'Ten years had elapsed since the Mutiny, but the Mutiny was, in the early years of my service, a living memory in the minds of all. That memory was not a benign influence on the future career of the young civilian. When I first arrived in the country it was duly enjoined on me as a matter of vital importance that I should insist on all the outward and visible signs of deference and respect which Orientals with a leaning to sycophancy, resulting from generations of subjection and foreign rule, are only too willing to accord.'—Sir HENRY COTTON, *Indian and Home Memories.*

'Nought remains
But vindictiveness here amid the strong,
And there amid the weak an impotent rage.'
THOMAS HARDY, *The Dynasts.*

CHRONOLOGICAL TABLE

Viceroy.		
LORD CANNING.	1859.	James Wilson appointed Finance Minister.
	1860.	Famine in North-West Provinces.
		Indian Councils Act.
		Penal Code passed.
	1861.	*Civil War in America.*
LORD ELGIN.	1862.	Formation of High Courts.
	1863.	Death of Dost Muhammad.
LORD LAWRENCE.	1864.	Bhutan War.
	1865.	*End of American Civil War.*
	1866.	Famine in Orissa.
	1867.	*British Reform Act.*
	1868.	Punjab Tenancy Act.
		Railway opened from Ambala to Delhi.
		Sher Ali, Amir of Afghanistan.
LORD MAYO.	1869.	Ambala conference with Sher Ali.
	1870.	*Forster's Education Act.*
	1872.	Lord Mayo murdered in Andamans.
LORD NORTHBROOK.	1872.	Seistan Boundary Report.
	1873.	Russians take Khiva.
	1874.	Bihar famine.
		Disraeli becomes Prime Minister.
	1875.	Gaekwar of Baroda's case.
	1876.	Royal Titles Act.
LORD LYTTON.	1876.	Treaty with Khelat.
		Deccan famine.
	1877.	Delhi Durbar. Queen proclaimed Empress.
		Extension of famine.
	1878.	Vernacular Press Act.
		Indian troops sent to Malta.
		Treaty of Berlin.
		Second Afghan War.
		Death of King Mindon Min of Burma.
	1879.	Treaty of Gandamak.
		Massacre of Burmese princes.
		Murder of Cavagnari at Kabul.
		Kabul reoccupied.
LORD RIPON.	1880.	Battle of Maiwand.
		Boer War.
		March to Kandahar.
		Recognition of Abdur Rahman.
		Gladstone's return to Office.
	1881.	Factory Act.
		Rendition of Mysore.
		Rebellion of Arabi Bey in Egypt.
	1883.	Ilbert Bill.
	1884.	Russians occupy Merv.
		Russo-Afghan Commission.
		Lord Ripon resigns.
LORD DUFFERIN.	1884.	
	1885.	Third Burmese War.

CHAPTER I

EFFECT OF THE MUTINY

Effect of Mutiny upon Indian opinion: opposition to Government: changed attitude of British: Crown government: reorganisation of army: new policy towards Indian States: issue of 'sanads': development of political law: interference by Government of India: Baroda case: rendition of Mysore.

THE Mutiny cannot be dismissed as an unhappy incident which ended with its suppression. It would be wiser to use a medical simile, and consider it as the primary symptoms of a deep-seated disorder—the reaction of India against the too rapid introduction of Western ideas and the limited scope left to the Muslim and Hindu upper classes. The primary symptoms were cured drastically and effectively, but the very success of the extremely ruthless methods employed added to the difficulty of diagnosing and treating the disease when the inevitable secondary symptoms began to appear a few years later. Opposition was driven underground. During the three-quarters of a century following the Mutiny there have been local disturbances, but few attempts at overt rebellion. The *izzat* of the Company, its reputation for invincibility, which had been badly shaken by the first Afghan War, were completely restored. The English were able to consolidate their position, until the danger of direct attack became negligible.

To Indians the Mutiny has remained a bitter memory. The extent to which this feeling has been ignored by English writers is a remarkable commentary upon the social estrangement between the two races. For a generation the events of those two years formed a subject for talk in every village and household. A war affects men's outlook far more rapidly than education or political agitation. Interminable discussions about the occurrences at Cawnpore, Delhi, and Lucknow, about the rising in Oudh, and the fate of Tantia Topi and of the Rani of Jhansi all helped to mould opinion throughout the peninsula. The two facts most firmly imprinted on the Indian mind were the failure of the rebel leaders to take advantage of their early successes, and the ferocity with which martial law was administered and the rebels were hunted down. Stories spread slowly from one *bazar* to another. The impression which

461

these caused was confirmed during the next few years by the changed outlook of most European officials and by the contemptuous brutality of less responsible Englishmen, such as planters and the rank and file of the army. Educated Hindus could read the virulent attacks, in the European Press, on Canning, Grant, and other 'humanity-pretenders' who were endeavouring to restore the rule of law. Muslims heard of the punishments meted out to their co-religionists. Trevelyan, writing from India shortly after the Mutiny, describes how

' after the capture of Delhi, every member of a class of religious enthusiasts named Ghazees was hung, as it were, *ex-officio*; and it is to be feared that a vindictive and irresponsible judge, who plumed himself upon having a good eye for a Ghazee, sent to the gallows more than one individual whose guilt consisted in looking as if he belonged to a sect which, probably, was hostile to our religion'.[1]

These things were not done in a corner, and it is absurd to imagine that they did not affect profoundly the millions who had remained passive, and had viewed events with the philosophy of a race which has seen many empires pass. Certain inferences forced themselves upon the minds of Hindu and Muslim alike. They had expected British rule to reach its zenith, and then to decline, like all the older dynasties. It was commonly held that England was a small island, and that a large proportion of the population had settled in India. After the Mutiny British rule seemed more solid than ever, its resources inestimable. Neither the Nana Sahib, nor the Mogul Emperor, nor the sepoy army had been able to provide an alternative government. The British, unlike any previous invaders, became more aloof the longer they stayed, more foreign, more efficient. They could neither be assimilated nor expelled, and thus naturally, if not logically, the idea of an Indo-European civilisation grew more remote and less desirable. From those formative years which followed the Mutiny it is possible to trace a swing back to the old religions, and a new attitude towards the English, who were in future the invincible adversary against whom Indians must combine to get what terms they could. The modern European knows from recent experience that an unsuccessful rebellion often leads to a revival of obscurantist religious nationalism; but few Victorian Englishmen foresaw a return to orthodox Hinduism, or expected that the small reformist element would be submerged under a wave of anti-European feeling. They still believed that Hinduism was a dying faith, and were surprised when the westernising *Brahmo Samaj* gradually receded, and the

[1] G. O. Trevelyan, *Cawnpore*, 109.

truculent proselytising *Arya Samaj* became a force in the land. With the religious revival came also a feeling of disgust at the ineptitude displayed by so many Indians during the Mutiny. The growing national desire for self-respect drove the educated classes to find some explanation for such incapacity. This led ultimately to a worship of the past, a 'back to the Vedas' movement, and the complaint, now grown tiresome from constant repetition, that the 'nation' had been 'emasculated' during the British occupation.[1]

The dissemination of these ideas was to take many years, but soon after the Mutiny there was evidence that discontented elements were ready to take action whenever they could find some nucleus round which to work. The *Wahabis*, a puritan but obscurantist sect, provided a rallying ground for the Muslims. A colony of these men had established themselves first at Sitana, and after being dislodged from there in 1858, had moved to Malka. Their agents travelled through India. They were active before and during the Mutiny, and afterwards made Patna the centre for a network of anti-British activities. A force under Sir Neville Chamberlain was sent against Malka in 1863, and after severe fighting captured this stronghold, but *Wahabi* activities continued throughout the 'sixties, ending in the trial of the ringleaders at Patna in 1871, during which the judge was murdered. It was a *Wahabi* prisoner in the Andamans who murdered Lord Mayo in 1873.

Poona was another centre of hostility to the Government. The nucleus in this case was provided by the Maratha Brahmins, who had attempted to revive the Peshwaship during the Mutiny, and who continued to work on the strong historical feelings of the Deccan Hindus. The actual conspiracy was discovered in 1862, and successfully checked by the Governor of Bombay, Sir Bartle Frere, who described it as 'an evident offshoot of the discontent which lost its chosen leaders in the Nana, Tantia Topi etc., and which still smoulders in Central India and the Maharatta country'. This traditional sentiment was in later years to form the basis of Tilak's political activities, of the 'Sivaji cult', and of the nationalist movement of Western India.

The extent of the change amongst the British in India is often overlooked, but there is abundant contemporary evidence that the Mutiny led to a new spirit in the administration, an almost complete break with

[1] As early as 1875 the Calcutta newspaper, the *Amrita Bazar Patrika*, referred as follows to the attempted murder of Colonel Phayre at Baroda: 'To emasculate a nation that a Government may rule without trouble. Surely to poison an obscure Colonel is by far a lighter crime'.—*Parl. Returns*, C2040, 1878, 41.

old traditions, and the formation of certain conventional habits of thought which have survived until modern times. The events in Northern India threw the small expatriated community together, rousing first their combative spirit and then a degree of vindictiveness and of racial solidarity not usually characteristic of the English, even after a war. 'Two months of Nana Sahib brought about an effect on the English character at the recollection of which Englishmen at home have already learned to blush, but the lamentable consequences of which will be felt in India for generations yet unborn or unthought of.'[1] Sir Bartle Frere, then member of the Viceroy's Council, wrote in 1860 to Sir Charles Wood that he had been 'shocked at the language of the Judges on the Army Bill. I am afraid that the antagonistic feeling of race is becoming a source of formidable danger.'[2] It is not surprising that Russell, the *Times* correspondent in India, should have felt that

' the mutinies have produced too much hatred and ill-feeling between the two races to render any mere change of name of the rulers a remedy for the evils which affect India, of which those angry sentiments are the most serious exposition. . . . Many years must elapse ere the evil passions excited by these disturbances expire; *perhaps confidence will never be restored*; and if so our reign in India will be maintained at the cost of suffering which it is fearful to contemplate'.[3]

The lessons which the English learnt from the Mutiny were not more logical than the reactions of the Indians, but from much repetition they gradually became axiomatic. The revolt of the Brahmin regiments caused the deepest resentment, for they had been the most favoured of all the sepoys, their religious privileges had been safeguarded at the expense of military efficiency, and their British officers retained till the very end an almost pathetic belief in their 'staunchness'. In future the Indian, above all the high caste Hindu, could never be completely trusted. This universal feeling elevated racial discrimination into a form of loyalty, and reinforced the promptings of self-interest in opposing the promotion of Indians to positions of responsibility. The early days of the Mutiny, especially the events at Meerut, were taken to justify quick and drastic action on the first signs of a revolt, and the British community came to consider itself as a garrison occupying a country which might always break out in a sudden rebellion. The heavy loss of lives and the great nervous strain also led to increasing caution,

[1] G. O. Trevelyan, *The Competition Wallah*, 283.
[2] Letter of September 2. Quoted by J. Martineau, *Life of Sir Bartle Frere*, i. 330.
[3] Russell, *My Diary in India*, ii. 259.

for it was believed that the civil rising was due to the reformist and innovating policy of Lord Dalhousie, and to the legislation which affected Hindu social life. The next eighty years were marked by an extreme unwillingness to interfere with religious and caste questions. The Englishman's duty was to keep the peace, maintain law and order, bring India some of Europe's material blessings, but not to worry about the Indian's family life or private morals.

The racial cleavage became more marked, though the extent of the difference before and after the Mutiny has sometimes been exaggerated.[1] It must be confessed that the growing number of English women who began to settle in India with their husbands increased the tendency of the white population to form not only a caste, but also a group of trade unions, and the recent vivid memories of 1857 inevitably encouraged a belief that these sacrifices merited 'some more substantial recompense than the privilege of governing India in a spirit of wisdom and unselfishness'. Amongst the better class of Englishmen this idea was translated into the belief that the British Empire in India was far more of a permanency than their predecessors had imagined, that the British element must be strengthened, and, as laid down by Sir John Strachey, 'in all departments of essential importance there must be selected Englishmen to maintain a standard of efficiency'. The rougher type of Englishman interpreted this prevalent feeling by classing all Indians into one opprobrious category, by a disregard for authority, and by a rudeness of bearing which was to be the cause of continual and growing friction during the next half-century.

Apart from the general developments in the administration which will be discussed in the next chapter, the Mutiny led directly to three important changes of policy. The Crown finally assumed control of the Indian Government, the army was completely reorganised, and a new attitude was adopted towards the Indian States. The first was 'rather a formal than a substantial change'.[2] The Company had for many years been in the position of mortgagees in possession, while the administration was shared between the President of the Board of Control in England and the Governor-General in India. The Directors were little more than an advisory council, and even their old powers of

---

[1] The population of mixed European and Indian descent—then known as Eurasians, now as Anglo-Indians—suffered severely during the Mutiny. Many fought with exceptional bravery for the Government. The struggle and its aftereffects segregated them almost entirely from Indians.

[2] H. S. Cunningham, *Earl Canning*, 170.

2 G

patronage had been reduced by the last Charter Act of 1853, which introduced the principle of competition for the Civil Service. The President was now replaced by a Secretary of State. A new and powerful Council of India, appointed 'during good behaviour', was constituted under the Act for the better government of India (1858).[1] For a few years Crown and Parliament showed a keen desire to supervise Indian affairs, but this gradually diminished. Power tended to concentrate in the hands of the Secretary of State and his technical advisers in the India Office. Towards the end of the 'sixties hardly a dozen members took any active interest in India, and only questions concerning the Indian States were referred to the Crown. An Act of 1869 reduced the status of the Council of India, and henceforward it was little more than a consultative body. About the same time certain other factors increased the importance of the Secretary of State and the control which he was able to exercise over India and over the Governor-General. The most important was the appointment of men like the Duke of Argyll, Lord Salisbury, and Lord Hartington to the Secretaryship, all of whom were of considerable political consequence, and of very different calibre to most Presidents of the pre-Mutiny era. Their position in the Cabinet led them to exercise an increasing control over the financial and political activities of the Government of India, and their ability to do so was immensely heightened by the opening of direct telegraphic communication in 1870. The days were over when a Governor-General, like Lord Wellesley, could get his own way by presenting the home authorities with a *fait accompli*. Lord Northbrook and many of his successors were to struggle against the tendency of the India Office to interfere in matters of administration, but by the end of the century Lord Elgin was telegraphing twice a day for instructions, and control from Whitehall probably reached its highest point when Lord Morley was Secretary of State.

The Indian army, as the primary cause of the Mutiny, had to undergo great changes. Many regiments had been disbanded, and the Company's methods of recruiting and of enforcing discipline had proved a failure. The Mutiny led to the introduction of an entirely new principle, that of balancing communities inside the army. The pre-Mutiny army had been

[1] The Act established a chain of responsibility from the Secretary of State to the lowest Indian official. 'The Governor-General in Council is required to pay due obedience to all such orders as he may receive from the Secretary of State.' 'Every local Government shall obey the orders of the Governor-General in Council.' See Ilbert, *The Government of India*, 94-6.

divided into three separate units, organised and controlled by the local governments of Bengal, Madras, and Bombay. But this had been merely a survival of the old system, and no attempt had been made to adopt the Roman policy of 'divide and rule'. The Indians, numbering in all over 200,000, were recruited as far as possible from the Presidencies in which they served, and were employed in all branches of the army, including the artillery. The European troops had been steadily reduced until they formed less than a sixth of the whole army.

For the next fifty years the idea of division and counterpoise dominated our military policy. The Presidency armies remained entirely separate until the Russian menace led to their partial consolidation under the Act of 1893.[1] The European troops were strengthened, and were reorganised so that certain essential services remained in their hands. By 1863 the European troops had been increased to 65,000, while the Indian troops had been reduced to 140,000, drawn from a wider range of caste and creed, and containing a strong element of the Sikhs and Gurkhas, who had proved so effective during the Mutiny.[2] The Commission of 1879 summarised and perpetuated this policy. 'The lessons taught by the Mutiny have led to the maintenance of two great principles, of retaining in the country an irresistible force of British troops and of keeping the artillery in the hands of Europeans.'[3] The proportion of about two Europeans to five Indians and the retention of the artillery in European hands remained as permanent features of the Indian army, which had two main functions, the protection of the frontier and what is euphemistically described as 'internal security'. In the course of time the former was to become much the most important, and led to the gradual modification of the post-Mutiny policy. The army was concentrated in the north, and was recruited chiefly from the Punjab, for reasons of convenience, prejudice, and climate, as well as for the martial qualities of the Sikh, the Punjabi Mussulman, the Dogra, and the Jat.

The reorganisation of the army had its counterpart in a new attitude towards the Indian States, based partly on a similar need for a better

[1] The troops were then formed into four territorial groups for Bengal, Madras, Bombay, and the Punjab under lieutenant-generals subordinate to the Commander-in-Chief. Lord Kitchener was responsible for the final unification.

[2] The Company's European troops, 15,000 in number, were transferred to the service of the Crown. The terms aroused great discontent, which gave rise to the so-called 'White Mutiny', a period of disaffection and insubordination.

[3] Report of Commission on Indian Army Reorganisation, 1879.

balance of power, partly on the idea of checking the too rapid and optimistic occidentalism of the pre-Mutiny period.

In view of the ultimate formation of an India federation, to include both States and provinces, it may now be regretted that the process of mediatising the smaller States was not continued during the latter half of the century, but such a conception of India's future was not in the minds of Lord Canning's generation. After the Mutiny there was a complete reversal of policy, which has had the effect of petrifying the India of 1858, with its confused boundaries and its conglomeration of over seven hundred States, covering two-fifths of the peninsula, and varying in size from Haidarabad, which is larger than Great Britain, to some tiny Orissan State of a few hundred acres.

The Government was actuated by several considerations in drawing up the Proclamation of 1858, and in the subsequent issue by Lord Canning of special *sanads* to all the important ruling chiefs. These documents assured the princes of Her Majesty's desire to see their rule perpetuated, sanctioning the practice of adoption for Hindus and for Muslims of 'any succession which might be legitimate according to their law'. It was argued that the uncertainty created by Lord Dalhousie's policy would prevent rather than encourage progress in the States, and it was felt that the Mutiny showed the value of the princes' co-operation, and the hold which they still had upon their subjects. Many officials considered that the process of modernising and unifying India had been pressed too hard, and that it would be better to allow development along different lines. They had lost the optimism of the early 'fifties, and had little ambition to administer the arid backbone of India which comprises so much of the States' territory. The Mutiny had again aroused the fear of invasion, which was always present in the minds of Victorian statesmen. Russia was now a potential enemy. Canning had, in his own words, 'seen a few patches of Native Government prove breakwaters to the storm which would otherwise have swept over us in one great wave', and it was felt that the States would be equally useful if any danger threatened from abroad at a moment when the country was disaffected.

Since 1860 there have been no further annexations. The only important change in what has been called the 'treaty map' of India occurred in 1881, when Mysore—a fertile area of some 30,000 square miles—was restored to a member of the ruling family. No new policy, apart from this rigid differentiation between 'British India' and 'Indian India,' was laid down at the time of the Proclamation, but an uncodified and extremely complicated kind of political 'law' gradually took shape during the post-Mutiny period. As the country settled down after the Mutiny the old difficulties with the States arose once more. Many officials felt that the Government had been precipitate in guaranteeing on their thrones these hundreds of ruling chiefs. Lord Lawrence, who had been a keen annexationist in Dalhousie's time, became Viceroy in 1864, and never hid his view that it was the Government's duty to level up the standard of administration in the States. 'At all his Durbars Lawrence used to harangue the chiefs, assembled out of all the corners of mediaeval barbarism, on the evils of infanticide and the blessings of female education.' There was continual friction about the size of the armies which many of the Central Indian States maintained. These were often far larger than necessary for internal security. Holkar had his gun foundry, and Sindhia his thousands of 'drilled soldiers'. Lawrence chafed at the restrictions laid down by the Proclamation of 1858, though in the case of the Nawab of Tonk, whom he deposed for abetting a murder, he duly placed an heir on the *gadi*. The attitude of the leading officials of that time has been described, not unfairly, as 'one of toleration of the States, reluctantly, without hope, and without any fixed intentions for the future'.[1]

The 'political law' which developed during the next half-century merely records the gradual incursions made by the Government upon the complete autocracy of the princes. The Government, though giving up all claim to escheatment in default of an heir, demanded a fuller paramountcy than had been exercised by the now defunct Company. No succession was valid until it received the sanction of the British authorities, and in cases of dispute the Government's decision was final. In the *sanads* granted by Lord Canning, as, for example, the one given to Patiala, the Government undertook not to receive complaints from the States' subjects, but the prince must 'execute justice and promote the happiness and welfare of his people'. In all cases of minority rule the Government claimed the right of approving, and ultimately of appointing, the Regent. British Residents were attached to the principal States, and their 'advice' became more and more authoritative. From time to time some new principle would be laid down, and gradually incorporated into the 'political law'. One of the most important was that 'treaties should be read together', and that the series of relationships which had developed between the Crown and the Indian princes should be assimilated. The States ceased to be isolated units, their rulers

[1] *The British Crown and the Indian States*, 59.

tending to become members of a body, all more or less in the same
semi-feudal relationship to the Crown, and all part of the imperial
organisation of India. This was an extremely slow process, carried
on piece-meal by successive Viceroys, whose personal predilections
played a larger part in these matters than in the ordinary administrative
work of British India.

Interference in the internal affairs of the States reached its zenith
under Lord Curzon, but a number of complicated problems have remained in dispute until to-day. Land-locked States always give rise to
difficult administrative and economic questions in regard to indirect
taxation, customs, currency, railway finance and policy, extradition,
and defence. Negotiations on such matters become impossible if they
have to be carried on with several hundred different authorities, and it
is easy to understand the temptation for a Viceroy to solve a deadlock
by a peremptory 'request', or to hasten a settlement by applying a precedent generally to all the States, irrespective of their different treaty
rights. During the thirty years which followed the Mutiny no attempt
was made to formulate a general policy, but the Government slowly
encroached upon sovereign rights as it strove to control the princes'
autocratic methods of dealing with their subjects and their finances.
Two important events, which occurred in this period, throw some light
on its attitude. The Gaekwar was deposed in 1875, and Mysore restored
in 1881.

The evil administration of Baroda had been the subject of protest,
but matters came to a head when Malhar Rao succeeded his brother in
1870. Three years later a commission of enquiry was appointed, and
subsequently the Gaekwar was warned that if certain reforms were not
carried out he would be relieved of his authority. Shortly afterwards
an attempt was made to poison the Resident, and the Gaekwar was
accused of abetting the offence. He was suspended, and publicly tried on
charges of misrule and disloyalty by a court which included two
princes. The Commissioners were divided, and the Government thereupon deposed Malhar Rao on the grounds of gross misgovernment.
The widow of his predecessor, Khande Rao, was allowed to adopt a
son, subject to Government approval, and a small boy was chosen from
another branch of the family. During his minority the administration
was conducted by the Resident and a staff of officials from British India.
The Government thus assumed the right of deposition for bad government, but there was no suggestion of annexation, and no alteration of
the treaties or status of Baroda.

The rendition of Mysore was 'practically a re-grant, and not merely a restoration of native rule after a temporary interruption'.[1] Lord Ripon took the opportunity of drawing up an instrument of transfer which amounted to a new constitution for the State, and presumably represents the ideal relations from the Government standpoint which should exist between the prince and the Viceroy. It marks a considerable derogation from the sovereign rights claimed by any of the larger States. Thus section 22 states that 'the Maharaja of Mysore shall at all times conform to such advice as the Governor-General in Council may offer him with a view to the management of his finances, the settlement and collection of his revenues, the imposition of taxes, the administration of justice. . . .' The final clause states that if any question arises about the fulfilment of the various conditions, 'the decision of the Governor-General in Council shall be final'. The Maharaja was, in fact, the agent of the Government, the position to which Lord Curzon would have liked to have reduced all the princes. The present administration, a model not only for other States, but in some respects for British India, suggests that Indians are well suited by an autocratic form of government in which the personal idiosyncrasies of the ruler are severely limited.

Considering the number and complexity of the Indian States, there were remarkably few occasions after the Mutiny when the Government had to interfere forcibly, either in support of the ruling prince or to settle a disputed succession. By far the most serious incident occurred in the little hill State of Manipur, where an inefficient raja had been expelled by one of his turbulent chiefs. The Government decided to confirm the heir apparent as raja, but insisted on the expulsion of the chief who had caused the revolution. The Chief Commissioner of Assam, when visiting the State in 1891 to enforce this decision, was captured, and put to death with four other officers. The Government treated this as an act of rebellion, not of war. A punitive expedition was sent, and those responsible for the murder were executed, but in accordance with post-Mutiny policy, troops were then withdrawn, and another member of the ruling family was placed on the throne.

[1] Sir William Lee Warner, *The Protected Princes of India*, 163.

CHAPTER II
PATERNAL ADMINISTRATION

Continuity of administration: financial reorganisation after Mutiny: Laing's reforms: growing importance of Europeans: their truculence: effect of Mutiny on administration: unification: the rule of law: growth of Services: departmentalism: agricultural prosperity after the Mutiny: the financial and commercial slump: the Orissa famine.

THE Mutiny did not cause any marked break in the administration. Most departments of the Government of India continued to function in the normal manner. During the worst crisis, in the latter half of 1857, Lord Canning summoned his Executive Council to discuss the necessary legislation for the foundation of Universities at Calcutta, Bombay, and Madras. The traditional phlegm of the British prevailed. The correspondent of the *Times* noticed that, while Lucknow was still held by the rebels, British officers going up-country from Calcutta wrote complaints about the absence of table-cloths and the 'incivility of the kitmutgar' in the *dak* bungalows. But the Mutiny was to leave its mark in many ways.

The cost of suppression shattered the Government's finances.[1] The four disturbed years left a deficit of about thirty-six millions, the equivalent of a year's revenue. This caused an alarm which seems incredible to the present generation. The Government of Madras wrote that 'according to our belief this is a more serious crisis than the Mutiny itself'.[2] The British had not accustomed themselves to the idea that India had any credit, and felt that it was unsound finance to borrow either for productive works, like canals, or for war expenses. The introduction of Crown rule into India thus coincided with the imposition of new taxes and the enforcement of rigid economies, a financial policy outlined by Mr. Wilson and continued by Mr. Laing, a British Member of Parliament brought out for the purpose. Some reforms were undoubtedly necessary.

' Until the appointment of poor Mr. Wilson, the public resources of India

---

[1] The whole cost of repressing the Mutiny was borne by the Indian Government. Nationalists have objected to this charge on the grounds that the rising was a war of independence.

[2] Despatch from Governor and Council of Madras, March 26, 1860.

were administered on the most happy-go-lucky system that perhaps ever existed in any civilised country.'[1]

Until 1846 the Bengal accounts had not even been separated from those of the Government of India, and many other anomalies survived the Mutiny. New accountancy methods were introduced, and the first tentative efforts were made to modify the earlier excessive centralisation. For Indians, however, the chief effect of the reforms was that the Government began to spend less and to demand more. The new taxation was not very high by modern standards. A uniform tariff of 10 per cent. was imposed on all imports, salt duties were increased, and a small income tax was imposed, an innovation so fiercely opposed by Sir Charles Trevelyan, the Governor of Madras, that he had to be recalled.

As Laing's financial reforms were to influence Indian policy for many years, it is important to notice certain limitations which he set to Government action. When he came to India great changes were taking place in the world's attitude towards the working classes. The Russian serfs were emancipated in 1861, and a few years later slavery was abolished in the United States. Other ideas of a far more radical nature were being bruited about in Europe. The Englishman of the upper classes, while proud of the part which the Empire had played in stopping the slave trade, felt instinctively that, once men were free, the State should not interfere any further between the rich and poor. Laing, a typical representative of his age and class, insisted that taxation should not be used to alter the existing social order. The income-tax was not graded, and the lowest incomes were only excluded for practical reasons. Laing was careful to explain why he discarded a policy which might have broadened the basis of taxation, and introduced the idea of equality of sacrifice.

' I do not put the case for the exemption of these persons on the ground that they are poor, for I have no sympathy with the socialist legislation which would place taxation exclusively on the rich. On the contrary, I believe the poor, as well as the rich, and often even more than the rich, are interested in the support of the State and the maintenance of social order.'[2]

The income-tax undoubtedly aroused opposition. The moneylenders especially objected to its inquisitorial character, and its assessment was complicated by the joint family system and the archaic

[1] G. O. Trevelyan, *The Competition Wallah*, 369. Wilson died after a few months' work.

[2] Financial Statement, 1862.

methods used in keeping private accounts. For thirty years the Government continually altered its ideas about this first experiment in direct taxation. The income-tax was dropped in 1865, and restored in 1869, and did not become a regular part of the Indian financial system until 1886. The result was that, during the important formative years which followed the Mutiny, the Government was still chiefly dependent on the land revenue, the salt duties, and the opium trade for the extra cost of the administration, while each department was hampered by a lack of funds.

The growing importance of the European settler was another source of embarrassment and root of many future difficulties. The Company had never encouraged the European 'interloper', and only reluctantly conceded the right of trading, and, subsequently, of acquiring land. The one exception was the indigo trade, for which the Company brought some planters from the West Indies, settling them in Bengal. These men successfully revived a dying industry, but they were a lawless set who combined some of the worst features of the eighteenth-century *Zemindars* with the tenacity of the Indian money-lender. Very few grew indigo themselves. They obtained their raw material by advancing money to cultivators, and gradually getting them completely under control. 'It matters little whether the *ryot* took his original advances with reluctance or cheerfulness, the result in either case is the same; he is never afterwards a free man.' [1]

Apart from the indigo planters, there were, in 1850, very few Europeans in India outside the Government services. A rapid change took place after the Mutiny. The Crown Government had no reason to discourage the settler, and may have felt that a larger European population was a safeguard against another rising. It was discovered that tea could be grown profitably in Assam, and coffee in the Nilgiris. Lord Canning issued 'Waste Land Rules' which made it easy for Europeans to take up this previously uncultivated hill land. From 1860 onwards development proceeded at a rate too fast to be healthy. The next decade saw the foundation of India's great textile industries, cotton in Bombay and

---

[1] *Bengal Indigo Commission Report*, 25. See also M. Wilson, *History of Behar*, and G. Watt, *Pamphlet on Indigo*. It is, however, only fair to quote an acute contemporary writer, the consul M. de Valbezen, *Les Anglais et l'Inde*: 'Le voyageur qui a parcouru les plantations du Mofussil doit attester, pour rendre hommage à la vérité, que s'il a souvent trouvé près de la maison du planteur un hôpital et une école, ses regards ont toujours cherché en vain les oubliettes et la salle aux tortures', 241. This work, published in 1857, is valuable because the author knew the country well, and seems to have been an impartial but by no means uncritical observer.

jute in Bengal. Railways and the growing foreign trade brought more business men to India. A flood of Englishmen came out East in the 'sixties, all of whom had been influenced by the wave of anti-Indian feeling which passed over Great Britain at the time of the Mutiny. Ignorant and contemptuous of all things Indian, they had a far stronger sense of racial superiority than their predecessors, and they were in sufficient numbers to develop a communal sense, and bring corporate pressure upon the Government. Gone were the days of Marshman and the *Friend of India*, when missionaries and reformers exerted their mild pressure on the Company. In their place was the raucous clamour of planters and business men vilifying 'Clemency Canning', demanding a criminal contract law to coerce the cultivator, indicting the unfortunate Mr. Long for 'libelling the general body of planters', agitating for the reprieve of the murderer Rudd, packing juries, fighting that very mild measure the 'Masters and Servants Act' of 1877, and finally joining in the uproar which was to defeat the Ilbert Bill in 1883.[1] It is impossible to understand the form which Indian nationalism was to take from the 'eighties onwards, or the temper of the Indian Press without some knowledge of this period. The lessons which the Indians learnt were that the Government could be moved by an agitation if it was sufficiently violent and uscrupulous, that the English criminal law as administered in India was ineffective in punishing crimes of violence, and that Indians could not expect racial impartiality from British judges.

British officials soon reacted against this extreme racialism. European business men might retain some influence upon the Government at Calcutta, the Supreme Court continued to display its bias against the Indian and against the cultivator, but no part of India, with the possible exception of Assam, has ever been a 'planters' colony'.[2] Indigo was the

[1] For Ilbert Bill, see below, page 498. Rudd was a planter's assistant who committed a peculiarly brutal and cowardly murder.

Mr. Long, the missionary, was fined and imprisoned for translating and publishing a vernacular drama—*Nil Durpan*, the 'Mirror of Indigo'. Sir Bartle Frere wrote of this trial and the Chief Justice's outrageous summing-up, 'It has been rather a shock to all my notions. I had much sympathy with the planters, which has been pretty well corrected by their un-English hatred of free discussion and vindictive alliance with the Press to punish a man for a libel not half as bad as the Press publishes daily on Government, and to punish him by a form of trial which does not admit of his pleading the truth or meeting the charge fairly. The sight of English judges behaving as —— and —— have done throws everything else into the shade.'—Martineau, *Life of Sir Bartle Frere*, i. 361.

[2] In 1881 the 'British-born' population was 99,738, over two-thirds being in the army. Planters and their friends numbered 1,119.

only crop which attracted the non-official European to interest himself in ordinary Indian agriculture, and vegetable dyes were already a failing industry. Nor was the indigo planter given much assistance by the Government. The Bengal Land Act of 1859 limited the powers of the *Zemindar*, and consequently of the indigo planter, over the *ryot*. It is true that the Lord Chief Justice did his best to nullify the Act by 'deciding broadly and roundly against the *ryot*'; 'the civilian magistrates and judges, however, so arranged matters that the planters have got very scant satisfaction from the decision of the Chief Justice'.[1]

The Mutiny had a more subtle effect upon district administration. The suddenness of the outbreak suggested that British officials were out of touch with the people, and that Indian officials could not be trusted. This led to a reaction in favour of the direct or personal system. The Punjab, which had been recently settled in a very direct and personal manner, had shown a remarkable loyalty to the Company, and the appointment of Sir John Lawrence as Viceroy, in 1864, completed the triumph of this school of thought. From 1860 the general policy was to build up a strong cadre of British officials, encouraging them to tour as much as possible. The decade which followed the Mutiny was the heyday of the paternal system. The new Government ruled according to European ideas without any serious attempt to gauge educated Indian opinion, depending for knowledge upon the District Officer, who was almost invariably a British covenanted servant. Three Indians were included in the Legislative Council, established under the Indian Councils Act of 1861, but the first three nominees—the Maharaja of Patiala, the Raja of Benares, and Sir Dinkar Rao—were all drawn from the Indian nobility, and it was not for some years that the Indian members could possibly be considered to represent the agricultural, professional, or business interests of British India. In the *mofussil* the British official became the invariable channel for all Government activities. If the Mutiny taught the danger of interfering too drastically in matters which had a religious significance, it also killed the 'filtration theory' of early English Liberals—the idea that India could be westernized by the spread of knowledge and ideas through the educated classes. The latter had very little place in the new structure which was built up on the ruins of the East India Company.

In spite of Lawrence's predilections, the supremacy of the District Officer was never complete, and was soon curtailed. District administration, at the time of the Mutiny, was of three types. In the Non-Regula-

---

[1] G. O. Trevelyan, *The Competition Wallah*, 315.

tion Provinces—Sind, the Punjab, Oudh, Nagpur, and Lower Burma—
the Commissioners and Deputy Commissioners resembled the old pre-
British officials, the *subadars* and *tarafdars* of Mogul times. They carried out all administrative orders, tried criminals, collected revenue and
decided civil cases. They had a rough criminal code, but civil cases
were settled by a mixture of custom, common sense, and a reference to
standing orders. The system was probably well suited to the rural
districts. As John Lawrence stated in 1856,

' we have a procedure without any pretension to exactitude; but a procedure
which provides for the litigants and their witnesses being confronted in open
court, for a decision being arrived at immediately, and for judgment being
delivered to the parties then and there'.

The first duty of the Deputy Commissioner was to be accessible, and
there was no form of public activity which was outside his purview.

In the older Regulation Provinces of Bengal, Madras, Bombay, and
Agra the District Officer had a very jealous rival in the District Courts.
These administered an elaborate series of regulations to which had been
given the authority of law. The Collector here was far less of an autocrat than the Deputy Commissioner in the Punjab, but in the *ryotwari*
districts of Bombay and Madras his duties took him into every village,
and his powers were various and comprehensive. In the *zemindari* areas
the Collector-Magistrate was still more limited in his activities. In
revenue matters he dealt through the *Zemindars,* and usually knew
little of his district. The Bengal and Punjab systems thus represented
the extremes of the rule of law and the rule of men.

During the twenty years which followed the Mutiny there was a
rapid process of assimilation and unification throughout British India.
Certain differences have never been eliminated, but the rule of law was
soon established throughout the provinces, chiefly by the legislative
activity of the Government of India, which from 1861 onwards poured
out a series of enactments covering every side of Indian life. Subsequently the various activities of the District Officer were further
whittled away by the establishment of highly centralised departments,
and later still by the transfer of certain powers to such elected bodies as
District Local Boards. The District Officer has remained an important
part of the administrative machine. He is responsible for the preservation of order, controls a large revenue establishment, and still wields
considerable influence and patronage, but the *subadari* system in its
more extreme form was only extended to a fraction of British India, and
did not last for more than a few years before and after the Mutiny.

It is natural that the British should look back upon this period as the golden age of their administration. The first officials sent into the Non-Regulation Provinces were picked men, and buckled to their task with enthusiasm. The despatch and efficiency of despotic methods are possibly more attractive to the rulers than to the ruled, but the system was remarkably effective in restoring order, and seems to have given the ordinary cultivator the type of government which he likes. Whether such methods could have survived into more settled times is doubtful. The growth of trade demands a more formal civil code, and despotism is apt to degenerate into bureaucracy. It was during the Governor-Generalship of Lord Lawrence, the great exemplar of personal rule, that the Chief Court was established in the Punjab; and the same year, 1866, saw the extension of the Code of Civil Procedure to the Non-Regulation Provinces, and the right of lawyers to plead in all courts. This meant the end of the District Officer's power to stand between the debtor and the creditor. The financing of agriculture by the money-lender, or *kirar*, was an established custom in the Punjab before the British went there, but the *kirar's* powers of recovery were strictly limited, and dependent on the good will of the village communities. The Punjab and the Non-Regulation Provinces were now to experience the rigid application of Western legal methods, and of civil legislation 'based on the assumption that the large majority of men are thrifty, intelligent, and business-minded'. One result of introducing Crown rule into India was a wide-spread belief that the Company's former actions had often been 'illegal', and must be regularised. The India Councils Act of 1861 was followed by the passing of Land Revenue, Tenancy, and Forest Acts, and by the three great codes—the Penal Code,[1] the Criminal Procedure Code, and the Civil Procedure Code. The Regulation Provinces were left some powers of subordinate legislation, but the Government of India rapidly filled up any gaps in the legal system, until the Cattle Trespass Act 'laid down the fine to be paid by an old woman whose cattle strayed anywhere between the Himalayas and Cape Comorin'.

All this legislative activity curtailed the executive authority of the District Officer, and his sphere of action was further reduced by the development of technical departments, not directly under his control and tending to become more and more centralised. These added to the rigidity of the administrative machine, and made it difficult for the

[1] The Indian Penal Code was drafted by Macaulay in 1837, but was only introduced, after revision by Sir Barnes Peacocke, in 1862.

District Officer to ease those hardships which must occur when illiterate villagers are first brought into contact with Western legal and commercial ideas. The district administration, instead of being centred in one man, was divided amongst a number of European heads of departments, nearly all of whom looked to their provincial headquarters for orders. The Police Act of 1861 laid the foundation of the existing constabulary, based originally on the Irish model, with each district force under the command of a British Superintendent of Police. The Crown Government showed none of the Company's reluctance to increase the European staff, and a number of new services were organised. These were entirely under European control, partly because they were nearly all technical, and intended to be run on Western lines, but chiefly because the Mutiny had left an unwillingness to use Indians in key positions. India has never been flooded with minor European officials in the manner of the French colonies, and the whole European staff in civil employ has never exceeded thirty per million of the population, but the heads of departments in each district remained predominantly British until the War.[1] An Educational Department under official 'Directors of Public Instruction' took the place of the amateur committees of pre-Mutiny days. A Public Works Department undertook irrigation work, roads, and buildings. The Sanitary Boards, founded originally in 1864 to look after the health of the European troops, were extended into a Public Health Department. Agriculture, forestry, and railways all required specialised services. In this way the great bureaucracy was built up, and because jealousy is the besetting sin of all officials, there was continual friction between departments about their proper spheres, and still more between the Government of India and the provinces, about supervision, expenditure, and control. Lord Mayo introduced some common sense into the relations between the central Government and the provinces, but until 1870 'the distribution of the public income', according to Sir Richard Strachey, 'degenerated into something like a scramble, in which the most violent had the advantage'.

Departmentalism was the outstanding weakness of the new bureaucracy. Half a century later Lord Curzon fought against it with little success. 'Departmentalism', he wrote, 'is not a moral delinquency. It is an intellectual hiatus—the complete absence of thought or appre-

[1] In 1913 there were 2501 administrative and judicial appointments with salaries of over Rs. 800 per month; 2153 were held by Europeans, 106 by Anglo-Indians, 242 by Indians.

hension of anything outside the purely departmental aspects of the matter under discussion.'[1] The division of authority, and the separate control from headquarters, discouraged initiative, and thus destroyed the great virtue of the personal and paternal method of administration. Climate and the instincts of the Indian clerical castes both incline the official to follow a routine, and for some years the newer services, not too well paid and with no traditions behind them, did not attract a very enterprising type of Englishman.

' On the first introduction of the Constabulary Police in 1861, the majority of the posts in the new department . . . were given to officers of the Indian Army, and they continued to be filled from this source for some time. These were the men who established the present police system in India. Side by side with them entered another type of man, a type which has been portrayed for us by Trollope and other lesser lights of the Victorian age—the amiable detrimental, the younger son, or the sporting public school boy, too lazy or too stupid for the Army, but prepared to go anywhere or do anything which did not involve prolonged drudgery.'[2]

For the Forestry Department it was difficult to find Englishmen with the technical training, and little could be done until Dr. Dietrich Brandis was brought out from Germany, and in 1864 became Inspector-General of Forests. The educational service suffered, during these early years, from the Government's desire to make a good showing for very little money. When it was proposed to start two schools for training teachers, the Government objected to paying 500 rupees a month to the staff.

' Cheaper men could be had for normal schools, and were recruited from the ranks of elementary teachers; so that men like Mr. Paul Bradley, of *Our Mutual Friend*, were responsible for the training of Indian teachers. It was an egregious blunder. Such men, however competent in a narrow way, had neither the education nor the imagination needed to train Indian teachers.'[3]

Education was to remain the Cinderella of the services. The new official Directors could do little more for the education of the masses than induce the indigenous schools to submit to inspection and advice in return for a grant in aid. The position was reviewed by the Hunter Commission of 1882, and it was only from about this date that local authorities were assisted to open new schools where most required. While it is true in a sense that India had a system of organised State education

---

[1] Lord Ronaldshay, *The Life of Lord Curzon*, ii. 321.

[2] J. C. Curry, *The Indian Police*, 54.

[3] H. Dodwell, *A Sketch of the History of India*, 204.

earlier than England, and half a century before the Dutch East Indies,[1] the scope of the Government's early activities was severely limited.

The other departments began to function with moderate efficiency. The expatriated Englishman is usually a conscientious worker, and the little groups of European officials gradually settled down to the routine of station life. They were just sufficient in number to form a society of their own, aloof from the Indian population. It was an administration fitted to deal with a static and contented population. Its weakness lay in its uniformity, which discouraged all experiments, and its lack of contact with Indian life, which made it difficult to use such indigenous forces as were available.

For a few years these deficiencies were not apparent. The post-Mutiny period began with a great increase in material prosperity, and of this the cultivator had his full share. The rapid development of communications, of metalled roads, railways, and ports, brought the *ryot* into the ambit of world trading conditions, and it so happened that his first experience was fortunate. The American Civil War made Lancashire turn to India for her raw cotton. Between 1859 and 1863 the export more than doubled, and prices increased fourfold. Simultaneously labour was in great demand for new irrigation canals, for the railways and roads, and for tea and coffee gardens. During the 'sixties the Punjab alone constructed 400 miles of railway and 1000 miles of metalled roads, neither of which were known in Northern India before the Mutiny. By 1872 some 2750 miles of irrigation canal had been made. It was a time of high prices, but also of high wages, of prosperity for the peasant, and of over-optimism in business. The present generation, reading of such a period, will turn the page confidently expecting an account of the subsequent depression. Our fathers knew little of trade cycles, the *ryot* knew nothing at all. Villagers were now introduced to a money economy, which was entirely new to them.[2] Few *ryots* knew how to use, or even how to hoard this new commodity. In parts of the Deccan the *ryots* are reputed to have put silver bands on their cart wheels. Undoubtedly much of the silver which found its way to the villages was converted wastefully into ornaments. The *ryot*, accustomed

---

[1] 'About 1900 Holland was still very far behind in this important direction. In India, Great Britain had half-a-century's start.'—Kat Angelino, *Colonial Policy*, ii. 195.

[2] Cf. Ludhiana Settlement Report of 1853: 'It would scarcely be saying too much to say that, excepting the village headman . . . none others possess the ordinary use of money'. Quoted in M. Darling's *The Punjab Peasant in Prosperity and Debt*, 207.

to save part of a good harvest in the form of grain, now invested his surplus in the form of bangles, forgetting that when the lean times returned it might be difficult to change them back into food.

The Government of India felt that Providence was rewarding them for their financial reforms, their legislative efforts, their free trade policy, and their expenditure on public works. Disillusion began about 1865, with the collapse of the speculative commercial 'boom' which followed the rise in cotton. Indian merchants were accustomed to trade movements being dependent on the monsoon, not on long term cycles, and their first contact with world trade encouraged the most extravagant ideas. The financial methods of Bombay company promoters were reminiscent of the South Sea Bubble, and the most flagrant malpractices were encouraged by the lack of an adequate commercial law.

' Companies were started for every imaginable purpose—banks and financial associations, land reclamation, trading, cotton cleaning, pressing and spinning companies, coffee companies, shipping and steamer companies, hotel companies, livery stables and veterinary companies, and companies for making bricks.' [1]

As in 1920, any share placed on the market rose to absurd heights, and to complete the parallel there was an ill-conceived scheme for reclaiming Back Bay. The crash came very rapidly. The Banks of Bombay and Agra went into liquidation, and much Indian money was lost when the firm of Overend and Gurney was ruined.

The financial cataclysm was followed by another and more tragic portent, the famine in Orissa. India had two crop failures in the ten years following the Mutiny, but the first, which affected the North-West Provinces in 1860, caused no great suffering. The country had recently been opened up by new roads, and by the East India Railway. Relief works were started, part of the population migrated into the adjoining area of newly irrigated land, and grain was moved into the provinces. 'It was a famine of work rather than of food.' [2] The Orissan famine presented a marked contrast. The area chiefly affected was a strip of territory between 'pathless jungle and an impracticable sea', intersected by short rapid streams which are very liable to flood. The line from Calcutta to Madras now runs through this country, but in those days there were neither roads nor railways. The inhabitants had been tempted by high prices to export much of their grain, and when

[1] *Report of Commissioners on Failure of Bank of Bombay*, 2. This bank was under Government supervision.
[2] Report of C. B. Smith, N.W.P. Famine, 1862, Pt. 1, para 25.

the monsoon of 1865 proved a total failure there was an alarming shortage of stocks. Some district officials seem to have suspected this in October,[1] but for seven months Sir Cecil Beadon, the Lieutenant-Governor of Bengal, refused to allow any Government importation of rice. He appears to have held very strong views against interfering with economic laws. By May the Viceroy, Lord Lawrence, had become seriously alarmed. It was then too late. Cargo boats were sent down the coast, but the monsoon had begun to blow, and it took one of them seven weeks to unload at Puri. The people 'were in the condition of passengers in a ship without provisions'. Heavy floods completed the damage which the drought had begun, and it is estimated that a quarter of the inhabitants died.[2] Seldom can official complacency and doctrinaire economics have combined to produce such a holocaust.

The famine and the financial slump only partially checked the general agricultural prosperity and the Government's passion for new legislation and new departmental activities. Paternalism remained unchallenged for some years, but these two events were a foretaste of the 'seventies, when world trade was unfavourable, and when the effect of bad harvests was accentuated by currency troubles and the Afghan War.

CHAPTER III

DECLINE OF PATERNALISM

The period of 'laissez-faire': its influence on Indian bureaucracy: effects on village life: agricultural debt: the money-lender: the origin of debt: famines and scarcity: famines of 1860, 1867, 1873 and 1877: experimental remedies: financial policy: fiscal issue: local government: indianization of services: control of Press: Ilbert Bill.

It is customary to trace the decline of the paternal system from the first meeting of the Indian Congress in 1885, but a marked change in the temper of the administration had occurred some years previously. The

---

[1] There is some doubt on this point. Cf. Cotton's *Indian and Home Memories*, 69: 'One of the local magistrates told me that his first knowledge of distress was when he found an old woman in his bathroom, eating his soap'.

[2] Orissa Report, 1867.

self-confidence of the post-Mutiny period began to dwindle after Lord Lawrence's departure in 1869. Neither new laws nor new technical departments were achieving the social and economic revolution expected from them. Brahminism showed signs of reviving rather than of declining. The educated classes, so far as they were articulate, were hostile, and the younger generation eager to take up the racial challenge implied in the behaviour of English planters and business men. In 1873 Sir George Campbell, Lieutenant-Governor of Bengal, was already suggesting the need of a Press Act, such as was afterwards passed by Lord Lytton. A similar disappointment was felt about government work in the districts. Four serious famines occurred between 1867 and 1877, and in no case did the administrative machinery function satisfactorily. By 1870 a severe agricultural depression had set in, after the exaggerated prices of the cotton shortage; and the sudden growth of agricultural debt and of litigation threw doubts on the whole system of land administration. There was a reaction against the optimism and aggressive efficiency of the 'sixties. Even the first census, taken in 1872, may have emphasised the impossibility of effecting much by direct methods applied to some two hundred and fifty million people. For the next thirty years the bureaucracy, now fully centralised and firmly in power, was strongly influenced by the *laissez-faire* theory of administration which was then popular in Europe. Lord Lawrence's successors, Lord Mayo and Lord Northbrook, were both products of Gladstonian Liberalism; and the latter reflected a wide-spread feeling amongst the higher officials when he declared that India needed a rest, and wrote, in 1873, that his 'chief aim was to take off taxes, and stop unnecessary legislation'.[1]

Lord Lawrence had entered into the minutiæ of administration in a manner which no subsequent Viceroy, except Lord Curzon, has even attempted. After his departure the internal administration became a huge machine, receiving little stimulus from outside. Viceroys, whether Liberal or Conservative, were chiefly occupied with foreign affairs, the frontier problem, their relations with the Indian princes, and questions arising from the growing demand of educated Indians for some share in the government. English interest in India had slackened soon after the Mutiny, and criticism was confined to a small group of Liberal members.[2] The influence of the Secretary of State, though tending to

[1] Bernard Mallet, *Thomas George, Earl of Northbrook*, 69.

[2] Mr. Baxter seems to have been the first of a long series of Members of Parliament who toured India in a critical spirit.

increase from 1870 onwards, was confined to matters of general policy, and especially to foreign affairs and finance. Indian opinion was almost entirely disregarded till after 1885. If the years immediately before and after the Mutiny were the heyday of personal and individual rule in India, the 'seventies saw bureaucracy in its purest form. The first years of the 'eighties brought misgivings and doubts. Certain aspects of Lord Ripon's administration and the remarkable demonstration of Indian feeling at its close showed that new forces were coming into play. The year 1885 may be taken as ending the two decades during which the Indian bureaucratic system was built up, with very little influence from outside.

Except for Disraeli's term of office, which had its Indian counterpart in Lord Lytton's aggressive foreign policy, the Liberals had been dominant in England throughout these twenty years. In a modified form their views had influenced the Indian administration. Translated into bureaucratic terms, Liberalism meant that Government should 'keep the ring', allowing complete freedom of trade, encouraging free competition, strictly enforcing all legal contracts, interfering as little as possible between different classes and interests, avoiding all activities which might be left to private enterprise or private charity. It was the exact antithesis of the attitude which would be adopted by the ordinary British District Officer when dealing with a scattered rural population, almost entirely illiterate and traditionally used to autocratic rule. One Punjab official has left a classic account of the hardships which necessarily follow the introduction of Western legal and commercial ideas into an Eastern agricultural country.[1] Throughout the villages of the *ryotwari* provinces, and especially in the Deccan and the Punjab, the following process was taking place during the quarter of a century subsequent to the Mutiny. Each individual *ryot*, after paying the assessment for two years, had become the recognised owner of the land under the Government. Then, during the 'sixties, the rise in prices, combined with an increase in population, gave ownership of land a definite value, while village economy was being slowly changed from barter to a cash basis. In the same decade a complicated civil code was introduced, and also a Law of Evidence modelled on the English system. Chief Courts were established by this time in each province, and could be relied upon, when a case was taken to them on appeal, to give a decision based on legal technicalities rather than on common sense and

[1] S. S. Thorburn, *Mussalmans and Moneylenders in the Punjab*, 1886.

knowledge of village conditions.[1] From 1870 the agricultural boom was followed by a slump. Owing to the pressure of population land still retained some value, but money prices fell rapidly, following the lead given by cotton, which was once more being exported from America. The *ryots,* whose first experience of money had given them exaggerated ideas of the amounts they could afford to spend on weddings, funerals, etc., now found the Government assessment a grievous burden. A series of famines added to their troubles, for even if a family could purchase enough grain, a failure in the monsoon meant a heavy loss in cattle, which had to be hastily replaced before the sowing season.

The next stage was inevitable in any peasant community. The *ryots* borrowed heavily from the grain merchants and money-lenders. The latter had also, as is the habit of middlemen, done extremely well during the boom period. They had money to invest, and lent freely. The law and the new land tenure placed them in a strong position. They no longer lent money on personal security, or depended upon the goodwill of the village community. In the Punjab 'the mortgage that was rare in the days of the Sikhs appeared in every village, and by 1878 seven per cent. of the province was pledged'.[1] The peasants, knowing nothing of the subtleties of mortgages with and without possession, were defrauded in every way. An appeal to the Court only meant their further undoing. Mr. Darling has described the sequel in the Punjab.

' By 1880 the unequal fight between the peasant proprietor and the money-lender had ended in a crushing victory for the latter, and as someone said, apropos of the wealth that was pouring into the country, the money-lender got the oyster, while the Government and the cultivator each got a shell. For the next thirty years the money-lender was at his zenith, and multiplied and prospered exceedingly, to such good effect that the number of bankers and money-lenders (and their dependents) increased from 53,263 in 1868 to 193,890 in 1911.' [2]

The same improvident borrowing and unscrupulous lending was occurring throughout the Deccan and Madras, and also in Indian States, like Baroda.[3] In those parts of the Bombay Presidency where rainfall is precarious, matters came to a head very rapidly, and riots

---

[1] As, for example, when 'the Chief Court, on the revision side, quashed a decision ... on the technical ground that as the officer giving the decision had signed himself "Magistrate of the District" instead of "Deputy Commissioner", he had acted "*ultra vires*".' See Trevaskis, *The Land of the Five Rivers,* 298-9.

[2] Darling, *The Punjab Peasant in Prosperity and Debt,* 208.

[3] See the *Report on Agricultural Indebtedness in Baroda State,* 1913.

broke out in 1874, leading to the appointment of the Deccan Riots Commission, and ultimately to the passing of the Deccan Agriculturists Relief Act of 1879.[1] This Act abolished imprisonment for debt, and enabled a Court to demand a full account of all transactions in cases brought before them, and to reduce interest to a reasonable rate. For some years it checked the worst evils of money-lending, and the Famine Commission, appointed in 1880, advised its extension to other provinces; but lawyers and money-lenders gradually learnt to evade its provisions. The legalism of the Chief Courts and the indifference of the Supreme Government had allowed the money-lenders to get into such a strong position that no preventive legislation, nor advances from Government under the Agriculturists' Loans Act, were likely to be of much avail. In 1880 the Famine Commission reported that 'one-third of the land-holding classes are deeply and inextricably in debt, and that at least an equal proportion are in debt, though not beyond the power of recovering themselves'.[2]

A controversy has arisen as to how far this state of affairs was due to such factors as heavy Government assessments, the machinations of lawyers and money-lenders, the difficulty of raising money to replace stock after famines, and the encouragement by Brahmins of heavy expenditure on religious ceremonies. The discussion has been embittered by political feeling, but the historian will find it difficult to avoid the conclusion which was reached by the tactless peace-maker. The accusations made by all parties seem to be correct. The first assessments in the Central Provinces, and the thirty years' assessments made in Bombay and Madras after the Mutiny, were undoubtedly influenced by the high prices and the general optimism of the time. The vague and unscientific rule about 'half the net assets' was still adhered to, and the Deccan assessments were roundly condemned as excessive by Sir Auckland Colvin, Sir William Hunter, and other officials.[3] Since 1875 the land

[1] *Report of the Committee on the Riots in Deccan*, 1876.

[2] *Report of Famine Commission*, 1880.

[3] The idea of extending the permanent settlement throughout India was brought forward after the Mutiny, and in 1862 Sir Charles Wood announced that the Cabinet had accepted the principle. The question was discussed, intermittently, for twenty years, and finally shelved in 1883. The most cogent argument against the idea was that if the assessments made at that period had been accepted they would have been fixed on a basis of abnormal prices. Subsequent fluctuations due to movements of currency and world prices emphasised the advantage—from the Government's and the *ryot's* standpoint—of some elasticity. Rates are now normally revised every twenty to thirty years.

revenue has probably taken a smaller share of the total agricultural produce, but the heavy assessments of the 'sixties played their part in the economic triumph of the money-lender. Later investigations do not suggest that land revenue demands are often the original cause of a peasant taking a loan, but the insistence on regular cash payments at certain fixed dates, irrespective of the state of the market, tempts any-one who is already in debt to borrow some more with the idea of re-paying a larger instalment when he has sold his produce. Michaelmas rent-day produces the same result in some parts of England.

Money-lenders throughout the world have so many enemies and so few apologists that it is hardly necessary to enumerate the ways in which they are apt to fail as good citizens. In India the *bania* caste has been singularly lacking in men of light and leading, and this may account for their failure either to defend their transactions in public or to repudiate the methods adopted by the many black sheep within their ranks. They seem to have little corporate feeling, due perhaps to the large numbers of outsiders who have joined their ranks. It is probably unfair to lay too much stress on the very high rates of interest which are charged, for this at least is a matter of bargaining, and the security is often very poor. The *bania's* worst offence is the manner in which he trades upon illiteracy and ignorance of the law. Sir Thomas Hope, in a speech made in 1879, summarised many of the ways in which the peasant is enmeshed once he has taken a loan.

' That the money-lenders do obtain bonds on false pretences; enter in them sums larger than agreed upon; deduct extortionate premiums; credit produce at fraudulent prices; retain liquidated bonds and sue on them; use threats and warrants of imprisonment to extort fresh bonds for sums not advanced; charge interest unstipulated for, over-calculated or in contravention of Hindu law, and commit a score of other rogueries—these are facts proved by evidence so overwhelming that I scarcely know what to quote out of the five volumes composing the Report of the Commission.' [1]

The burden of religious and social ceremonials—weddings, funerals, and purifications—became far more serious when the *ryot* had something more than his personal security to pledge. The high expense of marriages has long been a feature of Indian life, and was one reason for the prevalence of female infanticide. It remains a frequent original cause for taking a loan, and such a debt is the hardest to repay, for it is entirely unremunerative and very rapidly disbursed. Brahmins and money-lenders undoubtedly conspire to mulct the non-Brahmin Hindu,

[1] Speech in support of Deccan Agriculturists Relief Act. Quoted by Darling, *The Punjab Peasant in Prosperity and Debt*, 224.

especially over such grotesque and superstitious survivals as the insistence on ceremonial purification after certain diseases, or after an accidental breaking of caste. A quotation from Dr. Rabindranath Tagore's novel, *The Home and the World*, will be sufficient to explain how many debts are first incurred.

' Panchu's wife had just died of a lingering consumption. Panchu must undergo purification to cleanse himself of sin and to propitiate the community. The community has calculated and informed him that it will cost one hundred and twenty-three rupees.'

Amongst the landless poor, who form nearly two-fifths of the population—the village servants, craftsmen, factory workers, and wage-earning farm servants—these observances are almost the only reason for borrowing those larger loans for which a written bond is taken. The extent of indebtedness amongst the lower caste non-agricultural Hindus proves the importance of these social and religious demands.

The last but possibly the chief cause for the growth of agricultural debt is the occasional failure of the monsoon. This raises the question of famines, the subject of so much controversy. There is abundant evidence that a large part of the peninsula has been subject from the earliest times to the complete failure of crops and fodder. The normal annual rainfall varies from practically *nil* at one end of the Indo-Gangetic plain to 500 inches in parts of Assam, but it is also subject to great local variations which chiefly affect those areas with a low average precipitation— the Deccan 'about the Ghats', much of Bihar, the Punjab, and the United Provinces, and the northern parts of Madras. As the population increased it tended to spread from the safe but densely settled areas into the more precarious districts. Villages could survive one bad season from their accumulated stocks of grain, though most of the cattle would die and make the next year's sowing difficult. The second failure of the monsoon would complete the tragedy, and the only solution was migration. There was no economic urge to send grain into such areas, even if the practical difficulties of transport had not been overwhelming. A famine was generally the result of two successive bad seasons spread over a large area. Little is known about the fourteen major famines between 1660 and 1750.[1] These events were looked upon as natural calamities, and in those days of slow communications probably had little more effect upon other parts of India than the tragedy of the Yangtse inundations has had upon the modern world. Probably a century hence men will find our comparative indifference to wholesale starvation in China even

[1] Loveday, A., *History and Economics of Indian Famines*, App. A.

more surprising than the fatalism with which Indian rulers, and later the
East India Company, regarded the loss of life due to famine. The latter

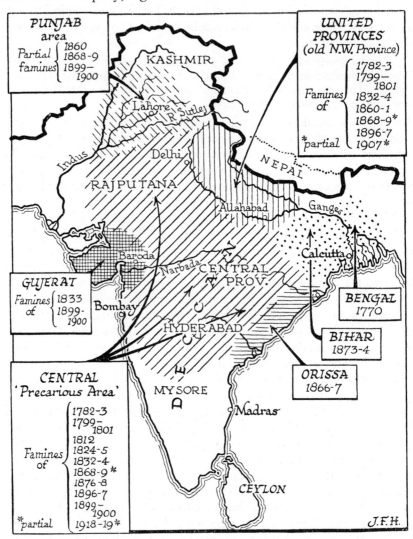

SKETCH MAP ILLUSTRATING FAMINES FROM 1770 ONWARDS.

had, at least, the excuse that they were dependent upon animal transport, and this made a drought-affected area almost impassable. Earlier
efforts at famine prevention and mitigation were limited to irrigation, to

regulating the grain trade, to the establishment of relief works and distribution centres, either outside the area or at places which could be
reached by water, and to setting an example of migration by withdrawing troops.

Some account has already been given of the Company's first introduction to these calamities, but for some years each famine was treated
as a separate problem, and the Government, after their complete failure
to cope with the 1770 famine in Bengal, made various experiments,
none very successful. The 1803 famine in the Deccan was mostly outside British territory, but relief works were opened near Bombay, and
according to one estimate, which is probably optimistic, 100,000 lives
were saved.[1] The conquests of Wellesley and Lord Hastings spread the
Company's rule over most of the precarious areas, except the extreme
north, and by 1837 the Government was faced by a widespread famine in
the Deccan, most of which was then within their territory; the new
civil administration seems to have been totally unable to rise to the
situation. Relief works were opened, but thousands crowded to them,
and the military had to be called in to stop rioting. Relief was given to
able-bodied men, and some food was distributed, but this only reached
an insignificant fraction. In the neighbouring non-British territories the
general policy adopted during the first half of the century was similar,
and equally unsuccessful.

Under Crown government famines began to be studied systematically, and it is possible to trace the development of a definite policy. The
factor of internal war, which complicated so many previous famines,
now disappears, and, with a settled administration, statistics become
more reliable. The 1860 famine in the North-West Provinces illustrates these points. The new East and West Jumna canals protected
nearly a million acres in the middle of the area, and about 160,000 of the
population migrated into the canal colonies. The new railway brought
grain in bulk from Calcutta. Two other principles were applied. Direct
relief in cash was given to those who were unable to leave their homes,
but work was demanded, mostly on the roads, from the able-bodied.

The Orissan famine of 1867 has already been described. It was a
reversion to earlier conditions, for Orissa had not been opened up, and
the only lesson learnt was that while the ordinary course of trade may
cause a movement of grain out of an area in times of plenty, it will not
bring grain back into an area of poverty, and it is necessary to forestall a

---

[1] James Forbes, *Oriental Memoirs*, iv. 291-5.

shortage. The influence of this failure was seen six years later in what has been called the 'panic famine' of 1873, when, on the threat of a food shortage in Bihar, some £6,500,000 was spent on the importation and distribution of grain. The Government was left at the end with 100,000 tons of unsaleable rice, and had to revise its ideas. After the Orissa fiasco, and during the more localised famine in Rajputana the next year, the principle had been laid down that local authorities would be personally responsible for any loss of life due to a drought, but the Bihar famine suggested that 'the task of saving life irrespective of cost is one which is beyond our power to undertake. The embarrassment of debt, and weight of taxation consequent on the expense thereby involved, would soon become more fatal than the famine itself'.[1]

These famines undermined the basis of paternal government. They showed that peace, an incorrupt judiciary, and an active administration would not necessarily bring security to the peasant, contentment to the townsman, or prosperity to the country as a whole. The final blow to the complacency of the early 'sixties came in Lord Lytton's unhappy term of office. The famine of 1877 struck the popular imagination, not only because of its severity, but because it coincided with the second Afghan War, and with the ostentatious and ill-timed *durbar* at which Queen Victoria was proclaimed Empress of India. The famine was due to a very widespread failure of the monsoon, causing a shortage of food all over India, but its relief was undoubtedly hampered by the army's demands on supplies and transport, and the absorption of the Council in other affairs.[2] Famine conditions affected 200,000 square miles and a population of thirty-six millions in Madras, Bombay, Mysore, and Haidarabad. The position was worst in Madras, where the population had increased very rapidly since the end of the Carnatic wars.

The Government was defeated by the area as well as the completeness of the crop failure. Works were opened for four hundred thousand people in Madras, but proved totally inadequate, and by September two millions were in receipt of relief.

In all provinces too much attention was concentrated upon relief works for the able-bodied. The Government was obsessed with the idea (which still survives in many countries) that there is something

---

[1] Sir R. Temple's *Report*, ii. 19.

[2] Lord Lytton insisted upon holding the durbar. 'If we are really threatened with a serious famine . . . the same opportunity will enable the Government of India to enter into timely and personal consultation with the heads of local administration.' See *Lord Lytton's Indian Administration*, Lady Betty Balfour, 115.

immoral in distributing public money to anybody except the completely infirm, without demanding some labour in return. A crop failure produces a sudden unemployment problem, and the Indian Government was faced with the question which has so disturbed the Governments of Europe and America since the last war, whether it is better to distribute relief directly, or encourage employment by undertaking more or less productive public works. In dealing with long-term unemployment there is much to be said for the second method, but for a short and violent dislocation the first is undoubtedly the best. The famine of 1877 proved that, though the railways could get grain into the famine area, there would be a heavy loss of life, due to starvation and all its consequences, unless some method of distribution was organised, village by village, either directly by parcelling out grain, or indirectly through the shops and a system of doles. Cholera and fever always follow in the wake of drought and underfeeding, and the 1877 famine, although eleven million pounds was expended on relief, resulted in between five and six million deaths. A Famine Commission, under General Richard Strachey, issued a report in 1880 which did something to systematise the granting of relief, and arranged for the assignment of an annual amount for the prevention of famine, as a kind of financial insurance. There was, however, no serious failure of monsoon for another twenty years.

The group of famines which occurred between 1865 and 1880 are important, not only for the suffering and loss of life involved, but because they happened at a transitional period when India was gradually changing on to a cash basis. The *ryot* had not had time to adjust his mind to the new order of things before he was faced by natural calamities which not only drained away his cash, but also destroyed his cattle. A slight fodder famine may do little harm, for it kills off some of the diseased and superfluous animals which are a feature of Hindu India, but 1877 left a vast tract without ploughing bullocks, and these had to be replaced. The Government accepted the principle of issuing *takkavi*, or loans at low interest, but most *ryots* were forced to go to their money-lenders, and the famine following the slump meant the final degradation and enslavement of the producer. Over much of India the moneyed classes now took the place of the landlords. The *ryots*, who had had a glimpse of a new world, sank back into their old fatalistic attitude, in which they expect nothing but a bare livelihood from the soil. The next twenty years were seasons of normal harvests, but prices remained low, and the years 1881-91 were marked by further pressure on the soil, due to an increase of population amounting to nearly ten per cent., of which only a very small proportion was absorbed by the towns.[1] Contact with the West brought little new life into the villages. A few new commodities made their appearance in the *bazars*, and the countryman slowly learnt to use the railways, but the land short-age and the caste system combined to keep life static and to kill ambition.

Something of this fatalism infected the Government of India in its dealings with economic questions. Each disaster confirmed its belief in Free Trade and non-interference. Sir John Strachey, who became Financial Member of Council in 1876, wished to make India 'a great free port, open to the commerce of the world'. He held the view, for which the present generation should not be too hasty in condemning him, that prosperity could only come from the rapid circulation of money and the easy movement of goods to their best market. He did away with that absurd anachronism, the inland customs line, a ditch and cactus hedge which stretched from Attock to the Mahanadi, a distance of 2500 miles. He cut down the tariff on many imported commodities and abolished the duty on sugar. Only on one economic question did any serious dispute arise, but this was important because it raised a consti-tutional issue, and later became a matter of political controversy. A five per cent. duty on manufactured cotton goods had been imposed for many years, in spite of continual demands from Lancashire for its reduc-tion. It was not considered as a protective measure, but merely a source of revenue. It would probably have been repealed as soon as financial considerations permitted, but in 1877 the House of Commons was ill-advised enough to pass a motion recommending its removal. This roused a kind of vicarious nationalism in the Council, which affirmed their view that it was purely an Indian question, and protested against any suggestion that pressure could be placed on them in the interests of Lancashire. In the end Lord Lytton was forced to use his overriding authority, almost the only instance of the exercise of this power. The removal of the duty—certainly too small to be protective according to modern standards—seems to have had little effect on the development of the Indian industry, which progressed steadily.[2]

The general 'policy of the open door' was continued under Lord

[1] See App. D.

[2]
Cotton Mills		1872-3	1879-80	1884-5	1889-90	1894-5
Number of Mills	-	20	58	81	114	144
Persons employed	-	—	39,537	61,596	99,224	139,578

These figures are taken from D. R. Gadgil, *The Industrial Evolution of India*, 80.

Ripon, and in 1882 Major Baring—afterwards Earl of Cromer—was able to give India a strictly 'free trade' budget, in which no import duties were charged except upon commodities which were subject to an internal excise, such as salt, wines, and spirits. In the same year the salt duties were lowered. The application of English Liberal principles to India has been criticised on the grounds that it was actuated by selfish motives, and that it injured India's development. Opinions on both subjects are unavoidably coloured by our reading of subsequent events, but there is no reason to question the sincerity of Victorian Liberals in their belief that free trade was a universal panacea, and it is doubtful if anything but completely prohibitive tariffs would have materially affected the growth of industrial India. Of the two textile trades, cotton and jute, the latter was almost entirely for export, and it is at least open to dispute whether Indians as a whole would have gained by a sudden rise in the price of cotton cloth at a time when agricultural prices were falling. It would probably have meant a repetition of the speculative mania of 1863-5. It would be a more valid criticism of the fiscal policy that it left the Government far too dependent on land revenue. The continuance of free trade in England was only made possible by the imposition of death duties and a steadily rising income-tax. The formation of Indian society makes it difficult for the Government to take a direct share in commercial prosperity, and until 1900 the land was still considered as the basis of all wealth. It is significant that in 1883 the idea of a permanent settlement throughout India was finally abandoned. Lord Ripon wished to pledge the Government that the only further enhancement of the land revenue would be based on a rise in prices, but even this compromise was not accepted by the Secretary of State.

British Liberalism found a more constructive field of work in the development of local government. The larger cities had had municipalities since shortly before the Mutiny, but they were in charge of nominated commissioners. The latter were gradually replaced by bodies, partly elected, partly nominated, under official chairmen. In 1883 the elective system was further extended and unofficial chairmen were permitted. Lord Ripon's policy was to 'substitute outside control for inside interference'. In rural areas district boards came into being about 1865, and Lord Mayo transferred the control of roads to them. Ripon extended the system by introducing 'taluka' or 'tehsil' boards, covering the divisions of the district.[1] Lord Ripon's resolution of

---

[1] District local boards correspond roughly to county councils, taluka local boards to rural district councils.

May 18, 1882, which extended the number and scope of these local boards, showed that their main purpose was educative. It was 'not primarily with a view to improvement in administration that the measure is put forward and supported. It is chiefly desirable as a measure of political and popular education.' Taking a long view, he was undoubtedly right, but the limited scope of these bodies, and their unrepresentative character, prevented these experiments having much effect. Liberal influence brought some reaction against the racial exclusiveness of this period. Since 1858 Indians had been permitted to enter the Covenanted Civil Service through the competitive examination, but very few had actually done so.[1] Some more definite policy was needed to give them a larger share in the administration. This change of outlook is often connected with Lord Ripon and the Liberal Party, but his predecessor Lord Lytton held strong views on the subject. Like Lord Canning, he believed it would be possible to enlist the services of the landed classes, and turn the *Zemindars* into magistrates and local administrators of the English type, while their sons could find their way into the Civil Service. Canning had appointed a number of honorary magistrates, and did his best to encourage their work, but the idea was never developed. Lord Canning foresaw, when Lawrence was suggested as his successor, how the official mind would react against such an innovation.

' He will go far to upsetting in a year all that I hope to have accomplished in my last three years, both in Oudh and in the Punjab. He will not do it by direct means—I can make that very difficult for any man—but by giving the cold shoulder to all measures for increasing the consequence of and placing trust in the native chiefs and gentry generally.'

Nearly twenty years later Lytton found himself opposed by this 'trade union mentality' amongst the officials, and in a well-known letter to Lord Salisbury he inveighed against 'the fundamental political mistake of able and experienced Indian officials . . . that we can hold India securely by what they call good government; that is to say, by improving the condition of the *ryot*, strictly administering justice, spending immense sums on irrigation works, etc.'[2] To Lord Cranbrook he wrote, in 1879, about 'the acknowledged failure to fulfil fairly the promises

---

[1] The first Indian to enter the Covenanted Civil Service was Mr. Satyendranath Tagore in 1863.

[2] Letter of May 11, 1877. It is quoted in Lady Betty Balfour's *History of Lord Lytton's Indian Administration*, 109.

given'. He had found that since 1870, when an Act of Parliament had been passed enabling the Government of India to appoint Indians to posts hitherto reserved for the Covenanted Civil Service, no serious attempt had been made even to frame regulations for putting the Act into operation. Accordingly in 1879 he produced his plans for the Statutory Civil Service, under which a fifth of the recruitment for the Civil Service could be made from Indians selected by the Provincial Governments, and a proportion of the posts reserved for the Covenanted Civil Service were to be held by men of Indian birth. Lord Ripon continued this policy, but partly from a lack of enthusiasm in the Provincial Governments, and partly because the wealthier *Zemindars* were not inclined to enter public service, the Statutory Civil Service was not a success. It was staffed almost entirely by Indians promoted from the uncovenanted service and was abolished in 1891.

Lord Ripon's Liberalism found an outlet in many fields. Only on one point did he directly reverse his predecessor's policy, but this was in a matter which will always get the maximum of publicity. The 'freedom of the Press' had been a controversial subject since the early days of the Company, when the British free merchants used journalists, like Buckingham, to attack the Government. The quarrel continued after the Mutiny, when the unofficial European Press transferred its attacks to the 'humanity pretenders', and to officials who interfered with the planters' claims to be above the law. By this time there were several Indian newspapers, published either in English or in the vernaculars, but all of them against the Government, and inheriting to the full the traditions of the *Eatanswill Gazette*. Their small circulation and precarious financial position encouraged an irresponsible violence, and they embarrassed the Government, whose own countrymen had been allowed for years to indulge their racial prejudices, and also to print the most astounding criticisms. Occasionally an editor had been deported, but the only Press Act was one introduced by Metcalfe in 1835, which insisted that every book and paper must bear the name of the printer and publisher. It was impossible to legislate against attempts to stir up racial and religious antagonisms without curbing the Anglo-Indian Press, and arousing opposition in England as well as India. Lord Lytton's Vernacular Press Act of 1878, which empowered a magistrate to take a bond from the publisher of any newspaper 'printed in an Oriental language', was too illogical to be either effective or permanent. It was only once put into operation—against the Bengali *Som Prakash* —and was repealed by Lord Ripon in 1882.

21

Another incident, which occurred in the following year, was to have a great influence on India's political development, though in itself it was of comparatively small administrative importance. By this date a few Indians, who had entered the Covenanted Civil Service by examination, had reached the rank of District Judges. No European at that time could be tried for a criminal offence by anyone except another European and the question was raised by an Indian covenanted servant as to his jurisdiction in such cases. Lord Ripon decided to abolish this racial discrimination altogether, and ordered the drafting of a Bill to this effect. This was undertaken by Sir Courtenay Ilbert, the legal member, and approved by the Council. The European community had been disturbed by other features of Lord Ripon's administration. The Ilbert Bill caused an immediate uproar, one of those curious outbursts of racial antipathy and the primitive herd instinct which are apt to afflict an expatriated community in an unsuitable climate. The tragedy of this agitation was that it succeeded, and that, after the Viceroy had been boycotted and insulted, a compromise was reached by which a European arraigned before a District Judge could claim to be tried by a jury of which half were Europeans.

No educated Indian has ever forgotten the lesson of the Ilbert Bill. They were accustomed to rulers who could be influenced by cajolery, entreaty, bribery, or threats of revolt, but it was an entirely new experience to see a Government, and especially the aloof and powerful British Government, deflected from its purpose by newspaper abuse and an exhibition of bad manners. In later days Indian nationalism was to acquire some of its technique from the suffrage movement in England, and more from Irish Home Rulers, but it was the successful agitation against the Ilbert Bill which decided the general lines upon which the Indian politician was to run his campaigns. It is significant that the two years which followed this agitation saw the foundation of the Indian National Congress and the European Association.

CHAPTER IV

THE NORTH-WEST FRONTIER AND BURMA

The imperial and local problems: nature of local problem: Lord Lawrence and the close border: limitations of non-intervention: punitive expeditions: Sandeman's policy: effect of frontier difficulties on administration and upon Indian opinion: relations with Upper Burma: death of King Mindon: Thibaw's misrule: third Burmese War: difficulties of pacification.

BY 1850 the British occupied most of the immense triangle of Northern India. To north-east of this wedge of territory lay the Himalayas. Behind these were Tibet and China. On this side impassable barriers divided India from a static and comparatively peaceful population.[1] The north-west was also mountainous, but by no means impassable. There are numerous passes leading into India, of which the most important are the Khyber, between Kabul and Peshawar, and the Bolan and Kohjak passes, some three hundred miles farther south, between Kandahar and Sind. For centuries these have been trade and military routes, with well-recognised advantages and limitations. The northern passage is the shorter and easier, but Kabul has little fertile land round it. Kandahar is the centre of a rich valley, but the southern route is stony and waterless, and is effectively controlled by any force which may occupy Quetta, on the tableland between the Bolan and Kohjak passes.

On this North-West Frontier the Government had to face two separate problems, one imperial and the other local. The first arose because the Empire was now brought into direct contact with Afghanistan, and behind this infertile unsettled country lay Central Asia, which was neither peaceful nor static. During the first half of the nineteenth century Russia had been expanding steadily southwards and eastwards, driven forward by much the same combination of frontier difficulties and the ambition of her local representatives as had led the British into Northern India. Russian aspirations, real or imaginary, became increasingly important as her outposts approached Afghanistan. After the Crimean War had ruined any prospect of an agreed policy for Central Asia, India was gradually drawn into the vortex of European rivalries about the same period as her peasants and workers were

[1] Post-Mutiny relations with Tibet and Bhutan are discussed in Book VII, chapter 3.

being brought within the sphere of world trade and world currency movements.

The local problem lay in the character of our immediate neighbours, the Pathan and Baluch tribes occupying the maze of hills and valleys between the Indus and Afghanistan. For centuries this had been a no man's land, inhabited by a mixed race of Muslims, who were too numerous and too pugnacious to live peacefully from the cultivation of their limited areas of fertile land. They had grown accustomed to take toll from the trade routes, and to make frequent incursions into the plains. The establishment of Sikh rule in the Punjab had added a religious fervour to these forays. Farther south a strip of desert separated the cultivated area of Sind from the Baluch hillman, but, along the Punjab border, crops and cattle are temptingly close to the Pathan raider. Ranjit Singh marked out a rough frontier, and placed a few lords of the marches in the narrow strip which he claimed on the far side of the Indus. Amongst these Hari Singh, in the Hazara district, and the Italian General Avitabile, at Peshawar, have left a reputation for the cold-blooded ferocity of their rule. The Pathans never threatened the stability of Sikh rule, but the frontier was frequently violated, and remained in a perpetual state of barbaric warfare. In some cases border villages were assigned to soldiers from the Punjab at an annual tribute of a hundred Pathan heads.

It will be convenient to describe separately the course of events and the policy of the Government in connection with each of these two questions—the local or small-scale problem of controlling the tribesmen, and the imperial or large-scale problem of relations with Afghanistan and Central Asia. They cannot, however, be entirely divorced, and no such clear distinction was made by contemporary politicians and officials. Our relations with Afghanistan were affected by the existence of these turbulent Pathans, over some of whom the Amir held a nominal suzerainty. The need of controlling them and the duty of civilising them were favourite arguments of the 'forward' school, who either wished to find a more suitable frontier somewhere in Afghanistan, or had, like Lord Lytton, 'painted a fancy prospect of . . . bequeathing to India the supremacy of Central Asia and the revenues of a first-class power'.[1] Their opponents, belonging to the 'non-intervention' school, considered that the block of mountainous and barbaric country between Russia and India formed a conveniently difficult barrier for a modern

[1] Letter to Sir James Stephen, April 7, 1880. Printed in Lady Betty Balfour's *Lord Lytton's Indian Administration*, 422.

army, and that it was best to interfere as little as possible with Afghanistan or the zone of independent tribesmen. In England the Liberal Party tended to be non-interventionists, and the Conservatives to support the 'forward' school. Neither side had, at first, much knowledge on which to base their views. Policy was decided on general principles, and this led to much confusion of thought. Arguments, suitable to local border questions, were applied to matters of general policy. Lord Lawrence's doctrinaire insistence upon the 'close border' proved impracticable in dealing with tribesmen who were completely impervious to European ideas of international behaviour, but this did not necessarily invalidate his view that in a contest with Russia 'the winning side will be the one that refrains from entangling itself in the barren mountains which now separate the two Empires'. The 'forward' school also mixed up the two problems, until Lord Salisbury was driven to warning his own party that excessive dread of Russia might be mitigated by using large-scale maps.

When British officials began to administer the frontier districts of Sind and the Punjab, only the local problem was important. For some years the policy of non-intervention was followed. General John Jacob, in North Sind, marked out his own frontier and defended it. On the far longer Punjab border we kept to the old Sikh frontier, which ran roughly across the first line of foot-hills on the west of the Indus, and across the ends of the valleys where the rivers debouched on to the plains. British officials remained strictly within this boundary, but, unlike the Sikhs, they encouraged trade across the frontier and removed all duties, including the unpopular capitation tax. A few years later trans-frontier Pathans were allowed to enlist in the army. Lord Lawrence, who had been an annexationist in respect to the smaller native States inside India, was strongly opposed to any further extensions of the boundary. During the Mutiny he had been prepared to evacuate Peshawar, and subsequently he advocated a partial withdrawal from the old Sikh boundary. This was a modification of the 'back to the Indus' policy, which still finds supporters, though for many reasons a river is an unsatisfactory frontier, especially when, like the Indus, it is apt to change its course. British officials of that period may be roughly divided into two schools. Some, like Lord Lawrence, wished to make India into a homogeneous unitary State. Their anxiety was to consolidate and centralise. Others, amongst whom Sir Bartle Frere was the most prominent, appreciated the diversity of India, the colour and variety of its life, the different stages of its civilisation. They had no wish to absorb and modernise the Indian States, or to force uniformity upon the provinces, but they also felt that this loosely-knit system could be advantageously extended into Central Asia, at any rate until India obtained a sound strategic frontier.

During the 'sixties Lord Lawrence's views were generally accepted in India, and by the Liberals in England. He was not able to withdraw to the Indus, but the 'close border' policy was strictly followed. After some years certain defects of the non-intervention policy became apparent, and towards the end of Lord Lawrence's term of office an opposition group had developed in India, and had the support of the Conservative Party in England. The Pathans soon proved themselves to be—as Sir Richard Temple had written in 1856—'savages, noble savages perhaps, and not without some tincture of virtue and generosity, but still absolutely barbarians nevertheless'. For centuries they had raided the plains, and the mere opening of the frontier to trade was not going to eradicate the habit. When cattle-driving and bazar-looting incursions were reported, and they happened every year after the tribesmen had gathered in their own harvest, the Government could only reply with military reprisals. There was no half-way house between war and strict neutrality. As the Government did not wish to occupy the trans-frontier territory, military actions took the form of a punitive expedition, followed by a withdrawal. This was irreverently known as the 'butcher and bolt' policy. Between 1850 and 1870 twenty-six such expeditions were made, and the British average yearly casualties numbered over a hundred. Apart from any ethical considerations, the policy was unsound. By destroying crops and property in the valleys, these expeditions added to the scarcity which was the main incentive to raiding. It was also impossible to be certain of attacking the guilty tribe, and the long series of little wars taught the tribes the art of fighting disciplined troops, and forced them to combine against the British. As early as 1860 Sir Bartle Frere was protesting against the system, writing as follows in a minute on the report of an expedition undertaken that year:

' We are told that the cultivation of the mischievous Nana Khail tribe was destroyed and trampled down by the troops when we could eat no more. . . . The Commissioner then calculates the damage at twelve hundred rupees per diem to the Wuzzeerees, "who depend entirely on it," and can only replace it by imported food. How this imported food is to be paid for, when their villages have been burnt and their cattle driven off, is not explained.' [1]

[1] Martineau, *The Life of Sir Bartle Frere*, i. 364.

The earliest modification of this policy came from Sind, and was chiefly due to the initiative of Sir Robert Sandeman. From the first there had been some difference between the methods used on the two frontiers, the officials in the south tending to establish relations outside their own territory. As early as 1854 a treaty had been made with the Khan of Khelat, to whom assistance was given on the understanding that he kept his tribesmen in order. Two years later, General Jacob had recommended the occupation of Quetta, but the Government of India felt that the position was too isolated. In 1866 the proposal was again brought forward, but by that time Lord Lawrence and the non-intervention school were in authority and no action was taken. Finally, in 1867, Sandeman, then a junior Deputy-Commissioner at Dera Ghazi Khan, started a new chapter in frontier administration by crossing the border and entering into direct personal negotiations with the Bugti and Marri tribes, which were then causing trouble. The success of his enterprise led to a gradual modification of the 'close border' policy. Civil officers were encouraged to learn Pashtu, and to get into touch with the tribesmen. A militia was organised to act as an auxiliary to the special Punjab Frontier Force, which had been detailed for work in this area. The Government took over the police administration of Tonk, where the local Nawab was unable to keep the Mahsuds in order. Similarly at Khelat, when trouble arose between the Khan and his vassal *sirdars*, Sandeman was empowered to negotiate a new treaty which allowed the construction of a railway through this territory, and in 1877 led to the occupation of Quetta. This marked the end of the 'non-intervention' period; but the triumph of the 'forward' school was short-lived. It was unfortunately bound up with the totally different question of the forward policy in Afghanistan, and by 1880 Lord Lytton had resigned. The Liberals were back in office, and Lord Ripon became Viceroy.

The change of Government did not lead to any permanent reversal of the local policy. British control was gradually extended over the whole of Baluchistan, and attempts were made to introduce the Sandeman method to other parts of the frontier. Sir Robert Warburton, in the Khyber district, came to terms with the local Afridis, under which they were allowed almost complete independence, but the Government had control of the pass. One part of the 'Sandeman system' was the granting of allowances in cash to the tribes for various duties, such as the protection of passes. As these were on a generous scale, but were withdrawn in case of misbehaviour, it was a little difficult to distinguish them from the payment of 'danegeld', but they were far cheaper than military reprisals, and they lessened the temptation to raid in bad years. Other efforts were made to relieve the pressure of population in the trans-frontier valleys. Waziris, Afridis, and other tribesmen were granted land in British India. Communications were improved near the border, and light railways built. In 1878 a special border police and militia were raised for the Kohat and Peshawar districts. The frontier, however, remained a storm centre, always liable to be disturbed, especially when relations were strained between the Amir of Afghanistan and the Government of India. Even in the 'eighties, when Abdur Rahman Khan was on good terms with the Government, six military expeditions had to be undertaken. A new phase began after 1890, and will be described later.

This local frontier problem has had important reactions upon the administration. Continual military and political activities added a new and uncertain burden to the Government's finances. Indian budgets, being dependent on land revenue, tend to be 'a gamble in rain'. From 1850 there was added the possibility of a frontier war, which was always liable to develop in some unforeseen manner. Frontier exigencies ultimately decided the constitution, size, and distribution of the army. The north attracted the enterprising and efficient officers, and the concentration of the army in the Punjab led to the excessive use of this province as a recruiting ground. The frontier, with its romantic associations, its virile and independent inhabitants, and its interesting problems, absorbed far too much of the time and thought, as well as the money, of the administration. Combined with the Mutiny tradition, it encouraged a war mentality amongst British officials, and a temptation to use 'frontier methods' in other parts of Northern India. The Maler Kotla case of 1872 was an example of this attitude, which has always had the sympathy of the European community. Some Sikh fanatics attacked a Punjab town, but were repulsed, and sixty-six of them fled into Patiala State. The State authorities handed them over to the nearest British Deputy-Commissioner, a Mr. Cowan, who wrote to his official superior, Mr. Forsyth, 'the entire gang has nearly been destroyed. I purpose blowing away from guns or hanging the prisoners to-morrow morning at daybreak'. Forsyth sent two letters to Cowan, telling him to keep the prisoners for trial, but he carried out his intention. Though the Government dismissed Cowan, he had the support of the entire Anglo-Indian Press, and Forsyth 'procured him a very good appointment in India'.[1]

[1] See *Autobiography and Reminiscences of Sir Douglas Forsyth*, 42.

For these and other reasons, frontier affairs have always exacerbated political feeling in India. The British were tempted to use the possibility of disturbances in the north as an excuse for drastic administrative action, and as an argument for the retention of a full complement of British troops. Hindu opinion has naturally tended to minimise the frontier problem. It is argued that for half a century the Sikhs had successfully confined the Pathans within their own valleys, and that a modern and expensively equipped army ought to achieve this with greater ease. The Marathas and the Sikhs especially object to the idea that they are dependent upon foreign assistance to protect them against the north-country Muslim.

Another problem arose on the far eastern frontier towards the end of the 'seventies. Mindon, King of Ava, had reigned over Upper Burma since 1853. For a quarter of a century his relations with British Lower Burma had been correct if not cordial. No great difficulties had been placed in the way of trade, and a British company held an important timber concession. In 1876 a dispute arose over court etiquette. The Government of India suddenly decided that it was not dignified for a British representative to kneel unshod at court. Mindon would not give way, and the Resident, no longer admitted to the palace, lost most of his influence. Two years later Mindon died. As happens so often in the East, disputes about the succession led first to anarchy, then to intrigues by European Powers, and finally to armed interference. Events in Upper Burma had a certain resemblance to those in Afghanistan after the death of Dost Muhammad, with France instead of Russia as the rival Power. There was, however, a tropical profusion about Burmese affairs. Mindon left forty-eight sons, not the paltry sixteen of Dost Muhammad. He intended that the three most efficient should succeed him and rule as joint kings. The ministerial party in the State, thinking this would lead to anarchy, placed a younger son, Thibaw, on the throne. They hoped he would prove pliable while they introduced Cabinet government on the European model. But Thibaw was a wastrel, and his court rapidly degenerated. In February, 1879, occurred the famous Massacre of the Princes, when eighty leading members of the royal family were clubbed to death. There was ample precedent for this drastic method of removing possible claimants to the throne, but it was hardly suited to a country with two European Powers as neighbours. Humanity and trade interest are a powerful combination; pressure was placed on both the British and French Governments to intervene, but at first neither showed much anxiety to take action. The British Resident was withdrawn later in 1879, chiefly because the Government feared a repetition of the murder of Cavagnari, which had occurred earlier in the year. Other massacres of princes occurred, but it was not till six years later that an ultimatum was sent by Lord Dufferin, of which the overt cause was an enormous fine imposed upon a British timber company, the Bombay-Burma Trading Corporation, after a forced loan had been refused. Another powerful motive was the activity of a French envoy, who was endeavouring to obtain a railway concession, and also the management of the important State monopolies, which would have placed the country under French control.

The first stage of the war was over in a fortnight. Thibaw surrendered, and the country with its three million inhabitants was annexed. There is evidence that the Government of India would have preferred to avoid this step, which, incidentally, was hardly foreshadowed by their ultimatum. Unfortunately Thibaw had killed off nearly every possible claimant to the throne, except Nyaungyan, who had died a few months before. The next five years justified the objections to annexation advanced by prominent officials, including Sir Charles Bernard, Chief Commissioner in charge of the annexation. Most of Thibaw's army joined the dacoits, and until 1890 many thousand British troops were operating amongst the jungles of Upper Burma.

An administration on the Indian model was erected in Upper as previously in Lower Burma, though an unusually high proportion of military officers were employed. Our complicated legal system was imposed within a few days of annexation. The old semi-feudal, semi-theocratic form of government was replaced by a modern bureaucracy of the most uncompromising secularity, while Indian officials, imported to fill subordinate posts, brought with them the departmental outlook as well as the 'files' which are the insignia of their office.

The administration gradually settled down to the orderly routine of a British province, but the distance from headquarters, the differences of race, religion, and language, have prevented Burma from being completely assimilated into the Indian system. The country has retained a character and patriotism of its own, and its history deserves separate study. It has developed commercially with great rapidity. Its timber, oil, and minerals have been exploited, and the Irawadi delta has become one of the world's great rice-growing areas. Much of the labour has been brought from India. Rangoon is now a huge commercial port, through which pass yearly a third of a million seasonal labourers. These have brought some prosperity, but also much crime and discontent. The Burmese have come to feel that they are being displaced by cheap Indian labour, and are not sufficiently used in administrative and clerical posts. Their nationalism has taken a double form, the desire for self-government being accompanied by an anxiety to be free from too much Indian competition.[1] After the war both sentiments were to become more intense. In 1931 an outbreak of a recurrent form of jungle superstition, coinciding with a confusion of agrarian, political, and economic grievances, gave rise to a rebellion which proved extremely difficult to suppress. But Burma, free from caste and Hindu inhibitions, from purdah and ideas of female inferiority, above all free from communal strife, has been happy in having little history since Thibaw's downfall.

The Burma frontier is uneventful but the frontier districts are important. They are excluded from the Reform Scheme and contain only one-seventh of the population—yet their races, though backward, are among the most intelligent and virile in Burma; they cover no less than two-fifths of her area, and they contain much of her minerals. The Shans, Karens, Kachins, Chins and other tribes have ancient feuds with the Burmese, but they are not as pugnacious as the Pathans, and a loose form of indirect rule, though it frequently means tolerating curious survivals, permits of a slower but truer line of evolution.

CHAPTER V

AFGHANISTAN AND RUSSIA

The imperial problem and Russia: belief in Russian ambitions: death of Dost Muhammad: war of succession: recognition of Sher Ali: Russian advance in Central Asia: Lord Northbrook and the Amir: Disraeli in office and reversal of policy: Lytton, Salisbury, and the 'forward' school: aggressive policy: Peshawar conference: Stolietoff's mission: Lytton's policy: advance upon Afghanistan: Treaty of Gandamak: British military deficiencies: Cavagnari mission and massacre: second campaign: Charasiab: occupation of Kabul and retributive action: recognition of Abdur Rahman: Maiwand: march to Kandahar and withdrawal: Abdur Rahman consolidates his position.

THE local problem of the North-West Frontier is limited to the prevention of raiding, and to the possibility of establishing settled govern-

---

[1] The census of 1931 gives Burma's population as 14,667,146, an increase of 11 per cent. over the last decade. Indians number rather more than a million.

ment on the near side of the passes into India. The tribesmen in the valleys between Afghanistan and the Indus have neither the numbers nor the organisation to penetrate far into modern India, unless supported by their Indian co-religionists. Some of the earlier Muslim conquerors, like Babar, entered India with only a few thousand men, but they were despotic rulers from Central Asia and brought their small but disciplined forces into a country where there was little organised opposition. Since British occupation the only danger to the established government could come from the far side of the passes. The threat of an overland invasion by France had perturbed the Company at the beginning of the nineteenth century, but after 1815 the imperial or 'large-scale' frontier problem was narrowed down to the possibility of a Russian invasion, or of Russia and Afghanistan becoming troublesome neighbours; either interfering with Central Asian trade or intriguing with hostile elements in India.

The modern Englishman may find it difficult to understand the Russophobia which periodically attacked his countrymen. The modern Indian is inclined to doubt its reality. The fear was genuine enough, though much of it was based on ignorance. *Omne ignotum pro horrifico.* British officials may have been tempted sub-consciously to exaggerate the fighting qualities of the Cossack, but the rapid advance of Russia through Central Asia was remarkable to a generation which knew little about the desiccation of those parts, or of the ruin which had befallen the country. Tashkent, Samarkand, Khiva, Bokhara, and Merv were names to conjure with in all the bazars of Northern India. As the news filtered through that one after another of these cities had been captured or was being threatened, that Khiva was reached in 1864, Bokhara reduced in 1866, a new province of Russian Turkestan formed in 1867, it is not surprising that every city in the Punjab was seething with rumours of another Timur coming from the north, and that the Government, with memories of the Mutiny a few years before, grew yearly more alarmed about their vulnerable north-west frontier, and the possibility of Afghanistan falling completely under Russian influence.

Russia's motives from 1860 onwards are still open to dispute. There was certainly a forward school amongst the Russian officers in Turkestan, and at times these exceeded their instructions. Abdur Rahman spent the years 1870 to 1880 in Russian Turkestan before he became Amir, and had no doubt that the Russian army was preparing to invade India.[1] The Tsarist Government also learnt, about the time of the

[1] See his autobiography, *The Life of Abdur Rahman*, i. 151.

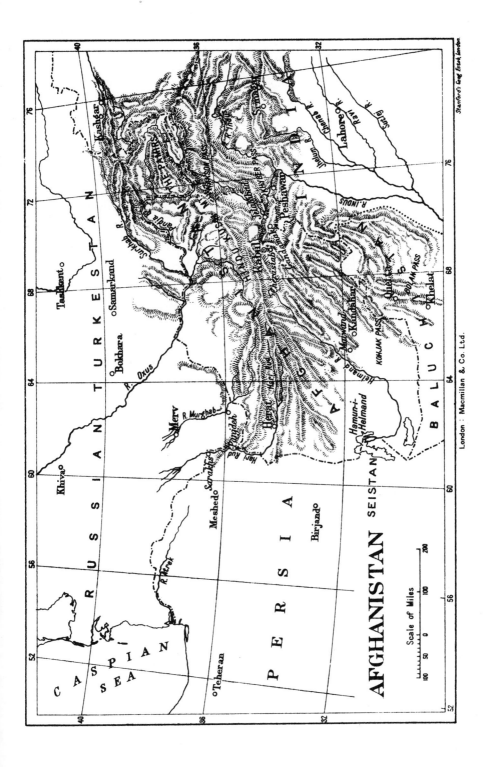

AFGHANISTAN

Scale of Miles

London : Macmillan & Co. Ltd.

Stanford's Geog Estab.London

Crimean War, that a show of activity in Turkestan was an easy method of putting pressure upon the Government in London. But it is more than doubtful whether any responsible Russian statesman ever intended an invasion of British India, or even of Afghanistan. The statesman does not discourage the dreams of his soldiers, but he need not believe in them. The main cause of the advance southwards was the lack of any satisfactory frontier north of the Hindu Kush. Like the Government of India, the Russians found how difficult it was to fix a boundary until they reached either an impassable territory or a settled government.[1]

The imperial problem became acute after the death of the Amir of Afghanistan in 1863. Relations with that country had improved during the twenty years which followed Dost Muhammad's return to the throne. Treaties had been made in 1855 and 1857, by which help in arms and money had been given to the Amir for his war against Persia. The British assisted in this war by sending Outram to capture Bushire in 1857, and one result of this co-operation was that Afghanistan did nothing to add to the Government's difficulties during the Mutiny. In 1862 the Amir aroused some misgivings in India by capturing Herat from an independent chieftain, but this did not alter the general policy of 'friendship towards the actual rulers, combined with rigid abstention from interference in domestic feuds'. Lord Elgin withdrew the British Agent from Kabul, but held that 'it was desirable to accept the *status in quo*, whatever it may be'. The following year was to place a greater strain upon the non-intervention policy. As often happens in Asia, a troublesome period began with a disputed succession.

Twelve of Dost Muhammad's sixteen sons took part in the five years' struggle which followed his death. The Government of India maintained a studiously correct attitude, but Lord Lawrence's position was made more difficult by appeals for recognition, and by the news that the two principal rivals had both applied to Russia for help, and one had opened negotiations with Persia. The 'forward' school in India and in England gained adherents during this period. Russia in 1867 moved its base forward from Orenburg to Tashkent, and captured Samarkand.

[1] This point is emphasised by Gortschakoff in his famous circular despatch of 1864. Schuyler, a foreigner very critical of Russian methods, gives a useful estimate of Russian ambitions in his *Turkestan*, almost the only contemporary and impartial account of Kaufmann's regime. See vol. ii. chap. xiv. Terentieff's *Russia and England in Central Asia* is a reply to the continual protests made from England against every Russian move in Turkestan.

The civil war and the appeals to Russia had shown how easily a disputed succession may lead to foreign intervention, and how vulnerable Afghanistan was from the west if Herat, its natural gateway, was held by some dissident chief.[1]

All parties recognised the danger of a further Russian advance; but Lord Lawrence believed that the proper place to apply pressure upon Russia was St. Petersburg, and not Kabul, while his opponents wished to undertake the defence of Afghanistan's western frontier and would have liked the Indian Government to play the rôle of king-maker. Lawrence remained in office until 1869, by which date Sher Ali had firmly established himself as Amir, and could be helped by money and official recognition. Non-intervention as an imperial policy had proved a success. We had avoided the expensive gamble of intervening on behalf of a claimant who would certainly have lost caste amongst the Afghans as soon as it was known that he was the British nominee. Such action during the 'sixties would not have retarded, and might have hastened, the Russian advance over the last two or three hundred miles to the western boundary of Afghanistan. Lawrence, like Sir Herbert Edwardes and many Indian officials, saw no objection to the spread of Russian rule over the 'nomad barbarism' of Central Asia. He did not believe that the Tsar would ever sanction such a hare-brained venture as the invasion of India, and while he saw the difficulties which must arise as Russia approached the Afghan frontier, he thought that they could be amicably adjusted. In a final despatch he urged the British Government to reach

' a clear understanding with the Court of St. Petersburg as to its projects and designs in Central Asia, and that it might be given to understand in firm but courteous language that it cannot be permitted to interfere in the affairs of Afghanistan, or in those of any State which lies contiguous to our frontier'.[2]

The policy of the buffer State was intrinsically sound. It was based on the instinctive xenophobia of the Afghan and the barrenness of his country. It was abandoned after 1874, following a change of government in England, but nothing occurred during the first five years of Sher Ali's rule to prove that non-intervention had failed as a large-scale policy. The various difficulties which arose were due to the new Amir's

[1] Holditch points out that 'there was nothing obligatory about Herat as a base of attack for India', but Herat dominates the more southerly routes through Kandahar. See *The Indian Borderland*, 48.

[2] *Afghanistan*, No. 1 (1878), 45.

character and antecedents. He was a man of inferior calibre, lacking the political acumen of his father, Dost Muhammad, or of his nephew and successor, Abdur Rahman. His long struggle for the throne had left him countless enemies, and he did not conceal his anxiety for English support. In 1869, during a visit to Lord Mayo at Ambala, he asked for a definite treaty, a fixed annual subsidy, and the recognition as heir of his younger son, Abdulla Jan, instead of his elder son, Yakub Khan, who had helped him to the throne but with whom he had quarrelled. Officials of the 'forward' school favoured such a treaty. Guaranteeing the western frontier of Afghanistan would have entailed some form of military supervision. Recognition of Abdulla Jan would have led within a few years to armed intervention in a dynastic quarrel, and ultimately to the occupation of the country, and to an Amir dependent on British bayonets. Sher Ali either did not understand this inevitable sequence or was sufficiently afraid of his compatriots to prefer a risky dependence upon British support. He was bitterly disappointed when Lord Mayo, and subsequently Lord Northbrook, made it clear that they would never send a British soldier across the frontier to coerce Afghan rebels. This feeling was mitigated at first by the personal regard which Sher Ali felt for Lord Mayo, and the effect of a glimpse at European civilisation upon a none too stable mind, but in Lord Northbrook's time there was no such contact, and the estrangement was increased by three incidents in each of which the Government of India erred by not adhering strictly to the policy of non-intervention. Lord Northbrook sent a letter and present to the Chief of Wakhan, from whom Sher Ali claimed allegiance. The Government unwisely agreed to arbitrate on a frontier dispute between Persia and Afghanistan, and the Seistan award grievously offended the Amir.[1] Finally the Viceroy not only refused to recognise Abdulla Jan, the chosen heir, but also wrote to Sher Ali about his treatment of Yakub Khan, whom he kept in prison.

In the meantime the Liberal Government in England brought such pressure as they could upon the Russians to define their Central Asian policy. Negotiations were opened between Lord Clarendon and Prince Gortschakoff, and Forsyth was sent to St. Petersburg in 1869 in order to explain the views of the Government of India. Allowing for the difficulty of discussing areas which were still unmapped, and occupied

[1] The Boundary Commission, under the presidency of Sir F. Goldsmid, was appointed at the end of 1871. The award divided Seistan, giving Persia the best-watered half.

by semi-nomadic tribes, the Russian Government seems to have been anxious for a settlement and ready to accept the integrity of Afghanistan as the basic factor in their relations with Great Britain. By 1873 the Russians had agreed to recognise Sher Ali's sovereignty south of the Oxus, and of a line through Badakshan which was suggested by the British Government. Certain arguments have been brought forward to prove Russia's bad faith in these transactions, but they are only valid on the assumption that the whole of Russia's policy was planned with India as an objective. From 1870 onwards, the Governor of Turkestan, General Kaufmann, sent occasional letters of a formal nature to Sher Ali, but these were shown to Lord Mayo and Lord Northbrook, who raised no objection. In 1873 the Russians took Khiva and retained control under a thin disguise, but Khiva is farther from Afghanistan than Samarkand, which was already occupied.

The Russian Empire continued to spread where there were neither physical obstacles nor a settled government, but the effect was to dissipate its energies. In the opinion of the British Government and of Lord Northbrook it made the possibility of an invasion even more remote. Consequently when an Afghan envoy came to Simla in 1873 and asked for a definite offensive and defensive alliance, the Viceroy would not go much farther than his predecessor in 1869. Lord Northbrook himself would have been willing to promise assistance with money, arms, and troops, in order to repel 'an unprovoked invasion', but even this was too definite for the British Cabinet and the final letter to the Amir, sent on September 6, 1873, was too guarded and diplomatic to be understood by the monarch, isolated and ill-advised, whom Lord Lytton was to describe five years later as 'a savage with a touch of insanity'. Sher Ali was undoubtedly disappointed, but he accepted a present of 20,000 rifles, and there is no evidence for the view put forward by Lord Roberts and others of the 'forward' school of thought, that he immediately 'decided to throw in his lot with Russia'.[1] The position deteriorated very rapidly, but this was due to the re-opening of the Near Eastern question, and to a change of Government in England, which combined to make any agreement with Russia impossible, and to inaugurate a more aggressive policy towards the Amir.

In March, 1874, Disraeli became Prime Minister, with Lord Salisbury as Secretary of State for India. Both combined a deep distrust of Russia with a belief that British policy in the East had been too cautious and

[1] Roberts, *Forty-One Years in India*, ii. 108.

too prosaic. The first view led to a strongly pro-Turkish attitude during the complicated series of events which began with the rising in Bosnia and Herzegovina, included the Russo-Turkish War and the Treaty of San Stefano, and ended with the Treaty of Berlin. By Disraeli's refusal to accept the Berlin Memorandum in 1876, England stood out as the chief opponent of Russia in Europe, and for the next two years relations grew steadily worse until, early in 1878, the two countries were on the verge of war, and Disraeli took the unprecedented and dangerous step of ordering 7000 Indian troops to Malta. In this great conflict of interests, when diplomacy was often on the verge of giving place to open war, Afghanistan was only a side issue, but it was clearly Russia's policy to use her position in Central Asia to create a diversion whenever affairs approached a crisis. Only once was any serious effort made by the British Government to reach an amicable settlement. The Powers met at the Conference of Constantinople, in December 1876, and Lord Salisbury—then Foreign Secretary—began to discuss terms with Russia, which would have included an agreement about Central Asia as part of the general treaty. This attempt was defeated by the obduracy of Turkey. Except for this interlude, when Russia showed her willingness to negotiate, she had every reason for distracting British attention by intrigues in Afghanistan. The final moves which led up to the sending of a Russian envoy, General Stolietoff, to Kabul in 1878 were the direct and natural consequence of the threat of war in Europe and the despatch of Indian troops to Malta.

Soon after taking over the India Office, Lord Salisbury began to bring pressure upon the Government of India to alter its policy towards Afghanistan. In this matter he was influenced by Sir Bartle Frere, then a member of the India Council and always a keen protagonist of the 'forward' school. Writing in June, 1874, Frere advocated the military occupation of Quetta and the establishment of British Agents at Kandahar and at Herat, then governed by Yakub Khan, the Amir's rebellious son. Lord Lawrence protested, but in January, 1875, Lord Salisbury sent a secret despatch to Lord Northbrook suggesting the advisability of establishing British Agencies at Kandahar, Herat, and ultimately at Kabul, because of the poor information then received from Afghanistan, and stating that Sher Ali had agreed to accept such envoys. Some correspondence followed in which Lord Northbrook pointed out that Sher Ali had not agreed to such a proposal, and that if he was forced to receive British envoys it would endanger his throne. In a final despatch sent to England in January, 1876, the Viceroy summed up the arguments of the non-intervention school, and stated that there was no reason to believe that the Amir 'has any desire to prefer the friendship of other Powers', and talked of his 'not unnatural dread of our interference in his internal affairs'.[1] The same mail carried home Lord Northbrook's resignation, and Lord Salisbury was able to replace him by a younger man, inexperienced in the East, but a convinced believer in the 'forward' school, and in Russia's 'anticipated conquest of the rich plains of British India'.[2]

Lord Lytton came to India charged with the immediate task of overcoming the Amir's 'apparent reluctance' to accept permanent British Agencies in his dominions in return for an increased subsidy, a more definite recognition of his chosen heir, and an explicit pledge of support in case of foreign aggression. Lord Salisbury's letter of instructions suggests clearly the kind of pressure which was to be brought upon Sher Ali. 'If the language and demeanour of the Amir be such as to promise no satisfactory result of the negotiations thus opened, his Highness should be distinctly reminded that he is isolating himself, at his own peril, from the friendship and protection it is his interest to seek and deserve'. For the next four years Lord Lytton set himself 'to the passionate pursuit of the object which he had been sent to India to effect—the virtual subordination of Afghanistan to India'.[3] The first move was a request that the Amir should receive a mission to announce the assumption by the Queen of the title 'Empress of India'. The Amir declined on the grounds that such a formal mission was unnecessary, and made it clear, through the British native Agent at Kabul, that he could not guarantee the safety of British officers, and that, if he accepted the British request, he would find it impossible to refuse a similar privilege to Russia. Lord Lytton continued his aggressive policy, although he was warned by three members of his Council—Sir William Muir, Sir Arthur Hobhouse, and Sir Henry Norman—that the Amir was fully within his rights. In October a further communication was sent through the Muslim Agent. This offered a subsidy, the recognition of Abdullah Jan as heir, and a pledge of protection against aggression; in return it demanded not only the establishment of British Agencies, but also the opening up of Afghanistan to Englishmen—official and non-official--and the reception of special missions when re-

---

[1] *Afghanistan*, No. 1 (1878), 147 *et seq.*

[2] Viceroy's minute, June, 1876, *Lord Lytton's Indian Administration*, 68.

[3] Colonel H. B. Hanna, *The Second Afghan War*, 96.

quired.[1] It was suggested that a new treaty should be drawn up, and the Amir sent Nur Muhammad to Peshawar to meet Sir Lewis Pelly.

The Peshawar Conference was held during the early months of 1877. Russia was then engaged in those disputes with Turkey which led up to a declaration of war in April. It is difficult to read an account of the claims put forward by Sir Lewis Pelly without thinking of the fable of the wolf and the lamb. The Government of India was clearly preparing for a forward movement along their boundaries, and for the possibility of an aggressive war in Afghanistan. Quetta was occupied by arrangement with the Khan of Khelat, and negotiations were opened with Kashmir to place a British Agent at Gilgit. There were military preparations on the Indian side to reinforce the meaning of these two threats to Kandahar and Kabul. This was the moment which Lord Lytton chose to complain about military activity in Afghanistan, and to inform Nur Muhammad that his country's relations with India were to be based on the treaty of 1855, made when the former Amir neither controlled Herat nor Kandahar. Nur Muhammad was an experienced and patriotic Afghan, who had carried on many negotiations for Dost Muhammad. He recognised, far more clearly than the incompetent Amir, the conspiracy to dismember his country, and his death at Peshawar was a fitting close to his dignified protest. Lord Lytton seized the opportunity to declare the conference at an end, although Sher Ali had already appointed a successor. For the next year relations were left in suspense. The Indian Agent was withdrawn from Kabul, and Lord Lytton justified his conduct in a long despatch [2] in which he accused the Amir of launching a *jehad* or religious war 'apparently only directed against his English, rather than his Russian neighbours'. The sole justification for this statement seems to have been the second-hand evidence of an anonymous Kandahari camel-dealer. The Amir undoubtedly moved some troops to Kandahar, but only as a reply to the garrisoning of Quetta.

Lord Lytton, faced by a severe famine in India, was not unwilling to defer a definite rupture with the Amir so long as the issue of the

---

[1] Lord Lytton's famous remarks about Afghanistan's position resembling that 'of an earthen pipkin between two iron pots', and the 'profound compassion' with which he regarded the Amir's position, were not included in the letter to the Amir, but in a statement made to the Agent, who was expected to repeat its substance to Sher Ali when he returned to Kabul. The demand for admission of British traders was a new departure in frontier policy.

[2] Despatch No. 13 of 1877, dated May 10. Addressed to the Marquis of Salisbury.

Russo-Turkish War was still uncertain and the probability of a war with Russia in Europe seemed imminent. His policy was explained in a letter to Lord Cranbrook, who in March, 1878, had succeeded Lord Salisbury as Secretary of State for India.

' I am persuaded that the policy of building up in Afghanistan a strong and independent State, over which we can exercise absolutely no control, has been proved by experience to be a mistake. If by war, or the death of the present Amir, which will certainly be the signal for conflict between rival candidates for the *musnud*, we should hereafter have the opportunity (and it is one which may at any moment occur suddenly) of disintegrating and breaking up the Kabul Power, I sincerely hope that opportunity will not be lost by us. . . . The best arrangement for Indian interests would be, *me judice*, the creation of a Western Afghan Khanate, including Merv, Maimena, Balkh, Kandahar, and Herat, under some prince of our own selection, who will be dependent on our support.' [1]

This was written in April, 1878, and in three months the opportunity had come. Tension between Russia and England had then reached its height. The refusal to recognise the Treaty of San Stefano had been followed by the occupation of Cyprus; and the movement of Indian troops to Malta. Russia thought the best counter-move was to embroil England with Afghanistan, and on June 13 General Stolietoff left Tashkent on a mission to Kabul and, after a strong protest from the Amir, was granted a safe-conduct. While he was moving slowly across Central Asia, a congress was sitting in Berlin. On July 13, before the mission had crossed the Hindu Kush, the Treaty of Berlin was signed.

There is some obscurity about Stolietoff's behaviour in Kabul. He was a professional soldier, a believer in a forward and belligerent policy for his country. He was sent to Kabul in anticipation of war with England, with a free hand to cause as much trouble as possible. It is probable that, like Lord Lytton at a later date, he exceeded his instructions. Certain points are clear. The Amir received the mission unwillingly, and resisted the attempt to drag him into the same kind of dangerous alliance which Lord Lytton had tried to force upon him. The first authentic news which Stolietoff received of the Berlin Treaty was in August, and with this intimation was an order to return to Russia, which he obeyed immediately. He took with him a draft treaty, and left a letter which suggested that he had been impressing upon Sher Ali the probability that in case of a war with Russia the British would overrun his country, a belief fully justified by the proposals contained in Lord Lytton's letter to Lord Cranbrook, written on August 3.[1] It is

[1] See *Lord Lytton's Indian Administration*, 247.

possible that Stolietoff was personally chagrined at the abrupt ending of his mission, and felt that he had made promises without letting the Amir know that they were really contingent upon an Anglo-Russian war. Stolietoff reached Tashkent on September 16, and wrote a letter to Sher Ali which was little more than the familiar Oriental gesture of 'saving face'. 'If God pleases, everything that is necessary will be done and affirmed. I hope that those who want to enter the gate of Kabul from the east will see the door is closed; then, please God, they will tremble.' [1] The Russian Government, as subsequent events proved, had no intention of binding itself to go to war with England because of some quarrel which might arise between the Amir and the Government of India.

Lord Lytton had the choice of two policies. He might have welcomed the Treaty of Berlin and the withdrawal of the Russian envoy as an opportunity for the quiet establishment of better relations with Sher Ali, while the British Government, now in a strong position, could reopen negotiations with St. Petersburg for a settlement regarding Central Asia. That this was Disraeli's intention is shown by a letter to Lord Cranbrook, written on September 26.

' He (Lord Lytton) was told to wait until we had received the answer from Russia to our remonstrance. I was very strong on this, having good reasons for my opinion. He disobeyed us. I was assured by Lord Salisbury that, under no circumstances, was the Khyber Pass to be attempted. Nothing would have induced me to consent to such a step.' [2]

Lord Lytton preferred to embark, on his own responsibility, upon a gigantic gamble. He saw, in Russia's virtual retirement, the chance of dismembering Afghanistan and establishing the 'scientific frontier' desired by the 'forward' school. Relying on the advice of his real counsellors, Colonel Colley, his private secretary, General Roberts, [3] General Lumsden, and Major Cavagnari, he determined to force a mission upon Afghanistan in a manner which would lead either to war or to the complete subservience of the Amir. He had no doubt about the result of a war, apparently sharing Colonel Colley's view that recent technical improvements had given an overwhelming advantage to British arms and that 'a thousand men armed with Martinis could march anywhere in Afghanistan'. In London was Lord Cranbrook,

[1] *Central Asia*, No. 1 (1881), 18.

[2] G. E. Buckle, *Life of Disraeli*, vi. 382.

[3] Afterwards Lord Roberts. He was then Quartermaster-General. Lumsden was Adjutant-General.

whom he could trust to keep the Cabinet quiet until he was sufficiently embroiled for it to be impossible to retract. Speed was essential, and a Muslim envoy was sent to Kabul on August 30, announcing that a British mission was on its way. A few days later Sir Neville Chamberlain set out from Peshawar.

Sher Ali, whose favourite son, Abdulla Jan, had just died, did not reply immediately, and an Afghan officer stopped the advance guard of the mission at Ali Masjid, informing them courteously that he must await orders from Kabul. This gave Lord Lytton the opportunity he needed. Lord Cranbrook won over the Cabinet by a virtual threat of resignation, and the Viceroy sent an ultimatum on November 2, demanding a full apology and the immediate reception of the mission. A reply came, dated November 19, but not received until November 30. The Amir accepted the mission, but the letter did not contain an apology. It is doubtful if any form of letter would have sufficed. By this date military operations had already been commenced. On November 21 three armies advanced upon Afghanistan—General Stewart from Quetta upon Kandahar, General Roberts through the Kurram valley, and Sir Samuel Browne through the Khyber. No serious resistance was offered to the occupation of Kandahar and of Jalalabad, on the road to Kabul. Sher Ali had lost his hold upon his people. He appealed to the Russians for help, but received no encouragement, and finally escaped into Russian Turkestan, where he died in February, 1879. His son Yakub Khan, whom he released from prison, opened negotiations with the British. He was recognised as Amir, and in May signed the Treaty of Gandamak, by which a British Resident was to be stationed at Kabul, with Agents at Herat and elsewhere. The Amir agreed to conduct his foreign relations under British guidance, and ceded the Pishin and Sibi districts. The Government of India undertook to grant him a subsidy, to defend him against foreign aggression, and to withdraw their troops, except from Kandahar, which was to be evacuated later.

From the English standpoint the treaty was entirely satisfactory. Lytton received the congratulations of the Home Government, though he himself still hankered after the immediate disintegration of Afghanistan. In a letter to Lord Cranbrook he argued against the theory of a buffer State.

‘ The primary condition of a strong independent Afghanistan is a strong, independent ruler. . . . Would not Afghanistan administered, by such a ruler, tend more and more to become a military State, held together by armed power? Would not the ambitious, energetic, and not over-scrupulous ruler of such a military State find, in the long run, his best account in alliance with the ambitious, energetic and not over-scrupulous Government of such a military empire as Russia, rather than in alliance with a Power so essentially pacific and sensitively scrupulous as our own.' [1]

It is not surprising that a Viceroy who could write such a letter did not see the weakness of his position. Anyone with a real knowledge of the East would have understood that no ruler in Afghanistan will be respected and followed by his own people if he is supported and 'advised' by a foreign Power. A month after the Treaty of Gandamak, Lord Lytton was assuring his Secretary of State that 'the Afghan people certainly do not view us with any ill will'. A capable administrator would have been warned by certain failures which had occurred during the short and easy campaign. The Duke of Wellington, speaking of the first Afghan War, said that 'the whole question is one of commissariat; that of commissariat, one of transport'. The ordinary baggage animals had suffered severe losses during two small frontier expeditions carried out early in 1878. The larger campaign made it necessary to collect camels and pack ponies from the whole north and west of India. This was done towards the end of a famine which had killed off most of the stock in parts of the Punjab, and had left the rest weakened and diseased.[2] Apart from the permanent injury caused to Indian agriculture, which Lord Lytton never seems to have considered, there was much inefficiency and some deliberate breaches of faith in the way in which the animals were acquired. Camels were hired on the distinct understanding that they would not be taken across the frontier, and were then sent on to Kandahar. The Quetta road into Afghanistan has little fodder, and most of the animals died.[3] Medical arrangements also failed, much as they did nearly forty years later in Mesopotamia.

The first Resident at Kabul appointed under the Treaty of Gandamak was Major Cavagnari, an enterprising and intelligent political officer, a keen advocate of the 'forward' school, who already exercised, as Deputy-

[1] *Lord Lytton's Indian Administration*, 311.

[2] See *Statement of Moral and Material Progress of India*, 1877-8. Some districts had already lost two-thirds of their stock. The old Deccani ponies, which had made the Marathas such formidable freebooters, were completely wiped out by the famine and the requisitions.

[3] "In 1878, during the first phase of the campaign in Afghanistan, the Punjabis had lost, from starvation, cold, and general neglect, 80,000 camels and other animals, and unascertained numbers of drivers."—S. S. Thorburn, The *Punjab in Peace and War*, 327.

Commissioner at Peshawar, some influence on the Viceroy. Colonel Hanna described him as

'a man of rash and restless disposition and overbearing temper, consumed by the thirst for personal distinction, and as incapable of recognising and weighing the difficulties, physical and moral, which stood in the way of the attainment of his ends as the Viceroy over whom he was thenceforward to exercise so pernicious an influence'.[1]

Apart from this criticism by a contemporary, there is abundant evidence that Sir Lewis Cavagnari soon dominated Yakub Khan, who had a weak character, probably enfeebled by long imprisonment. The Resident seems to have been at little pains to conceal the effective control which he exercised over such matters as appointments. Lytton reports that the Amir has

'at Cavagnari's suggestion restored to favour and office the Mustaufi who had been disgraced and imprisoned by his father, and whom he has now appointed finance minister. It is also on Cavagnari's recommendation that he has appointed General Daod Shah his Commander-in-Chief, and this he has done with a graceful alacrity which appears to have made a most favourable effect on all concerned'.[2]

Afghans are never inclined to accept a foreign *maire du palais*, but the inevitable outbreak was hastened by the Amir's inability to control his regular army, whose pay was many months in arrears. The soldiers, hearing that the British were subsidising the Amir, and recognising Daod Shah as a British nominee, not unnaturally concluded that the Residency was the best place from which to demand their pay. This seems to have been the real cause of the riots which ended in the massacre of Cavagnari, his staff, and escort on September 3. The soldiers precipitated a rebellion which would undoubtedly have taken place later. Abdur Rahman probably expressed the common sentiment when he wrote in his autobiography, 'I have heard that the British Envoy looked upon himself as Ruler of Afghanistan, and dictated to Yakub what he should do. This boasting was disliked by the Afghan people, and they attacked him.'[3]

The tragedy at Kabul was a defeat for the 'forward' school. Only a few optimistic soldiers saw in the murder an opportunity for 'setting the red line on the Hindu Kush'. It revived the worst forebodings of the

[1] Hanna, *Second Afghan War*, i. 119.

[2] *Lord Lytton's Indian Administration*, letter to Cranbrook, 334.

[3] *The Life of Abdur Rahman*, i. 152.

Cabinet in England. Lord Beaconsfield had grave misgivings about the state of the army.

' We may be only five days march from Cabul, but that would be as bad as the great desert, if we have no transport and inadequate commissariat. As for transport, I remember, with alarm, 50 or 60 thousand camels have already been wasted. . . . What alarms me is the state of the Indian Army as revealed in a letter from Lytton written to Cran. before the Catastrophe. Except Roberts, who he believes is gifted, and who is certainly a strategist, there seems no one much to rely on: Stewart respectable; Massey promising; but all the persons, with slight exceptions, to whom we have voted Parliamentary thanks, and on whom the Crown has conferred honours, utterly worthless. As for General Sam Browne, according to Lytton, he ought to have been tried by a court martial, and he goes thro' them all with analogous remarks. And these are the men whom, only a few months ago, he recommended for all these distinctions. I begin to think he ought to be tried by a court martial himself. . . .' [1]

Even the complacency which had carried the Viceroy through his earlier difficulties was shaken by this event. 'The web of policy', he wrote to the Prime Minister, 'so carefully and patiently woven has been rudely shattered. We have now to weave afresh, and I fear a wider one, from undoubtedly weaker materials.' [2]

The army was set in motion once more. General Roberts marched on Kabul, and Sir Donald Stewart reoccupied Kandahar, but they were no longer dealing with an apathetic people, and with a ruler supported by a few half-mutinous troops. The country was in a state of anarchy, but fear of British domination and the religious enthusiasm of the *mullahs* were sufficient to bring out thousands of Afghan villagers. Yakub Khan made no attempt to lead this movement. He abdicated at once, and fled to the British camp. Roberts, after a victory at Charasiab, entered Kabul on October 12, but he and Stewart were both surrounded by hostile levies under hastily elected leaders. The behaviour of the British destroyed any possibility of coming to terms with the Afghans. Roberts, from the day of his arrival in Kabul, considered the country as a rebellious province, and treated the men who had opposed him as if they were mutineers. In his Proclamation of October 12, he put a price on the head of those who had fought at Charasiab, and threatened to raze Kabul to the ground. The British claim to the country was based on the fiction of ruling in Yakub Khan's name, a claim which neither side

[1] Letter to Lord Salisbury. G. E. Buckle, *Life of Lord Beaconsfield*, vi. 485-6.

[2] *Lord Lytton's Indian Administration*, 358.

took seriously.[1] It was also a dangerous precedent, for Sher Ali had fled into Russian territory and his nephew, Abdur Rahman, was then in Russian Turkestan. On this doubtful and provocative basis a military Commission was set up in Kabul, which began operations in the spirit of the Government's order that 'punishment should be swift, stern, and impressive'. This was taken to justify the hasty execution of anyone whom an informer chose to accuse of complicity in the events of September 3, or of taking part in the fighting at Charasiab. An account left by Colonel MacGregor, a member of the Commission, shows that men were hanged on the most trivial evidence, sometimes of their avowed enemies.[2] Troops were sent into the neighbourhood to collect prisoners, and also to forage. They burnt any villages where there was the least show of opposition.

During the winter the fighting round Kabul was sufficiently fierce to cut Roberts' communications with India and force him to retire to Sherpur, where he was besieged until Stewart marched from Kandahar to relieve him. The spring of 1880 found the British in effective control of no more than the small strip of Afghanistan east of the Kabul-Kandahar road, but their enemies were still being treated as rebels and, in spite of General Roberts' denial, the policy of 'indiscriminate hanging and burning of villages' was continued into the new year. Opinion in England was now seriously alarmed at the heavy losses suffered, at the small progress made, and at rumours of barbarities committed by our troops. The Indian Government, better informed as to the weakness of the British position, received a further blow when it was discovered, towards the end of March, that the military accounts department had broken down. This administrative scandal completed the ruin of Lord Lytton's grandiose schemes. 'All other revelations,' he wrote to Lord Cranbrook, 'sink into insignificance before the tremendous discovery made by the Financial Department, that the war estimates prepared by the military department . . . were utterly worthless and will be inde-

[1] H. Hensman, *The Afghan War*, 1879-80. 'The Amir's authority is proclaimed as justification for many of our acts; yet, at the same time we loot his citadel, and seize upon, as spoils of war, all guns and munitions of war which for a few weeks only had passed out of his hands into those of the rebels.' 91.

[2] *Life of Sir C. MacGregor*, ii. 140 *et seq*. 'Saved five men's lives to-day—that is to say, if I had not inquired into their cases, they would have been hanged. . . . One of the accused was Abu Bakar, a merchant, against whom there was a regular got-up case, the principal witness being his deadly enemy.' See also Hensman, *The Afghan War*, 134. Hensman, a war correspondent and keen admirer of General Roberts, describes what were really wholesale executions of prisoners.

finitely exceeded'. The original estimate for the war had been under six millions. A further actual outlay of five millions had been incurred without the knowledge of the financial department, and another seven millions were required for the second campaign. In April Lord Beaconsfield resigned after a general election, and Lord Lytton, whose Afghan policy had contributed so much to this defeat, was replaced in June by Lord Ripon.

No rapid change of policy followed the fall of the Conservative Government. Lord Lytton had spent the last three months of office in an attempt to escape from the Afghan imbroglio, and had embarked upon a final and comparatively successful gamble. In February the Russian authorities permitted Abdur Rahman, the nephew of Sher Ali, to return to Afghanistan. Lord Lytton, who had failed to discover a suitable candidate for the Amirship, decided to open negotiations with a man who was known to have unusual abilities, and who would certainly have the advantage, from the Afghan standpoint, that he could hardly be considered as a British nominee. For once Lord Lytton's genius for self-deception proved fortunate for his country. Abdur Rahman was far from being the 'ram caught in a thicket' of the Viceroy's phrase. He had no intention of being sacrificed on the altar of British imperialism, but it happened that his interests coincided sufficiently closely with those of the Government of India to enable the latter to withdraw with dignity from an untenable position. The future Amir had learnt much about his two powerful neighbours during his ten years' exile, and was determined to use that knowledge in consolidating his position. He was as anxious as the Government of India to have the British troops safely out of Afghanistan, but in the interim he had no objection to the English fighting his enemies so long as the Afghans did not look upon him as a British nominee. In all this he was successful. While Sir Lepel Griffin was negotiating with him he slowly developed into 'the head of a united nation dictating terms to us, instead of accepting them from us',[1] but his influence was still confined to the Kabul district. Ayub Khan held Herat and the British had appointed an incompetent sirdar, Sher Ali, as Governor of Kandahar. Abdur Rahman had not long to wait before events gave him what he wanted, and the British were forced to fight his battles for him. The impetuous Ayub Khan, as he anticipated, left Herat and advanced on Kandahar. After routing a British force at Maiwand, he wasted his resources and the

[1] *Lord Lytton's Indian Administration*, 413.

patience of his followers by a fruitless siege of the city.[1] Abdur Rahman was able to ensure General Roberts an undisturbed march upon Kandahar from Kabul.[2] A remarkable military operation ended in the complete defeat of Ayub Khan. General Stewart then withdrew the British troops from Kabul. Kandahar, after some further negotiations, was evacuated in the following year. After the British troops had gone Ayub Khan made a final bid for the Amirship, but Abdur Rahman, to the great relief of the British Government, defeated him near Kandahar and became the acknowledged ruler of all Afghanistan.

Thus ended the second Afghan War. Like the first, it left on the Afghan throne a man who, from his previous history, had every reason to prefer Russian to English influence. Fortunately Abdur Rahman, like Dost Muhammad, was an astute politician, whose main interest was the integrity of his country; but England had failed in all the objects for which the war had been begun. India was the chief sufferer. Her debt had been increased, her live stock depleted, and her people taught that, at any moment, the imperial connection might involve them in some reckless and disastrous enterprise. The war had done nothing to solve the local frontier problem. The British retained Pishin, and pushed forward some other posts, but the trans-Indus districts grew more and more disturbed up till the end of the century. As to the Russian menace, the war brought enlightenment to at least one prominent advocate of the 'forward' policy. Sir Frederick Roberts wrote from Kabul in 1880.

'It may not be very flattering to our *amour propre*, but I feel sure I am right when I say that the less the Afghans see of us, the less they will dislike us. Should Russia, in future years, attempt to conquer Afghanistan, or invade India through it, we should have a better chance of attaching the Afghans to our interests if we avoid interference with them in the meantime.'

[1] For an amusing account of a Kabuli shopkeeper's accurate appreciation of the situation see Holditch, *The Indian Borderland*, 45.

[2] For evidence of Abdur Rahman's successful intervention see Kabul Diary, August 8, 1880. F.O. 65-1104.

BOOK VII

THE STRUGGLE OF THE NEW AND OLD: NATIONALISM AND VICTORIAN PATERNALISM

'The autumnal leaves are not more thickly strewn in Vallambrosa than the pigeon-holes of our Departments are filled with Resolutions on the subject (Education) inculcating the most specious and unimpeachable maxims in the most beautiful language.'—Lord Curzon, Opening of Simla Educational Conference, 1901.

CHRONOLOGICAL TABLE

Viceroys.

LORD DUFFERIN.	1885.	First Meeting of National Congress.
		Panjdeh incident.
		First Salisbury Ministry.
	1886.	Annexation of Upper Burma.
		Hindu-Muslim riots at Delhi.
	1888.	Hazara Expedition.
LORD LANSDOWNE.	1888.	
	1889.	Abdication of Maharaja of Kashmir.
	1891.	Factory Act.
		Age of Consent Act.
		Manipur Rebellion.
	1892.	Indian Council Act.
		Gladstone's Fourth Ministry.
	1893.	Durand's mission to Kabul.
LORD ELGIN.	1894.	Opium Commission.
	1895.	*Salisbury Ministry.*
		Chitral Expedition.
	1896.	Famine.
	1897.	Plague in Bombay.
		Murder of Rand and Ayerst at Poona.
		Frontier risings.
LORD CURZON.	1899.	Famine.
	1900.	North-West Frontier Province formed.
	1901.	Habib-ullah becomes Amir of Afghanistan.
	1904.	Expedition to Tibet.
		Co-operative Societies Act.
	1905.	Treaty with Amir.
		Partition of Bengal.
LORD MINTO.	1905.	Liberal Government.
		Morley Secretary of State.
	1907.	Anglo-Russian Convention.
		Refusal to allow Indians into Transvaal.
	1908.	Maniktollah trial.
		Tilak convicted of sedition.
	1909.	Morley-Minto reforms.
LORD HARDINGE.	1910.	Lord Crewe Secretary of State.
	1911.	Delhi Durbar.
		Transfer of capital to Delhi.
		Partition of Bengal modified.
	1912.	*Balkan War.*
	1913.	Hardinge's announcement about Indians in South Africa.
	1914.	Outbreak of the Great War.

CHAPTER I

BUREAUCRACY IN OPERATION

Bureaucracy: machinery of Government: Executive Council: controversy over Military Member: Legislative Council: legislative activity: finance: currency difficulties: effect on administration: education: district administration: industrial development: local self-government: Indians in Government service: military policy.

THE fifteen years following the second Afghan War mark the heyday of British-Indian bureaucracy. The various Services were fully organised in each province. The secretariats busily piled up precedents. Outside the judiciary, few Indians held responsible positions. Neither Viceroys nor the Home Government interfered with the official machine. The Nationalist movement was slowly becoming more vociferous, but the Government of India believed that they had the great bulk of public opinion behind them. Their attitude was shown in Lord Lansdowne's classic reply to a question about the 1890 meeting of the Indian National Congress.

' The Government of India recognise that the Congress movement is regarded as representing what would in Europe be called the advanced Liberal party, as distinguished from the great body of Conservative opinion which exists side by side with it. They desire themselves to maintain an attitude of neutrality in their relations with both parties, so long as these act strictly within their constitutional functions.'

From 1896 onwards came plague, frontier wars, famines, terrorist outrages, and the intense administrative activity of Lord Curzon's regime. The Government of India never regained the aloofness, conscious rectitude, and confidence of the 'eighties and early 'nineties, when it functioned, as it were, *in vacuo*.

This is a convenient place to examine the machinery of administration which had been built up after the Mutiny. Supreme authority was vested in the Governor-General in Council. The Executive Council had developed, by 1885, into a Cabinet of six British officials, each with his own portfolio.[1] The Viceroy could ultimately enforce his views, but

---

[1] A sixth member was added in 1874 to preside over the department of public works.

this was seldom necessary. The course of promotion brought to the Council senior men, efficient and cautious. On matters of general policy the Viceroy would strive to obtain their support, but his position was far stronger than that of a Prime Minister. If a member of Council resigned, it was the end of his career. He had no electorate to whom he could appeal, no alternative party to join. His hopes of rising to the better-paid and more honoured post of Lieutenant-Governor depended upon the Viceroy, and might be another motive for compliance. In small matters the Executive Council tended to be conservative, on larger issues it was little more than an advisory body. The Governor-General was his own Foreign Minister. The Council may have modified but was unable to prevent the rapid changes of frontier policy during the time of Lord Northbrook, Lord Lytton, and Lord Ripon. On two occasions only the Council unanimously opposed measures which the Viceroy introduced under pressure from Whitehall—Lord Lytton's abolition of a duty on certain kinds of cotton cloth, and Lord Elgin's levy of a countervailing excise on Indian cotton goods. In both instances the Council was protesting, though unavailingly, against an infringement of Indian fiscal autonomy.

The Executive Council remained entirely British, though not entirely official, until 1909, when an Indian barrister, Mr. (afterwards Lord) Sinha, was nominated as legal member. An important question of personnel had, however, arisen five years previously, when Lord Kitchener demanded the abolition of the military member of the Council, through whom all proposals of the Commander-in-Chief had passed. The military member was a soldier, and though the Commander-in-Chief was in practice appointed an extraordinary member of Council, the former was the Viceroy's official adviser. This, as Lord Kitchener complained, meant that the proposals of the executive head of the army would

' be criticised from the military point of view by the Military Member of Council, who must necessarily be both junior in rank and inferior in military experience to the Commander-in-Chief'.

Matters came to a head when Lord Kitchener sought to introduce some much-needed reforms of a technical nature. He found his work being held up by 'enormous delay and endless discussions', but Lord Curzon, as Viceroy, strongly objected to the removal of his official military adviser and his Council supported him. Matters reached a deadlock and the Home Government attempted a compromise whereby the Commander-in-Chief should alone have the right to advise on purely military matters, but a 'military supply member' should have charge of the subsidiary departments. This was an unsatisfactory arrangement, and introduced in such a manner that Lord Curzon resigned. Lord Morley subsequently decided that it was 'good neither for administration nor economy', and in 1910 the post was abolished. A new member was appointed to take charge of education and sanitation.

The Legislative Council, as constituted under the Act of 1861, was the Executive Council reinforced by six to twelve members, of whom half were not to be in Government service. Madras, Bombay, and Bengal also had their provincial legislative councils, with subordinate powers, and other councils were established for the North-West Provinces in 1886, and for Burma and the Punjab in 1898. From the first some Indians were included in both the central and provincial councils, but it was not until 1892 that the elective principle was introduced; then by Lord Cross's Act certain public bodies were allowed to elect members to the provincial councils, and four members were selected from these to attend the central legislature. No further attempt was made to give the councils a representative character until the Morley-Minto reforms, which will be considered in a later chapter. The Viceroy, and through him the Home Government, retained the same kind of overriding authority as on the executive side. He could frame and issue ordinances which would remain in force for six months, and in 1870, on a reference from Lord Mayo, it was laid down as a matter of abstract right, that the British Government could require the Governor-General to introduce a measure, and the members of the Indian Government to vote for it.[1] The first right was not used until 1909, when an ordinance was issued to regulate public meetings; the second was never actually enforced. The Legislative Council needed little encouragement to introduce an elaborate legal system into India, and the country

' was deluged with a steady flow of intricate, technical, and sometimes even mischievous Acts, the want of which had never been felt, and the meaning of which is a frequent subject of remunerative dispute to those who live by the law. Hardly any such Act passed between 1870 and 1884 is comprehensible to the layman'.[2]

Some of this legislation—notably the Specific Relief Act and the Easements Act—introduced new and unnecessary complications into

[1] The Duke of Argyll was then Secretary of State. See *Accounts and Papers*, 15, *East India*, 1876, lvi.

[2] Thorburn, *The Punjab in Peace and War*, 244.

2 L

Indian rural life, and was well described as 'ruffles for the shirtless'. The Council made a few cautious attempts at social and economic reform by legislation, but in this field they were handicapped by fear of offending religious prejudices, by financial stringency, and by their lack of contact with the people upon whom they were experimenting. On this last point Mr. Kipling, the best interpreter of his countrymen in India, has left an admirable commentary in his story, *Tod's Amendment*.

The Factory Acts of 1881 and 1891 illustrate the contemporary objection to any interference in business matters. During the last quarter of the nineteenth century a mill population was being collected in the most haphazard manner from the superfluous elements of the villages and from the unsettled tribes. These began to settle round the factories, living under appalling conditions, which were only relieved by the ability of some to escape periodically back to their villages. Neither Act mentioned conditions outside the factories, or recognised that employers have the least responsibility for the housing and the recruiting of their labour. The 1881 Act regulated the working hours of children under twelve, but only applied to factories employing over a hundred hands. The 1891 Act, introduced partly owing to pressure from Lancashire and Dundee, arranged for the inspection of factories, and included provisions for an eleven-hour working day for women, and a weekly holiday, but it left as a problem for the present day the whole question of settling and housing industrial labour.

The Legislative Council had some justification for avoiding questions involving religion. The tradition of non-interference still survived from the Mutiny period; and the one important incursion into family and social legislation—the Age of Consent Act of 1891 —raised almost as much outcry as Bentinck's abolition of 'suttee' sixty years before. It also brought a famous nationalist leader into public life, for Bal Gangadhar Tilak first appeared as a champion of the orthodox Hindu view. Lord Lansdowne insisted upon the passing of this measure, which forbids the consummation of marriage before the wife has reached the age of twelve; its practical effect was probably insignificant.

The Council was more effective in dealing with agrarian problems. The Bengal Tenancy Act was passed in 1885, and similar Acts defined the rights of cultivators in Oudh and the Punjab. The Land Improvements Act of 1883, the Agriculturists' Loans Act of 1884, were part of an attempt to deal with agricultural indebtedness by the issue of Government advances at a low rate of interest. These loans, known as *takkavi*, have led to many wells being sunk, but their utility was limited by a certain rigidity in their administration, and by the financial difficulties in which the Government was involved.

The shortage of money during a period of comparative prosperity was the result of a world currency movement by which India was specially affected. The rapid fall in the price of silver, due partly to increased production and partly to the demonetisation of silver in Germany, caused little inconvenience to the gold-standard countries, but it imposed an intolerable burden on a silver-standard country like India, which had heavy obligations in gold. The rupee sank steadily from 1873 onwards. By 1890 it had fallen to one shilling and fourpence instead of two shillings, and by 1892 it was little over a shilling. The effect of this was almost wholly injurious. It stimulated India's export trade, but this was chiefly in raw materials, and very little of this advantage reached the cultivator. It completely upset the Government's finances, which had already been severely strained by the Afghan and Burmese wars, and by the famine of 1876-8. Debt and home charges rose rapidly, and the uncertainty of the exchange made it impossible to forecast the budget. The inelasticity of Indian revenues under a free trade system again became apparent. Income tax was reimposed and the salt tax increased. These proved insufficient, and finally, in Lord Elgin's time, the general duty of five per cent. on all imports was revived. This comparatively mild form of protection immediately aroused the old Lancashire and India controversy. The first proposal, in 1895, was to omit cotton goods, but then the duty was imposed and a countervailing excise of the same amount was placed on the products of Indian mills. The next year this was reduced to three and a half per cent., where it remained to balance the budget, but also to be a continual source of irritation and political agitation for twenty years.

From 1895 the currency position slowly improved. Two years previously the Indian mints had been closed to the unrestricted coinage of silver, and gold coin was received in exchange for rupees at the rate of fifteen for a sovereign. This had little immediate effect, but from 1895, owing partly to this restriction and partly to world movements, the rupee gradually recovered until, from 1898 onwards, the Government was able to fix the exchange at 1s. 4d. It was found impracticable to establish a gold currency in India, though gold was made legal tender. Another method was adopted on the recommendation of a currency committee under Sir Henry Fowler. The profits made in coining silver were used to build up a Gold Standard Reserve, and by this means the exchange was kept steady until the War, when the question again became acute.

These financial complications, followed by the three disastrous years 1897 to 1900, were partly responsible for the marked ineffectiveness of the administration towards the end of the century. The bureaucracy, after Lord Lytton's departure, was favoured by a long series of good harvests and by fifteen peaceful years, little troubled by political agitation. The various departments were fully staffed, and the Executive Council could obtain all the legislative sanctions which it might need, but the machine did not function. The diffusion of responsibility prevented anyone, even with Lord Curzon's almost daemonic energy, from supplying the necessary motive force. Equally deadening was the obsession that efficient office work and legislative activity could accomplish substantial results without the expenditure of public money and without popular support. Every branch of the administration had fully equipped departments unable to work at more than half-speed because they were essentially spending departments with too little to spend. This was not only evil in itself, but it laid the Government open to the charge of employing unnecessarily expensive European staffs and concentrating too much on producing good statistical results.

Mass education provides a case in point. The obstacles are serious enough. The struggle against illiteracy is mainly a rural problem, and the *ryot* sees little use in his sons going to school, and still less his daughters. Even when children are spared from tending cattle, the education they receive usually fades away after a few years with nothing to read, no accounts to keep, and little occasion to write letters. Muslims often object to secular teaching, and all education is hampered by the social habits which prevent Hindu and Muslim women from acting as teachers. Free voluntary education is certain to produce disappointing results according to European or American standards, and progress in the latter half of the century was almost negligible. After 1871, each provincial Government was controlling its educational department, which had a Director, an establishment of inspecting officers, and a staff of teachers. The cadre was sufficient for an attack upon illiteracy along the lines of the 1854 despatch, but until the end of the nineteenth century provincial Governments had done little more than provide

' facilities for the castes and classes which by tradition and occupation desired education, and had always by hook or crook achieved a reasonable standard of literacy. What public money did was to substitute an organised system of schools, maintained by or aided from public funds and under regular inspection, for the miscellaneous methods by which these "literary" castes and classes had previously secured instruction. . . . Every year the Government conscience was salved by an increase in the "public" institutions due to the conversion of more "private" institutions. But the movement indicated no extension of education to classes hitherto untouched and no growth of a demand for education from such classes'.[1]

Lord Ripon, sensing this failure, appointed the Hunter Commission of 1882 to enquire into the state of elementary education, and 'the means by which this can everywhere be extended and improved'. The report, while recognising that primary education possessed 'an almost exclusive claim on provincial revenues', showed little appreciation of the magnitude of the problem. It suggested an increase of 10 lakhs (about £66,000) in the annual budget, which would allow for another 100,000 pupils. Outlay on education subsequently rose steadily from 132 lakhs in 1885 to 177 lakhs in 1901, but this merely covered a slightly higher standard in teaching and the natural increase in population. There was no appreciable difference in the proportion of literates amongst the population.[2] During the same period the number of college students had more than doubled, and pupils in secondary schools had risen from 429,093 to 633,728. Thus, until the coming of Lord Curzon, the problem of educating the masses had never been seriously tackled. The Government had even allowed the prejudices of upper caste Hindus to hamper the education of the few lower caste children who attended. A new era in mass education began in 1904. It was inaugurated by a Commission appointed by Lord Curzon, but its future was closely connected with the political developments which followed the Morley-Minto reforms, and will be considered later.

A similar lack of enterprise was apparent in other branches of the administration. District officers slipped easily into the routine of magisterial and revenue work, and at each 'station' a little group of British officials developed an exclusive social life. The Mutiny, the growth of the Services, and the Government's reluctance to admit Indians to the higher posts helped to turn the Europeans into a separate caste, the 'White Brahmins', with the usual features of the caste system—endogamy, commensality, and mutual control by members! This partly explains the stagnation of district life during the last twenty years of the century. A steadily increasing population was pressing heavily on the soil, agricultural debt was growing, and roads were needed almost as

[1] A. Mayhew, *The Education of India*, 229.   [2] See Census Report of 1901.

much as schools, but little was done, even experimentally, to improve agriculture, relieve indebtedness, or develop local self-government. An agricultural expert was appointed in 1882, and Dr. Voelcker drew up his famous report in 1890, but no serious efforts were made to improve agricultural research or education until 1906.[1]

The need for some constructive method of dealing with agricultural debt had been recognised in the 'eighties. Sir W. Wedderburn and Sir Raymond West both attempted to start agricultural banks, but were discouraged by their superiors.[2] In 1892 Sir Frederick Nicholson drew up a scheme for land banks in Madras, but nothing was done until after the passing of the Co-operative Credit Societies Act of 1904. Between 1881 and 1901 India's 500,000 villages absorbed nearly thirty million more inhabitants, but only where canal irrigation was undertaken was there any marked change in country life. The Lower Chenab Canal brought a large tract of desert under cultivation, and Lyallpur became the centre of a new colony which by 1901 had 800,000 inhabitants. The Jhelum, Betwa, Nira, and other canal schemes also belong to this period. It was in district administration rather than in constructive work that the bureaucracy was weak. So long as the country remained quiet, it was assumed that the machinery of control did not need either examination or improvement.

The Government's attitude towards industrial development was marked by the same disinclination towards active interference, but the motives were different and less open to criticism. Large-scale enterprise, tea gardens, textile factories, coal mines, and paper mills were mostly in European hands, but business men had singularly little influence upon the Government. The old distrust of the private trader or 'interloper' survived the Mutiny, and was confirmed by the orgy of speculation and the commercial disasters of 1865 onwards. Lord Lawrence voiced the feelings of the whole Civil Service when he cried, 'I know what private enterprise means. It means robbing the Government.' The authorities at least saved the country from wholesale exploitation. They watched

---

[1] Dr. Voelcker's views were embodied in his *Improvement of Indian Agriculture*. His remark that 'the improvement of cultivation is, in the main, not an agricultural need in India' was much misunderstood, and encouraged the belief that little could be done to help the *ryot*. Dr. Voelcker of course used the word 'cultivation' in its correct sense, the preparation of tilth. He was fully aware of the need for better seed and better manuring, and for improved methods of harvesting, preparation for market, and selling organisation.

[2] See S. K. Ratcliffe, *Sir William Wedderburn*, 37 et seq.

the unaided and fairly rapid development of the main industries, and saw no reason to give them artificial encouragement.[1] The theory of protecting 'infant industries' by tariffs was not so generally accepted as to-day, and, apart from cotton goods, there were few commodities to which they could have been applied. In one important field the Government deliberately discouraged the speculator. Mining and prospecting for minerals were hedged round by curiously obstructive rules, based on a far more socialistic conception of the State than was prevalent in Europe. One regulation, for example, insisted that premises and mines, when abandoned, should be handed over to the Government 'in a workmanlike state'. The same suspicion of private enterprise appeared in other departments, and from the days of the Company the Government has entered upon semi-commercial undertakings which in England would normally be left to contractors. The Government has its State railways with their own workshops, does its own printing, manages its forests and sells their products, worth three or four millions annually. Lord Curzon would have gone even farther, and in 1905 Sir John Hewett, as Director of the new Department of Commerce and Industry, started factories for making aluminium goods, for chrome tanning, and other minor industries. In this field the Government pursued a cautious but consistent policy; and much modern criticism is based on the assumption, which post-war experience scarcely justifies, that in a backward country successful industries can be built up *ab initio* behind a prohibitive tariff.

The two main defects of British rule during this latter part of the nineteenth century were the lack of any definite aim and the failure to associate Indians with such work as was being carried on. The bureaucracy, while unsuited for evolving any general policy, was remarkably effective in passively resisting any innovations of which the majority of officials did not approve. No Viceroy, with his limited term of office, could hope to accomplish much against them. Nor was there any continuity in the policy of Viceroys or of the Home Government. The

[1]					1880	1895	1914
Cotton mills	-	-	-	-	58	144	264
Persons employed	-	-	-		39,537	139,578	260,847
Jute mills	-	-	-	-	22	29	64
Persons employed	-	-	-		23,495	75,157	216,288
					1885	1894	1914
Coal (output in tons) -		-	-		1,294,221	2,800,652	15,738,153
Persons employed	-	-	-		22,745	43,197	151,376

history of rural self-government and of the employment of Indians in responsible official positions both illustrate this failing.

Lord Ripon had foreseen that ultimately a transfer of responsible government would have to take place, and that this could only be done through some form of democracy. On these grounds he extended local self-government in the rural areas. Most Englishmen would now agree that he was justified, but few nineteenth-century officials, and not many Secretaries of State, genuinely accepted either proposition. For the quarter of a century after Lord Ripon's reforms the rural boards were allowed to function in an almost farcical manner under the chairmanship and control of District Officers. The essentially sound proposal of the Bengal Provincial Government in 1883 to constitute purely unofficial bodies for areas smaller than the district was abandoned two years later, owing to the disapproval of the Secretary of State. The original purpose of these boards was forgotten, and by 1909 so little had been done to enlist Indian support that the Decentralisation Commission, while suggesting some modifications in official control, still recommended that the District Officers should remain at the head of the District Boards.[1] Official scepticism and unwillingness to work on equal terms with Indians had ruined a valuable educational experiment.

Opposition to Lord Ripon's innovations was based on the idea of efficiency. In the matter of admitting Indians to the higher posts the British officials had perhaps less excuse for resisting a long series of proposals made by Viceroys and the Home Government, though Civil Servants and Army officers were often sincere in believing that a mixed administration would not work. Two opinions may be quoted as representing the views of most Europeans in Government service. Mr. Seton Kerr, formerly Foreign Secretary to the Government of India, made a speech in London against the Ilbert Bill. This, he declared, outraged

' the cherished conviction which was shared by every Englishman in India, from the highest to the lowest, by the planter's assistant in his lowly bungalow and by the editor in the full light of the Presidency town—from those to the Chief Commissioner in charge of an important province and to the Viceroy on his throne—the conviction in every man that he belongs to a race whom God has destined to govern and subdue'.[2]

Lord Roberts equally believed in this fundamental racial superiority.

---

[1] *Report*, paragraph 795.

[2] Quoted in Bishop Whitehead's *Indian Problems*, 207.

'It is this consciousness of the inherent superiority of the European which has won for us India. However well educated and clever a native may be, and however brave he may have proved himself, I believe that no rank which we can bestow upon him would cause him to be considered as an equal by the British officer.' [1]

Holding these views, British officials were justified in expressing them, but not in using their exceptional position to block innovations, once they had been approved by Parliament and the Viceroy. Yet this was done habitually throughout the sixty years following the Mutiny.

Their resistance was the more important because most educated Indians regarded the gradual infiltration of their countrymen into the higher ranks of the Civil Service as their first political objective. The Civil Service rather than the Army seemed to them to personify British rule, and they possessed the clear but unfulfilled promise of the Queen's Proclamation of 1858: 'Our Subjects, of whatever Race and Creed, shall be freely and impartially admitted to Offices in Our Service'. Indians have a strong conception of a special ruling class, and many felt that the natural administrative genius of certain castes was being allowed to decay from lack of opportunity. The economic argument was also powerful in a country with a rapidly increasing educated class and very few available posts; for many castes do not take readily to commerce or engineering.

Indians had not made any serious inroad into the highest ranks of the Civil Service by 1885. A few had accomplished the difficult feat of going to London and competing successfully in the examination, but in 1878 even this avenue was practically closed by an order of Lord Salisbury which reduced the maximum age for candidates from 21 to 19. In 1870 there were seven Indian candidates, but in 1880 only two. The attitude of the British officials to those who did succeed was far from friendly. The very able Surendranath Banerjea, one of the three successful candidates of 1871, was soon afterwards dismissed for a small delinquency involving no 'moral turpitude'. In such an atmosphere Lord Lytton's experiment of a Statutory Civil Service was not likely to succeed, and only sixty-nine Indians were appointed to it before it was abolished. From 1885 onwards, the Congress in India and a small group of Liberals in England continually pressed for more Indians in the Civil Service. They might win an occasional victory in Parliament, as in 1893, when the House of Commons passed a resolution in favour of simultaneous examinations in India and England. They might sometimes

[1] Sir G. Arthur, *Life of Lord Kitchener*, ii. 177.

win the ear of a Viceroy. But the Government of India has a remarkable facility for deferring an unwelcome reform.

In 1886 Lord Dufferin appointed a mixed Commission, under Sir Charles Aitchison, to produce a scheme which should 'do justice to the claims of the native of India to higher and more extensive employment in the public services'. The effect of this Commission was to abolish the Statutory Service, and divide the administrative staff into three branches. The Indian Civil Service remained as it was before, recruited by an examination distinctively English in character and held in London. All the local Governments objected to the simultaneous examination, and repeated their objections after the House of Commons resolution. The two other branches—the Provincial Civil Service and the Subordinate Civil Service—were confined to those domiciled in India, and the Commission proposed giving the former a vested right to certain 'listed posts', which had formerly been reserved for the Indian Civil Service. These were supposed to be about a sixth of the total, but even this concession was resisted by the local Governments, and as late as 1923 only 88 posts had been listed instead of the 116 to which the Provincial Civil Service was entitled. The Commission advised the raising of the age for Indian Civil Service candidates, but this had little effect, and by 1915 only five per cent. of the Service were Indian. Throughout this period British policy aimed at keeping down the number of Indians in the Services on the grounds of efficiency, rather than insisting upon a certain proportion of Europeans as necessary to retain the Western character of the administration and the British connection. Lord Curzon, after his retirement, accepted the latter view:

' The question at issue is rather not what is the maximum number of offices that can safely be given to Indians, but what is the minimum that must of necessity be reserved for Europeans.' [1]

Unfortunately, by adopting the opposite line of argument, the Indian Government was continually forced to invent some excuse for not putting into practice a policy which it had accepted in theory. The British in India were in the position of an army fighting a rear-guard action instead of giving the country a lead towards some definite objective.

The same lack of purpose characterised our military policy. Successive Commanders-in-Chief took charge of the army. Many of them had

[1] Speech to Edinburgh Philosophical Society in 1909. Quoted in a valuable chapter on 'Indianisation' in *The Indian Civil Service* by L. S. S. O'Malley, 225.

little knowledge of India, and they considered that their sole duty was to bring this portion of the imperial troops to as high a state of efficiency as possible with the funds available. From a soldier's standpoint this was justifiable, but it meant that India's military policy was framed without any regard for the constitutional developments which were likely to take place. The desire for efficiency, combined with certain prejudices, made the Indian tax-payer provide for a force which was able to take a prominent part in the Great War, but which was very far from being a national army suitable for an autonomous Government.

The second Afghan War, especially the break-down of the transport arrangements and the defeat at Maiwand, had caused considerable misgivings about the fitness of the army to defend the frontier. The Panjdeh incident, in 1885, provided an opportunity to increase the British contingent by some 10,000 men. Subsequently the troops from Central and Southern India were steadily reduced, and those recruited from some lower castes were disbanded. The modern army was built up under one command, was recruited largely from Sikhs, Gurkhas, Punjabi Muslims, and Pathans, and stationed chiefly in the North of India. It was entirely a professional army, willing to fight in any part of the world. About half the personnel—the British, the Gurkhas from Nepal, the Pathans and Hazaras—could have little feeling of loyalty for India. The direction of the army remained entirely British. Until the War no Indian soldier in British India could rise higher than the Viceroy's commission. He could become a Risaldar or Subadar, but his position was scarcely above that of a glorified N.C.O., and he was junior to the youngest subaltern.

There was little constructive criticism of Indian army policy, either from Indians or from Liberals in England. No machinery existed by which the low caste Mahars or the Moplahs could make their objections heard when an order from Simla stopped their further recruitment or disbanded their regiments. From time to time a Viceroy would re-open the question of training some Indians to take the place of British officers in the Indian army, but such proposals were only tentative, and chiefly made with the idea of finding some occupation for the cadets of the princely families. A sufficient proportion of those in high places accepted Lord Roberts' views, to prevent anything being done. Lord Kitchener discussed with Lord Minto the formation of a training college for Indian officers, but the suggestion was not put into effect because of financial objections. Vocal Indian opinion concentrated almost entirely on the cost of defence. Moderate Indian politicians were still aiming at extending their influence into the Government of India, rather than replacing the bureaucracy by a democratic body. They employed their energies in capturing the control of local bodies and municipalities, and gaining some proportion of responsible civil posts. They criticised the general financial policy, took up cases of racial injustice, and agitated for better educational facilities, but they seldom argued that such and such actions by the Government of India would make it difficult later to develop a national government.

CHAPTER II

THE GROWTH OF NATIONALISM

Opposition to Government after the Mutiny: importance of newspapers: effect of Ilbert Bill controversy: growth of professional class: moderates and extremists: Indian National Congress: early extremists: Hindu revival: importance of Tilak: Bengal agitation: anti-Partition movement: economic boycott: terrorism.

A FOREIGN autocracy must ultimately arouse a nationalist opposition. The form this took in India was complicated by many peculiar factors, the structure of Hindu society, the importance and segregation of the Muslim minority, the large area covered by semi-autonomous States, the Western educational system, and the deep racial antagonism which developed after the Mutiny.

Such small revolts as occurred before 1870 were easily suppressed. The ruling princes, secure in their right of succession or adoption, were not disposed to place themselves at the head of any popular movement, and without their leadership there was no focus for local patriotism. The Muslims, who for some years after the Mutiny were considered the most dangerous opponents of British rule, showed neither the desire nor the ability to organise a rebellion. As the prospect of further armed risings seemed remote, most Indians accepted the British connection as a permanency; the more thoughtful began to consider how best they could influence the foreign government under which they and their children were fated to live. This attitude was most noticeable amongst the Bengalis. Their training and outlook, their long experience of British rule, and their propinquity to the seat of Government at Calcutta all helped to mark them out as political leaders.

Newspapers played an important part in these early formative years. Sir Thomas Munro, nearly half a century earlier, had foreseen 'a tremendous revolution, originating in a free press'. The daily or weekly paper proved the most effective way of bringing educated Indians into touch with each other, always a difficult problem in a country where distances are great, and caste and communal restrictions so powerful. In Bengal there was the *Hindoo Patriot*, the *Amrita Bazar Patrika*, and the *Bengalee*. The last was edited by Surendranath Banerjea, who took to journalism after his dismissal from the Indian Civil Service, and lived to be a Minister under the Montagu reform scheme. In Madras the *Hindu* was almost the only tangible evidence of anti-Government feeling. The *Mahratta* and the *Kesari* were to become equally important in the West. By the 'seventies the Indian Press was sufficiently influential to embarrass the Government, but they were protected by the equal vehemence of certain British papers, like the *Bengal Hurkaru*. The Vernacular Press Act, passed in 1878, caused much controversy at home, but was ineffective because it did not apply to papers published in English. These became relatively more important, and found easy targets for criticism in Lord Lytton's Government and the second Afghan War. From such newspaper activity the Indian Association developed. This group of educated Hindus was formed in 1876, held a few meetings, and was the forerunner of the Congress.

Political interest received a great stimulus from the European opposition to the Ilbert Bill. This unhappy dispute served to emphasise the inferior status of Indians. The point was driven home by a succession of cases where manslaughter of Indians was alleged against British soldiers and civilians. These cases were often treated by the Courts in a manner suggesting the half-conscious recognition that an Indian life was not so valuable as that of a European. The Nationalist movement began to take shape.

By 1884 British India had been peacefully administered as a unit for nearly a generation. Memories of rougher times had grown dim. A new professional class had come into existence, corresponding to the Effendis in Egypt, and had thriven as the older landowning class lost its former ascendancy. They were recruited partly from the Brahmins, partly from the children of the smaller *Zemindars*, and partly from families engaged in commerce and money-lending. Having received a semi-Western education and acquired some knowledge of English, they had a common language and some vestiges of a common though exotic culture. Much of this culture was based on ill-digested theories of democracy and political freedom, but it was rapidly assimilated and diffused. Railways, cheaper postage, and the growing use of the printing press combined to make communications easier between the different provinces for all who could afford travel, correspondence, and newspapers.

From the first there was much discontent. The old caste tradition encouraged the belief that a salaried and sedentary occupation was the right of anyone who was fully educated; but middle-class unemployment appeared very early in India. Those who did obtain situations were often brought into contact with Europeans who treated all educated Indians as clerks. Closely connected with the professional classes were other types, later to be drawn into politics. The Indian mill-owner and business man began to look about for allies to support a demand for fiscal change. At the other extreme were the older orthodox Hindus, the *gurus* and teachers, who had no reason to love the British. The 'eighties saw the growth of a politically minded and discontented middle class, able to communicate amongst themselves from one end of the peninsula to the other. They were the natural medium for any seditious movement. No longer was it necessary for the Wahabi fakir to wander surreptitiously from town to town, or for the *chaupatti*[1]—the Indian 'fiery cross'—to be passed secretly from village to village. Macaulay's theory about education filtering down from the upper classes had been mistaken, but political ideas were more fluid. They spread rapidly from one province to another, and brought with them a new conception of national unity and of racial pride.

A few of the middle classes became Anglophil and 'loyal'. The remainder tended to group themselves under leaders who may be described, in view of their later history, as Moderates and Extremists, though it must be remembered that the politically active were only a small proportion, and that the kind of party loyalty which characterised nineteenth-century England has little counterpart in India. The Moderates accepted, but wished to transform, British rule. The Extremists reacted against it. The first Moderate leaders were reformist in religious matters, many being members of the Brahmo Samaj. They were anxious to work with educated Muslims, a still smaller body, and with any sympathetic Englishmen. They were appreciative of their connection with Europe. Aiming ultimately at self-government within the Empire, they looked forward to so cautious a development of autonomy that they were not much in advance of English Liberal opinion as ex-

[1] Flattened cake of flour and water, not unlike the Australian 'damper'. It is possible that they were used for secreting messages.

pressed when the Liberal Party was not in office. Gopal Krishna Gokhale and Pherozeshah Mehta of Bombay; Dadabhai Naoroji, the Parsi Member of Parliament; Subramania Aiyar of Madras; Surendranath Banerjea and Bhupendranath Basu of Bengal—these were typical Moderates of the thirty years between the foundation of the Congress and its capture by the Extremists after Mr. Gokhale's death. The Moderates foresaw their country 'industrialised, socially emancipated and self-governing'.[1] They were prepared to concede to the British that

' the blessings of peace, the establishment of law and order, the introduction of Western education, and the freedom of speech and appreciation of liberal institutions that have followed in its wake—all these are things which stand to the credit of your rule'.[1]

In later days, condemned to perpetual opposition, they became more violent in their language, especially when they felt that the Extremists were stealing their thunder, but certain characteristics remained. They accepted and welcomed the spread of Western civilisation, they recognised that 'the continuance of British rule means the continuance of that peace and order which it alone can maintain',[1] and they wished to re-reform and finally transform the Government from within.

The Indian National Congress, which held its first meeting in 1885, was essentially an institution of the Moderates. Owing to the part played by the Congress Party in later days it is easy to exaggerate its early importance. It began as a body not unlike the Indian Association, but it had its committees scattered over the different provinces, and it was this fact which made it into an organisation worth capturing when nationalism had become more effective. A retired English civilian, Allan Hume, took a prominent part in its inception. Owing to his insistence it was planned in a manner which was to make it a powerful force in the future, but he can have had little conception of what would develop from the first meeting of seventy delegates, 'who had to be pressed and entreated to come'. The early limitations of nationalist ideals and the cautious tone of the first Congress can be inferred from the speech of the President, Mr. W. C. Bonnerjee. He mentioned as one of the objects of the Association 'the fuller development and consolidation of those sentiments of national unity that had their origin in our beloved Lord Ripon's memorable reign'.

The Congress rapidly lost its apologetic tone, but it retained for many years its close connection with sympathetic Englishmen, several of whom remained prominent in its counsels, especially Sir David Yule,

[1] The quotations are from Mr. Gokhale's speeches.

and later two retired Indian civilians, Sir William Wedderburn and Sir Henry Cotton. Allan Hume visited England and enlisted the support of John Bright, and, perhaps unfortunately, of Charles Bradlaugh. The Indian group in England were inclined to become a small set, suspected by their fellow-Liberals, but they were very active. They had considerable influence, they conducted for the Congress the propagandist paper *India*, and even got Dadabhai Naoroji a seat in Parliament.

There is little evidence about the strength of the Congress Party in its early years, but it was soon popular enough to attract over a thousand delegates to its yearly meeting. By 1892 it was criticising very frankly the new Councils Act, and concentrating upon obtaining some share in the direction of Government policy rather than upon the appointment of Indians to posts in the administration. The Government of India soon became definitely hostile. It withdrew its permission for Government servants to belong to the Congress, and in 1888 Lord Dufferin unwisely sneered at the pretensions of the 'microscopic minority' who supported it. This meant that for the next twenty years the Congress was left isolated between the growing forces of extreme nationalism and a totally unsympathetic Government. It says much for the calibre of the Moderates that they remained sensible and level-headed, and till the War maintained their principles and successfully defended the Congress from the attempts of the extremist sections to capture it, the most notable of these occasions being the 1906 Congress at Surat.

The agitation over the Partition of Bengal also placed the Congress in a difficult position, for it brought Muslim and Hindu interests into conflict, and for some years the Muhammadan element withdrew from its activities. In 1890 nearly a quarter of the delegates were Muhammadan, but by 1905 the number had fallen to about seventeen.

The Extremist philosophy made an early appeal to many sections, including nearly all the younger generation. It was a reaction against the threat of absorption into an alien civilisation, of losing their status as Indians for an indeterminate and subordinate position inside the British Empire, and of allowing the disintegration of the Hindu system without the substitution of anything to take its place. From the first the Extremist leaders have had to weld together two incongruous elements, the orthodox Hindus, who reacted against Western civilisation, and the younger men, who found the Moderates too cautious and too pacific. 'Scratch a Hindu', wrote Surendranath Banerjea, 'and you will find him a conservative.'[1] The career of Bal Gangadhar Tilak illustrates this

[1] *A Nation in the Making*, 397.

strange blending of obscurantism and modern revolutionary outlook. It was characteristic of this powerful leader that he should have first come to the fore as the bitter opponent of the Age of Consent Bill, which was designed to mitigate the evils of child marriage and had the full support of the Indian Liberals. The Bill was ultimately passed in a modified form, but during this struggle Tilak had made himself the acknowledged leader of the more aggressive nationalists, and he had behind him the growing force of orthodox Hinduism.

The Hindu revival, which marked the latter half of the century, was possibly strongest in the West, but was apparent in other parts of India. Its strength was largely due to the bitterness and estrangement which followed the Mutiny, and which made it easy to identify the new idea of nationalism with a zeal for the old religions. In Bengal, Ramakrishna Paramhamsa and his well-known follower Swami Vivekananda led a 'back to the Vedas' movement, based on the idea of a Hindu Golden Age and a totally uncritical reverence for the sacred books. Dayananda, who founded the *Arya Samaj*, and in 1877 moved to the Punjab, was more critical of Hindu usages, but equally determined that 'everything worth knowing, even in the most recent inventions of modern science, was alluded to in the Vedas. Steam-engines, railways, and steam-boats, —all were shown to have been known, at least in their germs, to the poets of the Vedas'.[1] A few English and American theosophists, like Mrs. Besant, Madame Blavatsky, and Colonel Olcott, ministered to this popular demand by praising the old Hindu civilisation, the perfection of which became an accepted doctrine amongst Indian Extremists. At first this Hindu revival was more religious than political, and was definitely anti-Muslim. Dayananda founded the Cow Protection Association in 1882, as an attack upon the Muhammadan sacrifice of cattle. Tilak began the cult of the Maratha chieftain Sivaji, who had successfully fought against the Muhammadans. Until the War Tilak and many extreme nationalists would class the Muslims as *mlecchas* or foreigners, but as the movement became more political and less religious this early tendency disappeared. It explains, however, why even those Muslims who were markedly anti-British were inclined to have their own organisations, and why the Moderate Muslims withdrew from the Congress, which after 1900 always had an extremist element in it.

Tilak in the Deccan, and Lajpat Rai in the Punjab, were chiefly instrumental in turning this religious enthusiasm into more political channels. The former was a learned and astute Chitpavan Brahmin, who

[1] Max Müller, *Chips from a German Workshop*, ii. 176.

2 M

combined a deep knowledge of Hindu literature with an ambition to revive the ancient glories of the Peshwas. It is probable that in his early days he did not envisage a united independent India, otherwise it would be difficult to explain his refusal to recognise Muslims as his countrymen, but he gradually developed into the personification of extreme nationalism. To him the English were always the enemy, and from the first he strove to develop a war mentality amongst his followers. As early as 1897 he began a bitter controversy with G. K. Gokhale, which not only emphasised the difference between Extremists and Moderates, but was to have important and unhappy consequences in later years. Gokhale, who was then in England, wrote a letter to the Press attacking the behaviour of the military during the anti-plague operations at Poona. He subsequently found that he had been misinformed and published an apology. Tilak at once accused him of being a traitor to his country, arguing that the truth or falsity of the charges was irrelevant, and that in a war any weapon is permissible. The Extremists, and afterwards the Congress, have accepted Tilak's view that their propaganda is war-time propaganda, and hence need not be accurate. Apart from any moral considerations, the policy has proved unfortunate, for it has gradually alienated all Congress sympathisers abroad except the uncritical and the unscrupulous, while within India it has led to a deplorably low standard of political and historical accuracy.

Within his own province of Bombay Tilak was a remarkable organiser, and he was the first to develop the technique of aggressive nationalism. He founded the *Kesari*, and proved that political invective could make a vernacular newspaper profitable. He went into the villages and, with the help of the Natu brothers, revived the old gymnastic societies and the annual festivals of Ganesh, perhaps the most popular deity in the western Deccan. When he developed the cult of Sivaji, he enlisted the support of the students, and he taught the younger generation that the only way to get what they wanted from the English was by incessant agitation, direct and indirect, and finally by the use of physical force. He used his immense energies to keep this agitation simmering, and the outbreak of plague in 1896 caused it to boil over. Little was known about this disease, and the first efforts of the Government to segregate it led to racial and religious ill-feeling, which the *Kesari* did its utmost to foment. Two officers, Mr. Rand and Lieutenant Ayerst, were murdered when on special plague duty. The two brothers Chapekar, who committed the murder, belonged to a society 'for removing obstacles to the Hindu religion', and the agitation against the plague restrictions was based on the idea that they outraged the religious susceptibilities of the people. The murderers were executed, and Tilak sentenced to eighteen months' imprisonment for incitement.

This ended the first chapter in the history of political extremism, but it had taught the other provinces the value of the vernacular Press, the importance of a religious appeal, and the ease with which students could be brought into a revolutionary movement. Tilak was the first great extremist leader. He adapted the methods of the Irish Home Rulers to Indian conditions, but he was himself too orthodox a Brahmin to become a successful national leader. His followers were Hindus and Marathas rather than Indians, and his limitations were apparent when he tried to extend the cult of Sivaji to parts of India in which memories still survived of the devastations caused by Maratha raids.

Bengal became the next centre of extremist activities. One result of the Permanent Settlement is that Bengal has an unusually high proportion of *bhadralog*, a *rentier* class recruited from the members of Hindu joint families with some financial interest in land. They are a class easily brought into political movements, and Bepin Chandra Pal and Arabindo Ghose began to organise from amongst them a party pledged to 'direct action' rather than the constitutional methods of the Moderates. In some respects they followed Tilak's methods. The *Yugantar*—edited by Bhupendranath Dutt, brother of Swami Vivekananda—was as successful as the *Kesari*. The revival of tantric ritual and the cult of the goddess Kali provided the popular religious basis for their work. In some respects the movement in Eastern India differed from that in the Deccan. It was Hindu, but certainly not Brahmin, for only a few of its leaders belonged to that caste. It aimed at arousing a local territorial patriotism instead of reviving old dynastic glories. In Bengal nature is more beneficent than in the arid Deccan, and it is easy to appeal to vague traditions of a Golden Age, and to portray the Motherland as once prosperous and self-supporting, but now despoiled by foreigners. The agitation was closely bound up with certain features in Lord Curzon's policy, which, combined with his off-hand methods of expressing his opinion, were well suited to bring Moderates and Extremists into the field against the Government. His resumption of control over the Calcutta municipality offended all who had taken part in local administration, his University Act annoyed the educated classes and the teaching profession. But the greatest challenge to the Hindus was the division of Bengal into two provinces.[1]

[1] See chapter iv. pp. 574-6.

This aroused all the local patriotism which the nationalists had been encouraging, and the manner in which the policy was evolved and forced upon the country emphasised the lack of any popular control over the administration. The formation of a separate Eastern Bengal Province, completed in 1905, also affected many practical interests. The new province was predominantly Muslim, which irritated leading Hindus without winning the Government any effective support. The professional and commercial classes were vexed because some of the trade and prestige of Calcutta were transferred to the new capital at Dacca. The anti-Partition movement was well calculated to embarrass the Government, and it remained one of the principal features of nationalist activities from about 1904 until the modification of the policy in 1911.

Certain changes in the nature of nationalism took place during this long agitation. Events outside India began to affect the standpoint of the educated classes. There were signs that Europe was losing its dominant position in the world. The long and doubtful course of the Boer War, the rout of the Greeks by the Turks, the massacre of Christians in the Near East, the resounding victories of Japan over Russia, all were noted with the keenest interest. The Russophobia which the Government of India had done so much to encourage during the nineteenth century now helped to embolden the nationalists, for it exaggerated the importance of the Japanese successes over a Power which has never been effective in attack, and was only partly European. The nationalist movement became less provincial and less religious, its adherents more interested in their status as Indians.

The Partition of Bengal was a convenient test case. Tilak's activities in the Deccan had had no definite object, and the Congress had busied itself with many small reforms. Moderates and Extremists could now work together to make the Government repeal or modify a definite decision. Twenty years earlier the Ilbert Bill had been modified as the result of a European agitation, and now the nationalists concentrated upon winning a similar victory. Two new weapons were used in this struggle. The first was the boycott of British goods, the second was political terrorism.

The economic boycott has been a feature of many nationalist movements, and is well suited to India, where foreign goods are easily recognised and are often of a luxury nature. There was already a strong *swadeshi* movement, closely connected with nationalism, aiming at the encouragement of home production and of business development by means of legislation and protective tariffs. The boycott campaign, formally inaugurated in August, 1905, was assured of the support, financial as well as political, of Indian mill-owners, and it could also make some appeal to village weavers. Its organisation was chiefly the work of Moderates, for it was a constitutional method, but the wearing of home-spun spread rapidly, bringing women into the movement for the first time.

The English hatred of political assassination is so strong that it is difficult to keep a sense of proportion in discussing this question. Life in India is held rather cheaper than in England, but the Indian has no natural proclivity for political murder, and those who have taken part in violent crimes of this nature have been few in number, and have been definitely influenced from abroad. Educated Indians had for many years been in the habit of comparing their nationalist movement with the Italian War of Liberation and the Home Rule struggle in Ireland. Political murders played a considerable part in both. If the Irish, who formed a large proportion of the official population in India, considered that shooting an unpopular official was a legitimate means of bringing pressure upon the Government, it is not surprising that many Indians accepted their view. The theoretical advocates of physical force amongst the Extremists found a section of the Bengali *bhadralog* ready to put these ideas into practice. The Bengali has a low emotional flash-point, and responded easily to the oratory of Bepin Chandra Pal and Arabindo Ghose, the tirades of the *Yugantar* and the historical arguments of Tilak, who in 1905 was again taking an active part in politics. There is also in Bengal a traditional tolerance for the crime of dacoity or gang robbery. Secret societies, like the *Anusilan Samiti* of Dacca, were formed amongst the students. They took to robbery in order to collect funds, and then developed the use of the pistol and bomb. As in Ireland, politicians, and in some cases religious leaders, gave them equivocally worded encouragement, and joined in the hero-worship of convicted assassins. It was not difficult to find suitable quotations from the sacred *Bhagavad-gita*—'he who regardeth the dweller in the body as a slayer, and he who thinketh he is slain, both of them are ignorant'.

The total number of outrages during the last twenty-five years would be insignificant if compared, on a population basis, with those which have occurred in Ireland, or in some other European countries, but from the first there was much popular sympathy with the murderers, though little belief in the efficacy of their methods. The terrorists, never numbering more than a few hundreds, have been careless of their own lives. Their relations with the Extremists have always been a matter of conjecture. One of the first outrages took place at Muzaffarpur in 1908, resulting in the accidental killing of two English ladies and leading to the discovery of a bomb factory at Maniktollah. During the subsequent conspiracy trial an informer was murdered, and the general attitude of the public was clearly sympathetic with the accused. Those who were executed were buried amidst those scenes of hysterical enthusiasm which have since become so familiar. From that date political crime has been endemic in Bengal, epidemic in the rest of India.

The Extremists, like the Moderates, began to build up connections outside India. The *Ghadr* movement in America was helped by many who were more interested in attacking the British Empire than in Indian affairs. Small groups were formed, in London and Paris, under men like Krishnavarma, editor of the *Indian Sociologist*, and Savarkar, who was a follower of Tilak. Dhingra, who murdered Sir Curzon Wyllie at the Imperial Institute in London, was one of Savarkar's pupils. This crime, which occurred in July, 1909, drew public attention in England to the existence of these secret societies and the activities of Indian Extremists. Like the Phoenix Park murders, it had a disproportionate effect on future political developments. From this time most Englishmen began to understand that there was an Indian 'problem', just as there was an Irish 'problem', and that, as in the case of Ireland, it was based on a national movement. Subsequent Indian history is chiefly concerned with the course of this movement and the policy of the Government towards it.

CHAPTER III

THE FRONTIER AND TIBET

Relations with Afghanistan: Panjdeh incident: Abdur Rahman and the Durand Mission: the North-West Frontier: Chitral: the 1897 outbreak: formation of North-West Frontier Province: Tibet: Younghusband's expedition: Lord Curzon and Habib-ullah: The Anglo-Russian Convention.

APART from the conquest of Upper Burma, the thirty years which preceded the Great War contained only one large-scale campaign, the Malakand expedition of 1897, but the problems of the North-

West Frontier, imperial as well as local, remained to embarrass the Government. These turned ultimately on our relations with Afghanistan.

The Amir, Abdur Rahman, succeeded in the double task of establishing his position, which he held till his death in 1901, and of maintaining his independence against his two powerful neighbours. He inclined towards friendship with the British, recognising that his country had more to fear and also more to gain from them, but if he had any feelings of gratitude it was for the Russians, whose guest he had been for ten years, and who had allowed him to return to Afghanistan at the critical moment. His autobiography shows that his only object was to preserve the integrity of his country and the stability of his throne. He accepted British subsidies, but successfully resisted every effort to reduce him to the level of a feudatory. He had no illusions about the English habit of extending their territory when it suited them for strategic or other reasons. 'Though England does not want any piece of Afghanistan, still she never loses the chance of getting one—and this friend has taken more than Russia has.'[1] He met such attempts by intrigues amongst the tribesmen rather than by force. The measure of his success was that he handed over his kingdom almost intact to his son Habibullah, who succeeded without any internecine war, and was able to enjoy a sovereignty far more complete than Abdur Rahman could claim when he first came to the throne.

The first frontier trouble, after Lord Ripon's retirement, was 'imperial'. The Russian capture of Merv in 1884 roused considerable excitement in England, and added to the difficulties of the joint Frontier Commission, which had been set up at the request of the Russian Government. The British Commissioners arrived to find both Afghans and Russians busily occupying as much of the debatable land as they could before the work of delimitation began. The British were placed in a very awkward position, for Abdur Rahman was then visiting Lord Dufferin, and the Viceroy was supposed to be maintaining not only the interests of the Indian Government, but also those of Afghanistan. The Commissioners, however, were subordinate to the Governments of London and St. Petersburg, and were kept a long time waiting for definite orders. The almost inevitable 'incident' occurred when Panjdeh, near which the British Commission was encamped, was forcibly seized by the Russian General Komaroff, though it was occupied by Afghan troops. The British Commission, who had a few soldiers with them,

[1] See his autobiography, *The Life of Abdur Rahman*, ii. 237.

withdrew. The Afghans, who suffered severe losses, felt that they had been betrayed.[1] It was widely believed that the Russians would advance against Herat, a place of far greater strategic importance. Strong pressure was put upon the Liberal Government to make Panjdeh into a *casus belli*. Gladstone, whose position had been much weakened by the Irish troubles and the death of General Gordon, gave way a little to the prevalent Russophobia. Lord Dufferin promised the Amir full military support in case of further aggression. The army in India was hastily mobilised and strengthened by an additional ten thousand British troops. The British members of the Commission encamped at Herat, which they helped to fortify.

After much diplomatic manœuvring the excitement gradually subsided. None of the three interested parties wanted a war. The Russians would not put their local representatives in the wrong by withdrawing from Panjdeh, but they waived their right to some other disputed territory. The English Government, after proposing arbitration, accepted the Russian offer and allowed the Commission to proceed with its work. Abdur Rahman, who had the most right to be aggrieved, did nothing to aggravate the dispute. He reckoned that the loss of a small town was a lesser evil than having his country overrun by two contesting Powers. In his own words, Afghanistan was the goat tied between the lion and the bear. It was not to the goat's interest that one of these jealous neighbours should establish a decisive superiority over the other. He was almost certainly right, for a victorious Russian or a victorious English Government would have found some excuse for making its strategic frontier on the far side of Afghanistan and bringing the mountain State under its protection. Abdur Rahman therefore expressed little concern over the fate of Panjdeh, but 'took the matter calmly as a lesson for the future'.[2] He had learnt that the belligerency of Russia and England contained a strong element of bluff, that promises of help were dependent upon political alignments in London, and that his most powerful weapon, especially against England, was intrigue amongst his co-religionists across the border. The Boundary Commission completed its work, and Russia ceased to be an important factor in Indian affairs. The Agents of the two local Governments continued to

---

[1] See T. H. Holditch, *The Indian Borderland*, 127. Holditch, who was with the Commission as surveying officer, says that it was the 'unanimous opinion of those present that the Russians would not have taken Panjdeh if the British had held on to their position'.

[2] *Life of Abdur Rahman*, i. 243.

intrigue against each other at Kabul, Chitral, and elsewhere, but it was the rivalry of Calcutta and Tashkent rather than of London and St. Petersburg.

For sixteen years after the Panjdeh incident Abdur Rahman continued his policy of steady but unobtrusive insistence upon his country's complete independence. His relations with the Government of India were frequently strained. He especially resented the extension of the Chaman railway, the occasional interference with his freedom to import arms, the general forward policy adopted on the frontier from about 1888 onwards, and the sending of British envoys to Gilgit in 1889 and to Chitral in 1893. About this latter date the two countries were on the verge of a conflict, for the Government of India, following an unhappy precedent, attempted to force the Amir to receive another 'military mission', and, as if to emphasise its aggressive nature, Lord Roberts was proposed as its head. Abdur Rahman handled a difficult situation with great skill. He had no wish to receive any mission, and, as he remarks in his autobiography,

' many of the relatives and friends of the Afghan people had been killed either in fighting against Lord Roberts, or in being punished by him at the time of the last Afghan war, a circumstance which made it unwise to allow him to enter Afghanistan with such a large force'.[1]

He had two great advantages in his relations with the British. He was a permanency, while his opponents, Viceroys, officials, even Secretaries of State, completed their term of office and might be succeeded by someone more amenable. It was also hardly necessary for him to intrigue actively in order to stir up trouble amongst the tribes—it was enough for them to know that his relations with the British were strained. A little diplomatic procrastination enabled the Amir to wait until Lord Roberts had left India. He then received Sir Mortimer Durand as an envoy. The mission resulted in the demarcation of an Indo-Afghan boundary—the Durand line. This, while not unsatisfactory from the Amir's point of view, was drawn without consulting the tribes affected, and was one of the causes of the 1897 outbreak. The Amir received an increased subsidy, but continued to aim at complete independence. In 1895 he made strenuous but unsuccessful efforts to be allowed direct relations with the British Government in London. He died in 1901 and was succeeded by his son Habib-ullah. This was the first peaceful and undisputed succession for generations, and provided the finest tribute to Abdur Rahman's wisdom.

[1] *Op. cit.* ii. 155.

The disturbed condition of the tribes on the North-West Frontier during the 'nineties can be ascribed to several causes, but there is scarcely enough evidence to decide their relative importance. The repercussions of political agitation in India can be traced in the events leading up to the great outbreak of 1897, while exaggerated reports of happenings in the Near East and North Africa encouraged talk of another *jehad* or holy war. Pressure on the land, which drives Pathans to raid, had possibly grown more acute, and a new economic grievance was added by the enhancement of the Kohat salt duty in 1896. During periods of tension between Afghanistan and the Government many irresponsible Afghans certainly helped to foment trouble over their border.

These all had their effect, but probably the most powerful influence was the forward policy adopted by Lord Lansdowne and Lord Elgin. Many small advances were made into tribal territory. In 1889 Sandeman extended British control over the Zhob valley, and in 1892 the Kurram valley was occupied at the request of the Turis, a Shiah tribe on bad terms with their Sunni neighbours. Expeditions were made against the Shiranis, the Orakzai and Isazai tribes, and an envoy sent to Gilgit. In 1892 a disputed succession in Chitral enabled the Government to send a mission under Dr. Robertson at the request of the successful claimant. Various reasons, including the usual excuse of Russian intrigues, were given for not withdrawing the mission. In 1895 the new Mehtar was murdered, and Dr. Robertson was besieged by the rival claimant, Sher Afzal. The garrison was relieved, after a heroic defence, by troops from Gilgit and by Sir R. Low, who marched over the Malakand, but the question remained whether Chitral should be evacuated. The retention of a garrison entailed building a road from Peshawar through Swat, and the occupation of fresh territory. Lord Rosebery's Government decided upon withdrawal, but Lord Salisbury reversed this policy, chiefly on the advice of Lord Roberts, and against the opinion of many experts, including Sir John Adye, Sir Neville Chamberlain, and others. The Chitral question became for a short time a political issue in England. It created far greater excitement on the frontier, where the final verdict was considered as pledging the new Government to a strong forward policy, and was an important factor in uniting the various Pathan tribes when war broke out in June, 1897, after an attack upon the Political Officer in the Tochi valley.

The Swatis were the first to rise, and were soon joined by the Mohmands, the Afridis and the Orakzais. The Punjab Government, which was still primarily responsible for the frontier, was completely unprepared for such general trouble. Conditions were reported as 'reassuring' when villages were being burnt almost up to Peshawar. The local military authorities were equally at fault in that unhappy incident when the Khyber forts, held by detachments of the Khyber Rifles, were left without a British officer and captured by Afridis after a siege during which no attempt was made to relieve them from Peshawar. Two large-scale campaigns had to be undertaken. Sir Bindon Blood led the Malakand force against the Mohmands. Sir William Lockhart operated against the Afridis. The Mohmands capitulated after severe fighting, but the Afridis, against whom some 35,000 troops were engaged, put up a stubborn and successful resistance, though they submitted in the following year on the threat of another expedition.

When Lord Curzon arrived in India in 1899 the fighting was over, but there were some 15,000 troops on the far side of the administrative boundary, many of them in small isolated detachments. The new Viceroy had keenly defended the retention of Chitral and the construction of the road from Peshawar, but, apart from continuing this policy, he proved a very moderate supporter of the 'forward' school. He gradually withdrew the British troops from the Khyber Pass and the tribal country. Their place was taken by tribal levies under British officers, or by military police, while British forces were concentrated in British territory and attention was paid to improving communications in the rear. Strategic railways were built as far as Jamrud and Dargai, the scene of the fiercest fighting in the Afridi War; another was taken to the entrance of the Khyber Pass. In some respects this policy was a return to the 'close border' system of earlier days, and it was combined with an important administrative reform, the creation of the North-West Frontier Province. The kind of dual control which had been exercised over frontier policy since the Mutiny had proved a failure since the latter part of the century. As the Punjab grew more settled and its canal system was developed, the local government found less time to deal with the highly specialised problems of the frontier. In a difficult crisis, like the summer of 1897, when action had to be taken by the Government of India and the army, the intervention of the Provincial Government only led to delay and inefficiency. Lord Curzon's method of introducing his new measure caused unnecessary friction with the local officials, but no one now doubts that it was a salutary and necessary reform. The Frontier Province included all the trans-Indus territory, except the settled district of Dera Ghazi Khan in the south, and stretched as far as the Afghan boundary. About a third of the area was administered, the remaining 25,000 square miles being occupied by the semi-independent tribesmen.

These civil and military reforms, following a period of severe fighting, brought comparative peace and a welcome check to heavy expenditure. It was found necessary to blockade the Mahsuds in 1900-2, and the Mohmands and Zakka Khel rose in 1908, but Lord Curzon could claim that, during his seven years of office, he only spent £248,000 on military operations on the North-West Frontier as against £4,584,000 in the years 1894-8. He did not 'solve the frontier problem', for many of its difficulties will remain as a legacy to the Federal Government, but he introduced a system which has proved to be a sensible compromise between conflicting views of experts.

He was less happy in his dealings with the North-East Frontier. Here he inherited no problems. The Nepalese Government had for nearly a century adopted a studiously correct and guardedly friendly attitude, while allowing many of their subjects to enlist in the Indian army. Relations with the Bhutanese had been difficult up to 1863, when a series of raids into disputed territory led to negotiations in which Lord Elgin's envoy was insulted and forced to sign a treaty which the Government immediately repudiated. Further quarrels led to an expedition in 1865, at the end of which the Bhutanese agreed to accept a subsidy in return for the eighteen Duars, part of the land under dispute. This arrangement, for which Lord Lawrence was much criticised, worked admirably. The Duars became a famous tea-growing district. The Bhutanese, who could hardly have developed this hilly tract, have remained contented with the yearly subsidy. The Tibet expedition of 1904 originated in a long series of disputes and negotiations painfully reminiscent of Lord Lytton's dealings with Afghanistan. For centuries the Tibetans had remained deliberately isolated. The Government—a monkish theocracy under the nominal suzerainty of China—had brought its inhabitants a fair degree of comfort, if not of civilisation. In the few fertile valleys, wrote an Irishman attached to the expedition, 'the standard of comfort amongst the very poorest is high, and indeed luxurious as compared with that of an Irish cottar'.[1] Attempts to open political and trade relations during the nineteenth century were unsuccessful, and almost the only contact with the Tibet Government was due to a dispute over the Sikkim boundary. An

[1] Capt. O'Connor, intelligence officer to the Younghusband expedition.

incursion by some Tibetans was repelled in 1887. The boundary was then marked out by a Sino-British Commission in 1890, but the Chinese did not encourage communications across the frontier, though a trade convention was made. Lhasa remained the forbidden city until the end of the century.

The British change of policy was due to two factors. Dorjieff, a Buddhist monk and a Russian subject, had acquired considerable influence over the Dalai Lama, who, unlike his predecessors, had managed to throw off priestly tutelage. The Russian Government undoubtedly used Dorjieff to keep on friendly relations with Tibet, but there is no evidence that this typical Asiatic intrigue was taken very seriously. The other factor was Lord Curzon's personality. Like Lord Lytton, he felt that the influence of the Indian Government should be predominant over its immediate neighbours, and the isolation of Tibet seemed to him incompatible

' with proximity to the territories of a great civilised power at whose hands the Tibetan government enjoys the fullest opportunities both for intercourse and trade'.

The presence of an alleged Russian Agent at Lhasa provided the necessary grounds for breaking down this one-sided reserve, and gave Lord Curzon his opportunity. In 1902 he pressed the Home Government to force a mission upon Tibet, urging as an excuse some very insignificant incidents which had occurred on the Sikkim frontier. Lord Lansdowne objected, pointing out that if any pressure was to be exerted, it should be upon Pekin. He had no desire to embroil himself with Russia on the doubtful grounds of a rumoured Russo-Tibetan treaty. Lord Curzon then deliberately forced the hands of the Home Government. He proposed that negotiations should be opened at Khamba Jong, some fifteen miles inside the Tibetan boundary, and in the summer of 1903 he obtained the Cabinet's consent to send Colonel Younghusband there with a military mission. The Tibetans, refusing conference until the British retired to the frontier, began to collect their totally inefficient troops. After further pressure from the Viceroy the Home Government permitted an advance to Gyantse. The Russian Government naturally protested, and Lord Lansdowne, pleading that the Tibetans had given great provocation, promised that no Tibetan territory should be permanently occupied.

Colonel Younghusband began his advance in March, 1904, and fought a lamentable battle at Guru, where his troops were able to shoot down some 600 Tibetans who were too badly armed to inflict any casualties.[1] Gyantse was reached in April, but the Dalai Lama refused to negotiate and the troops marched towards Lhasa. The Dalai Lama then offered to negotiate, but Colonel Younghusband advanced to Lhasa, which he captured in August. A treaty was then concluded with the Regent—the Dalai Lama having fled. Certain trading concessions were demanded, and a British commercial agent was stationed at Gyantse, where his successor still supervises an almost negligible exchange of goods. Other provisions gave the British the first claim to any concessions granted to foreigners, and ensured some control over Tibetan foreign policy. An indemnity of 75 lakhs was demanded, to be paid in seventy-five yearly instalments. The treaty enjoined that the Chumbi valley, in Tibetan territory, should be occupied until the payment was completed. Lord Curzon supported this disingenuous attempt to annex a part of Tibet without breaking our pledge to Russia, but the Secretary of State, Mr. St. John Brodrick, insisted on the reduction of the indemnity to 25 lakhs, and ordered that the troops should be evacuated after the payment of the third instalment. Thus ended one of the least justifiable of England's 'little wars', forced upon an essentially pacific and practically unarmed race. It merely interrupted the negotiations with Russia which ended three years later in the Anglo-Russian Convention of 1907. One term of this agreement was that neither Power would seek concessions in Tibet, or send representatives to Lhasa, or negotiate with Tibet except through China. China, in fact, was 'the one Power which has reaped solid advantages from the Mission'.[2] During the confusion which followed the withdrawal of the British troops, she was able to turn her vague suzerainty into practical sovereignty.

Lord Curzon was also involved in a dispute with Afghanistan, following the death of Abdur Rahman, and it is perhaps fortunate that he had a less bellicose Ministry in London than had Lord Lytton. The trouble arose over the renewal of treaties. Habib-ullah claimed that these were between countries, and did not need renewing on the death of the Amir. Lord Curzon wished to treat the Amir as a subsidiary ruler with whom personal agreements were necessary. For some years Habib-ullah stopped all communications with the Government of India. He did not draw his subsidy, and claimed the title of 'His Majesty'. He was then in a strong position, for in these years the relations between Russia

---

[1] For Colonel Younghusband's account, see his *India and Tibet*, 278.

[2] Lovat Fraser, *India under Curzon and After*, 146.

and England were frequently upset by disputes in the Persian Gulf, and by Russia's commercial and political activities in Persia and Central Asia. Habib-ullah could almost make his own terms when a mission, under Sir Louis Dane, was sent to Kabul. The treaty, signed in March, 1905, renewed all the engagements between the Government of India and Abdur Rahman, while not encroaching on Habib-ullah's assumption of sovereignty. Two years later the tables were turned. The Anglo-Russian Convention of 1907 ended a long series of disputes and intrigues ranging from Tibet to the Persian Gulf. Intended primarily to determine British and Russian interests in Persia, it was also extended to cover Afghanistan, which Russia agreed to be definitely outside her sphere of influence. The Amir was not even consulted, though some of the terms relating to equal commercial privileges were only operative with his consent. This he refused to give, although a visit to Lord Minto in 1906 had restored more cordial relations. His refusal made little difference. Russia stood by her agreement, and the Amir saw that he could no longer play off one powerful neighbour against the other. From that date until the overthrow of the Tsarist Government, Habib-ullah remained aloof, but in spite of pressure from the orthodox party and of intrigues by German Agents, his attitude during the War was strictly correct and neutral.

CHAPTER IV

BUREAUCRACY ON THE DEFENSIVE

End of the century: plague: famine: controversy over Government responsibility: famine economics: Curzon's term of office: administrative reforms: co-operative societies: police: education: Partition of Bengal.

FROM about the year 1896 it is possible to trace a change in the British attitude in India. Hitherto nearly every Englishman assumed that our work in the East was along sound lines, that steady progress was being made, and that there was no need for any great change and no likelihood of any sudden development. The few outside critics, English or Indian, could be disregarded, and there was far less effective criticism from within the administration than in pre-Mutiny times. Lovat Fraser, with his long Indian journalistic experience, notes the

' curious fact that all Indian reports were far better done under Company rule. . . . I believe the true reason to be that the servants of the Company had to justify their work, and that the obligation does not appear to lie in the same degree upon servants of the Crown. . . . The present craze of official secrecy was also then unknown'.[1]

The administration had been affected by Victorian complacency, and the last years of the century brought a full measure of those disasters which commonly await the self-satisfied. British arms received a severe set-back both in South Africa and on the frontier, from opponents weaker in number and equipment. In 1896 plague made its first appearance in Bombay, and led to a panic which suggested that neither our medical service nor our administration had the confidence of the people. A series of famines between 1896 and 1900 devastated much of the country, and cast doubt upon the agrarian system in which we took such pride. Attacks upon the administration, from inside and outside India, became more insistent and more pointed. Finally in 1899 Lord Curzon came to India as Viceroy. A believer in bureaucracy, who at that time could foresee no other form of government for India, he was also its sternest critic.[2] When he left, after six years of almost superhuman activity, but of limited achievement, a new era began, during which the bureaucracy was frequently modified and continually on the defence.

Lord Elgin, Viceroy at the beginning of this difficult transitional period, was a capable and cautious administrator. The disastrous years from 1896 to 1898, with their unhappy combination of famine and war, closely resembled the corresponding years of Lord Lytton's regime exactly twenty years earlier. But on this occasion India's troubles were not intensified by viceregal irresponsibility. The deficient rains of 1895,

[1] *India under Curzon and After*, 255. Written about 1910.

[2] Many years later Lord Curzon was responsible for the inclusion of a sentence about 'dominion status' in the announcement of 1917. When he left India, his farewell speech at the Byculla Club suggests that he did not then envisage any development of responsible self-government. 'I earnestly hope that the Viceroy of India may never cease to be head of the Government of India in the fullest sense of the term. It is not one man rule, which may or may not be a good thing—that depends on the man. But it is one man supervision, which is the best form of government, presuming the man is competent. The alternative in India is a bureaucracy, which is the most mechanised and lifeless of all forms of administration.'

the complete failure of the 1896 monsoon, and the frontier wars of 1897 would have placed an intolerable strain on any Government. Bubonic plague, first discovered in Bombay in August, 1896, completed the tale of misfortunes. Very little was then known about this curious disease, which seems to lie dormant for generations, only to break out again in some new area with the most devastating intensity. Its connection with rats was recognised in medieval times, but it was not till 1905 that research by the Indian Plague Commission established beyond doubt that the carrier of the disease was the rat-flea, *Pulex cheopis*. The plague was almost certainly brought to Bombay by rats on grain ships from Hong-Kong. At first the Government was working completely in the dark, though its system of quarantine, of evacuation of infected premises, and of disinfection was sound enough, so far as it went, for the fleas—which inhabit the nests and not the bodies of the rats—would be left behind or killed.

The disease got a good start. When it appeared in Bombay some 400,000 inhabitants fled to the villages, and it spread rapidly in the Deccan and then slowly through India. The first Punjab case was detected in the autumn of 1897, but there was no serious mortality till 1902. The incidence throughout India was curiously uneven. Madras suffered little, but the Punjab had lost over two millions by 1910. The villager's habit of storing grain in his house, his elementary ideas of sanitation, and the Hindu objection to taking life make it difficult to stamp out a disease in which vermin play such an important part. Haffkine's prophylactic was discovered and has done something to check the spread of the disease, though its general use was delayed by an unfortunate accident. Preventive measures gradually became more efficient and better understood, and Indian rats are probably growing more immune. Plague mortality has shown a steady decrease since the 'peak' year of 1907, when it amounted to 1,160,000. The total number of deaths in 1930-1 was just over 20,000, the lowest figure since the disease first established itself in India.

The plague left its mark on Indian history, apart from the eight million deaths which it had caused by 1921. In those parts, like the Punjab, which suffered most severely the disease had an effect similar to the Black Death in England. It raised the standard of living and wages amongst the poorer classes, and temporarily relieved the pressure on land. Its influence in this way was comparatively small and limited in area. A more general result was that it checked the movement to the towns which might normally have been expected in view of the intro-

2 N

duction of Western industries and ideas. It seems to have had a stultify-
ing effect, checking enterprise and keeping people in their villages. The
suddenness of the attacks and the lack of any effective remedies encouraged the characteristic fatalism of the Hindu.

The epidemic also intensified racial antagonism. Educated Indians,
knowing even less than the English about the nature of the disease,
resented the first drastic measures taken to segregate it. Tilak, as we
have seen, added to the difficulties of dealing with an excited and
frightened population. The comparative immunity of Europeans led to
absurd rumours about the British spreading the disease, a belief widely
held in the Punjab during the troubles of 1907.[1] On the other side, the
agitation against sanitary regulations provoked much hatred and contempt for the nationalists amongst the British in India. The Calcutta
Municipal Act of 1899, by which the Government took back much of
the local autonomy which had been delegated to the City Council, was
inspired by the feeling that educated Indians could not be trusted to
deal with the plague or to enforce proper measures for sanitation.

The series of droughts between 1895 and 1899 would also have taxed
the resources of any Government. The failure of the monsoon in 1899
was reckoned to be 'the greatest in extent and intensity which India has
experienced in the last 200 years'.[2] It came only three years after the
poor rainfall of 1895 and the wide-spread drought of 1896 had caused
famine conditions in the United Provinces, Bombay, the Central Provinces, and parts of the Punjab. The famine of 1899-1900 was the more
devastating because it extended not only over the 'precarious areas'
where population is comparatively light, but also over Gujarat and
Baroda, the 'garden of western India'. It was in these thickly populated
districts that mortality was heaviest. Neither famine was merely a
'work famine'; there was a real shortage of food, and a complete lack
of fodder over huge areas, amounting in 1900 to nearly a third of the
peninsula, and affecting a quarter of the population. The appalling
misery caused by these famines, the heavy loss of life, direct and indirect, and the fact that for the second famine Lord Curzon appealed for
assistance both within and outside the Empire drew upon the Government of India an unprecedented amount of criticism. The first accusation was that relief measures were begun too late, and were on too
parsimonious a scale. The second was that the Government's policy,

[1] Viscount Morley, *Indian Speeches*, 216.

[2] Report of Sir John Elliott, the Government meteorologist.

especially with regard to taxation and land revenue, had tended to weaken the villagers' ability to cope with famines.

Famine relief is primarily the responsibility of Provincial Governments, though in all cases their work is based on the Famine Codes which have been in existence since 1883. These laid down four principles: the establishment of public works as 'tests', the grading of labour into four classes, the payment of wages based on a subsistence level, and the grant of relief in villages to those who could not work. Attempts were made at revision in the light of the 1896-7 famine, but the next had begun before any general change in policy had been accepted.

The Commission of 1901 emphasised the lack of real preparation. 'In no province were well-considered programmes of public or village works ready at the beginning of the famine.'[1] The system of grading labour was too complicated for a wide-spread famine, and was generally abandoned. In some provinces, notably Bombay, there was a tendency to defer action until too late and to be too economical. The scale of relief had an undoubted connection with famine mortality, whether that mortality was due to starvation or to the indirect results of famine conditions.

' In four districts of Madras Presidency 20.8 per cent. of the population were in receipt of relief. Yet, in spite of the poverty of the cultivators in many localities, the mortality was only 4.1 per mille in excess of the normal. In Bombay, on the other hand, the percentage relieved did not exceed 17, while the mortality statistics rose to 15 per mille, above the decennial average. In the Central Provinces where, as has been seen, the relief was least adequate, it was 22 per mille above that of 1893. It is not without pertinence to add that the average wage as measured in food was 24 lb., 17 lb., 16 lb., in these districts respectively'.[2]

The heaviest mortality occurred amongst the aboriginal tribes, amongst whom it is difficult to organise relief. This accentuated the results of famine in the Central Provinces and Gujarat, but a large number of deaths were undoubtedly due to the low standard of relief in certain provinces, and to variations in the administration of relief works, especially the infliction of the 'penal minimum'.[3]

[1] *Report of 1901 Commission on Famines*, 10.

[2] Loveday, A., *The History and Economics of Indian Famines*, 69.

[3] A cut of 25 per cent. was made in the subsistence wage if the work done was considered insufficient. Vaughan Nash, in *The Great Famine*, discusses the unfortunate effect of this provision. See his chapter iii.

Official estimates place the number of deaths due to the two famines as between one and a half and two millions. This was in British India alone. Many of the States suffered severely, and their administration also varied between that of Mysore, which was a model for the British provinces, and that of some smaller States, which did so little that many of their inhabitants migrated into British territory. This adds to the difficulty of estimating the total mortality, but a study of the census returns gives some support to those who argue that famines cause a far greater loss than might be deduced from official reports.[1] The decennial figures—given in Appendix D—suggest a general tendency for the population to increase at a rate of about seven to ten per cent. over the ten year period. The three decades which show a far smaller rise are those ending in 1881, 1901, and 1921. The last was the War period, during which plague was severe, and the influenza epidemic of 1918 accounted for some eight million deaths. The other two included no epidemics, but the famines of 1873 and 1877-8, and of 1896-7 and 1899-1900.[2] In each decade the rate of increase is less than $1\frac{1}{2}$ per cent. Provincial figures are equally striking. The Bombay Presidency suffered from both famines, and the administration of relief was severely criticised. The 1901 census shows a drop in population of about three millions, though considerable numbers are supposed to have migrated into the area during the previous ten years. Some reduction in the birth rate follows inevitably from the general destitution, and from collecting labourers at the relief works, but these two factors and the pre-occupation of the administration must also tend to make the death statistics unreliable. It is difficult to avoid the conclusion that the mortality, due to the difference in the methods of administration, far exceeded the official estimates. If relief had been granted as quickly, and on as generous a scale in Bombay as in Madras, it would have resulted in an increased expenditure, but one still within the Code, and would have saved an indeterminate number of lives, certainly to be reckoned by the hundred thousand. This misplaced economy was not the fault of famine officers, but seems to have been due to an obsession about pauperising the *ryot* and a hesitation to apply emergency measures which afflicted certain senior officials. The actual famine administration was far more efficient than twenty years previously, the only serious

[1] The estimate of 19 millions in Digby's *'Prosperous' British India*, 317, has been frequently quoted. It was published without comment in the *Lancet*. The basis for this figure seems to be entirely supposititious.

[2] Deaths from plague had not amounted to a quarter of a million by 1901.

break-down being due to a shortage of rolling stock. The railways moved a sufficiency of grain into the famine area, but they failed completely over the transport of fodder. The stricken area was denuded of cattle, and the famous Gujarat breed of cows almost disappeared.

During the controversy which followed these disastrous years, effective criticism turned more upon the condition of the *ryot* before the famine, than upon the measures taken to relieve him. The widespread suspicion that his poverty, both in money and goods, was due to the land revenue system received some confirmation from an important memorial addressed to Lord George Hamilton, the Secretary of State, by ten retired British officials and Mr. R. C. Dutt, a distinguished Bengali civilian and writer. The essence of their demands was that the revenue should be limited to half the net profits in the *ryotwari* areas and half the net rental in the *zemindari* districts; that assessments should only be increased on the grounds of a general rise in prices, or the extension of irrigation facilities; and that settlements should have a currency of thirty years. Other critics pointed out, from abundant official evidence, that the enhancement of land revenue since the Mutiny had been accompanied by a great increase in indebtedness. They were able to quote Sir William Hunter, Sir Denzil Ibbetson, and other civilians to prove that in many areas the fixed assessment had not left the peasant enough upon which to live. Lord Curzon himself drafted a reply in the form of the Government resolution of January 16, 1902. Much of this document is special pleading, only effective against those who had argued that the rapid recurrence of famine after 1895 was due to the excessive demands of the Government rather than to the drought. The Government was unable to accept the very moderate demands of the memorialists, but there is no doubt that the criticism to which the Government was subjected hastened on certain reforms which will be considered later.

To the modern mind the controversy seems ineffective. It was confused by theories about 'rent' which have now been generally abandoned, and by the acceptance of certain 'economic laws' which have lately fallen into disrepute. The ability of the *ryot* to withstand a crop failure is dependent upon (1) his store of grain and fodder; (2) his cash reserve; (3) the possibility of buying grain and fodder imported into the drought-stricken district; (4) his freedom during the famine period from further demands upon his cash; and (5) his ability to earn or the Government's willingness to advance cash while his fields are still unproductive. India at the end of the century was in a transitional stage, and the *ryot* would very often get the worst of both worlds. For some years the revenue had been collected in money, most transactions were on a cash basis, and the peasant habitually sold a considerable part of his produce. Owing partly to his ignorance of the value and use of money, partly to improvidence which the *bania* and the priest encouraged, partly to an assessment which was heavy and only remitted in very bad seasons, the peasants seldom saved any money. Any surplus was normally kept in the form of ornaments, which involved a heavy loss if they had to be resold. The custom of keeping a grain and fodder reserve was slowly abandoned. The tendency was 'to exchange grain for money, and money soon flies, usually for unproductive purposes'.[1] The years preceding the droughts had not been very prosperous, as prices had remained low, and 1899 found the *ryots* in the precarious districts with little reserve either in the form of cash or of produce. The railways were still insufficiently developed to bring in full supplies at moderate prices. The money-lender demanded his interest, and the Government in certain areas was slow to remit assessment.[2] The *ryot*, therefore, was almost entirely dependent on money he could earn at the public works, or relief which was given to his family. He was in grave danger of losing his land to the money-lender even if he could keep his family alive through the famine. A lighter assessment during the previous thirty years would have given him a better cash reserve, but how much of this would have disappeared into the maw of the money-lender is a difficult question. So long as the Government was obsessed with the idea of freedom of contract and the rule of law, the position of the money-lender and merchant was unassailable. If the Government had returned a larger share of the land revenue in the form of relief and remissions during the bad years the heavy assessment might fairly have been considered as a form of insurance.

It was fashionable at this time to blame the railways for the disappearance of the village reserves of grain and fodder, and there was a long controversy over the respective merits of railways and irrigation. The two are not mutually exclusive, and large-scale irrigation for wheat in the Punjab would have been impracticable without proper transport

[1] *Report on Famine in Madras Presidency*, 1896-7, p. 48.

[2] The figures show great variations in policy:

	Land Revenue Demand	Suspensions
Bombay Presidency - -	Rs. 39,224,330	Rs. 7,146,000
Central Provinces (1st instalment)	Rs. 3,845,000	Rs. 2,528,000
Four famine districts of the Punjab	Rs. 2,105,160	Rs. 1,317,250

for the surplus grain. In the hilly areas of the Deccan irrigation facilities are definitely limited, and some form of mechanical transport not requiring fodder is needed to ensure a supply of food in bad seasons. The 1899 famine came when railway development had progressed considerably—there were about 22,000 miles of line—but the equipment was hardly sufficient to bear a sudden strain. By the later droughts of 1906-7 and 1918-19 these lines had been extended and improved. It was then clear that, with sufficient transport and a generous scale of relief, the ordinary trade channels should supply a sufficiency of food, though the more bulky fodder still remains an almost insoluble problem.

The lean years from 1896 to 1900 had a salutary effect upon the administration, and a new spirit was infused into the bureaucracy by the arrival of Lord Curzon in 1899. There is a tendency to ascribe all changes of policy to the Viceroy in office at the time, though he may only have assented to some proposals slowly evolved by permanent officials, which he has never seen until completed. In Lord Curzon's case this belief was justified. In some instances, notably the Partition of Bengal and the Calcutta Municipal Bill, he adopted policies which he had not initiated; but he was a man of very decided views, who came to India believing that many reforms were overdue. In his first Budget speech he referred to twelve important questions,

' all of them waiting to be taken up, all of them questions which ought to have been taken up long ago, and to which, as soon as I have the time, I propose to devote myself'.

His great capacity for work, his love of detail, his long term of office, which was extended beyond the usual period, his complete confidence in himself and in his mission, enabled him to make the bureaucratic machine function as it had never functioned before. He accomplished more than his predecessors, but he left India a disappointed man. The cause of his resignation—the controversy over the military member of Council—has already been mentioned. It was irrelevant to the rest of his work, and, before this dispute had occurred, the limitations of his policy and methods were becoming apparent.

For some years Lord Curzon enjoyed considerable popularity amongst educated Indians. They admired his independence of outlook, they liked the vigour which he infused into Government activities, and they appreciated the courage with which he insisted upon full investigation of cases in which British soldiers and civilians were alleged to have caused the deaths of Indians. The Bain case, and the disciplinary action taken against two British regiments which were considered to have burked an enquiry, did something to restore faith in British justice, though they brought Lord Curzon much abuse from his own countrymen. Yet in the end he helped to consolidate Indian opinion against British rule. Though he courted criticism, he was restive under it. He took the public into his confidence more than any previous Viceroy, but he was supremely contemptuous of views with which he did not agree. He recognised the growth of Indian public opinion, but, in the words of his biographer, he

' reserved the right to decide when public opinion was an expression of views based on sober reason and supported by obvious justice, and when it was a mere frothy ebullition of irrational sentiment'.[1]

His judgment was often at fault. He grossly underestimated the Indian desire for some voice in the control of the Government. 'My own belief', he wrote to the Secretary of State, 'is that Congress is tottering to its fall, and one of my great ambitions while in India is to assist it to a peaceful demise'.[2] Because of this weakness much of his work was destined to perish. Lovat Fraser, writing a few years after his resignation, rightly selected as his four principal achievements 'the Partition of Bengal, the solution of the problem of the North-West Frontier, the reform of the system of education, and the formulation of a land revenue policy'.[3] This was certainly the contemporary view, but the first was to be reversed in 1911 and the educational policy, which caused so much controversy, has not stood the test of time. Both failures were partly due to Lord Curzon's initial disregard for Indian opinion.

Lord Curzon's dictatorial methods and concrete ideas made him well suited to deal with the frontier question, unnecessarily complicated owing to differing schools of thought and personal rivalries, and he produced a moderate and sensible solution. India has even better reason to remember his agrarian reforms. District administration and the collection of land revenue had become stereotyped. The Agricultural Department was inefficient, little was done about the debt problem, and the revenue system was far too rigid. It was fairly said in those days that land administration in the States was of leather, but in British India it was of iron. A new procedure was introduced in 1905 for granting re-

[1] Lord Ronaldshay, *The Life of Lord Curzon*, ii. 328.

[2] Letter dated November 18, 1900.

[3] Lovat Fraser, *India under Curzon and After*, 18.

missions and suspensions in bad seasons, and it was extended to cover local crop failures and other disasters. The theoretical change was not great, and many regretted that the higher limit suggested by the memorialists had not been accepted, but the actual effect of this greater elasticity was considerable. The financial position in India was changing rapidly. With the development of industry and commerce new sources of taxation were becoming available, while currency reforms solved the more pressing needs of the Central Government. Provincial Governments had no longer the same urge to keep up their revenue receipts, and the new elasticity operated definitely in the *ryot s* favour. The principle of protecting cultivators from eviction was extended by the Punjab Land Alienation Act of 1900, and other measures.

On the constructive side Lord Curzon entirely reorganised the Department of Agriculture. Helped by a generous gift from an American friend, Mr. Phipps, he was able to institute research laboratories and experimental farms. The work which has been accomplished during the last generation in the improvement of seed and of cattle-breeding is seldom appreciated. Lord Curzon brought the same enthusiasm to the subject of irrigation, but he also knew, better than some of his critics, that its possibilities are strictly limited. The merit of the Commission, which he appointed under Sir Colin Scott-Moncrieff, was that it laid down a definite long-term programme for the whole of India in place of the piecemeal methods which had led to the irrigation of about twenty-one million acres by Government works. By 1920 the area had risen to 28,000,000 acres, by 1929 to 31,700,000. It is not work which can be pushed forward at too great a speed, and India has already some derelict schemes due to hasty planning. The systematic way in which this work has been carried through, and the small proportion of failures, are certainly due to the good foundations laid during Lord Curzon's term of office.

Another achievement, which may have a profound influence on India's future, was the Co-operative Societies Act of 1904. The father of co-operative credit in India was Sir Frederick Nicholson, a Madras civilian who was sufficiently enthusiastic to remain in India after his service was completed in order to spread his ideas amongst the villagers. Lord Curzon recognised the possibilities in his scheme, and must be given full credit for insisting upon the experiment in the face of much official incredulity. Success came slowly, but, by 1911, 3456 societies had been started with a membership of 226,000 and a working capital of £686,000, of which the Government had only contributed £46,000.

The movement gradually spread through British India and into some of the States. It has had its set-backs, and some provinces have had too high a proportion of societies which have had to be closed for irregularities. It has not put the money-lender out of business, but it has succeeded in building up an immense organisation which, apart from its economic effects, has taught millions of *ryots* to work with their neighbours and to make a better use of money. By 1929-30 there were 104,187 societies registered, with a working capital of 90 crores (about £67,500,000). The membership was over four millions, and the societies have now undertaken a wide range of activities besides the settlement of their members' debts and lending them money for new stock. In some cases they sell produce, purchase implements, and consolidate scattered agricultural holdings, thus undoing that minute subdivision of land which is an unhappy corollary of the Hindu law of inheritance.

Lord Curzon's careful overhauling of the bureaucratic machine extended into every department. The Police Commission was one of the most effective which he appointed, and it produced an indictment of the existing system so severe that the Government showed considerable courage in publishing it.

' The police force is far from efficient; it is defective in training and reorganisation; it is inadequately supervised; it is generally regarded as corrupt and oppressive; and it has utterly failed to secure the confidence and cordial co-operation of the people'.

The Commission proposed an increase in pay, some addition to the strength, the establishment of an entirely Indian provincial service, and the creation of a Criminal Intelligence Department. Many of these recommendations were carried out, and within a few years the force was increased from 150,000 to 175,000 officers and men. This, together with improvements in pay and training, raised the cost of the service from about two millions to over three millions. It is doubtful whether the police would have survived the strain of political and communal troubles during the next twenty-five years if this reorganisation had not been undertaken.

The force has received a full measure of criticism since Lord Curzon's time, and its future is none too certain. It has still 'failed to secure the confidence and cordial co-operation of the people'. A country may be said to get the police it deserves, and much of the trouble is due to the lack of any tradition in favour of helping the forces of law and order. This weakness was apparent before political feeling had become intense, but the position has grown worse since it has become necessary to use the police to check so many nationalist activities. Lord Curzon's reforms were sound, but limited in effect. He failed to enlist any popular support, though he might have done so more easily than any of his successors.

The same kind of stimulus was given to every Government department, and was assisted by the better financial position of India after 1901. Lord Curzon succeeded wherever results could be achieved by energy and the more generous use of public money. Railways were rapidly developed, and in view of the last famine the rolling stock was increased by over thirty per cent. The care of ancient monuments was a special interest. Innumerable buildings, from the Taj Mahal downwards, were cleared of rubbish and obstructions and placed under Government protection. No subject was too small for the personal consideration of a Viceroy who applied himself with the same attention to the formation of a new province or the suitability of hymns to be sung at the Durbar. This latter function was held at Delhi on New Year's Day, 1903, and was marked by great splendour, for Lord Curzon found time for that pageantry which suited his personal predilections and his ideas, possibly exaggerated, about Oriental fondness for display.

Lord Curzon was less successful when dealing with subjects which lay outside the ordinary official sphere, or were dependent upon some measure of Indian co-operation. His educational work showed his strength and also his weakness. It began with a conference to ascertain 'the trend of authoritative opinion', but every member was a British Government official except Dr. Miller, the famous principal of the Madras Christian College. The Viceroy's opening speech, an admirable survey,[1] covered the whole field of Indian education. His strictures on the University system, and on the Government's failures in the field of primary education, were irrefutable. He wished to change the Universities from examining into teaching institutions. He desired to enlarge the scope of secondary education. By primary education he understood 'the teaching of the masses in the vernacular', and agreed that 'Government had not fulfilled its duty in this respect'. He suggested, not altogether wisely, 'that the question is really in the main one of money'. The conference 'passed without a single dissentient voice no less than a hundred and fifty resolutions, every one of which was drafted by the Viceroy himself'.[2] The whole organisation of the Service was revised, and to some extent centralised under a new Director-General of Educa-

[1] The speech is given in full in *Lord Curzon in India*, 313.
[2] Lord Ronaldshay, *The Life of Lord Curzon*, ii. 191.

tion. The problem of the Universities, however, was not tackled immediately. A Commission was appointed in 1902. It contained only one Indian, a Muslim.[1]

Primary education was a direct function of the Government, and from 1904 an aggressive campaign was started. It was supported by large grants from imperial to provincial funds, and had the full weight of the bureaucratic machine behind it. The results were disappointing. Education was now being extended from the castes and classes which wanted it to those which were indifferent. 'Schools grew, and too often disappeared, like mushrooms. Harassed subordinates prepared maps and schemes and went round begging villages to accept schools.'[2] This and subsequent efforts have had comparatively little effect upon illiteracy. In 1921 nearly 230 millions out of a population of 247 millions in British India were still unable to read or write. The example of Russia suggests that in a backward agricultural country a mass attack on illiteracy must be based on some emotional or patriotic appeal. The Curzonian scheme was limited to the efficient provision of facilities for secular education. It failed to secure the support of those who might look upon the schools as a means of political or religious regeneration, and the educational enthusiast has usually preferred to work outside the official system.

There was little contemporary criticism of the primary education policy. This came later when its weakness was apparent. The real opposition centred on those proposals which dealt with higher education, especially the findings of the Universities Commission, from which the single Hindu member had dissented strongly. By the end of the nineteenth century the Universities were almost entirely free from State interference, but their Senates contained few men of academic distinction and they had degenerated into mere examining boards exercising little control over the schools and colleges subordinate to them, most of which were 'cramming establishments' having a lamentable effect upon the character and physique of their pupils. The need for reform was urgent and undeniable, but those engaged in this educational work could hardly be blamed for having invested their time and money in a system which was originally founded by the Government, and the proposals of the Commission were of that drastic character usual when people of one race pass judgment on the institutions of another. The Commission advised a measure of official control which led a later

---

[1] A Hindu judge was subsequently added.

[2] A. Mayhew, *The Education of India*, 231.

Commission—that of 1917—to describe the Indian Universities as amongst the most completely governmental in the world. The Senates were to be reduced in size, and to contain directors of public instruction. The Vice-Chancellors were to be appointed by Government, which would also determine questions of affiliation by colleges, and would approve the appointments of lecturers and professors. The Commission proposed that minimum rates should be fixed for college fees, that second-grade colleges should not be recognised, and that law classes should be abolished. Their object was to provide a better and wider education for a smaller number of students, with something of the corporate life of a European university, and with less concentration upon preparing for the Civil Service examinations and the legal profession.

The objects of the Commission may have been laudable enough, but their proposals, and the manner in which they were brought forward, were well calculated to rouse the hostility of every educated Indian. The extension of Government control ran counter to the growing nationalist sentiment. The restriction upon the enrolment of students was naturally unpopular, and the Commission spoilt their case by suggesting that this should be done by making education more expensive rather than by intelligence tests. The disaffiliation of the second-grade colleges would have ruined many teachers, and was not accepted by the Government. The legal profession were affronted by the Commission's obvious bias against their profession:

'To do away with the law classes will in many cases increase the expense of the law students' education; but the central school will have the scholarships; and even if the net result should be to diminish the number of lawyers in India, we are not certain that this would be an unmixed evil.'

Opposition, led by Surendranath Banerjea in Bengal and Pherozeshah Mehta in Bombay, was loud and bitter. The Universities Bill, embodying most of the Commission's recommendations, was finally passed in 1904, but it was condemned by the whole of the teaching profession, by the students, and by the parents of those likely to go to colleges. University reform cannot be effective in an atmosphere of suspicion and resentment, and everyone combined to make the new Act inoperative. When the position was reviewed by the Sadler Commission in 1917, Calcutta University was still mainly an examining body. Nearly the same proportion of students was engaged in legal or literary subjects, and the candidates for matriculation had risen to over 16,000. Most of them were still living in squalid and unhealthy conditions, and 'the foundations of a sound university organisation had not yet been laid'.[1]

The Partition of Bengal shows even more clearly the danger of initiating reforms without any attempt to secure the co-operation of those most affected. The case for some alteration was very strong. When Lord Curzon came to India, Bengal was not only the senior of the three Presidencies, with its capital the capital of India, but it was also the largest of the provinces, with some seventy million inhabitants scattered over an area of which much was very inaccessible. The Mofussil, especially the eastern portion, which is intersected by innumerable rivers, had undoubtedly suffered from the size of the province and the predominance of Calcutta. Dacca was the centre of a thickly populated area, chiefly Muslim by religion, whereas Western Bengal was mostly Hindu. There is nothing sacred about the boundaries of Indian provinces, which are satrapies carved out by its rulers as suited their convenience. Proposals for altering boundaries, to make better administrative or linguistic units, have frequently been discussed, though very few changes have actually been made until recently when the prospect of a federation has led to the division of Sind from Bombay and Orissa from Bihar. Bengal was a pressing case, and a correspondence had been started upon this subject, possibly in the same casual manner as the correspondence which ultimately led to the Ilbert Bill. Owing to the unauthorised publication of a confidential minute by Lord Curzon, the public was given a valuable insight into the working of Government departments. The Viceroy's note, which incidentally absolves him from the charge of initiating the policy, was long remembered for its amusing indictment of the system of 'files'.

' Round and round, like the diurnal revolution of the earth, went the file, stately, solemn, sure, and slow; and now, in due season, it has completed its orbit, and I am invited to register the concluding stage.' [2]

The proposal, which Lord Curzon accepted, was for the formation of a new province of Eastern Bengal, with Dacca as its capital.

Effective opposition was based on the widespread desire for a trial of strength with a Government which enforced vast changes without consultation with those affected, but the attack was supported by many

---

[1] *Report of the Calcutta University Commission*, 1917-19, i. chap. iii.

[2] The publication of this minute in the *Statesman* caused great official annoyance but much unofficial joy. It was long remembered as the 'round and round' minute from the quotation given above.

whose interests were more directly affected. The Hindus of Bengal resented the division of a province in which they were predominant. Nationalist sentiment had encouraged a belief in an historical Bengali nation, Hindu in religion and racially distinct. Many rather nebulous and sometimes inconsistent ideas were in the air. The Partition 'struck both at the dignity of the Bengalee "nation" and at the nationhood of the Indian Motherland, in whose honour the old invocation to the goddess Kali, *Bande Mataram* or "Hail to the Mother", acquired a new significance and came to be used as the political war-cry of Indian Nationalism'.[1] There is no need for an opposition to be strictly logical. The Partition formed a convenient ground on which to fight the Government of India, and Lord Curzon had to meet the attacks of those offended by the Universities Act, of Calcutta lawyers who objected to the establishment of a new High Court at Dacca, and of the mass of educated Indians, who disliked the hectoring manner in which he pointed out their short-comings and disapproved of the imperialist ambitions which had led to the expensive and unjustifiable Tibetan expedition.

The Partition and the agitation against it were the beginning of an unhappy period for this part of India. The new province was a difficult charge in view of the Hindu feeling against it, the backward character of the Muslim peasantry, the traditional aptitude of its inhabitants for land and river dacoity, and the long period of official neglect. Owing to the Permanent Settlement, district administration had never developed in Bengal as in other provinces, and Eastern Bengal especially lagged behind. Throughout the six years of its separate existence the new province was handicapped by lack of money—'every branch of education, every department of administration, makes urgent demands upon the revenues of this ill-equipped province'.[2] Matters were not made easier by the resignation of the first Lieutenant-Governor, Sir Bampfylde Fuller, after a dispute with Government over the disaffiliation of certain colleges which he suspected of being too active politically.

The administration had hardly settled down to its work before the Partition was reversed in 1911, and Eastern Bengal once more brought

---

[1] Valentine Chirol, *India Old and New*, 115. (The phrase *Bande Mataram* really owes its political significance to a song from Bankim Chatterjee's famous historical novel, *Ananda Math*, dealing with Muslim oppression.)

[2] Letter from Chief Secretary of Eastern Bengal and Assam to Government of India, May 18, 1908. See *Report of Bengal District Administration Committee*, 1913-14.

under Calcutta. Almost the only legacy of these six years was a great increase in communal tension and in crime. Reconstructed Bengal—less the provinces of Bihar and Assam—was left to work out its salvation under a Governor-General. With the removal of the capital to Delhi and the rapid development of higher education in other provinces, Bengal has lost its old leadership. The War gave unwelcome prominence to the essentially pacific nature of its inhabitants. Even the nationalist movement became centred in the west, and Bengal has contributed little to its development after the War, gaining its chief notoriety by irresponsible political murders. Finally time has had its revenge. The new Bengal under any democratic system will have a small Muslim majority, though its politically conscious classes are almost entirely Hindu. Its future as an autonomous province within a federation is probably more precarious than that of any other part of India.

CHAPTER V

REPRESSION AND CONCILIATION

Political activity of Curzon's period: Lord Minto: Morley: initiation of reforms: repressive measures: character of reforms: attitude of politicians: Muslim and Hindu: Indians abroad: South African question: Gandhi's campaign.

LORD CURZON's term of office had taught educated Indians to think politically, and to see their country in relation to the rest of the world. The rise of Japan drew attention to India's backward economic condition, her comparative poverty, her doubtful future under British rule, and the lowly status of Indians everywhere. Until the end of the nineteenth century very few Indians knew anything of other countries, partly owing to the Hindu prohibition against crossing the sea. Some of the lower castes had for centuries emigrated to East Africa as traders, or to Malaya as labourers, but it was a new experience for the higher castes to learn in what poor esteem they were held abroad. This lesson was brought home during the years preceding the War by Indian experiences in South Africa and by the rapidly increasing number of students and others who travelled in Europe, and were the victims of various forms of colour prejudice. A new school of writers helped to popularise the idea that India's poverty was due to her dependence on agriculture, and that this was the direct result of British rule. The need for high protective tariffs and the discouragement of exports, the evils of the 'drain', the balance of trade—now usually described as 'favourable'—due to payment of interest charges and pensions—these were the subject of economic disquisitions of doubtful validity, but accepted without question because they fitted in with nationalist sentiments and no one troubled to dispute them. There was a wide-spread feeling that an epoch had come to an end. The political awakening was accompanied by a widening of horizons and the quickening of spirit which follows the discovery of new worlds, but it was also embittered by the most vehement dissatisfaction with India's condition and the standing of her inhabitants.

These ideas spread until they affected other classes, land-owners, shopkeepers, and finally the workers and peasants. The process has been slow but continuous. Before the War vernacular newspapers were finding their way into the villages. Nationalist feeling has varied in intensity, but since 1905 it has been sufficiently strong and aggressive —except for the first two years of the War—to keep the internal political situation as the centre of interest in Indian affairs.

Towards the end of Lord Curzon's term some changes were also taking place in the English attitude towards India. Lord Minto, who succeeded him, was nominated by a Conservative Government, but within three months of his arrival Campbell-Bannerman had taken office at the head of a strong Liberal administration, and Morley had become Secretary of State. The change of Government was partly due to a reaction against the aggressive imperialism of the nineteenth century, and a desire to cut down our responsibilities. These tendencies were apparent during the negotiations over the South African constitution, but the usual 'time-lag' operated in the case of India, and the Liberals did not take the Indian nationalist movement very seriously. They had heard little about it, except from a few men like Sir William Wedderburn and Sir Henry Cotton, with first-hand experience but little influence. The rapid development of nationalist sentiment was not appreciated by a public which still believed in the 'unchanging East', and Morley was affected least of all. He was a doctrinaire Liberal who in his old age reacted unconsciously against the ideas of his youth. He longed to exercise that despotic authority from which his views and earlier manner of life had excluded him, and he has been rightly described as 'the most autocratic and the least constitutional Secretary of State ever seen in Whitehall'. Of his Liberalism little remained except a strong belief in free trade and the rule of law, neither helpful when nearly every educated Indian was a keen protectionist and the Government of India was faced with the breakdown of the criminal law imported from England. His positivist philosophy made him intolerant of Eastern mysticism and his humanitarianism hardly extended past Suez. 'The real truth', he wrote to Lady Minto, 'is that I am an occidental, not an oriental. . . . I think I like Indian Mohammadans, but I cannot go much farther in an easterly direction.'[1] When he took office at the end of 1905, he was probably more naturally antipathetic to the nationalist movement than the new Viceroy, Lord Minto—a soldier by profession, with little regard for political labels.

Minto's experience as Governor-General of Canada had accustomed him to exercise power by suggestion, rather than by the direct methods of Lord Curzon. His stalwart common sense and belief in his own countrymen revolted from the idea that the Government would collapse because Indians were admitted to a share in it.

A political 'swing to the left' in England usually produces some corresponding political activity in India. Hopes may have been awakened by speeches made when the in-coming party was in opposition, and Indians early recognised the advantage of pressing their claims when a sympathetic Government was in power. Mr. Dadabhai Naoroji was President of the Congress in 1906, and pointed the moral drawn from his European experience.

' Agitation is the life and soul of the whole political, social, and industrial history of England. . . . Agitate, agitate over the whole length and breadth of India, peacefully of course, if we mean to get justice from John Bull. The Bengalis, I am glad, have learnt the lesson and led the march. . . .'

Political discontent was reinforced by a suspicion that England was decadent, and that even commercially she was giving way to Germany and America. She was accused of pulling India down with her, and living on the poverty of the *ryot*. Mr. Bryan, who made a tour of India during Lord Curzon's time, ministered to Indian and American self-esteem by an eloquent if one-sided indictment of England along these lines.

Such economic arguments carry great weight with the middle classes. The enthusiasm over Japan's victories was a tribute less to her military

[1] Buchan, J., *Lord Minto*, 222.

prowess than to the way in which a backward Eastern agricultural country had by its own volition become a highly organised modern industrialised State. Lord Minto found a general feeling of expectancy, a country waiting for changes long over-due; and this vague unrest was accompanied by acts of violence in various parts of India. These were to increase in seriousness from 1907 onwards, the period during which the Morley-Minto reforms were under consideration.

Both Viceroy and Secretary of State early recognised the need for some constitutional changes. Within six months of taking office Morley was writing :

' I wonder whether we could not now make a good start in the way of reform in the popular direction. . . . Why should you not now consider as practical and immediate things—the extension of the native element in your Legislative Council; ditto in local councils; full time for discussing Budget in your L.C. instead of four or five skimpy hours; right of moving amendments. (Of course officials would remain a majority.) If I read your letters correctly, you have no disposition whatever to look on such changes as these in a hostile spirit: quite the contrary.' [1]

Minto wasted no time in setting the slow wheels of Government to work, and planned to supplement the changes in the Provincial and Central Legislatures by the inclusion of an Indian in that Holy of Holies, his Executive Council. But this took time, and India was waiting for some sign. A good opportunity was missed for absence of a settled policy before taking office. When the reforms were introduced two years later their benefits had already been discounted during a period of growing racial animosity accentuated by political outrages and by the estrangement of the Moderates. Ten years later a similar deterioration occurred between 1916 and the introduction of the Montagu reforms in 1919. On each occasion India suffered from the lack of any definite objective on the part of her rulers, the delays inseparable from the British parliamentary system, and the need of propitiating a House of Lords equally hostile to changes in India and Ireland.

The unrest which marked these intermediate years found many outlets. The formation of secret societies has been mentioned in a previous chapter. These carried on political dacoities and perpetrated murders. Between 1906 and 1909 over 550 political cases came before the courts in Bengal, two British magistrates were murdered, Mr. Allen at Dacca and Mr. Jackson at Nasik, and an attempt was made upon the life of Sir Andrew Fraser, the Lieutenant-Governor of Bengal. The

[1] Viscount Morley, *Recollections*, ii. 174.

bomb outrage at Muzaffarpur, followed by the Maniktollah conspiracy trial, caused great excitement. For his comments on this case Tilak was again arrested and sentenced to six years' transportation.

Apart from the Partition of Bengal, there was no specific grievance behind the movement in Eastern India and the Deccan. It was frankly anti-British, nationalist, and middle class. Its importance was due to the passive sympathy which it aroused amongst other classes of Indians, and to the reactions of the British in India and England to political murders.

In the Punjab the disturbances were less clearly political. They had their origin in definite agrarian grievances due to the Government's policy in the canal colonies, which more than savoured of bad faith, while land assessment had been too drastically revised in other parts. The agitation was increased by wild suspicions connected with the spread of plague in Northern India. Riots occurred in Lahore, Rawalpindi, and other towns. These may have been partly due to the activities of politicians, like Lajpat Rai and Ajit Singh, but it was essentially a popular movement. It constituted a serious danger, for it affected the classes from whom the bulk of the army is recruited; but it died down very rapidly after Lord Minto disallowed the unpopular Colonisation Act which threatened the rights of settlers in the Chenab canal area. To Lord Minto the Act seemed a clear breach of faith, but it required some courage to meet the official argument that (as he wrote to Mr. Morley) 'to refuse to sanction what we know to be wrong is a surrender to agitation, and an indication of weakness'.[1]

The anarchic crime of Bengal received far greater publicity, for an isolated murder has always had more effect upon opinion in England than riots involving a heavy loss of life. Lord Minto kept his head. He insisted upon continuing the preparation of his reform scheme, and using the ordinary processes of law, in spite of pressure from Conservatives at home and from the Calcutta European population.

' The worst of it is that the meaning of outrages is so enormously exaggerated at home. I wish the British public would understand that the troubles we have to deal with do not mean the possibility of rebellion.' [2]

The unrest placed a very heavy strain on the ordinary legal system, though the existing legislation dealing with political crime was reinforced by new Acts—the Seditious Meetings Act, the Explosives Act,

[1] Buchan, J., *Lord Minto*, 257.

[2] *Op. cit.* 301. Letter form Lord Minto to Secretary of State.

and the new Press Act of 1910. The same difficulties had to be met in India as in any country where an alien or an undemocratic Government is confronted with a popular movement. Unless all opposition is banned, the Government has to decide what forms of agitation are criminal and what are permissible. The Government of India has been driven to use unhappy and vague formulae, such as 'exciting hatred and contempt' of the Government, or 'taking part in a conspiracy to deprive the King-Emperor of his sovereignty in British India'.[1] The absence of any logical definition of sedition has hampered it for the last thirty years. A more immediate trouble was the difficulty of finding witnesses to give evidence about political crimes. As in so many other countries, their natural unwillingness was enhanced by a few cases in which informers were subsequently murdered.

When this feeling is general over a wide area, as in Bengal, the ordinary machinery of law breaks down. The Government, unless prepared to abdicate, is driven to undesirable extra-legal alternatives. It may declare martial law, which Kitchener advocated in 1909, or it may set up courts which can dispense with the ordinary rules of evidence, as has been done since the War. It may be driven to use *agents-provocateurs* and spies, or some form of *lettres de cachet* which will enable opposition leaders to be arrested and detained without trial. The mere enumeration suggests that few countries, even if democratic, have been able to dispense with such methods entirely during the last century.

Lord Minto preferred to use that of deportation without trial, under a Regulation of 1818, a device well understood in India and habitually employed by certain princes. In British India three of the original deportees under the Regulation had been Englishmen who had made themselves obnoxious to the Government.[2] Similar powers were presumably invoked to arrest and detain political prisoners, such as Yakub Khan, the ex-Amir of Afghanistan, and Sir Duleep Singh, who was arrested at Aden in 1886 after issuing a Proclamation claiming the

---

[1] The latter was the offence for which the accused in the Meerut conspiracy case were sentenced to heavy terms of imprisonment. An Indian judge has stated that even Indian Moderates could be brought within this formula. It must certainly include all workers for the Congress Party since the Lahore resolution in favour of complete independence.

[2] J. S. Buckingham, editor of the *Calcutta Journal*, was deported in 1823, and C. J. Fair, of the *Bombay Gazette*, in 1824. A little later another editor of the *Calcutta Journal* was deported from India. See S. M. Mitra, *Indian Studies*, chapter on 'Deportation.' For Buckingham, a very remarkable character, see above, p. 292, and a recent biography, R. E. Turner's *James Silk Buckingham*.

Punjab. Lord Minto arrested and deported Lajpat Rai and Ajit Singh from the Punjab, and detained a few Bengali political leaders. The action was successful, and probably prevented further disorders and loss of life, but was fiercely attacked in England by politicians entirely sceptical about any real constitutional advance in India. Lord Morley defended these proceedings with as good a grace as he could: 'In truth, if I did not happen to have a spotless character as an anti-coercionist in Ireland, our friends would certainly have kicked a good deal'.[1] Criticism came not only from Liberals and from the Irish members, but also from a group of Conservatives, led by a future Indian Secretary of State, Mr. F. E. Smith. It is an old and healthy English tradition that the opposition should stand upon the letter of the law.

Most of the changes—usually known as the 'Morley-Minto reforms' —were embodied in a new Indian Councils Act which superseded Lord Cross's Act of 1892. This measure, which was passed in February, 1909, referred only to the Provincial and Central Legislatures. It made no theoretical change on the executive side, though the legislatures' right of criticism was increased. Lord Minto was, however, able to introduce an Indian barrister into his Executive Council. Sir Satyendra (afterwards Lord) Sinha became Law Member in 1909. This was considered to be a great innovation. It was strongly opposed by the other members of the Council, and most officials objected to an Indian being admitted to the innermost counsels of the Empire, a view which was supported by English Liberals like Lord Ripon and Lord Elgin. Of less importance was the nomination of two Indians to the Council of India in London—Mr. Krishna Govinda Gupta and Mr. Saiyid Husain Bilgrami being its first Indian members.

The changes in the legislatures were cautious and tentative. The King's Proclamation of November 28, 1908, had foreshadowed reforms in which the 'principle of representative institutions' would be 'prudently extended', but Morley had no intention of introducing any system of democratic control into India. He even refused the suggestion of the Government of India which, under Lord Minto's influence, had declared its willingness to do without an official majority in the Imperial Legislature. From personal convictions as well as for parliamentary convenience he intended to keep the legislatures as advisory and not as independent law-making bodies. 'If I were attempting', he said in the House of Lords, 'to set up a parliamentary system in India, or if it could be said that this chapter of reforms led directly or neces-

[1] Letter to Lord Minto, May 16, 1907. Morley, *Recollections*, ii. 217.

sarily up to the establishment of a parliamentary system in India, I, for one, would have nothing at all to do with it'.[1] An indirect process of election was introduced, members being returned to the Provincial and Imperial Legislatures by municipalities and other bodies. In the Provincial Councils such members formed a majority, which gave them considerable negative powers, but they could not displace the Executive Councils. These usually contained one or two Indians, but they were also liable to be overruled by the Governor. In the Central Government elected Indians formed a minority of the Imperial Assembly; and there was one Indian in the Executive Council. The Government had thus organised for itself a perpetual opposition, with no function except to criticise, no chance of ever taking office, and no real responsibility to the rather vague electorate which they were supposed to represent.

The Councils and Assembly had some educational value in a country where little was known of the machinery of democratic government but when their work was reviewed ten years later it would have been difficult to avoid the conclusion that

' Parliamentary usages have been initiated and adopted in the Councils to the point where they cause the maximum of friction, but short of that at which by having a real sanction behind them they begin to do good'.[2]

Any hope of the Provincial Councils developing into autonomous units was defeated by the excessive centralisation which Morley encouraged, and the Decentralisation Commission of 1909 did little to modify.

The more active politicians soon tired of the Councils. The Moderates, who still dominated the Congress, returned to their demand for a larger share in the administrative work, and for more Indians in the highest Government posts, Lord Crewe, who had followed Lord Morley at the India Office, appointed a Public Services Commission in 1912, which spent two years taking evidence, mostly in public, and preparing a report which was not published until 1917. The Commission, which included Mr. Gokhale, Mr. Ramsay MacDonald, and Lord Ronaldshay, served to advertise the lack of any theory behind the apportionment of administrative posts between Indian and English, and gave the impression that the displacement of the latter was simply a matter of political pressure. The Muslims also began to take a new interest in politics after Lord Minto had been succeeded in 1910 by

[1] Morley, *Indian Speeches*, 91.
[2] *Report on Indian Constitutional Reforms*, 1918, 69.

Lord Hardinge. For many years their activities had been dominated by Sir Saiyid Ahmad Khan, the founder of Aligarh College, a man reformist in religious matters, with a keen appreciation of the British connection. He died in 1898, but the Muslim League, founded seven years later, was still animated by his spirit, and prepared to resist the Hindu domination which they believed would follow from the political concessions then under consideration. It was in this spirit that a deputation under the Aga Khan pressed upon Lord Minto the Muslim view about the Partition of Bengal. Other groups insisted upon the principle of separate community representation being included in the Indian Councils Act of 1909. An unfortunate precedent was thus established, and it has since been found impossible to get rid of the system of communal electorates.

The Muhammadans soon joined the Hindus in opposition. Even the older generation, Muslims first and Indians second, were forced to recognise that criticism was often more effective than tacit support of the Government. Certain events during Lord Hardinge's term of office confirmed this attitude. The revision of the Partition of Bengal in 1911 was inevitably hailed as a Hindu victory. Although Bihar was then separated from Bengal, Eastern Bengal was again merged into what was held to be a Hindu province. It was not till some years later that the importance of the slight numerical Muslim majority was fully appreciated. It was the first time that the Government had reversed an important decision as the result of an Indian agitation, and it emphasised 'the connection between bombs and boons'.

British foreign policy during these pre-War years added to Muslim discontent. One Muhammadan country after another was being absorbed by European Powers; and the British were either privy to the arrangement, as in Morocco and Persia, or made no protest, as in Tripoli. The Balkan Wars of 1912-13 were considered part of a general attack upon Islam. Meanwhile the younger Indian Muhammadans were increasingly affected by the racial nationalism of the educated classes, and their leaders were getting into touch with their co-religionists in other countries. Money was collected for a Turkish Red Crescent fund, while a common enmity brought a few Muslims into the extremist movement, which had lost most of its old Hindu bias.

Another sign of awakening national pride was the interest taken in the condition of Indians overseas. Following the abolition of slavery in 1834, there had been a demand for indentured labour in certain parts of the Empire, while Ceylon and Malaya absorbed large numbers of

Indian immigrants recruited by Indian agents for tea and rubber plantations. By 1901 there were some two and a half million Indians more or less settled abroad, about half of them in Ceylon and Malaya, and the rest scattered over such countries as Mauritius, British Guiana, Fiji, Natal, and East Africa. The bulk of these were manual workers, but there was a small sprinkling of traders, mostly Muslims and members of the *bania* caste. Only about 100,000 were outside the Empire, and this number has not increased. No country welcomed Indians except as semi-servile workers, and the indenture system was only practical inside the Empire. The tendency to treat Indians as a coolie race was increased by the Hindu restrictions against any but the lowest castes going overseas. Even Mr. Gandhi, who is of the *bania* caste, had great difficulty in obtaining the permission of his caste-fellows to leave India, first for England and later for South Africa.

At the beginning of the twentieth century the unhappy conditions of many Indians abroad had been forced upon the attention of the Government, and had become a favourite topic for nationalist critics. The reform of emigration to the Crown colonies was comparatively simple, for the officials on both sides were ultimately under the control of Whitehall. Officers were appointed who collaborated to check unscrupulous recruiting agents, and to arrange working conditions. They were effective in improving the conditions of those already settled in Fiji and other colonies. The indenture system was first modified, and then, being open to strong theoretical objections, was abolished in 1917. The emigration of indentured labour to Natal had already been stopped in 1910. The effect of these reforms will be considered later.

A more difficult problem arose with regard to the self-governing Dominions, and later in Kenya. The number of Indians involved was smaller, but their treatment raised in its acutest form the question of Indian status and the meaning of Empire citizenship. Nationalist politicians naturally seized the opportunity of pressing their claim to equal standing with the 'white' population. They had a strong theoretical case, especially in South Africa. Indians had been going to Natal as indentured labourers since 1860. They had been invited by the Natal Government to meet an acute labour shortage, and after their five year period of service was over some remained in the country and others moved into the Transvaal. They gradually became unpopular. Neither Dutch nor British wanted any further racial complications in South Africa, which already had too many. Indians were accused of lowering the standard of living by undercutting wages and by indulging in small-scale money-lending. In 1895 the Natal Government imposed a tax of £3 on all those who remained in the country and would not reindenture. In the Transvaal their treatment was such that the British Government protested, and this dispute was one of the minor causes of the Boer War.

Mr. Gandhi, who visited South Africa as a lawyer in 1893, led an agitation against the poll tax, and was involved in difficulties with the Transvaal authorities. Returning to South Africa shortly before the Boer War he became the leader of the Indian community, and advised those in Natal to take an active part on the British side. He believed that they would be better treated if South Africa became an Imperial Dominion. He wished to meet the charge that the Indian settler was a parasite, who 'would not render the slightest aid if the country was invaded or if homes were raided'.[1] He organised an Indian Ambulance Corps, which took part in the relief of Ladysmith, and after the war he settled in Johannesburg. A period of disillusionment followed, which had a marked effect on his subsequent career. South Africa under the British flag was no kinder to the Indian settler than the old Boer Government. Lord Milner, as Governor of the Transvaal, even proposed legislation which would have worsened their position. Though this was vetoed by the Secretary of State, the further entrance of Indians into the Transvaal was forbidden in 1907.[2] The British Government, anxious to conciliate Dutch opinion with a view to passing the Union Act of 1909, found that 'Home Rule' meant relinquishing the power to protect minorities, a dilemma which has arisen in other parts of the Empire. A complicated triangular dispute has continued until the present day. The Indian Government protests and sends delegations to South Africa, the British Government attempts to mediate, but the Union Government is entirely independent, and even when it agrees to some compromise Indians have no effective safeguard against administrative discrimination.

Mr. Gandhi organised a passive resistance movement, and the Indian Government took the only step in its power by stopping the further

---

[1] C. F. Andrews, Mahatma Gandhi, *His Own Story*, 142.

[2] The Government's action was indefensible. 'It is, indeed, impossible to resist the conclusion that either the protests made before the (Boer) war with the approval and aid of the High Commissioner, Lord Milner, were unjustified, or that the policy of leaving these wrongs unredressed after the war was unjustifiable.'—A. B. Keith, *Imperial Unity and the Dominions*, 203. The whole chapter on 'Coloured Immigration' is a valuable summary of events up to 1915. The Indian case in this dispute was admirably put by Mr. Gokhale in his speech to the National Congress (*Bankipur Congress Report*, 1912).

emigration of indentured labour. Mr. Gokhale went to South Africa to negotiate on behalf of the Government, and the Viceroy, in November, 1913, voiced the unanimous opinion of Indians in expressing 'the sympathy of India, deep and burning, and not only of India, but of all lovers of India like myself, for their compatriots in South Africa in their resistance to invidious and unjust laws'. These protests resulted in the appointment of a Commission of Enquiry and an Indian Relief Act, but further difficulties have arisen since the Great War.

Similar disputes on a smaller scale occurred with regard to emigration to Australia and to Canada, where a few Sikhs had settled on the western coastal belt. In the latter case the position was complicated by the activities of a few Indian revolutionaries who had settled in the United States, and were responsible for the murder of anti-revolutionaries and of Mr. Hopkins, then working on behalf of the Indian and Dominion Governments. The dispute culminated in the despatch of the *Komagatu Maru*, a Japanese boat requisitioned to make a direct journey from India to Vancouver with the object of defeating the immigration restrictions. The Sikhs on board were not allowed to land; returning after the commencement of the European War, they formed the nucleus of a revolutionary movement in the Punjab.

CHAPTER VI

ECONOMICS OF THE PRE-WAR PERIOD

Condition of the peasant: pressure on land: India's food supply: land revenue and other charges on the land: improved position of Government: the opium question: other financial changes: financial policy before the War.

THE ten years which preceded the War were comparatively prosperous. The lean period between 1896 and 1901 was followed by normal harvests, save in 1907-8, when the rainfall was so deficient as to necessitate local relief works. The peasant was being steadily brought into the Western economic system, a process which began in the 'sixties but had been hindered by famine and currency troubles. The twelve years from 1902 until the War were free from such disturbing influences, and make a convenient stage at which to examine the strength and weakness of India's economic position.

The rupee remained steady, the collection of land revenue was made more elastic and some of its inequalities were removed, the railway system was rapidly extended, the population, though partly checked by plague, increased at the rate of $\frac{3}{4}$ per cent. yearly, and nearly all cultivable land was occupied. The first point to notice is that the country remained predominantly agricultural, in spite of what might be considered rapid industrial development. Though the number of textile workers rose from 270,000 to 470,000 between 1900 and 1914, and the smaller industries increased even more quickly—so that India was soon to become one of the eight largest manufacturing countries in the world—no industrialisation could have absorbed any appreciable part of the eighteen million growth in population between 1901 and 1911. Ninetenths of these were born in the villages, and nearly all remained there.

As the usual village industries were contracting rather than expanding, the burden of this new population fell upon the land. The *ryot's* additional children remained to work the paternal acres. Others were forced to join the class of landless farm labourers. In some areas weavers and craftsmen took up small holdings.

The rise in population was partly met by cultivating a larger area. British India figures for 1901-2 and 1913-14 show that land cropped and fallow increased from about 242 million to 272 million acres. The irrigated portion had risen from 32 to 46 millions. There were signs that the limits of dry land farming were being reached—and much of the new land was of poor quality, the 'starvation acres' brought in by working further up the barren hills.[1]

In the older parts of the peninsula, like the Deccan, pressure on land had already become severe. Dr. Mann's study of a village near Poona was made in the early days of the War; his conclusions hold good for much of India:

' It is evident that in the last sixty or seventy years the character of the land holdings has altogether changed. In the pre-British days, and in the early days of British rule, the holdings were usually of a fair size, most frequently more than nine or ten acres, while individual holdings of less than two acres were hardly known. Now the number of holdings is more than doubled, and eighty-

[1] There is still much land officially described as 'cultivable' which is not occupied, but it is generally agreed that most of it is not worth ploughing. After the War many provinces found it difficult to find any vacant tillable land for returned soldiers.

one per cent. of these holdings are under ten acres in size, while no less than sixty per cent. are less than five acres.' [1]

Even in the Punjab, where conditions are relieved by irrigation, only one *ryot* in seven has the fifteen acres which are considered to be a suitable economic unit. The general position is made worse by the small migration between provinces. The density of population increases all over India, with little regard to the possibilities of making canals, or of opening up the few remaining areas of uncultivated fertile land. On the cultivated area live some 167 million peasants and their families, about 41 million landless farm servants, and at least 9 million landlords, agents, etc. In 1911 this huge population of 217 millions subsisted on the produce of 260 million acres, of which only 215 were cropped, and the remainder left fallow in rotation. Probably no land of such mediocre average quality is expected to do so much, and the position has grown steadily worse since that date. Canals allow closer settlement on the land, but their possibilities are limited, and in the race between irrigation and procreation the latter seems bound to win.

The increasing population was responsible for other changes in India's economic relations with the world. The proportion of different crops sown remained about the same, nine-tenths of the land being used for growing cereals and pulses. The *ryot* still aimed at supplying his family first, and then selling his surplus in order to meet the demands of the money-lender, of the landlord in the *zemindari* and the Government in the *ryotwari* districts. Many village servants continued to be paid in kind, and the caste system prevented most of the landless poor from selling their labour freely. The village had only gone part of the way, and that unwillingly, in establishing the cash nexus and freedom of contract. Perhaps a quarter of all food-stuffs were sold, while a tenth of the land was given up to growing inedible 'cash crops'—such as cotton, jute, and oil-seeds, nearly all of which would be sold.

Taking India, without Burma, as a unit, the period suggests that if nine-tenths of the cultivable area is under food crops, this about satisfies the very meagre requirements of some three hundred millions. Burma has a permanent rice surplus, nearly all of which is sold to Asiatic countries.[2] Apart from this, very little food was exported from the peninsula, except some wheat from the Punjab, the average for the pre-War decade being less than a million tons yearly, the product of

[1] H. H. Mann, *Land and Labour in a Deccan Village*, 46.

[2] For the five years previous to the War, the total export of rice averaged 2,398,000 tons. Of this 1,814,000 was from Burma; but Burma also sends some rice to Southern India.

about one per cent. of the total area. India was rapidly approaching the stage she has now reached, when she is just self-sufficing, sometimes importing and sometimes exporting small quantities of wheat. Of the tenth part of the land which is under 'cash crops', about half the produce is sold for export and half for local use—the mills of Calcutta and else-where taking a slightly larger share of the raw jute and cotton. Thus, only about five or six per cent. of the total cultivable area was being used for growing crops which would be exported, and the tendency was for this proportion to be reduced. The *ryot*, therefore, was ulti-mately dependent on the Indian market, and it was becoming most unlikely that he would ever share in an increase of prices due to world conditions, like the cotton boom of the 'sixties. For cash he could look only to the local corn-dealer, who usually combined this occupation with money-lending, and, in spite of the growth of the co-operative movement, the supremacy of the *bania* remained unchallenged.

By 1910 land revenue was practically stabilised, bringing in about £20,000,000 yearly, at assessments varying from about two per cent. of the gross output in Madras to eight per cent. in the Punjab, where irrigation charges had to be met.[1] The Government demand was now only a small proportion of the amount drawn in cash from the agri-culturist by various unproductive agencies. Rent and interest on debt are difficult to assess, for the landlord does not pay income-tax and the *bania* habitually evades it, but the total agricultural debt was rising steadily towards the figure of £400,000,000, a conservative estimate made in 1921.[2] This debt bore a high rate of interest, and since 1910 the total charges can never have been less than three times the land revenue. Some of this money-lending was done by agricultural castes, a tendency which was encouraged by various Acts passed to protect the *ryot* by preventing alienation of land to non-agriculturists. The pre-War period saw the development of a class of peasant who would hire labour and act as a middleman. In the Deccan

' it became a matter of general comment that whole classes of cultivators, who formerly used to do their own field work, have now ceased to take any active part in field operations. This is said of the Patidars in Gujerat, of the better-class Lingaiyets in the Southern Mahratta country, of the Havigs of Canara, and of the more substantial proprietors everywhere'.[3]

[1] See Pillai, *Economic Conditions in India*, 27. The stabilisation is general and only approximate. Districts in the *ryotwari* areas are liable to periodical reassessment.

[2] See M. L. Darling, *The Punjab Peasant*, and the reports of the Provincial and Central Banking Committees, 1931.

[3] G. Keatinge, *Agricultural Progress in Western India*, 145.

There was a corresponding increase in the number of landless farm labourers, whose numbers rose from 33 to 42 millions between 1901 and 1911. Although villages were still hardly on the cash nexus, the capitalist system was coming into full operation, draining away the surplus produce by a process as ruthless as that of the eighteenth century Mogul official and more efficient. The *ryot's* position was worse than that of peasants in most parts of the world, for hardly five per cent. of his debt had been incurred for productive purposes, and Indian landlords provide nothing in return for their rent. In most areas he had little prospect of taking up more land, the ambition which keeps the English small-holder alive and keen. Climate and religious inhibitions prevent keeping stock on European lines. Dry farming and rice growing are only seasonal occupations, giving employment for some 60 to 120 days a year, and the increasing pressure on the soil intensified all the evils of under-employment. We must trace to this time of peace and comparative national prosperity a marked pessimism about the future of the peasant, mitigated by the feeling that certain cheap industrial products were finding their way into the countryside for the first time. The politicians, free from any responsibility, could still pin their faith on rapid industrialisation and irrigation. The officials, with possibly a sounder appreciation of the position, had no solution to offer.

The stabilisation of the land revenue, though of little ultimate benefit to the cultivator, was a symptom of the healthier financial position which the Government enjoyed after the famine period of 1896 to 1901. The development of trade and of the railways made it possible to impose direct and indirect taxation over a far wider field, to reduce certain undesirable imposts, and to increase some kinds of beneficial expenditure. Land revenue, which had made up two-fifths of the total income till 1900, gradually sank to less than a quarter.[1] The unpopular salt tax was

[1] The last pre-War budget illustrates these changes :

Gross Revenue for 1913-14 (in thousands of pounds sterling)

Land Revenue	-	-	-	-	-	£21,391
Opium	-	-	-	-	-	1,624
Salt	-	-	-	-	-	3,445
Excise	-	-	-	-	-	8,894
Customs	-	-	-	-	-	7,558
Railways (less expenses)	-	-	-	17,625
Income Tax	-	-	-	-	-	1,893
Irrigation	-	-	-	-	-	4,713
Stamps	-	-	-	-	-	5,318
Miscellaneous	-	-	-	-	-	12,846
			Total	-	-	£85,307

halved between 1903 and 1907, and remained at the lower figure until after the War.[1] The revenue from opium was also becoming relatively unimportant. Sales abroad had been cut down since the first China convention of 1886, and the policy of reducing exports by agreement was extended to other countries which bought opium from India. The China trade, which was much the most important, was the subject of a new convention in 1907. The Chinese Government agreed to suppress cultivation within ten years, and the British Government to reduce exports so that they would finally cease in 1917.[2]

The sale of opium inside India—a source of revenue included under the head of Excise—continued to be a subject of controversy. Considerable pressure was brought upon the Government to prohibit its use, the same arguments being employed as for the suppression of alcohol in America—in fact, they sometimes emanated from the same source. The position was reviewed by a Royal Commission in 1893. It decided that opium-eating, which had been customary amongst certain classes for many generations, was 'for the most part without injurious consequences', and that opium was 'in universal use throughout India as the commonest and the most treasured of the household remedies accessible to the people'. The Government continued its policy of controlling production and distribution, aiming at 'the maximum of revenue and the minimum of consumption'. Following the Commission's recommendations, efforts were made to prevent opium-smoking, a comparatively recent innovation which was never common except in parts of Burma. The other abuse of opium, the giving of the drug to children, did not seem to justify embarking on a difficult and possibly unsuccessful experiment in prohibition. Forty years ago there was less anxiety to interfere with other people's private habits, and experience in America suggests the probable fate of such an heroic measure for which there was no support except amongst castes and classes which never use opium. India is cheaply but inadequately policed compared with Western countries. The illicit preparation of opium for eating is far easier than for smoking, and much simpler than making alcoholic drinks. Finally, some of the best poppy-growing land is in the States, and, even if the princes could have been cajoled or forced into a drastic system of prohibition in which they did not believe, the prevention of smuggling would have

---

[1] The reduction was from Rs. 2½ to Rs. 1 per maund of 82 lb. Annual consumption per head averages from 10 lb. in the Punjab to 18 lb. in Madras.

[2] Exports ceased at the beginning of the War. China has since developed a large illicit production, amounting to three-quarters of the world supply.

been almost impossible. The Government of India, with a wiser appreciation of the extra sweetness of stolen fruits, decided on a policy of steady discouragement. Since the Montagu Reforms excise has been transferred to the control of Indian Ministers, but by this time both production and consumption were declining rapidly. Between 1906 and 1922 the area under cultivation was reduced from 614,000 acres to 141,000 in British India, and from 146,000 to 64,000 in the States. Indian consumption decreased from 12,530 maunds in 1910-11 to 7406 in 1923-4. By 1922 the total production for export and home consumption was under 900 tons, which was about a seventeenth of the amount estimated by the International Anti-opium Association of Peking as the annual 'illicit' production in China.[1]

There were few important changes in financial policy before the War. The Government was still dominated by the Victorian tradition that its chief function was to keep the peace internally and externally, and that taxation was an evil. A lack of financial enterprise is a characteristic weakness in an alien government, and this natural cautiousness was enhanced by the type of criticism to which the Government was now exposed. Articulate opposition came from the lightly taxed professional and business classes, and from men with no serious prospect of having to form an alternative administration. They naturally took the popular line of inveighing against all taxation as tribute paid to the foreigner. The excise and salt duties lent themselves to an easy appeal to sentiment. In regard to expenditure they concentrated upon the large proportion taken for military purposes, and the small amounts assigned to the 'nation-building' services, such as education and sanitation. The middle-class bias of the opposition and of the Government left untouched large sources of revenue which should have been drawn upon and distributed. Agricultural debt and agricultural rent represented a capital value of several hundred million pounds, and an income which must have exceeded sixty million a year, but neither capital nor interest paid any real contribution to the Exchequer. No death duties were imposed, the Hindu family system proving an insuperable difficulty. On the basis of an obsolete theory agricultural rents remained immune from income tax even in areas under a permanent settlement, and the figures given above for the year 1913-14 show the extent to which the agricultural money-lender evades his share. The total income tax receipts were less

---

[1] The reduction has continued until the area under cultivation in British India was 36,537 acres in 1931-32. Bengal and other Provinces have passed special legislation against opium-smoking.

2 P

than two million pounds, of which a large proportion came from salaries and industrial enterprises. This basic weakness continues until the present time, though it has been partially obscured since the War by the rapid rise in custom receipts.

The annual budgetary 'turn-over' remained almost ludicrously small. Even when swelled by the inclusion of railway receipts, the total income did not reach eight shillings per head of the population. Revenue and expenditure were both disproportionate for a modern government.[1] The main items stood out like the bones of an ill-nourished horse. The thinness, if the metaphor may be pursued, was not a sign of any constitutional weakness. The financial position of the Government was from one standpoint very healthy. There was hardly any unproductive national debt. At the beginning of the War the Finance Minister could point to the result of many years of extreme caution in regard to loan expenditure.

'Of a total debt equivalent to £274,000,000 outstanding at the end of March, 1914, only about £13,000,000 represented ordinary or unproductive debt. Our total annual interest charges amounted to some £9,250,000. Railways and irrigation works in the same year yielded us a return of £15,250,000.'[2]

The old Liberal traditions still survived: the dislike of borrowing except for an immediately remunerative purpose, the inclination towards free trade and low taxes, the belief that any profitable occupation should be in private hands.

Unfortunately criticism, inside and outside India, has concentrated upon two items of expenditure, the army and the salaries for European officials and army officers. Lord Kitchener's reorganisation raised the army estimates from £20,415,787 in 1907 to £21,809,603 in 1914. This sum maintained a non-conscript army of about 220,000 effectives. The Mesopotamian campaign showed that it was ill-equipped by European

---

[1] The gross expenditure for the year 1913-14 is given below (in thousands of pounds sterling):

Interest and Direct Demands - -	£10,790
Military Services - - - -	21,265
Civil Departments - - - -	23,337
Famine Insurance - - - -	1,000
Irrigation and Public Works - -	10,542
Railways (Charges and Interest) - -	12,838
Miscellaneous - - - -	3,407
	£83,179

[2] Financial Statement and Budget, 1915-16.

standards, but the British connection and the British navy made it adequate for external defence, and it had been proved to be sufficient, though with no large margin to spare, for dealing with the frontier tribes and any internal troubles. For sixty years after the Mutiny India had never been invaded, no semi-independent Prince had ventured to disturb the peace, there had been no local or communal rising even on the scale of the Moplah rebellion of 1921. In 1913 Great Britain, with a seventh of the population, was spending over £72,000,000, the United States, with a third of the population and no serious frontier question, was spending £61,000,000, and nearly every European country had some form of conscription. High salaries and a tendency to spend too much money on headquarter and gubernatorial buildings provided sounder grounds for criticism, but the total expenditure which might have been saved in this way was not large, certainly not more than £2,000,000 yearly, an amount which would have made little appreciable difference to the budget.[1] The real weakness of the Government's financial policy was the failure to tap all the taxable resources of the country, an excessive caution especially in regard to social expenditure, and an unwillingness to use India's strong loan position to borrow money for development purposes which were not directly and immediately productive.

For many years the Government issued a yearly statement 'exhibiting the Moral and Material Progress and Condition of India'. Since the War a more modest and less question-begging title has been given to the compilation. Such caution is wise. The extent of the population, of trade and land under cultivation, the activities and finances of the Government, all these are easily ascertainable, but very little is known about the relative condition of the masses in 1860, and after half a century of Crown government. It used to be fashionable, especially in the decade before the War, to work out exact figures about the 'income per head' in British India. As these were based on statistics, of which some were definite but others highly conjectural, it was not surprising that the official estimates suggest a steady improvement, while those from the Government's critics showed a marked decline. Such controversies, in a country where most people are engaged in subsistence farming, are almost meaningless. We can estimate the increasing pressure on the land, we know there has been no radical change in

[1] Only a small proportion of senior officials in each of the services receive large salaries, and the higher grades scarcely numbered more than four thousand. An economy as suggested above would have made the services seem extremely lowly paid compared with business men, European or American, working in the East.

methods of cultivation or husbandry, but, apart from the land revenue, there is considerable doubt about the charges which the *ryot* has to meet and about the real value of his surplus. In some districts the villager seems to enjoy a few amenities which he did not have twenty years ago, but it is possible that he is not as well fed, and that there is more destitution.

In most countries the industrial worker provides a standard for the general condition of the people. The extent of the rural exodus shows the comparative attractiveness of factory life, and in the town exact figures for wages and cost of living are easier to obtain. In India industrial development is so abnormal that the half million urban workers are useless as a social barometer. Indian mills installed machinery requiring little skill, and no attempt was made to recruit from the better castes or the hereditary craftsmen. The factories collected the surplus population of the villages, unsettled tribesmen, superfluous agriculturists, Hindu widows, and the like. These, herded into single-room tenements, endured the disadvantages of barrack life without its cleanliness and discipline. The better-class men leave their wives in the villages, and return as frequently as they can afford, but by 1914 there was a large factory population, divorced from the land, unorganised, underfed, and riddled with disease. A few employers have endeavoured to collect a stable mill population, but the general mass of casual workers can give no lead to the countryman, and their living conditions, which have improved but little in the last twenty years, provide no standard for the manual worker in the village. They are merely an urgent problem for the future.[1]

---

[1] The war 'boom', in which the workers had little share, was followed by a slump which hit them severely. Factory legislation has been tightened up since the war, partly as the result of a commission of enquiry, but there has been no real mitigation of the social and housing evils, or of the prevalence of disease.

BOOK VIII

GREAT WAR AND POST-WAR

' We are trying within the Empire to foster the creation of a united India, sufficiently at one within herself in respect of those fundamentals on which every nation-State must rest, that we may devolve upon her people the power for the control of their own affairs, and the ordering of their own political life. And if the issue of what we seek to do is to reflect our aim truly and endure, this unity, at once the condition and criterion of success, must evoke not only the respect but the loyalty of an India, content and proud to realise its full destiny through imperial partnership.'—LORD IRWIN, Lecture at Toronto University, 1932.

CHRONOLOGICAL TABLE

Viceroy.

LORD HARDINGE.	1914. Outbreak of War.
	1915. Defence of India Act.
LORD CHELMSFORD.	1916. Home Rule League founded.
	Lucknow Pact.
	1917. Mesopotamian Commission Report.
	Mr. E. S. Montagu Secretary of State.
	Mr. Montagu's Visit to India.
	1918. Montagu-Chelmsford Report.
	Rowlatt Committee Report.
	1919. Rowlatt Acts passed.
	Murder of Habib-ullah.
	Punjab Disturbances.
	Third Afghan War (May).
	Death of Tilak.
	Expedition against Mahsuds.
	Royal Proclamation (December).
	1920. Hunter Commission Report.
	Elections to new Legislatures.
	Esher Committee Report.
	1921. Duke of Connaught Inaugurates Legislatures.
LORD READING.	1921. Moplah Rebellion.
	Prince of Wales' Visit.
	1922. Chauri-Chaura Outrage.
	Bardoli Resolutions.
	Mr. Gandhi's Arrest and Trial.
	Guru ka Bagh incident.
	1923. Certification of Salt Tax.
	1924. Bengal Ordinance.
	Swarajist Party enters Legislatures.
	1925. Reforms Enquiry Committee Report (Muddiman).
	Death of Mr. C. R. Das.
	1926. Royal Commission on Agriculture.
LORD IRWIN.	1926. Hindu-Muslim Riots at Calcutta.
	1927. Rupee Stabilisation (Currency) Bill passed.
	Appointment of Statutory Commission.
	1928. Deposition of Amanullah.
	All Parties Conference.
	Introduction of Mr. Haji's Bill.
	1929. Mr. Wedgwood Benn Secretary of State.
	Lord Irwin's Announcement of October 31.
	Lahore Congress.
	1930. Civil Disobedience Movement.
	Report of Statutory Commission.
	Rebellion in Burma.
	Round Table Conference (First Session).
	1931. Irwin-Gandhi Pact.
LORD WILLINGDON.	1931. Round Table Conference (Second Session).
	1932. Suppression of Congress.
	Round Table Conference (Third Session).
	1933. Publication of White Paper.
	Joint Select Committee.

CHAPTER I

THE WAR AND ITS EFFECTS

First reactions to the War: India's contribution: signs of disillusionment: Lucknow Pact: 1917 announcement: Montagu's tour: Rowlatt Committee: end of War: emergence of Mr. Gandhi as leader: Rowlatt campaign: Punjab disturbances: Jallianwalla Bagh incident and its effects: Hunter Commission: the Third Afghan War.

FOR over a generation after Lord Lytton's unhappy incursion into Afghanistan India had remained outside the orbit of European politics, and known no war more serious than a frontier expedition. The sudden conflagration of August, 1914, took everyone by surprise, and the first reaction was a genuine and immediate demonstration of loyalty towards the British connection. This enthusiasm extended not only to the Princes, who unanimously offered their help, and to classes accustomed to serve the Government as soldiers or officials, but it affected many who might have felt that England's difficulties were India's opportunity. It astonished those who believed that the outbreak of such a war would be followed by the rapid disruption of the Empire. Such a view, though shared by the German staff, was based on a misreading of recent Indian history. Apart from an insignificant section of extremists, few Indians at that time believed that it would be possible to establish an independent national government, fewer still wanted a change of masters; and there was a deep-seated confidence, which dated perhaps from the Mutiny, in the ultimate ability of the British to 'muddle through' a war.

The attitude of the middle classes, their offers of help and their avoidance of activities likely to embarrass the Government may be ascribed chiefly to the feeling that a war in which India took a prominent part would settle for ever the question of her status in the world. In two Provinces only the Government had to face troublesome opposition. The Bengal anarchists continued their murder campaign, and a conspiracy was discovered in the Punjab which was led by some of the Sikh emigrants who had returned in the *Komagatu Maru* after being refused admission by the Canadian Government.[1] Over most of India

[1] See page 587.

there was a truce from politics, and a general disposition to leave the Government free to concentrate on war work.

This attitude facilitated the recruiting, on a voluntary basis, of some 800,000 combatant and 400,000 non-combatant men. It ensured popular support for a financial policy by which the Indian Government contributed between twenty and thirty millions yearly, and later added a free gift of £100,000,000 to the British Government.[1] It brought in large contributions to the Red Cross, and helped the floating of a War Loan. The general good-will made it possible to denude the country of British troops, and to allow many British officials to join the army and do special war work. The garrison at one time included only 15,000 British soldiers. The ordinary administrative services were almost entirely in Indian hands. Tacitly the British had conceded two important points for which Indian politicians had been agitating for many years. The British garrison had been reduced, and the higher ranks of the civil services had been Indianized. If the British ever abdicated their position in India it was during these war years, and it is impossible to understand the general resentment and ill-feeling which followed the armistice without seeing that from the Indian standpoint this voluntary and peaceful abdication was succeeded by a determined if unavowed effort to return to pre-War conditions.

Popular enthusiasm gradually subsided. The Government, aloof and preoccupied, could not direct it into channels which might keep it alive. Offers of help were pigeon-holed, and little scope was given for voluntary civilian work. No new administrative methods were evolved, as in Europe, for carrying on the War, and the old machinery could not stand the strain. For this failure the long estrangement between the races must be blamed, rather than individual officials and soldiers. Within the first few months some 80,000 British and 200,000 Indian troops were despatched to France, East Africa, Egypt, and the Persian Gulf. It was a great achievement. The army, as laid down by the 'Army in India Committee' of 1913, was organised for the defence of the peninsula, and no previous expeditionary force had exceeded 18,000.[2]

[1] The Indian Government met the normal charges—pay, allowances, etc.—of Indian troops no longer employed within her boundaries. Further responsibilities were assumed in April, 1918, but the War ended before these amounted to more than £12,000,000.

[2] The policy formulated in the majority report, and accepted by the Government, based the strength and equipment of the army on the principle that India should provide for her own defence, but was 'not called upon to maintain troops for the

The weakness of this highly centralised organisation only became apparent later, when the Mesopotamian campaign, for which India had undertaken a special responsibility, proved disastrous, and the medical and commisariat arrangements collapsed in a manner reminiscent of the Afghan wars. By 1916 all hopes of speedy and conclusive victory had disappeared, and disillusionment had begun. It was accelerated by official methods employed in recruiting, especially in the North of India, and by the pressure brought upon the propertied classes to contribute to the Red Cross Funds and to invest in War Loan. Prices began to rise, and, as usually occurs in times of economic disturbance, a small section of the population enjoyed most of the benefit.

Soldiers returning from the War had a considerable influence. Some brought back tales of the European War, and of the prosperous French peasantry. Others confirmed the rumours of the administrative breakdown which was subsequently investigated by the Mesopotamian Commission, and did so much to discredit the Indian Government. The capture of Kut by the Turks, in April, 1916, followed immediately after Lord Hardinge had handed over the Viceroyalty to Lord Chelmsford. These two events mark the beginning of the second phase.

Specific grievances develop rapidly in such an atmosphere, and various political groups became active. Muhammadan troops fought staunchly against the Turks, but the War had never been popular amongst the Muslims. 'It was a sore point that the Government of our Caliph should be at war with the Government of our King-Emperor.' [1] Suspicions that the War meant the permanent disruption of their religious hierarchy were confirmed by the revolt of the Sherif of Mecca against the Sultan. The Calcutta Muslims passed a resolution condemning as enemies of Islam 'the Arab rebels headed by the Sherif of Mecca and their sympathisers'. From 1916 a movement can be traced amongst the orthodox which, four years later, culminated in the unfortunate Caliphate agitation. Educated Hindus also lost their early interest in the War. They could feel no responsibility for its conduct, and saw nothing of its realities, apart from the *Emden's* short raid into Indian waters and its surprising but ineffective bombardment of Madras. Nationalists were emboldened by the Irish rebellion and by the apparent collapse of

specific purpose of placing them at the disposal of the Home Government for wars outside the Indian sphere, although—as has happened in the past—she may lend such troops if they are otherwise available'. See the official *India's Contribution to the Great War*, chapter ii.

[1] Presidential Address, Muslim League, 1915.

Western civilisation. Many were swept into the Extremist camp, and were joined by business men of all creeds. The commercial classes were often at loggerheads with the Government over war-time restrictions, and a keenly protectionist industrial group became increasingly important in the nationalist movement, bringing the financial support which it had hitherto lacked. The Moderates were weakened by the death of Gokhale in the first year of the War. They received little encouragement from the Government, and Sir (afterwards Lord) Sinha, who had led the Congress in its support of the War, rapidly lost his following. Two years had elapsed since Mr. Asquith, as Prime Minister, had promised that 'henceforth Indian questions would have to be approached from a different angle of vision', but the Cabinet showed no sign of any alteration in its views about admitting Indians to some voice in the direction of policy, and no recognition of their new status.

The leader of the political revolt was Tilak. He had been released in 1914, and two years later emerged from his retirement. He chose his moment cleverly, and rapidly regained his old ascendancy, finding in Mrs. Besant a valuable lieutenant, who brought a knowledge of European political methods to the new 'Home Rule League', and whose perfervid admiration for Hinduism flattered the students and disarmed the orthodox. Tilak himself had grown less provincial in outlook, and less rigid in his religious views. He had learnt to see India as a unit, and rapidly came to terms with the Muslim League, which agreed to support his demand for Home Rule.[1] The capture of the Congress presented few difficulties. The Lucknow meeting, at the end of 1916, reflected the general disappointment with the achievements of the Moderates, and since that date Congress has remained an Extremist body. The Moderates have become a vague political group, important because of individual ability, but without effective organisation. Thus 1916 saw the beginning of a new wave of nationalist fervour which was to reach its peak three or four years later; and in 1917 the British Government, following closely the parallel of 1907, chose this period of growing disorder to institute a series of complicated and carefully balanced reforms. Mr. Chamberlain, before resigning over the Mesopotamian Report, had agreed to abolish the emigration of indentured labour to Fiji, and had removed an ancient grievance by allowing the

---

[1] The terms of agreement between the Muslim League and the Congress were embodied in the Lucknow Pact of 1916. These included, *inter alia*, an acknowledgment of the Muslim claim to separate electorates, the principle of which had already been conceded in the Morley-Minto reforms.

import duty on cotton goods to be raised to $7\frac{1}{2}$ per cent. without any equivalent rise in the excise duty of $3\frac{1}{2}$ per cent. He was succeeded, as Secretary of State, by Mr. E. S. Montagu, who was authorised by the Cabinet to make an important declaration in the House of Commons on August 20, which at last foreshadowed some definite transfer of responsible government. The object of British policy was defined to be 'not only the increasing association of Indians in every branch of the administration, but also the granting of self-governing institutions with a view to the progressive realisation of responsible government in India as an integral part of the British Empire'. A simultaneous announcement removed the bar to Indians receiving full commissions in the army.

This belated fulfilment of Mr. Asquith's pledge had little effect in India, partly because of its informality. It was undoubtedly the moment for a Royal Proclamation. The new Secretary of State was, however, an enthusiastic believer in the policy to which the new Cabinet had given its consent. He went to India in October to consult with the Viceroy and draw up the combined Report on which was based the Government of India Act of 1919.[1] Mr. Montagu could claim that his cold weather tour 'kept India quiet for six months at a critical period of the War',[2] but conditions became steadily worse during this period. His arrival in India coincided with severe communal rioting at Arrah. A financial crash in Bombay and a recrudescence of plague added to the general disaffection. Vocal Indian opinion grew more and more extremist in tone. Even the Moderates, who were co-operating with the Government, and at this time still included Mr. Gandhi, were beginning to use their position to bargain about political demands. In this unpromising atmosphere was evolved the policy of Dyarchy, a scheme of checks and balances. No important change was proposed for the central executive, but legislation was entrusted to the new Assembly and Council of State, each of which had elected majorities, though they also contained an official *bloc*. The Viceroy was also left with the power of 'certifying' any legislation which he might feel necessary and which the Legislatures did not pass. The Provinces also had their Legislative Councils, elected on a wider franchise, and the executive work was divided into two groups. The 'Reserved' subjects —including Finance and 'Law and Order'—remained under the control of the Governor and his Councillors, but the other 'Transferred' sub-

[1] Montagu-Chelmsford Report, 1918. Parl. Papers, 9109.
[2] Edwin Montagu, *An Indian Diary*, 208.

jects were entrusted to Ministers who were responsible to the Legislature. It was this delicate constitutional experiment which Mr. Montagu
had to place before a Cabinet chiefly concerned with the extreme likelihood of the Germans breaking the Western front. The Report was
published in July, and was received with hostility and suspicion in
India, with indifference in England. But the general principle had been
accepted by the British Government, and the preparation of a new
Government of India Bill began its usual slow course. A Franchise and
Functions Committee toured India in the cold weather of 1918-19, and
a Joint Select Committee sat in the following summer. After certain
modifications the Bill became law in December, 1919, some twenty
months after Montagu had returned from India.

The events which occurred during these twenty months left an im-
print on Indo-British relations comparable with the after-effects of the
Mutiny. The nationalist movement, aided by Mrs. Besant's skilful
propaganda, had become very troublesome to the Government, which
depended upon the Press Act and the Defence of India Act to curb
the opposition. The need for some less cumbrous procedure tempted
the Government to take a most ill-advised step. In 1917 a Committee,
under Mr. Justice Rowlatt, was appointed to enquire into the course of
criminal conspiracies. A peripatetic committee was not likely to eluci-
date much information not already possessed by the Criminal Investigation Department, and its appointment clearly foreshadowed some
more effective measures of repression, which would probably not be
confined to the anarchist organisation against which the Committee
was ostensibly directed. The Rowlatt Report was issued in the summer
of 1918, very shortly after the appearance of the Montagu-Chelmsford
Report. The two were read together, and educated Indians can hardly
be blamed for the conclusions which they drew. The Rowlatt Committee made some clear-cut proposals, speedily embodied in two Bills.
Judges were entitled to try political cases without juries in notified
areas, and Provincial Governments were given powers of internment.
Meanwhile the vague and tentative suggestions of the Montagu-
Chelmsford Report were being slowly incorporated into legislative
form. Indians, who had confidently expected that the end of the War
would bring a complete change in their status, now saw the Government of India taking new powers for repressive action, and found little
comfort in the prospect of Mr. Montagu's experimental reforms after
they had been whittled down by unsympathetic officials and a hostile
Parliament.

The Armistice added to the general exasperation. Victory brought a certain racial arrogance, accentuating the worst features of the British occupation. The commercial community indulged in an orgy of speculation and profiteering. Certain officials who had remained in India during the War seemed to take a delight in being rude to Indians who had done the same; others sullenly returned to routine work from a life where promotion had been rapid and their actions little trammelled by 'red tape'. No European showed any recognition of the political and social changes of the War period. It was treated as a mere interlude, and the chief anxiety was to resuscitate the old Anglo-Indian life. From the Indian standpoint the War had finally killed the idea of European superiority, and roused new ambitions and new hopes. Both races were in the exasperated mood which precedes a fight. The new Sedition Bills provided the incentive. When they were brought before the unreformed Legislature in January, 1919, political Indians saw in them a direct challenge, not unlike the Partition of Bengal, but providing better grounds for a struggle because it was a challenge which would unite every party and every creed.

A number of factors, more or less connected with the War, carried nationalist sentiments into classes which had been previously almost immune from political influence. The influenza epidemic, which affected so many parts of the world in 1918, swept across India, attacking about a third of the population, and resulting in some twelve or thirteen million deaths. It caused more havoc in a few months than bubonic plague during the previous twenty years. The disease ran its course unchecked, leaving a feeling of depression and uncertainy which was intensified by the poor harvest of 1918, and the rapid rise in price of the villagers' small requirements. A partial break-down of the railway system added to the difficulties of the villagers and to the opportunities for rapacity on the part of dealers and middlemen. Soldiers and men from Labour Corps returned with grievances of their own due to the hasty demobilisation and unfulfilled promises. They formed a critical and discordant element in the villages. Factories were making enormous profits, but owners, British as well as Indian, kept wages low, and did not attempt to use the surplus wealth to effect permanent improvements in housing and settling the mill population.[1]

[1] Between 1917 and 1924 most of the larger cotton and jute mills repaid their shareholders several times the value of their original stock. A small proportion of the money, thus irretrievably lost to the industry, would have sufficed for the rebuilding of settlements for the factory hands along modern lines, and the removal of some factories from areas where rebuilding is impossible owing to congestion.

It was a period which showed Indo-British civilisation at its worst, and it produced a reaction which helped to bring to the front a new leader whose philosophy of life was based on a revolt from Western morality and Western industrialism.

The activities by which Mohandas Karamchand Gandhi had won his reputation in South Africa have been touched upon earlier. The difficulties in which he had been involved, first with the Natal and Transvaal Governments, and later with the Union of South Africa, had not made him an extremist in Indian politics, though they had taught him much about organising a popular movement and harassing a modern government. In pre-War India he was known as a Moderate, as a friend of Mr. Gokhale, and as a keen social reformer with somewhat heretical views about caste. As late as July, 1918, he was defining *swaraj* as equal partnership within the Empire, and taking part in a recruiting campaign, in which he urged the Gujarati peasants to win *swaraj* by joining the army. He seems to have been favourably impressed by the Montagu-Chelmsford Report, and served as a member of the Government Commission which investigated labour and agrarian troubles in the Champaran district. There is no reason to believe that the sudden revulsion of feeling which threw him so violently against the Government immediately after the War was a mere politician's *volte-face*. It must be chiefly ascribed to the selfish and hubristic attitude of the European population, an attitude of which the Rowlatt Bills were only one manifestation. Mr. Gandhi, like millions of his politically-minded compatriots, thought that Indians were being tricked. They saw Europeans coming back to take up their posts, and the Government apparently bent upon restoring pre-War conditions. Mr. Gandhi's South African reputation and wide experience made him pre-eminent amongst the politicians, and speedily gained him a far greater hold upon uneducated Indians than could be claimed by any former nationalist leader. This position he owed to his obvious sincerity, his close approximation to the Hindu ascetic ideal, his knowledge of industrial questions, and his reputation as a negotiator on behalf of the factory workers, the plantation coolies, and the depressed classes.

He had other qualifications for leadership which were not immediately apparent, but were to make him the greatest force in Indian politics for over a decade. His lowly *bania* caste saved him from the Brahmin's inhibitions, and brought him many supporters amongst the business men and shopkeepers. These had received little encouragement from the older politicians, who were drawn from the professions and from the higher castes. He co-operated easily with the wealthy commercial element then joining the nationalist movement, and gained humbler supporters in every market town. In his youth he had had close connections with the Jain community, and acquired the extreme pacificist and humanitarian outlook which won him sympathy from similar elements all over the world during those post-War years before the recent revival of aggressive and ruthless nationalism. His experiences in England and South Africa had taught him how to appeal to non-Indians, he had learnt much from the British suffrage movement and more from Irish nationalism. The former showed how easily a Government with some regard for the decencies can be made ridiculous by any group which indulges in passive resistance and does not mind imprisonment. From the Irish he learnt how a modern government can be goaded into repression, and how this can be exploited in other countries in order to complicate international relations. The United States formed the obvious field for such an appeal, owing to their post-War importance as a creditor nation, their strong 'mugwump' elements, and their old hatred of British imperialism. With this knowledge and a decided flair for publicity, Mr. Gandhi became the first Indian nationalist to gain an international reputation, which was later an important asset in ensuring his pre-eminence in the movement.

The campaign against the Rowlatt Acts proved that Indian nationalism had acquired a new and effective technique, which combined Western political methods with a religious appeal peculiar to India. The propaganda was as deliberately mendacious as any used during general elections in Europe or America. Ever since 1897, when Tilak violently attacked Gokhale for withdrawing a statement which he could not verify, the Congress had accepted the view that nationalist propaganda was a war-time weapon, and there was no need for it to be based on truth.[1] Though ultimately this has disillusioned many of their friends abroad, the method is effective in India, where fact and fancy are liable to be confused, and there is little serious political controversy. The successful political propagandist appeals to the fears or the cupidity of the masses, and the comparatively limited and innocuous proposals of the Rowlatt Acts were translated into provisions for inspecting all couples before marriage, and for preventing festive assemblies of more than two or three people, or the possession of more than two plough bullocks. Mr. Gandhi now introduced two Hindu religious conceptions —satyagraha, the vow to hold to the truth, and ahimsa, or harmless-

[1] Supra, p. 546.

ness. These he welded into a policy of passive resistance to the Government, and added another Hindu idea, the *hartal*, or day of fasting and suspension of business, a very ancient method of protesting against the vagaries of an autocrat. Although Mr. Gandhi's appeal was primarily to Hindus, there was much which attracted Muslims, most of whom still retain that veneration of asceticism which they have inherited from their Hindu forbears.

The disturbances which occurred in March and April, 1919, seem to have been spontaneous outbursts of popular feeling, due to economic as well as political discontent. They were characterised by violent racial bitterness, and occurred in those parts where war-time measures or post-war profiteering had pressed heaviest on the people—in the Punjab and Western India. There was no evidence of any serious attempt to set up an alternative government or to win over the army. Rioting took place in a number of cities, Delhi, Virangaum, Lahore, Kasur, and Amritsar, but the mobs, while attacking isolated Europeans and Government buildings, showed few signs of organisation or objective, and accepted no leadership. In Lahore the ostensible cause of the outbreak was the declaration of a *hartal* of April 6, *satyagraha* day. The arrest of Mr. Gandhi, on his way to the Punjab, was announced on April 10, and precipitated trouble at Ahmadabad, where he was well known amongst the mill-hands, and also at Kasur and Amritsar. There was, however, no evidence that the Satyagraha League either foresaw events taking this course, or desired that they should do so, and Mr. Gandhi, with his committee, helped to restore order at Ahmadabad. Martial law was declared in the Punjab on April 15, a measure justified by the growing tension with Afghanistan, as well as by the condition of the Province, although definite hostilities on the frontier did not begin till May, by which time the active unrest in India had subsided. The historical importance of these disorders does not lie in their direct results, but in the racial animosity aroused by the action of the commanding officer at Amritsar, by the methods employed in enforcing martial law, and by the subsequent controversy.

Two nationalist leaders, Dr. Kitchlew and Dr. Satyapal, were arrested at Amritsar on April 10, and deported. A large crowd attempted to enter the civil lines, but was turned back, and began rioting in the city. Two banks were attacked, and the European agents murdered. The railway station was gutted, and a European railway guard killed. Some other Europeans in the city were attacked, including a missionary, Miss Sherwood, who was left for dead. Order was restored by

General Dyer, who was in command at Jullundur, and arrived on the 11th. All public meetings were then forbidden by proclamation. It so happened that the 13th was the date of the annual horse fair, when many countrymen come into the city. That evening a prohibited meeting was held in a large, but completely enclosed space, known as the Jallianwalla Bagh.[1] General Dyer, hearing of this, marched a small detachment to the entrance. He had with him 65 Gurkhas, 25 Baluchis, and two armoured cars. Without giving any warning, he ordered fifty of his men to open rifle fire on the densely packed crowd. According to his own account, he fired 1605 rounds while the crowd was endeavouring to disperse, and then withdrew his men. The armoured cars remained in the street outside, as they were not able to enter. Casualties in the crowd were afterwards officially estimated at 379 killed, of whom 87 were villagers. The troops were not molested, but no attempt was made then or subsequently to assist the wounded, who numbered at least 1200. This action was approved by the Provincial Government, and on the following day aeroplanes were sent to Gujranwala, where a crowd was burning and rioting. Bombs were dropped and a machine-gun turned on to groups of men in the town and also in surrounding villages. Martial law was proclaimed on April 15, and continued until June 9. During this period a number of orders were given with the obvious intention of humiliating the inhabitants. Men passing through the street where Miss Sherwood was attacked were forced to go on all fours. At Gujranwala all Indians had to 'salaam' any commissioned officer. Flogging, often in public, was the favourite punishment, and it was inflicted for minor offences, such as 'the contravention of the curfew order, for failure to salaam a commissioned officer, for disrespect to a European, for taking a commandeered car without leave, or refusal to sell milk, and for similar contraventions'.[2] These facts are taken from the majority report of the Hunter Committee, which investigated the disturbances in the Punjab. An unofficial Indian committee also examined these incidents. They were the subject of debate in Parliament, and of legal proceedings, which, for reasons discussed in the preface, prevent anything but a bare recital of events which have

---

[1] 'The Jallianwalla Bagh is in no sense a Bagh as understood by those familiar with India. . . . it can best be described as resembling a very large sunken swimming bath with perpendicular sides.' General Sir Geo. Barrow, *Life of Sir Charles Carmichael Munro, Bt.*, 184.

[2] *Report of Hunter Committee*, 1920, Cmd. 681, p. 85. See also chapters iii., v. and xi. of the Report.

2 Q

been the subject of much dispute conducted along painfully racial lines.

Certain points must be noted, for the bitterness aroused over this controversy has had a marked effect on recent history. It formed a turning-point in Indo-British relations almost as important as the Mutiny. The Duke of Connaught, when opening the new Legislatures some two years later, rightly said that 'the shadow of Amritsar lengthened over the fair face of India'. The reason for this was not merely the number of the slaughtered at Amritsar, or even the brutality displayed in subsequent proceedings, so much as the assumption, implied in the behaviour of responsible Englishmen and in their evidence before the Hunter Commission, that Indians could and should be treated as an inferior race. If the events described in the last paragraph had occurred in any part of the 'white Empire', it is inconceivable that they would not have been the subject of immediate judicial or official enquiry. For some months little notice was taken of the Punjab disturbances in England, and it was not until October that the Hunter Committee was appointed. Besides Lord Hunter, the Committee included four British and four Indian members, three of the British being Government servants. Although the Indians were men of moderate political views, the Committee divided along racial lines, but both majority and minority reports severely criticised General Dyer's action and the administration of martial law.

The point in the enquiry which brought the racial issue to a head was General Dyer's defence. He made it clear that he went down to the Jallianwalla Bagh intending not only to disperse an illegal assembly, but also to punish the crowd in a manner which would be an example to the whole Province.

'I fired and continued to fire until the crowd dispersed, and I consider this is the least amount of firing which would produce the necessary moral and widespread effect it was my duty to produce if I was to justify my action. If more troops had been at hand the casualties would have been greater in proportion. It was no longer a question of merely dispersing the crowd, but one of producing a sufficient moral effect from a military point of view not only on those who were present, but more especially throughout the Punjab.'[1]

This statement, which was amplified under cross-examination, constituted a direct challenge. Shooting down an unarmed crowd in one town in order to have a moral effect upon the rest of the country was a measure which could not conceivably have been employed in any part

[1] *Report of Hunter Committee*, 30.

of the 'white' Empire, even in Ireland during the War, when local terrorism and the general situation afforded stronger justification. The Government of India promptly and definitely repudiated this use of force, but General Dyer had only blurted out the view commonly held by a high proportion of military and civil officers in India. When disciplinary action was taken against him and certain other officers, his action and his attitude were supported by a large section of the Press, by many members of the House of Commons, by an overwhelming majority of the Lords, and later in the *obiter dictum* of a judge.[1]

The Hunter Committee agreed that there was no evidence 'to show that the outbreak in the Punjab was part of a pre-arranged conspiracy to overthrow the British Government in India by force', but British and Indian members were divided over the effect of war-time administration in the Punjab, and over the necessity of enforcing martial law. On this latter point Indian opinion showed its usual tendency to minimise the frontier danger. It is true that martial law was not enforced in the Bombay Presidency, where unrest almost as severe was far better handled, but the frontier situation was serious, and the Government had no means of knowing that the third Afghan War was going to be a curiously abortive affair.

For the first time in Indo-British history the Afghans were the aggressors, and proved that, like the Russians, they were feeble in attack though powerful in defence. The new Amir, Aman-ullah,[2] was probably forced into war by a desire to divert attention from the discreditable means by which he had risen to the throne, and to satisfy those fanatical supporters who had chafed against Habib-ullah's neutral attitude during the War. There is evidence that he was completely misled about contemporary events in India and Europe, and was influenced by Russian emissaries. He not only declared his absolute independence of any control by the Government of India, but began an attack on the frontier. The whole affair was over in a few weeks. The Afghan plan was to march columns to the frontier with the object of raising the tribes, but Aman-ullah's commanders were not aware of the immense recent development in the technique of war. Although the British can hardly have raised any enthusiasm for the war, and there was a breakdown in the medical arrangements which resulted in heavy losses from cholera, the only partial success of the Afghans was in the Tochi valley,

[1] This judge's habit of commenting upon social and political topics was subsequently the subject of a rebuke by the Lord Chief Justice.

[2] Habib-ullah had been murdered in February, 1919.

where British troops in advance of Miram Shah were withdrawn and the Mahsuds and Waziris joined the enemy. Aeroplanes, high explosives, and wireless gave the Indian army a decisive advantage, which was clinched by the capture of Spin Baldak fort in the south. Peace was signed on July 26. The Indian Government stopped its former subsidies, and withdrew permission to import arms through India, but abandoned its now illusory claim to control Afghan foreign policy.

Subsequently more cordial relations were established with Amanullah, but he only retained his Amirship until 1928. A visit to Europe inspired him with an excessive admiration of Western civilisation. He attempted but failed to imitate Kemal Pasha, and modernise his country. He was succeeded by the more moderate Nadir Shah, under whose rule relations with Afghanistan were correct and friendly.[1]

Peace with Afghanistan did not mean the pacification of the frontier, and a new period of trouble began in 1919, involving expeditions against the Mahsuds and into Waziristan. The war had vastly increased the number of arms in the tribal area, which by 1920 was estimated to contain at least 140,000 modern rifles. The raiding nuisance and the expense of frontier administration led to the appointment in 1921 of a committee to examine the problem. The old battles of the 'close' and 'open' borders, of the 'forward' and the 'half-way' schools were again debated, and this time political India took a prominent part in the discussion. A compromise was finally adopted, which combined external supervision by regular troops at Razmak and Manzai with the opening up of the Mahsud country and Waziristan by making roads and protecting them with locally recruited levies, or Khassadars. In spite of some unfortunate incidents, murders and kidnapping, the frontier remained fairly settled until towards the end of Lord Irwin's viceroyalty.

---

[1] Nadir Shah was assassinated in November, 1933, but this did not involve a break in the succession. His son appears to be following his father's policy towards England.

CHAPTER II

DYARCHY IN OPERATION

The reform scheme: internal troubles: Moplah rising: dyarchy: its partial success: effect of financial difficulties: Mr. Gandhi displaced as leader: Muddiman Committee: South African dispute: indianisation of the Services: the Swarajist Party: communal disturbances: the Akali movement: Hindu-Muslim friction: later developments.

THROUGHOUT the disturbances of 1919 the Government had been slowly maturing its reform scheme, and by December the Government of India Bill had passed through Parliament. A Royal Proclamation announced the coming changes. It also declared an amnesty for many political prisoners, but the effect was negligible. Political India was still dominated by memories of martial law in the Punjab, and by the growth of the Caliphate agitation.[1] Congress decided to hold its annual meeting at Amritsar, and Mr. Gandhi threw himself, with his usual uncritical fervour, into the Muslim movement. The confused and dishonest policy of England towards Turkey—from the harsh Treaty of Sèvres to the abject surrender of Lausanne—was matched by a confused and politically dishonest agitation in India.

The Ali brothers, Muhammad and Shaukat, had been interned during the War. On their release they took up the cause of Turkey, and thus gave a religious bent to the Muslim post-War grievances, but in a form which did not alienate the Hindus. They expatiated on the danger to Islam of curtailing the temporal power of the Caliph, though Indian Muhammadans had never acknowledged his spiritual authority, and in 1924 the Angora Assembly ended an anomaly by abolishing the Caliphate and sending the Caliph into exile. The movement, however, embarrassed both the English and Indian Governments, and brought about Mr. Montagu's resignation. In India its effects were deplorable. The finances of the movement became a scandal, which helped to lower the tone of Indian nationalism. Under its auspices thousands of Muslim peasants sold their land, and emigrated to Afghanistan, although no arrangements had been made to receive them, and they finally drifted back to India. Later, in August, 1921, the Moplahs, a partly Arab Muslim community in the Malabar territory of Madras, who had

[1] The usual Indian spelling is Khilafat, but the title Caliph is known in England.

broken out frequently in the nineteenth century, began a kind of holy war which rapidly developed into attacks upon the local Hindus, marked by massacres, forcible conversions, and desecration of temples. Mr. Gandhi was ill-advised enough to minimise the first reports, and describe the 'brave God-fearing Moplahs' as 'fighting for what they consider as religion, and in a manner which they consider religious'. This rebellion combined with the collapse of the Caliphate movement to intensify the growing communal tension of the next ten years.

The first elections for the Provincial Councils, the Legislative Assembly, and the Council of State were held in November, 1920. The Congress Party boycotted them; but sufficient candidates were forthcoming, and about a third of the six million voters went to the poll, in spite of the scattered constituencies, the lack of any definite political issue, and the high proportion of illiteracy.[1] The machinery of dyarchy was set in motion. In each Province Indian Ministers were appointed to hold the portfolios of the 'transferred' subjects, such as Education, Local Self-Government, Sanitation, and Agriculture. They were chosen from the various political and communal groups. Only in Madras, where the non-Brahmin Party won a decisive victory and the Muslims are few in number, could any feeling of corporate responsibility be introduced, and Lord Willingdon formed his Ministers into a kind of Cabinet.

Certain weaknesses of the reforms were soon apparent. The ten-year limit, which had been included in the Act to appease Conservative opinion, discouraged Indians from taking too seriously a measure clearly intended as an experiment. It was also difficult to fix ultimate responsibility. Ministers with no voice in financial policy did not feel themselves answerable to the Legislature for the efficiency of their departments.

Dyarchy was born under an unlucky star. Political troubles were closely followed by the slump of 1920. This completely upset the finances, both of the Central Government and of the Provinces. After the reforms these had been entirely separated. The Provinces had certain sources of revenue assigned to them, but remained liable to contribute to the Central Government under a scale laid down by the Meston Committee—'the Meston Award' which caused much inter-Provincial controversy subsequently. The Afghan War and the partial failure of the 1920 monsoon increased the difficulties due to world con-

---

[1] For figures see Appendix to *India in 1920*. Polling was as high as 70 per cent. in Madras urban districts. The boycott was only effective in preventing voting in Bombay. The average proportion was little lower than in France.

ditions. The rupee, after soaring to nearly three shillings, fell below 1s. 6d., and the ordinary balance of trade was suddenly reversed. The Government of India had to demand the full contributions from the Provincial Governments, which had themselves suffered heavily from the slump, from the poor harvest, and from nationalist activities, which added to the cost of the police and reduced the excise receipts.

In spite of complaints about the starving of the 'nation-building' services, such as education and sanitation, the reforms were far from being a complete failure. Useful work was done in the Provinces by Indian Ministers, and there was no break-down during the first three years. The process of indianisation within the Government was proceeding quickly if unostentatiously. An important departure from precedent was the appointment of the first Indian Provincial Governor, Lord Sinha being given charge of Bihar and Orissa in 1920. The Legislative Assembly functioned successfully within its limits. When Lord Reading took over the Viceroyalty in April, 1921, it was already proving itself an effective critical body, with views which had to be considered in administration as well as answered in debate. Interest at first centred on those two closely connected subjects, finance and the army. Criticism was directed to four main points—fiscal policy, loans and currency, direct taxation, and military expenditure. In each case the elected members established the important principle that these questions were to be considered only from the Indian standpoint, and that the Assembly had the right to modify policy.

India ended the War without an overwhelming unproductive debt, but with her full share of inflated expenditure and currency troubles.[1]

After three deficit years the Budget was balanced by means of severe retrenchments, by increasing the salt tax, and by raising customs duties to a level which made India a protectionist country. As in seventeenth-century England, the financial difficulties of the Executive had important constitutional results. Once India and England had both ceased to be 'free trade' countries, the latter could hardly deny the Government of India fiscal autonomy. It became a convention that 'the Secretary of State should normally refrain from interference in fiscal matters', and a Tariff Commission, appointed in 1921, led to the permanent Tariff Board, which has now been in operation long enough to destroy the rather naïve belief of most Indian politicians in the

---

[1] In March, 1921, the Indian national debt amounted to £383,000,000 (taking the rupee at 2s.), but only a quarter was unproductive.

immediate benefits of high protection.[1] It also finally closed the old controversy about cotton duties and excise.

The Government's currency and loan policy had been equally suspect, because dictated from Whitehall. Matters came to a head over the floating of a 7 per cent. loan in 1921 under conditions which proved far too favourable to the investor, while the break-down of the ordinary machinery of foreign exchange concentrated attention upon the irresponsible manner in which the Secretary of State could conduct India's finances. No formal convention was reached upon this point, but the appointment of the Currency Commission, and an undertaking about future loans transferred some measure of control to India. The question of voting supplies arose in an acute form during the last session of the first Assembly. Sir Basil Blackett proposed to double the salt tax in 1923, a most unpopular measure. When it was defeated in the Assembly the Viceroy had to choose between allowing another 'deficit year', or 'certifying' the tax under the special powers allowed by the 1919 Act. He chose the latter course, but the stir which this caused showed that such action could not be repeated often or lightly under the new constitution.[2]

The last and perhaps the most important target for criticism was military expenditure. Like every country which had participated in the War, India was left with a swollen military budget, and this was made worse by the war with Afghanistan, the Moplah rising and troubles on the frontier. In 1921 the army estimates came to 82 crores of rupees as against a pre-War average of about thirty. The Assembly's attack was along three lines. The army was more expensive than India needed or could afford. The excessive cost was due to the unnecessarily high proportion of British troops. The Government was not seriously trying to build up a national army with an entirely Indian personnel and officers. Added force was lent to the opposition by the Esher Committee, which was appointed to enquire into the Indian military system. Its composition was perhaps unfortunate, and its recommendations—published in October, 1920—were never adequately explained to the public. The Report gave the impression, not altogether unjustifiable, that it was intended to treat the army in India as part of an Imperial Defence

---

[1] The reality of this convention was later disputed. In the Budget Speech of 1930 Sir George Schuster emphatically stated that 'the fiscal autonomy convention is a reality'.

[2] The Viceroy had previously certified a Bill, thrown out by the Assembly, for protecting the Indian Princes against hostile propaganda conducted in British India.

Force under the British War Office. The position was the more obscure because the Government had never, since the Mutiny, enunciated any clear policy. Lord Rawlinson, Commander-in-Chief until his premature death in 1925, was fortunately a man who combined great practical ability with an appreciation of the Indian point of view.[1] He cleared up a number of misunderstandings, and although his reforms were far from satisfying Indian politicians, they represented a considerable departure from pre-War ideas in the most independent and conventional department of the administration. In 1921 he explained to the Assembly that the modern army was divided into a Field Army, organised for foreign service; Covering Troops, for maintaining order on the frontier; and Internal Security Troops, which acted as a garrison. Within four years the estimates were down to 56 crores, British troops were reduced from 75,000 to 57,000, and Indian troops from 159,000 to 140,000. The territorial force, started in 1921, gave middle-class Indians an opportunity of learning something of military life. Arrangements were made for training Indians as fully commissioned officers in the Indian army, and eight regular regiments were chosen for complete indianisation. The Indian Sandhurst Committee, which reported in 1927, recommended accelerating this process, and founding an Indian equivalent to Sandhurst, proposals which have subsequently been adopted.

When the first Assembly was prorogued in July, 1923, it had achieved some useful legislation.[2] It had also begun that process of establishing precedents and conventions by which the British constitution was developed. It is a method admirably suited to a people with a genius for compromise, with old political traditions, and a cheerful disbelief in official panaceas, but it was not much appreciated in India. Nor did her politicians pay much heed to other evidence of their country's new position in the world. Her representatives had signed the Paris Peace Treaty, and India was admitted an original member of the League of Nations. Already her participation in the work of the International

[1] Lord Rawlinson's attitude towards expenditure was very sane. 'When I come away from meetings of Council after fighting for a little more money to provide for India's security, and I pass the huge palace which is being built for the Viceroy, I am tempted to curse and swear.' See *Life of General Lord Rawlinson*, Major-General Sir Frederick Maurice, 310.

[2] E.g., the Indian Factories Amendment Act, the Indian Mines Act, the Workman's Compensation Act. The Press Act of 1910, and several other measures, including the 'Rowlatt Acts', were repealed.

Labour Office was having its repercussions. Almost the first business of the reformed Assembly had been to consider the Washington Conventions, which formed the basis of the Factory Act of 1922. Similarly, at the Imperial Conference of 1921, the British Government had been at pains to insist upon the equality of India with the self-governing Dominions, and a resolution affirmed that 'there is an incongruity between the position of India as an equal Member of the Empire, and the existence of disabilities upon British Indians lawfully domiciled in some other parts of the Empire.' These events were too remote from Indian life, and the basic weakness remained. Representatives, like the Maharaja of Bikaner and Mr. Srinivas Sastri, might be prominent Indians noted for their independent judgment, but they were nominated by the Government of India, a body ultimately responsible to the Imperial Parliament.

Educated Indians wanted a new status in the world and a break with the past. They had taken very seriously the promises of their politicians, especially about economic nationalism. But the weakness and dangers of the non-co-operation movement were apparent, and by 1923 there had been a definite revolt against Mr. Gandhi's leadership, which had been notably unsuccessful. He had been foolish enough to promise *swaraj* by the end of 1921. His plans for Hindu-Muslim unity had been ruined by the Moplah rising. The riots which occurred at Bombay and elsewhere, when the Prince of Wales visited India in the autumn of 1921, showed the dangers of *satyagraha* as a popular creed. He failed to propitiate the Marathas by the Tilak Swaraj Fund, which was grossly mismanaged. His 'National Volunteers' were responsible for the horrible affray at Chauri-Chaura, in February, 1922, when twenty-one policemen were murdered. It was after this disaster that he published his Bardoli resolutions, which were a confession of failure, and annoyed the Congress leaders, who had not been previously consulted. A few weeks later the Government saved him from an anomalous position by arresting him. He was sentenced to six years' imprisonment, but released after a year.

His leadership had passed from him. A new Swaraj Party, under Mr. C. R. Das and Pandit Motilal Nehru, had won over most of the Congress to a new policy of entering the legislatures and obstructing the Government constitutionally. At the second elections they were successful, they dominated two of the Provincial Councils, and their forty-five members formed a powerful block in the new Assembly.

Intransigent nationalism had entered the legislatures and another phase began. No longer was there any question of a new constitution developing from dyarchy, or of liberty broadening down from precedent to precedent. From 1924 began the interminable series of Commissions of Enquiry, of formal and informal consultations with leading Indians, which were to culminate in the Round Table Conference and the Bill of 1934. Less effective legislative work was undertaken than during the first session, and the Assembly was frequently interrupted by 'scenes', which were followed, in 1925, by the formal withdrawal of the Swaraj Party and discussions as to the constitutional position of the legislature after this had occurred.

Hopes of a rapid change in India's status were encouraged by the first Labour Government. The Labour Party had passed resolutions about the need for Indian self-government, and the new Prime Minister had expressed very strong and definite opinions on this subject. These were taken more seriously in India than in England, and when a Committee of Enquiry was appointed under Sir Alexander Muddiman, it was widely considered as preparatory to a new constitution which would be introduced before the end of the experimental ten-year period laid down in the Act of 1919. The Committee did not report until the Labour Party were out of office, and for a time there was a lull in politics. The last years of Lord Reading's term of office were marked by the periodic quietening of nationalist agitation which so often follows a phase of extreme activity. Only in Bengal did a fresh outbreak of terrorism necessitate the passing of a special Ordinance.

The tendency of politicians to concentrate upon constitutional issues brought into prominence two old and embarrassing problems —the position of Indians in the Empire, and the proportion of Indians in the Services. The Swaraj Party had public opinion unanimously behind them in protesting against anti-Asiatic legislation in South Africa, Kenya, and elsewhere. Sir Tej Bahadur Sapru had brought this question before the Imperial Conference in 1923, and though the British Government accepted his proposal for a Committee of Enquiry, General Smuts had refused on behalf of the South African Government. Two measures, the Class Areas Bill and the Natal Boroughs Ordinance, were clearly aimed at the Indians; the first arranged for their segregation, and the second prevented any more Indians being enfranchised. Negotiations were subsequently opened in 1926. Mr. Sastri, who had previously visited and come to terms with the Governments of Canada and Australia, went to Cape Town as the first Agent for the Government of India, but the general basis of his work, and of

Sir K. V. Reddi, his successor, was to prevent further emigration, to encourage repatriation, while maintaining the status of those Indians who are fully domiciled.

Kenya raised an equally acute difficulty, though the number of Indians involved was small. It was a Crown colony, but, unlike some, it had no need of cheap Indian labour, and the Government of India could exert no pressure by merely restricting or preventing emigration. After a long controversy, which did much to weaken Moderate opinion in its wish to remain within the Empire, a compromise was reached by which the franchise was conceded, but on a communal basis, segregation was stopped in the towns, and immigration not finally barred. No settlement has been reached about the position of Indians in the Empire, and apart from Ceylon it would seem that no country, within or without the Empire, welcomes Indians on terms which they consider satisfactory. They are tending to return to their own country in spite of the pressure of population. Seventy thousand were, for example, repatriated from Malaya in 1930 at Government's expense. The two and a half millions settled abroad seem likely to diminish rather than increase. The feeling of not being wanted anywhere, except as coolies, is a very powerful factor in the spread of extreme nationalism, economic as well as political.[1]

The report of the Lee Commission raised the question of Indians in the Civil Services. The War almost stopped British recruitment, and the number of candidates subsequently showed a considerable decline, due to the changes which seemed to be impending. The Lee Commission had been appointed by Lord Peel in 1923, with the double task of laying down the rate of indianisation and of making the Services more attractive. Their Report appeared when the Labour Party had taken office, and was fiercely attacked in India as a reactionary document out of tune with the new era ushered in by Mr. MacDonald's Government. Actually it suggested a rate of indianisation more rapid than proposed by the pre-War Public Services Commission, of which Mr. MacDonald had been a member. The opposition was due to racial antagonism and the desire to press home a political advantage rather than to any fear lest the Lee Commission, with its possibly unnecessary financial

---

[1] See *India in 1930-31*, 49. 'The actual number of Indians settled abroad is about 2,406,000, of whom 800,000 are in Ceylon, 628,000 in Malaya, 281,000 in Mauritius, 279,000 in British Guiana, Trinidad, and Jamaica, 165,000 in South Africa, 73,000 in Fiji, and 69,000 in East Africa. The total number for the British Empire as a whole being about 2,305,000.'

concessions to the Services, would check the steady disappearance of Europeans from Government service, which has been such a marked feature of the post-War period.[1]

The Muddiman Committee reported in 1925, when Mr. Baldwin had taken office, and Lord Birkenhead was Secretary of State. The Majority Report, signed by the three British and by two Indian members, took the view that their terms of reference did not permit suggestions for any fundamental changes in the system, and was confined to detailed recommendations for facilitating the working of dyarchy. The Minority Report, signed by four Indian members, including Sir Tej Bahadur Sapru, held that dyarchy was unworkable and that the various defects pointed out by provincial governments were inherent in the scheme. This latter Report was adopted as a manifesto uniting all types of politically minded Indians. Dyarchy was left without a defender, either in India or England. The Conservatives were as delighted to hear of its failure as the Congress, and the English Liberals, who alone might have sponsored Mr. Montagu's schemes, had almost ceased to count politically. Lord Birkenhead spoke of dyarchy as

' the kind of pedantic hide-bound constitution to which Anglo-Saxon communities had not generally responded, and . . . unlikely to make a successful appeal to a community whose political ideas were . . . so largely derived from Anglo-Saxon models'.[2]

Dyarchy was faring even worse in India. The activities of the Swarajists in the Provincial Councils of Bengal and the Central Provinces led to a break-down of the constitution and the resumption of authority by the Governor. Both of the Muddiman Reports had emphasised the basic weakness of the 1919 reforms, even as an experiment in political education. The Moderates suspected that they had wasted their energies in trying to work the scheme, and hankered to return to free and irresponsible criticism of the Government. The Congress leaders began to beat up nationalist enthusiasm throughout the country, and organised a 'National Demand' movement for a Round Table Con-

---

[1] The extent of this change is hardly appreciated in England. There are comparatively few Europeans in civil employ outside the Indian Civil Service, the Indian Police, and a few special services like irrigation engineering. In 1928 there were 922 Europeans in the Civil Service, 569 in the Police. By January, 1932, the corresponding figures were 843 and 528. The Government adopted the Lee Commission proposals that two-fifths of the candidates should be selected in England, two-fifths in India, and one-fifth promoted from the Provincial Service.

[2] Speech in the House of Lords, July 7, 1925.

ference, which would draw up in legal form a constitution granting India full dominion status.

Although the end of Lord Reading's term of office was marked by a general revolt against dyarchy and a return to nationalist politics, there were certain cross-currents visible. The Swarajist Party itself had split over the question of taking office, or at least of serving on committees, a powerful group being in favour of undertaking the usual activities of a constitutional opposition. Mr. V. J. Patel set the fashion by being nominated President of the Assembly in August, 1925. Mr. C. R. Das, who had died two months earlier, had been in communication with Lord Birkenhead, and in a speech at Faridpur showed an appreciation of the difficulties in establishing home rule and the value of the imperial connection, which suggested that he was getting past the dialectical stage in politics. His early death was a disaster, for it left only Pandit Motilal Nehru as a possible leader of those nationalists who were prepared to take a realist view. The rising tide of national feeling, which was to sweep Mr. Gandhi back into power by 1928, involved the Congress and the higher caste Hindus in a maze of fanciful economics and metaphysical politics. Meanwhile other groups, seeing that a real transfer of power might take place in the next decade, began staking out their own claims, and thus belying the vague and optimistic generalisations of the Mahatma.

This sense of impending change was a powerful factor in the bitter communal antagonism which developed after the War. The Akali movement amongst the Sikhs was as symptomatic as the Hindu-Muslim riots a year or two later. The Sikhs are a comparatively small sect, numbering less than four and a half millions, but their former supremacy in the Punjab and their martial traditions give them an importance greater than their numbers might justify.[1] The Akalis were a puritan group, bent on eradicating certain abuses, especially those connected with the management of their holy places. They forced the incumbent of Amritsar to resign, but the Mahant of Nankana Saheb collected a Pathan guard, and some 130 Akalis were killed in a treacherous affray on March 5, 1921. The Punjab was still in an uneasy condition, after the events of 1919, and the Akalis soon fell foul of the Government, which was endeavouring to keep the movement within legal bounds. Conflicts with the police occurred, the most important being at Guru ka Bagh; the Akalis adopted with considerable success Mr.

[1] The number of Sikhs is given as 4,335,771 in the census of 1931. Just over three million are in the Punjab.

Gandhi's passive resistance methods. The excitement spread and involved the States of Patiala and Nabha, whose rulers were at enmity. Ultimately the movement subsided, after an Act had been passed for the better management of the shrines. The outbreak was of historical importance, for it showed how any group of religious fanatics can embarrass the Government in modern India by adopting the technique which has been developed by the nationalists during the last generation.

Communalism is an old Indian problem which time does little to solve. Only to a small extent is this enmity based on race or religion. It may be better regarded as the revolt of emancipated lower caste Indians against the social and financial domination of the higher castes. The Muslim invaders brought very few of their own countrymen into India, and it is only in the extreme north of the peninsula that Central Asian types are common. According to census reports hardly a sixth of the Muhammadans, even in the Punjab, are of a different race from the Hindus. The great bulk of Indian Muslims are descendants of converts, in nearly every case of converts from the lower caste Hindus. Many Hindu customs, and sometimes even the caste system, still survive amongst them,[1] but their new religion gives them a self-respect and class consciousness which was denied to those who remained in the Hindu system. Recently the work of Dr. Ambedkar and others has had a similar effect upon the depressed classes amongst the Hindus.

Almost invariably there is some economic basis to Hindu and Muslim rivalry. In many parts the Hindus are the shopkeepers and money-lenders, the Muslims peasants. In cities the petty employers and shopkeepers may be Hindu and their labourers chiefly Muslim. Sometimes, as in Bombay, north-country Muslims have been brought in as strike-breakers. Where such rivalry exists disturbances usually follow some religious provocation—the sacrificial killing of cows or the playing of music in front of mosques—but the underlying force is an economic grievance.

Of later years all religions and castes have found it expedient to organise politically, and they have also discovered that disturbances are an easy way of attracting the attention of the Government to any grievances. The worst trouble is likely to occur where communities are comparatively equal, and are anxious to display their strength. Recent political developments have added to this temptation, while doing nothing to ease the old economic differences. Perhaps the best evidence of the political nature of much communal trouble is to be found in the

[1] See Census Report of 1921, section 198.

Indian States. Until the last decade they were almost free from this scourge. Under strictly autocratic rule no one is likely to gain from such demonstrations. It was useless for a Hindu *sabha* or Muslim league to agitate against a Muslim or Hindu Prince. It was better to take thankfully what they could get, and the Prince could afford to be generous to his subjects of another religion. Now that some semblance of democracy has been introduced into most of the larger States, and the inhabitants have learnt that the Government of India may intervene in case of a well-advertised quarrel, Hindu-Muslim troubles have occurred in Kashmir, Alwar, and other States, and these have been almost as serious as any in British India.[1]

The 1919 scheme retained the communal electorates of the Morley-Minto reforms, for which neither political group could blame the Government. The Muslims specifically demanded separate electorates, and the Hindu leaders conceded the principle in the 'Lucknow Pact' of 1916. Their effect has been altogether bad. It is not only that they have led Indians to organise along sectarian lines, for this was probably inevitable, and caste grouping occurs even within the Hindu constituencies, but the system throws up the worst type of pugnacious fanatic, who loves to 'prove his doctrines orthodox, by apostolic blows and knocks'. The feeling that great changes were going to take place, and the prospect of some actual transfer of responsibility and control over appointments, have combined to rouse all the meaner political passions, especially in those Provinces, like Bengal and the Punjab, where the two communities are nearly equal in number. Middle-class unemployment, and a family system which elevates nepotism into something like a virtue, have also helped to embitter the politico-religious struggle. A further and very grave disadvantage of the communal electorate is that an alteration in the balance of the parties can only occur through wholesale proselytism or through differences in the birth-rate. And both sides are stirred to new missionary enterprise, when the reward is not only a soul but also a permanent addition to one's voting strength. The activities of the Arya Samaj amongst the poorer Muslims, and of various Muhammadan bodies amongst the lower caste Hindus, have caused the greatest bitterness. The politicians get all the support they need from an irresponsible Press, while ill-feeling amongst the educated classes is kept alive by scurrilities like the *Rangila Rasul*.[2]

[1] For the present distribution of Hindus and Muslims throughout India, see Appendix E.

[2] A libellous attack upon the Prophet, published in 1924. The conviction and

Towards the middle of the decade two other political developments tended to accentuate communal feeling. The movement to organise the depressed classes and outcastes was a severe blow, not only to the Brahmins, but also to certain wealthy but more lowly castes. It has added to the missionary fervour of both the Hindu and Muslim communities, for here are potential converts being snatched away into another fold. Less justifiable and far more dangerous is the revival of pan-Islamic ambitions amongst certain sections of educated Muhammadans. The emergence of Federation as a serious political proposition has given a new meaning to old and vague aspirations. The fear that the Central Government will be dominated by caste Hindus has revived the idea of a great northern Muslim country, including and possibly centring round Afghanistan, and having Karachi as a port. Propaganda of this kind added significance to the Kashmir troubles, where a Muslim State is profoundly discontented under a Hindu Prince. When Lord Irwin succeeded Lord Reading in 1926, communal tension, due to these various factors, had become acute, and his arrival was heralded by fierce Hindu-Muslim rioting.

CHAPTER III

PROGRESS BY CONFERENCE

Feeling at beginning of Lord Irwin's term of office: Currency Commission: Simon Commission: growth of ill-feeling: All-Parties Conference: return of Mr. Gandhi to Congress leadership: Government disputes with Assembly: Lord Irwin's visit to England: invitation to Round Table Conference: Congress decision in favour of complete independence: Civil Disobedience Movement: first session of Conference: decision in favour of federation: points at issue: the safeguards: minorities: the Irwin-Gandhi Pact: second session: the proscription of Congress: third session and White Paper.

THE idea of an all-Indian federation was introduced into Indian politics in the same casual manner as dyarchy. It did not develop logically from previous constitutional experiments, nor was it the fruit of long political

subsequent acquittal of the author, after complicated and protracted legal proceedings, did much to intensify Hindu-Muslim anatagonism. The author was murdered in 1929, an act which led to reprisals and more ill-feeling.

2 R

agitation. Like dyarchy, it was hastily conceived in a time of great political excitement. Many individuals, including the Gaekwar of Baroda,
had long foreseen that a federation of the Provinces and States was the
only method by which any real transfer of responsibility could be made,
but their views aroused little more than an academic interest. Of the
two groups most directly concerned, both Indian politicians and British
officials expected the latter to be gradually replaced by the former in
controlling the Government of India, which they imagined would continue to exercise much the same functions in respect to the Provinces
and the States. The politicians ignored the claims of the States, and also
overlooked the friction which would occur between a highly centralised
Assembly, dominated by higher caste Hindus, and Provinces with a
Muslim majority. British officials were sceptical about all change, and
expected the administration to deteriorate until some drastic remedy
was needed. Dyarchy had deadened executive enterprise. A common
attitude amongst the British might be summarised in the phrase, 'It will
last my time'. The administration, like many business enterprises, suffered from the slackening hand of men who had no intention of ending
their lives in the country, and who no longer expected their sons to
continue their work. The tendency was accentuated by the rapid fall in
the number of Europeans employed in the country. The little groups
of ten or more British officials, who formed the nucleus of the old civil
'station', had now dwindled down to two or three. Economic troubles
in England, and the doubtful fate of European civilisation, helped to
destroy the last remnants of that buoyant self-confidence upon which
the Indian Empire had been founded.

   The usual periodic wave of nationalist enthusiasm came when the
English were disillusioned and tired of an Empire which brought little
credit or profit. It so happened that the next Viceroy after Lord Reading
was a man of remarkable character, whose personality left an impression
upon Indian life only equalled by that of Lord Ripon and Lord Curzon.
Lord Irwin won the immediate interest of many Indians because he was,
what is unusual in official circles, a keen practising Christian. For five
disturbed years he maintained his peculiar political austerity, and when
he left, Englishmen and Indians were discussing the future of India on
equal terms. Memories of the past and the chances of political life combined to nullify part of his work, but he did as much as any Englishman has done to raise the status of Indians, and to ensure that the future
constitution of the country should be evolved on the basis of conference rather than dictation.

As soon as he arrived he was brought face to face with obstacles to constitutional advance, but he held that they had to be overcome and not treated as reasons for inaction. Hindu-Muslim riots broke out, involving heavy loss of life, and one of his first tasks was to bring the leaders of the two communities together to discuss certain differences. Meetings at Calcutta and Delhi were not very fruitful, and from 1927 onwards the rising political or anti-British feeling was accompanied by a marked increase in communal animosity, especially in Northern India. Serious economic troubles also followed, and encouraged a belief amongst those engaged in commerce that India was disadvantageously tied to Great Britain, with its declining industrial and financial standing in the world. This idea was fostered by Americans, with motives not entirely disinterested, and it had a great influence upon Indian business men, especially in the West. The fall in production also caused much labour unrest in Calcutta and Bombay, and India's new 'landless proletariat' began to organise itself, though with little success.

The year 1927 began inauspiciously with a bitter dispute over a highly technical currency measure, intended to stabilise the gold value of the rupee. The Currency Commission had recommended stabilisation at 1s. 6d., the price at which the rupee had settled after wide fluctuations. One member, Sir Purshotamdas Thakurdas, in a minute of dissent, had argued in favour of the pre-War rate of 1s. 4d. This mildly inflationary proposal was open to several objections, but it rapidly developed into a political battle-cry. The cotton manufacturers of Western India, claiming without much justification to be fighting for the agriculturist, headed a violent opposition, and though they just failed to gain a majority in the Assembly, the agitation brought the Hindu monied interest solidly behind the Congress. With their backing the Congress was recovering its former energy. The party sponsored a youth movement, under the leadership of Jawaharlal Nehru and Subash Chandra Bose, and began a systematic campaign in certain rural areas. Politicians, as ten years previously, were looking about for a definite issue on which to fight the Government—the Currency Bill had been too technical for more than a preliminary skirmish. They found it, towards the end of 1927, in the appointment of the Statutory Commission, with Sir John Simon as chairman.

The Montagu Reforms had included a provision for parliamentary reconsideration of the position after ten years. This had been inserted to pacify those Conservative members who felt there should be an opportunity of reviewing, possibly unfavourably, the first results of applying democracy in the East. Indians also had taken this clause as evidence of the experimental nature of the Reforms, but looked upon the Commission merely as delaying the last stage in transferring full responsibility. Its appointment and its terms of reference were bound to reveal the immense difference between these two points of view. The first struggle came over its personnel. To the English it was a parliamentary enquiry, and the Conservative Government appointed Sir John Simon and six members of Parliament, none of whom were known in India or had any experience of the East. There was an arguable case for the appointment of an all-British Commission; the inclusion of two Indian members of the House of Lords would have been a useful gesture, but little more.[1] The essential point was the standing of the Commission, whether its seven members were to conduct an inquisition into India's 'fitness for self-government', or to be *rapporteurs*, who would epitomise for the British Parliament the best Indian and official opinion about future constitutional developments. Unfortunately little attempt was made to keep Indians informed about the object and scope of the Commission.

The educated Indian, with his ingrained suspicion of British motives, naturally assumed from the personnel that the old dictatorial methods were to be pursued. Even the Moderates, led by Sir Tej Bahadur Sapru,[2] decided that it was impossible to co-operate. Lord Irwin did his best to ease the position by informal conversations, but he received little assistance from the Home Government, which was culpably vague in defining the scope of the Commission, or its relations with the central and provincial legislatures. In the end Sir John Simon went to India with power to include six elected Indian members of the Central Legislature, who would sit with the Commission, and report together, but not jointly, with the British members. It is probable that if this procedure had been laid down from the first, and had been explained in the parliamentary debate on the appointment of the Commission, much of the Indian opposition would have been averted. Certainly many Moderates, Hindu and Muslim, would not have joined in boycotting the Commission.

Ill-feeling was accentuated by other factors, and within a few months the tide of racial animosity was running strongly. Even such minor incidents as the publication of Miss Mayo's *Mother India*, an attack upon

[1] Lord Sinha was already a member of Parliament. It would have been easy to create a Muslim peer, and appoint both to sit on the Commission.

[2] Law Member of the Viceroy's Executive Council, 1921-3.

Indian social and family life, had an entirely disproportionate effect.[1] Terrorism does not always accompany political activity, for the *failure* of politicians may be an excuse for the bomb, but at this period the outburst of anarchic crime in Bengal and the Punjab was closely connected with Congress propaganda, and received the open approval of the local Congress leaders. The Bengali Hindus have sometimes been described as 'the Irishmen of India'. They certainly take more readily than most of their countrymen to the formation of murder societies and the adoration of the murderer, but for two or three years the methods of their terrorists were to become popularised over much of British India. The young Sikh, Bhagat Singh, who killed a police officer in the Punjab, and subsequently threw a bomb into the Central Assembly, was a popular hero, the attitude of educated Indians towards him closely resembling that of middle-class Germans towards the murderers of Herr Rathenau.[2] Racial antipathy reached a stage at which nearly all social intercourse ceased. This reinforced the boycott of the Simon Commission, a boycott observed by the chief political groups and by the Central Assembly, though not by most of the Provincial Legislatures. A further symptom of the general disaffection was the prevalence of strikes, some thirty million working days being lost during the year 1927-8. About this time it became customary to ascribe all labour disputes to communist origin, though the evidence for this was generally nugatory, and no worker in the world has more cause to demand higher wages and better conditions than the Indian textile worker. From this date, however, the 'communist menace' began to take the place of the old 'Russian menace' of the nineteenth century, and added to the general confusion and insincerity of post-War Indian politics.

Three important developments occurred in 1928. An 'All Parties Conference' drew up a Constitution; Mr. S. N. Haji introduced a Coastal Reservation Bill, which Europeans considered confiscatory; and Mr. Gandhi returned to active politics. These events were not unconnected, and followed from the boycott campaign. The Conference was a reply to Lord Birkenhead's challenge when he sought to justify

[1] It was believed to have been inspired by the Government. The history of its publication shows that this idea was without any foundation.

[2] Bhagat Singh was arrested immediately after the bomb outrage of April 8, 1929, and was sentenced to death for complicity in this and in the murder of Mr. Saunders in the previous December. The *hartal* following his execution in April, 1931, led to the Cawnpore riots. It is, perhaps, worth noting that he was widely known as the 'Michael Collins of India'!

the personnel of the Simon Commission by a reference to India's communal and other dissensions. Pandit Motilal Nehru and Sir Tej Bahadur Sapru drafted a valuable report, which had only a partial success. Muhammadans were not prepared to tie their hands by accepting the terms of a document of little more than academic interest, and traversing many of the Muslims' 'fourteen points' drawn up by Mr. Jinnah (himself a signatory of the Report). Its publication led to the more definite grouping of Hindus and Muslims into opposing camps. At the Lucknow Congress meeting Maulana Shaukat Ali and other Congress Muslims bitterly attacked the new proposals with regard to joint electorates and reserved seats. Subsequently the Muslim League regained much of its old independence and standing.

The boycott had not rid Indian politics of the communal taint, but otherwise it was successful, and the Haji Bill showed the strength and unanimity of racial as opposed to communal feeling. Hindus and Muslims could join in the demand for economic nationalism, even when translated into the crudest terms for popular consumption. The Congress, troubled by Muslim dissensions, and by a personal dispute between its two leaders, Pandit Motilal Nehru and Mr. Srinivasa Iyengar, turned to someone who they hoped might personify intransigent nationalism and also exploit this economic demand. Only one man seemed capable of lifting Congress politics out of the rut, and the difficulties likely to arise from Mr. Gandhi's leadership were forgotten or ignored. At the Calcutta Congress, in December of 1928, he was welcomed back to a body in which it was impossible that he should take second place. For the next five years he dominated the extremer nationalists, and made for himself a unique position in Indian life.

Conditions had changed since the days of the Rowlatt agitation. In some ways Mr. Gandhi's position was stronger. The object of the Congress was to bring the Government of India into 'hatred and contempt', especially abroad. Some even hoped that matters might come to such a pass that a foreign country would intervene. Mr. Gandhi, with his sense of publicity, was admirably fitted to win support in America, where a generation educated on headlines and traditionally hostile to England was captivated by the picture of the small and ascetic Mahatma defying the might of the British Empire, or in later days parleying on equal terms with the tall Viceroy. Within India, Mr. Gandhi's connection with the industrialists had become even more important. Indian business men had sampled the commercial possibilities of political action during the early years of the fiscal autonomy convention. Tariffs had not proved so effective as they had hoped, and they hankered after control of currency and finance. Many genuinely believed in the importance of the cheaper rupee, though it appealed to them primarily as a means of cutting down their production costs, including labour. Whatever their motives, they were now ready to pay for their politics. When the civil disobedience movement was formally launched in March, 1930, the Congress was being backed financially to the tune of several lakhs of rupees monthly, and was thus enabled to pay a subsistence allowance to thousands of volunteers, and to organise in a manner impossible ten years before. Mr. Gandhi was an invaluable asset in the agrarian campaign. The taluka of Bardoli, in the Surat district, was chosen for a 'no tax' agitation, (conducted by Vallabhai Patel), because the 'Mahatma' was well known there, and many of the *ryots* were emigrants returned from South Africa.

In certain respects Mr. Gandhi's supremacy was less unchallenged than in the years immediately following the War. The Muslims, apart from a rather amorphous group under Dr. Ansari, were either hostile or aloof. Other sections began to group themselves under leaders, who were usually fervent nationalists, but were independent and often critical of the Congress. The Hindu Mahasabha took a communal line of its own. Even more significant was the political emergence of the 'depressed classes' under the leadership of Dr. Ambedkar and Rao Bahadur M. C. Rajah. Events in 1929, notably the return of a Labour Government, persuaded the most sceptical that great changes were imminent, acting as a spur to the keener nationalists, but busying the minorities in the work of staking out their claims and getting together some kind of political organisation. Popular expectation was further aroused by Lord Irwin's visit to England, after a session of wrangling over the Public Safety Bill and the Trades Disputes Bill, two Government measures which met with great opposition.[1] A new complication had arisen in the Assembly owing to disputes with the Speaker, Mr.

---

[1] In order to win some popular support for these measures the Government was ill-advised enough to initiate a communist conspiracy trial. Three Englishmen and twenty-six Indians, who had been engaged in some rather ineffective industrial agitation at Bombay and Calcutta, were arrested and incarcerated. Their case was allowed to drag on for four years. The conduct of the case and the savage sentences injured the reputation of British justice in India and abroad. On appeal some of the accused were acquitted, and all the sentences were greatly reduced.

The 'Meerut Case' was, of course, only one of many post-war conspiracy trials, but in all the others the object of the conspiracy was immediate acts of terrorism.

V. J. Patel, brother of the Vallabhai Patel who was leading the Bardoli agitation. Mr. Patel had always been a violent and very bitter nationalist, whose venerable appearance concealed a considerable fund of sheer *gaminerie*. His position and his comparative leisure enabled him to devise innumerable tricks for harassing the leading officials in the Assembly, and making the Government of India ridiculous. This session may have helped to convince the Viceroy that it was hopeless to combine an elected legislature with an official executive ultimately responsible to Parliament. He left behind this welter of inconsequent politics, and took leave to consult with Mr. Wedgwood Benn in England.

A completely new orientation in the British attitude towards political India began during the autumn of 1929. The extent of the change was not immediately appreciated either in India or England. Lord Irwin came back authorised to invite Indians to meet representatives of the British Government at a Round Table Conference. This marked the end of the old system, whereby each stage of Indian development was the result of inquisition and dictation from England. It was probably unfortunate that the Government of India simultaneously issued a Declaration—that of October 31, 1929—in which it was stated that the attainment of 'dominion status' was the 'natural issue of India's constitutional progress'. The importance of the first point was obscured by the controversy which followed the Declaration. Although Lord Irwin had only reaffirmed the statement of 1917, which mentioned dominion status as the goal of British policy, his action gave many prominent British politicians an opportunity of attacking a minority Government, which they thought was proceeding too fast.

The vague phrase 'dominion status' has played an important but not a happy part in recent politics. The future government of India, a federation embracing some 360 or more millions, will be an authority *sui generis*, unlike anything in the rest of the world. Whether it will be totally or only partially responsible to its legislatures, there seems little advantage in linking its future development with the changing relations existing between England and self-governing dominions like Australia or South Africa. In spite of Sir Malcolm Hailey's official disclaimer, the phrase represents to most Indians a complete change in their status, which must include, as the greater does the less, full responsible government. Mr. MacDonald had added to the confusion by a speech made shortly before taking office for the second time.

' I hope that within a period of months rather than years there will be a new Dominion added to the Commonwealth of our Nations, a Dominion of another race, a Dominion which will find self-respect as an equal within the Commonwealth. I refer to India.' [1]

On the strength of this and similar statements by members of the Government, Indian leaders assumed that the Round Table Conference would draw up a constitution raising India to the status of the self-governing Dominions. A prompt denial, by Liberal as well as Conservative leaders, was followed later by some ill-judged remarks from the Under-Secretary for India, and led to a rapid and excessive reaction in India. The East is always ready to suspect that the English Party system is an elaborate façade behind which England can carry on her imperial designs, and break her word when convenient.[2]

The good effect of Lord Irwin's constructive effort was lost in a maze of words. Revolutionary crime became more frequent, the Congress more intransigent. The Viceroy's train was bombed on December 23, a few hours before he granted an interview to Mr. Gandhi and other leaders which ended all hopes of a peaceful setting for the Conference. The Moderates and certain Congress politicians were prepared to co-operate, but Mr. Gandhi now began the fashion of 'dictating terms', often irrelevant or impossible, which was to react so fatally upon himself and his followers. On this occasion he insisted that the Viceroy should promise that the Round Table Conference would draw up a scheme for full dominion status, to become operative immediately. He must have known that the Viceroy could not make such a promise, and the inevitable result was seen a few days later when the Congress passed resolutions at Lahore in favour of complete independence. From that moment the Congress Party separated itself from all other political groups. Most Indians were ready to applaud Mr. Gandhi while he was harassing the Government of India, or winning sympathy for nationalism abroad, but they did not necessarily intend to let him decide the future of their country. This brought an atmosphere of make-belief into Indian politics. Few, even amongst Mr. Gandhi's immediate followers, accepted his Tolstoyan ideas, or imagined that the Government would capitulate to his demands for 'purna swaraj', full self-government, itself a phrase of doubtful meaning.[3] The business men who financed the

[1] British Commonwealth Labour Conference, July 2, 1928.

[2] Cf. Abdur Rahman's views, *supra*, p. 552.

[3] It was usually taken to mean complete independence, presumably for British India only. A year later Mr. Gandhi defined it to Lord Irwin as the discussion of the future constitution *on equal terms* between Indians and Englishmen.

civil disobedience movement treated his spinning-wheel and muddled economics with amused tolerance.

In launching his civil disobedience movement, Mr. Gandhi showed that mixture of subtlety and irresponsibility which have characterised his leadership. He chose a most effective line of attack when he broke the salt laws. The monopoly had always been unpopular, and Lord Reading's certification of the higher salt tax had aroused considerable political feeling a few years previously. The march to Dandi, and the formal manufacture of salt received great publicity, in India and also in America, where imperial relations are still viewed in terms of the Boston Tea Party. The Government, which had never worried about the non-commercial manufacture of salt, did not choose to accept this challenge. The Congress almost immediately went to the other extreme, though it is doubtful how far its leaders—or even Mr. Gandhi, except in his immediate vicinity—had any control over events. Instead of a small-scale peaceable demonstration against the Government there followed, more or less under the inspiration of the Congress, a series of violent attacks upon Government and private property, and a marked increase in the isolated murders of British and Indian officials and policemen. Simultaneously a commercial boycott was organised throughout India, while interference with liquor shops and obstruction of the police led to frequent collisions with authority. The Chittagong armoury was raided, six Government servants being killed and much ammunition taken. In Peshawar and Sholapur the mob gained the upper hand for some days, and looted the bazaar. Disturbances occurred in hundreds of towns, and agrarian trouble was rife in the United Provinces. Later in 1930 conditions amounting to open rebellion prevailed on the frontier and in Burma, both entailing protracted military operations.

The issue of ten special Ordinances, the arrest of many Congress leaders and supporters, including Mr. Gandhi, the use of the military, and the local application of martial law were sufficient to restore order, except in Burma and the Frontier Province. But the delegates for the Round Table Conference left an India in which there was probably more suppressed political and racial bitterness than at any period in the British occupation. Certain features of this outbreak are worthy of note, because they are likely to recur in the future. Educated women took an active part, being used to hamper the police, and rouse ill-feeling against them. Subsequently, in Bengal two girl students committed an unusually cold-blooded murder of an English official, and another made an attempt on the Governor's life. Equally remarkable were the rapidity with which the agitation spread, and the effectiveness of the boycott. Both were due to better communications, to an appeal which aimed far wider than the educated classes, and to the financial backing which made it possible to pay volunteers. The intensity of the boycott, which was extended to British institutions like banking and insurance, owed much to the technical knowledge supplied by Indian business men, who actively directed the movement against their trade rivals. Finally, the most ominous feature of the disturbances was that the rioting took a communal turn as soon as the weak civil authority had been overcome, and before military assistance had arrived. The confusion of the two impulses, racial and communal, was very noticeable on the frontier, where Abdul Ghafur Khan organised a 'red shirt' movement, pan-Islamic in sentiment but closely allied with the Congress Party.

In this atmosphere the Round Table Conference held its first session. The Viceroy had been able to collect a more representative personnel than might have been expected. The Indian States sent a strong contingent, led by the Maharaja of Bikanir, and containing such able Ministers as Sir Akbar Hydari from Haidarabad, Sir Mirza Ismail from Mysore, Colonel Haksar of Gwalior, and others whose experience and independence enabled them to take a leading part. There was no important group in British India (except the Congress) which had not sent its acknowledged leader, though the effect, inevitable under any quasi-democratic system, was to accentuate communal differences. The task of the Conference had not been made easier by the publication, a few months previously, of the Simon Report, a document unhappy in its form and in the circumstances of its appearance. Like the White Paper of three years later, it was written for British politicians, but chiefly read and discussed by Indians, amongst whom it could only arouse hostility. The first volume reiterated, in somewhat sententious fashion, facts known to most people interested in India. But the emphasis was laid deliberately upon the diversity of the Indian people and their communal dissensions, while the account of recent events wholly disregarded the depth and intensity of nationalist feeling. The second volume surprised all Indians by being practically unanimous, although the three English parties were equally represented on the Commission. This confirmed the idea that all Englishmen, once they are in office, take the same view about India. The proposals of the Commission were of a conservative character, and such innovations as they contained had already been discounted by moderate opinion both in England and

India. Dyarchy was condemned, but the provincial autonomy which was to take its place was carefully safeguarded by the special powers of the Governor, and by the authority left to the Central Government. No effective change was suggested in the Central Executive until the States were prepared to come into a Federation and the country was capable of defending itself, two provisos which were taken as clearly deferring any transfer of authority for a generation or more. Indian nationalists could not be expected to consider such proposals seriously. Their status was left unchanged, and their future would have been dependent upon two factors, neither of which was under their control. The Report suggested an endless series of disputes between provincial legislatures and a British-controlled Central Government which in each Province would have its own representatives in the person of the Governor and the members of the imperial services.

The Round Table Conference rendered a great service by raising the discussion on to a higher plane. The Princes' delegation declared at once that they were prepared to come into a Federation so long as it was an independent authority not controlled from London. They were willing to accept certain limitations on that authority—the 'safeguards' of subsequent controversy—but only as features of a defined period of transition. The rest of the Indian delegates agreed with practical unanimity that they wanted a change on this scale and along these lines; and they had the guarded support of the representatives from the European community in India. The latter, like the Indian Moderates, wanted a settlement of the racial dispute which was poisoning Indian life, and preventing orderly progress or commercial development. This unanimity surprised both officials and politicians in London. They had assumed that the expatriated business man must be intensely conservative and short-sighted. They had learnt to ascribe the enlightened self-interest of the Princes to some innate 'loyalty', and to believe that a natural dislike for the British Indian politician must preclude them from any sympathy with Indian nationalism. These were superficial views. The European community had learnt much since the War. A more intimate knowledge of India might have suggested that some aspects of 'Gandhi-ism' would profoundly affect many Hindu Princes, while English history has shown that the local autocrat is often a keen patriot and intensely jealous of the supreme authority.

The Simon Report was quietly shelved, and the Conference began working out the terms of an early federation. The Government and permanent officials were placed in an unaccustomed position. Instead of doling out 'instalments of self-government', they had now to suggest limitations to a complete transfer of authority. The main lines of federation were rapidly sketched out. It was to include the whole of the peninsula, but not Burma, unless the Burmese specifically voted in favour of being incorporated in the scheme. It was to be a comparatively 'loose' federation, suitable for a heterogeneous collection of democratic Provinces and autocratic States. The initiative of the Princes in suggesting a federation, and the ability of their representatives, enabled them to make very favourable terms in regard to their participation and the curtailment of their sovereignty. Since 1920, when the Chamber of Princes—the Narendra Mandal—had been formed as part of the Montagu Reform scheme, their attitude towards the Government of India had changed rapidly. The meetings of the Chamber were of no great importance, but they had given the Princes a corporate feeling, and encouraged that unofficial co-operation amongst their ministers which was so important at the Conference. Many difficulties had arisen after the War. The activities of British Indian politicians had alarmed and annoyed the Princes, and the Government of India, while making concessions to Indian opinion, had shown a tendency to assert its paramountcy over the States. The Maharaja of Indore was forced to abdicate in 1926, as an alternative to accepting a Commission of Enquiry into his alleged connection with a murder and abduction in Bombay. A few years previously, the Nizam of Haidarabad chose to revive the old controversy over Berar, which had been originally ceded in 1853, and in 1902 was leased in perpetuity to the Government of India, a transaction which the Nizam now affirmed to have been forced upon his father. Lord Reading in 1926 closed the correspondence with a letter in which he was at pains to point out that 'the Sovereignty of the British Crown is supreme in India, and therefore no Ruler of an Indian State can justifiably claim to negotiate with the British Government on an equal footing'. In supporting the idea of an immediate Federation the Princes' motives were obviously mixed. They saw nineteenth-century India disappearing, and like other minorities they were determined to stake out their claim while they could do so to the best advantage. Many of them preferred to see India free from British control; but they had no intention of allowing a British Indian legislature to assume the Viceroy's powers.

By the end of the first session it would have been possible to make a rough draft of the future constitution, the allotment of seats in the Central Legislature, the powers of the Central Government, the financial arrangements between the Federal Government and its members. There were innumerable details to be settled, for each group wished to leave opportunities for bargaining until the last possible moment. Relations with the States presented complicated problems, for little had been done since the time of Lord Curzon to regularise and simplify them. Many disputes on fiscal and other matters were still outstanding, but these formed no insuperable bar to federation, and the Conference showed how quickly a new authority could arrange matters which had lain for years unsolved in the files of the Political Department. The most controversial subjects at the Conference turned upon the limitations to the complete autonomy of this new authority— the so-called 'safeguards'. They can be roughly divided into three groups. (1) Those intended to secure the stability of the Federation, internally and externally, during its early years. (2) Those demanded by minorities, like the Muslims and the depressed classes, which distrust the working of a rigid democracy. (3) Those arising from the long British connection, from the need of further British support, and from the vested interests acquired and the liabilities incurred. It was generally agreed by all delegates that India would not be able to defend herself for some years to come without the help of a British garrison, and the ultimate support of the British navy.

Unfortunately these groups of safeguards were found to be inter-dependent, and this led to much confused thinking, to bargaining and cross-bargaining between the different sections of the delegates. The Muslims objected to reaching definite conclusions about the jurisdiction of the Central Government until they knew their exact representation in the legislatures, a question on which they could not come to terms with the Hindus. The European community appeared as a racial minority, and also as representing vested business interests. Their claims for protection against expropriation were bound up with India's foreign relations. The control of finance continually recurred in con-nection with the different forms of safeguard. It was agreed that De-fence could not be transferred to a responsible Minister until an Indian national army had been organised, and so long as any considerable body of British troops remained, but the cost of defence absorbs the major part of the central revenue, and the future of the army is inti-mately bound up with central taxation and currency policy. So also is the security of Government loans. This subject affects England directly, because all the earlier loans were raised in London. But India's ability to borrow money at moderate interest is vital to her future prosperity and stability.[1] The financial relations between the Federal Government and its members were also found to divide Hindus and Muslims, the former favouring a strong central Executive with ultimate financial control, at least over the Provinces, for the Central Legislature must be predominantly Hindu. Owing to these cross-currents it was never possible to say that certain safeguards were in the interest of India and others in the interest of England, a classification which Mr. Gandhi demanded, but did not attempt to elaborate.

The first session evolved certain principles. Two subjects, Defence and Foreign Relations, were to remain in the hands of the Viceroy. Suggestions for securing the Legislature some control over army policy were still in dispute. It was agreed that the Viceroy, but not the Provincial Governors, should have special powers and responsibilities in regard to finance, though the machinery by which these were to be exercised was left unsettled. Governor-General and Governors were to be given wide emergency powers, and special responsibilities in connection with minorities, and the prevention of commercial discrimination. Apart from the question of the army, there was little in these safeguards for which parallels could not be found in the early constitutions of the self-governing dominions. In all of these the British Government had reserved rights which had long been exercised by the Government of India, and would be automatically transferred to the Federation.[2] Under favourable circumstances the safeguards might be expected to atrophy from want of use, or be waived by the Home Government. Unfortunately, there were other factors more disturbing than in the case of Australia or New Zealand. Ancient grievances and racial differences were as acute as in Ireland and South Africa. An important political party, with the only effective organisation covering British India, had refused to take part in the Conference, and bitterly attacked the credentials of the delegates. Finally, the exclusiveness of the various groups, which had held up work in the first session, was becoming more intense. Each of these, the Princes, the Hindu Moderates, the Muslims, and the smaller minorities, could exercise what amounted to a veto, and both Muslims and Princes had shown themselves prepared to endanger

[1] Indian loans are usually trustee stock, and are considered, though the matter admits of some doubt, to be backed by the British Government. This enables India in, say, 1933 to borrow at about half the rate of a Central European Power.

[2] E.g., in Canada where the disposal of public land was reserved until late in the nineteenth century. The South African constitution contains various safeguards, some designed to protect native rights, but they have not been used.

the Conference in this way. Hindu Moderates, like Sir Tej Bahadur Sapru and Mr. Jayakar, had shown great political wisdom and constructive statesmanship, but they were weakened by the feeling that they had not the support of the higher caste Hindus, whose case they defended.

These considerations persuaded the Viceroy to take a very bold step soon after the delegates from the first session had returned to India. Following the Irish precedent, Lord Irwin decided to enter into negotiations with the Congress leader, Mr. Gandhi, who was then in gaol. This complete reversal of traditional methods marked a great change in the British attitude, and a determination to follow out the conference method to its logical conclusion. It was justified on general grounds by the uneven balancing of the parties at the Conference, where the minorities tended to be over-weighted, and by the danger to the new constitution if the Congress continued to hold aloof. The whole country was suffering from the civil disobedience movement, which was ruining trade in the towns, upsetting finance, and throwing too much strain on the police and civil administration. The arguments in favour of Lord Irwin's action were powerful enough, but he possibly underrated the purely racial basis of Congress politics, and overrated Mr. Gandhi's control over his party. The Pact, which was signed in March, was a satisfactory document from the Government standpoint. The civil disobedience movement was called off, though 'peaceful picketing' was allowed for a *swadeshi* campaign, a concession which was inevitable, as England, like many other countries, was then engaged in a similar campaign to stimulate home production. Political prisoners, not convicted of violent crime, were to be released, but this was something of a relief to the authorities, whose accommodation had been strained to the uttermost. Temporary ordinances were to be withdrawn, and the Congress agreed to participate in the Conference.

The Pact in the end proved Mr. Gandhi's undoing, and it also hindered the natural development of the Federation. Within a year Mr. Gandhi was back in prison, the Congress was a proscribed body, and the inter-communal tension was definitely worse. The experiment, which was almost Lord Irwin's last act before handing over his office to Lord Willingdon, had been a fine conception, and its failure must be ascribed first to the weakness of the Congress leaders, and later to political changes in England. The Karachi meeting, called to confirm Mr. Gandhi's action, showed the Congress at its worst, emotional, short-sighted, and ineffective, though it also proved that advanced nationalism was appealing to a far wider range of people than a few years previously. It was perhaps inevitable that Mr. Gandhi should have been hailed as the dictator of an alternative government, which had called a truce in a successful encounter. But statesmen should not be deceived by their own pose, and it was a fatal mistake when he insisted upon being the sole representative of the party at the Conference.[1] It would only have been defensible if the Congress had had settled views about the complicated issues raised by the Federation proposals. This was palpably not the case, and the weakness of the Congress on the constructive side was emphasised by the last-minute production of an elaborate and irrelevant charter, which no one took seriously and which was never discussed. Instead of sending a solid group of men and women to the Conference who would represent its many-sided interests and varied membership, the Congress threw its future organisation and the shaping of its policy into the hands of a man who had never succeeded as a disciplinarian and who, apart from his nationalism, held distinctly individual views on social and economic questions. The process of disillusionment began at once.

By an unfortunate coincidence the execution of Bhagat Singh occurred when the Karachi Congress was sitting, and anger at Mr. Gandhi's failure to obtain his reprieve was the beginning of the party's rapid disintegration. Immediately afterwards one of the worst communal riots in Indian history occurred at Cawnpore, beginning in an attempt by Congress volunteers to enforce a *hartal* amongst the Muslim shopkeepers. Mr. Gandhi's subsequent efforts to ease the general communal situation only aroused worse feeling. He adopted the old political artifice, for using which he had so often attacked the British Government. He promised the Muslims their full demands, if they were made unanimously, although he knew that he could count on the support of one section, under Dr. Ansari, and this would make unanimity impossible. The reaction amongst a public tired of certain aspects of civil disobedience had its counterpart inside the Congress. Disputes occurred in several Provinces, due to accusations of peculation and to the hasty demobilisation of the volunteers, who claimed, with some justification, that they had been badly treated financially. In Bengal Mr. Subash Chandra Bose and Mr. Sen Gupta began a quarrel which was to lower the reputation of Congress locally. When Mr. Gandhi left

[1] Three prominent Congress leaders—Pandit M. M. Malaviya, Mrs. Naidu, and Mr. A. Rangaswami Iyengar—attended the second session of the Conference, but as individual delegates, not as Congress representatives.

2 S

India his party was already out of hand, and an important group was determined to prevent him from pledging the Congress to support a scheme of federation along the lines of the Conference proposals. By the time he arrived in England the Labour Party was out of office, and India had been almost forgotten in the political and financial confusion which marked the autumn of 1931.

Although Mr. MacDonald and Lord Sankey, the Chairman of the Conference, retained their offices in the new Government and after the General Election, the second session was marked by a decided stiffening in the British attitude towards safeguards, and by an attempt on the part of the new Secretary of State, Sir Samuel Hoare, to divide the question of provincial autonomy from that of the transfer of authority to the Federal Government. This latter proposal was abandoned in the face of unanimous opposition from the delegates, but the changed atmosphere inside the Conference had its counterpart in the renewed activities of those who opposed Federation in India and in England. Mr. Gandhi, presumably sensing this change, and feeling that he could not carry the Congress in support of a scheme emanating from the new Government, decided not to take any serious part in the Conference. His few speeches were irrelevant, and clearly intended for the Press in India and abroad. He deliberately precluded any idea of co-operation, by attacking the credentials of the other delegates, and threw all the minorities together by claiming to speak both for the Muslims and the depressed classes.[1] His open dispute with Dr. Ambedkar was to have unfortunate results later. Its immediate effect was to prevent any possibility of an agreed communal settlement, and the second session closed with the Government decision to issue a communal award after a stated period.

Subsequent developments were rapid and rather confused. It is probable that Mr. Gandhi returned to India with no intention of reviving the civil disobedience movement, but anxious to use such a possibility as a means of putting pressure on the Government, and keeping the Congress in hand. The situation did not permit such manœuvres. Various sections nominally affiliated to the Congress, notably Abdul Ghafur Khan and his followers in the Frontier Province, were determined to bring matters to a head, and they began an agitation which forced the Government to intervene. On the other side Lord Willingdon was equally determined not to begin a series of bargains

---

[1] He claimed to represent 95 per cent. of India—presumably British India. Muslims number 22 per cent., and the depressed classes about 16 per cent.

with Mr. Gandhi, and perfectly willing to accept the Congress challenge. Within three weeks of Mr. Gandhi's return, in January, 1932, Congress was a proscribed organisation, and he himself was back in prison. Whatever may be the ultimate result, the Government had undoubtedly chosen an effective moment for repressive action. The Congress had lost its financial backing, and much of its popular support. The shopkeepers were tired of *hartals*, peasants were disillusioned by no-rent campaigns which were run for political rather than economic reasons, the minorities and many educated Hindus were alienated by Mr. Gandhi's egoism and inconsistencies. The Government proceeded by the method of preventative arrests and sequestration of Congress funds, a double attack which, in the altered circumstances, was not only successful in itself but aroused curiously little feeling in India or abroad. There were the usual accusations of police tyranny, some probably well founded, but the Congress suffered from its recent past and from its long adherence to Tilak's theories about propaganda. Within a year the Government of India had been able to release the bulk of the prisoners.[1]

In the meantime the British Government continued with the preparatory work of the Federation, though somewhat in the manner of a schoolmaster who has undertaken reforms of which he does not really approve. Three mixed Committees toured India to settle outstanding questions with the States, and to draw up recommendations about the franchise. The Lothian Committee, rejecting the idea of indirect election, made proposals for an extended franchise which were substantially accepted in the White Paper of the following year. The electorate for the Provincial Councils would be about 27 per cent. of the adult population, but the Federal Assembly would be chosen from a very limited electorate of about seven to eight million voters. Shortly after the report of the Lothian Committee the Prime Minister announced the communal award. It retained, as was now inevitable, the special communal electorates, and assigned a number of special seats to the depressed classes. The allocation of seats had been discussed for so many years, that the British Government had done little more than register a bargain which both sides had frequently approached, but never actually accepted. The Government expressed its willingness to modify the terms, but only by general agreement between the parties concerned.

---

[1] The highest figure for prisoners interned for offences in connection with civil disobedience was 34,458 in April, 1932. By May, 1933, the number had been reduced to 9144; by July, 1933, to 4683.

This led to a curious incident. Mr. Gandhi, who strongly objected to the depressed classes being considered separately from other Hindus, began a 'fast to death' in order to get the terms altered. The reason for this action, which established a dangerous precedent, was widely misunderstood, especially abroad. Appreciating the fact that he had placed himself in a false position, Mr. Gandhi came to terms with Dr. Ambedkar, under which the depressed classes, while voting for the general constituencies, also formed 'electoral colleges' to choose their representatives for the reserved seats, which, according to this 'Poona Pact', were to be increased. It was a bargain to which none of the minorities were likely to object, and it was accepted by the Government. The only group whose interests are injuriously affected are the higher caste Hindus, now seriously under-represented in certain Provinces, notably Bengal.[1] They had been manœuvred into a position where it was difficult for them to protest, and they had also spoilt their case by supporting the Sikh demands in the Punjab, although this community had already received an allocation of seats far in excess of its numerical standing.

The third and final session of the Conference was something of an anti-climax. Not only was the Congress unrepresented, but the British Labour Party also took no part in the proceedings. In March, 1933, the official 'White Paper' was published, and a Parliamentary Joint Select Committee was appointed, preliminary to the drafting of a Government of India Bill. Although some Indian representatives sat with this Committee, the procedure marked the end of the Conference method, and the resumption of parliamentary responsibility. It forms a convenient point at which to end the narrative account of British rule in India.

The White Paper accepted a Federation for the whole peninsula, but the future of Burma was left uncertain. Politically Burma was divided into two groups: the Separationists, who wished to form a separate State, but only on certain terms, and the Anti-Separationists, who wished to come into the Federation, but only if allowed a freedom to secede which no Federation could permit. The Government had been against the inclusion of Burma, and on general grounds there is much to be said for excluding an area which would bring another race, another religion, and another frontier under a Federation which is already unwieldy and troubled by racial, religious, and frontier problems. An election gave the Anti-Separationists a small majority, chiefly because the official world was believed to favour the other side, but the majority

---

[1] See Appendix E for the allocation of seats, according to the White Paper.

showed no enthusiasm for coming into the Federation, and their only desire was to get as complete a measure of home rule for their country as possible. On other questions the White Paper followed roughly the lines laid down during the Round Table Conference, but the attitude of the National Government showed itself in three ways. The document was written for the British politician with the whole emphasis laid upon the safeguards against dangers implicit in the new experiment, and without any attempt to win Indian support or interest. The safeguards were made as full and explicit as possible; on most disputed points the Government decided against the Indian delegates. There was no concession to Indian demands for some voice in military policy, while the future of the Civil Service was left to be reconsidered after five years. Finally the question of a future 'time-table' was to remain in the hands of the British Government. There was no suggestion that safeguards would automatically come to an end, either after a period of time or after fulfilment of conditions. Inauguration of the Federation was made subject to a number of vague conditions which would be interpreted by the Government—that a Reserve Bank should be set up, which must be 'already successfully operating', that 'the Indian Budgetary position should be assured, that the existing short-term debt . . . should be substantially reduced, that adequate reserves should have been accumulated, and that India's normal export surplus should have been restored'. A document of this kind was not likely to rouse much enthusiasm in India, and the future Federation of India, one of the greatest experiments which the world has ever seen, seems likely to begin its life amidst the recriminations of its two parents.

CHAPTER IV

EPILOGUE

THE writer of Indian history must recognise the narrow limits of the world which he has described. The little groups of alien officials and leading Indians, who have moved across the stage, draw too much attention from the vast audience, silent and seldom moved, which has watched their activities, at first with indifference but of later years with a growing interest. Centuries of subjection, the Hindu caste system, in many cases an inadequate diet, and finally the British domination, have all combined to keep these millions in the background. Peace and the pressure on the soil have also been great levellers. No longer can the ambitions of a Prince offer rewards for courage and skill at arms, irrespective of birth, while in the overcrowded districts the industrious peasant can hardly hope to raise himself by adding acre to acre. It would be impossible to write a history of any European country during the last two centuries without mentioning some who had begun life working on a farm or on a factory bench, but in India neither *ryot* nor craftsman have learnt to look upon the world as their oyster, and society remains static except in a few large europeanised cities.

Generalisations about the mass of villagers and poorer townsfolk, vague talk of their 'loyalty' or of their united demand for certain reforms, these must be dismissed as part of the stock-in-trade of politicians. Apart from the call of religion, itself illusive and indeterminate, it is doubtful whether any common purpose or sentiment animates the Maratha and the Lingaiyat of the West, the Muslim peasant of the Punjab or of Bengal, the sturdy Jat, the Tamil of Southern India, the Dogra of the northern hills. Territorial patriotism and feudal loyalties have never affected more than a small proportion of the population. It would be unwise to presume more about the villagers' political views than a certain weariness of a Government which after a century still remains alien and largely incomprehensible, which has failed to curb the money-lender, the landlord, and the policeman, or to ease the country's most pressing economic troubles. Personal feeling about the European is not an important factor. Outside the great cities only an infinitesimal part of the population is brought into contact with the English, and probably most Indians live and die without even seeing one.[1] Recent events suggest that many parts of the country are ready to listen to an appeal, half religious and half political, so long as it comes from someone, like Mr. Gandhi, whom they can reverence personally, and who promises a way out of the economic depression in which they are sunk. If they do not take the lawyer type of politician very seriously, it is because they suspect him of being the ally of the money-lender and the landlord. It may well be that when future demo-

[1] The ordinary Mofussil district, of about one or more million inhabitants, has seldom more than one or two Englishmen in it, and may have none. Of the 1300 English civil servants and police officers, about a quarter are normally on leave, and half the rest doing some kind of 'headquarters' job.

cratic leaders suggest revolutionary changes, social as well as economic, it will be the peasants who will support them, and the landlords, business men, and professional classes who will organise to circumvent them. This has already occurred in Ireland, where nationalism was once regarded as a middle-class movement.

The Indian villager's difficulty is that of slum dwellers in other parts of the world. He has no means of escape, and his standard of living is continually being lowered by the pressure of population. The census of 1931 impressed the urgency of his case on all but the most superficial. Every year about three million new inhabitants are being absorbed into India's half-million villages.[1] None of the three obvious methods of relieving that pressure are having much influence. Emigration has almost ceased, the number of Indians abroad remaining about the same, and the present tendency is for them to drift back to their own country. Certainly no other country seems ready to accept Indians by the million; yet this is the only form of emigration which would have an appreciable effect. Industries and trade barely absorb the urban surplus. Factories increase in number, but without a corresponding rise in the numbers employed, for better machinery and organisation keep down the labour requirements. In 1929 the total number of factories rose from 7863 to 8129, but the factory population only from 1,520,000 to 1,553,000, which is a smaller increase than the pre-War average of about 40,000 yearly. Irrigation seems to promise more than either industrial development or emigration. By 1930 some 32 million acres were under canal irrigation, and several large schemes are now in hand. The Lloyd Barrage in Sind, the Bandadara and Bhatgar Dams in the Deccan, the Kavari Reservoir in Madras, and Satlej Valley Project are all works on a scale which would hardly have been possible before the War, and when completed will water another ten million acres, much of it land which is at present waste. Unfortunately, it would seem that after these works are finished the law of diminishing returns will operate, and physical conditions will make each further development more difficult and more risky.

The development of irrigation should check, for a decade at least, any marked tendency for the population to outgrow its food supply, though with the separation of Burma, India will definitely become a food-importing country.[2] Irrigation will also slow down the increasing

[1] See Appendix D.

[2] For the year 1930-1, when 'the monsoon had been, generally speaking, satisfactory', India—apart from Burma—exported about 280,000 tons of rice, 13,000

pressure on the land in certain parts of India, but it cannot prevent India gradually sinking into a kind of rural slum, definitely below the general standard of living in most of the world, a reserve of cheap labour whose people and whose products will be excluded by countries wishing to maintain a higher standard. The urgent need for reforming village life is accepted by politicians and officials, but specific remedies have either proved inadequate or else involve revolutionary changes which must certainly wait until India is autonomous. Experiments in 'village uplift' have been tried on a small scale round Dr. Tagore's college, Santiniketan, and by various charitable and missionary institutions.[1] A magnificent work is Sir Daniel Hamilton's co-operative colony in the Sandarbans below Calcutta.

A still more ambitious attempt was made in the Gurgaon district by Mr. Brayne, the District Officer. The basis of all this work is a double attack, first on the inefficiency of village life, which is partly due to religious and traditional inhibitions, and then on the waste of time, due to the purely seasonal nature of the *ryot's* work. The Gurgaon experiment aimed at the more scientific collection and use of manure, the redivision of holdings into larger and better shaped blocks, the more economical use of money (reducing, for example, expenditure on weddings, funerals, and jewellery), improvements in methods of keeping village cattle and prevention of breeding by immature bulls and heifers. Such practical reforms were combined with lessons on the more rational treatment of women and children, and the need for cleanliness and better sanitation. An energetic official or social worker can undoubtedly accomplish much in his immediate neighbourhood, but so far this work has been like a cutting planted in uncongenial soil. It is not a strong growth, even when carefully nurtured, and shows little tendency to take root and spread. Mr. Brayne would be the first to agree that much of his work disappeared in a lamentably short time after his departure.

The Dutch methods of improving cultivation in Batavia were drastic, and more effective in a limited field, but the time for such compulsion by the British is past, and it is only in a few parts that the same

tons of wheat, 50,000 tons of wheat flour, and imported 357,000 tons of wheat from Australia and other countries. India, however, still exports some three to four million tons of oil-seeds and ground-nuts, and will probably continue to do so, while slowly increasing her grain imports.

[1] For Santiniketan see Prem Chand Lal's *Reconstruction and Education in Rura India*. The Y.M.C.A. have also established several educational centres.

problem arises, of the wasteful use of good land. It is the general village economy which is at fault, and this is based on religious feelings which are hardly likely to be modified by extraneous persuasion. It is also probable that the introduction of the cash nexus into a population of small-scale peasants is a disadvantage, especially when, as in India, the villagers have attached to them a great mass of outcastes, criminal and wandering tribes, jungle folk like the animists, and some five million religious mendicants. When there is little understanding of the use of money, and the amounts in circulation are ludicrously small, cash becomes a poor instrument of compulsion, or of inducement to attain a higher standard of living. The Russian experiment is still inconclusive, and is complicated by irrelevant factors, but a return to some form of communal village economy may well be an essential feature of any permanent reform. It would have to be accompanied by the wholesale amortisation of agricultural debt, and probably preceded by an attack upon the landlord system in the *zemindari* districts. Perhaps some compromise will be reached between those, like Mr. Gandhi, who wish the revival of village life to be accompanied by greater simplicity, and those more orthodox economists who believe that the first essential is that the peasant should 'want more wants'.

Whatever may be the form of democracy introduced in 1934, or evolved in the subsequent decade, the moulding of India's future will depend, as in other countries, upon the wealthy and the educated. It must be many years before the villager gains a direct and decisive voice in provincial and federal affairs. Generalisations about the educated classes are dangerous, if not impertinent. At the lowest estimate they form a population of between ten and twenty millions, always changing in outlook and rapidly increasing. It includes men and women of great ability, considerable achievement, and vast possibilities. For nearly all of them political nationalism remains the great motive force, in spite of the temporary eclipse of the Congress Party. The influence of the Brahmo Samaj and the Prarthana Samaj is now waning, a grievous thing for India. Though never numbering more than a few thousand in actual membership, they were the channel through which the best of Western civilisation reached Bengal and the West of India. These two small communities produced a galaxy of talented men, like Sivanath Sastri, Akshaykumar Datta, Pratapchandra Majumdar in Bengal and Justice Ranade and Sir R. G. Bhandarkar in Bombay. From the Prarthana Samaj was evolved that admirable educational and philanthropic society, the 'Servants of India'. Since the days of the Maharshi—

Debendranath Tagore—the Brahmo Samaj suffered from internecine disputes. The ill-fated marriage of their great leader Keshab Chandra Sen's daughter into the 'idolatrous' Kuch Bihar family was the beginning of much trouble.[1] Latterly the Brahmo Samaj, though still producing men like Dr. Rabindranath Tagore and Sir P. C. Roy, has suffered the fate of many liberal institutions in an era of extreme political and economic nationalism.

The neo-Hindu revival of the 'eighties has also lost much of its early force. The Arya Samaj, aggressively nationalist and anti-Christian, still wields some influence in the North, but has found no leader to succeed Lala Lajpat Rai. The Ramkrishna Mission, which Vivekananda founded to commemorate his great teacher Ramkrishna Paramhamsa, does much practical good in a limited sphere, but neither of these bodies justifies the extravagant hopes of those early Western exponents of the new Hinduism, like Colonel Olcott and Mrs. Besant, who believed that they heralded a speedy and complete reformation. Mr. Gandhi has been more effective in attacking untouchability and other crudities along political and social lines. But orthodox Hinduism still remains a force in the land, and those of the younger generation who oppose its influence seem inclined to attack it from outside rather than inside the fold. The educated Hindu of to-day is apt to find himself lost between two worlds. A keen nationalist, he is beginning to see that success may mean an obscurantist reaction, and is afraid of losing all contact with the West. Such contact has lessened considerably of recent years, owing to racial estrangement and the far fewer Englishmen of the professional classes who now go to India.[2] An instructive commentary was provided by the nationalist schools, founded after the War as rivals to the Government institutions. These insisted on an exceptionally high standard in English, though Mr. Gandhi was advocating a return to the vernaculars.

The problems of Hinduism demand solutions which no conferences can evolve. The Untouchables have found leadership and have learnt their power, wringing out of Mr. Gandhi (reluctantly supported by his orthodox followers) concessions of far more practical value than mere

[1] For this unhappy affair, for which Keshab deserved to be pitied rather than blamed, see Mr. S. K. Ratcliffe's article in the *Fortnightly Review* of February, 1933.

[2] The educational and many other services have almost ceased to recruit from England. British entrants to the Civil Service average under twenty yearly (in 1933 the number was seventeen). Few Englishmen now go to India as lawyers, doctors, or clergymen.

'temple entry'. Many in the higher ranks of Hindu society are as sceptical of inherited religious custom and ritual as are their contemporaries in Europe and America. An increasing proportion of the best Indian minds, of all religions, are ignoring religious quarrels and enthusiasms, and are putting their energy into science and economics. Both Hinduism and Islam seem to be on the eve of drastic reconstruction, and those who continue to believe in an 'Unchanging East' are destined to a shock as great as when Russia—known to those now only middle-aged as 'Holy Russia', equally spiritual and conservative with India—swung to the extreme of secularism.

The Muslim community was long depressed by its economic inferiority, and by the belief amongst Europeans that it had been the mainspring of the Mutiny. But Indian Islam has rich traditions and has been built up by centuries of courage. Its awakening, when it came, showed that these finer qualities were still present. Saiyid Ahmad Khan accomplished for Muhammadanism a task not unlike that which the Brahmo Samaj did for Hinduism. His favourite statement was that 'Reason alone is a sufficient guide', and he was determined that his community should be laid open to the influences which invigorated the Western world. In 1876 he founded the Muslim University of Aligarh, and ten years later the Muhammadan Educational Conference, which still meets annually. His modernist views about the Quran brought him much unpopularity, but, owing possibly to the weaker influence of nationalism amongst his community, his work has survived better than that of the early Brahmo leaders. Saiyid Amir Ali and Mr. S. Khuda Buksh are his spiritual descendants, and the community is fortunate in the number of its centres of culture. In Peshawar, Lahore, Delhi, Agra, Allahabad, Haidarabad, as well as Aligarh, it has scholars and writers whose appeal goes far beyond provincial borders; critics as catholic and sane as Sir Abdul Qadr, novelists as stirring as Abdul Halim Sharar,[1] poets like Saiyid Reza Ali Wahshat, Shabir Hasan Khan Josh, and above all Sir Muhammad Iqbal.

Indian Islam, after a long period of disillusionment, is growing realist at last. For the rebuilding of its strength it looks towards those countries, Turkey, Persia, and Afghanistan, which have remained Muhammadan and independent. Above all it has been moved by the example of Turkey.

' The truth is that among the Muslim nations of to-day Turkey alone has shaken off its dogmatic slumber, and attained to self-consciousness. She

[1] Died in 1926.

alone has claimed the right of intellectual freedom; she alone has passed from the ideal to the real.'[1]

This last phrase deliberately echoes (and traverses) a famous prayer in the *Upanishads* of Sir Muhammad Iqbal's ancestors. Afghanistan is in closer touch with Indian Islam than ever before in British-Indian history, and is seeking the co-operation of the latter's leaders in bringing her people into the modern age. The vision which these leaders are cherishing and spreading is not one of gradual unexciting approximation, along the lines of the White Paper, to democracy of the established English pattern. They may desire a 'steel framework', but not one made of a civil service on an alien model.

During the last century neither the ruling Princes nor the great landlords have done much for Indian progress. Certain individual States are exceptions, and in some instances—notably Mysore, Baroda, and Travancore—are ahead of British India. The foreigner sceptical of Indian advance, and believing in the 'unchanging East' should spend some days at Baroda, a city of wide streets and amenities. It is true that Baroda is exceptionally lucky in its soil, and that the capital has been enriched far beyond anything done outside it, but its libraries, reading rooms, picture galleries are influences reaching out irrespective of caste and religion, and increasingly touching a whole people. Best of all, the Gaekwar has been happy in finding servants to whom this educational work is a vocation and delight. Although 'Indian India' remains a backward patch, the Round Table Conference confirmed the general impression that some of the ablest Indian administrators are to be found in the States, where federation should encourage the growth of an enlightened Indian bureaucracy even if it does not lead to the extension of democracy. We believe that, no matter what the Paramount Power may 'guarantee' to Indian Princes of their former status and unimpaired authority, they must come to terms with the majority, as nobles did in mediaeval Europe and the Samurai in Japan; and it is obvious that they know this themselves.

The Federation will depend primarily on these three main groups, the Princes and their advisers, the educated Hindus, and the educated Muslims. But minorities such as the Europeans, the Sikhs and the Parsis will have considerable influence because these communities are comparatively united and intelligent. Prophecy is not the historian's business. But a forward glance of surmise and interrogation cannot be

[1] Mohammad Iqbal, *The Reconstruction of Religious Thought in India*, 154.

altogether avoided. The White Paper possibly represents the greatest measure of agreement amongst politicians of both races and both schools of thought, the 'Imperialist' and the 'Nationalist'. Neither extremist wing, British or Indian, has produced an alternative measure which offers any prospect but that of renewed exacerbation. Its production, however, took time, and slow cautious thought and bargaining, while the political progress of country after country, other than India, has been marked by volcanic explosions. The face of affairs throughout the world has shifted so quickly that the Federation already wears an obsolete appearance, as being based on a system of compromise, of check and counter-check, and the preservation of native governments medi-aeval in their main characteristics. Neither Hindu nor Muslim India is looking too closely towards it. Those Indian politicians who might have been expected to work it are men advanced in years, and with little following though of great ability and reputation.

Young India, like Young Everywhere, is moving away from politics of a constitutional kind. We cannot expect India to be exempt from tendencies that are growing even in our own land. In some respects the reaction against the excessive optimism of the nineteenth-century nationalism may be a healthy symptom. We may expect a vigorous provincial life, with threats of secession if the central Government is too expensive or too domineering. Already such slogans as 'Bengal for the Bengalis' have made themselves heard, and the effect of the new constitution will be to leave the more interesting 'nation-building' subjects to the provincial legislatures. The greatest immediate danger is that the long period of internal peace under British rule has induced the belief that there will always be an outside authority ready to restore order, while the politician, unable to redeem his pledges, will be tempted to raise constitutional questions and revive racial or religious animosities. Ireland and Germany bear witness to the ease with which both can be done on very slender grounds.

The position, therefore, at the end of a century and a half of British rule, can at best give grounds for a guarded optimism about the future of the Indian race. Its economic difficulties remain unsolved and possibly insoluble. The villager is still prevented by traditional and religious inhibitions from making the best of his limited resources. The vast majority of townsmen and industrial workers live in abject squalor. Socially the people are still divided into strictly segregated groups, with no intermarriage and little ordinary intercourse. 'When inter-marriage is out of the question social equality cannot exist; without social equality political equality is impossible.'[1] It must be doubtful whether a rigid Federation can long survive without great economic and social changes which would normally precede rather than follow the establishment of such an immense democratic organisation. For a period the British connection, the great bureaucratic machine, and the presence of British troops will combine to prevent fresh patterns being shaken in the Indian kaleidoscope; but events in other parts of the Empire show that once England has given up complete and direct responsibility for a territory there is little urge to interfere in subsequent developments. Possibly the future will see a number of almost autonomous units, based roughly on the existing Provinces and larger States, but each developing along its own lines, and merely sacrificing a measure of its sovereignty to a body like a miniature League of Nations.

Whatever the future may hold, the direct influence of the West upon India is likely to decrease. But it would be absurd to imagine that the British connection will not leave a permanent mark upon Indian life. On the merely material side the new Federal Government will take over the largest irrigation system in the world, with thousands of miles of canals and water-cuts fertilising between thirty and forty million acres; some 60,000 miles of metalled roads; over 42,000 miles of railway, of which three-quarters are State-owned; 230,000 scholastic institutions with over twelve million scholars; and a great number of buildings, including government offices, inspection bungalows, provincial and central legislatures. The vast area of India has been completely surveyed, most of its land assessed, and a regular census taken of its population and its productivity. An effective defensive system has been built up on its vulnerable North-West frontier, it has an Indian army with century-old traditions, and a police force which compares favourably with any outside a few Western countries. The postal department handles nearly 1500 million articles yearly, the Forestry Department not only prevents the denudation of immense areas, but makes a net profit of between two and three crores. These great State activities are managed by a trained bureaucracy, which is to-day almost entirely Indian.

The spiritual heritage is far more difficult to estimate, and for many years most people will have their judgment warped by the racial animosities of the last half-century. How much of the common language

[1] Goldwin Smith's *Commonwealth or Empire*. For the Indian position see a recent pamphlet by K. M. Panikkar on *Caste and Democracy*.

and common culture which we have introduced will survive under the new constitution? Will the three per cent. of 'English educated' Indians cling to their knowledge when the present racial animosity has become less acute, and will a happier relationship begin when English administrators go East only at Indian invitation? Many special virtues, as well as failings, went to the building up of the British Empire and its retention by a minute force. A high sense of duty, incorruptibility, a passion for improving, a recognition of social responsibility, these may be remembered and be better appreciated when the friction due to disputed authority, economic grievances, and social differences has been forgotten.

A bewildering host of facts beset the historian; yet we may conclude our story of storm-ravaged years with an expression of hope. We live in a world where the gallows and shooting file have again become political arguments; and we reflect that no controversy has been more miraculously preserved from irreconcilability than this one between England and India. We have criticised Mr. Gandhi as politician. But he will be remembered as one of the few who have set the stamp of an *idea* on an epoch. The idea is 'non-violence' which has drawn out powerfully the sympathy of other lands, and has also set a reciprocal quality on the Government's 'repression'. The struggle in India has been accompanied by bloodshed and savagery. Yet, when all has been said by the extreme protagonists of both sides, its conduct justifies a guarded belief that its outcome may be a sane and civilized relationship between the two countries.

The moral and social prestige lost to the West by the War can never be recovered, but there is no reason why a far healthier relationship should not develop, and the great sub-continent of India form part of a noble comity of nations within the British Commonwealth. It is in this belief that this book has been written. We cannot expect it to 'be anything but unacceptable to those who do not believe in the proximity of a deluge or the necessity of an ark. We address ourselves, therefore, to those who believe in both, for the simple reason that they are already afloat'.[1]

[1] George Tyrrell, *Through Scylla and Charybdis*. We have changed the 'I' to 'we'.

APPENDIX A

ECONOMIC THEORIES OF THE EARLY PERIOD OF COMPANY ADMINISTRATION

WE shall be unfair to our forefathers if we do not understand the economic and political theories which they inherited and lived with. The Duke of Wellington, during his brother's governor-generalship, weighed the pros and cons of the current financial policy with characteristic care,[1] and concludes:

' If the question were, whether the people of Bengal would not be more happy and comfortable if they did not pay more revenue than is necessary to defray the expenses of their establishment, there could be no doubt upon the subject; and if their own comfort were alone to be considered, the surplus revenue ought to be remitted to them as soon as possible. But, as I shall show hereafter, Great Britain has a right to expect this tribute from them; it is impossible to devise means by which a revenue can be drawn from a people so little to their injury, as that which Great Britain draws is injurious to the natives of Bengal.

' If specie were not essentially necessary for all the purposes of commerce, and if a drain to the amount of the surplus above stated would not be felt severely in all transactions of barter and exchange in the country, there would be no harm in sending this revenue home in money. . . . As the case stands at present, there is a large revenue raised from this people: it is spent in the first instance in defending them, and in paying the usual expenses of government; in the next, in paying the expenses of their dependencies, which may be called their defence; in the third, in paying the interest of debts contracted for their defence and security; and in the fourth, in a tribute to Great Britain. The three last may be stated to be laid out in the country in encouragement of agriculture and manufactures. Supposing the sums laid out for the support of Madras, Bombay, &c., for the interest of debts, or for the tribute, were remitted in the revenue, and that the tenantry still continue to pay the same sums as at present, which is more than probable, it is doubted whether the proprietors of land, into whose hands they would go, would encourage the agriculture and manufactures of the country to the degree that they are at present encouraged by the present application of the revenue; and in that case if the demand for the produce of Bengal, upon the coast, &c., and in England were to cease, the country would indeed be in a ruinous condition.

[1] Sidney Owen, *Despatches of the Duke of Wellington*, 498-50.

656

'Therefore, upon the whole, although the peasants may complain of the amount of what they pay, and that so little is left to them, they have no reason to complain of the manner in which what is taken from them is applied. There is another question upon this part of the subject which has been treated with a considerable degree of asperity in the "Remarks"; it is whether it is just or right for Great Britain to take any tribute whatever from Bengal? The first question ought to be, whether it is just or right for one country to conquer another? . . . After a conquest has been made, and the Government is in the possession of the conqueror, it is said in the "Remarks" he has no right to any advantage but the Government. That would be true in some instances, but otherwise in many others.'

He goes on to argue that Britain had not gained a better frontier, a monopoly of trade, or men or provisions for her fleet and army.

'Therefore I conclude, that in return for the protection which that country undoubtedly receives, Great Britain has some right to expect remuneration. In fact, all conquered countries give the conquerors an advantage in some point of view; and Bengal gives none to Great Britain, excepting in tribute, which therefore, the latter ought to take.'

APPENDIX B

OPINIONS OF SIR THOMAS MUNRO AND OTHERS ON PRE-MUTINY ADMINISTRATIVE PERSONNEL

SIR THOMAS MUNRO'S views are too important for the historian to omit any fair chance of calling attention to them; but they merit such extensive quotation that we do it here, rather than break up the main narrative further than it is already broken up by contemporary quotations. In 1817 Munro sent Lord Hastings long minutes[1] pleading against the now settled policy of granting no employment but the most mechanical and trivial to even the ablest Indians. To the *cliché* that Orientals were 'too corrupt to be trusted', he retorted:

'This is an old objection, and one which is generally applicable, in similar circumstances, to the natives of every country. Nobody has ever supposed that the subordinate officers of the Excise and Customs in England are remarkable for their purity. But we need not go home for examples. The Company's servants were notoriously known to make their fortunes in partnership with native agents, until Lord Cornwallis thought it advisable to purchase their integrity by raising their allowances. Let this be done with regard

[1] Gleig, *Life of Sir Thomas Munro*, 269-85, *passim*.

2 T

to the natives, and the effect will be similar, though not perhaps in a similar degree; for we cannot expect to find in a nation fallen under a foreign dominion the same pride and high principle as among a free people; but I am persuaded that we shall meet with a greater share of integrity and talent than we are aware of. While we persist in withholding liberal salaries from the natives, we shall have the services of the worst part of them. . . .'

' Foreign conquerors have treated the natives with violence, and often with great cruelty, but none has treated them with so much scorn as we; none have stigmatized the whole people as unworthy of trust, as incapable of honesty, and as fit to be employed only where we cannot do without them. It seems to be not only ungenerous, but impolitic, to debase the character of a people fallen under our dominion. . . .'

' The strength of the British Government enables it to put down every rebellion, to repel every foreign invasion, and to give to its subjects a degree of protection which those of no Native power enjoy. Its laws and institutions also afford them a security from domestic oppression, unknown in those states; but these advantages are dearly bought. They are purchased by the sacrifice of independence, of national character, and of whatever renders a people respectable. The Natives of the British provinces may, without fear, pursue their different occupations . . . and enjoy the fruits of their labour in tranquillity; but none of them can aspire to anything beyond this mere animal state of thriving in peace. . . . none of them can look forward to any share in the legislation or civil or military government of their country. . . . The effect of this state of things is observable in all the British provinces, whose inhabitants are certainly the most abject race in India. No elevation of character can be expected among men who, in the military line, cannot attain to any rank above that of subahdar, where they are as much below an ensign as an ensign is below the commander-in-chief, and who, in the civil line, can hope for nothing beyond some petty judicial or revenue office, in which they may, by corrupt means, make up for their slender salary.

' The consequence, therefore, of the conquest of India by the British arms would be, in place of raising, to debase the whole people. There is perhaps no example of any conquest in which the Natives have been so completely excluded from all share of the government of their country as in British India.

' Among all the disorders of the Native states, the field is open for every man to raise himself; and hence among them there is a spirit of emulation, of restless enterprise and independence, far preferable to the servility of our Indian subjects. The existence of independent Native states is also useful in drawing off the turbulent and disaffected among our Native troops.'

' Their exclusion from offices of trust and emolument has become a part of our system of government, and has been productive of no good. Whenever, from this cause, the public business falls into arrear, it is said to be owing to the want of a sufficient number of Europeans; and more European agency is recommended as a cure for every evil. Such agency is too expensive; and, even if it was not, it ought to be abridged rather than enlarged, because it is, in many cases, much less efficient than that of the natives. For the discharge

of all subordinate duties, but especially in the judicial line, the natives are infinitely better qualified than Europeans. I have never seen any European whom I thought competent, from his knowledge of the language and the people, to ascertain the value of the evidence given before him. The proceedings in our courts of judicature, which in our reports make a grave and respectable appearance, are, I know, frequently the subject of derision among the natives.' [1]

' In all original suits they are much fitter to investigate the merits than Europeans. The European judges should be confined almost entirely to the business of appeals. In criminal cases the fact should be found by a native jury, who are much more competent than either the European judge or his officers to weigh the nature of the evidence. . . .' [1]

Sir John Malcolm, politically a rigid Conservative with a horror of 'radical' tenets, equally deplored the exclusion of the inhabitants of the country from their own government. He writes to a friend (1829):

' I regret as deeply as you, or any man, can, that there is no opening for natives. The system of depression becomes more alarming as our power extends . . . we must, or we cannot last, contrive to associate the natives with us in the task of rule, and in the benefits and gratifications which accrue from it.' [2]

As the opinions of Elphinstone, Sleeman and other distinguished civilians and soldiers have been made sufficiently plain in the text, we conclude with Bishop Heber's evidence of the unhappy contrast between people who had some say in their own administration and those who were mere subjects for the exercise of power, however beneficent. In a letter (1826) he says:

' In Bengal, where, independent of its exuberant fertility, there is a permanent assessment, famine is unknown. In Hindustan, on the other hand, I found a general feeling among the king's officers, and I myself was led, from some circumstances, to agree with them, that the peasantry in the Company's provinces are, on the whole, worse off, poorer, and more dispirited, than the subjects of the native Princes; and here, in Madras, where the soil is, generally speaking, poor, the difference is said to be still more marked.'

[1] *Op. cit.* 269-70 (to Governor-General, November 12, 1818).

[2] Kaye, *Life of Malcolm*, ii. 392-3.

APPENDIX C

MACAULAY'S MINUTE ON EDUCATION, 1834

'NEITHER diffident nor inactive',[1] Macaulay possessed unique advantages for the battle between Westerners and Orientals, and almost instantaneously drove his foes pell-mell and seized all the spoils: he was profoundly ignorant of the other case (always an advantage, joined to decisiveness such as his), he saw clearly and entertained no shadow of misgiving as to his own rightness, and he had an almost unequalled knack of guessing, if not the whole truth, at any rate a large and essential part. His *Minute* conveys its own gusto; it was obviously intensely enjoyable in the writing, and is very good fun to read:

' . . . It is argued, or rather taken for granted, that by literature the Parliament can have meant only Arabic and Sanscrit literature, that they never would have given the honourable appellation of "a learned native" to a native who was familiar with the poetry of Milton, the metaphysics of Locke, and the physics of Newton; but that they meant to designate by that name only such persons as might have studied in the sacred books of the Hindus all the uses of kusa-grass and all the mysteries of absorption into the Deity. This does not appear to be a very satisfactory interpretation. To take a parallel case; suppose that the Pasha of Egypt . . . were to appropriate a sum for the purpose of "reviving and promoting literature and encouraging learned natives of Egypt", would anybody infer that he meant the youth of his Pashalic to give years to the study of hieroglyphics, to search into all the doctrines disguised under the fable of Osiris, and to ascertain with all possible accuracy the ritual with which cats and onions were anciently adored? . . .

' The admirers of the Oriental system of education . . . conceive that the public faith is pledged to the present system, and that to alter the appropriation of any of the funds which have hitherto been spent in encouraging the study of Arabic and Sanskrit would be downright spoliation. It is not easy to understand by what process of reasoning they have arrived at this conclusion. . . . We found a sanatorium on a spot which we suppose to be healthy. Do we thereby pledge ourselves to keep a sanatorium there if the result should not answer our expectations? We commence the erection of a pier. Is it a violation of the public faith to stop the works if we afterwards see reason to believe that the building will be useless?'—

arguments which with trivial change we hear to-day, against the protest that to set back political progress in India, after the repeated promises of pushing it to full freedom, would be a breach of faith. It sometimes

[1] Boulger, *Lord William Bentinck*, 151.

seems as if no human controversy has so little changed as the Indian one. Macaulay says disarmingly:

' I have no knowledge of either Sanscrit or Arabic. But I have done what I could to form a correct estimate of their value. I have read translations of the most celebrated Arabic and Sanscrit works. . . . I am quite ready to take the Oriental learning at the valuation of the Orientalists themselves. I have never found one among them who could deny that a single shelf of a good European library was worth the whole native literature of India and Arabia . . . when we pass from works of imagination to works in which facts are recorded and general principles investigated the superiority of the Europeans becomes absolutely immeasurable. It is, I believe, no exaggeration to say that all the historical information which has been collected from all the books written in the Sanscrit language is less valuable than what may be found in the most paltry abridgments used at preparatory schools in England. . . .

' In India, English is the language spoken by the ruling class. It is spoken by the higher class of natives at the seats of Government. It is likely to become the language of commerce throughout the seas of the East. It is the language of two great European communities which are rising, the one in the south of Africa, the other in Australasia; communities which are every year becoming more important and more closely connected with our Indian Empire. . . .

' The question now before us is simply whether, when it is in our power to teach this language, we shall teach languages in which by universal confession there are no books on any subject which deserve to be compared to our own; whether, when we can teach European science, we shall teach systems which by universal confession whenever they differ from those of Europe differ for the worse; and whether, when we can patronise sound philosophy and true history, we shall countenance at the public expense medical doctrines which would disgrace an English farrier, astronomy which would move laughter in girls at an English boarding-school, history abounding with kings thirty feet high and reigns 30,000 years long, and geography made up of seas of treacle and seas of butter. . . .'

As for the argument that Sanscrit and Arabic are the languages of sacred literature, 'on that account entitled to peculiar encouragement', he exclaims:

' It is confessed that a language is barren of useful knowledge. We are to teach it because it is fruitful of monstrous superstitions. We are to teach false history, false astronomy, false medicine, because we find them in company with a false religion. We abstain, and I trust shall always abstain, from giving any public encouragement to those who are engaged in the work of converting natives to Christianity. And while we act thus can we reasonably and decently bribe men out of the revenues of the state to waste their youth in learning how they are to purify themselves after touching an ass, or what text of the Vedas they are to repeat to expiate the crime of killing a goat? . . .'

By the Resolution of March 7, 1835, English became the official language of British India.

It is usual to-day to pour scorn on all that Macaulay said or thought, a mistake never made by those actually familiar with his writings. If we sift out exaggerations and misunderstandings, sound fact underlay his vigorous certainty. Moreover, Indians themselves were clamouring to be taught English, and given modern Western knowledge.

The policy for which Macaulay, Metcalfe and Bentinck were responsible has not been the sweeping failure so often casually alleged. 'Babu English' does not exhaust its field of achievement. Indian mastery of our difficult and intricate tongue has been perfect in such a multitude, that the world's whole history can show no parallel conquest. And the system of education has imparted a wide culture to a painstaking and intelligent people, as well as easily-parodied absurdities and stupidities. Indians have learnt to think our thoughts, to see with our eyes, and to express themselves with a nervous and sensitive exactness and beauty which have made them free citizens of the kingdom of English thought and expression, fellow-citizens with ourselves and not strangers inhabiting it on sufferance and temporary licence.

APPENDIX D

POPULATION (IN MILLIONS) SINCE 1872

Year of Census	Total Population	Apparent Increase	Due to New Areas	Due to New Methods	Real Increase	Rate per cent. Real Increase
1872	206·1	—	—	—	—	—
1881	253·8	47·7	33	11·7	3	1·5
1891	287·3	33·5	5·7	3·8	24·3	9·6
1901	294·3	7	2·7	·2	4·1	1·4
1911	315·0	20·7	1·8	—	18·9	6·4
1921	318·8	3·8	·1	—	3·7	1·2
1931	352·8	34	—	—	34	10·6

Real increase since 1881 is approximately 85 million, on a population of about 263 million (allowing for areas added since that date). This is at the rate of about 32 per cent.

APPENDIX E

RELIGIOUS CENSUS IN 1931

(Figures given in millions)

	Hindus	Muslims	Buddhists	Christians	Sikhs	Tribal and other Creeds
BRITISH INDIA -	177·7	67	12·7	3·9	3·2	16·8
INDIAN STATES -	61·5	10·7	·1	2·4	1·1	5·5
Major Provinces						
Bengal - -	21·6	27·5	·3	·2	—	·3
Bihar and Orissa	31	4·2	—	·3	—	2
Bombay -	16·6	4·5	—	·3	—	·5
Burma - -	·6	·6	12·3	·3	—	·7
Central Provinces	13·3	·7	—	—	—	1·4
Madras - -	41·3	3·3	—	1·7	—	·4
Punjab - -	6·3	13·3	—	·4	3·1	·4
United Provinces	40·9	7·2	—	·2	—	·1
Assam - -	4·9	2·8	—	·2	—	·7
N.W. Frontier Prov.	·1	2·2	—	—	—	—

PROPOSED COMPOSITION OF FEDERAL ASSEMBLY AND PROVINCIAL LEGISLATURE.

(The 'Communal Award', White Paper, Cmd. 4268.)

	Total	General (Hindu)	General (Reserved for Depressed Classes)	Muslim	European and Anglo-Indians	*Other Religions	†Special Seats
Federal Assembly (British India) -	250	86	19	82	12	14	37
Provincial Legislatures							
Bengal - -	250	50	30	119	15	2	34
Bombay - -	175	104	15	30	5	4	17
U.P. - -	228	124	20	66	3	2	13
Madras - -	215	122	30	29	5	10	19
Punjab - -	175	35	8	86	2	34	10
Bihar - -	152	74	15	40	3	8	12
C.P. - -	112	67	20	14	2	1	8
Assam - -	108	41	7	34	1	10	15
‡Sind - -	60	19	—	34	2	—	5
N.W. Frontier	50	9	—	36	—	3	2
‡Orissa - -	60	42	7	4	—	3	4

*Other Religions includes seats for Sikhs, Indian Christians, and representatives of the backward areas.

†Special Seats includes those reserved for Labour, Landholders, Commerce, etc.

‡These are to become separate Provinces.

BIBLIOGRAPHICAL NOTE

[This note is intended for the general reader. The student may be referred to the classified lists of books, occupying scores of pages, in the later volumes of the Cambridge History of India.]

FOR the earliest period consult the *Minutes and Despatches of the East India Company*, edited by Sir George Birdwood, P. Sainsbury, Ethel Sainsbury and Sir William Foster. These run to many volumes, and are still incomplete. Early travels, Herbert's, Sir Thomas Roe's, and others', are edited by Foster. It may be said once for all that anything edited by him should be read, and that the editing is as near perfection as we are likely to get. Ralph Fitch's story is retold in Foster's *England's Quest of Eastern Trade*, R. C. Locke's *The First Englishmen in India*, and J. H. Ryley's *Ralph Fitch, England's Pioneer to India and Burma*. Colonel H. D. Love's *Vestiges of Old Madras* is valuable. Some early voyages and records are in Hakluyt.

Of general histories of British India, those written a century or more ago are, with hardly an exception, franker, fuller, and more interesting than those of the last fifty years. In days when no one dreamed that anyone would ever be seditious enough to ask really fundamental questions (such as 'What right have you to be in India at all?'), and when no one ever thought of any public but a British one, criticism was lively and well informed, and judgment was passed without regard to political exigencies. Of late years, increasingly and no doubt naturally, all Indian questions have tended to be approached from the standpoint of administration: 'Will this make for easier and quieter government?' The writer of to-day inevitably has a world outside his own people, listening intently and as touchy as his own people, as swift to take offence. 'He that is not for us is against us'. This knowledge of an overhearing, even eavesdropping public, of being *in partibus infidelium*, exercises a constant silent censorship, which has made British-Indian history the worst patch in current scholarship. Orme, Elphinstone, Montgomery Martin, Marshman, Thornton, Keene, Beveridge, Mill and Wilson, and most of the earlier historians of separate episodes, are vivacious reading, and kept the subject alive. There are four recent standard histories, Vincent Smith's *Oxford History of India*, the several-volumed *Cambridge History of India*, Mr. P. E. Roberts's *History of British India*, Professor H. H. Dodwell's *British India*. The second of these includes work by some contributors whose record ensures that it will be good; and Mr. Roberts's volume is far superior to the *Oxford History*, as also is Professor Dodwell's.

For the end of the seventeenth century and early part of the eighteenth, there are some first-rate authorities: *Keigwin's Rebellion*, by Ray and Oliver

665

Strachey, a lively and excellent little book; the *Diary of William Hedges*, edited by Sir Henry Yule; Captain Alexander Hamilton's *New View of the Indies*, edited by Sir William Foster; E. R. Wilson's *Early Annals of the English in Bengal* (an account of Surman's embassy). These all merit the highest praise, for matter, manner and editing. See also Professor H. G. Rawlinson's books on the Marathas. From the Indian side, the student now has *English Records of Sivaji* (Poona), and Dr. Surendranath Sen's admirable studies of the Marathas. As we get on in the eighteenth century, these are reinforced by the *Diary of Ananda Ranga Pillai* (12 volumes, edited by Sir J. F. Price and H. Dodwell), and the *Seir-ul-Mutaquerin* of Ghulam Husain Khan, in Sir H. M. Elliot and J. Dowson's *History of India as told by its own Historians*. J. Talboys Wheeler's *Madras in the Olden Time* can be consulted; and for Bombay, Malabari, Masani, Shafaat Ahmad Khan.

From the beginning of the Anglo-French wars there is an abundance of first-hand evidence. Orme's *Transactions* is the chief one, but may be supplemented by Clement Downing, R. O. Cambridge, Surgeon Edward Ives's book on the siege of Calcutta, Colonel Wilks on the South Indian wars, etc. Professor Dodwell's *Dupleix and Clive* is a good study. See H. E. Busteed's *Echoes from Old Calcutta*. The India Office Library, the Madras Record Office, the Admiralty and War Office Records, the *Archives de Pondichéry* and *Archives du Ministère Colonial* (Paris) contain much unpublished matter, to which may be added such printed English records as *The Records of Fort St. George, Military Consultations*, 1752-56, *The Siege Diary*, 1757-9. The available material is almost endless, and is still increasing.

There is a continuous stream of pamphleteering on trade and political questions, all along from the Company's foundation. In the late eighteenth century this is changed to one of almost solely political controversy. Everything to Clive's discredit (including much that is invented) may be found in Charles Caraccioli's *Life* (London, 1775, 1777), inspired by the officers disgruntled by his handling of their mutiny; Caraccioli does not even allow Clive courage or the slightest ability, which greatly detracts from his plausibility when he is right. For nearly a century pamphlets flew to and fro, often bearing names prominently attacked in the cause which they were defending, such as those of Bolts, Verelst, Vansittart. We begin to get memoirs also— Mrs. Fay, William Hodges, etc. Selections from the official despatches of Clive and Warren Hastings have been edited by Sir George Forrest.

There is no good full-dress *Life* of any Indian statesman or soldier of the front rank. Of shorter *Lives*, those in the series 'Rulers of India' are often good. Of longer *Lives*, Gleig's *Warren Hastings* is almost unreadable; Sir George Forrest's *Clive* is badly arranged. For the controversies centring on Hastings's actions the reader may be referred to Sir James Stephen, Sir John Strachey, H. Beveridge, Burke and Macaulay. For Hastings's impeachment, see the contemporary full report published by Debrett. The *Oxford History* is almost uniformly unsatisfactory on Hastings; Miss 'Sydney Grier' is a special pleader but informing; Mr. P. E. Roberts is good.

For the wars with Tipu the best authorities are Wilks's *History of Mysoor*;

and for Cornwallis's campaign A. Dirom (*Narrative of the Campaign*), and for the last campaign A. Beatson's *View of the Origin and Conduct of the War with Tippoo Sultaun*. Mr. Roberts's *India under Wellesley* is an example of the kind of book that is badly needed on each of the Governors-General of first importance. The best authority for the Marathas is Grant-Duff's *History*. We now get very valuable material in individual biographies: those of Elphinstone, Munro, Malcolm, presently of Metcalfe. Malcolm's own writings should be noted. The correspondence of most Governors-General has been published; for example, that of Cornwallis and Shore. Wellesley's despatches, edited by Montgomery Martin, and the Duke of Wellington's, edited by S. J. Owen (see also J. Gurwood's eight-volume edition), are full and illuminating. The Duke is an extremely 'seditious' writer (by recent standards) and illustrates what we have said about the greater freedom which the earlier writers allowed themselves. For Minto, read *Lord Minto in India* and *Life and Letters*, 1751-1806, 3 volumes, both edited by his grand-niece the Countess of Minto. See Sir C. P. Ilbert, *The Government of India*. For Lord Hastings, see his *Private Journal*, a book of high value as literature and deserving of reprint; H. T. Prinsep's *History of the Political and Military Transactions in India during the Administration of the Marquess of Hastings*, and Colonel Blacker's account of the Maratha War; also, the biographies of the leading soldiers and statesmen of the period, freely cited in our text. Material on the next two Governors-General is very scanty. We need full *Lives* of both Lord Amherst and Lord William Cavendish-Bentinck; it is a pity that Lady Amherst's journal has not been printed. See Bishop Heber's *Narrative of a Journey*. Sir W. H. Sleeman's *Rambles and Recollections* and Meadows Taylor's *Confessions of a Thug*, and General Campbell's privately printed *Narrative* of his work in suppressing *Human Sacrifices and Female Infanticide*, supply the background of Bentinck's reforms; perhaps we may be permitted to refer to *Suttee* (Edward Thompson), as there is no other book dealing with the subject. Peggs's *India's Cries to British Humanity* is a sufficiently appalling indictment to make the reader willing to overlook a great many of the Company's sins. Such journals as *The Calcutta Review* now become important. From now on, biographies of great missionaries (Carey, Duff) should not be neglected. See Miss Collett's books on Rammohan Roy and Keshab Sen. For Lord Auckland and the First Afghan War, see Miss Eden's books, especially *Up the Country* (latest edition, Oxford University Press), Sir H. M. Durand's *The First Afghan War and its Causes*, Havelock's *Narrative*, and especially J. W. Kaye's *History of the War in Afghanistan*. Kaye, like Colonel Wilks on Mysore, is an admirable writer, excellent reading and excellent history. It is a pity that he is often confused with Colonel Malleson, who completed his *History of the Sepoy War*, for the difference in their quality is immense. Lady Sale's book is a grim little commentary, vividly preserving the suffering and passionate longing for vengeance of the period. Lieutenant Vincent Eyre's book is another good contemporary witness. Lord Colchester's *History of the Indian Administration of Lord Ellenborough*, a Governor-General very meagerly represented in publications, gives official letters only. The reader may care to compare the two blue-books on the Afghan War, that issued in 1839 and that issued (after Kaye had exposed its garbled character) in 1859. For the Sind campaign and pacification, see Sir William Napier's *The Conquest of Scinde* and *History of Sir Charles Napier's Administration of Scinde*; also his *Life* of his brother. Outram's *Rough Notes on the Campaign in Sinde and Afghanistan in 1838-9* is a dry little book. See a blue-book, *Correspondence relative to Sinde*, 1838-43. The Sikh Wars called out a mass of contemporary matter: J. D. Cunningham's *History of the Sikhs*, memoirs by the two adventurers Honigberger and Steinbach, narratives by soldiers who took part in the operations. There are some valuable books by travellers; e.g. by Drew and Vigne. For Ranjit Singh, see Sir Lepel Griffin's little book, and the Hon. W. Osborne's *The Court and Camp of Runjeet Singh*, as well as the books already mentioned. See also Major S. Carmichael Smyth's *History of the Reigning Family of Lahore* (1847), Syad Muhammad Latif's *History of the Panjab*, W. M'Gregor's *History of the Sikhs*. See the official biographies of Lord Gough, Herbert Edwardes, John and Henry Lawrence, and others. Few important figures on the British side, from this time onwards, are unrepresented by either autobiographical matter or *Lives* after their death. See J. A. Baird's *Private Letters of the Marquess of Dalhousie*, Sir Edwin Arnold's *Marquis of Dalhousie's Administration*, and Sir W. Lee Warner's *Life of the Marquess of Dalhousie*. For the Raja of Satara, see Major Basu's book, and *Debates at the India House on the Case of the Deposed Raja of Sattara and the Impeachment of Col. C. Ovans (of the East India Company)*, 1845; there is a good deal of other material on this episode.

The Mutiny called forth a flood of controversy and, still more, printed reminiscences, to an extent that can hardly ever have been approached. Kaye and Malleson's book is still the best general history. Books that for one reason or another stand out are Cooper's *The Crisis in the Punjab*, W. H. Russell's *My Diary in India*, G. O. Trevelyan's *Cawnpore*, Forbes-Mitchell's *Reminiscences*. This literature is enormous; and it can be supplemented by biographies, which exist of all the great soldiers who either won fame now or began careers which led to fame hereafter.

The post-Mutiny literature is mostly reflective or explanatory, and not so largely narrative as the literature dealing with the exciting events which resulted in the full establishment of British rule everywhere. We now get abundant autobiographical material, the practice having become usual of writing your reminiscences after retirement, even if you had done little beyond big game shooting. Most of these books, however, contain something of historical value, and a considerable proportion justify their publication. Official documents now keep a high standard; gazetteers, reports, are often excellent, though their authors had no thought of producing literature. For an example, see Colonel W. F. Eden's *Report on the Political Administration of Rajputana*, 1865-1867. There are biographies of many Indian rulers and statesmen. Indians begin to produce books of reminiscences, some of which are available in English. There is a *Life* of Michaelmadhusudhan Datta, the originator of modern Bengali poetry and drama, which is partly in English. Very good books, which have had a wide Western circulation, are the *Autobiography* of the 'Maharshi' (Debendranath Tagore, the poet's father), and Rabindranath Tagore's *Reminiscences.* There are *Lives* of all post-Mutiny Governors-General, and some of these, as those of the twentieth century Lord Minto and of Lord Curzon, are by recognised living men of letters (John Buchan and Lord Zetland).

Some Viceroys, like Lord Dufferin and Ava, have themselves written on Indian affairs, and Lord Curzon's monumental *British Government in India* contains much information difficult to obtain elsewhere. Lord Lytton's curious mentality is laid bare in Lady Betty Balfour's edition of his letters. Colonel H. B. Hanna's *Second Afghan War* and Abdur Rahman's *Autobiography* can be read in connection with that period. As we come to our own time, politicians, soldiers, and officials have produced a mass of polemical literature, partly apologetic and partly autobiographical. Such are Lord Roberts's *Forty-One Years in India*, Sir Surendranath Banerjea's *A Nation in the Making*, Edwin Montagu's *An Indian Diary*, published posthumously, Sir M. O'Dwyer's *India as I knew it*, Tilak's Writings and Speeches, M. K. Gandhi's various autobiographical volumes, and Mrs. Besant's *India, Bond or Free.* Two distinguished journalists, Lovat Fraser and Sir V. Chirol, wrote admirably of India just before and after the last War.[1] Since their time the flood of political and journalistic works has been unceasing. D. Graham Pole's *India in Transition* and J. Coatman's *Years of Destiny* give a consecutive narrative of post-war history.

The best side of British administration appears in the semi-technical studies written by officials, usually with an impartiality and knowledge which make it regrettable that their books appeal to so small a public. Such were the works of Sir William Hunter, Sir Alfred Lyall, and Sir Richard Temple in the era after the Mutiny. A generation later S. S. Thorburn's *Mussulmans and Money-lenders in the Punjab* and *The Punjab in Peace and War* reflect the independence and sound sense of their author. Important administrative studies of agriculture and village life have appeared during the last thirty years. G. Keatinge's *Rural Economy in the Bombay Deccan*, H. H. Mann's *Land and Labour in a Deccan Village*, J. C. Jack's *The Economic Life of a Bengal District*, M. L. Darling's *The Punjab Peasant* and *Rusticus Loquitur*, while F. L. Brayne has explained the Gurgaon experiment in *Village Uplift in India*, and *Socrates in an Indian Village*. Other sides of the administration are dealt with in Mr. Mayhew's admirable *The Education of India*, and L. S. O'Malley has written a useful book on the *Indian Police*. The vexed question of Indian India has an extensive literature, but Sir W. Lee Warner's *The Native States of India* still remains the classic work. Recent developments are discussed by K. M. Panikkar in his *Indian States and the Government of India*. The same author's *Federal India*, written with

[1] Lovat Fraser's *India Under Curzon and After*, and Chirol's *Indian Unrest, India Old and New*, and *India*.

Colonel (now Sir) K. N. Haksar, is important as showing the genesis of the Federation scheme. The frontier question has also a large bibliography of its own. A useful modern book is C. C. Davies's *The Problem of the North-West Frontier*.

The nationalist standpoint can be studied in many works, of which Lajpat Rai's *Unhappy India* is a good example. Mrs. Besant's *How India Wrought for Freedom* gives a sketch of the earlier period of the Congress. Indian publishers, such as Natesan of Madras or the *Modern Review* office (Calcutta), could supply lists of nationalist works, including many short biographies. Some Indian Congress literature is proscribed, or has sought comparative immunity by being published only in a vernacular. We have consulted books in both classes, but few show signs of original thought or research. William Digby's *Prosperous British India*, a voluminous but ill-arranged work, remains the mine from which many Indian and most American authors have dug their material for attacks upon the British administration.

Studies of Indian religions and customs, of economics, ethnology and literature suggest an immense field of study. This cannot be included in a note which, in any case, only skims the ocean of available material.

INDEX

Abbott, Sir James, 376, 386.

Abdul Ghafur Khan, 635, 642.

Abdulla Jan, son of Sher Ali, 511, 514.

Abdur Rahman, Amir of Afghanistan, 504, 508, 520, 522-4, 551-3, 558.

Aboukir, battle of, 202.

Achin, 6.

Adam, John, 286; acting Governor-General, 291-3; action against Press, 292.

Adams, William, 7.

Adye, Sir John, 554.

Afghanistan and Afghans, 104, 128, 158, 242-4, 264, 303, 435, 437; First Afghan War, 335-54; continuance of, in Sind campaign, 354, 367, 381, 385, 395; treaty with, 414; Second Afghan War, 483, 507-24, 531, 539, 551-5, 599, 608; Third Afghan War, 611-12, 613-14, 625, 651.

Afridis, 504, 554-6.

Aga Khan, 584.

Age of Consent Act (1891), 530, 545.

Agra, 10, 16, 198; surrenders to Lake, 220; 224, 326, 353; Bank of, 482; 651.

Agricultural debt, 429, 474, 486-9, 493, 530, 534, 566, 590.

Agricultural holdings, 422, 588 ff.

Agriculture, Department of, 479, 568-9, 614.

Agriculturists' Loans Act (1884), 487, 530.

Ahalya Bai, 180, 213, 215.

Ahmad Khan, Sir Saiyid, 584, 651.

Ahmad Shah sacks Delhi, 89; defeats Marathas at Panipat, 97.

Ahmad Ullah, the 'Moulvi of Faizabad', 441, 457-8.

Ahmadabad, 16, 431, 608.

Ahmadnagar stormed, 221.

Aiyar, Subramania, 543.

Aix-la-Chapelle, Treaty of, 72.

Ajit Singh, 580, 582.

Akali movement, 622-3.

Akbar, 5, 123, 127, 143, 147, 166, 206.

Akbar Khan, 348-9.

Akram Khan, execution of, 345.

Albuera, battle of, 372.

Aleppo, 4 ff.

Ali Masjid, 518.

Ali, Muhammad, 613.

Ali, Shaukat, 613, 630.

Aligarh, battle of, 219; University, 584, 650-1.

Aliwal, battle of, 373.

'All Parties Conference', 629.

Allahabad, 105; Treaty of, 125; 185, 301, 445, 451, 453.

Allahvardi Khan, Nawab of Bengal, 81 ff., 99.

Allen, Mr., murder of, 579.

Alley, Captain, interloper, 44.

Almora, 367.

Aman-ullah, Amir of Afghanistan, 611-12.

Ambedkar, Dr. B. R., 623, 631, 642, 644.

Amboyna, massacre of, 16 ff., 27, 96.

American Civil War, 481.

American War of Independence, 143, 145, 150, 171.

Amherst, Lord, Governor-General, 265, 286, 293-7; and Oudh, 298; established custom of summering at Simla, 300, 317, 319; and suttee, 328.

Aminchand, 82, 85, 88; deceived by Clive, 89 ff., 139.

Amir Ali, Seiyid, 651.

Amir Khan, 239, 241 ff., 270, 274 ff.

Amrita Bazar Patrika, 463, 541.

Amritsar, 243, 391, 608-11, 622.

Amurath II, 4.

Ananda Raz, 94.

'Anglicists', 314 ff.

Anglo-Russian Convention (1907), 558-9.

Angria, Kanhoji, 56 ff.; Tukoji, 56 ff.

Anjidiv, 30.

Ansari, Dr., 631, 641.

Anson, General, 447, 449.

Anusilan Samiti, 549.

Anwar-ud-Din, 69 ff.; death of, 72.

Apa Sahib, Raja of Nagpur, 272, 275 ff.

Apa Sahib, Raja of Satara, 401.

Arakan, 293; annexed, 294 ff.

Aras, battle of, 142.

Archbishop of York, William Markham, 160, 164.

Arcot, 63, 73; siege of, 75 ff., 187, 412.

Argaon, battle of, 222.

Argyll, Duke of, 466.

Terry, Edward, 11, 15.

Tezin, battle of, 351.

Thagi (thuggee), 302, 318; suppression of, 323 ff., 388, 429.

Thakurdas, Sir Purshottamdas, 627.

Thibaw, King, 505-6.

Thomason, Sir James, 409, 417 ff., 444.

Thornton, Edward 132, 145, 298.

Tibet, 499; expedition against, 556-8.

Tilak, Bal Gangadhar, 61, 463, 544-8, 562; as defender of orthodox Hinduism, 530; imprisonment, 547; return to politics, 602 ff.

Times, the, 244, 329, 439, 464, 472.

Tilak Swaraj Fund, 618.

Tinneveli, 149.

Tipu Sultan, 112, 149; war of Cornwallis with, 176 ff., 183, 187; war of Wellesley with, 200 ff.; death, 205; character, 206; family of, 208 ff., 241, 249; 216, 219, 235, 237, 258.

Tochi valley, 554, 611.

Tod, Colonel James, 212, 278, 303, 394.

Todd, Captain, murder of, 223.

Tonk, Nawab of, 275, 469.

Towerson, Gabriel, 16.

Trafalgar, battle of, 237.

Transferred subjects, 603-4.

Transvaal, 586, 606.

Travancore, attacked by Tipu, 177, 242, 652.

Treasury, British, payments to, 68, 109, 125.

Trebeck, 303.

Trevelyan, Sir C. E., 318, 473.

Trevelyan, Sir G. O., 192, 455, 462.

Trichinopoli, siege of, 75 ff.

Trimbakji, 275.

Trinomali, battle of, 112.

Tripartite Treaty, 336, 342, 350.

Tukoji. *See* Holkar, Tukoji, and Angria, Tukoji.

Tulsi Bai, 278.

Turkestan, 242, 303, 305, 508 ff.

Turkey, 1, 5, 613, 651.

Turkey Company, 4.

Twenty-four Parganas, 91, 95.

'Tyger, a vain superfluous charge', 36.

Tyger, sailing of the, 4 ff.

Udaipur, 239, 303, 405.

United Provinces, 301, 490, 562.

United States of America, 550, 578, 627, 630, 634.

Universities, 472, 572-3; Commission, 572-3.

Untouchables, employed in Maratha forces, 57. *See under* Depressed classes.

Utrecht, Peace of, 59.

Van Cortlandt, General, 381.

Vansittart, Henry, Governor of Bengal, 99 ff., 117.

Venice, 3.

Verelst, Governor of Bengal, 113, 434.

Vernacular Press Act (1878), 497, 541.

Versailles, Treaty of, 164.

Vickars, Captain, murder of, 223.

Victoria, Queen, 360, 363, 388, 492.

Virangaum, 608.

Virgil, 76.

Vishnupur, 62; Raja of, 120, 154, 191.

Vivekananda, Swami, 545.

Vizagapatam, 94.

Vizier, 94 ff. *See* Oudh, Nawab of.

Voelcker, Dr., 534.

Voltaire, 97.

Wahabi sect, 463, 542.

Wakhan, Chief of, 511.

Walpole, Horace, 95.

Walsh, 91.

War Loans, 600.

Warburton, Sir R., 503.

Wargaon, Convention of, 143 ff.

Waring. *See* Scott, Major.

Waste Land Rules, 474.

Watson, Admiral, 81, 85 ff.

Watts, Agent at Murshidabad, 90 ff.

Wazir. *See* Oudh, Nawab of.

Waziris, 502, 504, 612.

Weavers, 18, 23, 430-4.

Webbe, W., 299.

Wedderburn, Sir William, 534, 544, 577.

Wellesley, Arthur. *See* Wellington, Duke of.

Wellesley, Gerald, 268.

Wellesley, Henry (Lord Cowley), 198, 212, 234.

Wellesley, Richard, Marquess, 6; his subsidiary system anticipated by Dupleix, 81, 185, 187; founds Fort William College, 190; interferes with Hindu religious customs, 195; his governor-generalship, 197 ff.; forbidding character of, 190 ff.; on Sir John Shore, 198; subsidiary system, 199 ff.; war with Tipu, 200 ff.; rewards for success, 205, 208; pushes his brothers, 212; approbation of Nana Farnavis, 213; on balance of power, 214; war with Marathas, 214 ff.; magnanimity to Monson, 224; treatment of Emperor, 227 ff.; settles Tanjore and Surat, 229; treatment of Oudh, 230 ff.; annexes Carnatic, 235; treatment of Haidarabad, 236; proposed action with regard to shipping, 237, 238 ff., 248, 250, 254, 261 ff., 271, 273;